MW01256019

Mr. BOOKS
Ph. 278843-45
Islamabad-Pakistan

Mr. BOOKS
Ph: 2543-45
Islamabad-Pakistan

JINNAH OF PAKISTAN

JINNAH
of
PAKISTAN

Stanley Wolpert

New York   Oxford
OXFORD UNIVERSITY PRESS
1984

Copyright © 1984 by Oxford University Press, Inc.

Library of Congress Cataloging in Publication Data

Wolpert, Stanley A., 1927–
  Jinnah of Pakistan.

  1. Jinnah, Mahomed Ali, 1876–1948. 2. Statesmen—
Pakistan—Biography. I. Title.
DS385.J5W64   1984   954.9′042′0924 [B]   83–13318
ISBN 0–19–503412–0

      Printing (last digit): 9 8 7 6 5 4 3 2 1

    Printed in the United States of America

for

Dorothy

with love

Preface

Few individuals significantly alter the course of history. Fewer still modify the map of the world. Hardly anyone can be credited with creating a nation-state. Mohammad Ali Jinnah did all three. Hailed as "Great Leader" (*Quaid-i-Azam*) of Pakistan and its first governor-general, Jinnah virtually conjured that country into statehood by the force of his indomitable will. His place of primacy in Pakistan's history looms like a lofty minaret over the achievements of all his contemporaries in the Muslim League. Yet Jinnah began his political career as a leader of India's National Congress and until after World War I remained India's best "Ambassador of Hindu-Muslim Unity." As enigmatic a figure as Mahatma Gandhi, more powerful than Pandit Nehru, Quaid-i-Azam Jinnah was one of recent history's most charismatic leaders and least known personalities. For more than a quarter century I have been intrigued by the apparent paradox of Jinnah's strange story, which has to date never been told in all the fascinating complexity of its brilliant light and tragic darkness.

Many people have helped make this book possible. To the late Lord Louis Mountbatten I am indebted for his having so generously given me a morning in the last year of his life to recall personal meetings with and impressions of Jinnah. To Begum Liaquat Ali Khan I am equally indebted for her gracious hospitality and assistance in Karachi. Professor Z. H. Zaidi of London University most warmly encouraged me to write this book more than a decade ago and helped in many ways; he shared his Jinnah letters with me, and his own cogent articles, and introduced me to his old friend and one of Jinnah's closest colleagues, Mr. M. A. H. Ispahani, who was still living in London then. Vice-Chancellor Sir Cyril Henry Philips of London University kindly assisted me during the early stages of my long search for Jinnah.

My dear friend, the late Professor B. N. Pandey of London, helped by inviting me to participate in his "Leadership in South Asia" seminar in 1974. Warmest thanks to my mentor, Professor Holden Furber, for inspiration and generous criticism.

Professor Sharif al Mujahid, the director of the Quaid-i-Azam Academy in Karachi, was most generous in assisting me during my visit to Pakistan in 1980 as a Fellow of the American Institute of Pakistan Studies. I thank him and AIPS Director Professor Hafeez Malik for all of their invaluable help. I gratefully acknowledge the aid provided by the AIPS and its board in awarding me a fellowship to complete my research in Pakistan. My sincere thanks also to Dr. Charles Boewe, Mr. Arshad, Mr. Afaqi, and Akbar, of the United States Educational Foundation in Islamabad for their kind hospitality.

Dr. A. Z. Sheikh, the director of the National Archives of Pakistan, and his fine staff were most cooperative in opening the full resources of their archives to me during my visit to Islamabad. I am especially grateful to Mr. S. M. Ikram, the microfilming and photostating officer of the NAP, for expediting the filming of Jinnah papers for me. Vice-President Khalid Shamsul Hasan of the National Bank of Pakistan in Karachi was most helpful in granting me full and immediate access in his office and home to the excellent Shamsul Hasan Collection of primary Jinnah papers. I am deeply grateful to him, and to Dr. M. H. Siddiqi, the director of the University of Karachi's Freedom Movement archives, who introduced me to his very impressive collection.

My continuing gratitude and appreciation to the librarian and staff of the excellent India Office Library in London, with special thanks to Deputy Archivist Martin Moir and to Dr. Richard Bingle, both of whom were singularly helpful in steering me toward new material. For this book I have interviewed a great number of Jinnah's colleagues and contemporaries in Pakistan, India, and Great Britain, as well as in the United States, over the past fifteen years; and although there is not space to mention each by name, I wish to thank them all for helping me to better understand this singularly secretive and complex man.

To the Rt. Hon. S. S. Pirzada, the minister of law of Pakistan and chairman of the Quaid-i-Azam Biography Committee, my sincere thanks for sharing with me his personal memories and writings on the Quaid-i-Azam. To Admiral S. M. Ahsan I am most warmly indebted for historic insights and generous hospitality. My grateful appreciation also to Mian Mumtaz Daultana, Sardar Shaukat Hayat, Justice Javid Iqbal, Brig. N. A. Husain, former Chief Minister of Sind Mumtaz Ali Bhutto, former Karachi Mayor Hashim Raza, and former Ambassador Mohammad Masoor, for many helpful insights concerning Jinnah's personality.

To Lady Dhanavati Rama Rao, Srimati Pupal Jayakar, and Srimati Sheela Kalia I am deeply indebted for singularly sensitive keys to the character not only of Jinnah, but of his wife and daughter as well. I thank Ved Mehta for sharing with me his father's memory of Jinnah. I am most thankful to Professor Fazlur Rahman for recalling all that he did about Jinnah, and to Professor Khalid Bin Sayeed for his help. Many colleagues and students at the University of California have helped me stay the course in this long search, and I especially thank Professors Damodar Sar Desai, Nikki Keddie, John S. Galbraith, H. Arthur Steiner, Steven Hay, Peter Loewenberg, and Ismail Poonawala. For the past decade and a half, my seminar students have posed useful questions about Jinnah, each stimulating deeper investigation into his life and motivations; and for this I especially thank Ravi Kalia, Juan Cole, Roger Long, Anand Mavalankar, David Kessler, Sasha Jamal, Nasir Khan, Rajan Samtani, and Professor Saleem Ahmad.

I spoke many times by phone with Jinnah's only daughter, Mrs. Dina Wadia. In 1980 I was to have interviewed her at her Madison Avenue apartment in Manhattan, but unfortunately, perhaps because of her acute shyness or illness, the meeting was canceled at the last moment. One question she asked in a conversation has often echoed in my memory as illustrative of their relationship, "Why so much interest in my father's life, after all these years?" Mrs. Wadia's only son, Nusli, was unavailable to meet with me in Bombay, both in 1978 and in 1982, but he did write: "My grandfather died when I was four. . . . My memory of him is vague indeed." Nusli's father was equally elusive, writing from Switzerland in 1982 to inform me that "As Mr. Jinnah disapproved of my marriage to his daughter on religious grounds [Wadia was born a Parsi and converted to Christianity], I saw very little of him & therefore regret I cannot help. . . . My daughter was too young to remember him & saw little of him so there would be no use in contacting her." In 1980, Jinnah's last surviving sister was bedridden in Karachi; I was unable to see her, and she died shortly after my visit there.

I thank my editor, Nancy Lane, and my copy editor, Kathy Antrim, for their help in bringing this book to press, and I thank Kate Wittenberg as well. To Faye Fauman, who typed the manuscript, and to my friend Elaine Attias, who so kindly photographed me, heartfelt thanks.

As for my dearest wife, who has nurtured, sustained, and inspired me and my works throughout the past thirty years, I confess that no good thing I have ever done or written would have been possible without her co-authorship.

Los Angeles   S. W.
September 1983

Contents

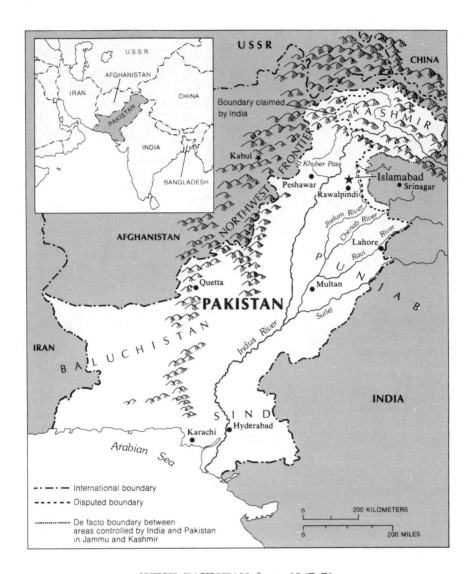

WEST PAKISTAN from 1947–71

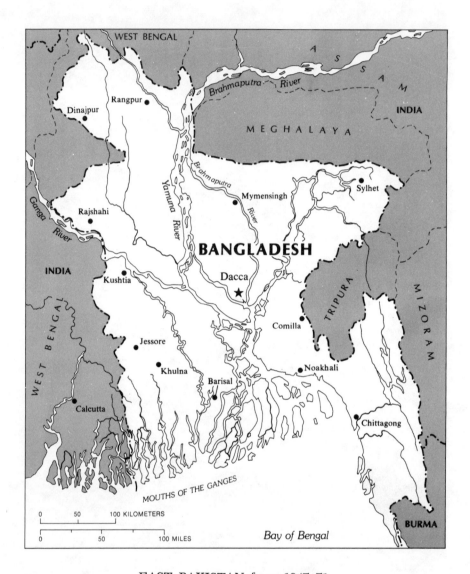

EAST PAKISTAN from 1947–71

JINNAH OF PAKISTAN

1

Karachi

Students, barristers, and benchers rushing in and out of Lincoln's Inn nowadays rarely glance at the oil painting, hung since July 1965, on the stone wall over the entrance to their Great Hall and Library in London. Those who do may wonder why on earth the gaunt, unsmiling face of "M. A. Jinnah, Founder and First Governor-General of Pakistan" should be staring down at them. Tall, thin, monocled, astrakhan-capped, the portrait's subject was, so the strip of brass secured to its frame attests, "born 25 December 1876 and died 11 September 1948." Nothing more is revealed of M. A. Jinnah's history. The anonymous artist captured his upright, unbending spirit, as well as his impeccable taste in clothes, yet Jinnah's face is almost as enigmatic and spare as the shining brass plate beneath. His eyes, opened wide, are piercing; his lips, tightly closed, formidable. One would guess that he was a man of few words, never easily thwarted or defeated. But why is he there—in so honored a place on that hallowed wall of British jurisprudence?

Across the timeworn stairs of stone that supported Queen Victoria and Her Majesty's entourage when she came to dedicate that Great Hall and oak-beamed Library in 1845 are two portraits of Englishmen who obviously do belong. Sir William Henry Maule was baron of the Exchequer, a judge of the Common Pleas, and a bencher, one of four officers elected to administer Lincoln's Inn. Lord Arthur Hobhouse was legal member of the Executive Council of India's Viceroy in 1875, the year Prime Minister Benjamin Disraeli persuaded Queen Victoria to add "Empress of India" to her regalia. Two marble busts flank M. A. Jinnah's portrait, like horseguards, their unblinking eyes staring ahead. These also seem appropriate to the setting, for one is Lord Macnaghten, who was "Lord of Appeal in Ordinary" and not only a bencher but treasurer, while the other immortalizes Sir Francis Henry

Goldsmit, "First Jewish Barrister," bencher and member of Parliament. Jinnah, however, held no office at Lincoln's Inn, nor was he ever elected to Parliament or appointed to preside over any British court, nor did he even serve on the cabinet of a single British viceroy.

Yet the story of Jinnah's unique achievement was so inextricably the product of his genius as a barrister, perhaps the greatest "native" advocate in British Indian history, that his portrait richly deserves the place of high honor it holds. During the last decade of his life, in fact, Jinnah may have been the shrewdest barrister in the British Empire. He was certainly the most tenacious. He crossed swords with at least as many great British-born as Indian barristers, defeating them all in his single-minded pleas for Pakistan. He burned out his life pressing a single suit, yet by winning his case he changed the map of South Asia and altered the course of world history.

Jinnah (in Arabic, "wing" as of a bird or army) was born a Shi'ite Muslim Khoja (*Khwaja,* "noble"). Disciples of the Isma'ili[1] Aga Khan, thousands of Khojas fled Persian persecution to Western India, among other regions, between the tenth and sixteenth centuries. The exact date of the flight of Jinnah's ancestors is unknown, but as a minority community within Islam, itself a religious minority in India, the Khojas of South Asia remained doubly conscious of their separateness and cultural difference, helping perhaps to account for the "aloofness" so often noted as a characteristic quality of Jinnah and his family. Khojas, like other mercantile communities the world over, however, traveled extensively, were quick to assimilate new ideas, and adjusted with relative ease to strange environments. They developed linguistic skills and sharp intelligence, often acquiring considerable wealth. Mahatma Gandhi's Hindu merchant (bania) family, by remarkable coincidence, settled barely thirty miles to the north of Jinnah's grandparents, in the state of Rajkot. Thus the parents of the Fathers of both India and Pakistan shared a single mother tongue, Gujarati, though that never helped their brilliant offspring to communicate.

Jinnah's father Jinnahbhai Poonja (born c. 1850), the youngest of three sons, married Mithibai, "a good girl" of his own community,[2] and soon moved with his bride to Sind's growing port of Karachi to seek his fortune. After completion of the Suez Canal in 1869, Karachi enjoyed its first modern boom as British India's closest port, only 5,918 nautical miles from Southampton, two hundred miles nearer than Bombay. The population was as yet under 50,000, a far cry from the more than 6 million who inhabit that premier city of Pakistan today, but enterprising young people, like Jinnahbhai and Mithibai, flocked to its municipality's commercial heart, pulsating along both banks of the Lyaree River. There Jinnahbhai rented the second floor apartment of a three-story house, Wazir Mansion (since rebuilt and made into a national monument and museum), in the bustling cotton mart on Newnham Road still cluttered with camels and laden with bales of raw cotton.

Here sometime in the 1870's Mohammad Ali Jinnah was the first of seven children born to Mithibai and her husband.[3] Certificates of birth and death were not issued by Karachi's municipality prior to 1879, and though Jinnah in later life would claim December 25, 1876, as his true date of birth, the birthday officially celebrated throughout Pakistan, there is reason to doubt its accuracy. Unlike Hindus of comparable wealth and social status, who would have been careful to record the precise date and moment of a child's birth for astrological purposes, Muslims generally did not concern themselves with birthdates and no records were kept prior to their enrollment in a public school. The register preserved at the first such school Jinnah attended, the Sind Madressa-tul-Islam of Karachi, notes October 20, 1875, as the birth date of "Mahomedali Jinnahbhai."[4]

At birth, in fact, "Mamad" (his pet name at home) was "small and weak," his devoted sister Fatima (July 31, 1893–July 9, 1967) recalled. "His health caused concern as he weighed a few pounds less than normal."[5] Mamad was approximately six when his father hired a private tutor to start his son on alphabets and mathematics, but the boy proved "indifferent" to studies, "positively loathed" arithmetic, and could not wait to go outdoors as soon as his tutor arrived. Those private lessons were one indicator of how Jinnahbhai Poonja's business had prospered by the early 1880's. The annual value of Karachi's trade almost doubled since he had arrived scarcely a decade earlier, climbing to above 80 million rupees. Jinnahbhai handled all sorts of produce, cotton, wool, hides, oil-seeds, and grain for export, and Manchester manufactured piece-goods, metals, and refined sugar imports into the busy port. Business was so good, in fact, with profits soaring so high, that he became a "banker and money-lender" as well for his customers. Despite Islam's prohibition against lending or borrowing money at interest, banking was clearly how Jinnahbhai made his fortune, and subsequently lost it.

Early in 1887, Jinnahbhai's only sister, Manbai, who had married an even more successful Khoja named Peerbhai and lived in metropolitan Bombay, came to visit. Mamad loved Auntie's witty, vivacious, cosmopolitan good humor, and she in turn adored her bright, handsome young nephew. "Night after night," Fatima remembered, Manbai told them "wonderful tales of fairies and the flying carpet; of *jins* and dragons." She lured Mamad back to Bombay with her that year, introducing him to the great city that was to become his chosen home most of his adult life. Even as provincial Karachi's commercial houses clung in those days "to Bombay as the ivy clings to the oak,"[6] Jinnah followed his Aunt Manbai, who must have symbolized for him the beauty, glamor, and endless fascination of that presidency capital.

Little is known of Mamad's life in Bombay during his first tantalizingly brief visit to the big city, as far advanced culturally from Karachi as the latter was from Paneli village. He lived with Auntie and was enrolled at school, but whether it was at the Muslim Anjuman-i-Islam as Fatima recalled, or in the secular Gokul Das Tej Primary School as his secretary, Mr. M. H. Sayyid, reported,[7] remains uncertain. Perhaps he attended both schools, joining the latter after quitting the former.

Young Jinnah's tolerance for formal education was never high. Sitting at home, learning things by rote, was bad enough. It is not hard to imagine that spirited young brain rebelling inside a typical Indian primary school classroom. Especially in Bombay. India's most beautiful port was adorned with crescent beaches of white sand topped by lofty palisades sprouting royal palms. The usually placid sparkling waters of Back Bay were dotted with sugar-loaf islands. In spacious covered bazaars like Crawford Market, Englishmen and their ladies strolled amid the world's riches, all on display, all for sale. Round the Maiden and Oval, the high court, and the university he must have gaped in awe at the Victorian gothic monuments to all that the British raj and its modernization brought to India. Elphinstone Circle and the town hall, the imperial bank, and chamber of commerce building were doubtless included in the many carriage tours Auntie arranged for her young visitor's delight on their holidays. Had he rusticated in Karachi for another decade before visiting Bombay, Jinnah might well have been persuaded simply to follow in his father's footsteps, content with inheriting the booming provincial business of Jinnahbhai Poonja and Company. But having seen Bombay he would never forget it, and though he went back to Karachi after little more than six months, it was hardly out of boredom with his new environment.

His mother, Fatima noted, "had been miserable" without her "darling son." Mamad enrolled in the Sind Madressa on December 23, 1887, but a few years later his name was "withdrawn" from the roster because of "long absence."[8] He enjoyed riding his father's Arabian horses more than doing arithmetic, and he cut classes regularly with his friend, Karim Kassim, to gallop off on "adventures" across Sind's barren sands. Mamad "loved" horses, as he did "minarets and domes." He liked reading poetry, too, but at his own pace and leisure, not harnessed to any Karachi pedagogue's lesson plan. Jinnah was never intimidated by authority, nor was he easy to control, even as a child. His parents sent him to Karachi's exclusive Christian Mission High

School on Lawrence Road, close to home, in the hope that that might prove a more congenial stimulus for his restless mind. He stayed only a few months, however, and perhaps the legacy of that Mission school was to stimulate his interest in and attraction to the importance of December 25.

By 1890 business was good enough for Jinnahbhai Poonja to buy his own "stables" and several "handsome carriages." His firm was closely associated with the leading British managing agency in Karachi, Douglas Graham and Company. Sir Frederick Leigh Croft, Graham's general manager may have inherited his job with his baronetcy. Sir Frederick's influence on Jinnah's life was, indeed, so significant that it is unfortunate so little is known of him. A "kinswoman" remembered Croft, thirty-two at the time, as a bachelor and "something of a dandy, with a freshly picked carnation in his buttonhole each morning; a recluse and a wit, uncomfortable in the presence of children, whom he did not like."[9] And a decade later, this thumbnail description might also suffice for his provincial apprentice, though instead of the carnation, Jinnah chose a monocle, borrowed from another of his British models of high style, Joseph Chamberlain. Sir Frederick obviously liked Mamad, thinking highly enough of his potential to recommend the young man for an apprenticeship to his home office in London in 1892. That single letter to London lifted young Jinnah from provincial obscurity into the orbit of British imperial prominence, accessible at that time to fewer than one in a million Indians. Paradoxically, Karachi proved a far better launching pad for Jinnah's career than Bombay would have been, since there were hundreds (if not thousands) of young men in Bombay at least as well connected, if not as bright as Jinnah, all of whose parents doubtless tried to convince men like Croft there to do as much for their sons. Karachi, however, had only one Jinnah.

When his mother learned of her favorite child's latest travel plans, she cried out bitterly against the trip. Bombay with Auntie had been far enough, and much too long a separation. Now London? Alone and for two years at least? To her it was out of the question, impossible, and intolerable—perhaps intuition told her she would never see him again. Her tears, imprecations, and arguments continued for weeks, but Jinnah had made up his mind. His mother could not change it. Finally, "after much persuasion," she surrendered, consenting—on one condition. "England," she said, "was a dangerous country to send an unmarried and handsome young man like her son. Some English girl might lure him into marriage and that would be a tragedy for the Jinnah Poonja family."[10] He protested at first, yet saw how much it meant to her and finally "behaved like an obedient son," accepting her arranged marriage as the price of his passage to England. His mother found a suitable Khoja girl in Paneli village, fourteen-year-old Emibai, "a good girl," as she herself had been. The matchmakers and parents decided everything for Jinnah and his bride, even as young Gandhi's parents had done a few years before, the way countless other teenage Indian couples were married in the nineteenth century.

"Mohammad Ali was hardly sixteen and had never seen the girl he was to marry," Fatima reported of the wedding. "Decked from head to foot in long flowing garlands of flowers, he walked in a procession from his grandfather's house to that of his father-in-law, where his fourteen year old bride, Emi Bai, sat in an expensive bridal dress, wearing glittering ornaments, her hands spotted with henna, her face spotted with gold dust and redolent with the fragrance of attar."[11] How did young Jinnah feel about this stranger child bride? He really had no time in which to learn much about her. Only days after their marriage he sailed out of her life, never to see her again. Long before Jinnah would return from London, Emibai, like his mother, was dead.

In January 1893, Jinnah left for England, "unaccompanied and unchaperoned," aboard a Pacific & Orient steamship. During that sea voyage he was befriended by an "elderly Englishman," who "took to him like his own son," giving young Jinnah his London address when he disembarked at Marseilles. "During the next four years, whenever this Englishman came back to his native land from India he would call my brother to his house and ask him to have a meal with him and his family," recounted Fatima.[12] Mohammad Ali landed at Southampton, catching the boat train to Victoria Station. "During the first few months I found a strange country and unfamiliar surroundings," he recalled. "I did not know a soul and the fogs and winter in London upset me a great deal."[13] At Graham's he sat at a small desk surrounded by stacks of account books he was expected to copy and balance. The agency's head office was in the City of London near Threadneedle Street, a short walk from historic Guildhall, the Bank of England, and the old East India Company's original headquarters along the River Thames on Leadenhall Street. Jinnah kept no diary and wrote no autobiography, as did Gandhi and Nehru, yet he must have felt at once elated and depressed to find himself in the cold, remote, inspiring heart of the mighty empire into which he had been born. "I was young and lonely. Far from home. . . . Except for some employees at Grahams, I did not know a soul, and the immensity of London as a city weighed heavily on my solitary life. . . But I soon got settled to life in London, and I began to like it before long."[14]

His father deposited money enough to his account in a British bank to allow Jinnah to live in London for three years. There is no record of precisely how many hotel rooms or "bed and breakfast" stops he rented before moving into the modest three-story house at 35 Russell Road in Kensington

that now displays the County Council's blue and white ceramic oval showing that the "founder of Pakistan stayed here in 1895." Now rather run-down,
that block of attached buildings must have looked quite fashionable in
Jinnah's day. The flat he lived in was owned by Mrs. F. E. Page-Drake, a
widow with "an attractive daughter who was about the same age" as Mohammad Ali and "liked my brother." Perhaps to reassure herself, the spinster
Fatima added, "but he was not the flirtatious type and she could not break
through his reserve."[15] "She would sometimes arrange mixed parties in her
mother's house, and among the various games she would organise was one
in which the penalty for a fault was a kiss. Mohammad Ali always counted
himself out of this kissing game. 'One Christmas Eve,' he recalled, 'Miss
Page-Drake threw her arms around me as I was standing under some mistletoe, the significance of which I did not then know, and said that I must kiss
her. I told gently that we too had our social rules and the mistletoe kiss was
not one of them. She let me go and did not bother me again in this manner.' "[16] Most puzzling perhaps about so innocuous an incident is why Miss
Jinnah should have considered it important enough to report in detail. Was
it simply a prudish sister's way of embellishing the historic record to keep
her great brother's image immaculate?

Jinnah anglicized his name in London, replacing the cumbersome Mohammed Ali Jinnahbhai of Karachi with its streamlined British version,
M. A. Jinnah, which he first used for crossing his Royal Bank of Scotland
checks. He also traded in his traditional Sindhi long yellow coat for smartly
tailored Saville Row suits and heavily-starched detachable-collared shirts.
His tall, lean frame was perfectly suited to display London's finest fashions.
Jinnah was to remain a model of sartorial elegance for the rest of his life,
carefully selecting the finest cloth for the 200-odd hand-tailored suits in his
wardrobe closet by the end of his life. As a barrister he prided himself on
never wearing the same silk tie twice. The very stylishness of his attire extended to the tips of his toes, which were sheathed in smart two-tone
leather or suede. Few Englishmen ever developed as keen an interest in
dress as did Jinnah. His perfect manners and attire always assured him
entry into any of England's stately homes, clubs, and palaces. Like Anthony
Eden and the Duke of Windsor, Jinnah became a model of fashion the world
over, rivaled among his South Asian contemporaries only by Motilal Nehru.

Mr. M. A. Jinnah did not take long to abandon the drudgery of his
Graham's apprenticeship. He arrived in London in February 1893 and on
April 25 of that year "petitioned" Lincoln's Inn and was "granted" permis-
sion "to be excused the Latin portion of the Preliminary Examination."[17]
The grand and petty lures of London dislodged him from his musty desk in
the old city. Walking toward the spires of Westminster, Jinnah sauntered

down Fleet Street, past Chancery Lane and the old Temple Bar, into the spacious fields of Lincoln's Inn, then still bared by winter's bite but having the promise of forsythia, lilac, and wisteria. Half a century later, addressing Karachi's Bar he recalled, "I joined Lincoln's Inn because there, on the main entrance, the name of the Prophet was included in the list of the great law-givers of the world."[18] It was a fascinating trick of memory he played on himself, for no such inscription exists over the main, or indeed any other entrance of Lincoln's Inn, nor did it then. What Jinnah recalled seeing, how-ever, was G. F. Watt's fresco in Lincoln's New Hall called "The Law Givers," depicting the Prophet with Moses, Jesus, and other great spiritual leaders of civilization. A London tour guide or Inn guard must have pointed out Mu-hammad's visage within earshot of young Jinnah, who possibly decided then that this was the Inn he would like most to attend. For orthodox (Sunni) Muslims, of course, any human depiction of the Prophet was an anathema, heresy to iconoclastic Islam. Jinnah's message to Pakistan's young Sunni barristers was naturally meant to be inspirational, yet how could he admit to them that the holy Prophet's *image* had early inspired him? Subconsciously, therefore, he deleted the face from memory, "inscribing" Muhammad's "name" over Lincoln's "main entrance" instead.

Young Jinnah was fascinated by the glamorous world of politics that he glimpsed as often as possible from the visitor's gallery of Westminster's House of Commons. Lord Cross's India Councils Act, passed after heated debate in 1892, stimulated the first full-dress discussion of Indian affairs in London since 1888. That act introduced, albeit indirectly, the elective prin-ciple into British India's constitution, thus serving as an historic thin-edge of the wedge of representative government that was soon to force open offi-cially dominated council chambers throughout British India. Jinnah himself soon was elected as one of Bombay's representatives to Calcutta's Central Legislative Council and later served for decades on New Delhi's expanded assembly, where he played an important parliamentary role.

The Liberal tide that brought William Gladstone back to 10 Downing Street for a third time in 1892 also carried Bombay Parsi Dadabhai Naoroji (1825–1917) into Parliament. Dadabhai, who had started a firm in London and Liverpool in 1855, was elected to the House of Commons from Central Finsbury on a Liberal ticket by so slender a margin (three votes) that he was commonly called "Mr. Narrow-Majority" by his peers. To India's youth, however, Dadabhai was the Grand Old Man of national politics, a veritable Indian Gladstone. Dadabhai presided over the second session of the Indian Congress in 1886, crying out then: "No matter what it is, Legislative Coun-cils or the Services—nothing can be reformed until Parliament moves and enacts modifications of the existing Acts. Not one single genuine Indian voice is there in Parliament to tell at least what the native view is on any question."[19] Lord Salisbury, the ousted Tory prime minister, characterized fair-skinned Dadabhai as a "black man" during the campaign, a racist slur that backfired, contributing to Parsi Dadabhai's victory. The volunteer ward labors of energetic young Indians like Jinnah helped bring the voice of a leading Indian nationalist to echo through the mightiest chamber of the British Empire.

"If Dadabhai was black, I was darker," Jinnah told his sister. "And if this was the mentality of the British politicians, then we would never get a fair deal from them. From that day I have been an uncompromising enemy of all forms of colour bar and racial prejudice."[20] Jinnah listened from the Commons gallery to Dadabhai's maiden speech in 1893 and "thrilled" as he heard the Grand Old Man extol the virtues of "free speech." As Jinnah noted, "there he was, an Indian, who would exercise that right and demand justice for his countrymen." Without freedom of speech, Jinnah wisely understood any nation would remain "stunted" or wither "like a rose bush that is planted in a place where there is neither sunshine nor air."[21] Thanks to Dadabhai's inspiring example, Jinnah entered politics as a Liberal nationalist, joining Congress soon after he returned to India.

Did Jinnah embark upon his study of the law in preparation for a political career? No record survives of the thoughts that passed through his mind in the spring of 1893. We know only that he did decide to sit for his "little go" preliminary examination, a "relatively simple" test for admission to the Inns of Court; he took it without the Latin portion and "passed" on May 25, 1893. Had he procrastinated he might not have been able to complete his legal apprenticeship, for next year a number of prerequisites were added and the process of professional legal certification was substantially prolonged. Jinnah's funds would have run out before he finished his studies. Nor could he have received any further support from home, since his father's fortune, tied to the vagaries of world market and monetary exchange cycles that plunged India's silver rupee into deep depression relative to British gold-backed sterling after 1893, then collapsed.

Even if Jinnahbhai Poonja could have afforded the luxury, it is doubtful that he would have contributed another rupee to his son's support in London. The old man was "furious" when he learned of Jinnah's impulsive decision to abandon his business career. Nor is it very likely that Sir Frederick, or any of his elders at Graham's home office, would have lifted a further finger to help this "Sindhi upstart ingrate." As Jinnah well knew, he was on his own. No pillars of support remained to fall back upon. Nor would this be the only time in life that he would find himself isolated, cut off in so perilous a position. Still he never faltered, acting with surgical swiftness to alter his career. If he had any fears or doubts about his future, he left no record of them. On June 25, 1893, he embarked upon his study of the law at Lincoln's Inn.

Lincoln's Inn had a most imposing list of graduates and dropouts, including Thomas More, William Pitt, and half a dozen other British prime ministers from Lord Canning to Asquith. Two of Britain's greatest prime ministers, Disraeli and Gladstone, went there but neither completed his course of study. In 1893 when Jinnah enrolled, John Morley (1838–1923), who first entered Lincoln's premises thirty-one years earlier, was elected a bencher. Author of *On Compromise*, John Stuart Mill's greatest disciple, Gladstone's Irish Home Rule secretary and Liberal lieutenant, "Honest John" (later Lord) Morley then had his most important half decade as secretary of state for India (1906–10) still ahead of him. One of Britain's most brilliant Liberals, Morley became one of Jinnah's heroes. The uncompromising idealistic fervor of *On Compromise* went through Jinnah's mind "like a flame,"[22] igniting his imagination with arguments such as that which insisted upon placing "truth" first among any choice of "principles." Jinnah quoted Morley to student audiences later in life, and he personally tried to adhere to the Liberal ideals early imbibed from Lincoln's great bencher.

M. A. Jinnah's legal education was, with minor modification, the medieval guild apprenticeship method launched with the founding of Lincoln's Inn, which was named for the King's Sergeant of Holborn, Thomas de Lincoln, in the latter half of the fourteenth century. Records of that self-governing society's council meetings and business affairs have been preserved at the Inn's library in annual "Black Books" since 1422, when the students all still lived within the Inn's somber walls. After the enrolled number of students became too great to accommodate inside, the hostel tradition was only symbolically retained through the requirement that all students enrolled at a university eat a minimum of three dinners in the Great Hall, or those not enrolled, as in Jinnah's case, eat six. The collegial environment of those dinners, where barristers and benchers sat close enough to students to engage them in conversation, argument, or debate, was deemed an important aspect of legal training. For how better could young men sharpen their wits and develop forensic skills, after all, than in debate with their guild elders? The conviviality of table talk was, moreover, a shortcut to friendship or antipathy, and if a young apprentice was alert as well as wise he soon learned what was best said or left unsaid in the company of lawyers.

The Great Hall was used not only for dining, however, since "moots" and "bolts" were also held there; barristers debating legal issues and questions in the former, students following suit in the latter. The most important element in Jinnah's legal education, however, was the two years of "reading" apprenticeship he spent in a barrister's chambers. He would follow his master's professional footsteps outside chambers as well, through all the corridors of Temple Court, up every creaking stair of Holborn's crowded pubs. With slight exaggeration one might say that if, in addition to the above, a bright lad read William Blackstone's *Commentaries* on common law he could cram enough information into his head to pass the final examination prior to admission to the Bar. Jinnah's class still belonged to that old school of young gentlemen who were deemed fit for a career in law as long as they knew the jargon, dressed properly, and ate with the right utensils.

When he was not in chambers or dining in Great Hall, Jinnah passed much of his time in London strolling or studying in the book-lined Reading Room of the British Museum, a Mecca for scholars the world over. On Sundays, when that haven closed, he went at times to Hyde Park corner at the Marble Arch to listen to the open-air oratory of anyone who had a box to stand upon and the courage to speak his mind on any subject. Irish Home Rule was one of the burning issues of the day, and Irish Parliamentary party M. P. Alfred Webb, whom Jinnah had heard from Westminster's gallery, was elected to preside over the Madras Congress in 1894. "I hate tyranny and oppression wherever practised, more especially if practised by my own Government, for then I am in a measure responsible," Webb said to his Indian audience that December. And until the "Irish question" was resolved, President Webb insisted, India, like the rest of the British Empire, would suffer, for Parliament "is paralysed with . . . the affairs of under five millions of people, and ministries rise and fall on the question of Ireland rather than great Imperial interests."[23] It was an important lesson for Jinnah, one he subconsciously assimilated during those early lonely years in London, of how a small minority and its insistent demands could "paralyze" a huge empire. He learned to appreciate all the weaknesses as well as strengths of British character. Whether or not he ever rose the requisite minimal height above the sacrosanct soil at Hyde Park corner to harangue any London audience himself, he learned many useful debating tricks merely by listening there, and engaging speakers in argument.

Not every weekend was spent in London, however. He went at least once to Oxford with friends, later recalling that his first "friction with the police" occurred during the annual Oxbridge boat race, when "I was with two friends and we were caught up with a crowd of undergraduates. We found a cart in a side street, so we pushed each other up and down the roadway, until we were arrested and taken off to the police station . . . [and] let off with a caution."[24] It was the closest this remarkably law-abiding Indian would ever come to being placed behind bars—another polar difference that separated him from Gandhi, Nehru, and most other nationalist leaders who spent years in British prison cells.

Young Jinnah fell in love with theater while living in London. His secret ambition, he later confessed, was "to play the role of Romeo at the Old Vic."[25] Exactly when he started to dream of an acting career is unclear, though it was obviously after he had begun to study law. Perhaps law bored him at first, or it may have been watching the performances of barristers, the greatest of whom were often spell-binding thespians, that stimulated his interest in going on stage. At any event, it was no mere whim or passing fancy, but a love affair that lasted till the end of his years. "Even in the days of his most active political life," Fatima reminisced, "when he returned home tired and late, he would read Shakespeare, his voice . . . resonant." The ubiquitous monocle remained his major courtroom prop later and those who witnessed his dramatic interrogations and imperious asides, whether to judge or jury, often commented that he was a born actor. Many a political opponent made the mistake of believing, however, that Jinnah was "only acting" when he was most serious.

On June 7, 1895, Jinnah wrote a check for £138/19/— covering all fees for admission to the Bar. He had ignored his father's letters ordering him to "come home" to help save the fast-failing business and paid the full Bar expenses early to not be tempted later to spend any of that sum. He was charged only £10 a month for his room and half board at the home of Mrs. Page-Drake, and would always be very careful with money. The habits of frugality he developed in those early London years never left him. He even managed to save £71/1/10 of the sum his father had initially turned over to him, after three years of living in the heart of what was then surely the most tempting marketplace on earth. Still he dreamed of a life in art, and of remaining in London.

"After I was called to the Bar, I was taken by some friends to the Manager of a theatrical company, who asked me to go up to the stage and read out pieces of Shakespeare," Jinnah reminisced. "I did so. His wife and he were immensely pleased, and immediately offered me a job. I was exultant, and I wrote to my parents craving for their blessings. I wrote to them that law was a lingering profession where success was uncertain; a stage career was much better, and it gave me a good start, and that I would now be independent and not bother them with grants of money at all. My father wrote a long letter to me, strongly disapproving of my project; but there was one sentence in his letter that touched me most and which influenced a change in my decision: 'Do not be a traitor to the family.' I went to my employers and conveyed to them that I no longer looked forward to a stage career.

They were surprised, and they tried to persuade me, but my mind was made up. According to the terms of the contract I had signed with them, I was to have given them three months notice before quitting. But you know, they were Englishmen, and so they said: 'Well when you have no interest in the stage, why should we keep you, against your wishes?' "[26]

The signed contract indicates how serious Jinnah's commitment to London's stage and acting had been. It was obviously his first love at this time. His father's "long letter" had dissuaded him, forcing him to change his mind on a matter of major importance, but that was the last time he would ever do so. The charge of familial "treason" cut his conscience to the quick, leaving him sorely wounded. Apparently that letter also informed him of his mother's death, and possibly of his wife's as well. For in reporting how "exultant" he had felt after landing the job, he noted, "I wrote to my parents craving for their blessings." What a shock that letter from his father must have been, full of dread news and reprimand. And what a cloud it must have cast over his last days and weeks in London.

On May 11, 1896, "Mahomed Ali Jinnah Esquire, a Barrister of this Society," petitioned the benchers of Lincoln's Inn for a "certificate" attesting his "Admission Call to the Bar and of his deportment."[27] With that talisman he would be welcome to join the Bar of any court in British India. Now he was ready to go home, but not to Karachi. There was nothing left in Karachi that he truly cared for any more. So before leaving London he transferred the total balance of his bank account to a new account in his name to be opened at the National Bank of India, Ltd., Bombay. That was done on July 15, 1896. Next day he climbed the gangway of the P & O liner that sailed east. Karachi would be nothing more than a brief stop en route to the city he chose as his new permanent home. His father had lured him from London with its matchless wonder, but nothing short of the partition of India would bring him back to live in Karachi—and then only briefly, to found a new nation, before dying.

2

Bombay
(1896-1910)

Jinnah was enrolled as a barrister in Bombay's high court on August 24, 1896, precisely one decade after the Karachi country boy was first driven past that Victorian palace of law. His richly variegated London experiences, tempered by the traumas of his brief return home, had made a man of him. He was bereft of mother and wife; his most powerful ties to Karachi had been cut with surgical finality. M. A. Jinnah, Esq., borne out of the bitter disappointment and pain that shrouded his last few months, was launched into orbit on his own.

For Bombay, as for Jinnah personally, it was a time of tragedy and mourning. Bubonic plague from China reached that busy port in the autumn of 1896. The Black Death that claimed millions of Indian lives in the ensuing decades remained most severe in the crowded, bustling cities of Bombay, Poona, and Ahmedabad, at least until the ingenius Dr. W. M. Haffkine (1860–1930) developed his vaccine in 1899. Jinnah's preoccupation with cleanliness, scrubbing his hands many times daily at almost obsessive length, seems to date from this pre-Haffkine era, when the only known "antidotes" to the Black Death were soap, water, and whitewash. His lifelong obsession with clean, meticulous dress as well as personal hygiene and privacy seem rather more sensible than surprising, given the humid heat and health hazards prevalent in Bombay, especially at this time. Jinnah rented a reasonable room in the Apollo Railway Hotel on Charni Road within walking distance of the high court, where he spent most of his days auditing the advocacy of others and awaiting his first client.

Virtually nothing is known of the young barrister's first three years in practice. By 1900, however, his professional promise was held "in high esteem" by a most influential "friend,"[1] who introduced him to Bombay's acting advocate-general, John Molesworth MacPherson. The latter took immediate liking to young Jinnah and invited him to work in his office. It was the first such invitation MacPherson "ever extended to an Indian," Sarojini Naidu (1879-1949), one of Jinnah's most devoted friends, recalled.[2] MacPherson's confidence and support came "as a beacon of hope" at a low point in Jinnah's early struggles to establish himself. Auntie Manbai Peerbhoy, her husband, and their circle of friends, assisted him socially, of course,[3] and having come through Lincoln's Inn gave him the proper credentials; but MacPherson did for Jinnah's legal career what Croft had done for his life—removed it from the humdrum realm of local competition to a more exalted plateau of power and possibility. In MacPherson's chambers Jinnah had access to information long before it reached the ears of penurious pleaders plodding through dim corridors of the court. Within a few months of going to work for MacPherson, he learned, for example, that one of Bombay's four magistracies (a municipal judgeship) was about to fall vacant. His response to the acquisition of this valuable news offers a glimpse of young Jinnah in action. "Gazing through the window and smoking a cigarette" in the advocate-general's office, Jinnah saw a "Victoria cab . . . slowly passing by," rushed outside, and "jumped into it and drove straight to the office of Sir Charles Ollivant."[4] Sir Charles was then judicial member of the provincial government of Bombay and found MacPherson's handsome ambitious young assistant so impressive that he hired him to serve as "temporary" third presidency magistrate.

Jinnah sat for six months on the municipal bench, hearing every sort of petty criminal case, from charges brought against two Muslim "opium eaters" from Basra of concealing their dope under their turbans, to complaints by the Great Indian Peninsula Railway brought against riders accused of failing to pay any fare, to accusations against ordinary Chinese seamen for refusing to work on their ships while in port. Jinnah proved himself fair and fearless as a judge but found the Bench a much less attractive professional prospect than the Bar. Was it the pugnacity of youth that made advocacy more fascinating for him? Or the lure of more lucrative rewards? Fame as well as fortune went to great barristers, of course, and Jinnah longed for both. When Sir Charles offered him a permanent place on the bench, therefore, at the perfectly respectable starting salary of 1,500 rupees a month in 1901, Jinnah declined, replying, "I will soon be able to earn that much in a single day."[5] As soon he did.

The dawn of the Edwardian era, coinciding with that of the twentieth century, found Jinnah firmly established in his chosen career, earning enough money to rent a "new office." He "spared no expense" to furnish that "elegant and attractive chamber," his sister recalled, in a manner which "any lawyer would have been proud to call his own."[6] Jinnahbhai Poonja's health had declined with his business fortune, and so the old man moved with his remaining children to Bombay, renting a small house in the Khoja district of *Khajak*. Jinnah appears not to have seen much of his father in this interlude, however, and by 1904 Jinnahbhai moved off to Bombay's Ratnagiri coast, where he spent his final years in quiet retirement. The only sibling with whom Jinnah established a close, continuing relationship was Fatima, who enrolled as a boarding student in Bombay's Bandra Convent School thanks to her brother's munificent support. Mission schools were still the best primary and secondary centers of education in India at this time, and because of her excellent early education Fatima was able to gain admission to the highly competitive University of Calcutta, where she attended the Dental School. Jinnah visited his adoring sister on Sundays, taking her for carriage rides around Bombay which she learned to love as much as her brother. Almost as tall and lean as he, Fatima's appearance was an arresting replica of her brother's, the noble brow as high, the cheek bones as prominent, the luminous eyes as wide and probing, and the hair, initially as warm and raven black, would later become just as coldly white.

Though religion never played an important role in Jinnah's life—except for its political significance—he left the Aga Khan's "Sevener" Khoja community at this stage of his maturation, opting instead to join the less hierarchically structured *Isna 'Ashari* sect of "Twelver" Khojas, who acknowledged no leader. One of Jinnah's most admired Bombay friends, Justice Badruddin Tyabji (1844–1906), first Muslim high court judge and third president of the Indian National Congress, was an *Isna Ashari*. Tyabji, like Jinnah, was a secular liberal modernist, who argued in his presidential address to the Madras Congress: "I, for one, am utterly at a loss to understand why Mussulmans should not work shoulder to shoulder with their fellow-countrymen, of other races and creeds, for the common benefit of all . . . this is the principle on which we, in the Bombay Presidency, have always acted."[7] Jinnah's other closest friends and admired elders in Bombay were Parsis, Hindus, and Christians, none of whom took their respective religions as seriously as their faith in British law and Indian nationalism.

Most of the leaders of the one-fourth of British India's population that adhered to Islam, however, were either orthodox (Sunni) fundamentalists, who continued to look to the *Qur'an* and prophetic practices as their twin sources of appropriate daily behavior, or modernist disciples of Sir Sayyid Ahmad Khan (1817–98), who rejected Congress's claim to institutional direction of a single united Indian national movement as vigorously as they denied Islamic orthodoxy's infallibility. In 1875, a decade before the Indian National Congress was founded, Sir Sayyid started his potent Muhammadan

Anglo-Oriental College at Aligarh, some sixty miles southeast of Delhi. Modeled on the Oxbridge residential and tutorial collegiate system, Aligarh taught generations of wealthy young Muslim males of British India Western science, moral philosophy, and the dual virtue of loyalty to the British raj as well as to Islam. Aligarh's cricket fields and commons rooms served as breeding grounds for the Muslim League. Sir Sayyid himself, knighted in 1870, devoted his mature life to service in the British Empire. Appointed by the viceroy to his Imperial Legislative Council, Sir Sayyid argued from that powerful platform in 1883 against "the introduction of the principle of election, pure and simple" into the body politic of "a country like India, where caste distinctions still flourish, where there is no fusion of the various races, where religious distinctions are still violent."[8] A decade later he denounced the "aims and objects" of Congress as "based upon ignorance of history and present-day realities; they do not take into consideration that India is inhabited by different nationalities; they presuppose that the Muslims like the Marhattas, the Brahmins, the Kshatriyas . . . can all be treated alike, and all of them belong to the same nation."[9] That was the earliest modern articulation of the two-nation theory, which was to become the ideological basis for Pakistan.

Barrister Jinnah of Bombay remained as remote from such feelings, as out of tune with such reasoning, as he had been in London in 1893, when Sir Sayyid first spoke of Hindus and Muslims as "different nationalities." Jinnah's universe at this time was the law, though his singular success as an advocate was not unrelated to his acting talent. "He was what God made him," a fellow barrister of Bombay's high court put it, "a *great* pleader. He had a sixth sense: he could see around corners. That is where his talents lay . . . he was a very clear thinker. . . . But he drove his points home— points chosen with exquisite selection—slow delivery, word by word."[10] Another contemporary noted, "When he stood up in Court, slowly looking towards the judge, placing his monocle in his eye—with the sense of timing you would expect from an actor—he became omnipotent. Yes, that is the word—*omnipotent.*" Joachim Alva said he "cast a spell on the court-room . . . head erect, unruffled by the worst circumstances. He has been our boldest advocate."[11] Jinnah's most famous legal apprentice, M. C. Chagla, the first Indian Muslim appointed chief justice of Bombay's high court, reminisced that his leader's "presentation of a case" was nothing less than "a piece of art."[12]

In politics, Jinnah's heroes remained Dadabhai Naoroji and another brilliant leader of Bombay's Parsi community, Sir Pherozeshah Mehta (1845–1915), in whose chambers he worked for some time during this early interlude. Mehta presided over the Congress in 1890 and stressed the role of all minorities in India's nation-building process. "To my mind, a Parsi is a better and a truer Parsi, as a Mahomedan or a Hindu is a better and truer Mahomedan or Hindu, the more he is attached to the land which gave him birth," Sir Pherozeshah insisted. "Is it possible to imagine that Dadabhai Naoroji, for instance, true Parsi that he is, is anything but an Indian? . . . Can any one doubt, if I may be allowed to take another illustration, that Sir Syed Ahmed Khan was greater and nobler when he was devoting the great energies and talents with which he is endowed . . . for the benefit of all Indians in general, than when, as of late, he was preaching a gospel of selfishness and isolation?"[13] Mehta was India's first Parsi barrister, called to the Bar from Lincoln's Inn in 1868, and served as a member of Bombay's Municipal Corporation for forty-six years, four times in its chair. Elegant, imperious, a fierce advocate, hailed as "Uncrowned King of Bombay," Sir Perozeshah was more the Bombay model for Jinnah's early career than Dadabhai. In 1890 he labeled the "supposed rivalry" between Hindus and Muslims nothing more than "a convenient decoy to distract attention and to defer the day of reform."[14] Young Jinnah felt much the same way.

The first annual session of Congress attended by Jinnah was its twentieth, held under canvas on Bombay's Oval in December 1904. Sir Pherozeshah chaired the reception committee, his welcoming "remarks" taking longer than Sir Henry Cotton's entire presidential address, indicative of their relative positions within the Congress as well as their rhetorical styles. Responding to Viceroy Lord Curzon's patronizing advice, "I do not think that the salvation of India is to be sought in the field of politics," Mehta asked, "How can these aspirations and desires be even gradually achieved, unless we are allowed to play at all times a modest and temperate part on the field of politics?"[15] Surely not through the "dubious labors" of British India's "secret and irresponsible bureaucracy," argued Mehta, agreeing with Walter Bagehot that all bureaucracy tended to "under-government in point of quality" and "over-government in point of quantity."[16] Mehta proposed that two of his trusted disciples from Bombay be sent as Congress deputies to London the following year to lobby what he and other well-informed observers of Britain's political climate correctly anticipated would be the new Liberal government in Westminster and Whitehall. His choices for so important a task were Gopal Krishna Gokhale (1866–1915) and M. A. Jinnah. Mahatma ("Great-Souled") Gokhale, who was to preside over the next session of Congress, seemed an obvious choice to everyone, but Jinnah was still unknown to most Congress delegates, and enough questions were raised to hold up release of any funds for his passage.[17] He did, however, sail to England with Gokhale eight years later, when both were appointed to the same royal commission. The 1904 Congress was Jinnah's first meeting with Gokhale, whose wisdom, fairness, and moderation he came to admire so that he soon stated his "fond ambition" in politics was to become "the Muslim Gokhale."[18]

Jinnah's involvement in Congress politics was as integral a by-product of his flourishing legal career and social life in Bombay as his earlier commitment to Dadabhai had been in London. Lord Curzon's paternalistic viceroyalty helped to stimulate growing political impatience among India's swiftly expanding pool of educated young men, fired with the liberty-loving ideals of British literature while faced with the depressing realities of Indian unemployment, political dependence, and abysmal poverty. Internationally, 1905 was a year of revolutionary surprises. Japan's electrifying victory over Russia's titanic fleet, the Petersburg Revolution that moved the tsar to appoint a representative duma, the Chinese boycott of British goods in many port cities, and Britain's turbulent national election that ushered in a decade of Liberal party rule in London, sent shock waves of excitement throughout the Indian subcontinent. Internally, the most dramatic and far-reaching act during Lord Curzon's half decade of viceregal rule was the partition of Bengal, British India's premier province.

With a population of over 85 million, Bengal was certainly "unwieldy" to administer, but the line drawn to divide it ran through the Bengali-speaking "nation" of that sprawling province, dividing its predominantly Hindu Bengali-speakers in the West from the mostly poorer Muslim Bengali-speakers east of Calcutta. A new Muslim-majority province, Eastern Bengal and Assam, was created with its capital in Dacca. West Bengal, administered from Calcutta, continued to have a Hindu majority but contained so many Bihari and Oriya-speaking people that it no longer had a Bengali-speaking Hindu majority. Calcutta's Bengali Hindu elite, who had been Curzon's loudest critics since 1903, viewed this partition of their "motherland" as British *divide et impera* with a vengeance. The half decade of violent anti-partition agitation that started in Calcutta's crowded bazaars and narrow alleys spread fires of national protest and boycott against British goods across India to ignite Bombay, Poona, Madras, and Lahore. Millions of Indians hitherto untouched by political demands were politicized by the impassioned anti-government speeches and actions of Bengal's revolutionaries, who left British classrooms by the thousands to march through Calcutta's streets singing the Congress's new anthem "Bande Mataram" ("Hail To Thee, Mother") with clenched fists held high.

Jinnah personally voiced no traceable reaction to Bengal's first partition, though the political impact of its explosive aftershock was to change his life as much as it altered the map of India. As a Congress moderate, friend, and disciple, he must have agreed, however, with President Gokhale's characterization of partition as "a cruel wrong, . . . a complete illustration of the

worst features of the present system of bureaucratic rule—its utter contempt
for public opinion, its arrogant pretentions to superior wisdom, its reckless
disregard of the most cherished feelings of the people."[19] As a Bombay
Muslim, however, Jinnah was perhaps most remote among all subsets of
Indian nationalists from the feelings of outrage and betrayal shared by so
many Bengali Hindus. He well understood, of course, how shrewd a British
political move this was, weaning Bengali Muslims from dependence on Calcutta's landlord and moneylending as well as political Hindu leadership, ex-
alting sleepy little Dacca to equal provincial status with Calcutta, Bombay,
and Madras. That first partition ignited Muslim political consciousness
throughout the subcontinent, providing a provincial cradle in Dacca for the
birth of the Muslim League in 1906.

Curzon's successor, Lord Minto (1845–1914), was also a Tory, entrenched
in Calcutta shortly before the British general elections that would depose his
party from power in London for the next decade. Paradoxically, British
India's Liberal secretary of state, John Morley, contributed as much as
Minto did to dividing the empire he ruled from 1906 to 1910 by promising,
for the noblest of reasons, to initiate parliamentary constitutional reforms
soon after he took Whitehall's helm. Morley's council reforms, intended to
liberalize and expand the base of secular representative popular government
throughout India, planted the seeds of religious partition in the heart of
British India's emerging constitution.

On October 1, 1906, thirty-five Muslims of noble birth, wealth, and
power, from every province of British India and several princely states,
gathered in the regal ballroom of the viceroy's Simla palace in the Hima-
layas. The fourth earl of Minto, an avid horseman nicknamed "Mr. Rolly,"
entered precisely at 11:00 A.M., the Aga Khan introduced each of his fellow
deputies to the viceroy, and then Lord Minto read aloud the address, which
was printed on vellum and had earlier been sent to his secretary, J. R. Dunlop Smith (1858–1921). The address contained a warning that

> The Mohamedans of India have always placed implicit reliance on the
> sense of justice and love of fair dealing that have characterised their
> rulers, and have in consequence abstained from pressing their claims
> by methods that might prove at all embarrassing, but earnestly as we
> desire that the Mohamedans of India should not in the future depart
> from that excellent and time-honoured tradition, recent events have
> stirred up feelings, especially among the younger generation of Mo-
> hamedans, which might, in certain circumstances and under certain
> contingencies, easily pass beyond the control of temperate counsel
> and sober guidance.[20]

And none of the ominous implications of that warning were lost upon the viceroy or his staff.

> We hope your Excellency will pardon our stating at the outset that representative institutions of the European type are new to the Indian people; many of the most thoughtful members of our community in fact consider that the greatest care, forethought and caution will be necessary if they are to be successfully adapted to the social, religious and political conditions obtaining in India, and that in the absence of such care and caution their adoption is likely, among other evils, to place our national interests at the mercy of an unsympathetic majority.

This was the first use of the words "national interests" by Indian Muslims in appealing to British rulers for help against the "unsympathetic" Hindu majority. The address went on to spell out Muslim hopes for more positions within every branch of government service, arguing: "We Mohamedans are a distinct community with additional interests of our own which are not shared by other communities, and these have hitherto suffered from the fact that they have not been adequately represented. . . . We therefore pray that Government will be graciously pleased to provide that both in the gazetted and the subordinate and ministerial services of all Indian provinces a due proportion of Mohamedans shall always find place." Thanks to increased educational opportunity, "the number of qualified Mohamedans has increased," but "the efforts of Mohamedan educationists have from the very outset of the educational movement among them been strenuously directed towards the development of character, and this we venture to think is of greater importance than mere mental alertness in the making of a good public servant." Separate seats for Muslims were requested to be reserved on viceregal and provincial councils, high court benches, and municipalities, as well as on university senates and syndicates.

The deputation received a "hearty welcome" from Minto. He praised Aligarh and its student body, "strong in the tenets of their own religion, strong in the precepts of loyalty and patriotism." He congratulated the deputation for the "loyalty, common-sense and sound reasoning so eloquently expressed in your address." He also thanked the Muslims of Eastern Bengal and Assam "for the moderation and self-restraint they have shown" in the wake of partition, promising them they could rely as firmly as ever on "British justice and fair play." Since he shared none of Morley's deep-rooted Liberal democratic convictions and was a conservative landlord himself, Minto assured his aristocratic audience that "I should be very far from welcoming all the political machinery of the Western world amongst the hereditary instincts and traditions of Eastern races."

> Finally, Minto announced that "any electoral representation in India
> would be doomed to mischievous failure which aimed at granting a
> personal enfranchisement, regardless of the beliefs and traditions of
> the communities composing the population of this continent . . . the
> Mahomedan community may rest assured that their political rights
> and interests as a community will be safeguarded by any administrative re-organization with which I am concerned."

The viceroy's remarks were greeted with "murmurs of satisfaction" and cries of "hear, hear" from the delighted deputation. At a garden tea party that afternoon, delegates assured Lady Minto that "now we feel the Viceroy is our friend." Minto and Dunlop Smith considered it a most important day's work, and it was probably the latter who told Her Ladyship that evening that he viewed it as "nothing less than the pulling back of sixty-two millions of people from joining the ranks of the seditious opposition."[21] Calcutta's leading nationalist newspaper, *Amrita Bazar Patrika*, reported the deputation and its reception as "a got-up affair . . . fully engineered by interested officials . . . to whitewash their doings . . . the authorities wanted a few simple-minded men of position to give them a certificate of good conduct. They knew the Hindus would not do it, so they began operation among the older classes of Mussalmans."[22] Both assessments were exaggerated, though the deputation did win the promise of "separate electorates" for Muslims—a major historic landmark on the road to Pakistan. From the nucleus of that Simla deputation, however, the Muslim League would be born before the year's end. Jinnah, who had so recently quit the Aga Khan's Isma'ili fold, had nothing to do with the Muslim deputation or its historic Dacca aftermath.

In November, Salimullah Khan, the leading landowner of Dacca, whose vast holdings won him the title "Nawab," invited Aligarh's Mohammedan Educational Conference to Dacca for its annual meeting, suggesting at the same time that a "Muslim All-India Confederacy" be convened in his city. The "Nawab of Dacca" had been "sick" during the Simla meeting but chaired the reception committee for the founding meeting of the Muslim League in Dacca's *Shah Bagh* ("Royal Garden") on December 30, 1906. Sleepy Dacca's backwater thus suddenly emerged as *the* center of South Asian Muslim politics, hosting fifty-eight Muslim delegates from every corner of the subcontinent.

"The Musalmans are only a fifth in number as compared with the total population of the country," noted the Muslim League's first president, Nawab Viqar-ul-Mulk Mushtaq Hussain (1841–1917), of Hyderabad, and it is manifest that if at any remote period the British Government ceases to exist in India, then the rule of India would pass into the hands of that community which is nearly four times as large as ourselves. Now, gentlemen, let each of you consider what will be your condition if such a situation is created in India. Then, our life, our property, our honour, and our faith will all be in great danger. When even now that a powerful British administration is protecting its subjects, we the Musalmans have to face most serious difficulties in safeguarding our interests from the grasping hands of our neighbours . . . woe betide the time when we become the subjects of our neighbours. . . . And to prevent the realization of such aspirations on the part of our neighbours, the Musalmans cannot find better and surer means than to congregate under the banner of Great Britain, and to devote their lives and property in its protection.[23]

Thus founded by conservative loyalist Muslim nobility, frank in their confession that British imperial protection was indispensable to their continued well-being, if not sheer survival, the Muslim League emerged without stated nationalist ambitions. "It is through regard for our own lives and property, our own honour and religion, that we are impelled to be faithful to the Government . . . our own prosperity is bound up with, and depends upon our loyalty to British rule in India," President Hussain frankly admitted. He was, after all, reared in the autocratic service of the nizam of Hyderabad, who permitted no political agitation, tolerated no dissent.

I do not hesitate in declaring that unless the leaders of the Congress make sincere efforts as speedily as possible to quell the hostility against the Government and the British race, . . . the necessary consequence of all that is being openly done and said to-day will be that sedition would be rampant, and the Mussalmans of India would be called upon to perform the necessary duty of combating this rebellious spirit, side by side with the British Government, more effectively than by the mere use of words.[24]

Nawab Salimullah Khan moved four resolutions in Dacca, all carried unanimously, creating the "Muslim League." Destined to remain Muslim India's major political organization, emerging in less than four decades as standard-bearer for Pakistan, the League was created to "protect and advance the political rights and interests of the Musalmans of India, and to respectfully represent their needs and aspirations to the Government."[25] The nawab of Dacca called it "a turning of a corner of the course" set two decades earlier by Sir Sayyid Ahmad Khan when he founded his Muhammadan Educational Conference.

The Aga Khan was elected first honorary president of the Muslim

League, though he did not attend the Dacca inaugural session, and later
wrote it was "freakishly ironic" that "our doughtiest opponent in 1906" was
Jinnah, who "came out in bitter hostility toward all that I and my friends
had done and were trying to do. He was the only well-known Muslim to
take this attitude. . . . He said that our principle of separate electorates
was dividing the nation against itself."[26]

Jinnah had joined forty-four other like-minded Muslims in neighboring
Calcutta, meeting together with some 1,500 Hindus, Parsis, and Christians
at the 1906 annual session of Congress. Dadabhai Naoroji presided with
Jinnah serving as his secretary. Old Dadabhai was too weak to read the
address himself that Jinnah had helped write, so Gokhale read it for him,
beginning with several quotations. One, from Liberal Prime Minister
Campbell-Bannerman, called for self-government, "Good government could
never be a substitute for government by the people themselves." And as
practical immediate steps toward attainment of this goal, the Dadabhai-
Gokhale-Jinnah address "earnestly" called for employment of more Indians
in every branch of the services to help eliminate the "three-fold wrong" in-
flicted on India by retaining so many British officers

> depriving us of wealth, work and wisdom, of everything, in short,
> worth living for. . . . Alteration of the services from European to
> Indian is the keynote of the whole. . . . Co-ordinately . . . educa-
> tion must be most vigorously disseminated among the people—free
> and compulsory primary education, and free higher education of
> every kind. . . . Education on the one hand, and actual training in
> administration on the other hand, will bring the accomplishment of
> self-government far more speedily than many imagine.[27]

Dadabhai's speech replete with quotes from Morley, included one
equating "the sacred word 'free'" with "the noblest aspirations that can
animate the breast of man." Such were the feelings and aspirations animat-
ing Jinnah as he celebrated his thirtieth birthday from the platform of India's National Congress. The speech called the Bengal partition "a bad
blunder for England," but one Dadabhai hoped "may yet be rectified"
through "agitation." And addressing himself to the growing distance between
Hindus and Muslims in the aftermath of partition, Dadabhai called for

> a thorough political union among the Indian people of all creeds
> and classes. . . . I appeal to the Indian people for this because it is
> in their own hands. . . . They have in them the capacity, energy and
> intellect, to hold their own and to get their due share in all walks of
> life—of which the State Services are but a small part. State services
> are not everything. . . . Once self-government is attained, then will

there be prosperity enough for all, but not till then. The thorough union, therefore, of all the people for their emancipation is an absolute necessity. . . . They must sink or swim together. Without this union, all efforts will be vain.[28]

This theme of national unity was to be echoed by Jinnah at every political meeting he attended during the ensuing decade, in which he emerged as India's true "Ambassador of Hindu-Muslim Unity."[29]

Jinnah first met India's poetess Sarojini Naidu at that Calcutta Congress, when he was "already accounted a rising lawyer and a coming politician, . . . fired," as she recalled, by a "virile patriotism." She was instantly captivated by his stunning appearance and "rare and complex temperament" and has left a most insightful portrait of young Jinnah.

Tall and stately, but thin to the point of emaciation, languid and luxurious of habit, Mohammad Ali Jinnah's attenuated form is a deceptive sheath of a spirit of exceptional vitality and endurance. Somewhat formal and fastidious, and a little aloof and imperious of manner, the calm hauteur of his accustomed reserve but masks, for those who know him, a naive and eager humanity, an intuition quick and tender as a woman's, a humour gay and winning as a child's—pre-eminently rational and practical, discreet and dispassionate in his estimate and acceptance of life, the obvious sanity and serenity of his worldly wisdom effectually disguise a shy and splendid idealism which is of the very essence of the man.[30]

Jinnah left Calcutta inspired with his mission of advancing the cause of Hindu-Muslim unity, perceiving as few of his contemporaries did how indispensable such unity was to the new goal of *swaraj* ("self-government") that Congress had adopted. He was politician enough to realize, of course, that his only hope of succeeding his liberal mentors and friends Dadabhai, Pherozeshah, and Gokhale as leader of Congress was by virtue of his secular constitutional national appeal, not through his double minority status. He had risen above all parochial roots and provincial prejudice, a Shakespearian hero in modern garb, with the noblest imprecations of Burke, Mill, and Morley ringing in his mind, stirring his heart. Congress's national political platform had become his new dramatic stage, grander and more exciting than Bombay's high court. In one short decade after returning from London he had virtually emerged as heir-apparent to the Bombay triumvirate which led Congress's slow-moving, political bullock-cart toward the promised land of freedom.

A more militant, revolutionary faction within Congress, led by Maharashtra's *Lokamanya* ("Friend of the People") Bal Gangadhar Tilak (1856–

1920) and Bengal's fiery Bipin Chandra Pal (1858–1932), competed, however, by then with the moderate "old guard" for control of India's premier
nationalist organization. Though Tilak and Gokhale both started as Poona
colleagues in public education and national service, they differed fundamentally in many ways, especially with respect to political tactics and philosophy. The *Lokamanya* and his "new party" had no faith in Morley's
promised reforms, rejecting reliance on "pleas or petitions" to British officialdom for anything. *Boycott* was their battle cry—first of British machine-
made cloth and other manufactured imports, later of all British institutions,
including schools, courts, and council chambers. The other side of their
economic plank of boycott was *swadeshi* ("of our own country"), stimulating indigenous Indian industry, especially cotton cloth woven and spun both
by hand and machine. They made *swaraj* their goal, but the "self-rule" they
demanded was not that of British citizens but of totally independent Indians. The symbols popularized by Tilak in rousing the mass following he
won among mostly illiterate peasants and urban workers were drawn from
the religious ocean of Hinduism and regional lore, and usually served to
alienate Muslim and other minorities as it won Hindu adherents. British
officials on the spot vainly tried harsher techniques of repression to silence
this mounting opposition—"Pills for the Earthquake," Morley called that
method of dealing with nationalism. The most popular leaders were arrested
and deported, including a new "martyr" from the Punjab, Lala Lajpat Rai
(1865–1928), who became a hero as soon as he was arrested in the spring
of 1907 and shipped off to Mandalay prison. The new party immediately
proposed Lajpat Rai as their candidate for next president of Congress.
Pherozeshah and Gokhale had their own candidate, however, the mild-
mannered moderate Calcutta educator, Dr. Rash Behari Ghosh.

The factional split that left Congress torn apart for almost a decade exploded at the session in Surat in 1907. Next to Bombay, which had so recently hosted the Congress, Surat was the strongest bastion of moderate
leadership power, Gujarat's center of mercantile wealth. Sir Pherozeshah felt
confident that he could keep the peace and control of his organization in
the port of Surat. He had, however, underestimated the passion and stubbornness of Tilak and his followers. As Rash Behari Ghosh moved toward the
rostrum inside the Congress pandal to read his presidential address, Tilak
rose to shout, "Point of order." He had indicated earlier his intention of
introducing Lajpat Rai's candidacy from the Congress floor. No one on the
platform "recognized" him, however, yet that did not stop the *Lokamanya*.
He mounted the platform himself and headed for the rostrum. Several tough
young "guards" moved to intercept Tilak, but Gokhale warded them off,
jumping to his old colleague's defense and protectively extending his own

arms around Tilak's body. Most of the delegates were on their feet, shouting and gesturing. A stiff Maharashtrian slipper was then tossed vigorously onto the stage, hitting both Pherozeshah and Bengal's venerable Surendranath Banerjea (1848–1926). Panic and pandemonium ensued. The tent had to be cleared by police and hired guards. For the next nine years Congress remained divided into angrily conflicting moderate and revolutionary parties, each claiming to be sole rightful heir to India's national movement.

In the wake of the Surat split, revolutionary violence and official repression intensified. Tilak was arrested in the summer of 1908, charged with "seditious writings" for several editorials published in his popular Poona newspaper, *Kesari*. Tilak represented himself before the high court in Bombay, but immediately after his arrest when he was held without bail, he secured the services of Jinnah to plead for his release pending trial. Jinnah argued valiantly but to no avail, for British justice had closed its mind to Tilak long before his trial began. And although Jinnah's argument fell on deaf ears, it attests at once to his brilliance as a barrister and the strength of his national leadership potential. A pettier man might have found some excuse for refusing to plead on behalf of the leader of a political party opposing his own. Jinnah, however, not only stood up for Tilak at this juncture but defended him on another charge of sedition in 1916 and won, thus earning the gratitude as well as affectionate admiration of Hindu India's foremost conservative leader.

The legislative council reforms proposed by Morley and Minto initially provided for four separately elected Muslim members on the expanded Imperial Council of the Viceroy. By the time the Indian council's bill was finished in 1909, however, no fewer than six such seats were reserved on a central legislative council of sixty, more than half of whom remained British officials. Minto, moreover, had promised to "appoint" at least two additional Muslim members as nominees off his own bat if they were not elected by special constituencies such as landholders or municipalities, raising Muslim membership to eight out of twenty-eight non-official members on the viceroy's council, more than the actual ratio of India's Muslim minority to the total population of the subcontinent. By 1909 even Minto complained of "the excess of representation granted to Mahomedans."[31] Morley retorted, "It was *your* early speech about their extra claims that started the M. [Muslim] hare."[32] The secretary of state was by then convinced that "It passes the wit of man to frame plans that will please Hindus without offending Mahometans, and we shall be lucky if we don't offend *both*."

The separate electorate formula, which Jinnah initially rejected on grounds of national principle, served, in fact, to raise his personal consciousness of Muslim identity. Jinnah was one of the first half dozen Muslim members specially elected, in his case from Bombay, to sit on the viceroy's Central Legislative Council in 1910, three years before he actually joined the Muslim League. At thirty-five, he was one of the youngest members elected to that high council and would have stood no chance but for the fact that two much older knighted Muslim candidates, equally matched and antipathetical, ousted one another in preliminary skirmishes to choose the "Muslim candidate." Jinnah's secretary recalled that "Discussions went on for hours and in the end both of them decided that none of them should seek election, but should send a third candidate, and after careful scrutiny the choice fell on the 'young lawyer.' "[33] That singular honor catapulted Jinnah to the side of Gokhale, whose "general" Bombay seat had been held before him by Sir Pherozeshah. The legislative center of India's government, first in Calcutta and Simla, later in Delhi, soon became one of Jinnah's most important and powerful stages.

Morley's reforms also introduced Indian participation in British India's powerful executive councils, both at Whitehall and in Calcutta-Simla. Two Indian members were appointed to the secretary of state's Whitehall Council of India in 1907, and the first Indian to hold the post of law member of the government of India, Satyendra P. Sinha (1864–1928), took his seat in 1909. A Hindu Brahman by birth, Sinha was, like Jinnah, a barrister and moderate Congress leader. His legal practice in 1908 was so lucrative that accepting the government's invitation meant a cut in his annual income of £10,000. Sinha's first inclination, therefore, was to turn down the viceroy's invitation, but Jinnah and Gokhale convinced him to accept the job. His role in this matter further attests to Jinnah's strong personal commitment to the principle of finding the candidate best qualified for any job, regardless of race, religion, caste, or creed. Muslim League leaders had lobbied for a Muslim jurist to fill that powerful position in India's central government. The League's president at its 1908 Amritsar session, Syed Ali Imam (1869–1933), was himself a barrister of London's Middle Temple and would succeed Sinha as law member after the former resigned in November 1910, establishing the precedent of alternating Hindu Muslim appointees and subsequent communal parity in all executive appointments. Born as the League was out of the separate electorate Muslim "affirmative action" demand, that organization remained most firmly committed to its founding principle, proposing names of Muslim candidates for every important official vacancy. Congress, on the other hand, always viewed this principle as anti-national and undemocratic, even as English liberals like John Morley did. Any "religious register," after all, whether Muslim, Catholic, or Calvinist, was dangerously subversive to the egalitarian foundations of a modern secular nation. Barrister Jinnah believed that as much as his great bencher mentor had and was to rise in the Allahabad Congress of 1910 to second a resolution that "strongly deprecates the expansion or application of the principle of Separate Communal Electorates to Municipalities, District Boards, or other Local Bodies."[34]

Paradoxically, Jinnah spoke at the end of his first year as the Calcutta council's Muslim member from Bombay.

3

Calcutta
(1910-15)

On January 25, 1910, the Honourable Mr. M. A. Jinnah took his seat as
"Muslim member from Bombay" on the sixty-man legislative council con-
vened in the capital of British India. The old council chamber in the palace
Lord Wellesley had built more than a century earlier was freshly gilded for
this historic meeting, filled to capacity with bejewelled visitors as Viceroy
Minto pompously addressed his government's newly elected advisers, in-
cluding Gopal Gokhale, Motilal Nehru, Surendranath Banerjea, and M. A.
Jinnah, predicting, "I am glad to believe that the support of an enlarged
Council will go far to assure the Indian public of the soundness of any
measures we may deem it right to introduce."[1]

Minto's pious hopes were soon shattered. Jinnah clashed with the viceroy
the very first time he rose to speak in the council, addressing himself to a
resolution that called for an immediate end to the export of indentured Indian laborers to South Africa. The violent repression of *Satyagrahis* ("Non-
cooperators") led by Gandhi in the Transvaal had ignited feelings of indignation and grief throughout India the year before. Congress then resolved
to "press upon the Government of India the necessity of prohibiting the
recruitment of indentured Indian labour for any portion of the South African
Union, and of dealing with the authorities there in the same manner in
which the latter deal with Indian interests."[2] This matter came before Calcutta's council on February 25, when Jinnah spoke out saying: "It is a most
painful question—a question which has roused the feelings of all classes in
the country to the highest pitch of indignation and horror at the harsh and
cruel treatment that is meted out to Indians in South Africa."[3] Minto reprimanded him for using the words "cruel treatment," which the viceroy
deemed "too harsh to be used for a friendly part of the Empire" within his

council chambers. "My Lord!" Jinnah responded. "I should feel much inclined to use much stronger language. But I am fully aware of the constitution of this Council, and I do not wish to trespass for one single moment. But I do say that the treatment meted out to Indians is the harshest and the feeling in this country is unanimous."

That first brief exchange reflected Jinnah's courtroom as well as council style. He always chose his words carefully and never retracted any once uttered. His critics, whether judges, viceroys, or pandits usually received humiliating tongue lashings for any barb aimed at him. He was not known to sit silent for the slightest reprimand, honing his razor-sharp mind and words on the generally duller weapons of logic or wit drawn against them. Lord Minto, appalled at Jinnah's response, was struck dumb by it. "Mr. Rolly" left India that summer, replaced by a much sharper Liberal statesman, Sir Charles Hardinge (1858–1944), who became one of Jinnah's foremost official admirers. A career diplomat by training, Hardinge's sophistication and intelligence set a new tone of urbanity and responsibility in Calcutta's council. He was John Morley's choice for India. Lord Kitchener, then commander-in-chief of the Indian army, had lobbied energetically for the viceroyalty he coveted, but when King Edward VII died in May 1910, Kitchener lost his most powerful ally. Morley offered India to Hardinge at the royal funeral. The new viceroy was quick to recognize, shortly after reaching Calcutta, how debilitating a thorn Bengal's partition remained in his new domain's body politic. His first major policy recommendation to Morley's successor at Whitehall, Lord Crewe (1858–1945), was to reunite Bengal, creating the separate province of Bihar and Orissa at the same time.

On March 17, 1911, Jinnah introduced his first legislative measure, the Wakf (tax-exempt Muslim endowments) Validating Bill that was to emerge two years later as the very first non-officially sponsored act in British Indian history. London's privy council had invalidated testamentary gifts of Muslim property left in tax-free "trusts" (wakfs) for ultimate reversion to religious charity in 1894. Jinnah called for legislative reversal of that decision charging it was "opposed to the fundamental principles of Islamic Jurisprudence."[4] Probate law became Jinnah's most lucrative special field of knowledge and legal interest, one he remained master of at least until 1941, as is attested by his handsome leather-bound set of probate court law reports from 1888–1941, still preserved in his Wazir mansion library in Karachi. His probate clients were to include many of India's wealthiest princes, among them the nizam of Hyderabad, the nawab of Bhopal, and the raja of Mahmudabad.

Even as Bengal's partition did so much to help create the League, King George's surprise announcement in Delhi that partition was annulled in December 1911 jolted that organization out of its loyalist rut. The nawab of

Dacca read in Britain's reversal of partition, the government of India's capitulation to Congress "agitators," and a simple new message to all Indians—"No bombs, no boons!" Together with his announced annulment of partition, King George V proclaimed his government's decision to shift the capital of British India from Calcutta to Delhi's historic plain, where a new imperial city was to be built. Delhi had been the capital of Muslim sultans and Mughal emperors, who reigned over most of the subcontinent since the early thirteenth century. Delhi remained at the hub of North India's Muslim population, educational centers, and historic monuments, within easy reach of Lahore, Agra, Deoband, Aligarh, and Lucknow. On December 23, 1912, however, when Lord Hardinge passed through Delhi's Chandni Chawk ("Silver Market") atop the elephant leading a viceregal procession to the new capital, Delhi almost became that viceroy's graveyard. A bomb hurled into Hardinge's howdah, killed one of his guards, and lacerated the Viceroy's back, exposing the shoulder blade. The would-be assassin of one of India's most popular viceroys was never apprehended.

Jinnah attended the annual meeting of Congress as well as the council meeting of the Muslim League, both held in Bankipur in December of 1912. He had not as yet actually joined the League but was permitted to speak to its council at Bankipur, supporting a resolution that expanded the League's goals to include "the attainment of a system of self-government suitable to India," to be brought about "through constitutional means, a steady reform of the existing system of administration; by promoting national unity and fostering public spirit among the people of India, and by co-operating with other communities for the said purposes."[5] A few months later he went to Lucknow, joining Mrs. Naidu on the platform as an honored guest at the larger League meeting, where a new more liberal constitution was adopted. President Shafi in presenting the new constitution noted that "I am in entire accord with my friend the Hon'ble Mr. Jinnah in thinking that the adoption of any course other than the one proposed by the Council would be absolutely unwise."[6] The League's first resolution congratulated "the Hon. Mr. M. A. Jinnah for his skillful piloting" of the Wakf Validating Act through the Imperial Legislative Council. Faced with such acclaim, Jinnah could hardly resist renewed appeals to join the Muslim League pressed upon him that year by its new permanent secretary, Syed Wazir Hasan (1874–1947), and Maulana Mohammad Ali (1878–1931), revered Pan-Islamic alim and editor of *Comrade*, both of whom were deputed to London to lobby there for Muslim demands. Jinnah did agree to join in 1913, but he insisted as a prior condition that his "loyalty to the Muslim League and the Muslim interest would in no way and at no time imply even the shadow of disloyalty to the larger national cause to which his life was dedicated."[7]

In April 1913, Jinnah and Gokhale sailed together from Bombay for Liverpool to meet with Lord Islington, under secretary of state for India and chairman of their Royal Public Services Commission, on which Ramsay MacDonald (1866–1937) also served. That leisurely trip was their longest interlude alone, but no record was preserved by either of the subjects they discussed, though the commission agenda, general council reforms, and ways of attaining Hindu-Muslim unity and ultimately of achieving Indian independence were surely among them. Gokhale later told Sarojini, who often visited him at his Servants of India Society in Poona before he died, that Jinnah "has true stuff in him, and that freedom from all sectarian prejudice which will make him the best ambassador of Hindu-Muslim Unity."[8] How ironic that prediction sounds, yet in his late thirties Jinnah seems to have personified that tragically elusive spirit of communal unity.

Jinnah returned to India in September 1913 and attended the Karachi Congress two days after celebrating his thirty-seventh birthday. He had not visited his place of birth for over seventeen years, and he now warmly expressed his pleasure at finding a number of "personal friends with whom I played in my boyhood."[9] He drafted and moved a resolution for reconstructing the Council of India that called first of all for charging the salary of the secretary of state and his department to the English Home rather than Indian budget, thereby seeking to save Indian taxpayers the burden of maintaining Whitehall's entire English staff. The new council, Jinnah argued, should consist of not fewer than nine members, at least one-third of whom should be "non-official Indians chosen by a constituency consisting of the elected members of the Imperial and Provincial Legislative Councils."[10] Half of the remaining nominated members of the council should be "public men of merit and ability" unconnected with Indian affairs, the other half, ex-Indian officials with at least ten years of Indian experience, no more than two years old. The council was to be purely advisory rather than administrative, and tenure on it would be limited to five years. Thanks to his work on this resolution, and indicative of his rising position of leadership within Congress, Jinnah was chosen to chair a Congress deputation to London in the spring of 1914 to lobby members of Parliament and Whitehall on Lord Crewe's own proposed new Council of India Bill. Jinnah also seconded a Karachi Congress resolution, congratulating the League for adopting "the ideal of Self-Government for India within the British Empire," and expressing "complete accord with the belief that the League has so emphatically declared at its last sessions that the political future of the country depends on the harmonious working and co-operation of the various communities in the country."[11]

From Karachi, Jinnah entrained for Agra, where the Muslim League met on December 30–31, 1913, in the former twin capital of the Mughal Empire. He was busily at work seeking a formula for bringing his two political organizations together on a single national platform. His position was unique, for not only did he belong to Congress and the Muslim League, but he was also inside the government's camp, both in London and Calcutta. Not even Gokhale or Sir Pherozeshah were as strategically positioned to hear all the views on the major issues affecting India's political future. At the Agra session of the League, Jinnah proposed postponing reaffirmation of faith in the principle of "communal representation" for another year, urging his coreligionists that such special representation would only divide India into "two watertight compartments."[12] Congress had just deferred action on that question, and Jinnah explained there were "many other reasons" for his urging postponement upon the League, though he "could not give any of these reasons in public." The latter probably alluded to his shipboard conversations with Gokhale or London talks with Wedderburn and other M. P.s of the British Committee of Congress. At any event he was obviously pursuing a joint platform, such as the one he would help fashion for Lucknow in 1916. The Muslim League voted, however, to reject Jinnah's first formal appeal to them, deeming the principle of their affirmative action separate electorate formula "absolutely necessary" to the League's immediate future. It was one issue on which a majority of the League's members would long remain at odds with Jinnah.

He sailed again for London in April of 1914. Other members of Jinnah's prestigious deputation included Congress's Bengali president-elect, Bhupendra Nath Basu (1859–1924), and Lal Lajpat Rai, who arrived a few weeks later. Lord Crewe met with the Congress deputation soon after they arrived, finding Jinnah "the best talker of the pack," though he considered him "artful" for having "remarked (as it were casually) that they would be glad if dissents in my council now be recorded and laid before Parliament on the motion of a Member."[13]

By historic coincidence, Jinnah and Mohandas K. Gandhi (1869–1948) were both in London at the start of World War I. Barrister Gandhi had gone to Natal in 1893 to work for an Indian Muslim trading company in South Africa, and he remained more than two decades, devising and testing his *Satyagraha* ("Hold fast to the Truth") technique of nonviolent non-cooperation in the Transvaal as well as in Natal from 1907–14. The war's outbreak diverted Gandhi's ship "home" from South Africa to London; when he arrived there, however, the first message he uttered to the world was to urge his countrymen to volunteer for military service, and "Think Imperially."[14]

Jinnah attended the gala reception for Gandhi at London's Cecil Hotel but joined neither the army nor the Field Ambulance Training Corps raised by the Mahatma. Jinnah's own mission had ended in total failure, all English hearts and minds were preoccupied with war, with no one giving a moment's thought to Indian reforms. The work of the Islington Commission went down the same tubes of indifference that swallowed change for the Council of India. Morley quit the cabinet in frustration and disgust at how eagerly his younger Liberal colleagues led by Lloyd George, Edward Gray, and Winston Churchill rushed toward the precipice of Armageddon. Passionately impulsive, self-righteous, puffed up with pride and dreams of glory, they all expected a swift, easy victory. Kitchener alone, who took charge of the War Office with waxed moustaches as sharp as the top of the Kaiser's helmet, envisioned a long, blood-drenched battle of titans almost equally matched in manpower and armor. Initially, India became a warmly supportive, totally loyal Allied mine of troops, wheat, money, and vital materiel, including leather goods, uniforms, and pig iron shipped west throughout the war.

In November of 1914, however, when the Ottoman caliph opted to link his empire's fortune and forces with the Central Powers, rather than joining the Allies who had courted him, Indian Muslim loyalties were sorely challenged. As Islam's world leader and "deputy of God," the caliph was revered far beyond the limits of the Ottoman Empire. British intelligence feared that the nizam of Hyderabad, India's leading prince, was soon trying to buy Turkish rifles for possible use in a South Asian "Pan-Islamic Revolt." Such rumors proved, in fact, completely groundless, and though a few Muslim units had to be disarmed the following year in Singapore, virtually every Muslim soldier in the British Indian Army proved "true to his salt," and Pathan North-West Frontier as well as Punjabi Muslims remained with Sikhs and Gurkhas the backbone of British India's army. Muslim regiments were used without defection in Mesopotamia itself, as well as on the Egyptian and Western European fronts. The Muslim League held no meeting, however, in December 1914, reflecting the deeply divided feelings of its leaders, and their fears of inadvertently providing a forum for expressions of Pan-Islamic, anti-British sentiment.

By January of 1915 Jinnah was home. The Gujarat Society (*Gurjar Sabha*), which he led, gave a garden party to welcome Gandhi back to India. The Mahatma's ambulance corps had sailed for France without its founder after he had a slight nervous breakdown in London and decided to return home to India instead, thus prolonging his life by some three decades. Gandhi's response to Jinnah's urbane welcome was that he was "glad to find a Mahomedan not only belonging to his own region's Sabha, but chairing it."[15] Had he meant to be malicious rather than his usual ingenuous self, Gandhi could not have contrived a more cleverly patronizing barb, for he was not actually insulting Jinnah, after all, just informing every one of his minority religious identity. What an odd fact to single out for comment about this multifaceted man, whose dress, behavior, speech, and manner totally belied any resemblance to his religious affiliation! Jinnah, in fact, hoped by his Anglophile appearance and secular wit and wisdom to convince the Hindu majority of his colleagues and countrymen that he was, indeed, as qualified to lead any of their public organizations as Gokhale or Wedderburn or Dadabhai. Yet here, in the first public words Gandhi uttered about him, every one had to note that Jinnah was a "Mahomedan." That first statement of Gandhi's set the tone of their relationship, always at odds with deep tensions and mistrust underlying its superficially polite manners, never friendly, never cordial. They seemed always to be sparring even before they put on any gloves. It was as if, subconsciously they recognized one another as "natural enemies," rivals for national power, popularity, and charismatic control of their audiences, however small or awesomely vast they might become.

Gokhale's death in February 1915, followed a few months later by the demise of Sir Pherozeshah, left Jinnah virtually alone (Dadabhai remained in London for his final two years) at the head of Bombay's moderate Congress. Tilak, released from Burmese prison exile in June of 1914, was the undisputed hero and national leader of the "New Congress" party. The Lokamanya's popularity was unrivaled, yet he was almost sixty and ailing, and would rely more on legal remedies—some entrusted to Jinnah—than revolutionary agitation for the last half decade of his life. A new luminary in the constellation of India's nationalist leadership was Mrs. Annie Besant (1874–1933), who came to Madras to preside over the Theosophical Society founded by her guru, Madame Blavatsky, and stayed to edit New India and start her Home Rule League in 1915, thus inspiring Tilak to do the same a year later in Poona. Mrs. Besant's Irish temper, silver-tongued oratory, and inexhaustible energy were focused in 1914–15 on seeking to reunify the still divided Congress. Jinnah did his best to help, working dexterously at the same time to bring Congress and the Muslim League together for their annual meetings in Bombay.

The December 1915 sessions of Congress and the League were the first held within walking distance of one another, facilitating attendance at both by members interested in fostering Hindu-Muslim unity and hammering out a single nationalist platform. Satyendra Sinha, who presided over that Congress, was not as yet appointed undersecretary of state in Whitehall. He

and Jinnah now worked together to fashion a formula agreeable to all political factions and communities. While reiterating Congress's general major
demands for reform, Sinha focused on three specific matters concerning
which he had found "practical unanimity of opinion." The first called for
army commissions for qualified Indians and "military training for the people," the second for extension of local self-government, and the third for
"development of our commerce and our industries including agriculture."

The Muslim League met under the presidency of Bengali barrister
Mazhar-ul-Haque (1866–1921), another Congress liberal committed to
fashioning a joint platform acceptable to both organizations. Several League
leaders had argued against holding any meeting this year, fearing that what
was said at it might "embarrass" the government during the war; but President Haque argued that

> Our silence in these times would have been liable to ugly and mis-
> chievous interpretation. . . . There is no such thing as standing still
> in this world. Either we must move forward or must go backward.
> . . . It is said that our object in holding the League contemporane-
> ously with the Congress in the same city is to deal a blow at the
> independence of the League, and to merge its individuality with that
> of the Congress. Nothing could be further from the truth. Commu-
> nities like individuals love and cherish their individuality. . . . When
> unity is evolved out of diversity, then there is real and abiding na-
> tional progress.[16]

There were, nonetheless, many members of the League who strongly resisted any effort at rapprochement. Angry dissidents led by the mercurial
Maulana Hasrat Mohani (1875–1951), moved to adjourn this meeting of the
League at the start of its second sitting on December 31, 1915. Jinnah had
just been recognized by the chair when Maulana Mohani jumped up to
shout, "Point of order!" The president ordered him to "please sit down."
Other Urdu-shouting orthodox Muslims rose inside the huge tent erected
near the seashore on Marine Lines to support Mohani's attempt to adjourn
the meeting before Jinnah could move the creation of a special committee
to draft a scheme of reforms. Some angry mullahs, who filled the visitor rows
of seats started yelling at President Haque: "If you are a Mohammedan,
you ought to appear like a Mohammedan. The Holy Quran asks you to dress
like a Mohammedan. You must speak the Mohammedan tongue. You pose to
be a Mohammedan leader, but you can never be a Mohammedan leader."[17]
Similar anti-Western, revivalist sentiments would be hurled at Jinnah for
the rest of his life, even after he was hailed the League's Quaid-i Azam

("Great Leader"). A number of bearded Pathans in the audience rushed the dais, shouting angrily in Pashtu. Hasrat Mohani called Urdu the only "proper language" in which to hold Muslim League proceedings. Every one in the crowd of several thousands was standing, many shouting at once, some wildly waving their arms. Jinnah helped escort the ladies in attendance outside and found Bombay's commissioner of police, Mr. Edwardes, nonchalantly standing near the tent, keeping his men inert. Jinnah told Edwardes that the crowd inside had become so disorderly the meeting could not proceed and that those causing the disturbance were public "visitors," who had been admitted "out of courtesy and by ticket."[18] He asked the commissioner's help to clear the tent of nonmembers, offering "to refund the money instantly" of anyone who had paid for a ticket. Edwardes refused to be of such sensible service, however, insisting he would use his force only to clear the tent entirely if informed that the situation inside was "out of control." Jinnah preferred to urge President Haque to adjourn the meeting and he met with the League's leaders later that day in the president's house to plan for the next day's session.

The Muslim League was reconvened on New Year's Day 1916 in Bombay's elegant Taj Mahal Hotel. Attendance was strictly limited to regular members and the press. President Haque opened the meeting at 10:00 A.M., commenting briefly on the previous disorders, then called upon "Mr. Jinnah," who was "received with loud cheers."[19] As president of the Bombay Muslim Students' Union, Jinnah was the "idol of the youth," and "uncrowned king of Bombay."[20] Raven-haired with a moustache almost as full as Kitchener's and lean as a rapier, he sounded like Ronald Coleman, dressed like Anthony Eden, and was adored by most women at first sight, and admired or envied by most men. He reported Commissioner Edwardes's pig-headed behavior to cries of "shame" from his audience, then moved the unanimously carried resolution to appoint a special committee "to formulate and frame a scheme of reforms" in consultation with other "political" organizations—the two parties of Congress—which would allow them to "demand" a single platform of reforms "in the name of United India."[21] That resolution was greeted with loud applause. A committee of seventy-one leaders of the Muslim League was appointed, representing every province of British India, and chaired by Jinnah's close friend and client, Raja Sir Mohammad Ali Mohammad Khan Bahadur, the raja of Mahmudabad (1879–1931). Committee members from Bombay included the Aga Khan (1877–1965) and Jinnah; those from the Punjab were led by Mian Sir Muhammad Shafi (1869–1932) and Mian Sir Fazl-i Husain (1877–1936); while the Bengal contingent had A. K. Fazlul Haq (1893–1962) in its ranks. Before that meeting in the Taj ended, President Haque remarked upon "the great work done for the League ('risen Phoenix-like from the ashes') by his friend Mr. Jinnah," adding: "The entire Mohammedan community of India owed him a deep debt of gratitude, for without his exertions they could not have met in Bombay." In a unique tribute, the president then turned to Jinnah, saying, "Mr. Jinnah, we the Musalmans of India thank you."[22] It was the first such tribute Jinnah received from the Muslim League, but would not be his last.

4

Lucknow to Bombay (1916-18)

For Jinnah, 1916 was a year of national fame and good fortune. After helping to save the Muslim League from dissolution in Bombay he was elected to lead it to new heights of hope in Lucknow, capital of the once mighty Mughal nawabs of Oudh. While Europe tore itself apart all along the poison gas-filled western front, India advanced, under Jinnah's inspiring leadership toward a political horizon that seemed ablaze with the golden dawn of imminent freedom.

Jinnah was re-elected for a second term to Bombay's Muslim seat on the Central Legislative Council and used that forum to good advantage in presenting the Congress-League proposals, once drafted, to London. Congress had appointed its own committee headed by Motilal Nehru (1861–1931), who invited its members to his palatial Allahabad house in April to discuss the proposed reforms with League leaders. Part of the fortune he had earned as a lawyer was lavished on hospitality and support for Congress and for Mrs. Besant's Home Rule League, which Motilal funded most generously. The elder Nehru admired Jinnah, introducing him to friends at this time as "unlike most Muslims . . . as keen a nationalist as any of us. He is showing his community the way to Hindu-Muslim unity."[1] For a while they supported one another in the Central Legislative Council, but by the late 1920's Motilal and Jinnah became bitter rivals. Motilal, a fierce advocate and tenacious wrestler, wanted personally to lead India's nationalist movement to independence, or hoped at least to bequeath such power to his son. Jinnah, the Lincoln's Inn barrister, would never rest content simply to assist a provincial pleader, no matter how great his fortune happened to be.

That April, as Congress and the League labored in Allahabad to draft the "Freedom Pact" that was to be sealed at Lucknow, Dublin lay shattered in ruins under martial law. The Easter Rising of 1916 was as brutally crushed by Kitchener's army in Ireland as was General John Nixon's Indian army, by disease, incompetence, and Turkish troops in Mesopotamia that same month. Contrary to all rational expectation, shattering every civilized hope and dream, the war continued, intensifying rather than abating in its blind fury with the incredible death toll of its rage mounting every moment. Indian demands for direct representation with the self-governing dominions at the Imperial Conference intensified. Crewe left the India Office, replaced by Austen Chamberlain (1863–1937) in May. Hardinge found it impossible to ignore Indian demands for a greater role in deliberations, agreeing that India's claim to a representative voice at all imperial conferences was just. With Curzon and Kitchener still dominating the War Cabinet, however, Hardinge was ignored. By mid-1916 he left India and was replaced as viceroy by an uninspired and uninspiring cavalry captain, Lord Chelmsford (1868–1933).

From his meeting in Allahabad, Jinnah went north to Darjeeling to escape the next two months of intense Bombay heat by vacationing at the summer home of his client and friend, Sir Dinshaw Manockjee Petit (1873–1933). The Petits were one of Bombay's wealthiest Parsi families, textile magnates, whose vast fortune was begun by Sir Dinshaw's enterprising great grandfather, who came to Bombay from Surat in 1785 and worked as a shipping clerk and *dubash* ("two-language" interpreter) for the British East India Company. French merchants who dealt with this bright, very small Parsi clerk dubbed him *"Le petit Parsi."*[2] The nickname became his descendants' surname. His son Manockjee Petit founded Bombay's first successful cotton mill, which grew into the sprawling Manockjee Mills complex in Tardeo. The first baronet Sir Dinshaw started Bombay's powerful Mill-Owners' Association in 1875, which he chaired from 1879–94. He also served as one of five trustees of the Bombay Parsi community's most sacred matters—marriage, succession laws, and proper disposition of the dead upon the Towers of Silence. The elder Sir Dinshaw had been instrumental in securing British legal recognition and public promulgation of the Parsi Succession and Marriage acts, which he personally helped administer. The Petit family was thus not only among the richest, but also one of the most devout, orthodox Parsi families in Bombay by the end of the nineteenth century.

With the death of the first Sir Dinshaw in 1901, his entire name, fortune, and religious duties and responsibilities passed on to his son, whose first child and only daughter, Ratanbai, had been born the previous year, on February 20, 1900. Ruttie, as she came to be called, was a thoroughly enchanting child, precociously bright, gifted in every art, beautiful in every way. As she matured, all of her talents, gifts, and beauty were magnified in so delightful and unaffected a manner that she seemed a "fairy princess," almost too lovely, too fragile to be real. And her mind was so alert, her intellect so lively and probing that she took as much interest in politics as she did in romantic poetry and insisted on attending every public meeting held in Bombay during 1916, always sitting, of course, in "the first row," chaperoned by her "multimillionaire philanthropist" maiden aunt, Miss Mamabai Petit.[3]

That summer when Ruttie was sixteen and Jinnah at least forty, they shared the Petit chateau within view of Mount Everest, perched 7,000 feet high in the idyllic "Town of the Thunderbolt"—Darjeeling—where only the choicest tea plants and the silent snow-clad mountain peaks and isolated trails witnessed the passionate glances of longing and love that passed between these two.

That October in 1916, Jinnah presided over the Bombay Provincial Conference in Ahmedabad, the textile capital of Gujarati wealth and power. Jinnah proposed transforming provincial governments, such as that of Bombay, into virtually autonomous administrations responsible to elected representatives of the people, "Muslims and Hindus, wherever they are in a minority" having "proper, adequate and effective representation." As to all district and municipal governments, Jinnah reiterated the arguments of Liberals Ripon and Morley, insisting they "should be wholly elected . . . that the present official control exercised by the Collectors and Commissioners should be removed; that the Chairman should be elected by the Boards and the *ex officio* President should be done away with; that a portion of Excise revenue or some other definite source of revenue should be made over to these Bodies so that they may have adequate resources at their disposal for the due performance of their duties."[4] It would have meant no less than transforming the all-powerful Indian Civil Service into true servants of responsible Indian opinion. Jinnah's radical proposals for change did not, however, stop there. He also demanded an end to "the unjust application of the Arms Act to the people of India from which the Europeans are exempted"; called for the repeal of the Press Act; less resort to the "martial law" Defence of India Act, specifically denouncing its recent application in banning Mrs. Besant from Bombay; and immediate enactment of a "free and compulsory" measure of elementary education. He insisted that Indians should have long since been admitted to royal commissions in the army and navy, asking, "If Indians are good enough to fight as sepoys and privates, why are they not good enough to occupy the position of officers?"[5]

Jinnah concluded his Bombay Conference address with the "all-absorbing question" of Hindu-Muslim unity.

I believe all thinking men are thoroughly convinced that the keynote of our real progress lies in the goodwill, concord, harmony and co-operation between the two great sister communities. The true focus of progress is centered in their union. . . . But the solution is not difficult. . . .[6]

Jinnah was speaking as an advocate for the Muslim community as a whole. He was not expressing his own political ideology or reflecting his own experience. The burden of sacrifice, he argued, fell upon the majority community, yet their reward would be commensurate.

I would, therefore, appeal to my Hindu friends to be generous and liberal and welcome and encourage other activities of Muslims even if it involves some sacrifice in the matter of separate electorates. . . . It is a question . . . of transfer of the power from the bureaucracy to democracy. Let us concentrate all our attention and energy on this question alone for the present. The Hindus and the Muslims should stand united and use every constitutional and legitimate means to effect that transfer as soon as possible. . . . We are on a straight road; the promised land is within sight. "Forward" is the motto and clear course for young India.[7]

Never was Jinnah more optimistic. The future for India seemed as bright, as full of life, hope, and light as did his own future with Ruttie. They were born to different communities, yet love scaled every height, reduced to rubble all barriers. So at least it must have seemed to him then, at the peak of his creative political powers, on the road to his triumph at Lucknow.

First he went to Calcutta, where the Imperial Legislative Council still met for its winter session, the New Delhi of Luytens and Baker rising so slowly on the spacious plain south of the old city's massive wall and gates that it would not be ready for council use till the late 1920's. Before October ended, Jinnah was able to convince eighteen other elected members of Calcutta's council to sign his "Memorandum of the Nineteen," which was then presented to the viceroy and sent on to Whitehall. The memorandum[8] demanded that elected representatives of legislative councils should select all Indian members who would, in future, serve on executive councils. Legislative councils, moreover, "should have a substantial majority of elected representatives," and the franchise should be "broadened," with "Muslims or Hindus, wherever they are in a minority, being given proper and adequate representation." A supreme council of not fewer than 150 members, and provincial councils of from 60 to 100 members were recommended. Councils were to enjoy greater responsibilities and parliamentary freedoms, and the position of the secretary of state should be abolished, replaced

by two permanent undersecretaries, with one being Indian, with salaries
"placed on the British estimates." In any scheme of imperial federation,
"India should be given through her chosen representatives a place similar
to that of the self-governing Dominions." Provincial governments should be
made autonomous, a "full measure" of local self-government was demanded
"immediately," the "right to carry arms" should be granted to Indians "on
the same conditions as to Europeans," and Indian youths should be equally
eligible for royal commissions in the armed forces.

The memorandum provided a skeletal constitution for an Indian dominion which, had this proposal been accepted by the British after World
War I, could have taken its place within the British Commonwealth, united,
loyal to every ideal for which the Allies had fought, progressively modern-
izing under responsible leadership. The war was still far from over, however, and the full report of how Indian arms had sustained their worst
defeat in Mesopotamia was as yet to be disclosed, reducing British faith in
anything Indian to its lowest point, even as the Revolution soon to rock
Russia would strip the Allies of their eastern wing. The British War Cabinet
tragically lacked the vision, or desire, or energy, to focus attention upon and
take the outstretched hand of united India. The winter of 1916 had offered
Great Britain, as well as India, one of those rare opportunities in history
when a cresting wave could be caught and ridden toward a welcoming
shore, but if missed, left to crash with murderous impact on the heads of
those too preoccupied, timid, or ill-prepared to seize the swiftly changing
moment.

Jinnah caught a spectacular ride on the crest of a formula his ingenious
legal mind had fashioned, and which he was able to convince Congress
President A. C. Mazumdar to accept, after meeting with him for two days
in Calcutta in mid-November. The key to their Lucknow Pact lay in agreeing upon percentages of guaranteed "Muslim members" for each of the
legislative councils, one-third at the center and in Bombay, one-half in the
Punjab, 40 percent in Bengal, 30 percent in the United Provinces, 25 percent
in Bihar and Orissa, and 15 percent in the Central Provinces and in Madras.
Except for the Punjab and Bengal, where Muslim representation was slightly
less than the fraction demographic equivalence warranted, the minority
community received a louder legislative voice than population estimates
alone would have dictated. As an even more vital safeguard to reassure
Muslims who feared losing Islamic identity within a future "Hindu Raj,"
the pact provided that

No bill, nor any clause thereof, nor a resolution introduced by a non-
official member affecting one or the other community, which question

is to be determined by the members of that community in the Legislative Council concerned, shall be proceeded with, if three-fourths of
the members of that community in the particular Council, Imperial or
Provincial, oppose the bill or any clause thereof or the resolution.[9]

Jinnah left no loopholes in the contracts he drafted.

"All that is great and inspiring to the common affairs of men, for which
the noblest and most valiant of mankind have lived and wrought and suffered in all ages and all climes, is now moving India out of its depths,"
declared President Jinnah from the Muslim League's rostrum on December
30, 1916.

> The whole country is awakening to the call of its destiny and is scan-
> ning the new horizons with eager hope. A new spirit of earnestness,
> confidence and resolution is abroad in the land. In all directions are
> visible the stirrings of a new life. The Musalmans of India would be
> false to themselves and the traditions of their past, had they not
> shared to the full the new hope that is moving India's patriotic sons
> to-day, or had they failed to respond to the call of their country.
> Their gaze, like that of their Hindu fellow-countrymen, is fixed on
> the future.
>
> But, gentlemen of the All-India Muslim League, remember that the
> gaze of your community and of the whole country is at this moment
> fixed on you. The decisions that you take in this historic hall, and at
> this historic session of the League, will go forth with all the force and
> weight that can legitimately be claimed by the chosen leaders and
> representatives of 70 million Indian Musalmans. On the nature of
> those decisions will depend, in a large measure, the fate of India's
> future, of India's unity, and of our common ideals and aspirations for
> constitutional freedom.[10]

Jinnah would never again speak so passionately from a public platform. He
spoke of bureaucratic British "shallow, bastard and desperate political max-
ims" often "flung into the face of Indian patriots," noting such clichés as
"Indians are unfit to govern themselves," and "Democratic institutions cannot thrive in the environment of the East," rejecting them all as "baseless
and silly."

President Jinnah hailed "the living and vigorous spirit of patriotism and
national self-consciousness . . . this pent-up altruistic feeling and energy of
youth" that was surging through India's "pulse." He said, "the most significant and hopeful aspect of this spirit is that it has taken its rise from a
new-born movement in the direction of national unity which has brought
Hindus and Muslims together involving brotherly service for the common

cause."[11] This vital portion of his Lucknow address later proved so embarrassing to the League's goals that it was excised from the official pamphlet
subsequently published and reproduced by advocates of the Pakistan Movement. Such censorship was, however, surely as misguided as misleading, for
to ignore the potent power of Jinnah's commitment to Hindu-Muslim unity
in 1916 would make it impossible fully to appreciate the tenacity of his later
determination to bring Pakistan to fruition. Jinnah understood perfectly that
India's only hope of emerging as a national entity, independent and strong,
from under the heel of British imperial rule was through prior abatement
of communal fears, suspicions, and residual anxieties. His standing within
Congress was such that he managed to persuade colleagues there of the
overriding national value of conceding a large enough quota of elected
legislative council seats to Muslims, to be able to convince the League that
joining forces with Congress in articulating a single national set of demands
was, in fact, in their own best "communal" interest. This delicately negotiated settlement attested as much to his remarkable legal talents as it did
to his passionate nationalist commitment.

Dynamic optimism made Jinnah predict that at least half "our constitutional battle" had been "won already." The "united Indian demand, based
on the actual needs of the country and framed with due regard to time and
circumstances, must eventually prove irresistible. . . . With the restoration
of peace the Indian problem will have to be dealt with on bold and generous
lines and India will have to be granted her birth-right as a free, responsible
and equal member of the British Empire."[12] It all seemed so clear and
simple then, so rational. The Congress-League plan, called the Lucknow
Pact, provided a blueprint for independent India's constitution. Jinnah had,
moreover, worked out every step for translating his scheme into legislative
reality.

> After you have adopted the scheme of reforms you should see that
> the Congress and the League take concerted measures to have a Bill
> drafted by constitutional lawyers as an amending Bill to the Govern-
> ment of India Act which embodies the present constitution of our
> country. This Bill, when ready, should be adopted by the Indian Na-
> tional Congress and the All-India Muslim League and a deputation of
> leading representative men from both the bodies should be appointed
> to see that the Bill is introduced in the British Parliament and
> adopted. For that purpose we should raise as large a fund as possible
> to supply the sinews of war until our aim and object are fulfilled.[13]

His mind raced years ahead of most of his contemporaries, British and
Indian alike. Unfortunately, the Lucknow Pact was never implemented, but

its adoption marked the high point of Indian nationalist unity and provided as liberal and rational a constitutional framework for governing the subcontinent of South Asia as any subsequent plan devised after years of labor, vast expenditure, and much precious blood had been wasted. British rulers were not quite ready, however, to apply the Wilsonian principle of "self-determination" to their Indian empire.

Congress met just a few days before the League in the same historic *Kaisar Bagh* ("Royal Garden") of Lucknow, its first reunified session since the 1907 split at Surat, attracting more than 2,300 delegates. "Blessed are the peace-makers," said President Mazumdar, welcoming Tilak and his aging "new" party back to the fold. Turning to the Hindu-Muslim "question," Mazumdar announced it

> has been settled and the Hindus and Mussalmans have agreed to make a united demand for Self-Government. The All-India Congress Committee and the representatives of the Moslem League who recently met in conference at Calcutta have, after two days' deliberations, in one voice resolved to make a joint demand for a Representative Government in India. . . .[14]

Tilak, ever the political realist, remarked, "We are ready to make a common cause with any set of men. I shall not hold back my hand even from the bureaucracy if they come forward with the scheme that will promote the welfare of our Nation."[15]

Jinnah's triumph was unmarred. The complete contract he had written was accepted by both parties. Now he was ready to put it to the acid test of personal application. He found a way to unite the two subjects uppermost in his mind and approached Sir Dinshaw Petit with a seemingly abstract question of "what his views were about inter-communal marriages."[16] Caught "fully off his guard," Ruttie's father "expressed his emphatic opinion that it would considerably help national integration and might ultimately prove to be the final solution to inter-communal antagonism." Jinnah could not have composed a better response! He wasted no words in further cross-examination, informing his old friend that he wanted to marry his daughter. "Sir Dinshaw was taken aback," as Justice Chagla, who was then assisting Jinnah in his chambers, so vividly recalled, "He had not realised that his remarks might have serious personal repurcussions [*sic*]. He was most indignant, and refused to countenance any such idea which appeared to him absurd and fantastic."

Jinnah argued as eloquently, as forcefully as he alone could, but to no avail. At its first test his dream of spreading communal harmony and loving unity was thus rudely jolted. Sir Dinshaw never agreed, indeed, never spoke as a friend to Jinnah after that hour of such a bitter and rude awakening to what everyone else in Bombay already knew. Nor would he sanction the marriage under any circumstances. First he forbid Ruttie ever to see Jinnah again—at least while she remained a minor under his palatial roof of fine marble. Then he sought legal remedies, filing an injunction to prevent their marriage once she came of age, based on the Parsi Marriage Act; but he was pitted against a barrister who rarely lost any case and would gladly have died before surrendering in this matter. Predictably perhaps, Ruttie's passionate devotion to her self-chosen husband-to-be only intensified, thanks to her father's adamant insistence that she never see him again. Juliet-like, she would not be deterred by prejudice or the preference of her parents. Sir Dinshaw met his own match in stubborn resolution twice over in this long-suffering committed young couple. Silently, patiently, passionately they waited till Ruttie would attain her majority at eighteen and married just a few months after that, as soon as the last legal obstacle could be slashed aside by Jinnah's invincible courtroom sword.

The German and Ottoman armies proved as frustratingly difficult and far more deadly than Ruttie's father. The Mespot Disaster, or Bastard War, as the dreadful Iraqi desert tragedy to British Indian arms came to be called, led to many angry questions in Parliament and long inquiries that revealed utter incompetence in the shipment of military medical supplies and other vital materiel from Indian ports to the Persian Gulf. Secretary of State Chamberlain accepted the entire "blame," though hardly deserved, as his own, resigning from command of the India Office in mid-1917. Thanks to that sacrificial act, however, Liberal Edwin Montagu (1879–1924) was placed in charge of India and rose in the House of Commons on August 20, 1917, to announce that the new, inspiring "policy of His Majesty's Government, with which the Government of India are in complete accord, is that of the increasing association of Indians in every branch of the administration and the gradual development of self-governing institutions with a view to the progressive realisation of responsible government in India as an integral part of the British Empire." Here, at last, appeared to be the promise of "dominion status" that political leaders throughout India had awaited since the war began. Nationalist eyes glossed over the "gradual development" and "progressive realisation," reading only the "self-governing institutions" and "responsible government" mantras in Montagu's formula. Imperialist Curzon rather than Montagu sat on the Home government's all-powerful inner circle War Cabinet and managed with various official "safeguards" adroitly to sabotage every major reform that was to emerge during Montagu's tenure at Whitehall. In the winter of 1917, however, Edwin

Montagu became the first secretary of state for India actually to visit the subcontinent while holding that high office.

The ancient complexity of India, its pluralism and paradox affected Montagu deeply as it did most visitors from afar, though he had toured the country once before in 1913, and, as a Jew, considered himself "an Oriental." He had never seen so many people, so much poverty, amid so ostentatious a display of wealth and luxury. India fascinated and terrified him so that by the end of his journey he was thoroughly exhausted, frustrated, and drained. In fact, poor lugubrious Montagu was traumatized by India, flattered by the magnanimity of her welcome, shocked at the magnitude of her problems and plight, and disoriented by the official royal treatment he received.

Of all the political leaders Montagu talked with in India, Jinnah impressed him most: "Young, perfectly mannered, impressive-looking, armed to the teeth with dialectics, and insistent upon the whole of his scheme. . . . [Viceroy] Chelmsford tried to argue with him, and was tied up into knots. Jinnah is a very clever man, and it is, of course, an outrage that such a man should have no chance of running the affairs of his own country."[17] Montagu confided to his diary:

> My visit to India means that we are going to do something, and something big. I cannot go home and produce a little thing or nothing; it must be epochmaking, or it is a failure; it must be the keystone of the future history of India. . . . Nothing is wanting in comfort . . . I am not the stuff to carry this sort of thing off. For the first time in my life I wish I looked like Curzon. . . . I wish Lloyd George were here; I wish the whole British Cabinet had come; I wish Asquith were here. It is one of India's misfortunes that I am alone, alone, alone the person that has got to carry this thing through.[18]

Annie Besant, fresh out of prison thanks to Jinnah's personal appeal to the Home minister on her behalf, invited Montagu to attend the Calcutta Congress over which she was to preside that December. "Oh, if only Lloyd George were in charge of this thing!" Montagu moaned to his diary. "He would, of course, dash down to the Congress and make them a great oration. I am prevented from doing this. It might save the whole situation. But the Government of India have carefully arranged our plans so that we shall be in Bombay when the Congress, the real Indian political movement, is in Calcutta!"[19] Mrs. Besant was the first woman, the only Englishwoman, to be elected president of the Congress, her reward for the suffering she experienced after her arrest in mid-year for "seditious journalism." Jinnah took charge of the Bombay branch of her Home Rule League immediately after

Mrs. Besant's internment on June 15, 1917, and Ruttie was one of her most ardent admirers. Just under 5,000 delegates and almost as many visitors attended the Calcutta Congress, where Jinnah moved the most important resolution calling for implementation of the Lucknow Pact reforms, a resolution carried by acclamation. A few days later Jinnah moved much the same resolution before the Muslim League, which "strongly urges upon the Government the immediate introduction of a Bill embodying the reforms contained in the Congress-League Scheme of December, 1916, as the first step towards the realization of responsible government." As the prospect of responsible government appeared to draw closer, many of his League colleagues were growing more concerned that Muslim interests would be ignored by the Hindu majority. Jinnah reassured them, arguing: "If seventy million Muslims do not approve of a measure, which is carried by a ballot box, do you think that it could be carried out and administered in this country? Muslims should not have the fear that the Hindus can pass any legislation, as they are in a majority, and that would be the end of the matter."[20] He strongly advised the Muslim League not to be "scared away" by "your enemies . . . from the co-operation with the Hindus, which is essential for the establishment of self-government."[21]

Maulana Mohammad Ali had been elected to preside over the Muslim League's Calcutta session, but his chair was empty throughout the meeting as he remained interned under house arrest with his brother Shaukat Ali (1873–1938). Since 1915 the Ali brothers had been under arrest by the government under its martial emergency powers. The newspapers they edited, *Comrade* and *Hamdard*, had argued favorably on behalf of Caliph Abdul Hamid of the Ottoman Empire, but British officialdom retained sphinxlike silence for over two years concerning the precise reasons for arresting these two alims, till Jinnah pressed the question in the Central Legislative Council in 1917 and was told that "they were interned because they expressed and promoted sympathy with the King's enemies."[22] The Ali brothers became a rallying cry, not just for Muslims but for Hindus as well, and were singled out by Mahatma Gandhi as his first great national cause in opposition to the British raj.

While Gandhi courted popular Muslim support by allying himself most outspokenly with the struggle on behalf of the Ali brothers, he sought simultaneously, and won, official confidence by urging all Indians to enlist in the British army. Both positions appeared paradoxical to disciples who had never considered the Mahatma enamoured either of Muslims or of war, yet in late 1917 and throughout 1918 those causes proved to be Gandhi's most important springboards to political power.

Jinnah at this juncture was most vocal in his criticism of Britain's intensified recruiting drive in India, insisting first of all that Indians "should be put on the same footing as the European British subjects" before being asked to fight. Specifically, he demanded that royal commissions be made available "to the people of India." Chelmsford angrily rebuked that position as "bargaining," to which Jinnah irately replied, "Is it bargaining, consistently with my self-respect as King's equal subject in my own country, to tell my Government face to face that this bar must be removed? Is it bargaining, My Lord, to say that in my own country I should be put on the same footing as the European British subjects? Is that bargaining?"[23] As an elected member of the council, Jinnah was, of course, invited to the war conference the Viceroy planned to hold that April in Delhi, but first he had a much more important engagement to attend in Bombay.

Jinnah married Ruttie on Friday, April 19, 1918, at his house, South Court, on Mount Pleasant Road atop Malabar Hill in Bombay. She had converted to Islam three days earlier, though she remained a nonsectarian mystic all her life. None of Ruttie's relatives attended her wedding. She had fled from her father's palatial prison less than a mile away on the day she turned eighteen and was mourned as if dead by Sir Dinshaw until she and Jinnah separated less than a decade after they had married. The raja of Mahmudabad and just a few other intimate Muslim friends of Jinnah attended the quiet wedding. "The ring which Jinnah gave to his wife on the wedding day was my father's gift," Mahmudabad's son and heir recalled. "The Jinnahs spent their honeymoon at Nainital in our house."[24] It was not quite Darjeeling, yet perched over a mile above sea level, Naini was the cool hill station that the Nehrus as well as Mahmudabads liked best, and Jinnah and Ruttie rode their horses over miles of lovely trails through rich forests of pine, relishing the freedom, the perfect liberation and joy of being together, alone in an environment whose natural beauty seemed barely to reflect the bliss they found in one another.

After less than a week of honeymooning in the hills, the young couple motored down to Delhi, where they stayed in Maidens, a magnificent hotel just outside the old city gate beyond the Red Fort, an ideal hideaway replete with Mughal gardens, fountains and pools, a regal staircase, a crystal chandelier, and a palatial dining hall. The perfect mixture of imperial elegance and British privacy, Maidens was to remain Jinnah's favorite hotel retreat in Delhi. They were a stunning couple. Ruttie's long hair was decked in ever-fresh flowers, her lovely lithe body draped in diaphanous silks of flaming red and gold, pale blue, or pink. She wore headbands replete with diamonds, rubies, and emeralds, and smoked English cigarettes in long ivory and silver filters that added a flamboyance to her every graceful gesture, bend, and twirl of arm or body, even as the musical ring of her uninhibited laughter reminded the world of her beautiful presence. Jinnah, with his bristling black moustache and brilliantly luminous eyes, dressed as smartly as any British lord inside Buckingham, seemed the perfect consort for his bride, and they looked in that spring of 1918 as happy and fulfilled as they felt. With a start that perfectly beautiful, surely they had reason to expect that the future might be one long life of continuing happiness, if not eternal bliss.

The Delhi war conference was the first battleground on which Jinnah confronted the man who was to become his foremost contender for national prominence and political power. With his honeymoon not yet over, Jinnah could hardly be blamed perhaps for underestimating just how potent a force was arrayed against him that April, seated half-naked across the viceroy's conference table. "In response to the invitation I went to Delhi," Gandhi recalled, gratuitously protesting, "It was not in my nature to placate anyone by adulation, or at the cost of self-respect."[25] Recounting this event almost a decade later, as the Mahatma whose *Experiments With Truth* would inspire millions of young Indians and students the world over to emulate his virtues, Gandhi could not, of course, ignore what he had done, nor could he erase it from his conscience. Yet, how was he to explain himself? "I had fully intended to submit the Muslim case to the Viceroy," he insisted, arguing his "principled objections" to participating in a conference that perforce excluded the Ali brothers. Thus, after reaching Delhi, he wrote to Lord Chelmsford "explaining my hesitation to take part in the conference. He invited me to discuss the question with him. I had a prolonged discussion with him and his Private Secretary Mr. Maffey. As a result I agreed to take part in the conference."[26] Gandhi's "part," however, was to be confined to seconding the key resolution on recruiting Indians for the army, and "As regards the Muslim demands I was to address a letter to the Viceroy." Having capitulated to Chelmsford, however, the Mahatma was so conscience-stricken at what he had agreed to that he resolved to do it as briefly, as palatably as possible. His second would be one short sentence, "With a full sense of my responsibility I beg to support the resolution." He delivered that sentence, moreover, first in Hindi and then translated it himself into English. Then in his *Autobiography* he focused on the initial language he had used, not on the words spoken, or the meaningful support they rendered to martial violence and the British war machine.

Many congratulated me on my having spoken in Hindustani. That was, they said, the first instance within living memory of anyone having spoken in Hindustani at such a meeting. The congratulations and the discovery that I was the first to speak in Hindustani at a Vice-regal meeting hurt my national pride. I felt like shrinking into myself.

What a tragedy that the language of the country should be taboo in meetings held in the country, for work relating to the country, and that a speech there in Hindustani by a stray individual like myself should be a matter for congratulation! Incidents like these are reminders of the low state to which we have been reduced.[27]

Unable to admit how wretched he felt at receiving the congratulations of so many imperialists for having abandoned nonviolence to curry favor with a viceroy, Gandhi expressed his true feelings as "a *stray* individual" whose "national pride" was "hurt" but justified them to his own memory and the world purely on national-language grounds. There was, in fact, no "taboo" on Hindustani, which seems hardly the reason Gandhi "felt like *shrinking*" into himself! His commitment to recruiting for the war would, however, indeed, drive him to severe mental breakdown before the end of 1918. But Gandhi's loyalist role at the war conference proved devastating to Jinnah's anti-government stand and caught the entire nationalist leadership in attendance at Delhi off balance.

Jinnah had tried to move a substitute nationalist resolution but was ruled "out of order" by the viceroy. In a telegram he had sent Chelmsford, Jinnah boldly insisted, "We cannot ask our young men to fight for principles, the application of which is denied to their own country. A subject race cannot fight for others with the heart and energy with which a free race can fight for the freedom of itself and others. If India is to make great sacrifices in the defence of the Empire, it must be as a partner in the Empire and not as a dependency. Let her feel that she is fighting for her own freedom as well as for the commonwealth of free nations under the British Crown and then she will strain every nerve to stand by England to the last. . . . Let full responsible government be established in India within a definite period to be fixed by statute with the Congress-League scheme as the first stage and a Bill to that effect be introduced into Parliament at once."[28] Had Gandhi been willing to close ranks behind Jinnah's leadership in Delhi in 1918, Jinnah would have mistrusted him less a year later. Together they might not have persuaded the British to grant India freedom overnight, but they could certainly have accelerated the transfer of power timetable. They might even have avoided partition.

Tilak and Annie Besant marched shoulder to shoulder with Jinnah. Bombay's governor, Lord Willingdon, denounced the three of them in a letter to Montagu for having "no feeling of what is their duty to the Empire at this crisis."[29] A few months later, Chelmsford would further poison his secretary of state's mind about Jinnah and several other of his nationalist colleagues in the legislative council, labeling them "irreconcilables" with whom "it is no use thinking that we can do anything. . . . There is a root of bitterness in them which cannot be eradicated, and for my part I am not going to attempt the task."[30]

Governor Willingdon convened his own provincial war conference in Bombay's town hall on June 10, 1918. Jinnah was there and must have felt the blood rush to his face as Willingdon remarked: "There are a certain number of gentlemen, some of whom have considerable influence with the public, many of them members of the political organisation called the Home Rule League whose activities have been such of late years, that I cannot honestly feel sure of the sincerity of their support."[31] Tilak tried to amend Willingdon's proposed resolution, insisting there could be no "Home Defense" without Home rule, but he was ordered to leave the conference. Jinnah then rose to speak and said he was

> pained, very much pained, that His Excellency should have thought fit to cast doubts on the sincerity and the loyalty of the Home (Rule) Party. He was very sorry, but with the utmost respect he must enter his emphatic protest against that. They were anxious as any one else to help the defence of the motherland and the Empire. . . . The difference was only regarding the methods, for, Government's methods the Home Rule Party did not want. He was only making suggestions for the improvement of the scheme. The Government had their own scheme, namely, for the recruitment of sepoys, but that was not enough to save them from the German menace. . . . They wanted a national army or, in other words, a citizen army and not a purely mercenary army. . . . I say that if you wish to enable us to help you, to facilitate and stimulate the recruiting, you must make the educated people feel that they are the citizens of the Empire and the King's equal subjects. But the Government do not do so. You say that we shall be trusted and made real partners in the Empire. When? We don't want words. We don't want the consideration of the matter indefinitely put off. We want action and immediate deeds.[32]

Jinnah's public conflict with Willingdon was reflected in their acerbic social relationship. The Jinnahs had been invited to dinner at Bombay's Government House soon after returning from their honeymoon. Ruttie wore one of her lowest-cut Paris evening gowns, and Lady Willingdon was quick to order her servant to bring a "wrap to cover up Mrs. Jinnah . . . in case she felt cold." Jinnah did not wait for the servant's return, jumping up from table to inform his hostess, "When Mrs. Jinnah feels cold, she will say so, and ask for a wrap herself."[33] He escorted his wife from the room. They did not set foot inside the Government House again till the Willingdons had moved out.

Less than a week after the provincial war conference broke up, Jinnah's league celebrated Home Rule Day, on June 16, 1918, with a mass rally in Bombay, at which Jinnah said:

> Lord Willingdon has said that the support of the Home Rule Party is half-hearted. My answer is this. . . . Your methods and policy are all wrong. I cannot believe that even a bureaucrat is so blind as not to see it . . . they do not trust us and, therefore, are not prepared to allow us to take up arms for the defence of our own motherland and of the Empire. They want us to continue an organisation, which they call an army, which is a sepoy army and nothing else, and they then turn round and tell us that we are not helping them. I say what Mr. Montagu in his speech on the Mesopotamia Report has said . . . that the Government of India is "too wooden, too iron, too antediluvian to be of any use for the modern purpose we have in view."[34]

Less than a month later, Gandhi wrote to urge Jinnah to "make an emphatic declaration regarding recruitment," arguing:

> Can you not see that if every Home Rule Leaguer became a potent recruiting agency whilst at the same time fighting for constitutional rights we should ensure the passing of the Congress-League scheme? . . . "Seek ye first the recruiting office and everything will be added unto you."[35]

It was one of Gandhi's strangest letters and appears to have left Jinnah too shocked to respond. Gandhi came to appreciate the wisdom of Jinnah's position on recruiting as soon as he started going from village to village in Gujarat, to the beat of a soldier's tin drum.

> As soon as I set about my task, my eyes were opened. My optimism received a rude shock. We had meetings wherever we went. People did attend, but hardly one or two would offer themselves as recruits. "You are a votary of Ahimsa, how can you ask us to take up arms? What good has Government done for India to deserve our co-operation?" These and similar questions used to be put to us.[36]

By August, Gandhi wrote Maffey, quoting even tougher common peasant questions, such as, "How can we who can hardly bear the sight of blood and who have never handled arms suddenly summon up courage to join the army?"[37] Before September was over, Gandhi's health broke down, permitting him to abandon this most difficult, uncongenial work.

> I very nearly ruined my constitution during the recruiting campaign. I felt that the illness was bound to be prolonged and possibly fatal. . . . Whilst I was thus tossing on the bed of pain . . . Vallabhbhai [Patel] brought the news that Germany had been completely de-

feated, and that the Commissioner had sent word that recruiting was
no longer necessary. The news that I had no longer to worry myself
about recruiting came as a very great relief. . . . Vallabhbhai came
up with Dr. Kanuga, who felt my pulse and said, "Your pulse is quite
good. I see absolutely no danger. This is a nervous breakdown due to
extreme weakness." I passed the night without sleep. The morning
broke without death coming. But I could not get rid of the feeling
that the end was near.[38]

Montagu's report on Indian constitutional reforms was published in July
1918, recommending "partial control of the executive in the provinces by the
legislature, and the increasing influence of the legislature upon the executive
in the Government of India," and "as far as possible, complete popular control in local bodies."[39] Jinnah studied this initial report and issued his
reactions to the press on July 23, 1918, noting that

The proposals are not like the laws of the Persians and the Medes, but
they may be modified upon further discussion. . . . Great effort has
been made to face the problem. I know that great difficulties were put
in the way of Mr. Montagu in India and he was called upon to deal
with one of the most intricate and complicated problems that any
country had ever to face . . . but, I think, he has been unduly influenced by the alarmist section, which has resulted in innumerable re-
strictions being put on the concessions that have been made to the
people. . . . The advancement would be worthless unless in major
provinces like Bombay all the departments, except the Police and
Justice, are transferred. I am willing to accept this only as a transi-
tional stage with a view to show that for the present the maintenance
of law and order may be reserved to the Government, since the argument has been advanced that, after all, we are going through an ex-
perimental stage.[40]

Again, Jinnah proved himself eminently moderate and flexible, a brilliant
constitutional lawyer and negotiator. Had his efforts to deal directly with
Montagu not been sabotaged by the government of India and its "Black"
Rowlatt acts, the years of tragedy that were to ensue in the wake of the
war need not have derailed the process of responsible transfer of power set
so patiently in motion by Britain's two greatest Liberal secretaries of state,
John Morley and Edwin Montagu.

Jinnah served on the joint Congress-League committee to coordinate
both responses to Montagu's proposals, which emerged as a qualified acceptance of the report combined with reaffirmation of the Lucknow Pact,
and urged rapid strides toward attainment of full responsible government.
Congress leaders differed widely in their assessments of the report. Surendra

Nath Banerjea was willing to support it, C. R. Das, anticipating "the failure of Dyarchy," wanted "real Responsible Government in 5 years," while Motilal Nehru was ready to wait "another two decades." The regular annual sessions of Congress and the Muslim League were scheduled to be held in Delhi in December.

As World War I sputtered to its end that November, so did Willingdon's tenure over Bombay. The Jinnahs could hardly wait for that governor to leave, and when they learned of plans by some of Willingdon's Parsi friends to host a public function at Town Hall honoring him on the eve of his departure, they launched a mass opposition movement to that function. It was Jinnah's first and most vigorous public demonstration against a British official. The Willingdon Memorial Committee timed their meeting to start at 5:00 P.M. on December 11. Some 300 of Jinnah's youthful followers started camping out near the steps of Bombay's town hall the night before. Police kept the broad steps themselves clear of crowds till 10:00 A.M. when the hall opened, shortly before which Jinnah himself arrived to take a place saved for him at the head of the queue. He raced up the steps as fast as his long legs could carry him and secured the very first rows, with his Home rule comrades. About noon, Ruttie arrived with a tiffin basket filled with their sandwiches, for they dared not leave those choice seats, knowing Willingdon's supporters would start to show up in the early afternoon. The large hall was filled, in fact, hours before the robed sheriff of Bombay called the meeting to order. Sir Jemsetjee Jeejeebhoy, one of Bombay's leading Parsis whose family fortune was made in the opium trade, "presided" over that meeting, but from the moment he rose to address the audience, Jinnah and his claque were on their feet, shouting "No, no!"[41] Raucous protests continued for about twenty minutes, and though no one could hear him do so, Sir Jemsetjee supposedly moved the "resolution of appreciation" for Lord Willingdon. The commissioner of police then ordered the hall to be "cleared," and Jinnah as well as Ruttie and their friends were hustled forcibly outside. It was the first and only time Jinnah would be roughed up and bruised by any one in uniform. He emerged from the town hall, however, a uniquely popular Bombay hero.

"Gentlemen, you are the citizens of Bombay," Jinnah told his adoring audience that stretched across Apollo Street that evening. "Your triumph today has made it clear that even the combined forces of bureaucracy and autocracy could not overawe you. December the 11th is a Red-Letter Day in the history of Bombay. Gentlemen, go and rejoice over the day that has secured us the triumph of democracy."[42] That night a huge demonstration was held in Shantaram's Chawl, and soon no fewer than 65,000 rupees were raised, much of it in one-rupee contributions, to build "People's Jinnah

Memorial Hall" which still stands in the compound of Bombay's Indian National Congress Building, commemorating the "historic triumph" of the citizens of Bombay "under the brave and brilliant leadership of Mohammad Ali Jinnah."[43] After Jinnah left Congress, and especially after the birth of Pakistan, that hall appeared strangely anachronistic and is now anonymously referred to only by its initials as P. J. Hall. Few Indians remember that People's Jinnah Hall was erected to honor the fearless leadership of Bombay's most inspiring ambassador of Hindu-Muslim unity.

5

Amritsar to Nagpur
(1919-21)

Armistice brought not peace but the sword of harsh repression and bitter disillusion to India. Martial law "Defence of India Acts" passed in 1915 had suspended civil liberties and all legal due process throughout the war, allowing the government of India to arrest, detain, intern, or expel any Indian without trial, warrant, or stated cause. The Allied victory was, naturally, expected to restore all such rights and legal safeguards. Such was not the case, however, for an ominous report written by the government's sedition committee, chaired by King's Bench Justice Sir Sidney Rowlatt, had just been published, recommending immediate extension of the Criminal Law (Emergency Powers) Act for at least six months. Such was the very first bill introduced to the postwar Central Legislative Council. It soon came to be known and hated throughout India as the "Black" or Rowlatt Act.

"This was a wrong remedy for the disease, the revolutionary crimes," warned the Hon. Mr. Jinnah, as Rowlatt's Bill was tabled on February 6, 1919.

> To substitute the Executive for the Judicial will lead to the abuse of these vast powers. . . . There was no precedent or parallel in the legal history of any civilized country to the enactment of such laws. . . . This was the most inopportune moment for this legislation as high hopes about momentous reforms had been raised. . . . If these measures were passed they will create unprecedented discontent, agitation and will have the most disastrous effect upon the relations between the Government and the people.[1]

His warnings fell on deaf ears. Chelmsford, Rowlatt, and the others were determined to steam full ahead despite the unanimous opposition of all twenty-two Indian members on the council. There were thirty-four official members willing to rubber stamp the Black Act that was passed into law in March 1919.

"By passing this Bill," Jinnah wrote Chelmsford a few days later from his Malabar Hill house, to which he had returned as soon as the vote was announced,

> Your Excellency's Government have actively negatived every argu-
> ment they advanced but a year ago when they appealed to India for
> help at the War Conference and have ruthlessly trampled upon the
> principles for which Great Britain avowedly fought the war. The fun-
> damental principles of justice have been uprooted and the constitu-
> tional rights of the people have been violated at a time when there is
> no real danger to the State, by an overfretful and incompetent bureau-
> cracy which is neither responsible to the people nor in touch with real
> public opinion. . . . I, therefore, as a protest against the passing of
> the Bill and the manner in which it was passed tender my resignation
> . . . for I feel that under the prevailing conditions I can be of no use
> to my people in the Council nor consistently with one's self-respect is
> co-operation possible with a Government that shows such utter dis-
> regard for the opinion of the representatives of the people in the
> Council Chamber, and for the feelings and sentiments of the people
> outside. In my opinion, a Government that passes or sanctions such a
> law in times of peace forfeits its claim to be called a civilised Gov-
> ernment and I still hope that the Secretary of State for India, Mr.
> Montagu, will advise His Majesty to signify his disallowance to this
> Black Act.[2]

The resignation, further attesting to Jinnah's courageous national leadership at this time, made no impact on Chelmsford, while Montagu's own
influence in London continued to deteriorate. Jinnah had no way of knowing on how impotent a secretary of state he pinned his hopes for India's
future, and he decided to sail for London to seek to persuade his faltering
friend to override the government of India. Ruttie was pregnant; and though
their love would never be as strong again and the aftermath of the war
proved so politically frustrating, the future never seemed as promising to
both of them as it did that winter at the start of 1919.

The Muslim League had appointed Jinnah to lead a deputation to Prime
Minister Lloyd George that year to plead for at least one Muslim delegate
to the forthcoming Paris Peace Conference. Most Indian Muslims felt, as
League President A. K. Fazlul Haq put it, that "Muslim countries are now
the prey of the land-grabbing propensities of the Christian nations, in spite
of the solemn pledges given by these very nations that the World War was

being fought for the protection of the rights of the small and defenceless minorities."[3] Sir Satyendra P. Sinha and the Maharaja of Bikaner (1880–1943) had been appointed to represent India at the Imperial War Conference in 1917, but since neither was Muslim, the League feared that Islamic interests were being shortchanged or ignored. With the Ali brothers and other popular Khilafat leaders, including Delhi's scholarly devout Maulana Abul Kalam Azad (1887–1958), still under detention without specified charges, Muslims felt more intensely than ever a sense of communal alarm and second-class subjectship under British rule. Khilafatists feared that British wartime pledges and promises to protect Islam's holy places would be broken, now that Turkey was a defeated enemy power at the mercy of Christian victor states, determined to crush it for all time.

The Jinnahs reached London in May and rented a flat near Regent's Park. Friends visited them there, including Bombay's diwan Chaman Lal, who recalled Jinnah's "uninhibited laughter when telling a funny story which was often in the category of a parable."[4] One evening in mid-August, Jinnah took Ruttie to the theater, but they were obliged to leave their box hurriedly. Their only child, a daughter named Dina, was born in London shortly past midnight on August 14–15, 1919, oddly enough precisely twenty-eight years to the day and hour before the birth of Jinnah's other offspring, Pakistan. Jinnah's mission for the League proved less successful, however, for though he presented the Muslim case vigorously to Lloyd George, the prime minister granted him no satisfaction. Montagu and Bikaner alone represented India at Versailles, where Britain and France formally assumed their protectorate mandates over Iraq, Palestine, Transjordan, Syria, and Lebanon, carved out of the dismembered Ottoman Empire. Jinnah must have hoped for an invitation to attend the peace conference himself, especially since he had come so far and was *the* "delegate" of the Muslim League, but the distrust, hatred, and suspicion of him so recently expressed by Chelmsford, Willingdon, and other leading experts on India sufficed to keep Britain's cabinet cold to his overtures. More doors remained closed than open to him this time round. Bombay's new governor, George Lloyd, did his best to poison Montagu's mind against Jinnah, writing of him that June as "fair of speech and black of heart," a "real irreconcilable," and "of all the agitators . . . the only one who has consistently said one thing and gone straight away and done the other."[5] There were fewer smiles on those robust London faces he met, as Whitehall closed ranks behind Simla, Delhi, and Bombay. He had, after all, resigned his "honorable" position. Best not to encourage that sort!

Since April, moreover, non-cooperation and violence had spread across India like brushfire in the wake of anti-Rowlatt Act mass protests and the

British massacre at Jallianwala Bagh. Gandhi chose April 6, 1919, as the first "sacred" day of a nationwide business strike (hartal) to protest the Black Acts, which he urged his *Satyagraha* followers to "refuse civilly to obey." It was a totally nonviolent day, but a week later, on April 13, 1919, Amritsar ("Nectar of Immortality"), a city sacred to the Sikhs of the Punjab, was transformed shortly before sundown into India's first national urban shrine. Two of Gandhi's lieutenants had been arrested a few days earlier and deported, thus stirring up a protest march toward the British commissioner's bungalow in the cantonment. Several soldiers panicked and opened fire, killing a few marchers and turning the peaceful crowd into a raging mob bent on retaliation. They burned British banks and attacked a few Englishwomen as well as Englishmen in Amritsar's old city. A British brigadier and his force were called in to restore order. The general banned all public meetings. On April 13, when he learned of a meeting of thousands taking place inside Jallianwala *Bagh* ("Garden"), he drove to that almost totally enclosed site with some of his troops, ordering them to open fire without uttering a word of warning to the peacefully assembled crowd inside. It was a Sunday, a Hindu festival holiday. The crowd, mostly villagers, had come to the city to celebrate. The soldiers fired 1,650 rounds of live ammunition at point-blank range for ten minutes at the terror-stricken human targets, who found no exits from that nightmare in the garden, leaving some 400 Indians dead and over 1,200 wounded. The general and his troops beat a hasty retreat as the sun set on the bloodiest massacre in British Indian history, which Chelmsford later termed an "error of judgment."

"India has got to keep her head cool at this most critical moment," Jinnah advised his readers in an interview the *Bombay Chronicle* published on his return home in mid-November 1919, "Unless at the next session of the Congress in December a thoughtful programme is laid down by our leaders and accepted by the people, an incalculable amount of harm would be done to our cause."[6] Jinnah still felt "confident that Mr. Montagu will not fail us" but termed Chelmsford's administration "a failure" and argued that "the sooner he is recalled the better for all concerned." As to the prime minister's "promises" on behalf of "poor Turkey," he called those "a scrap of paper" and did not believe the Allies stood ready to concede "self-determination and independence" to Arab states. He was, however, more optimistic about India, envisioning a true "renaissance" through education, commercial, industrial, and technical progress and growth, and a nationalized military policy. Asked if he had any "message to the people" as the Amritsar Congress was approaching, Jinnah replied: "The attitude of the Congress will have to depend upon the Reform Bill which I think will be passed before the middle of December." Jinnah had written Gandhi from London in June asking what he thought of Montagu's bill then in Parliament, and Gandhi replied:

> I cannot say anything about the Reforms Bill. I have hardly studied it. My preoccupation is Rowlatt legislation. . . . Our Reforms will be practically worthless, if we cannot repeal Rowlatt legislation. . . . And as I can imagine no form of resistance to the Government than civil disobedience, I propose, God willing, to resume it next week. I have taken all precautions, that are humanly possible to take, against recrudescence of violence.[7]

It epitomized their different approaches to political process, Jinnah still relying upon moderate legislative change, Gandhi preoccupied with civil disobedience. The vectors of their widely divergent paths led them ever further apart.

"If India were to send her real representatives, say half-a-dozen, who will carry on propaganda work there [in London] backed up by substantial financial help and public opinion," Jinnah suggested in his *Bombay Chronicle* interview, "a great deal can be done. But it must be a continual and permanently established institution carried on by men, not only who go there for a few months, but permanently, settled." Was he hoping for such a chance himself? He was now a father, after all, and had to plan for his daughter's future, as well as his young wife's. India was less secure than usual, less safe a land to raise a family in than it had been since the terrible war of 1857–58. The influenza epidemic alone had claimed more than six million lives since 1918, and with the frontier rumbling, the Punjab bleeding, and the rest of the land poised on the verge of *Satyagraha,* prospects for the immediate future seemed dismal. Nor had Ruttie's father relented, continuing to refuse to acknowledge them socially despite the birth of his granddaughter. So the lure of London remained, growing more romantic perhaps as its permanent realization became less plausible. Jinnah's Bombay practice continued to prosper, demanding and receiving more and more of his time and attention, evenings as well as days and often seven days a week. The law was an exacting mistress, as Ruttie soon learned. What little free time was left to him, politics consumed. "Mercurial, dashing, impulsive,"[8] and lovely, lonely young Ruttie found herself daily with more time than she could possibly devise ways to spend.

The long-awaited Montagu reforms were passed into law as the Government of India Act on December 23, 1919, the day of King-Emperor George V's royal proclamation granting amnesty to all political prisoners. It was His Majesty's "earnest desire at this time that so far as possible any trace of bitterness between my people and those who are responsible for my

Government should be obliterated," but the new act fell far short of that mark. Had it come a year earlier perhaps it would have sufficed to satisfy expectations roused by the war. Though it did provide some measure of provincial responsibility to elected representatives of India by "transferring" certain departments and their revenues to popular control, while "reserving" other, more important matters, to official hands. This newly devised technique of half-and-half rule, called dyarchy, was Britain's formula for devolving political power "by successive stages," to India. The Central Legislative Council was greatly enlarged into a bicameral mini-parliament with an elective majority lower house to be called the Legislative Assembly. The expense of the secretary of state for India's salary and those of his assistants was taken off India's budget and transferred to Parliament, as Congress and the League demanded. A public service commission was to be established in India, thanks to which simultaneous recruitment to the coveted civil services would begin in New Delhi as well as in London by 1923. Finally, the act provided for further statutory inquiry "into the working of the system of government, the growth of education, and the development of representative institutions, in British India . . . as to whether and to what extent it is desirable to establish the principle of responsible government" after ten years. Had these come before the Rowlatt Act and Amritsar such constitutional concessions would surely have sounded generous, and, have been more warmly welcomed throughout India.

Both Congress and the Muslim League held annual meetings in Amritsar in 1919. Hindu-Muslim unity was seen by the League to be "the secret of success," not just of the newly proposed reforms, but of all work done by Indians at home and abroad; and thanks to the "Congress-League Compact of 1916" the major political obstacle to such unity had been resolved. The Ali brothers appeared before the Amritsar League to a standing ovation and "reverberating chorus of joy."[9] Mohammad Ali assured his joyously tearful audience that "there was no Government but the Government of God." Jinnah was elected to preside over the League for the following year.

Jinnah called a special meeting of the Muslim League that September in Calcutta, where Congress met as well in emergency session to consider the radical change of political posture caused not only by announced Allied peace terms but also by harsh, callous British reactions to the Jallianwala *Bagh* massacre and published reports of its atrocious aftermath throughout the Punjab.

We have met here principally to consider the situation that has arisen owing to the studied and persistent policy of the Government since the signing of the Armistice. First came the Rowlatt Bill—accompanied by the Punjab atrocities—and then came the spoliation of the

Ottoman Empire and the Khilafat. The one attacks our liberty, the other our faith. Now, every country has two principal and vital functions to perform—one to assert its voice in international policy, and the other to maintain internally the highest ideals of justice and humanity. But one must have one's own administration in one's own hands to carry it on to one's own satisfaction. As we stand in matters international . . . notwithstanding the unanimous opinion of the Musalmans, and in breach of the Prime Minister's solemn pledges, unchivalrous and outrageous terms have been imposed upon Turkey and the Ottoman Empire has served for plunder and broken up by the Allies under the guise of Mandates. This, thank God, has at last convinced us, one and all, that we can no longer abide our trust either in the Government of India or in the Government of His Majesty the King of England to represent India in matters international.

And now let us turn to the Punjab. That Star Chamber Legislation named after the notorious Chairman of the Rowlatt Committee was launched by the Government of Lord Chelmsford, and it resulted in those "celebrated crimes" which neither the words of men nor the tears of women can wash away. "An error of judgment," they call it. If that is the last word, I agree with them—an error of judgment it is and they shall have to pay for it, if not to-day then tomorrow. One thing there is which is indisputable, and that is that this Government must go and give place to a completely responsible Government. Meetings of the Congress and the Muslim League will not effect this. We shall have to think out some course more effective than passing resolutions of disapproval to be forwarded to the Secretary of State for India. And we shall surely find a way, even as France and Italy did—and the new-born Egypt has. We are not going to rest content until we have attained the fullest political freedom in our own country. Mr. Gandhi has placed his programme of non-cooperation, supported by the authority of the Khilafat Conference, before the country. It is now for you to consider whether or not you approve of its principle; and approving of its principle, whether or not you approve of its details. The operations of this scheme will strike at the individual in each of you, and therefore it rests with you alone to measure your strength and to weigh the pros and the cons of the questions before you arrive at a decision. But once you have decided to march, let there be no retreat under any circumstances.[10]

Ruttie sat behind him on the platform, a vivid reminder of all that he personally risked from so revolutionary a step. He would, of course, be expected to give up his lucrative legal practice as long as *Satyagraha* continued, if he endorsed it, which he never did. He must have sensed now, as well, that the unique role of rising political power he had enjoyed at Lucknow was starting its rapid descent. Gandhi's star burned so bright that now lesser luminaries could barely be seen in India's political firmament. Jinnah tried, nonetheless, to recapture the position he had held little more than a year ago, castigating British rule for its broken promises.

Jinnah noted how the majority of the royal commission appointed to investigate the Punjab atrocities exonerated the hate-crazed general Dyer and his minions as "one more flagrant and disgraceful instance that there can be no justice when there is a conflict between an Englishman and an Indian. The Government of India, with its keen sense of humour and characteristic modesty," he added trenchantly, "proceeds to forward a resolution in its despatch to the Secretary of State commending its conduct, blind to the fact that they were in the position of an accused passing judgment. Now, let us turn to the great 'error of judgment,' the judicious finding of the Cabinet which itself is no less an error. . . . I must mention the Parliamentary debate. . . . Of course Mr. Montagu hadn't the time to put India's case before the House, being far too busy offering personal explanations. And then the blue and brainless blood of England, to their crowning glory, carried the infamous resolution of Lord Finlay." Viscount Finlay of Nairn had proposed honoring the deranged brigadier, General R. E. Dyer, hailed by the lords as "Hero of the Hour," presented with a large purse and jewelled sword inscribed "Saviour of the Punjab," and was backed by eight British dukes, six marquesses, thirty-one earls, ten viscounts, and seventy-four barons.

"These are the enormities crying aloud, and we have met to-day face to face with a dangerous and most unprecedented situation. The solution is not easy and the difficulties are great. But I cannot ask the people to submit to wrong after wrong." Jinnah was clearly torn, his heart and mind rent by the grave problems he tried to face rationally, doggedly seeking to avoid the abyss of civil war. "Yet I would still ask the Government not to drive the people of India to desperation, or else there is no other course left open to the people except to inaugurate the policy of non-cooperation, though not necessarily the programme of Mr. Gandhi."[11]

Jinnah thus moved as close as ever he dared to the far side of his personal faith in British justice and the noblest principles of Western civilization. He could not take that final stride into the vale of total rejection, however, as Gandhi and tens of millions who followed him would do, for that would have been a repudiation of himself, of all he stood for and had become. Jinnah was no more of a maulana than a mahatma, and could no sooner have relinquished his elegant legal chambers and clubs for village or prison life than Gandhi could have abandoned spinning to start a probate practice. The patterns of both personalities were by then set too firmly in fundamentally different molds to be altered without mortal damage. Each became the perfect prototype of a style of leadership suited to different con-stituencies, attuned to different languages and goals, fashioned by different worlds. Jinnah was the model of urban Westernized India at its cleanest and sharpest. Gandhi reflected India's ocean of peasant wisdom and village life with its infinite capacity to endure poverty and patiently suffer any hardship.

The Calcutta Congress gave Gandhi his first major victory, for though his non-cooperation program was strongly opposed by Bengal's leading poli-ticians, C. R. Das (1870–1925) and B. C. Pal (1858–1932) who joined forces with Jinnah and Annie Besant against him, the Mahatma, with the Ali brothers and Motilal Nehru in his corner, emerged with a clear majority mandate to lead the march against the government. Khilafat trainloads of delegates, hired by Bombay's merchant prince Mian Mohamed Chotani, one of Gandhi's leading supporters, had been shipped cross-country to pack the Congress pandal and vote for their hero's resolution, transforming Congress into a populist political party. It marked a revolutionary shift in Congress's base of support to a lower-class mass, funded by wealthy Hindu Marwari and Muslim merchant-industrialists. *Lokamanya* Tilak died the day Mahatma Gandhi launched his first nationwide *Satyagraha*, August 1, 1920. Tilak him-self refused to accept Gandhi's lead and was too orthodox a Brahman to em-brace the Khilafat cause. Annie Besant, who never trusted Gandhi, openly denounced his movement as a "channel of hatred," while Gokhale's moderate successor at the head of the Servants of India Society, V. S. Srinivasa Sastri (1869–1946), considered the Mahatma "fanciful." Pherozeshah Mehta's most conservative disciple, Dinshaw E. Wacha (1844–1936), a leader of the National Liberal Federation, called Gandhi a "madman . . . mad & arro-gant." Montagu, who could not for the life of him understand Gandhi's "saintly" politics, by now suspected that perhaps his *Satyagraha* as well as the Khilafat movement were both part of a "Bolshevik conspiracy." The secretary of state wrote Chelmsford the very day Gandhi won his Calcutta victory: "The Bolsheviks, in their animosity to all settled government, are using the grievances of the Mohammedans, and what frightens me is the way in which Pan-Islamism . . . is taking charge of the extremist move-ment."[12]

From Calcutta, both Jinnah and Gandhi went by rail to Bombay, to at-tend a Home Rule League (*Swaraj Sabha*) meeting there on October 3, 1920. Gandhi chaired that meeting and proposed changing Annie Besant's former organization's constitution to bring its goals more fully into line with his *Satyagraha* campaign—"To secure complete Swaraj for India according to the wishes of the Indian people." Jinnah argued against the motion, insisting that "Attainment of self-government within the British Commonwealth . . . by constitutional methods" remained the *Sabha's* best goal, and the only one he could accept. Gandhi remarked that anyone was "free" to "resign" from the *Sabha* who could not accept the majority's decision. Only sixty-one members attended that meeting, which had been called at short notice, but of those less than one-third, eighteen, agreed with Jinnah, including his loyal Bombay Parsi lieutenants, the brothers Jamnadas and Kanji Dwarkadas. The defeated minority left the meeting and before month's end, Jinnah wrote "with great sorrow"[13] to resign from the League he had once led. Gandhi then wrote to seek to win Jinnah back, asking him to take his "share in the new life that has opened up before the country, and benefit the country by your experience and guidance."[14] Jinnah's reply to that letter indicates how passionately apprehensive he felt on the eve of the Nagpur Congress about the course Gandhi charted for India.

> If by "new life" you mean your methods and your programme, I am afraid I cannot accept them; for I am fully convinced that it must lead to disaster. But the actual new life that has opened up before the country is that we are faced with a Government that pays no heed to the grievances, feelings and sentiments of the people; that our own countrymen are divided; the Moderate Party is still going wrong; that your methods have already caused split and division in almost every institution that you have approached hitherto, and in the public life of the country not only amongst Hindus and Muslims but between Hindus and Hindus and Muslims and Muslims and even between fathers and sons; people generally are desperate all over the country and your extreme programme has for the moment struck the imagination mostly of the inexperienced youth and the ignorant and the illiterate. All this means complete disorganisation and chaos. What the consequence of this may be, I shudder to contemplate; but I for one am convinced that the present policy of the Government is the primary cause of it all and unless that cause is removed, the effects must continue. I have no voice or power to remove the cause; but at the same time I do not wish my countrymen to be dragged to the brink of a precipice in order to be shattered.[15]

Was that "shudder" of apprehension in 1920 Jinnah's first rude awakening to the death knell of his dream of national leadership and unity? Clearly, he had no faith in Gandhi or his judgment to save India from being "shattered." Was this possibly his first premonition of partition? "The only way for the Nationalists," Jinnah warned in his revealing letter, "is to unite and work for a programme which is universally acceptable for the early attainment of complete responsible government. Such a programme cannot be dictated by any single individual, but must have the approval and support of all the prominent Nationalist leaders in the country; and to achieve this end I am sure my colleagues and myself shall continue to work." While conceding his own weakness, on the one hand, Jinnah thus reaffirmed his commitment to the same goal, the same struggle for responsible government through Hindu-Muslim unity, to which he had devoted himself since long before Lucknow. His wounded pride was palpable, perhaps more in those concluding remarks even than in his pained confession, "I have *no* voice or *power*."

Central India's Nagpur hosted both regular sessions of the Muslim League and Congress after Christmas in 1920. That ancient parched strong-hold of Hindu religious sentiment, fueled by Nag-Vidarbha regional mili-tancy gave birth to a new Congress under Gandhi's revolutionary leadership. The Mahatma first moved his credo resolution at a meeting of the subjects committee on December 28, proposing "the attainment of swaraj by the people of India by all legitimate and peaceful means." Jinnah immediately objected that it was impractical and dangerous to dissolve "the British connection" without greater preparation for independence, but Gandhi argued:

> I do not for one moment suggest that we want to end the British con-nection at all costs unconditionally. If the British connection is for the advancement of India we do not want to destroy it. . . . I know, be-fore we are done with this great battle on which we have embarked . . . we have to go probably, possibly, through a sea of blood, but let it not be said of us or any of us that we are guilty of shedding blood, but let it be said by generations yet to be born that we suffered, that we shed not somebody's blood but our own; and so I have no hesita-tion in saying that I do not want to show much sympathy for those who had their heads broken or who were said to be even in danger of losing their lives. What does it matter?[16]

Jinnah argued as best he could against the resolution in committee, but was told his caution betrayed "a want of courage" and was shouted as well as voted down the next day. As that fateful year rushed to its end, the new creed was placed by Gandhi before the more than 14,500 delegates, who flocked to Nagpur and crowded the Congress tent, more than twice the num-ber at Amritsar a year earlier. The Mahatma's resolution was greeted with deafening, prolonged cheers and applause. Lala Lajpat Rai seconded the motion amid further raucous acclamation. Jinnah alone rose and demanded to be heard in opposition, striding to the dais. "Mr. Jinnah with the usual smile on his face mounted the platform with an ease suggestive of self-confidence and the conviction of the man, and opposed in an argumentative, lucid and clear style, the change of creed,"[17] reported the *Times of India*.

He was "howled down with cries of 'shame, shame' and 'political im-poster.' "[18] He referred to "Mr. Gandhi's resolution," but the irate audience

yelled "*No. Mahatma Gandhi.*"[19] He repeated "Mister," then finally abandoned any preface, seeking a way to inject some air of logical reasoning into
an atmosphere charged with passionate emotion. "At the moment the destinies of the country are in the hands of two men," Jinnah argued, "and one
of them is Gandhi. Therefore, standing on this platform, knowing as I do
that he commands the majority in this assembly, I appeal to him to pause, to
cry halt before it is too late." Jinnah's appeal went unanswered by Gandhi,
however, as the boos, hisses, and catcalls of the audience finally drove the
author of the Lucknow Pact and ex-president of the Home Rule League and
the Bombay Conference from that Nagpur platform. As the Central Provinces' Commissioner Frank Sly quite accurately reported of the Nagpur Congress to Chelmsford two days later, "Jinnah carried no influence."[20] It was
the most bitterly humiliating experience of his public life. He left Central
India with Ruttie by the next train, the searing memory of his defeat at
Nagpur permanently emblazoned on his brain. Whatever hopes he had had
of National leadership were buried that day. Gandhi had scaled the heights
of political popularity; Jinnah plummeted over the precipice to a new low,
reviled by fellow-Muslim Khilafat leaders even more than by the Mahatma's
devoutest Hindu disciples. Shaukat Ali hated him and made no secret of his
sentiments wherever he went.

Though he had presided over the Muslim League only three months
earlier, Jinnah did not even bother to attend its Nagpur session, rightly
gauging the futility of his opposition to the Gandhi-Khilafat express. He had
no more heart for raucous confrontations that bitter December, no stomach
left for the names he had been called. He had warned them openly of the
futility of their battle plan, told them honestly of the havoc he correctly anticipated would be unleashed by and against the suddenly politicized
masses. Yet every jury, Khilafat Conference, *Swaraj Sabha*, Congress, and
Muslim League had rejected his arguments as outmoded, cowardly, or invalid. There was no court of appeals left for the moment, so Jinnah went
silently home—his "career" in politics a shambles, though hardly at an end.

6

Retreat to Bombay
(1921-24)

Jinnah's withdrawal from the political stage in 1921 left him totally preoccupied with the law. He poured all his energy and talent into his work then and for the last half of his fifth decade devoted himself, day and night, to that demanding mistress. His quiet chambers and the Bar became his protective walls from the noisy, muddy field of public life. Safely removed from the fray, he watched as violence and stupidity stirred up dark clouds of public rage and official repression. The death of his nationalist career in politics coincided with changes in his relationship to Ruttie. Their lives were less glamorous now, less exciting. Jinnah was no longer the rising political hero. Gone forever were the days of his leading a charge up any town hall steps or addressing mass meetings on streets named for Greek gods. After Nagpur he aged much faster. The rakish beau of forty-two was transformed—overnight it seemed—into an elder statesman, a careful barrister of forty-five, who had precious little time for the whims or fancies of a young wife and infant daughter.

Ruttie tried in many ways to recapture his interest and attention, using all the natural gifts and allure she possessed. But she belonged to his Lucknow era, those days of heady promise and infinite possibility. That mirage was behind him, almost as remote and strangely romantic a dream as his London stage career. "In temperament they were poles apart," Jinnah's legal assistant in this interlude recalled. "Jinnah used to pore over his briefs every day. . . . I remember her walking into Jinnah's chambers while we were in the midst of a conference, dressed in a manner which would be called fast even by modern standards, perch herself upon Jinnah's table, dangling her feet, and waiting for Jinnah to finish the conference so that they could leave together. Jinnah never uttered a word of protest, and carried on with his work as if she were not there at all."[1] She had not as yet turned to the "spirit world" for company, still desperately seeking friendship among the living. Spoiled child that she had been, once the center of her father's universe, having been cast out of that world doubled her demands on her husband's time. She was obliged to rely more on his human support and friendship than most Indian women of her class, who usually retained the closest ties with parents, siblings, cousins, and all distant members of the extended family, especially after becoming a mother. Ruttie had no one. Sir Dinshaw never spoke to her again, even refusing to attend her funeral just over a decade after her marriage. "No husband could have treated his wife more generously," Justice Chagla noted, summing up Jinnah's relationship with Ruttie, yet he could "well imagine how the patience of a man of Jinnah's temper must have been taxed" by so demanding, so lonely, a wife.[2]

Jinnah's first public address after Nagpur was on February 19, 1921, at the Poona Servants of India Society, which Gokhale had founded. Each year, a distinguished disciple of Gokhale's was invited to speak on the anniversary of his death. Jinnah launched into an analysis of the then paralyzing confrontation between "a Government which had persistently and deliberately followed a policy that had wounded the self-respect of the country," and Gandhi's non-cooperation movement, which "was taking them to a wrong channel."[3] Two and a half months of abstinence from politics had been withdrawal enough for him. He could not bring himself to follow "Mr. Gandhi's programme," calling it "an essentially spiritual movement," based on "destructive" methods "opposed to the nature of an ordinary mortal like the speaker himself." Jinnah made clear his own readiness to return to the public stage, but only to lead "a real political movement based on real political principles." His critique of Gandhi, though scathing, was not totally negative, concluding that "Undoubtedly Mr. Gandhi was a great man and he [Jinnah] had more regard for him than anybody else. But he did not believe in his programme and he could not support it." Jinnah ventured to "guess" that were Gokhale still alive, he too "would not have endorsed this programme."

The *Satyagraha* boycott proved less effective than Gandhi envisioned. British courts remained busy as ever, though some Indian lawyers abandoned their practices. Schools and colleges continued to function. Most trains ran on time. Jails were filled, police did not stop working, and the army remained entirely loyal to the British raj that paid it. There were signs of seismic cracking in the wall of Hindu-Khilafat unity that started to crumble with the mass flight of Muslims to Afghanistan in the summer of 1920, and kept toppling deadly communal rubble on the heads of Muslims who fought Hindu neighbors in the south as well as the north during the rest of the decade. "God only knows how often I have erred," admitted Gandhi by mid-August 1921. "Those who charge me with infallibility simply do not know me . . . Life consists in struggling against errors."[4]

Chelmsford's successor, Rufus Daniel Isaacs (1860–1935), the first Marquess of Reading, arrived in India on April 2, 1921. Ex-lord chief justice of Britain, Viceroy Reading had much more in common with fellow barristers like Mr. Jinnah than had cavalry captain Chelmsford. Before the end of 1921, Reading enlisted Jinnah's assistance in seeking to reopen lines of communication with political India.

Jinnah attended the Ahmedabad Congress that December and worked with Bombay's liberal M. R. Jayakar (1873–1959) and several other moderate leaders, trying to convince Gandhi to call a halt to *Satyagraha* in order to allow all of them to explore the new viceroy's promise of "full provincial autonomy" and of a Round Table conference to discuss possible extension of dyarchy to the center. Gandhi pondered that remarkable viceregal offer "silent in deep thought" for a while,[5] as Jinnah and Jayakar waited. Finally, the Mahatma agreed to give Reading a chance to prove himself, but within the hour, pressed hard by the misgivings of his more militant lieutenants, Gandhi changed his mind. Had he adhered to his initial response, the transfer of power from Imperial British to national Indian control might have been advanced a full decade and a half. Gandhi feared, however, that Reading was trying to "emasculate" him. "I am sorry that I suspect Lord Reading of complicity in the plot to unman India for eternity," wrote the Mahatma in his "private notes" at this time.[6] Was the fifty-year-old Mahatma possibly losing confidence in his own "manhood" at this critical hour of severe tribulation?

The Muslim League also met in Ahmedabad that December, with Maulana Hasrat Mohani, Jinnah's *bête noire* presiding. It was a low point in the League's history, for most Muslims either expended their political energies on the Khilafat movement, or, like Jinnah and the raja of Mahmudabad, abandoned the League in disgust at its uninspiring postwar leadership. "The present condition of the League appears to be very weak indeed," admitted Mohani, confessing "the League remains nothing more than an old calendar."[7]

Jinnah convened an All-Parties Conference in Bombay for mid-January of 1922, hoping to chart an alternative course to that set by Gandhi's insistence that intensified *Satyagraha,* including non-payment of taxes, was the only way of achieving *Swaraj.* Some 300 political leaders from all of India's major parties attended that conference, including Gandhi, who participated "informally," claiming as he told the press to do so only "To see if he could bring round his Moderate friends."[8] The "Leaders' Conference" was chaired

by Madras' Sir Sankaran Nair (1857–1934), former Congress president, now
law member of the viceroy's council, who called upon Jinnah to propose the
draft resolutions. Those began with a strong condemnation of the government's repressive policy, and an equally strong urging of Congress to
abandon non-cooperation. A compromise resolution ultimately agreed upon
called for a Round Table conference to settle outstanding differences between the government and the Congress and Khilafat movements. Gandhi
addressed the conference, insisting that before any Round Table meeting
could be held government would have to issue "a proper declaration of peni-
tence" and "retrace their steps."

The Mahatma met with a subjects committee of twenty leaders to help
draft the final resolutions, changing Jinnah's proposals enough to drive conservative Sir Sankaran Nair from his chair the next day when the new resolutions were submitted. Sir M. Vishveshvaraya, ex-diwan (prime minister)
of Mysore State, then took the chair. The resolutions all passed unanimously,
but Gandhi had not yet abandoned his call for accelerating the pace of civil
disobedience and considered "the idea" of a Round Table conference "for
devising a scheme of full *swaraj* premature. India has not yet incontestably
proved her strength," Gandhi argued.[9] Two weeks later, however, the fatal
immolation of twenty-two Indian policemen inside their station in a United
Provinces town named Chauri Chaura by a mob of *"Satyagrahis"* convinced
Gandhi that his countrymen were not ready for a nonviolent movement.
Early in February of 1922, the Mahatma called a halt to the campaign he
had launched with such confidence. "God has been abundantly kind to me,"
he wrote at this time.

> He has warned me the third time that there is not as yet in India that
> truthful and non-violent atmosphere which and which alone can
> justify mass disobedience which can be at all described as civil, which
> means gentle, truthful, humble, knowing, wilful yet loving, never
> criminal and hateful. . . . God spoke clearly through Chauri Chaura.[10]

Soon after this about-face by the Mahatma, Jinnah and Jayakar met with
him, the latter noting that Jinnah's "strong dislike of Gandhi" grew more
"manifest" at each of their meetings.[11] Immediately following news of the
violence at Chauri Chaura, "Jinnah and (Sir Hormusji) Wadia's treatment
of Gandhi was most discourteous."[12] Little more than a year since Nagpur,
then it was Gandhi's turn to swallow the bitter potion of humiliation. There
was no sweetness, no satisfaction for Jinnah, however, in the defeat of his
foremost rival. The collapse of *Satyagraha* which he had anticipated, the
violence and resurrected Hindu-Muslim antipathy, brought him no joy, for
all that was left of Lucknow and the laurel wreath of national leadership

snatched from his brow before it could settle there, were ashes. Like those wretched, dismembered corpses at Chauri Chaura, his countless hours of patient Bombay negotiation and careful Calcutta formulation of parliamentary schemes confirmed at Lucknow had gone up in the smoke of Nagpur's display of wild enthusiasm. For what? Now it was even too late to bring Reading round again to where he had been just a few months before. Why should any viceroy in his right mind negotiate a new constitution after mayhem and abject surrender? Jinnah's "discourtesy" to Gandhi was hardly surprising.

By mid-1922 Jinnah was trying to organize a new moderate party from which he would have excluded Gandhi entirely, speaking out more "strongly" against the Mahatma.[13] He invited Jayakar and Motilal Nehru to join forces with him in this ambitious venture, but both "declined," thus leaving Jinnah isolated from his former Congress Hindu colleagues. The old "Ambassador's" bridge of communal unity broke down. Jinnah's political isolation and frustration at this time were compounded by his alienation from Muslim Khilafat leadership as well. The Ali brothers and Maulana Azad considered him a spokesman for the government and virtual "traitor" to their cause. His only political friend was Muslim League fellow barrister and Sindhi, Ghulam Mohammed Bhurgri (1881–1924), who continued to visit him in Bombay, where they often talked politics atop Malabar Hill well into the night. Jinnah's former Home rule secretary, Parsi Jamnadas Dwarkadas, and his younger brother Kanji were often there too. Kanji, who became Ruttie's closest friend, wrote:

One night in May (1922) I had a dream in which I saw Ruttie lying on a peculiarly shaped old fashioned sofa . . . and in that dream Ruttie said: "Kanji, help me." Next morning as I woke up I remembered the dream, but . . . I took no notice of it. The next night the same dream appeared . . . including Ruttie's call for help. . . . On the 3rd afternoon at about 5, returning from office and without remembering the dream I called at Jinnah's "South Court" . . . I had not seen Ruttie for some weeks and this was the first time that I went to Jinnah's house without a previous appointment. As I got out of the car, Jinnah's servant met me and told me that Ruttie was ill. I gave him my card. . . . In a minute he came back and said that Ruttie wanted to see me and I was taken to the back varandah [sic] where she was lying. Imagine my surprise when I saw her lying on the sofa. . . . We kept on talking and Jinnah returned home from his Chamber at about 7.30, asked me to have a drink with him and to stay on for dinner. I said I was there since 5 o'clock and I did not stay for dinner[14]

That September, Ruttie left Bombay with her daughter, pets, and nurse for London. Kanji sent her a bouquet of "beautiful roses" from Poona's Empress Gardens as a bon voyage gift, and Ruttie wrote to thank him from her P. & O. cabin before reaching Aden, on September 25, 1922: "It will always give me pleasure to hear from you, so if you ever have a superfluous moment on your hands you know how now—" and she gave her London address, adding somewhat cryptically it "will find me if I don't lose myself— And just one thing more—go and see Jinnah and tell me how he is—he has a habit of habitually over-working himself, and now that I am not there to bother and tease him he will be worse than ever."[15] Her perception of his "habit of habitually over-working himself," while couched in a wife's language of concern, revealed their growing isolation from one another. As did her coy reference to her own demands upon his time as "to *bother* and *tease* him." A streak of gray emerged now from the middle of Jinnah's forehead, visual proof of how fast he was aging. He no longer sported his handsome Lucknow mustache, and pictures from this era never show him smiling. His dress remained meticulous, and it was always pinstripes in hues of gray, black, or navy blue.

In September 1923, Jinnah issued an appeal to Muslim voters of Bombay. "The duty of the Muslim voters of this city who will take part in the election to the Legislative Assembly is . . . to give their entire support to Mr. M. A. Jinnah," editorialized the *Bombay Chronicle*, whose board Jinnah chaired. Congress split into opposing council-entry Swarajist party factions led by Motilal Nehru and C. R. Das, and "no-changer" non-cooperators loyal to Gandhi. The Swarajists selected their own candidates for the general Bombay seats. Jinnah ran as an independent Muslim candidate, and his popularity and prestige within Bombay were such that he stood unopposed and on November 14, 1923, was easily returned to the seat he had resigned after passage of the Rowlatt acts.

Ruttie tried to see more of him after she returned from abroad, but nothing she attempted ever seemed to work. During that election campaign, for example, one afternoon as Jinnah and Chagla were going out for lunch,

> Mrs. Jinnah drove up to the Town Hall in Jinnah's luxurious limousine, stepped out with a tiffin basket, and coming up the steps . . . staid . . . "J"!—that is how she called him—"guess what I have brought for you for lunch." Jinnah answered: "How should I know?" and she replied: "I have brought you some lovely ham sandwiches." Jinnah, startled exclaimed: "My God! What have you done? Do you want me to lose my election? Do you realise I am standing from a Muslim separate electorate seat, and if my voters were to learn that I am going to eat ham sandwiches for lunch, do you think I have a

ghost of a chance of being elected?" At this, Mrs. Jinnah's face fell. She quickly took back the tiffin basket, ran down the steps, and drove away. . . . We decided to go to Cornaglia's, which was a very well-known restaurant in Bombay. . . . Jinnah ordered two cups of coffee, a plate of pastry and a plate of pork sausages. . . . As we were drinking our coffee and enjoying our sausages, in came an old, bearded Muslim with a young boy of about ten years of age, probably his grandson. They came and sat down near Jinnah. It was obvious that they had been directed from the Town Hall. . . . I then saw the boy's hand reaching out slowly but irresistibly towards the plate of pork sausages. After some hesitation, he picked up one, put it in his mouth, munched it and seemed to enjoy it tremendously. I watched this uneasily. . . . After some time they left and Jinnah turned to me, and said angrily: "Chagla, you should be ashamed of yourself." I said: "What did I do?" Jinnah asked: "How dare you allow the young boy eat pork sausages?" I said: "Look, Jinnah, I had to use all my mental faculties at top speed to come to a quick decision. The question was: should I let Jinnah lose his election or should I let the boy go to eternal damnation? And I decided in your favour."[16]

Jinnah never permitted religious taboos to alter his tastes in food or drink, but from this point in time he was more sensitive to the concerns and feelings of orthodox Muslims. Not that he abandoned his commitment to secular reform and national independence, or refused to cooperate with Hindus, Parsis, and all other Indians. As late as 1925, in fact, he reproached the young raja of Mahmudabad, who had by then come to think of himself as a "Muslim first," with a stern, "My boy, no, you are an Indian first and then a Muslim."[17] But now he would never forget or underestimate the political importance of his Islamic identity. Many doors had been slammed in his face since Nagpur, some on his toes. The public humiliation and personal rejection he had felt drove him back deeper into himself, and to the enduring community that still valued his advice. That helped him grow strong again, but in a different way. A new phase of his political life had begun, a more cautious ascent, by another route. He had climbed very high, but too swiftly. Were it not for the rope of his separate electorate constituency there might have been no return. This time he would cut each toehold with great care, cleaving to the rock that sustained him.

7

New Delhi
(1924-28)

British India's newly elected National Assembly met for the first time in New Delhi on January 31, 1924. Jinnah wasted no time, inviting all twenty-three "independents" to confer with him immediately after the viceroy's opening address. Ingenious negotiator, practical politician that he was, he managed to define a program of basic reforms that he convinced all his prima donna colleagues to join forces and work toward achieving. He was then in position to go to Motilal Nehru and C. R. Das, offering to merge his powerful swing-bloc of "independent" votes with their plurality of forty-two Swarajist party members, who could rout the phalanx of thirty-six official appointees whenever they wished. A new Nationalist party was thus born within the assembly overnight, much to Reading's amazement and dismay. This powerful Indian bloc of elected representatives committed to achieving dominion status and fully responsible provincial government at the earliest possible date, had been conjured into existence, miraculously it seemed, from the disparate dross of individuals who posed no threat, no political challenge to officialdom till touched by the welding fire of Jinnah's brilliant alchemy. So he repeated in New Delhi much the same feat of political unification he had achieved at Lucknow. Only the magic formula did not extend as far this time, nor last quite as long.

Jinnah's assembly strategy bore fruit in February 1924, when a resolution on constitutional reforms recommended the "early" summoning of a Round Table conference "with due regard to the protection of the rights and interests of important minorities" to "take steps to have the Government of India Act revised with a view to establish full responsible Government in India."[1] That resolution carried by a vote of 76 to 48, and as a result, Lord Reading appointed a Reforms Inquiry Committee, chaired by Home member Sir

Alexander Muddiman. Jinnah served on that committee with four other Indians: Madras' Sir P. S. Sivaswamy Aiyer (1864–1946), president of the National Liberal Federation; Poona educator Dr. R. P. Paranjpye (1877–1969); Allahabad's barrister Sir Tej Bahadur Sapru (1875–1949); and the Punjab's Sir Muhammad Shafi, law member of the government of India. The committee soon came to be referred to among the elected members within the assembly as "the Jinnah Committee."[2] Jinnah drafted a "national demand" minority report by the year's end, but official fears of the growing effectiveness and escalating demands of the united elected majority were by then so strong that the viceroy vetoed several attempts to debate the Reforms Inquiry Committee reports, thus squelching Jinnah's recommendations.

The Pakistan movement and its singular impact on recent Indian history have tended to obscure Jinnah's positive contributions to the evolution of parliamentary government in India. Much of his time and talent, however, were lavished on fashioning legislation, arguing for or against budget items, and trying to keep officials as well as nationalist colleagues intellectually honest. Just as Gokhale had been for the Central Legislative Council of Calcutta, Jinnah emerged in this interlude as the gadfly of Delhi's assembly, speaking to most resolutions, perusing every document and report with the precision of a lawyer, and expressing himself without fear or hope of favor. Speaking, for example, to a resolution designed to empower the assembly to review government contracts, strongly opposed by officialdom, Jinnah argued: "What is the difficulty? It is only an excuse, it is the same old story; the Executive does not wish to stand the searchlight of this House in entering into engagements of a serious character—I say there is absolutely no justification."[3] And to a bill proposed to require passports for entry into British India, Jinnah remarked: "Sir, I think that all regulations which impose passports are the biggest nuisance and the sooner they are done away with the better."[4]

In February of 1924 he introduced an important resolution that went to the heart of India's struggle for economic independence, insisting that the government of India be allowed to purchase its vast and valuable "stores" through "rupee tenders" submitted in India, rather than only through sterling bids made in London. "Although this Resolution of mine may not interest every Member of the House, it being a very dry subject," Jinnah began wryly, "I have no doubt that when Honourable Members understand this question . . . they will realise that it affects India most vitally."[5] He then reviewed the history of some seventy-five years of imperial purchases that inhibited Indian economic development, concluding "it gives a tremendous advantage to the British manufacturers who are on the spot, who get the information first, and invariably it is really for all practical purposes confined to the tenders coming from the British firms in England." Moreover, Jinnah argued that during the war "necessity" dictated the purchase of many stores in India. Jinnah's resolution carried and probably did more to stimulate Indian economic development prior to independence than any other measure passed by the assembly.

Jinnah remained a great civil libertarian, always outspoken in defense of individual rights and equal justice. "Sir," he insisted, on behalf of readmitting the deported editor of the *Bombay Chronicle*, B. G. Horniman,

> I do maintain, and I have drunk deep at the fountain of constitutional law, that the liberty of man is the dearest thing in the law of any constitution and it should not be taken away in this fashion. If you have any case, if Mr. Horniman has committed an offence, place him before a tribunal. . . . I speak very feelingly, because I feel that no man should be deported and certainly not on such fabricated allegations as these, which, to my knowledge, are absolutely false.[6]

That September in Simla, Jinnah reiterated his firm belief in "this principle that no man's property or liberty should be touched without a judicial trial."[7] In debating another bill the same day, Jinnah objected to the Home minister's motion, remarking: "I am not standing here merely as a person who distrusts Government, but I am standing here as a representative of the people and the Government have got to do what is best for the people and not as it pleases their whims."[8]

That May, Jinnah presided over a special session of the Muslim League in Lahore. "Since the commencement of 1923, it was realized and admitted that the triple boycott was a failure, and that the mass Civil Disobedience could not be undertaken successfully in the near future," Jinnah argued. His return to active political life had diminished his recent pessimism:

> Boycott of Councils, as desired by Mahatma Gandhi, was far from being effective or useful . . . the Khilafat organization, which was carried on, could not claim any better position. . . . The result of the struggle of the last three years has this to our credit that there is an open movement for the achievement of *Swaraj* for India. There is a fearless and persistent demand that steps must be taken for the immediate establishment of Dominion Responsible Government in India.[9]

And returning to the theme he stressed since first joining the League in 1913, Jinnah cautioned India never to forget "that one essential requisite condition to achieve *Swaraj* is political unity between the Hindus and the Mohammedans; . . . I am almost inclined to say that India will get Dominion Responsible Government the day the Hindus and Mohammedans are united. *Swaraj* is an almost interchangeable term with Hindu-Muslim unity."[10]

The Muslim League resolved at this important meeting to work for *Swaraj*, defined as a federal union of provinces "fully autonomous," except for a minimal number of central government functions "of general and common concern." "Full religious liberty" was to be "guaranteed to all communities," and "separate electorates" were to remain for Indian Muslims, since joint electorates were deemed a "source of discord and disunion" as well as "wholly inadequate to achieve the object of effective representation." Nor was any "bill or resolution" affecting "any community" to be passed in "any legislature or in any other elected body" if three-fourths of that community's elected members opposed it. The League also appointed a special committee headed by Jinnah to frame a scheme for a constitution for the government of India. Viewing with "great alarm the deplorable bitterness of feeling at present existing between the Hindus and Musalmans," the League further resolved to cooperate in establishing "conciliatory boards" on which members of all communities could meet regularly to resolve communal differences and try to alleviate causes of conflict. Jinnah moved the above resolutions as well as one deploring "the present scandalous state of disorganization existing among Muslims in all spheres of life, which not only prevents all healthy interchange of ideas and co-operation for the good of the Community, but also seriously handicaps the Muslims in shouldering their proper share of responsibility in the national struggle for progress and self-government."[11] One committee was to stimulate "internal solidarity among the Musalmans of India" and another, also chaired by Jinnah, would confer with the Central Khilafat Committee. Jinnah was elected "permanent" president of the League for the next three years to give him time to carry out this ambitious plan of revitalization of Muslim India. Three years was not enough, but it was a beginning.

The cornerstone was blasted out of the Khilafat movement by Turkey's President Mustafa Kemal Ataturk (1881–1938) who formally abolished the caliphate in October 1924. The fallout in India from that shattered pillar of Pan-Islam included accelerating Hindu-Muslim riots. From the Pathans of the North-West Frontier to the Moplahs of Malabar, from Kashmir to Dacca, outraged Muslims the length and breadth of South Asia turned against neighboring Hindus to vent frustrations at having lost their khalif. Hindus, in turn, retaliated, with militant revivalist organizations, like the Mahasabha, launching programs of forced "conversions" (*shuddhi*) of unwilling Muslims to Hinduism. Paramilitary "organizations" (*sangatan*) drilled and marched through Hindu-dominated cities, noisily luring Muslims from prayer in their mosques, indiscriminately attacking leatherworkers or cow slaughterers.

Each flurry led to more retaliatory raids, provoking full-fledged riots, leaving countless dead, wounded, and embittered.

Motilal Nehru, as head of the Swarajist faction within Congress (Das fell mortally ill in 1924), was Gandhi's only competitor for leadership of that organization. In August 1924, in a *"Very Confidential"* letter, the Mahatma wrote Motilal to inform him that he was "prepared to facilitate your securing the Congress machinery, actually assisting you to do so," and would "In no case . . . be party to vote-catching," claiming "no interest in anything but promoting a peaceful atmosphere," and adding "If you are not prepared to take over the whole of the Congress machinery, I am quite prepared to facilitate your taking over those Provinces where you think you have no difficulty in running it." Almost as an afterthought, however, in the very same letter, Gandhi named those who have been "insistent" that *he* [Gandhi] should become president himself, concluding: "The only condition that will make me reconsider my position would be your desire that I should accept. Will you please consult Messrs. Das, Kelkar and others and let me know what you would advise?"[12]

The Mahatma's continued boycott of all councils undermined Motilal's position within both Legislative Assembly and Congress. Gandhi had published a statement of "Fundamental Difference" with the Swarajists that May, concluding that "Council-entry is inconsistent with Non-co-operation, as I conceive it."[13]

Motilal was thus faced with the need to choose, by mid-1924, between continuing his party's assembly alliance with Jinnah and risking the loss of Gandhi's confidence and erosion of his Congress position, or moving the other way. It was not an easy decision. The elder Nehru wrestled with it all summer, inviting Gandhi to stay as his guest at the family beach house in Bombay's Juhu during August, trying to convince the Mahatma of the "nation-building utility" of Swarajist work within the assembly. Motilal's son, Jawaharlal, who was Congress secretary that year, joined them for those vacation summits but recalled that he and his father "did not succeed in winning Gandhiji, or even in influencing him to any extent." The Mahatma's only match for stubbornness in recent Indian history was Jinnah. "Behind all the friendly talks and the courteous gestures, the fact remained that there was no compromise," wrote the younger Nehru. "I also returned from Juhu . . . disappointed, for Gandhiji did not resolve a single one of my doubts. As is usual with him, he refused to look into the future, or lay down any long-distance program."[14] Jawaharlal rightly called it a tug-of-war between his father and Gandhi.

Capitulating to Gandhi's position, Motilal got his assembly Swarajists to agree after mid-year to "throw out all proposals for legislative enactments by which the bureaucracy proposes to consolidate its power." While admitting "It is conceivable that some good may incidentally result from a few of such measures," Motilal insisted, "we are clearly of opinion that in the larger interest of the country it is better to temporarily sacrifice such little benefits rather than add an iota to the powers of the bureaucracy."[15] That "Swarajist statement" presaged the death of the Nationalist party, for Jinnah and his independents refused to engage in "obstructionist tactics" within the assembly, continuing to consider each motion on its merits, voting for or against a measure only because they believed it might advance or retard the economic or constitutional development of India.

During his visit to Bombay that summer, Gandhi spoke to the "Parsi circle" at Excelsior Theatre to raise funds for Malabar flood relief. Kanji Dwarkados attended the meeting and walked in Jinnah's Nagpur footsteps, addressing Gandhi as "Mister" and noting that a great deal of "dirty work" had been done under the mantle of "Mahatma." Kanji was loudly heckled from the audience, but Gandhi rose on this occasion to his critic's defense, stating that

> The word "Mahatma" stinks in my nostrils; and, in addition to that, when somebody insists that everyone must call me "Mahatma" I get nausea, I do not wish to live. Had I not known that the more I insist on the word "Mahatma" not being used, the more does it come into vogue, I would most certainly have insisted. In the Ashram where I live, every child, brother and sister has orders not to use the word "Mahatma."[16]

It was the closest he came to a public apology to Jinnah for what had happened at Nagpur almost four years earlier. He must have known that Kanji would report what he said to Mr. and Mrs. "J."

Ruttie saw almost as much of Kanji by now as she did of her busy husband, and "communicated" more openly and more intimately with him. She had turned to mysticism for solace, and Kanji was her guide in the realm of seances, magnetizing, and thought transference. Wrote Kanji: "Ruttie was intensely interested in contacting the non-physical world and she made difficult and dangerous experiments to verify her beliefs and convictions. She wanted first-hand knowledge."[17] Just how difficult or "dangerous" her "experiments" were is unclear, but she seems to have been taking drugs for some time, initially to help her cope with insomnia and depression perhaps. Opium, morphine, hashish, and cocaine were, of course, readily available in the port of Bombay. She wrote Kanji in November 1924:

> There is a matter about which I am most anxious to speak with you, as I think you can help me. Lately I have been very much drawn to-

wards the subject of Spirit Communication and I am *most* anxious to know more and to get at the Truth. It is such an elusive Subject and the more I hear of it the more puzzled do I become, though still more passionately interested. I have some sort of an idea that you must be cognisant of spiritual circles in our City, whose Seance one may join. I don't profess any creed nor do I subscribe to a belief, but . . . I am too deeply immersed in the matter now to give it up without some personal satisfaction for I cannot content myself with other peoples' experiences . . . I would prefer my identity, however, to remain unknown while you make enquiries. And I sincerely hope that you will be able to assist me.[18]

A month later, Ruttie wrote again to remind him that "What I am after is a Seance controlled by some experienced medium . . . as I am most anxious to get a personal experience of this matter in which I so passionately believe."[19] Her loneliness, her desperate need for some one to talk with and to discuss questions that interested her "so passionately" was palpable: "Do come and see me soon so that we may resume our chat of the last occasion.

"My dear Kanji," she wrote the following April, "Yes, I know of the dream travels of which you speak. But I do all my dreaming in my waking hours. . . . There is nothing I would welcome with greater rejoicing than an experience of the sort to which you refer in your letter, but in my heavy druglike sleep there is no redeeming feature . . . five or at most six hours rest . . . a restive mind, and a correspondingly restless physical state . . . I don't dream excepting very rarely." She was now twenty-five years old. "My soul is too clogged! and though I aspire and crave, God knows how earnestly, my researches remain uncrowned—even by thorns! I am feeling peculiarly restless and wish one with psychic powers could come to my assistance."[20]

She tried her best to arouse her husband's interest in such things. Writing to report to Kanji, she even thought she had succeeded.

I am slowly, but surely drawing J's interest into the matter and by alternate bullying and coaxing I got him to read that book "The Spirit of Irene." . . . J. had to admit that it was remarkable and irrefutable. . . . The incident deals with the tracing of a murder . . . it revolves round a poor girl—a cook—who was decoyed from London to Boscomb and then done to death, the details of the crime are horrible, it having been a crime of lust. The police being baffled by the cunning of the man, were at their wits end, or you may be sure they would not have consented to hold Seance. Anyway they got the needed clue and the evidence was of such a nature that the unfortunate man was hanged. . . . J. was not at all events able to find any flaw in the case."[21]

One can hardly imagine Jinnah devoting much time or attention to "Irene." His legal practice alone remained so demanding that Ruttie added in this letter of April 12, 1925, "It doesn't look as if we were going to Kashmere after all, as J. is engaged in the Bawla case." Kanji kept her well supplied with books of all kinds, his own literary reviews, and plays (she specially enjoyed Noel Coward). Throughout 1925 he saw her regularly, three or four times a week. Dina was now six, and Kanji tried to convince Ruttie to send her to school in Madras, at the headquarters of Mrs. Besant's Theosophical Society. Jinnah resisted that move, sensing no doubt, that it would further alienate his daughter from her own community. He may have feared he would soon "lose" his only daughter, as Sir Dinshaw had lost his. By June 1925, Ruttie was "ill again" and wrote "dear Kanji" as it was "nearing 2 A.M. I am frightfully tired and sleepy but the thought of you having come to me I simply had to crawl out of bed to write to you—to ease my conscience if nothing else. Will you excuse me and let me get back now."[22] She told Jinnah in July that she would go with Kanji to the Theosophical Society's Jubilee Convention in Madras that December. The Muslim League would meet in Aligarh. She was to have been initiated as a theosophist by Mrs. Besant at the jubilee, but then Ruttie's cat "fell ill," delaying her departure a week. She did, however, meet Annie Besant at Adyar before year's end, and the older woman immediately perceived how "unhappy" she was, reproving Kanji's amazement at that verdict with: "Don't you see unhappiness in her eyes? *Look at her.*"[23]

Despite his disclaimers of interest, Gandhi finally did preside over the Congress in 1925 but, as he insisted, "only as a businessman presides at business meetings." The 1921 census figures revealed such rapid growth among Muslims in both wings of the north that they were now a majority in the Punjab (54.8 percent) and in Bengal (52.7 percent). This development stimulated demands for renegotiating the Lucknow Pact formula, with many League leaders from both Muslim-majority provinces no longer willing to rest content with the prospect of mere minority council status. The wedge of communal separation was thus driven deeper, irreversibly dividing the Muslim League from Congress, even as Muslim disillusion with Gandhian methods of non-cooperation grew.

It was Reading's final year in India. The viceroy valued Jinnah's assembly work highly enough to offer to include his name that December on the coveted list he was recommending for knighthood, if only Jinnah would agree to accept that honor. "I prefer to be plain Mr. Jinnah," he replied, "I have lived as plain Mr. Jinnah and I hope to die as plain Mr. Jinnah."[24] Ruttie reportedly responded to a query of how she would like being addressed "Lady Jinnah," by snapping—"if my husband accepts knight-hood I will take a separation from him." The latter course may have been an option she contemplated by now. It was one she would, at any rate, exercise a few years later, even though Jinnah was never knighted. His increased conservatism and growing Islamic consciousness contributed to the ideological gulf that divided them. There were more personal gulfs as well. He was practically fifty, she was half that age, and they were attuned to different harmonies. Not that he ever stopped loving her—he hoped, in fact, that they might recapture the magic of their early years in the spring and summer of 1926, when he took her abroad with him on a tour that included London, Paris, Canada, and the United States.

Jinnah had been appointed to the assembly's Sandhurst Committee in 1925, chaired by then army chief of staff Lieutenant General Sir Andrew Skeen, to study the feasibility of establishing a military college like Sandhurst in India. He was one of three Indian subcommittee members invited to undertake the grand tour of inspection of military colleges and installations overseas, leaving Bombay early in April and returning home in August. Ruttie was nervous about the trip and wrote her friend shortly before leaving, "Kanji, I am going away to Europe and U. S. A. for a few months. You will not be with me to protect me and help me. Do please, therefore, magnetise something for me to keep me in touch with you."[25] She gave him a beautiful jade brooch she wore, and he "magnetised it with thoughts of love and protection." (Jinnah never believed in such things and used to laugh at her for putting faith in amulets, Ruttie reported to Kanji after her return home.) But instead of being a second honeymoon, it was their final trip together.

Ruttie's health deteriorated rapidly after their trip abroad. "I suppose we all have our moments of melancholy and moments when everything seems to be impending and yet nothing happens—a sort of waiting mood, and one just waits and waits and grows distrustful of life," she wrote her best friend early in 1927. "I am always glad when you come. So don't please let any idea of my not being strong enough and well enough keep you away. . . . P.S. I am quite alright again and were it not that my feet are ugly and swollen I should be getting about as usual. As it is I go calling at my friends and to-night I am going to cinema—in bedroom slippers as no shoes are large enough to accommodate my elegant and lily-like feet!! Had X-rays taken and find that the broken needle is still there, so am trying to make up my mind to undergo another operation."[26] She lavished most of her time and emotional energy now on her numerous pets, cats and dogs, each of which she pampered, nursed, and treated as a child. For unlike Dina, who was out all day at school or preoccupied with friends, the pets were hers alone to fondle, spoil, and project all of her feelings and fears upon.

The Muslim League's devoted secretary, Syed Shamsul Hasan, wrote that "After the shifting of the League Office to Delhi in February 1927, I acted as a sort of chamberlain to the Quaid [Jinnah] whenever he visited Delhi. His relations with his wife, Mariam [Ruttie's Muslim name], were estranged during this period . . . and he resided alone, sometimes at the Cecil [one of Old Delhi's best hotels] or Maiden's and sometimes at the Western Courts—the accommodation provided by the Government for the members of the Legislative Assembly. He was not as careful about his health as in other matters. The Delhi winters did not suit him; and he often suffered from severe attacks of cold and flu. In spite of his poor health, he attended the Assembly . . . and devoted most of his time and energy to political activities."[27] This may have marked the beginning of the complex and compounded malignant lung disease that would take his life twenty-one years later. Was it coincidence that Jinnah's powerful constitution should have suddenly started to deteriorate then? His separation from Ruttie was surely a severe blow. (Her lungs and body were more afflicted than his and too frail to survive another two years.) And the combination of the Delhi winters, knowing he had lost the one love of his life, and the collapse of his faith in the *bona fides* of an imperial system he had always trusted irreparably wounded him. He would never breathe easily again.

For India as a whole, as well as for Jinnah personally, 1927 was a year of shattered hopes and dreams. A full decade had expired since Montagu's ringing words had given wings to soaring nationalist expectations. Yet dominion status, independence, *Swaraj*, seemed more remote than ever. Indian Secretary of State Lord Birkenhead (1872–1930) and his Tory clique knew that their own days of Westminster power were numbered, making them all the more determined to burn their brand of narrow imperial rule into India's hide. Ramsay MacDonald's Labour opposition was growing stronger with every by-election, and rather than wait for the inevitable Labour victory that would come in 1929, the Tory cabinet decided to jump the gun by appointing its own Royal Statutory Commission in 1927, carrying out the mandate of the Act of 1919, well before the deadline expired to chart the "next step" in constitutional advance for India. Birkenhead could now choose the membership of that mighty commission and appointed his barrister friend, Sir John Simon (1873–1954), and six other Englishmen, all equally uninformed about India.[28] Reading's successor as viceroy, Edward Wood, Lord Irwin (later Halifax) (1881–1959), more sympathetic and sensitive to Indian feelings, had urged the appointment of at least two Indian members on this blue-ribbon body, but Birkenhead wanted his "jury," as he thought of them, to do their research in India "without any preconceived prejudice."[29]

Jinnah had written the viceroy in June explicitly to warn him that "the personnel of the Commission is far more important than any other factor in this matter."[30] Had he hoped to be appointed himself? Most probably. He was always generous in helping government with his time and deep understanding of what needed to be done to reform India's constitution, and work was his only solace now. Doubly bitter was the draught of rejection Jinnah was obliged to swallow then with the rest of India's ignored and wasted leadership, which was so publicly rejected, repudiated that November by Lord Birkenhead's lily-white list. As if with one impassioned voice, India would respond, "Simon, go back!" when the commission reached Bombay's port February next, its years of projected labor doomed, torpedoed before it ever got underway, by the pig-headedness of a narrow-minded coterie of imperial managers who put their selfish interests above the needs, aspirations, and just demands of most of humankind.

The Muslim League divided over the Simon Commission issue. A small group, mostly from the Punjab, lined up behind ex-Law Minister Shafi and met in Lahore, where they voted to welcome and cooperate with the commission. Most members of the League's council, however, joined the "Jinnah Group" in Calcutta, meeting on December 30, 1927, and New Year's Day, 1928. Annie Besant and Sarojini Naidu attended as honored guests and the Aga Khan was to have presided, but he withdrew at the last moment. Maulvi Mohammad Yakub took his place and delivered his presidential address extempore in Urdu. The most important resolution, carried by acclamation, declared "emphatically" that "the Statutory Commission and the procedure, as announced, are unacceptable to the people of India. It [the Jinnah League] therefore resolves that the Musalmans throughout the country should have nothing to do with the Commission at any stage or in any form."[31] Jinnah was re-elected permanent president of the League for another three years and thundered:

> A constitutional war has been declared on Great Britain. Negotiations for a settlement are not to come from our side. Let the Government sue for peace. We are denied equal partnership. We will resist the new doctrine to the best of our power. Jallianwalla Bagh was a physical butchery, the Simon Commission is a butchery of our souls. By appointing an exclusively white Commission, Lord Birkenhead has declared our unfitness for self-government. I welcome Pandit Malaviya [a leading Congress Hindu in attendance], and I welcome the hand of fellowship extended to us by Hindu leaders from the platform of the Congress and the Hindu Mahasabha. For, to me, this offer is more valuable than any concession which the British Government can make. Let us then grasp the hand of fellowship. This is indeed a

bright day; and for achieving this unity, thanks are due to Lord Birkenhead.[32]

The outgoing Tory secretary of state thus achieved in a single act more than Gandhi and Jinnah alone could accomplish at the peak of their popularity and powers, momentarily at least reuniting a country still bleeding from communal wounds, breathing fresh life into the all-but-abandoned corpses of boycott and non-cooperation, and bringing Gandhi, Jinnah, the Nehrus, and even old Annie Besant back into harness at the head of a single mass national movement resolved to reject Birkenhead, Simon, and the morally bankrupt company they represented.

8

Calcutta
(1928)

The euphoria Jinnah felt at the start of 1928 was to dissipate long before the year ended. His joy was a brief remission. By year's end the castle of Hindu-Muslim unity, built on shifting sands of communal mistrust, suspicion, and doubt would be washed away by tides of frustration and discontent. There was no true turning back, no restoration of that balmy climate before Nagpur. It was but momentary delusion Jinnah experienced, induced by the enormity of Birkenhead's contempt for all Indian politicians. How insignificant such English arrogance suddenly made his conflicts with Congress colleagues seem.

Immediately after Calcutta, Jinnah returned to Bombay to organize the boycott of Simon and his commission's imminent entry there. Jinnah chaired the local boycott committee, and his assistant, Chagla, was its secretary. "I must say," Chagla recalled, "Jinnah was as firm as a rock as far as the question of the boycott of the Commission was concerned. Proposals were made that the boycott should be only political and not social. Jinnah would not agree and did not give an inch. He said a boycott was a boycott, and it must be total and complete. We held many meetings in connection with boycott campaign. We had a mass meeting at the Chowpatty sands."[1]

Simon arrived on February 3, 1928, and Jinnah's boycott proved totally effective. Gandhi wrote to "tender my congratulations to the organizers for the very great success they achieved. . . . It did my soul good to see Liberals, Independents and Congressmen ranged together on the same platform."[2] Birkenhead had briefed Simon on the eve of his departure from London; he wrote to remind Viceroy Irwin the next day: "We have always relied on the non-boycotting Moslems; on the depressed community; on the business interests; and on many others, to break down the attitude of boy-

cott. You and Simon must be the judges whether or not it is expedient in
these directions to try to make a breach in the wall of antagonism."[3] Officialdom cracked down with a vengeance as the nationwide boycott proved more
effective than Birkenhead dreamed it would be.

The primacy of Jinnah's role in this boycott was underscored by Birkenhead's singling him out as the leader to be undermined. "I should advise
Simon to see at all stages important people who are *not* boycotting the Commission," Birkenhead urged Irwin, "particularly Moslems and the depressed
classes. I should widely advertise all his interviews with representative
Moslems." He then announced, as baldly as it had ever been put into writing
by a British official, the "whole policy" of *divide et impera,* advising that
Simon's "obvious" goal was "to terrify the immense Hindu population by
the apprehension that the Commission is being got hold of by the Moslems
and may present a report altogether destructive of the Hindu position,
thereby securing a solid Moslem support, and leaving Jinnah high and dry."[4]

On February 12, Jinnah attended the All-Parties Conference chaired by
Congress president Ansari in Delhi. Motilal and Jawaharlal were there, as
were Lajpat Rai, Malaviya, Jayakar, and most of the other leaders of political India. Gandhi did not attend; he remained at his Sabarmati ashram,
placing as he did so little faith in constitutional planning. The conference,
however, was convened to do just that, seeking to provide a single Indian
alternative to whatever formula Simon and the others might fashion. "The
first question discussed by the Conference was the objective to be aimed at
in the constitution. It was proposed that the constitution should aim at establishing what is called a dominion form of government in India. Objection
was taken by some members to this on the ground that the Congress had
decided in favour of independence as the goal and no lesser goal should be
aimed at."[5] Jawaharlal Nehru and ex-Congress president S. Srinivasa Iyengar
(1874–1941) led the latter group, differing sharply from Motilal as well as
Jinnah on this point. The formula finally agreed upon was to frame a constitution "for the establishment of full responsible government." The problem of Muslim rights and representation was less easily resolved. Wrangling
and haggling continued for over a week till "The strain was too great for
me and I fled to avoid riot and insurrection!" Jawaharlal reported to Gandhi.[6]

Jinnah tried to remain optimistic. The budget session of Delhi's assembly
had started before the All-Parties Conference was over, and he convinced a
number of his independent colleagues there to sign a communal unity "appeal" he drafted. Ten fruitless days after the conference had begun, however, it ended without agreement on any Muslim question. Jayakar, Malaviya, and Lajpat Rai wanted to eliminate separate electorates entirely, yet
they were unwilling to concede any of the compensating constitutional

changes Jinnah demanded in return. Jinnah's position on separate electorates had always been equivocal. They were a necessary evil, the sort of protection required by Muslims only as long as the community remained too weak and too educationally backward to aspire to anything approaching equality with Hindus. There were, however, ways of assuring Muslims sufficient real security and constitutional leverage to make such affirmative action crutches dispensable. Jinnah had, indeed, formulated just such proposals in 1927. They were accepted by the then still united League in March and "substantially accepted" by Congress in May of 1927.

Those Delhi Muslim Proposals, as they came to be called, "agreed to the institution of joint electorates under certain conditions."[7] This strictly conditional concession and the proposals that followed were, like the Lucknow Pact, unique products of Jinnah's ingenious constitutional lawyer's mind. He was actually able to get twenty-nine leading Muslims, including conservatives like Shafi and Abdul Rahman, to agree to abandoning the League's separate electorate foundation stone, which gave Muslims alone the right to vote for Muslim candidates and would have obliged all Muslim politicians to appeal to the entire electorate of their constitutency in future contests. Minimal numbers of Muslim candidates would still have to be elected in all provinces where Muslims remained minorities, as under the Lucknow Pact, but similar numbers of Hindu representatives would be required in each Muslim majority province. Since every candidate would be obliged to appeal to joint electorates for support, they would all have to tone down, if not entirely abstain from, narrow communal rhetoric, and run only on national issues and appeal more often to secular interests of economic development and reform. All Muslim candidates elected under such a scheme might conveivably be congressmen, or Khilafatists, rather than Muslim leaguers. It was a bold political concession and proved how broad and selfless Jinnah's commitment to national principles and the goal of helping India attain full independence remained.

Nor were the constitutional concessions he demanded in return any less appropriate, though they would have given Muslim majorities control of three new full provinces (Sind, the North-West Frontier, and Baluchistan) and the proportional control they deserved by virtue of their recent population strides in two long-established provincial governments (the Punjab and Bengal). Sind had till then remained administratively under Bombay's provincial control, a relatively recent anomaly of British conquest, which was hardly justified on deeper historic, geographic, religious, or ethnic grounds. The North-West Frontier and Baluchistan were still deemed "too backward," tribal and turbulent, by the British to enjoy the freedoms of full provincial status, hence they continued to be administered by centrally-appointed martial autocrats, without any provincial assemblies. Since the 1921 census, Punjabi and Bengali Muslims had gained absolute majorities within both of those powerful provinces, but such demographic advance was not reflected in the composition of their legislatures. Jinnah's proposals would, therefore, have given Muslims elective majority control in five provincial governments. The final demand was for "not less" than one-third Muslim representation in the central legislature also to be chosen by mixed electorates.

Jinnah sensed well before the end of February 1928 that Hindu Mahasabha pressure had persuaded Congress to back off from its acceptance the previous May of his new constitutional compromise. He had to remain in Delhi, however, till the assembly concluded its budget session that March, and Jinnah convened his League council, which officially "regretted that the Hindu Mahasabha has practically rejected the Muslim League proposals."[8] Forced to face the sobering reality of his own countrymen's parochialism, Jinnah now looked to Lord Irwin for help. He had observed the lean, long-suffering viceroy closely in the assembly's chamber during the past two months and had developed respect for his intellect, diligence, and integrity—virtues Jinnah always admired. The longer the All-Parties Conference "riot" continued, in fact, the more attractive Irwin's cool but competent manner must have seemed to Jinnah, who finally approached the viceroy in March, suggesting "two ways" of resolving the current constitutional impasse. "One was by turning Simon's Commission into a Mixed Commission," Irwin reported to Birkenhead, "and the other was by establishing a twin Indian Commission with parallel authority."[9] Irwin liked both ideas and found them especially appealing, since Jinnah promised to "take the brunt of the attack in India" if either of his cooperative options was implemented. Birkenhead refused, however, to consider such changes, pig-headedly insisting, "It does not do to take these people too seriously; indeed I find it increasingly difficult to take any Indian politicians very seriously."[10] Once again, Jinnah found himself without effective allies.

Weary and depressed, he went home to Bombay on March 30, 1928. Ruttie was not waiting for him in South Court. She had moved to the Taj Mahal Hotel, renting a suite there by the month. They were never again to reside under the same roof. Still she kept track of his whereabouts, writing Kanji that day: "J returns today at 2.30 p.m.—so I understand."[11] She could never quite let go. She sailed on the P. & O. for Paris on April 10, with her mother. Jinnah steamed out of Bombay a month later aboard the S.S. *Rajputana*. Srinivasa Iyengar and diwan Chaman Lal were his fellow-passengers that May. Chaman was headed for an I.L.O. conference in Geneva and wrote that he found Jinnah

frankly disgusted. Minor differences over Sind and majority represen-
tations by reservation and Reforms for the North-West Frontier Province have wrecked, for the moment, all chances of unity. "Give me,"
says Mohammad Ali Jinnah, "three leaders to join me over a united
programme, which was all but accepted at Delhi, and Swaraj will not
be a mere dream but a matter brought within the realm of real politics." . . . Jinnah is frankly in a despondent mood. He is one of the
few men who have no personal motives to nurse or personal aims to
advance. His integrity is beyond question. And yet he has been the
loneliest of men.[12]

Jinnah had no official business in London that summer but met with old
Liberal and Labour friends, including Ramsay MacDonald and Lord Reading, and he visited Dublin at the invitation of Fenner Brockway, Ireland's
leading pro-Indian member of Parliament, who had just toured India. Jinnah
was in Ireland when Chaman Lal, who had visited Paris after his work in
Geneva ended, conveyed an urgent message about Ruttie. She was "deliri-
ous" with "a temperature of 106 degrees."[13] He reached Paris in two days
and spoke with Lady Petit immediately after checking into the George V.
Ruttie's mother informed him that her daughter was feeling "better," but
then Chaman Lal arrived to report that he had just come from her hospital
bed, where she was "dying."[14]

He sat still for a couple of minutes, struggling with himself and asked
me to telephone the clinic which I did. He spoke to the nurse in
charge who confirmed what I had told him. Thumping the arm of his
chair, he said: "Come, let us go. We must save her." I left him at the
clinic for nearly three hours, waiting at a nearby cafe and when he
returned, the anxiety had vanished from his face. He had arranged
for a new clinic and a new medical adviser and all was going to be
well. But alas! although Mrs. Jinnah recovered, she did not stay on
with her husband but returned ahead of him to Bombay and I do not
think they met again.[15]

While Jinnah was abroad, Congress president Dr. Ansari chaired a May
18 meeting in Bombay of some members of the February All-Parties Conference who resolved to appoint a "commission" led by Motilal Nehru to
draft a nationalist constitution by July 1. This Nehru commission, the Congress counterpart to the Simon commission, proved equally ineffectual,
however, completing its deliberations without powerful Muslim representation and failing to win the support of Muslim India's leading luminaries,
even as Simon had failed in India as a whole. The Nehru commission could
not complete its work on time. Motilal was quite busy that summer with
politics, still seeking what Gandhi called the "Crown" of the Congress presi-

dency, more for Jawaharlal than himself. Motilal would agree in December to wear that crown rather than allow it to elude his family altogether.

The Nehru commission met in Lucknow during the last week in August to hammer out a report based on proposals drafted by Motilal and Jawaharlal in Allahabad that summer. Motilal tried to anticipate Jinnah's objections and to adopt positions acceptable to him on the most thorny issues; he invited Chagla to Lucknow, where Sarojini Naidu and Annie Besant met with the Nehrus and Sir Tej Bahadur Sapru, then leader of the National Liberal Federation. "I think my main contribution to the Report was my steadfast adherence to the belief in joint electorates," Chagla noted. "Motilal Nehru for a moment thought, that in order to get the minorities to accept the Report, we should agree to separate electorates. I argued we were drafting a Constitution not for the present but for the future [Chagla was then 27]—a document which was expected to endure for a long time, and we must not therefore incorporate into it any principle which on the face of it was anti-national. Ultimately Motilal agreed."[16] Chagla "accepted the Report" at Lucknow "on behalf of the Muslim League." When Jinnah returned to Bombay, his young assistant was the first person to greet him in his ship's cabin and found Jinnah "furious" with him. Instead of acting impetuously Jinnah said he would "reserve judgment, and we will consider the report at a regular meeting of the League."[17] For Jinnah and Chagla, however, there would be no return to earlier days of cordial friendship and trust. Nor would Jinnah ever agree to accept the Nehru report as anything other than the "Hindu position" on his Delhi Muslim Proposals of the previous year.

Democratic though the Nehru report may have been in principle, it fundamentally repudiated the Lucknow Pact and offered no compensatory advantages to the Muslim community. There were platitudinous exhortations such as: "The doing away of communal electorates is intended to promote communal unity by making each community more or less dependent on the other at the time of the elections."[18] Such words must have sounded disingenuous to those who had lived through years of violence and communal discrimination. Jinnah, at any rate, was not prone to accept superficial promises nor to express himself prematurely. His first pronouncement concerning the Nehru report came late in October: "My position as President of the All-India Muslim League is one which does not permit me to anticipate decisions of the League."[19] At the same time he appealed to all Muslims "not to be alarmed. I see no reason for consternation and stampede. Muslims should organise themselves, stand united and should press every reasonable point for the protection of their community."[20] The day after Jinnah's remarks hit the headlines, Motilal wrote to invite him to join the committee and attend its forthcoming Delhi meeting.[21]

Jinnah refused Motilal's invitation. The Muslim League had not as yet had a chance to meet to consider the Nehru proposals, he argued, and "As the President of the League . . . it would not do for me to anticipate their decisions."[22] It was one of his most effective negotiating techniques, part of the secret of his singular power, for he always magnified himself by the force of his entire party whenever he felt unhappy about the terms of an offer. He was just then leaving for Sind to take charge of the defense of a wealthy and powerful Muslim pir of its northernmost district.

Pir Pagaro had been jailed at Sukkur for "allegedly wrongful confinement of some one and for keeping a large number of arms un-authorizedly in his possession."[23] His trial was held in a special magistrate's court in the Sukkur district. There Jinnah stayed in the government circuit house, Sukkur's only decent accommodation, on a hilltop overlooking the Indus and the massive dam that spanned it. He commanded 500 rupees a day, a very handsome fee at the time. Although the magistrate convicted Pagaro, Jinnah appealed two years later, and had his client's sentence reduced.

Two significant things occurred while Jinnah was in Sind. He met young Mohammed Khuhro, who then worked for Pir Pagaro and was destined to become independent Pakistan's chief minister of Sind. And Mian Sir Haji Haroon, a princely ruler of neighboring Khairpur State and one of Jinnah's Independent party assembly colleagues, held a fete in his honor at the ornate Khairpur House, which Jinnah attended in a most fashionable modern Sindhi costume—black sherwani, *choridar* pyjamas, and pump shoes. Jinnah took this occasion to speak to the Muslim elite of Sind, several of whom would become his strongest backers and lieutenants during the two remaining decades of his life.

Before leaving Sind on November 10, Jinnah had openly discussed his grave concerns and pessimism about Motilal's committee and its report with fellow Muslims. He would be going to Calcutta in December but anticipated—quite accurately as it turned out—that the convention there might prove "the parting of the ways." Had he decided, in fact, prior to December in Calcutta that it was time to abandon the indigenous all-parties search for a constitutional "solution" acceptable to every shade, caste, and religious community of India's pluralistic spectrum? Had he concluded that it might be more profitable—and less hazardous—for the Muslim League to go it alone in negotiating with the British? For what had all the time spent in all-parties haggling accomplished, after all? Were he and the leaders of the Hindu Mahasabha any closer to consensus than they had been five years ago? With increasingly fragile health he must have felt more keenly the futility of long meetings with hundreds of shouting, importunate delegates, some of whom could hardly speak the English language, most of whom had never drafted a legal document. Nor was he simply being middle-aged and irritable, though he would soon be at least fifty-two!

At Lucknow, the meeting of Jinnah's League council did not go as he hoped it would, and to his personal disappointment he found many good Muslim colleagues so enamoured of the Nehru report that he dared not call for a vote on it in early November. Even the maharaja of Mahmudabad, who was elected that year's president of the Muslim League, liked the report and was ready to accept it. Chagla was overjoyed to find so many allies and hoped Jinnah would see the wisdom of his earlier actions, but Jinnah remained set against the Nehru "constitution," viewing it only as a "Hindu" document.

Motilal, Dr. Ansari, and Maulana Azad met with him in Lucknow, urging him to attend a special meeting of the Nehru committee before the League or Congress met in December, and before the All-Parties Convention would be convened in Calcutta, to try to fashion a compromise formula on communal issues. Jinnah turned them down. He still insisted that first his League had to meet and officially take its stand. He asked Motilal to postpone the convention till early next year after both annual sessions of League and Congress. Then he returned to Bombay and prepared for a provincial League meeting, which was held on November 23, hoping at least to win a majority in his home town. But Chagla stood up and argued so effectively for the Nehru report that Jinnah adjourned the meeting without putting the question to a vote. Had he sensed once again that on this issue he sided with a minority of his own party? Jinnah was growing short-tempered, feeling more isolated and dispirited.

In an earlier "confidential" letter to his own committee, Motilal had reported, after meeting with Jinnah in Lucknow, that Jinnah "objected to the Convention being held before the meeting of the Muslim League on the ground that the authority to represent the League at the Convention could only be derived from the League . . . I may mention that had the Report of the Committee and the Lucknow decisions been taken into consideration they would have been approved by a greater majority [of the Muslim League's Council] than that which elected the Maharaja of Mahmudabad as President of the League. It is expected that the result will be the same at the open session of the League."[24] Motilal was obviously kept well informed of Jinnah's plight within his own party and felt less need to cater to his demands than he might otherwise have done. He misjudged Jinnah's resilience, however, by underestimating his powers. It was a fatal error, not only for his report, but for his hopes of retaining India as a united entity. The All-India

National Convention started as scheduled in Calcutta on December 22, but
no officially appointed representatives of the Muslim League arrived to attend its crowded sessions till December 28.

Following recitations from the *Qur'an*, Abdul Karim, the chairman of the
League's reception committee, welcomed its delegates on December 26, at
the opening of Jinnah's League's annual meeting in Calcutta "on the eve of
momentous changes in the Constitution and administration in India." Karim
regretted that "some forces were at work to divide the political strength of
the Muslims of India at a time when vital interests, both of the community
and the country, required that there should be solid unity."[25] On December 27, the League voted to appoint twenty-three delegates to represent
it and "take part in the deliberations of the Convention called by the Indian National Congress." That deputation, led by Mahmudabad and Jinnah, included thirty-two-year-old Nawabzada Liaquat Ali Khan (1896–
1951), who was to become Pakistan's first prime minister, and Chagla, who
was to be India's minister of external affairs (1966–67). Chagla recalled that
"Jinnah was in favour of outright rejection [of the Nehru report]. . . . After
a long and protracted debate, we ultimately decided . . . three important
amendments. One was that separate electorates should remain, second, that
there should be reservation of one-third of the seats in the Central Legislature, and third, residuary powers should be vested in the Provinces."[26]

Jinnah presented the Muslim case before the national convention on
December 28. He insisted it was "absolutely essential to our progress that a
Hindu-Muslim settlement should be reached, and that all communities
should live in a friendly and harmonious spirit in this vast country of ours."[27]

Allahabad's Sir Tej Bahadur Sapru, ex-law member of the viceroy's council, rose to respond to Jinnah's plea.

> If you examine the figures you will find that, including nominated
> members, Muslim representation in the Central Legislature is 27 per
> cent and Mr. Jinnah wants 33. . . . Speaking for myself, I would like
> you to picture Mr. Jinnah, whom I have known intimately for fifteen
> years. If he is a spoilt child, a naughty child, I am prepared to say,
> give him what he wants and be finished with it.[28]

However, Poona's M. R. Jayakar, then deputy leader of the Nationalist party
in the assembly, spokesman for the Hindu Mahasabha at the convention, was
less willing to "pamper" Jinnah than Sapru had been.

> I have also known Mr. Jinnah for the last sixteen years in close asso-
> ciation as a colleague in nationalist life and I can assure you that he
> comes before us today neither as a naughty boy nor as a spoiled

child. . . . One important fact to remember . . . is that well-known Muslims like the esteemed patriots Maulana Abul Kalam Azad, Dr. Ansari, Sir Ali Imam, Raja Sahib of Mahmudabad and Dr. Kitchlew have given their full assent to the compromise embodied in the Nehru Committee Report. It is further to be borne in mind that even in the Muslim League a large body of members have given their assent to the Nehru Committee Report. Mr. Jinnah, therefore, represents, if I may say so without offence, a small minority of Muslims.[29]

He knew, of course, just how offensive a slap that was to Jinnah's ego and sensitivity, and there was applause and many a thump of approval as Jayakar sat down.

Jinnah responded softly, yet spoke with an intensity of control he had not publicly displayed since Nagpur.

We are engaged to-day in a very serious and solemn transaction. . . . We are here, as I understand, for the purpose of entering into a solemn contract and all parties who enter into it will have to work for it and fight for it together. What we want is that Hindus and Muslims should march together until our object is attained. Therefore it is essential that you must get not only the Muslim League but the Musalmans of India and here I am not speaking as a Musalman but as an Indian. . . . Would you be content with a few? Would you be content if I were to say, I am with you? Do you want or do you not want the Muslim India to go along with you? . . . Minorities cannot give anything to the majority. It is, therefore, no use asking me not to press for what you call "these small points." I am not asking for these modifications because I am a "naughty child." If they are small points, why not concede? It is up to the majority, and majority alone can give. I am asking you for this adjustment because I think it is the best and fair to the Musalmans. . . . We are all sons of this land. We have to live together. We have to work together and whatever our differences may be, let us at any rate not create more bad blood. If we cannot agree, let us at any rate agree to differ, but let us part as friends. Believe me there is no progress of India until the Musalmans and Hindus are united, and let no logic, philosophy or squabble stand in the way of coming to a compromise and nothing will make me more happy than to see a Hindu-Muslim union.[30]

He must have sensed that the restless jury he addressed had made up their minds against him long before he reached the end of his argument, surely by the time he said "let us part as friends." For this marked a major point of departure in Jinnah's life, an even sharper veering off from the road

of Congress and all it represented than Nagpur had been eight years earlier.
He had delivered his swan song to Indian nationalism. The dream stirred by
Dadabhai's ringing voice in Westminster's Commons, nurtured by Morley
and Pherozeshah, enriched by Gokhale and Montagu, all those long lost
Liberal giants was dead. Born thespian that he was, Jinnah spoke his lines
to a packed, if not always friendly, house before each curtain fell on a major
act of his political life. Nagpur had ended Act One. Calcutta finished Act
Two. This time there would be a longer intermission.

9

Simla
(1929-30)

Jinnah adjourned his faction of the Muslim League after a stormy session that followed the Calcutta convention debacle. He left Mahmudabad, Chagla and their youthful allies, and Bengal behind, entraining for Delhi before the year's end. On New Year's Day of 1929 he entered the All-Parties Muslim Conference presided over by the Aga Khan in the ancient capital of Turco-Afghan sultans and Mughal emperors. Shafi was there with his Punjabi cohort when Jinnah walked into the silken pandal pitched on the parade ground of the Red Fort that Shah Jahan had built. Bearded mullahs and knighted bejewelled princes of Islam sat side by side. Jinnah entered late, and sat alone. He was as yet undecided how long he would remain back among his fold, who must have seemed almost as foreign and uncongenial to him as the other, larger crowd from which he had just fled. The radical Ali brothers were there, together with nawabs and rajas from many a Muslim state. Was this really his home? Were these truly his people?

"It was a vast gathering representative of all shades of Muslim opinion," wrote the Aga Khan, recalling the conference. "I can claim to be the parent of its important and lasting political decisions. After long, full and frank discussions we were able to adopt unanimously a series of principles which we set out in a manifesto."[1] The first of these was that "the only form of government suitable to Indian conditions is a federal system with complete autonomy and residuary powers vested in the constituent states." The next reaffirmed separate Muslim electorates, and others asserted further Muslim "weightage" demands in provincial and central governments, as well as for the civil services. It was not yet Pakistan, but almost its early embryo, within a weak federal womb. The League's weighty royal father, driven from the bridge of his communal vessel a decade and a half earlier, was at the helm of Muslim India again. His nationalist mutineer was welcomed effusively aboard. "The unanimity of this conference was especially significant," reflected His Highness, "for it marked the return—long delayed and for the moment private and with no public avowal of his change of mind—of Mr. M. A. Jinnah to agreement with his fellow Muslims. Mr. Jinnah had attended the Congress party's meeting in Calcutta shortly before, and had come to the conclusion that for him there was no future in Congress or in any camp— allegedly on an All-India basis—which was in fact Hindu-dominated. We had at last won him over to our view."[2]

Well might the Aga Khan gloat over that victory, though Jinnah did not become his malleable vassal, or ever rejoin the Khoja fold. His Highness understood, however, the value of so priceless a prodigal's return. Nor was it the royal "we" he used in that last sentence. Shafi and Sir Fazl-i Husain and others had helped him win Jinnah "over to our view." They could not have achieved it without Jayakar's unwitting aid. That there would be "no public avowal" of his "agreement" indicates at least Jinnah's ambivalence about joining forces with so conservatively pro-British a team. He had, indeed, concluded there was "no future" for him in Congress or any "Hindu-dominated" political party. Shifting into reverse to keep pace with the Aga Khan and Shafi could hardly be accomplished without first idling, however, in neutral gear.

By mid-January he was back in Bombay. Ruttie was virtually bedridden at the Taj Hotel, going out rarely and then only "for short walks" with Kanji. Jinnah went to visit her there—he must have known she was near the end. Kanji remained at her side, and till the assembly budget session started early in February, Jinnah dropped in "every evening" and talked with them both "as in the old times."[3] Naïvely, Kanji believed that "they were getting reconciled to each other." But that was even more an illusion than the reconciliation of Congress and the League had been. "Look after my cats and don't give them away," she asked Kanji on February 18, 1929, being too weak to say any more. Two days later, on what would have been her twenty-ninth birthday, Ruttie Petit Jinnah died.

Chaman Lal was chatting with Jinnah in his Western Court apartment in New Delhi "when a trunk call was put through to him from Bombay. He spoke calmly saying he would leave that night. He came towards me, after the conversation was over and said: 'Rati is seriously ill. I must leave tonight'—and then there was a pause. 'Do you know,' he added, 'who that was? It was my father-in-law. This is the first time we have spoken to each other since my marriage.' I persuaded him to leave the next morning by the Frontier Mail as the night train would not get him to Bombay any quicker.

I did not know then but learnt only later that Rati was not merely seriously ill but she was actually dead."[4]

The funeral was held at Bombay's Muslim cemetery on February 22. Kanji met Jinnah's train at Grant Road Station and drove him there, trying to convince him "that Ruttie would have liked to be cremated," but "she was buried under Muslim rites."[5] It was a painfully slow ritual. Jinnah sat silent through all of its five hours. "Then, as Ruttie's body was being lowered into the grave, Jinnah, as the nearest relative was the first to throw the earth on the grave and he broke down suddenly and sobbed and wept like a child for minutes together."[6] Chagla was also there, and he too recalled "there were actually tears in his eyes," adding, "That was the only time when I found Jinnah betraying some shadow of human weakness."[7]

By early March he was back in New Delhi's assembly, responding to Motilal's cut motion on "touring expenses" for the viceroy's cabinet, which raised the constitutional question of redress of grievances before granting supplies and hence opened the door to debate on the Nehru report. "The differences between Hindus and Muslims over the Report remain unresolved and, therefore, the attempt of making an agreed Constitution for India has become a dead issue," Jinnah rejoined. Motilal tried his best to elude that objection, but Jinnah drove home his point, hammering tight the lid over that report's coffin: "I know, the Nehru Report is my Honourable friend's pet child, but I am speaking dispassionately and I want him to realise, and the sooner he realises it the better—that it is not acceptable to the Muslims."[8]

Jinnah decided to prove to Motilal, Jayakar, and the rest that he spoke, in fact, for more than a "small minority," but that was not an easy task. His own faction of the Muslim League remained riddled with dissension. He reconvened the adjourned session of his League in Old Delhi on March 30, 1929, and had met with some of his rivals "till the early hours of the morning" the night before, trying to hammer out a new platform on which all of them could stand. The formula he produced, which came to be known as the Fourteen Points of Mr. Jinnah, was opposed by Dr. Ansari, Tassaduq Ahmed Khan Sherwani, Dr. Mohammad Alam, and Dr. Syed Mahmud, all of whom favored supporting the Nehru report. Maulana Mohammad Ali, however, totally disenchanted with Gandhi, supported Jinnah "wholeheartedly" that evening, "paying glowing tributes" to his "unique feat of statesmanship and, in a lighter vein, calling him the 'arch compromiser.'"[9] Jinnah was now trying to achieve with India's Muslims what he had accomplished in 1916 with the entire nationalist movement. He took the Aga Khan's "four principles," patched them together with his Delhi Muslim proposals of 1927, hammered a few more planks onto either end, and hoped it would float, an ark in which all of them might survive the coming flood. Asaf Ali and Dr. Saifuddin Kitchlu joined, "believing it to be the best solution under the circumstances." But there was no enthusiasm for his makeshift craft, little chance that those fourteen points[10] would survive the first rough squalls of any storm-ravaged sea. Nor could his "coalition" hold together—even for one day.

Next morning, the League was to have met at the Rowshan Theatre near Ajmer Gate in Old Delhi. Jinnah was to have opened the meeting at 10:30 A.M. but arrived late, doubtless exhausted after the long night of bickering. Dr. Ansari's supporters were in the front rows, and "Dr. Alam forcibly occupied the presidential chair. He presented a resolution approving the Nehru Report, and called upon Tassaduq Ahmad Khan Sherwani to second it. The gathering, however, did not allow Dr. Alam to conduct the proceedings. Maulana Mohammad Ali demanded that he should vacate the chair. As Dr. Alam refused, the audience rushed towards the platform and a general *melee* followed."[11] Just then Jinnah arrived, and his appearance seemed to have had some sobering effect; but gauging the futility of the enterprise on which he had embarked, he immediately adjourned the session without attempting to move his fourteen points. Had the audience awaiting him been less hostile, he had intended to introduce his many-pointed platform by admonishing them that if "the will of Muslim India" was to be "registered, then it can only be accomplished by a united decision."[12]

No one was in a mood to listen. The Jinnah league had, in fact, ceased to exist, its last few meetings adjourned either for lack of a quorum or because of wild behavior. The rest of "Muslim India" was either within Congress, where Maulana Abul Kalam Azad remained, or impotently divided into smaller and smaller "parties," none of which attained more than provincial status. Shafi's league remained a force in the Punjab. Dr. Ansari convinced Asaf Ali and Choudhry Khaliquzzaman to help him start a new Nationalist Muslim party that was influential in the United Provinces. The Aga Khan founded his own All-India Muslim Conference, a continuing seminar of conservatives such as Sir Fazl-i Husain, Sir Shafa'at Ahmad Khan, and the nawab of Chhatari. It was less than three months since the All-Parties Muslim Conference, and they were all running again, in different directions. How realistic were Jinnah's prospects of pulling them back together? "Except for a few personal friends, such as Malik Barkat Ali, Abdul Matin Choudhry and Sir Mohammad Yakub," his loyal helper in running the League, Syed Shamsul Hasan, rightly noted that "others were reluctant to work with the Quaid. His strict attachment to principles and independent approach to problems were the main reasons which kept the others away from him."[13]

Jinnah had no place left to turn but to his British friends. The political climate in London was rapidly liberalizing, and his old Islington Commission colleague, Ramsay MacDonald, was about to become Westminster's new polestar. That May the Tory government fell, and Prime Minister Mac-Donald appointed his Labour colleague, William Wedgwood Benn (1877–1961) (later Viscount Stansgate), secretary of state for India. Jinnah wasted no time, traveling to Simla as soon as he learned of the Labour victory, for "a long personal talk" with Lord Irwin.[14] The viceroy would be returning to London in a few weeks to meet with his new chiefs at Whitehall and 10 Downing Street. Jinnah urged him to press for a strong declaration by the Home government that dominion status was the goal of British policy for India, suggesting a Round Table conference in London to draft such a constitution.

But the "present system" was again coming under heavy siege. Gandhi had returned to Congress's center stage during its final hours in Calcutta, to prepare to mount a new national *Satyagraha* campaign if Parliament failed to implement the Nehru report within the calendar year 1929.

The Mahatma moved the Congress resolution accepting Motilal's report for one year only in order to avert a fight between the forces of Motilal and Jawaharlal on the Congress floor over whether the national goal should be dominion status or complete independence. "This Congress will adopt the [Nehru Report] constitution in its entirety if it is accepted by the British Parliament on or before December 31st, 1929," that resolution stated, "but in the event of its non-acceptance by that date or its earlier rejection, Congress will organise a non-violent non-co-operation by advising the country to refuse taxation and in such other manner as is settled."[15] Despite the sanctity of that resolution's mover, Subhas Bose proposed an amendment, calling for "complete independence" without further delay. "What is the fundamental cause of our political degradation?" cried Bose, the future Indian National Army's *netaji* ["leader"] and later twice Congress president. "It is the slave mentality. If you want to overcome this slave mentality, you will do so only by inspiring our countrymen with a desire for complete independence."[16] He was cheered wildly. Young India was ready to shed its blood for freedom. The darkest days of 1922 were by now forgotten.

On June 19, 1929, Jinnah wrote to Ramsay MacDonald, his old friend and the new prime minister, "The present position is a very serious deadlock and if allowed to continue it will, in my judgment, prove disastrous both to the interests of India and Great Britain."[17] He then briefly outlined political events of the preceding few years, especially since the appointment of the Simon Commission and the futility of awaiting its report, since "So far as India is concerned, we have done with it." Noting that "India has lost her faith in the word of Great Britain," Jinnah advised, "The first and foremost thing that I would ask you to consider is how best to restore that faith and revive the confidence of India in the 'bona fides' of Great Britain."[18] He warned that "there is a section in India that has already declared in favour of complete independence, and I may tell you without exaggeration that the movement for independence is gaining ground, as it is supported by the Indian National Congress." To diminish the momentum of such a movement, which Jinnah considered no less dangerous a threat to India's security than did the viceroy, he suggested as step one, a declaration "without delay" by His Majesty's government that "Great Britain is unequivocally pledged to the policy of granting to India full responsible Government with Dominion status. The effect of such a declaration will be very far-reaching and go a great way to create a different atmosphere in the country." As to practical actions to implement such a declaration, he urged his friend to "invite representatives of India, who would be in a position to deliver the goods (because completely unanimous opinion in India is not possible at present)" to London to meet with British officials till they could reach a constitutional "solution which might carry, to use the words of the viceroy, the 'willing assent of the political India.'" The proposals thus formulated could then be placed before Parliament.

Lord Irwin reached London at the same time as Jinnah's letter and went directly to the India Office to meet with Wedgwood Benn, suggesting "the two ideas of Round Table Conference and formal declaration of Dominion Status as the goal of British policy for India."[19] The new secretary of state "was disposed to concur, but wished to be satisfied that we were not going behind the backs of Simon and his Commission, who were then preparing their report. I accordingly discussed both suggestions with Simon and was much interested in his reaction to them," Irwin recalled.

Somewhat to my surprise, he at first saw no objection at all to the declaration about Dominion Status, but felt difficulty about the Round Table Conference, principally on the ground that it would be likely to affect adversely the status of the Commission's report, when it appeared, by making this only one among other papers that the Conference would presumably have before it. . . . A little later, again to my surprise, his position changed on both points, and I have always surmised that he was much influenced by Reading. Anyhow, whatever the cause, he finally expressed himself satisfied with the Round Table Conference, and fell in with the plan of an exchange of letters with the Prime Minister, by which the Conference would appear as an idea put by the Commission to the Government and readily accepted by them, on the very proper ground of the need to take account of the Indian States as well as of British India.[20]

So much for historic duplicity seeking to salvage Simon's face. Actual credit for both ideas belongs not to Irwin but to his new unacknowledged adviser, Jinnah.

Soothing Simon's ruffled feathers took time. It was not until August 14 that Ramsay MacDonald could reply in a "private letter."

Dear Mr. Jinnah,

I am very sorry, but owing to a mistake [sic] your letter of the 19th of June was not put immediately before me. Let me say at once how much I appreciate the spirit in which it was written and how glad I would be to meet it in any way possible. The report of the Simon Commission you need have no hesitation in assuming was never intended to be anything more than advice given for the guidance of the Government and that the intention of the Government is, as soon as that report is in its hands, to consider it in the light of all the facts. The suggestions which you make in your letter will be pondered over with a desire to use them in every way that circumstances will allow. But one thing I can say here,—because I have said it before repeatedly and it still remains the intention of the Government,— that we want India to enjoy Dominion status.

There will probably be announcements made very soon regarding future proceedings.[21]

Jinnah was very pleased and optimistically replied on September 7, "If you carry out my suggestion with which I am glad to find that you are in accord, it will open up a bright future for India and the name of Great Britain will go down in history as one nation that was true to its declarations.[22]

Lord Irwin wrote Jinnah from his "viceroy's camp" the following month announcing that

His Majesty's Government are greatly concerned to find means by which the broad question of British Indian constitutional advance may be approached in co-operation with all who can speak authoritatively for British Indian opinion . . . and I am authorised to say that in the judgment of His Majesty's Government it is implicit in the Declaration of 1917 that the natural issue of India's constitutional progress as there contemplated is the attainment of Dominion Status. In the full realisation of this policy the States must ultimately have their place . . . and His Majesty's Government accordingly propose . . . to invite representatives of different interests in British India and of the Indian States to meet them, separately or together as circumstances may demand, in regard both to British India and all-India problems. They hope thus to be able to submit eventually to Parliament proposals commanding a wide measure of general assent.[23]

The first steps that would lead to three major Round Table conferences in London were thus taken, and Jinnah was not only the prime minister's personal friend and adviser in initiating that complex process, but had now become the viceroy's key emissary as well.

Irwin's historic statement appeared on the front page of every major Indian newspaper on November 1, 1929. Jinnah was in Bombay that day and met with eighteen others in Sir Chimanlal Setalvad's chambers to issue a joint public statement in response to Irwin's announcement, welcomed as a

> fundamental change of procedure whereby the representatives of India will be invited to meet His Majesty's Government in conference for the purpose of arriving at the greatest possible measure of agreement regarding the proposals to be submitted to Parliament for the attainment of Dominion Status by India and thereby reaching a solution which might carry the willing assent of political India.[24]

Sarojini Naidu, Bhulabhai Desai, Sir Homi P. Mody, Chagla, Kanji Dwarkadas, and his brother were among those who signed that statement. In New Delhi, at a meeting chaired by Motilal Nehru, including thirty leaders of many parties other than Congress, a "policy of general conciliation" was called for, together with the grant of "general amnesty" for political prisoners, and the "predominant representation" of the Indian National Congress at the forthcoming Round Table conference. This leaders' Manifesto, as it soon came to be called, further insisted that "the [Round Table] Conference is to meet not to discuss when Dominion Status is to be established but to frame a scheme of Dominion Constitution for India."

No sooner did Jawaharlal Nehru sign that Manifesto than he regretted doing so, however, instead of walking out with Subhas Bose and his comrades. Feeling himself "an interloper," Jawaharlal now wanted to "resign" from the presidentship of Congress, which he had just accepted. Gandhi responded to Jawaharlal's anxious ambivalence by insisting: "You must not resign . . . it will affect the national cause. There is no hurry and no principle at stake. About the crown, no one else can wear it. It never was to be a crown of roses. Let it be all thorns now."[25] Nehru did not, in fact, resign, but his emotional threat of resignation stiffened both Gandhi and Motilal in their resolve to stand by the leaders' manifesto as the most they would be willing to do by way of "accommodating" the viceroy and His Majesty's government. Irwin, however, had secured as much promise of change as Ramsay MacDonald was prepared to offer. Jinnah, therefore, found himself in the unenviable, yet not unfamiliar position, of having to try to bridge the gap remaining between both sides.

Jinnah, Gandhi, Motilal Nehru, Sapru, and Patel met with Irwin at the viceroy's house in New Delhi at 4:30 P.M. on December 23, 1929. Irwin had just returned from his viceregal tour that morning, and, as his train approached Delhi station, a bomb exploded under one of its carriages. Fortunately, neither the viceroy nor his escort was injured. Gandhi was first to speak that afternoon, expressing "the horror he and those who accompanied him felt at the attempt on His Excellency's train," offering "congratulations on Their Excellencies' escape."[26] He then asked Lord Irwin whether the interpretation of his announcement published in the Congress leaders' manifesto ("The [Round Table] Conference is to meet not to discuss when Dominion Status is to be established but to frame a scheme of Dominion Constitution for India.") was accurate. Gandhi explained that "unless agreement was reached on this point he felt it fruitless to proceed to any other questions." Irwin insisted "he thought that the wording of his announcement made the position plain." The object of the conference "was to thresh out the problems which arose out of His Majesty's Government's definite declaration of policy." He then quickly added that here at last was a chance "of doing something big and the danger of losing a great opportunity." It "was obviously impossible to lay it down that the Conference was to draft any particular Constitution," Irwin argued, but "it would have the fullest opportunity to discuss any proposals put before it. He emphasized that the Conference would be absolutely free. . . . There would be no closure to the freest discussion; the Conference would not, he took it, proceed to definite voting, but would rather follow the lines of the Imperial Conference, a record being kept of the general sense of the members."

> *Mr. Gandhi* felt that the Imperial Conference was on a different footing. There all the parties to the discussions were more or less of one mind. At the Indian Conference this would not be so. However much they argued they could not reach a policy which would be acceptable to all.[27]

It was a remarkably prophetic conclusion, coming as it did almost eighteen years prior to partition and anticipating hundreds of thousands of man-hours wasted on conferences and in cabinets, and millions of futile words, whether printed on parchment or paper. Gandhi admitted there could be no actual voting at the conference; but he argued that unless the establishment of dominion status could be "presumed as an immediate result of the Conference," he could not take part in it. He demanded "complete freedom at once" and said India was capable of "solving her own problem of defence." Motilal agreed, adding that "British people exaggerated the difficulties in the way of Dominion Status for India. There was no difficulty about having full Dominion Status at once, though he did not mean that the Indian form of it would necessarily be exactly the same as any particular form of Dominion Status already in existence."[28]

Lord Irwin thought that "unreasonable" and looked to Jinnah and Sapru at this point for more effective support. Both "reasoned at some length with Mr. Gandhi and Pundit Motilal Nehru. They argued that those who went to the Conference would be at liberty to propose Dominion Status. Supposing from the opposite side somebody pointed out the difficulties, that would at least narrow the issues, and the true function of the Conference would be to discuss the difficulties in the way of immediate conferment of full Dominion Status and to argue about safeguards."[29] But Gandhi and Motilal remained true to their promise to Jawaharlal and others who had signed the Delhi manifesto, refusing to attend another conference to "argue" about issues "unacceptable" to all the parties with their divergent perspectives.

> *Pundit Motilal Nehru* gave it as his opinion that no Indian would be satisfied with less than Dominion Status. He saw no difficulties in the way himself. But if there were any, they could be solved after the central point was admitted; India could solve them for herself. The whole crux was the transference of power from Great Britain to India.[30]

The bitterness and cold inflexibility later noted by those who were to meet with Jinnah emerged in the wake of this aborted conference more than as the aftermath of Ruttie's death. Once again he had permitted his hopes to take wing, for what *he* had "arranged," after all, was no negligible affair. He had extracted from Ramsay MacDonald and Lord Irwin no ordinary promise. Within five years, perhaps India could have taken her place beside Canada and Australia as an independent dominion helping "the progress of the world at large," as Jinnah put it to the prime minister, whom he had also assured "a great success" in response to his announcement. And he had actually brought them all into the same room, though that alone had taken almost two months of "negotiating." Then to watch everything disintegrate before the stone wall erected by Gandhi and Motilal as spokesmen for Jawaharlal and his friends—how else could it leave Jinnah but bitter? Tired. Frustrated. Furious. Alone and bitter. He understood precisely what Motilal meant when he said that he saw no difficulties in the way to winning dominion status. Gandhi had been more forthright, insisting there was, in fact, "the lack of unity" and that *did* present a problem. Motilal, however, was not even prepared to concede that a "Muslim problem" existed, even as his son would still refuse to admit it eight years later. Jinnah knew how much they resented him. His mere presence in so select a group, though he had been the most instrumental in bringing it together, must have been singularly offensive to Motilal, for Jinnah was the living reminder to him of why the "constitution" he had labored so hard to write last year was about to pass into the trash bin of history. Nor could Jinnah have helped feeling as the sun set upon that long and weary afternoon that he was, at heart, closer to Lord Irwin than to Motilal or the Mahatma seated beside him. He had no Muslim League left to meet with this year. Nor would the ocean now dividing him from Congress ever be bridged again.

Congress met that week in Lahore. The "complete independence" (*purna swaraj*) resolution passed at this Congress marked a radical departure for the Indian nationalist movement, now in its forty-fourth year. This would be the last annual session of Congress held during the Christmas holiday, President Jawaharlal Nehru announced, "Inasmuch as the Congress is intended to be representative of the poor masses, and inasmuch as the holding of the Congress at the end of December involves very considerable expense to the poor people in providing for extra clothing for themselves and is otherwise inconvenient to them." The revolutionary changes initiated by Gandhi a decade earlier had matured to the point where Congress and its younger generation of leadership wanted no longer to be tied in any way to the British Empire, its habits, institutions, traditions, or timetable. Sunday, January 26, 1930, was proclaimed *Purna Swaraj* Day by the Working Committee of Congress, and a resolution stating that "We believe . . . that India must sever the British connection and attain Purna Swaraj or Complete Independence"[31] was posted and read out to millions across the subcontinent.

From his lofty, lonely Malabar Hill home, Jinnah watched the rising of this new revolutionary tide lash against official indifference and repression, massed like mighty breakwaters athwart every gateway to India. The irresistible force of those waves would keep shattering themselves against these immovable objects till the tide turned back again. Imperceptibly, the rocks would erode or shift, some would settle and others sink. With the next high tide more of the ocean would break through, and still more with the tide after. Jinnah was wearied, bored by the futility of it all. Was it perhaps time for him to abandon India altogether, for what really kept him there? He could practice law just as easily in London, confining himself to appeals before the Privy Council, if he liked. There were enough such briefs in his reach, and they would prove just as rewarding—and far less exhausting.

Jinnah blamed Gandhi "for this sudden outburst of political hysteria," as he publicly characterized the new Congress program.[32] Sapru agreed, writ-

ing Jinnah on January 5, 1930, "I have today read your interview in the
Press. I entirely agree with you. The Congress has gone mad, but the worst
of it is that in its madness it is going to involve the country in disaster."[33]
Sir Tej was ready to start afresh, enthusiastically adding: "We must act and
act together and with a determination that we will solve our differences. I
have no doubt that on this occasion you can be of the greatest possible use
to the country." He wanted to organize another all-parties conference and
assured Jinnah, "I personally think that we should not find it difficult to
bring about a settlement of the Hindu Mohamedan question. But without
flattering you I do say that it is impossible to get a settlement effected without your cooperation and guidance." Jinnah agreed to give it a try, as did
Shafi and Mahmudabad. Hindu Mahasabha leaders were also willing to join
such a conference, after much persuading and cajoling by Sapru. Jinnah
selected most of the Muslim representatives to the conference in Delhi that
met on February 26, 1930. More than fifty delegates were invited, including
leading Liberals, Mahasabhites, Christians, Anglo-Indians, and Madras Justice party "Untouchables" as well as Muslim leaguers. Early in February
Jinnah met with Madan Mohan Malaviya, the Hindu Mahasabha's leader in
the assembly, to discuss communal problems and felt "the atmosphere has
improved" for possible settlement. Yet nothing had really changed since
February 1928, except that Congress was not in attendance at the latest
futile "all-parties" conference.

Jinnah had not expected much of Sapru's conference; rather he focused
his own attention on the London arena and pressed Irwin to announce an
opening date of the Round Table conference, urging the viceroy to send out
official invitations.

The Mahatma had almost completed his heroic march from Sabarmati
to the sea where he then symbolically made salt in open violation of the
British salt monopoly, launching a new nationwide *Satyagraha*. Jinnah
feared that the rising tides of *Satyagraha* and British repression would serve
only to destroy the fragile constitutional craft he had launched, even before
it could clear Bombay's harbor. Why would Irwin not commit himself to a
date? His legal instinct sensed the viceroy was trying to back away from
signing the contract they had orally agreed upon. Called back to Sukkar for
the Pir Pagaro appeal, Jinnah wrote from the circuit house there to Lord
Irwin on April 26. Two weeks later Irwin replied, reporting that the Round
Table conference was set to start in October, asking what Jinnah thought of
holding the Simla assembly session in July instead of the usual September.
Jinnah felt "no useful purpose will be served" with such a session at all.
Anyway, most of the assembly's elected members had resigned in response
to Congress's boycott call. But, he wrote Irwin from Sind, "I think I shall

get back to Bombay about the end of this month, and if it would suit you, I can run up to Simla for a few days in the first week of June."[34]

Gandhi's march, from his ashram in Ahmedabad 240 miles south to Dandi on the sea, had started March 12 and ended April 5, with the eyes of the world focused upon this latter-day Moses leading his "children of India" out of bondage. April 6 was the date set by Gandhi for the "simultaneous beginning" of the nationwide *Satyagraha*, when hundreds of thousands of Indians broke the government's salt tax monopoly law by "stealing" natural salt for themselves from India's thousands of miles of coastline. "There is no alternative but for us to do something about our troubles and sufferings and hence we have thought of this salt tax," Mahatma Gandhi said, speaking at Surat on April 1. Gandhi was arrested on May 5 and taken to Poona's Yeravda prison, which he renamed "palace" and "mandir" ("temple") in his letters.

Less than two weeks after entering prison, the Mahatma wrote to Lord Irwin, addressing him as "Dear Friend," and began to negotiate with him, reiterating the "eleven points"[35] he had communicated to Ramsay MacDonald in January, which he deemed essential prerequisites to calling off his "civil disobedience" campaign before it had started. The first of these was "Total prohibition," the fourth called for "Abolition of the Salt Tax"; others demanded "Reduction of Land Revenue at least by 50 per cent and making it subject to Legislative control," "Reduction of Military expenditure at least by 50 per cent to begin with," "Reduction of salaries of the highest grade services by half or less," "Protective tariff on foreign cloth," amnesty for political prisoners, abolition of the Criminal Intelligence Division of police, "or its popular control," and the issuance of "licenses to use fire-arms for self-defense, subject to popular control." In a prison interview he granted, Gandhi insisted:

> I have taken what has been called a mad risk. But it is a justifiable risk. No great end has been achieved without incurring danger . . . I am an optimist. In forty years of struggle I have frequently been told I was attempting the impossible, but invariably I proved the contrary.[36]

Soon after that interview appeared in the press, Sapru and Jayakar launched their "peace mission" with the viceroy's private approval. Jinnah hoped Irwin was not going "soft" on the eve of the Round Table conference he now viewed as his only ray of political light, guarding it with almost proprietary jealousy. "I am very anxious that the names of the representatives who are going to be invited to the Conference should not be published till the end of August or the beginning of September and I may re-

quest you to let me see the list of the invitees before you finally decide upon
the names, so that I may be in a position to make such suggestions as it may
strike me. Of course it will be for you ultimately to decide who should be
invited. This can be done while I am at Simla."[37] The viceroy had insisted
on having his assembly meet in Simla that July despite Jinnah's advice to
the contrary. Jinnah's relationship with Irwin thus became increasingly intimate but did not always run smoothly. Both gaunt, elegant, and punctilious,
these two men were so alike they must have found one another at once
attractive and exasperating.

Sapru and Jayakar came to the Yeravda prison to meet with Gandhi on
July 23–24, and the Mahatma wrote a "note" for hand delivery by the viceroy's emissaries to Motilal and Jawaharlal in Naini prison, stating that his

> personal position is that if the Round Table Conference is restricted to
> a discussion of safeguards that may be necessary in connection with
> full Self-Government during the period of transition, I should have no
> objection, it being understood that the question of independence
> should not be ruled out if anybody raises it. I should be satisfied be-
> fore I could endorse the idea of the Congress attending the Confer-
> ence about its whole composition.[38]

Gandhi sent a covering letter to Motilal on the same day, adding, "My position is essentially awkward. . . . But after all, Jawaharlal's must be the final
voice. You and I can only give our advice to him."[39] Then Sapru and Jayakar
met with both Nehrus in Naini on July 27–28. Motilal's health had deteriorated since his incarceration in June; he ran a high fever during the long
interviews with the two peace missionaries. The elder Nehru did not live
another year.

On July 28 Irwin wrote Jinnah to inform him of the Labour government's
decision to invite members of London's Liberal and Conservative opposition
parties to the Round Table. Jinnah wrote him in reply, stressing, "May I
once more urge you not to forget the suggestion I made in the course of our
conversation at Simla that Your Excellency should do your utmost to arrange and be present in London at the time of the Conference? I am more
anxious and more convinced than ever that it is absolutely essential to the
success of the Conference."[40] Jinnah also pressed in this letter for the release
of more prisoners, especially Khan Abdul Gaffoor (Ghaffar) Khan, one of
his two recommended delegates to the conference from the North-West
Frontier Province, though as Jinnah noted, he "has no or very little knowledge of English language." That "Lion of the Frontier" was, however, the
most popular leader of the Pathans and would become a staunch Congress
ally, soon to be hailed as the "Frontier Gandhi."

Sapru returned to Naini prison on August 8 to inform the Nehrus that Lord Irwin had "no objection" to sending them to Poona to meet with Gandhi in Yeravda. Two days later a special train rushed them to Maharashtra, and from August 13–15 Congress's three leaders met with Sapru and Jayakar inside the Mahatma's "palace temple" cell. Several other members of the Congress party's working committee, including Vallabhbhai Patel and Sarojini Naidu, joined them. On August 15 the Congress prisoners wrote to Sapru and Jayakar, concluding that "the time is not yet ripe for securing a settlement honourabe for our country."[41]

Jinnah's anxiety over the fate of *his* conference mounted as he followed news reports of the Yeravda prison "all-parties" conference, from which he and the Muslim League by his own choice were excluded. He wrote again to Irwin on August 19 what was a most remarkable letter not only for the impatience and irascibility bordering on petulance it revealed, but because it reflected what was actually a reversal of roles, with Jinnah urging the viceroy to be more "firm and definite" in his dealings with Indian nationalists.[42]

Jinnah had taken upon himself, as it were, the full burdens of viceroy and secretary of state, internalizing those roles in what he truly believed to be the best interests, not only of the Muslim minority, but of the entire population of India, Great Britain, and, indeed, the world. He considered Gandhi quite mentally unbalanced by now, believed Jawaharlal Nehru a dangerous young radical, whose judgment could not be trusted, and knew that Motilal's fever was higher since the Yeravda "summit." He sensed that the older Nehru's will had fallen hostage to his son's more powerful resolve to march toward "complete independence." Isolated, cut off from the "peace talks" entirely, Jinnah saw no ray of hope left in India, only in the distant glow of London's Round Table conference, the thoughts of which sustained him.

Lord Irwin wrote to Sapru and Jayakar from his viceregal lodge in Simla on August 28:

> I fear as you will no doubt recognize that the task you had voluntarily undertaken has not been assisted by the letter you have received from the Congress leaders. In view both of the general tone by which that letter is inspired and of its contents, as also of its blank refusal to recognize the grave injury to which the country has been subjected by the Congress policy, not the least in the economic field, I do not think any useful purpose would be served by my attempting to deal in detail with the suggestions there made and I must frankly say I regard discussion on the basis of the proposals contained in the letter as impossible. I hope if you desire to see the Congress leaders again you will make this plain.[43]

So ended Round One of the peace talks. Irwin wrote to notify Jinnah of his firm response on September 1. Jinnah's reply a week later continued to sound like a communication from a higher official to his subordinate: "I am in receipt of yours of the 1st September, 1930 and I thank you very much for it. This is just to inform you that I am going to Sind on a professional engagement tonight and shall return to Bombay on the 18th or 19th. I have now booked my passage for the 4th October in view of the fact that the Conference does not meet till the middle of November. More when I return."[44]

He had much to arrange in what was to be his last full month in India for several years. Almost thirty-five years had gone by since his return from London to make Bombay his home. The would-be thespian had reached stardom as Bombay's most successful barrister, a viceroy's alter ego, and the prime minister's friend. It was time to go back then to London—not to retire exactly, but to settle in and to enjoy an atmosphere less frenzied, less perilous than India's had become. Ever guarded and secretive about his private life, Jinnah made no pronouncement of future plans on the eve of his departure. Those who knew him assumed, of course, that he was merely packing in preparation for the Round Table conference. But he was planning his next step up the ladder of the law, to transfer his practice entirely to appeals before London's Privy Council, the highest court in the empire. In mid-August he had invited Dr. Muhammad Iqbal (1877–1938) to preside over the Muslim League's annual session, which he would not himself attend. He had lost almost as much faith in his Muslim colleagues as in the Hindus. They could agree on virtually nothing. Jinnah was fed up with petty conflicts and nights of endless argument. The Round Table would serve as the setting for his final act on British India's political stage. And should the curtain there descend on a flop, at least that would leave him in London.

10

London
(1930-33)

Jinnah had sailed aboard the P.&O. *Viceroy of India,* leaving Bombay on October 4, 1930. As the first stroke of noon reverberated from Big Ben on November 12, 1930, King Emperor George V, standing before his throne in the Royal Gallery of the House of Lords, inaugurated the first Round Table conference on India, with his message being broadcast throughout the world by wireless. Rays of morning sun filtered through the high stained-glass windows of that cathedrallike hall filled with the fifty-eight well-dressed delegates from British India, among whom stood Jinnah, the Aga Khan, Sapru, Jayakar, and sixteen "representatives" of the Indian states, including Patiala and Baroda, Bhopal, and Alwar in his vivid green turban, plus a phalanx of officials led by Prime Minister MacDonald, Mr. Benn, and Lord Sankey, the chancellor of the lords. Ex-viceroys Hardinge and Reading were there, as were the prime ministers of most dominions of the British Commonwealth, all of whom remained standing during His Majesty's brief address. King George departed as soon as he concluded his speech. The maharaja of Patiala, the chancellor of the Chamber of Princes, then proposed that Prime Minister MacDonald take the chair of the conference, and the Aga Khan seconded the motion, which was carried by acclamation. Liberal V. S. Srinavasa Sastri spoke first for the British Indian delegation. Then Jinnah, as spokesman for the sixteen Muslim delegates, rose, introducing what the *Times* reported as "the first suggestion of controversy," "I am glad, Mr. President [MacDonald], that you referred to the fact that 'the declarations made by British sovereigns and statesmen from time to time that Great Britain's work in India was to prepare her for self-government have been plain.' . . . But I must emphasize that India now expects translation and fulfilment of these declarations into action."[1]

This was a stage more glorious than any he had ever spoken from before, the culmination, not simply of a year-and-a-half's lobbying and labor from half a world away, but of his current political career. To utter a few adulatory platitudes as timorous Sastri had done, to say nothing of substance, nothing momentous or historic, was unthinkable for Jinnah. Emphasizing as he already had the need for "action" was electrifying enough for most of them, more than any of the princes who had preceded him dared, but Jinnah had a still more powerful bombshell to drop in that hallowed hall. "In conclusion," he said, "I must express my pleasure at the presence of the Dominion Prime Ministers and representatives. I am glad that they are here to witness the birth of a new Dominion of India which would be ready to march along with them within the British Commonwealth of Nations." Did any of those who heard him dream it would, in fact, be Jinnah's destiny to lead another as yet unborn dominion into that commonwealth?

Certainly not Sir Malcolm Hailey, ex-governor of the Punjab as well as of the United Provinces, the government of India's senior consultative official at the conference.

"As a whole the Moslems seem up to the present to be fairly well combined," Hailey reported to Lord Irwin from Whitehall. "The Aga Khan does not give them a lead, but professes himself willing to follow the majority. Jinnah is of course a good deal mistrusted; he did not at the opening of the Conference say what his party had agreed, and they are a little sore in consequence. He declined to give the Conference Secretariat a copy of his speech in advance as all the others had done. But then Jinnah of course was always the perfect little bounder and as slippery as the eels which his forefathers purveyed in Bombay market."[2]

The conference reconvened in St. James's Palace on the afternoon of Monday, November 17. The night before, Jinnah, Shafi, and the Aga Khan had met with Sapru, Setalvad, Jayakar, and Dr. B. S. Moonje, Nagpur's president of the Hindu Mahasabha, in the nawab of Bhopal's London residence on Upper Brook Street.[3] They had achieved "a surface harmony," as the Aga Khan put it, "but underneath there were deep and difficult rifts of sentiment and of outlook whose effect was bound to be felt.[4] Nothing had changed. Jinnah and most of the Muslims wanted all of his fourteen points, only half of which Sapru and Setalvad were ready to concede, and none of which Jayakar or Moonje would fully accept.

As Jinnah had feared, the conference proved much too large. There was time only for three addresses to the first plenary session, six on the next day, and four on the third. Those speeches were so prolix, redundant, and rhetorical that future statements were strictly limited by the chair to no more than ten minutes, for it soon became obvious to everyone that precious time was being frittered away listening to oft-repeated arguments, while the magic moment of world interest and attention was being wasted. Virtually all the Indian speeches, however, echoed a single theme—the "whole future" was at stake. "The time has long since passed by when India could be told to hold its soul in patience,"[5] as Sapru put it. And speaking for the princes, the gaekwar of Baroda was even more forthright. Even Sir Muhammad Shafi warned against further "tardy measures." But Lord Peel (1867–1937), former secretary of state for India under Baldwin's Tory government from 1922–24, who led the Conservative party's delegation, ignored all the appeals, urgent, impassioned, and quite accurate though they proved to be, arguing for implementation of the timid Simon Commission proposals.

Jinnah spoke for only ten minutes on November 20 but addressed himself directly to Lord Peel, insisting that the Simon Commission's Report was "dead." He spelled out in his brief address, moreover, what was later to become his strategy for achieving Pakistan. Evelyn Wrench subsequently reported that when he asked Jinnah "when he first got the vision of Pakistan . . . he told me it was in 1930,"[6] but there is no evidence that he seriously contemplated leading the struggle toward its attainment as yet. Two points he made at the Round Table in November 1930, however, offer important insights into his strategic thinking on the subject. ". . . I have no hesitation in conceding this proposition—that you [Great Britain] have a great interest in India, both commercial and political, and therefore you are a party, if I may say so, gravely interested in the future constitution of India. But . . . I want you equally to concede that we have a greater and far more vital interest than you have, because you have the financial or commercial interest and the political interest, but to us it is all in all." And as to the question of "parties," Jinnah stated that ". . . there are four main parties sitting round the table now. There are the British party, the Indian princes, the Hindus and the Muslims."[7]

Jinnah had long recognized a wide range of Muslim special interests, needs, and demands, but this was a new departure and became a major theme of his Pakistan strategy, that is, that the *Muslims* were a "party," a distinct bloc, separate from, if not actually equal to, the Hindus, the princes, and the British. His second point was at least as important but remained still a veiled warning, a threat construed by most who heard it as nothing more than Jinnah's "language of the bargainer," the sort of thing a scion of "eel-purveyors" might lightly say. He warned that unless this Round Table negotiated a "settlement" to "satisfy the aspirations of India" then the seventy million Muslims and all others who had "kept aloof" might be tempted to "join" the "non-co-operation movement."

Jinnah then stated "the cardinal principle," which he hoped British members of the conference would keep uppermost in mind, that "India wants to be mistress in her own house; and I cannot conceive of any constitution that you may frame which will not transfer responsibility in the Central Government to a Cabinet responsible to the Legislature."[8] It was, he argued, the least that would now suffice to satisfy political leaders throughout the subcontinent, those who came to London, as well as those who had remained in British India's crowded prison cells. He reminded MacDonald that two years earlier, at a Labour conference, the future prime minister had said, "I hope that within a period of months, rather than years, there will be a new Dominion added to the Commonwealth of our nations, a Dominion of another race, a Dominion that will find self-respect as an equal within the Commonwealth—I refer to India." Trenchantly, he added, "Since 1928 two years have passed."[9]

Jinnah was assigned to the federal structure subcommittee chaired by Lord Sankey, before which he and Shafi both "made it clear" that "no constitution would work unless it embodied provisions which gave a sense of security to the Muslims and other minorities."[10] Hailey reported to Irwin after the failure of every London attempt at resolving the Hindu-Muslim conflict, on December 4, 9, and 15. The last of these meetings was at the prime minister's country house, Chequers, to which "Hindus and Muslims are being conveyed in motor-buses," wrote Hailey on the 13th. "I had a long talk with some of them last night. . . . So far as one can prophesy, the indications are that the Muslims will give up separate electorates but will get a bare majority in the Punjab and Bengal and weightage in the other Provinces."[11] Hailey's predictions proved premature. "The Muslims, acting on renewed pressure from India, now refuse to go back on their insistence on separate electorates and demand not only these but all the terms which they have included in their fourteen points. The Hindus, led by Moonje, went back on their agreement to concede the fourteen points. There was, in fact, a complete deadlock."[12] Ramsay MacDonald was so depressed by the Chequers fiasco that he decided to turn to Lord Willingdon (1866–1941), then governor-general of Canada, for help in augmenting a new tough line toward India. Irwin's term as viceroy expired in April 1931, and on December 23, 1930, Britain's prime minister wrote to Canada's prime minister, Richard Bennett, asking him to let go of his governor-general, explaining: "A solution of this problem is essential to the future government of India, and it must now be sought in India itself. I know no man who can conduct these negotiations better than Willingdon."[13]

Jinnah's bête noire as governor of Bombay during World War I would thus return to take the helm of India's government at New Delhi from

1931–36. It was not entirely coincidental perhaps that for most of Lord Willingdon's term as viceroy, Jinnah remained out of India, though by then he more closely resembled the formidable marquis in temperament as well as appearance than he did that radical young nationalist leader of the 1918 anti-Willingdon protest. Willingdon's feelings toward Jinnah sufficed to keep the latter off the joint committee appointed to fashion final Round Table conference proposals into a new government of India bill for Parliament. Jinnah opted to live in London, however, despite Willingdon's presence in India (a "target" who must have tempted him sorely at times to return to the legislative assembly), as much as because of it. Jinnah did not hesitate to return, periodically, for visits to Simla, Delhi, and Bombay during his half decade of "permanent" residence in London.

Before Ramsay MacDonald's admission of failure to resolve the communal problem could reach Canada, however, a new proposal of the Muslim position was being articulated at a poorly attended meeting of the Muslim League in Allahabad, on December 29, 1930. That meeting was presided over by Dr. Muhammad Iqbal (1877–1938), a mystic Urdu poet-philosopher of the Punjab. Though a barrister of Lincoln's Inn, educated in Heidelberg and Munich University, and a graduate of Trinity College, Cambridge, *Allama* ("Islamic Scholar") Iqbal remained deeply religious throughout his turbulent life. He joined the Muslim League's British committee when it was first started in London in 1908, served as secretary of Shafi's league, and was a leading force in the Punjab's legislative council from 1926–30. In Allahabad Iqbal was first to articulate the two-nation theory of irreconcilable Hindu-Muslim difference. He was not calling for complete national separation as yet but insisted that "The principle of European democracy cannot be applied to India without recognizing the fact of communal groups. The Muslim demand for the creation of a Muslim India within India is, therefore, perfectly justified." He then went further than any previous president of the league had ever gone, spelling out his vision of the future "final destiny" of the Muslim community of his own Punjab and its neighboring provinces. "I would like to see the Punjab, the North-West Frontier Province, Sind and Baluchistan amalgamated into a single State. Self-government within the British Empire, or without the British Empire, the formation of a consolidated North-West Indian Muslim State appears to me to be the final destiny of the Muslims, at least of North-West India."[14] Iqbal did "not feel optimistic" about the Round Table conference and, in the concluding section of his Allahabad speech, criticized Ramsay MacDonald for refusing "to see that the problem of India is international."

On January 14, 1931, the Aga Khan, Jinnah, and Shafi called on Ramsay MacDonald to warn him that "unless his statement of the Government's policy is accompanied by an announcement of satisfactory safeguards for the communities, most of the Moslem delegates will dissociate themselves from the findings of the Conference."[15] Kanji Dwarkadas reported that Ramsay MacDonald tried, by this time, to win greater cooperation from Jinnah during the conference by "casually" remarking to him in "the course of conversation" that

> in view of the forthcoming changes in India the British Government would be looking for distinguished Indians for appointment as Provincial Governors. The obvious implication of this suggestion was that "Jinnah would have an excellent chance if he proved to be a good boy." Jinnah at once made it clear to Ramsay MacDonald that his services were not available for sale and firmly rejected the offer which he believed was nothing less than "an attempt to bribe him."[16]

Jinnah's legal acuity proved, moreover, at least as important a factor by now as his "unpurchasability" in helping account for the leadership he attained over the Muslim deputation in London and later over all of Muslim India. At the end of the first Round Table conference,

> The Muslim delegation was anxious to learn beforehand what safeguards were to be incorporated for the protection of minorities. . . . A letter was received by the Aga Khan and the delegation met immediately in his room. Jinnah was delayed and the letter was discussed and had been approved of when Mr. Jinnah arrived. He went through it and pointed out the flaw where none seemed to exist—a flaw that would have meant the annulment of most of what had been conceded. All were amazed. The result: Muslims secured for their nation 12 out of the 14 points.[17]

In mid-January, on the eve of the concluding plenary session of the conference, the Muslims were therefore united in presenting their "last offer" to the minorities subcommittee, one proposing Hindu-Sikh and Muslim parity for Punjab and Hindu-Muslim parity for Bengal, but both reasonable suggestions failed to win Punjabi Sikh or Bengali Hindu approval. Significantly, neither Jinnah, Shafi, nor the Aga Khan spoke at the concluding plenary session, when most other delegates, including Shafi's lovely daughter, Begum Shah Nawaz, delivered congratulatory speeches of thanks to the prime minister and their British hosts, optimistically hailing the work of the conference as marking "the dawn of a new era."[18] Not so for Jinnah. The hope that had buoyed his spirits on arrival at Westminster two months earlier had dissolved in the acid of fermenting misgivings as to the possibility of ever settling the Hindu-Muslim conflict. He had sent for Fatima and his daughter Dina to live with him in London and began looking for a home for the three of them. He was ready to leave the League to Iqbal and his Punjabi friends. Jinnah's only remaining political ambition was to enter Parliament—through whichever party would have him. Perhaps he thought he could still be of service to Muslim India from there, or if not—the Privy Council remained, possibly even its Bench, as the crowning achievement of his career. And the news he read and received from India served only to confirm the wisdom of his withdrawal from that scene of chaos compounded.

Jinnah applied to London's Inner Temple to let chambers that had just fallen vacant within its walls. The Temple's treasurer was none other than Sir John Simon, who wrote to assure a mutual barrister friend Bhugwandin Dube that his Inn would "be very glad to have so distinguished a man within our own boundaries. . . . He need not trouble about recommendations, as, of course, I know all about him, but I think there is, according to our ordinary rule, a surety in connection with the actual lease."[19] Jinnah secured his chambers in King's Bench Walk before the winter was over. It would take several more months of estate hunting to locate the appropriate house, "a three-storied villa, built in the confused style of the 1880's, with many rooms and gables, and a tall tower which gave a splendid view over the surrounding country,"[20] set in the middle of eight acres of garden and pasture on Hampstead's West Heath Road. (This house was torn down soon after his death, however, and the unobscured view he enjoyed has also long since disappeared.)

Lord Willingdon was sworn in as viceroy on April 18, 1931. Before leaving London he had been "so pleased" to meet with Jinnah at his home on Abbey Road on the morning of Saturday, March 21.[21] Though no record of their conversation has as yet come to light, it was hardly a social chat between old friends. Jinnah doubtless reiterated the Muslim position, briefing the new viceroy on all of the latest demands that had been added since he first drafted his fourteen points. Willingdon's response can well be imagined, for he was always vocal in support of every minority and encouraging to Muslim demands. He must have been pleased to see how much Jinnah's political point of view had "matured" since their last heated confrontation.

Jinnah hoped initially to enter Parliament as a Labour M. P., desiring "to try the fortune of the ballot box in a party which in the main" agreed with his own "political creed."[22] His uncooperative stance on several key issues at the First Round Table conference had, however, left Ramsay Mac-Donald less than eager to further this erstwhile friend's political ambitions, and by June the prime minister wanted nothing whatsoever to do with Jinnah, actually refusing to see him by pleading "it is absolutely impossible for me to fit in another engagement."[23] Jinnah had by then gone so far as to join the Fabian Society,[24] yet even that did not make him sufficiently attractive to Labour's leadership as a Commons candidate. To British workingmen dapper Jinnah hardly looked like a trustworthy representative—one Yorkshire Labourite was reported having said, after listening to Jinnah talk to his party's selection committee, "We don't want a toff like that!" By June, therefore, Jinnah decided to try securing the nod to run for a Tory constituency; he abandoned Labour and turned to the Aga Khan for help. Though the Conservative party was traditionally opposed to all Indian political aspirations, Jinnah, much like the Aga Khan himself, hoped to appeal to their growing interest in Muslim demands as the only effective internal counterpoise to Congress revolutionaries.

Even with such high-level help, including the Aga Khan's personal coaching, however, Jinnah never managed to find a Tory constituency willing to back his candidacy. Had he been elected to Parliament, he might never have returned to India's political stage, except for brief visits, such as the one he undertook in August 1931 when he ventured east to defend a large landowning client in a Talukdari case before the chief court of Oudh in Lucknow. Jinnah spoke at Lucknow University's union one evening during that trip, reporting on the Round Table conference and "his disappointment at the attitude of the Hindu leaders." Karachi's former mayor, Syed Hashim Raza, recalled how he "raised his fore-finger . . . revolving it with the words:—'We went round and round in London. We are still going round and round in India without reaching the straight path that would lead us to freedom.' "[25]

During this sojourn in India, Jinnah visited Simla, conferring with old Assembly colleagues who were there for the fall legislative session. Sind's Mian Sir Haji Haroon had written earlier to report that "There is no cohesion or discipline of any kind. . . . Needless to say we are all feeling your absence keenly."[26] Sir A. P. Patro, the leader of Madras's Non-Brahman Justice party, had written Jinnah in much the same vein: "There is no outstanding leader among the Moslems, there are many lieutenants but no general. From this point of view I thought you would have been very helpful to Indian Unity . . . Intrigue and jealousy rampant on all sides. . . . We feel your absence very much."[27] Jinnah met briefly with Willingdon in Simla.

By the evening of August 27, Gandhi, who had been released from prison by Irwin had made up his mind to go to London for the second Round Table conference, as he reported to Willingdon, not "without fear, trembling and serious misgivings. Things from the Congress standpoint do not appear to be at all happy but I am relying upon your repeated assurances that you will give personal attention to everything that is brought to your notice."[28] Willingdon sent his "blessings and all good wishes," informing

Gandhi, "You can entirely rely upon my assurance to you."[29] To Ramsay MacDonald, the viceroy had recently written of Gandhi, "He is a curious little devil—always working for an advantage. In all his actions I see the 'bania' predominating over the saint!"[30] Gandhi embarked for London as sole representative of the Congress. Jawaharlal wanted to accompany him, and many "friends" urged Gandhi to take Nehru along but the Mahatma refused to allow any of his colleagues to share his London limelight.

Jinnah returned "home" by early September. The new passport he had taken out in 1931 "gave England, not India, as his place of residence."[31] Fatima was waiting in Hampstead, and Dina was safely enrolled in her private boarding school nearby. Secretary of State Wedgwood Benn invited Jinnah to sit on the Federal Structure Committee at the second Round Table conference that started on September 7, 1931, but his role was much diminished from what it had been the previous year. All eyes were on Gandhi in 1931, for his was the voice of Congress on every committee as well as at the plenary sessions where he spoke. The Federal Structure Committee met from September 7–27 under Lord Sankey's chairmanship. The next day the Minorities Committee was reconvened by Ramsay MacDonald, with Gandhi joining its ranks; it met till November 18, ten days after which the entire Conference gathered again in St. James's Palace in plenary session.

The second Round Table conference achieved no greater unity than the first had done for all its strenuous, wordy labor and well-meaning leaders, Sankey, Sapru, Gandhi, Ambedkar (the leader of the Untouchables), and Jayakar. The ranks of the Muslim delegation remained firm behind the line of their as yet unmet demands of the previous year. Though Lord Sankey reported that his committee had concluded its lengthy deliberations with the hope that an all-India federation was possible, Jinnah spoke for the entire Muslim deputation when he insisted, "I am still of the opinion that the achievement and completion of the scheme of all-India Federation must, with the best will in the world, take many years. No outstanding vital ingredient of the scheme has yet been agreed upon."[32] Sir Shah Nawaz Bhutto, one of Sind's wealthiest landowners and the father of Pakistan's future prime minister, voiced much the same feeling, noting before Ramsay MacDonald's concluding statement, "The Conference has come to an end without achieving any tangible result."[33]

Mr. G. D. Birla, one of India's wealthiest millowners and Congress supporters, represented the Federation of Indian Chambers of Commerce and Industry at this second conference and "frankly" stated, "we are not at all satisfied with what has taken place."[34] Birla's critique of the Indian budget and financial situation was as brilliantly scathing as any made to the face of a British cabinet minister. Birla suggested a number of ways in which to reduce the British "mortgage" to 40 or 50 percent of India's annual budget but then voiced the strongest attack of the conference against constitutional "safeguards," warning "you should not ignore the Indian investor." The Indian investor, Birla argued, himself one of their leaders, "detests these safeguards, because these safeguards which are proposed are not in his interest; they are in the interests of City financiers."[35]

Gandhi was last to address the conference, starting his speech after midnight on December 1, 1931. "All the other parties at this meeting represent sectional interests," argued the Mahatma.

> Congress alone claims to represent the whole of India, all interests. It is no communal organisation; it is a determined enemy of communalism in any shape or form. . . . And yet here I see that the Congress is treated as one of the Parties. . . . I wish I could convince all the British public men, the British Ministers, that the Congress is capable of delivering the goods. The Congress is the only all-Indiawide national organisation, bereft of any communal basis. . . . Believe me, that (Mussulman) problem exists here, and I repeat . . . that without the problem of minorities being solved there is no Swaraj for India, there is no freedom for India. . . . But I do not despair of some day or other finding a real and living solution in connection with the minorities problem. I repeat . . . that so long as the wedge in the shape of foreign rule divides community from community and class from class, there will be no real living solution, there will be no living friendship between these communities. . . . Were Hindus and Mussulmans and Sikhs always at war with one another when there was no British rule, when there was no English face seen there? . . . This quarrel is not old; this quarrel is coeval with this acute shame. I dare to say it is coeval with the British advent.[36]

The Aga Khan himself did not feel confident about the true strength of the Muslim majority either in Bengal or in the Punjab, since as he had earlier written to Jinnah, "in view of the fact that Moslem women are under purdah and many are not prepared to go to the poll—and also the economic indebtedness of Moslems to Hindus—the mere fact of giving them a majority on the register does not get rid of the trouble."[37] Jinnah felt even more gloomy about the second conference and its prospects, as he told an old journalist friend, Durga Das, at lunch in Simpson's, "What can you expect from a jamboree of this kind? The British will only make an exhibition of our differences."[38] He anticipated that nothing would come of Gandhi's appearance on the scene, predicting that the British "will make a fool of him, and he will make a fool of them" and asking, "Where is the Congress claim that it represents the Muslims as well? . . . I expect nothing to come out of this conference."

"The discussions . . . during the past two months have been of value in showing us more precisely the problems we have to solve," concluded Prime Minister MacDonald in his closing remarks.[39] And as positive and immediate steps, MacDonald announced his government's decision to bring the North-West Frontier province into full governor's status, and to create a new equally advanced province of Sind, two direct concessions to Muslim demands that helped convince the Muslim delegation of the wisdom of its political strategy to date, though the North-West Frontier, under the leadership of "Frontier Gandhi," Abdul Ghaffar Khan would align itself with Congress rather than the Muslim League in future elections.

In moving his vote of thanks to the prime minister, on behalf of the conference, Gandhi warned that it was "somewhat likely" that "so far as I am concerned we have come to the parting of the ways," and, indeed, soon after reaching Indian soil he would be arrested again in Bombay on Willingdon's order. Jinnah, on the other hand, urged Britain's government to "give Provincial Autonomy without delay simultaneously with responsibility at the Centre in British India," recognizing, as he did, the total impossibility of getting the princes to agree to any federal scheme. He further advised his British friends, as MacDonald intimated, to "decide the communal question provisionally. I say this because, if the British Government settle the communal question and make a substantial advance towards real responsibility at the Centre in British India, both Hindus and Mahommedans will realise the earnestness on the part of the Government and the bulk of the people will accept their decision."[40] The stage was thus set for the next decade of political tug-of-war, with Jinnah's constitutional formula proving in part prophetic in anticipating British intentions, while Gandhi and his side braced themselves for longer incarcerations and stiffer revolutionary resistance.

The next few years in London would be the quietest, least political years of Jinnah's adult life. His daily routine rarely altered. Breakfast at nine, then off to chambers in the City. He had an English chauffeur, Bradbury, who drove the Bentley. He quickly established a reputation for excellence before the Privy Council. Yet in spite of this, he was never invited to serve as a judge on it as Jayakar would later be. Justice Chagla reported that "He did not succeed in his practice in the Privy Council as he had expected,"[41] which "chastened" Jinnah, predisposing him to return to India in 1934.

Durga Das confirmed this, noting that during their "excellent meal" at Simpson's, "Jinnah confessed he was not enamoured of his legal practice in

London; what he coveted professionally was a seat on the Judicial Committee of the Privy Council. Or he might try to enter Parliament."[42] The
truth, in fact, seems to be that he *did* succeed as well as any lawyer could,
but that simply was not enough to keep him occupied. Parliament, of
course, was his goal, yet every constituency remained closed to him. The
judicial committee of the Privy Council, had it been offered, would probably have proved as much of a bore as did appealing to its tribunal. In less
than a year he must have paced off every inch of Hampstead Heath and
had probably eaten in every decent restaurant in London. Even if the
theater continued to lure him to the West End and old friends to Oxford or
Cambridge, there was really nothing to tax his talents, no challenge left to
his life, no summits to win, no opponents worthy of his genius to vanquish.
At fifty-five he appeared to have achieved a routine resembling the perfect
tranquillity of the grave.

Dina was his sole comfort, but Dina was away at school most of the
time and home only for brief holidays. She was a dark-eyed beauty, lithe
and winsome. She had her mother's smile and was pert or petulant as only
an adored, pampered daughter could be to her doting father. He had two
dogs, one formidable black Doberman, the other a white West Highland
Terrier. And there was always Fatima, of course, but she was much too
somber, too busy worrying, ever "guarding" him from "intruders," and especially women. "She hated any woman he ever liked," Begum Liaquat Ali
Khan recalled. "Oh, how she hated Ruttie! I think she must have been
jealous of us all! We used to call her the wicked-Witch!"[43] In November of
1932, Jinnah read H. C. Armstrong's life of Kemal Ataturk, *Grey Wolf*, and
seemed to have found his own reflection in the story of Turkey's great
modernist leader. It was all he talked about for a while at home, even to
Dina who nicknamed him "Grey Wolf." Being only thirteen, her way of
cajolingly pestering him to take her to High Road to see Punch and Judy,
who surfaced in Hampstead every Sunday, was, "Come on, Grey Wolf, take
me to a pantomime; after all, I am on my holidays."[44]

There were other distractions as well, yet all too few and far between.
Begum Shah Nawaz returned to London to help transform the recommen-
dations of the first two conferences into a bill for Parliament, the sort of job
Jinnah was best equipped to carry out, yet he was not even invited to at-
tend the third Round Table conference or to meet with Parliament's Joint
Select Committee, which the second Marquess of Linlithgow (1887–1952)
chaired. The Aga Khan and Zafrulla Khan, Sapru and Jayakar, Patro and
Ambedkar were there, cheek by jowl with Hardinge and Irwin, Attlee and
Zetland, the Lord Chancellor and the Archbishop of Canterbury. However,
there was no Jinnah, no Gandhi, no Nehru. (Jawaharlal had been arrested

again in Allahabad before Gandhi reached Bombay, and by mid-January 1932 both heads of Congress were left to languish behind British bars. Jinnah's London retreat could hardly be compared to the harsh, enforced isolation of a prison cell, yet he must have felt almost as lonely and cut off at times in Hampstead.

Government's "Communal Decision" was presented to Parliament in August 1932, in keeping with the prime minister's promise at the end of the second Round Table conference, and in response to pressure from Willingdon urging swift action to placate India's Muslims. That communal award assured Muslims some 51 percent of the legislative seats in the Punjab, and just under 50 percent in Bengal, where special interest Europeans would hold the balance of power, retaining separate electorates and Muslim representation in excess of total population proportions in all Hindu majority provinces. The third Round Table conference ended on Christmas eve 1932 with Secretary of State Sir Samuel Hoare (1880–1950) announcing that Muslims would be assured the full 33⅓ percent representation they demanded at the All-India Federal Centre, and that Orissa as well as Sind would become separate new provinces of British India.

In Cambridge a pamphlet was published that year, written by a thirty-five-year-old Muslim "student" from the Punjab, Choudhary Rahmat Ali (1897–1951). Now or Never was its title; it was subtitled Are We to Live or Perish for Ever? The shadowy Rahmat Ali identified himself as "Founder of the Pakistan National Movement" and named three associates, also Cambridge "students," Mohammad Aslam Khan, Sheikh Mohammad Sadiq, and Inayat Ullah Khan, who apparently contributed to the contents of this pamphlet, which first publicized the name "Pakstan." Rahmat Ali's "proposed solution of the great Hindu-Muslim problem" was written "on behalf of the thirty million Muslims of PAKSTAN, who live in the five Northern Units of India—Punjab, N.W.F.P. [Afghan Province], Kashmir, Sindh, and Baluchistan, embodying their inexorable demand for the recognition of their separate national status as distinct from the rest of India."[45] While this early 1933 demand clearly derived inspiration, at least in part, from Iqbal's Allahabad address of December 1930, the Cambridge founders of this "Pakstan national movement" insisted that their plan was "basically different from the suggestion put forward by Doctor Sir Muhammad Iqbal," whose Northwest "unit" was to have remained within an all-India federation, by insisting: "These Provinces should have a separate Federation of their own. There can be no peace and tranquillity in the land if we, the Muslims, are duped into a Hindu-dominated Federation where we cannot be the masters of our own destiny and captains of our own souls."[46]

Soon after the Pakistan pamphlet was printed, testimony by several conservative British officials before Parliament's Joint Committee on proposed Constitutional Reforms echoed that as yet obscure demand. Sir Michael O'Dwyer (1864–1940), who ruled the Punjab during the Jallianwala Bagh massacre and its martial law aftermath, testified before that committee in mid-June, arguing against an all-India federation since "if the Federal Government, with a Hindu majority, endeavours to force its will on provinces with a Muslim majority, what is to prevent a breakaway of the Punjab, Sind, Baluchistan and the N.W.F. *as already foreshadowed* and their possibly forming a Muslim Federation of their own." [Italics added][47] Sir Michael did not explain where that "Muslim Federation" was "foreshadowed," but he appears to have received one of Rahmat Ali's pamphlets. Or could he perhaps have helped inspire it?

Sir Reginald Craddock (1868–1937), former Home member of the government of India, a conservative member of Parliament (from 1931) appointed to Linlithgow's Joint Committee on Indian Constitutional Reforms, also knew about the Pakistan idea by August 1, 1933, when he asked Abdullah Yusuf Ali, of the North-West Frontier Province, "whether there is a scheme for Federation of Provinces under the name of Pakistan?"[48] Yusuf Ali's answer was, "As far as I know, it is only a student's scheme; no responsible people have put it forward." Sir Reginald was more sanguine about its prospects, however, stating: "They have not so far, but . . . you advance very quickly in India, and it may be, when those students grow up it will be put forward; that scheme must be in the minds of the people anyhow." Mr. Zafrulla Khan (1893–1981), the previous year's president of the League, destined to become Pakistan's foreign minister, had never heard of the word or movement. Mr. Isaac Foot, a Liberal member of Parliament, who, unlike Craddock, had no prior India experience, asked, "What is Pakistan?" To this Yusuf Ali, who served as spokesman for the joint five-member Muslim delegation of the Muslim League and the All-India Muslim Conference to the Parliamentary commitee, replied: "So far as we have considered it, we have considered it chimerical and impracticable. It means the Federation of certain Provinces." Yet Craddock was still not willing to drop this "chimerical" subject, pressing on with, "I have received communications about the proposal of forming a Federation of certain Muslim States under the name of Pakistan." Another member of the Muslim deputation, Dr. Khalifa Shujauddin, insisted, "Perhaps it will be enough to say that no such scheme has been considered by any representative gentlemen or association so far."

If Jinnah knew about the Pakistan scheme at this date, there was no indication in his papers of such knowledge or of any personal interest expressed in it. Nor would he agree to meet with Rahmat Ali the following year, despite several attempts by the latter to discuss his ideas with Jinnah in London.[49] Nor was Jinnah willing as yet to accept the Muslim League's invitation to return to India to preside over its annual deliberations in Delhi in April of 1933. "I cannot return to India before December next," he replied to that telegraphic invitation from Abdul Matin Choudhury in March.

> Besides I don't see what I can do there at present. You very rightly suggest that I should enter the Assembly. But is there much hope in doing anything there? These are questions which still make me feel that there is no room for my services in India, yet I am sorry to repeat, but there is no chance of doing anything to save India till the Hindus realise the true position. . . . The Hindus are being fooled . . . by chance any scheme goes through, it will be worse than what is at present. . . . Thank you for your suggestion that I should try and stand for election as Sir Ibrahim [Rahimtoola] is going to resign. Well! I can't say till I come to India as I am due in December, at any rate for a few months.[50]

The scheduled December visit was for business, yet the prospect of re-election to the assembly clearly tempted him. It was not Parliament, though one day soon it might almost be. Perhaps he was simply getting bored with Hampstead. Liaquat Ali Khan and his beautiful begum arrived that summer to add their voices to those seeking to lure Jinnah home. They had come to London for their honeymoon and met Jinnah at a reception, where he invited them to dinner in Hampstead. "You must come back," Liaquat urged. "The people need you. You alone can put new life into the League and save it." Begum Liaquat, much like Begum Shah Nawaz, appealed to him with the same vital glowing beauty, idealistic enthusiasm, and hero worship that Ruttie had displayed during their exciting early years of marriage. His heart's fire, his ambition began to burn again with the revitalized brilliance of the twilight glow of fifty-seven years. Liaquat's imprecations, offers of assistance, and flattery were, of course, an added factor, for Jinnah always responded to appeals aimed at his ego, his unique capacity to "save" the situation. In London, the only round table left to him was one at which he and Fatima dined alone, rarely speaking to one another and never smiling. Most evenings, except in those scarce interludes when a beautiful begum appeared, the house lights at Hampstead Heath Road remained dim. And what great actor, after all, would not find the prospect of an eagerly awaiting vast audience tempting enough to lure him back home, at least for part of each year?

II

London – Lucknow
(1934-37)

Jinnah returned to Bombay in 1934, but did not close his Hampstead establishment or abandon his City chambers. The next few years would be spent sailing back and forth between the two worlds that claimed him, seeking to parcel out his days between those basically incompatible lands, and trying to keep himself attuned to both time zones while living mostly in limbo.

On March 4, 1934, the Muslim League met in New Delhi and resolved to heal the second major split, which had fragmented the party one year earlier, when its acting president, barrister Mian Abdul Aziz of Peshawar, "fired" all the secretaries and "attempted to transform the League into a party of his own."[1] The Aziz Group, as it came to be called, met in Howrah across the Hughli from Calcutta in October 1933; it claimed legitimacy, but a month later the Hidayat Group, named after its president Khan Bahadur Hafiz Hidayat Husain, branded Aziz and his followers "rebels." Hidayat Husain had attended the Round Table conferences, where he had regularly met with Jinnah, Shafi, and the Aga Khan and had supported the unified Muslim demands. One of the resolutions passed by his group in 1933 authorized the League Council to meet with Jinnah and the Aga Khan to discuss plans for "bringing about unity in the ranks of the League."[2] Aziz readily agreed to bring his group back to the League's fold if Jinnah presided over a unified party. Hidayat was at first reluctant to surrender his post as president but finally agreed to step down for Jinnah, remaining honorary secretary of the League. Jinnah was authorized by the council in March to set the date and place of the 1934 annual session, but he had already booked passage to sail for London on April 23, so he could meet with the council only on April 1 and 2 in New Delhi.

Jinnah was given "an enthusiastic welcome" by the forty-odd members of council who attended the proceedings that were closed to the press. After the council meeting ended, Jinnah granted the Associated Press an interview, stating: "The League is perfectly sound and healthy, and the conclusion I have come to is that Musalmans will not lag behind any other community in serving the very best interests of India. To condemn the White Paper, one does not require special arguments, one has only got to read the White Paper proposals . . . that is enough."[3] Sir Samuel Hoare had presented his proposals for Indian constitutional reform, known as the White Paper, to Parliament in March 1933. The federation of India was to be a union of governors' provinces and Indian states, all of whose "powers" would remain vested in the (British) Crown. Executive authority over the federation was to be exercised on behalf of Britain's king emperor by a governor-general appointed at His Majesty's "pleasure," whose powers included supreme command of the military, naval, and air forces in India, and who would personally direct and control the departments of defense, external affairs, and ecclesiastical affairs. Such extraordinary powers were unique under any system of government deemed "constitutional," and Jinnah was one of their most outspoken critics. A bicameral federal legislature was envisioned, consisting of a council of state with not more than 260 members, 150 of whom would be elected from British India, and an assembly with not more than 375 members, 250 of whom would be elected from British India, with the rest appointed to represent the princely states. There were to be eleven governors' provinces (including Sind and Orissa), with the appointed governor over each representing the British king. The governor would be empowered to select ministers to assist him in running his province "during his pleasure." He would, however be "enjoined" to seek to select such executive aid "in consultation with the person who, in his judgment, is likely to command the largest following in the Legislature" and to appoint those "best in a position collectively to command the confidence of the Legislature."[4] Such was the nature of provincial "autonomy" envisioned by the White Paper. There were many elaborate safeguards and emergency powers provided for the governors "in the event of a Breakdown in the Constitution." Winston Churchill led a vigorous Tory opposition to the White Paper on March 17, 1933, but it passed through Parliament with a comfortable 3 to 1 margin, indicative of how secure most Englishmen felt with the new Indian reforms.

Jinnah's strategy at this point was to turn back toward the Congress to see if its leadership might not, in fact, be prepared to concede all that MacDonald's Communal Award had promised to Muslims,[5] thus clearing the way for Hindus and Muslims to join forces in a common front against the White Paper. Angered at the Tory party's rejection of his bid for a parliamentary ticket, disgusted at the high-handed way in which Willingdon and Hoare were running India, Jinnah hoped the time was ripe for communal peace and was ready to launch a new series of talks aimed at weaning Congress from its dependence upon the Hindu Mahasabha position. "Can we even at this eleventh hour bury the hatchet, and forget the past in the presence of imminent danger," Jinnah asked Congress in his statement to the Associated Press.

> . . . nothing will give me greater happiness than to bring about complete co-operation and friendship between Hindus and Muslims; and in this desire, my impression is that I have the solid support of Musalmans. . . .

> Muslims are in no way behind any other community in their demand for national self-government. The crux of the whole issue, therefore, is: can we completely assure Muslims that the safeguards to which they attach vital importance will be embodied in the future Constitution of India?[6]

Jinnah's willingness to continue to work toward a united national platform terrified the more pro-British leaders of the League like Sir Fazl-i-Husain and Hidayat Husain, who joined with the nawab of Chhatari in trying to muster a Muslim majority against Jinnah as soon as his ship disappeared over the Arabian Sea's horizon. They met to form a "Parliamentary Majlis" that was convened by the nawab of Chhatari,[7] but it did not prove very effective, since they failed, despite Hidayat's vigorous exertions, to convene an emergency meeting of the Muslim League's council to validate the new group's claim to represent most Muslims. Old Hidayat's strenuous labors and frustrations were responsible for his death before the year ended, thus removing the mainspring from that Majlis "revolt" against Jinnah's leadership. Jinnah's "pendulum strategy" of swinging the ballast of Muslim support from Congress to the British and then back again, which thus won the greatest concessions for Muslims at every stage of the long, tough struggle toward a negotiated transfer of power, remained his most effective long-range technique.

While in London, Jinnah was re-elected that October by the Muslims of Bombay City to represent them in New Delhi's assembly. There was, in fact, no contest since his was the only name nominated for the seat he had first taken before World War I, and to which he would return as leader of the assembly's Independent party. He sailed back to Bombay in December 1934 and entrained to New Delhi in January 1935. Jinnah soon thereafter met with Congress president Rajendra Prasad (1884–1963), a Bihari lawyer destined to become India's first president, but their "heart-to-heart" talks failed to resolve the communal deadlock. Pandit Madan Malaviya, leader of the Hindu Mahasabha, who had also been president of the Congress, still adamantly refused to accept Jinnah's Muslim demands despite their equity. Thus, once again, the fate of helpless millions was sealed by a few stubborn leaders who refused to stretch that extra inch of representational concession to close the gap dividing India's pluralistic society and keeping it constitutionally fragmented. The Jinnah-Prasad talks came to "an infructuous end," as Prasad put it, alienating the one Muslim leader capable of reining his impatient, high-spirited community into harness with Congress's bullock team.

In February 1935, Jinnah stood on the floor of New Delhi's assembly to introduce an amendment in the debate that had just begun on Indian constitutional reform. His three-part proposal was to accept the Communal Award segment of the White Paper "until a substitute is agreed upon by the various communities concerned"; to urge the removal of "objectionable features" from the provincial government section, "particularly the establishment of Second Chambers, the extraordinary and special powers of the Governors, provisions relating to Police rules, Secret Service and Intelligence Departments, which render the real control and responsibility of the Executive and Legislature ineffective"; and to reject the all-India federation scheme proposed for the center as "thoroughly rotten, fundamentally bad and totally unacceptable."[8] Bhulabhai Desai (1877–1946), leader of the assembly's Congress party spoke against Jinnah's proposal to support the Communal Award, but Congress did not vote against part one—it merely abstained. Jinnah proved himself the most brilliant parliamentarian in British India.

> My amendment accepts the Communal Award . . . until a substitute is agreed upon between the communities concerned. Now, it may be that our Hindu friends are not satisfied with the Communal Award, but at the same time I can also tell the House that my Muslim friends are not satisfied with it either . . . and, again speaking as an individual, my self-respect will never be satisfied until we produce our own scheme. . . . But why do I accept it? . . . I accept it because we have done everything that we could so far to come to a settlement . . . therefore, whether I like it or whether I do not like it, I accept it, because unless I accept that no scheme of Constitution is possible. . . . Sir, this is a question of minorities and it is a political issue. . . . Minorities means a combination of things. It may be that a minority has a different religion from the other citizens of a country. Their lan-

guage may be different, their race may be different, their culture may
be different, and the combination of all these various elements—
religion, culture, race, language, arts, music, and so forth makes the
minority a separate entity in the State, and that separate entity as an
entity wants safeguards. Surely, therefore, we must face this question
as a poliical problem; we must solve it and not evade it.[9]

Jinnah's argument carried the House by a vote of 68 to 15, with the official bloc and elected Europeans voting with him. As for parts two and three
of his proposal, they were voted upon together, with Congress supporting
him and the government opposed, and those amendments carried by an
even greater majority. Jinnah realized full well that his was but a "paper
victory," one that Britain's Parliament could ignore with impunity; but he
had at least demonstrated both to Britain's Tory party and to the Congress
that his "tiny minority" voice could still be magnified, and if modulated
properly, win enough strategic support to carry India's "Commons"—transforming Muslim minority demands into a majority position. Yet it remained
an uphill struggle, trying to recapture and retain a position of national
leadership in a land where he lived only for a few months of each year. He
sought to win back former disciples, like Chagla, in Bombay, but Chagla
would not rejoin the Muslim League, rejecting his old boss' appeals and
countering them by urging Jinnah to organize a "thoroughly non-communal
. . . strong party . . . to recapture his position as a tribune of the people."[10]
On the eve of his sixtieth birthday, however, Jinnah was hardly prepared
to abandon the one party that retained enough faith in him to elect him to
lead it. He returned aboard the S.S. *Conte Verde* to London again in late
April of 1935, continuing to divide his year between the poles of his estab-
lishments. For the next six months Jinnah was preoccupied with his legal
work, which had by this time become so lucrative that he reportedly earned
40,000 rupees per month (£ 2,000) at the Bar alone.

Before the end of October 1935, he returned to Bombay to help re-
organize his Muslim League in preparation for the elections that would
bring a fresh cadre of representatives to British India's provincial and central legislatures under the Government of India Act of 1935. That act was
passed into law on August 2, 1935, and though its all-India federation section would never be implemented, the other portions of it served for the
most part as the constitution for British India after 1937 and remained the
skeletal framework for both India and Pakistan for years after each attained
independence a decade later. The inimitable Winston Churchill dismissed
the act as the rotten fruit of half a decade of "tumultuous confabulations"
that "has brought us nothing that has been good for this country or India,"
marking "no advance towards efficiency, no advance towards finality, and,

above all, no advance towards agreement."[11] Jinnah felt about the 1935 act precisely the way he had about the White Paper that sired it. "We all know that the new Constitution has been forced upon us," he said, on returning to India late in 1935. "It is now the duty of the various leaders to put their heads together and chalk out a definite and common policy with regard to the Constitution."[12] Jinnah's critique of the all-India federation in New Delhi's assembly in 1935 had been the strongest attack against it expressed in India, for Gandhi, who had announced his "retirement" from Congress in September 1934, devoted himself to the abolition of untouchability and village reforms as part of his *sarvodaya* ("uplift of all") socialism.

> I believe that it [the proposed federation] means nothing but absolute sacrifice of all that British India has stood for and developed during the last 50 years, in the matter of progress in the representative form of Government. No province was consulted as such. No consent of the princes has been obtained whether they are willing to federate as federating units on the terms which are laid down . . . by the British Government. My next objection is that it is not workable.[13]

And before retaking his seat in that important debate, Jinnah explained why he proposed accepting the provincial autonomy section of the new constitution:

> First of all, the franchise, enlargement of the electors and voters. That is the foundation-stone of any Constitution. . . . Next, all members of the Provincial Legislatures will be elected: that is an advance. Your cabinet in the provinces will be of the elected members responsible to the Legislature and the Legislature will be responsible to the electorates. That framework of the Provincial Constitution is undoubtedly an advance.[14]

Jawaharlal Nehru had been released from prison in September 1935 and permitted to leave India to join his tubercular wife Kamala then living in Germany. Nehru remained in Europe till Kamala's death on February 28, 1936, but visited England for brief interludes, where he avoided meeting with British officials. However, Lord Lothian (1882–1940), the liberal parliamentary undersecretary of state for India who had chaired the reforms franchise committee, tried very hard to lure Nehru to his country house, where he and the Earl of Halifax (formerly Lord Irwin), Britain's new foreign minister, hoped, unsuccessfully, to convince Nehru of the value of their Indian constitution. Then Nehru returned to India to take charge of Congress once again, succeeding Prasad as president in 1936.

The Muslim League met in Bombay that April, with Jinnah as permanent president introducing his old Lucknow Pact colleague, Sir Syed Wazir Hasan, the retired chief justice of Lucknow's high court, to preside over the League's 1936 session. Fazl-i Husain should have presided, but the illness resulting in his death later that year forced him to withdraw. Sir Fazl-i bitterly disliked Jinnah and wrote in his diary a month earlier, "I will not now go out of my way to be nice to him."[15] Jinnah gave him no opportunity to test that resolve, however, twice postponing the last meeting they had scheduled for Saturday, March 7, 1936, then calling to say "he was too busy." Sir Fazl-i concluded, "It appears that he was avoiding seeing me."

The Bombay session of the League initiated the slow process of transforming that small fragmented party into a mass movement with district branch volunteers throughout the country, who could nominate candidates and spread the League's message in every Muslim town and village of South Asia. An initial fund of half a million rupees was to be raised by the League council to pay for expanded secretariat needs, but student volunteers were recruited from Aligarh and other universities to carry on the political spade work. Jinnah's idea, voiced by Sir Syed Hasan in his presidential address, was to issue a joint Congress-League invitation to all "other progressive political parties in the country, to find such minimum measure of agreement as would enable us to act together . . . to draft a Constitution for India." It was one more try for the original Lucknow Pact approach and the pre-Nehru report All-Parties Conference concept. He had even gone so far as to draft four points that would serve, he hoped, to lure Jawaharlal's Congress, liberals, and possibly even the Mahasabha to a Round Table—this time on Indian soil.

1. A democratic responsible government, with adult franchise, to take the place of the present system
2. Repeal of all exceptionally repressive laws and the granting of the right of free speech, freedom of the press and organization
3. Immediate economic relief to the peasantry; State provision for educated and uneducated unemployed; and an eight-hour working day, with fixed minimum wages for the workers
4. Introduction of free, compulsory primary education[16]

Jinnah moved the resolution stating his League's "emphatic protest against forcing the Constitution as embodied in the Government of India Act of 1935, upon the people of India against their will, and in spite of their repeated disapproval and dissent." In speaking to this resolution, Jinnah advised his followers, indeed, all "Indians" to treat the new federal scheme the same way as the Germans had reacted to the Treaty of Versailles. He viewed "constitutional agitation" as the only sound approach for pressuring the

British into changing their scheme, since, as he put it, "Armed revolution was an impossibility, while non-co-operation had been tried and found a failure."[17] To effect such a constitutional transformation, however, "required all communities to stand shoulder to shoulder."

Supreme strategist of pendulum negotiations that he was, Jinnah probed first at the weak points of one opponent, then rushed to the opposite side's exposed flank, always seeking as he shifted his ground to rally his former "enemy" to his side. Small wonder both sides mistrusted him! Yet each underrated him, failing to see that he was, in fact, the most ingenius advocate, then of India as a whole and later of its Muslim minority alone, extracting for each client the greatest constitutional concession which the British, and Congress, were willing to grant at every turn. Just when one side thought it had him securely in its corner, Jinnah twirled with agility totally out of reach. For example, in New Delhi's assembly in March 1936, the Congress party had tabled an adjournment motion of censure against the government for having arrested Subhas Chandra Bose. The British confidently faced that "no-confidence" challenge, assuming they had more than enough independent party votes to put it down. But as Jawaharlal jubilantly wrote in a letter to Subhas, the censure motion "was passed by a majority of three votes—Jinnah and some of his colleagues remaining bravely neutral."[18]

A month later Lord Linlithgow replaced Lord Willingdon as viceroy, coming out to inaugurate the Constitution he had been most instrumental in helping to complete as chairman of the joint parliamentary committee. In his first broadcast to India, Linlithgow tried to assure his pluralistic audience of his personal impartiality, stating: "God has indeed been good to me for he has given me five children. . . . I love them all most dearly. But among my children I have no favourite."[19] The viceroy's son, who reported that speech, also wrote of Jinnah's "reaction" to it as "ominous," adding in what must have been Linlithgow's perception of the League leader's policy, that he "told his followers that the new Viceroy's pledge of impartiality was a poor reward for Muslim loyalty to the Government."

That same month Jinnah stood before the Muslim League, almost six years after Iqbal's Allahabad address and a full three years after the first Cambridge call for Pakistan, urging his followers to stand "shoulder to shoulder" with Congress and other Hindu-majority parties in the nation. This made it far more difficult, of course, for him to win or maintain the allegiance of Muslim colleagues, especially powerful provincial barons like Sir Fazl-i in the Punjab, Sir Ghulam Hussain Hidayatullah (1879–1948) of Sind, Sir Mohammad Saadullah (1886–1950) of Assam, or Abdul Qayum Khan (b. 1901) of the North-West Frontier, who thought only in terms of special provincial privileges for Muslims under the shield of a British wing of central power. Jinnah's vision went beyond that, soaring to encompass a future of complete equality among nations, English and Indian—or Pakistani, if Congress remained as churlish as some of its leaders persisted in being toward his Muslim demands.

To strengthen the League, bolster its bargaining position, and help prepare it for contesting elections, Jinnah was authorized at its Bombay meeting to appoint and preside over a new Central Parliamentary Board and affiliated provincial parliamentary boards. These boards, similar to those earlier established by Congress, were to become Jinnah's organizational arms in extending his power over the entire Muslim community. It was not before late May that he managed to win acceptance from fifty-four prominent Muslim politicians to serve on his central board, which met for the first time in Lahore from June 8–11, 1936. Sir Fazl-i died on July 9, removing Jinnah's foremost rival from the venue of his board's birth. Jinnah was, moreover, careful to court and win the support of Iqbal, with whom he met in Lahore during the last week in May.

Jinnah took "all the trouble that was possible in doing my utmost to see that the Central Board is made as truly representative of the Musalmans of India as possible," he reported, after his board's first meeting.[20] He consulted in Delhi with members of the council of the All-India Muslim League and various representatives of different provinces, who were invited "for that purpose" and spent four days in the Punjab recruiting various leaders there. In addition to Iqbal, that first list included three future premiers of Pakistan; Liaquat Ali Khan of the United Provinces, H. S. Suhrawardy (1893–1962) of Bengal, and Ismail I. Chundrigar (1897–1960) of Bombay. Thanks to Jinnah's unique status and singular ability to attract and retain the loyal support of young men of such talent, intelligence, and integrity, the "scattered crowd of Muslims" were soon "welded into a nation."[21] Jinnah's lieutenants included men of wealth and business experience as well as wisdom. Before 1936 the League had always been in financial trouble; most members never bothered to pay their annual "subscriptions," even though "Value Payable Parcels" were posted at considerable expense. "In a majority of cases," Secretary Hasan recalled, "they were returned unpaid!" The maharaja of Mahmudabad came to the League's rescue when it was still relatively small by providing 3,000 rupees annually to support its activities after 1911, but other patrons had to be recruited to share the burden of running a full-time national party. One of those financiers, who later remained among Jinnah's closest personal friends in the party, was Mirza Abol Hassan Ispahani (b. 1902), the scion of the wealthy Calcutta commercial and financial empire, M. M. Ispahani Ltd.

Ispahani first met Jinnah during his "fresher" term at Cambridge in 1920.

"It was in the Michaelmas term," Ispahani recalled, "that Mr. Jinnah accepted the invitation of the Indian Majlis . . . to address its members. He wore with distinction a thin streak of grey hair right in the middle of his head. . . . At the time I could well appreciate why women of diverse ages fell captive to his charm and personality."[22] They met again in London several weeks later at Ispahani's uncle's house on Putney Hill. Ruttie's youngest brother, Jamshed Petit, was Ispahani's Cambridge classmate and friend. Jinnah and his bride were invited to a "grand dinner" there, where a "jazz band performed" and most of the guests "cut capers"—except for Jinnah and the young Ispahani, who went off to play billiards while Ruttie and her brother did the Charleston. Despite such early intimacy, Jinnah and Ispahani rarely saw one another again till 1936, when Ispahani was "astonished" to be invited by Jinnah to join the League's new Central Parliamentary Board. After becoming a barrister of the Inner Temple, Ispahani had gone into his family's business, and, though elected to the Calcutta corporation in 1933, took little time from business for either provincial or national politics. He did not, however, hesitate to accept Jinnah's call and emerged as the League's major backer in Bengal.

Jinnah's League was faced in 1936 with two parties competing for Bengali Muslim allegiance; the nawab of Dacca's United Muslim party, and Fazlul Haq's *Krishak Proja Samiti* ("Peasants and Tenants party"). The nawab scheduled a three-day convention of his party in Calcutta's town hall, but Ispahani and his friends engineered a "dispute" there in early August, by getting Fazlul Haq and his followers to attend the conference and to demand to be heard, which lead to the conference's dissolution. "It was agreed between the United Muslim Party leaders and Fazlul Haq's group to invite you to settle same," Ispahani wired Jinnah, adding: "Wonderful opportunity created please leave for Calcutta immediately advise date departure."[23]

Jinnah reached Calcutta a week later and addressed a meeting of Bengali Muslim leaders in the town hall. The United Muslim party agreed to merge with the League. The merger brought such vital leaders into Jinnah's ranks as H. S. Suhrawardy and Khwaja Nazimuddin, who would serve Pakistan both as governor-general and prime minister, respectively. Initially, Fazlul Haq also agreed, and Jinnah named him to the Central Parliamentary Board, but by September 1 he had changed his mind. Always more radical than Jinnah and equally ambitious, Fazlul Haq proved his most mercurial ally, never long remaining in harness with anyone. The ostensible causes of his change of heart in 1936 were his party's twin demands that Bengal's zamindari (landlord) class be abolished without compensation, and that free and compulsory primary education be introduced throughout the province without raising additional taxes. Jinnah favored both measures but insisted on appropriate legal payment for each. Fazlul Haq's *Krishak Proja Samiti* ran its own slate of candidates for Bengal's Muslim seats and managed to capture almost as many as Jinnah's League did—thirty-eight to his forty. It was not until just before the new provincial assembly met that Jinnah could negotiate an agreement with Haq, merging their parties and luring enough Muslim independents to join them in order to give the new Bengal ministry, which Fazlul Haq himself headed, a comfortable majority. And Jinnah made one other important addition to the League. Next to Liaquat Ali Khan, who served Jinnah most effectively as honorary secretary of the League, the young raja of Mahmudabad (1914–73), Amir Ahmad Khan, was Jinnah's foremost supporter in the United Provinces. As the largest Muslim landlord of Lucknow, the raja enjoyed an estimated income of some 2 million rupees annually. Jinnah appointed him treasurer of the League's central board.

The platform adopted by Jinnah's central board on which Muslim League candidates stood for election in January–February 1937 was much the same as that of Congress, including these advanced nationalist demands:

> To make every effort to secure the repeal of all repressive laws; To resist all measures which are detrimental to the interest of India, which encroach upon the fundamental liberties of the people and lead to economic exploitation of the country; To reduce heavy cost of administrative machinery, central and provincial, and allocate substantial funds for nation building departments; To nationalise Indian Army and reduce the military expenditure; To encourage development of Industries, including cottage industries; To regulate currency, exchange and prices in the interest of economic development of the country; To stand for the social, educational and economic uplift of the rural population; To sponsor measures for the relief of agricultural indebtedness; To make elementary education free and compulsory; To take steps to reduce the heavy burden of taxation.[24]

Each of these had long been integral to the Congress national demand, and all were anathemas to more conservative Muslim parties, such as the Agriculturist party of the United Provinces landlords, formed at Governor Sir Malcolm Hailey's instigation. The one clear divergence between the League's socioeconomic position and that of Congress, however, which reflected a basic difference in philosophy dividing Jinnah from Nehru and Subhas Bose, was the League's firm opposition "to any movement that aims at expropriation of private property." Even as Jawaharlal placed increasing faith in socialist solutions for India's problems of poverty, Jinnah retreated more than ever behind the bastions of private property. His growing passion for real estate and his constant preoccupation with details concerning the daily management of his ever-proliferating portfolio of properties were, in fact, soon to rival his interest in politics. Private property, most of it forever rooted on Indian soil, became, ironically enough, almost as fascinating a diversion for Jinnah's mind and energies during the last lonely decade of his life as Pakistan itself.

By this time Rahmat Ali, the founder of the Pakistan National Movement, was residing at 16 Montague Road in Cambridge, from which a massive quantity of strange religiopolitical pamphlets and letters appealing mostly to British lords poured forth between 1935 and his death in 1951. For example, "May I venture to address this appeal to your Lordship on behalf of the people of PAKISTAN at this critical hour," he wrote on July 8, 1935, urging "My Lord's sympathy and support in our fateful struggle against the ruthless coercion of PAKISTAN into the proposed Indian Federation. The Government of India Bill, based on the Indian Federal Scheme, has created an acute crisis in the national life of PAKISTAN and has raised a supreme issue—an issue of life or death—for its national future." He continued:

I earnestly hope that you kindly will lend your fullest support to the inexorable demand of PAKISTAN—a demand based on justice and equity—for the recognition of its sacred right to a separate national existence as distinct from HINDOOSTAN. . . . PAKISTAN is not Hindoo soil nor are its people Hindoostani citizens. . . . The very basis and content of our national life is founded on fundaments essentially different from those on which Hindooism lives and prospers. . . . We, the Pakistanians, have, more than once, emphatically repudiated the most shameful surrender of our national future made by the State-nominated Muslim delegates to the Round Table Conferences in agreeing to the Indian Federal Scheme. They were neither the delegates of PAKISTAN, nor the representatives of the Pakistanian people. . . . These distinguished exponents of the art of surrender, in complete disregard of the warnings of history, sold our nationality and sacrificed our posterity. They will have to answer for this—the most contemptible betrayal of PAKISTAN—before history.[25]

Jinnah continued assiduously to ignore Rahmat Ali and his angry attacks, which were to become even more personal and virulent by the eve of Pakistan's birth. He would not, however, be able much longer to ignore the political demand of Rahmat Ali's obviously well-funded movement sponsored from the heart of Cambridge. The platform adopted by the League's central board in 1936 included, indeed, a number of important concessions to Islamic fundamentalist groups within India, if not as yet to the extremist ad-

vocates of a Pakistan National Movement. Three out of fourteen planks
were drafted exclusively to appeal to special concerns of the Muslim minority, whose 482 separate electorate seats alone were among those contested
by League candidates. The League's first plank was: "To protect the religious rights of the Mussalmans. In all matters of purely religious character,
due weight shall be given to the opinions of Jamiat-ul-Ulema Hind [Indian
Ulema Party] and the Mujtahids." Two later planks were: "to protect and
promote Urdu language and script," and "to devise measures for the amelio-
ration of the general conditions of Muslims." The Indian *Ulema* party, born
during the Khilafat Movement and then relatively dormant under the leadership of Maulana Husain Ahmad Madani and Maulana Ahmad Said, had
merged with the Muslim Conference party in the United Provinces to contest elections as the "Muslim Unity Board," presided over by the raja of
Salempur, with brilliant Choudhry Khaliquzzaman as its secretary. In February of 1937, Khaliquzzaman and several members of his board met with
Jinnah in Delhi and were promised a majority on the League's United
Provinces parliamentary board if they joined forces. It was one of Jinnah's
most creative political coups—surrendering numerical for nominal power.
The one thing he demanded was that Unity Board candidates all run as
Muslim leaguers, thus enhancing his party's stature while broadening the
base of its support. He knew that to build a national party capable of asserting effective demands both to Congress and the British raj he might have
to surrender provincial powers to any number of local magnates. He never
balked at such demands, readily negotiating from weakness today and tomorrow so that on the day after his party would be in position to battle
from a vantage point of strength.

Liaquat Ali Khan was, however, furious at having lost control over
choosing Muslim League candidates from his own province and tried his
best to regain the power of selecting members for the UP's Board, despite
the fact that he was in a minority among the Lucknow seven on the League's
central board. Jinnah gave his verdict against Liaquat, who was so annoyed
after their July meeting in Bombay that he resigned from both parliamentary boards and sailed off to England for a few months. Jinnah thus almost
lost the support of the man who would become his right arm in transforming
the League into a party second only to Congress, and Pakistan's first prime
minister. Yet he would rather risk so important a loss than go back on his
word once it was given. Oxford-educated Liaquat later hailed him as "the
Disraeli of Indian politics," admiring his "unpurchasability" and recognizing
the wisdom of his political judgment even when he most disliked its impact
on his personal base of power. Liaquat looked to Jinnah the way a British

public school boy looked to a headmaster, with emotional ambivalence but ultimate admiration.

Jinnah's judgment paid off handsomely by the year's end; his League and its allies captured 29 out of 35 Muslim seats for which its candidates competed, while Congress returned not a single Muslim member on its own. Rafi Ahmed Kidwai was elected only because of Khaliquzzaman's help. It was an impressive show of strength, and had the League done nearly as well elsewhere, Jinnah might have wrested some real concessions from Congress's haughty leadership. In the Punjab, however, only 2 out of 7 League candidates were elected, in Assam 9 out of 34, in Bengal 39 out of 117. Most of the League's minority in Bombay and Madras were returned, and 109 Muslim League seats were captured for British India as a whole. By Jinnah's own estimate his party returned from 60–79 percent of its total number of candidates. Congress alone won 716 out of the 1,585 seats in all eleven provinces, however, enjoying absolute majorities in most of the country; but it elected only 26 Muslim members, an Achilles heel it hoped to remedy through working much harder in future Muslim "mass contact."

Nehru, stalking the campaign trail in 1937, made the mistake of refusing to take the Muslim League and the communal problem seriously, insisting:

> There are only two forces in the country, the Congress and the government. . . . To vote against the Congress candidate is to vote for the continuance of British domination. . . . It is the Congress alone which is capable of fighting the government. The opponents of the Congress are bound with each other by a community of interests. Their demands have nothing to do with the masses.[26]

"I refuse to line up with the Congress," Jinnah insisted, when he heard Nehru's simplistic analysis in Calcutta early in January. "There is a third party in this country and that is the Muslims."[27] A few days later Jinnah publicly warned Nehru and the Congress to "leave the Muslims alone"; but sensing victory, Nehru refused to be intimidated and decided, instead of backing away from India's Muslim electorate, to seek to convert the vast mass of them to Congress's platform. "Mr. Jinnah . . . objects to the Congress interfering with Muslim affairs in Bengal and calls upon the Congress to let Muslims alone. . . . Who are the Muslims? Apparently only those who follow Mr. Jinnah and the Muslim League."[28] "What does the Muslim League stand for?" Nehru asked, with gratuitous insult and acerbity he would long live to regret. "Does it stand for the independence of India, for anti-imperialism? I believe not. It represents a group of Muslims, no doubt highly estimable persons, for functioning in the higher regions of the upper middle classes and having no contacts with the Muslim masses and few even with the Muslim lower middle class. May I suggest to Mr. Jinnah that I come into greater touch with the Muslim masses than most of the members of the Muslim League."[29]

It would not be the last of Nehru's political errors of judgment in his dealings with Jinnah, but it was one of the most fatal mistakes he ever made in a moment of hubris. More than Iqbal, it was Nehru who charted a new mass strategy for the League, prodding and challenging Jinnah to leave the drawing rooms of politics to reach down to the hundred million Muslims who spent most of each day laboring in rural fields. There was, of course, only one possible way for the League to stir that mass, to awaken it, and to lure it to march behind *Muslim* leadership. The cry of Islam—in danger—of *din* (religion) alone could emerge as *the* unique stand of the Muslim League. "No common principle or policy binds them," Nehru had taunted, referring to Jinnah's independent "party" in the assembly. And for Jinnah this was as significant a turning point, traumatically triggered by public humiliation, as the Congress non-cooperation resolution rebuke he had sustained at Nagpur in 1920. Only, then *his* was the secular rational leadership, seeking in vain to reduce a "Mahatma" to mere "Mr." Now Nehru had used "Mr." before Jinnah's name as a sarcastic form of rebuke, for that title was the badge of British-identity Jinnah appeared to epitomize, despite his claims to Muslim leadership. It was a more scathing attack than Jayakar's had been at the All-Parties Conference a decade earlier. Jawaharlal was more eloquent than Jayakar, after all, and had reason to feel more confident of his supreme power over the masses, more hopeful about Congress's future, and more bitter about the pains and punishment of the past, for neither his father nor his wife had lived to see his triumph, to hear the hoarse thunder of millions of voices cry "Jawaharlalji-ki-jai" ("Victory to Honored Jawaharlal"). He, moreover, was a man of many moods and the victim of strong passions, often swept from his mental moorings of sounder judgment by a surging impulse of the moment. It was Nehru's greatest weakness, a fatal flaw in a man who aspired to political leadership over all of India and indeed believed that he was "fit to rule . . . the world."[30]

Jinnah, however, never lost his temper except for calculated political advantage. He used anger as a barrister or an actor would, to sway his jury audience, never from an uncontrollable flaring of passion. For personal passion had all but died in him and was never to be rekindled. The hatred he felt toward Nehru was cold, born of contempt rather than rage. "What can I say to the busybody President of the Congress?" Jinnah remarked of Nehru in an interview several months later. "He seems to carry the responsibility of the whole world on his shoulders and must poke his nose into everything except minding his own business."[31] As Congress president,

Nehru called a national convention in Delhi that March, following the elections, to decide whether in fact Congress would allow its successful candidates to take the provincial offices they had won when the new constitution went into effect on April 1, 1937. For Jawaharlal this was another sore point of pride, since he had often declaimed against that "charter of slavery" and insisted he would never have anything to do with helping implement any part of it. Gandhi, however, urged giving the constitution a try, as most members of the Congress Working Committee wanted to do, and Nehru bowed to their advice. He refused absolutely, however, to invite any elected Muslim League or other non-Congress candidates to his conference, calling it "a dangerous thing to revert to an all party attitude" and insisting that Congress should not cooperate with "semi-Imperialist groups."[32]

Khaliquzzaman, who belonged to Congress for two decades before merging his Unity Board with the League in 1936, hoped that a Congress-League coalition government, including himself, might be appointed to administer the United Provinces. Muslim Rafi Kidwai, their leader of the Congress at this time, had been Motilal's secretary and remained Jawaharlal's confidant in Nehru's home province. Kidwai and Khaliquzzaman were old friends, and it was hardly surprising, therefore, for them to discuss a coalition ministry with Kidwai promising Khaliquzzaman "two Muslim Leaguers to join the Congress Ministry" prior to his election.[33] Nehru "turned down" the League after his victory. Maulana Abul Kalam Azad was the only Muslim on the Congress Working Committee and managed to wean the provincial *Ulema* party away from its commitment to the League in mid-May of 1936. Azad used the classic lures of a provincial cabinet office with all its seductive perquisites to achieve that dramatic defection. He, of course, won Nehru's gratitude and trust and was to preside over the Congress throughout World War II, serving in Nehru's first cabinet as minister of education. But he won Jinnah's undying enmity. To Jinnah, Azad's political treachery placed him beneath contempt. "This is war to the knife," Jinnah remarked, after learning of the *Jamiat-ul-Ulema*'s flip-flop.[34]

That July, Azad visited Lucknow and tried to negotiate a settlement with Khaliquzzaman, offering to bring him into the United Provinces cabinet if "The Muslim League group in the United Provinces Legislature shall cease to function as a separate group," its members all becoming "part of the Congress Party," the League's provincial Parliamentary Board thus, in effect, agreeing to "dissolve."[35] Khaliq rightly read those terms as a "death warrant" of the provincial party over which he presided and refused to agree. Meanwhile, Nehru called upon Congress committees throughout India to intensify recruitment among "the Muslim masses."

Jinnah had never liked the younger Nehru but at this point lost all hope of trying to reach any agreement with him, appealing instead to Gandhi who had withdrawn from active politics to his Wardha ashram retreat. That May, Jinnah sent a message to Gandhi through B. G. Kher, the leader of the Congress in Bombay's legislature and chief minister-designate there, who had asked Jinnah "to give him two members of his Muslim League to join the Ministry."[36] The League had done brilliantly in Bombay, capturing twenty out of twenty-nine Muslim seats, and Kher had the good sense to know that with Jinnah's cooperation his administration would be a powerful and efficient one; without it, a hopeless, thankless task. As to Jinnah's request that Gandhi personally enter negotiations to seek some sort of Hindu-Muslim agreement nationwide, the Mahatma replied: "I wish I could do something but I am utterly helpless. My faith in unity is as bright as ever; only I see no daylight out of the impenetrable darkness and, in such distress, I cry out to God for light."[37]

The forthcoming session of the League was to be held in Lucknow, and Jinnah knew that his presidential address must either galvanize his party to march toward a new destiny, or would serve as its death knell. He must have sensed, moreover, that for him personally as well as for the League, time was running out. "He was always coughing," Ispahani recalled, "smoking and coughing. We thought it just 'smoker's cough' or bronchitis. None of us realized how bad it was—until it was too late."[38] He spent that summer in Simla and Srinagar, Kashmir; the legal demands on his time increased with his growing fame as Muslim India's premier advocate. Fatima joined him on his trip to Kashmir, accompanying him virtually everywhere from then on till the end of his life, as sister-confidante, nursemaid, sounding board, and defender-against-the-outside-world. He pleaded before the Jammu and Kashmir high court in four cases—two criminal matters, two civil—that summer. The most famous was the disputed marriage case of Hanifa Begum v. the State, where Jinnah won his client's appeal by forcefully asserting his personal knowledge—"My Lord, I am the Authority!"—as an accurate interpretor of Islamic law.[39] His prestige in the community was such that no one dared deny his claim, and, as usual, he won every case he appealed.

Wherever Jinnah went that summer and early fall he invited Muslim leaders he met to come to Lucknow to attend the forthcoming League session. Besides Shafi's son-in-law, Mian Bashir Ahmad, other powerful non-League leaders, including the new premiers of the Punjab and Bengal, Unionist Sir Sikander Hayat Khan (1892–1942) and Fazlul Haq, also came to Lucknow at Jinnah's behest; and before leaving that fateful session of the League they would agree to join forces in what was about to become a revitalized united Muslim movement, alarmed by Congress's victories and

Nehru's attempts to cut the mass base of their constituencies out from under their very feet if they failed to respond with alacrity and unity to that clear and present Hindu-atheist challenge.

Jinnah came by rail from Bombay, and as his train steamed into Cawn-pore (Kanpur) Central Station "a vast crowd of Muslims mobbed his compartment," Jamil-ud-Din Ahmad recalled.

> So exuberant was their enthusiasm and so fiery their determination to resist Hindu aggression that Mr. Jinnah, otherwise calm and imperturbable, was visibly moved. . . . His face wore a look of grim determination coupled with satisfaction that his people were aroused at last. IIe spoke a few soothing words to pacify their inflamed passions. Many Muslims, overcome by emotion, wept tears of joy to see their leader who, they felt sure, would deliver them from bondage.[40]

He arrived that evening, October 13, 1937, in Lucknow, where twenty-one years before he had forged the pact that brought Congress and the League together for the first time, heralding a bright era of Hindu-Muslim unity that lasted little longer than World War I. This time storm clouds of conflict darkened the horizon replacing that dawn, even as the pallor of age gave a sepulchral look to Jinnah's drawn and tired face. Khaliquzzaman and Mahmudabad had gathered a small army of League volunteers to await him at the station, and they led their president and his sister on a torchlight carriage procession through the winding streets of the former capital of Nawab-Viziers of Oudh, where many a Mughal emperor had journeyed on bejewelled elephants. "There was a scuffle at one place between the volunteers and some hot-headed Congressmen," Khaliquzzaman reported,[41] noting one of the opening salvos of what was soon to become the Congress-League civil war, India's political prelude to partition.

The Punjab's Sir Sikander met with Jinnah and the League council next morning, listing his demands for merging his powerful Unionist party forces with the League. He essentially insisted upon the retention of his party's totally autonomous control over the Punjab, where the League had elected only two out of eighty-six Muslim members to the legislature. Jinnah had no option but to accept mighty landlord Sikander's terms, gladly "stooping" to embrace and conquer that Punjabi baron. The pact concluded that October 14 between British India's two most powerful Muslims was approved "with thunderous cheers" by the council of the Muslim League. And well should they have cheered, for without the Punjab, the League had no real heartland of power, no core around which to build its potential claim to nationhood. The Punjab was more than just a bare Muslim majority province—the Punjab meant Pakistan, made Pakistan possible. Bengal was too remote from the rest of Muslim India, as was Hyderabad. Sind, the North-West Frontier, Baluchistan, and Kashmir, were islands of Muslim dominance, yet none was large enough, none strong enough to stand alone. The Punjab was the mortar that integrated, unified, and bridged every one of those other northwest provincial units. The Punjab was Pakistan's first and most important capital letter; and by luring Sir Sikander into his party's tent, Jinnah raised the green flag with its giant "P" over the League's Kaisar Bagh ("Royal Garden") outside Mahmudabad House, signaling the birth of an inchoate nation that was to remain in the womb of British India for precisely one decade. Fazlul Haq closed ranks as well that fateful day in 1937, adding a remote Eastern wing to the nation of South Asian Muslims now in the making. By sundown Jinnah knew that this second Lucknow pact he had negotiated would tear asunder the subcontinent just as his first pact had almost led to independent but united rule for all of India. Soon Jawaharlal and the Mahatma would know it as well. Soon the whole world would see what one seemingly frail Muslim, a minority-among-that-minority, white-haired and weary, could accomplish once he had set his mind to it. He had been taunted, ignored, humiliated, and dismissed as insignificant long enough. Now he had the premiers of the Punjab and Bengal to stand between. The next day he would speak for them all. His was going to be the one mighty, magnified, final voice of Muslim South Asia.

To symbolize the dramatic change marked by this Lucknow session, not only in the League's platform and political position, but in Jinnah's personal commitment and final goal, he changed his attire, shedding the Saville Row suit in which he had arrived for a black Punjabi sherwani long coat, donned by the Quaid-i-Azam ("Great Leader") for the first time in public on the morning of October 15, 1937. He had spent the night at Mahmudabad House; and after breakfasting with the raja was about to leave for the packed meeting outside when his eye was attracted to a black Persian lamb cap worn by Nawab Mohammad Ismail Khan (1886–1958), one of the greatest provincial League leaders. He asked his friend if he might try on that compact cap, which would soon be known throughout the world as a "Jinnah cap." When he saw how handsome it looked over the white of his sideburns in a mirror, he knew that it was just the headgear needed to give his Muslim costume its crowning touch. At the 1916 Lucknow session over which he had presided, Jinnah had worn a red fez, but since Ataturk banished the fez from modern Turkey it was out of style. The Jinnah cap resembled the fez but was softer, yet equally Islamic in its symbolic significance. It soon became as famous as the flatter "Gandhi cap" of hand-spun cotton, which the Mahatma and Jawaharlal wore. That cap came to symbolize Congress membership, just as the Jinnah cap helped immediately to distinguish and identify Muslim League leaders.

"This Session of the All-India Muslim League is one of the most critical that has ever taken place during its existence," Jinnah began, addressing the estimated 5,000 Muslims from every province of India, crowded into the huge tent erected in Mahmudabad's garden.

> The present leadership of the Congress, especially during the last 10 years, has been responsible for alienating the Musalmans of India more and more, by pursuing a policy which is exclusively Hindu; and since they have formed Governments in the six provinces where they are in a majority, they have by their words, deeds and programme shown, more and more, that the Musalmans cannot expect any justice or fair play at their hands. Wherever they were in a majority and wherever it suited them, they refused to co-operate with the Muslim League parties and demanded unconditional surrender and the signing of their pledges.

> To the Musalmans of India in every province, in every district, in every tehsil, in every town, I say: your foremost duty is to formulate a constructive and ameliorative programme of work for the people's welfare, and to devise ways and means for the social, economic and political uplift of the Musalmans. . . . Organize yourselves, establish your solidarity and complete unity. Equip yourselves as trained and disciplined soldiers. Create the feeling of an *esprit de corps,* and of comradeship amongst yourselves. Work loyally, honestly and for the cause of your people and your country. No individual or people can achieve anything without industry, suffering and sacrifice. There are forces which may bully you, tyrannize over you and intimidate you, and you may even have to suffer. But it is by going through this crucible of the fire of persecution which may be levelled against you, the tyranny that may be exercised, the threats and intimidations that may unnerve you—it is by resisting, by overcoming, by facing these disadvantages, hardships and suffering, and maintaining your true convictions and loyalty, that a nation will emerge, worthy of its past glory and history, and will live to make its future history greater and more glorious not only in India, but in the annals of the world. Eighty millions of Musalmans in India have nothing to fear. They have their destiny in their hands, and as a well-knit, solid, organized, united force can face any danger, and withstand any opposition to its united front and wishes. There is a magic power in your own hands. Take your vital decisions—they may be grave and momentous and far-reaching in their consequences. Think a hundred times before

you take any decision, but once a decision is taken, stand by it as one man.[42]

As their great leader sat down every Muslim in that pandal rose to cheer, sensing a new League had been born, that by some "magic power" Jinnah had taken his most "grave and momentous" decision and knew its consequences would be "far-reaching," that there would be no turning back. Not for him. Not for his party. The Jinnah who had come to Lucknow still in limbo was torn between two worlds no longer. He left the old capital of Mughal power firmly rooted in his Muslim party's soil as its new Quaid-i-Azam.

12

Toward Lahore
(1938-40)

Building a mass party became the Quaid-i-Azam's primary occupation during 1938 and 1939. From its winter session at Lucknow in 1937 to the spring League meeting at Lahore in 1940, the Muslim League's membership multiplied from a few thousand to well over half a million. Membership dues were dropped after Lucknow to half the purely nominal four-anna fee charged by Congress, inviting any Muslim of India with two annas to his name to join the All-India Muslim League. The League's constitution was revised in many other ways as well and modernized into a vehicle of mass national capability under its inspiring new great leader.

At Lucknow, the League resolved to work toward "establishment in India of full independence in the form of a federation of free democratic States in which the rights and interests of the Musalmans and other minorities are adequately and effectively safeguarded."[1] Congress was denounced for imposing its own party anthem, "Bande Mataram" ("Hail to Thee, Mother"), as the official new anthem of government, wherever Congress ministries took provincial power, "in callous disregard of the feelings of Muslims." The League considered that "song not merely positively anti-Islamic and idolatrous in its inspiration and ideas, but definitely subversive of the growth of genuine nationalism in India."[2] The League further resolved to do everything possible to make Urdu, rather than Hindi, "the universal language of India." Finally, a comprehensive program of socioeconomic and educational reforms was proposed, committing the League "to fix working hours for factory workers and other labourers; to fix minimum wages; to improve the housing hygienic condition of the labourers and make provision for slum clearance; to reduce rural and urban debts and abolish usury; to grant a moratorium with regard to all debts, whether decreed or otherwise," and ultimately "to devise measures for the attainment of full independence and invite the co-operation of all political bodies working to that end."[3]

The week of demanding meetings at Lucknow took its toll on Jinnah's health. He ran a fever on his way home to Bombay, and a hacking cough continued to plague him. It was more than a month before he felt strong enough to respond to letters from any provincial lieutenants, including Malik Barkat Ali, the League's only elected member of the Punjab legislature. "I have not been well enough to tackle the various details that are referred to," Jinnah replied in late November 1937, referring to Barkat Ali's many complaints against Sir Sikander and his Unionist cohort.

Sir Sikander and the true nature of the Unionist-League "pact" would remain Jinnah's thorniest problem, for as Barkat, Iqbal, and others with political awareness in Lahore plainly saw, the Unionists remained precisely as they had been before Lucknow, Punjab's ruling party. Sir Sikander assured his Hindu and Sikh colleagues that Jinnah was now in *his* pocket, not the other way round. Had Jinnah, in fact, "capitulated" to the Unionist chief as the price of enhancing his League's status? Was the cost of Sikander's cooperation really higher than the League stood to gain from his nominal affiliation? Jinnah, at least, believed it was not; yet the Punjab conundrum would not disappear, even after Sir Sikander's death in December 1942.

Jinnah decided to shift the venue of his council's April meeting from Lahore to Calcutta, where he had been in late December 1937, to inaugurate the All-India Muslim Students' Federation. Born out of a merger of the Lucknow Muslim Students' Conference with the Aligarh University Union and All-Bengal Muslim Students' League, that federation was organized by Mohammad Noman (1914–72) of Aligarh. Noman had gone to Bombay to invite Jinnah to preside over his federation's first annual session. "To my great surprise," Noman recalled, "it did not take more than a minute to get his consent. I immediately requested him to allow me to release the news to the Press. He got up and said 'Do it just now.' . . . From Calcutta onwards the Muslim students marched under his guidance."[4] Jinnah and Fatima stayed at Ispahani's house in Calcutta, and some 300 Muslim students from the North-West Frontier province to Assam assembled to hear Jinnah speak at 8:30 P.M. on December 29. He talked softly without dramatic gesture or emotion, explaining that at Lucknow, "I have only rung the alarm bell. The bell is still ringing. But I do not see the fire brigade. I want you to produce the fire brigade. And God willing, we shall extinguish the fire."[5] The most memorable of his statements to that newly organized Muslim fire brigade was that "We do not want to be reduced to the position of the Negroes of America." Jinnah now had the youthful muscle and cadre of energetic volunteers his League required. The older All-India Students' Federation, which identified closely with Congress, branded the new Muslim federation "reactionary and communal." The raja of Mahmudabad was elected president of the All-India Muslim Students' Federation, and Noman served as general secretary. The federation's constitution listed among its objectives: to arouse political consciousness among the Muslim students and to prepare them to take their proper share in the struggle for the freedom of the country; to work for the advancement of the economic and social conditions of the Musalmans; and to popularise Islamic culture and studies and to strengthen the Islamic religion and faith by combating anti-Islamic forces.

Soon after returning to Bombay in January 1938, Jinnah entrained again for Aligarh, where he received "a right royal reception" from admiring students, who insisted on hauling his carriage themselves from the station to Aligarh campus three miles away. The Quaid-i-Azam delivered a more eloquent than usual speech to his vociferously cheering audience in that intellectual cradle of the Muslim League. "You, Mr. President, have said, the Muslim is born free," Jinnah began. "When was he free? In this country at any rate we have been slaves for 150 years."[6] This was the first time Jinnah used the word "slave" in a public address, and he went on further dramatizing the plight of Muslims. Since 1936, however, Jinnah assured his wildly cheering audience, the Muslim League had revitalized itself, and "has freed the Musalmans from the clutches of the British Government. But now there is another power which claims to be the successor of the British Government. Call it by whatever name you like, but it is Hindu and Hindu Government." He closed with the glowing promise that they were "gathering the precious stones, rubies, sapphires and diamonds, the scattered energies and talents of the Muslim community; and when you have got an artistic jeweller to set them it will be a jewel which you will be proud of."[7]

In March 1938 Jawaharlal was succeeded as Congress president by Bengal's Subhas Chandra Bose, only forty-one years of age and heroically fresh from British detention. On the eve of passing his mantle of leadership to Bose, Nehru wrote Jinnah: "We are eager to do everything in our power to put an end to every misapprehension and to endeavour to solve every problem that comes in the way of our developing our public life along right lines and promoting the unity and progress of the Indian people."[8] Nehru asked Jinnah to "let me know what exactly are the points in dispute which require consideration," to which Jinnah replied, "But do you think that this matter can be discussed, much less solved, by and through correspondence?"[9] Jawaharlal agreed that it was "always helpful to discuss matters and problems face to face," but "Correspondence helps in this process and sometimes is even preferable as it is more precise than talk. I trust therefore that you will help in clarifying the position by telling us where we differ and how you would like this difference to end."[10] Jinnah, however, was most reluctant to be lured into written debate of differences, insisting it was "highly undesirable and most inappropriate," trenchantly arguing: "You prefer talking at each other whereas I prefer talking to each other. Surely you know and you ought to know what are the fundamental points in dispute."[11]

By rejecting Jawaharlal's repeated appeal for an updated brief on the Muslim argument, Jinnah was not merely saving vital energy when demands on his time had escalated from his own lieutenants. He was also holding out till Gandhi was ready to invite him to talk, knowing that ultimately the Mahatma would be called on to approve any formula accepted by his Congress disciples, whether it was Jawaharlal, Subhas, Azad, Patel, or Prasad. All of them made regular pilgrimages to the Wardha ashram, but it was Gandhi he wanted to deal with. By late February 1938 Gandhi himself did write: that he had accepted Abul Kalam Azad as his guide and that "conversation should be opened in the first instance as between you and the Maulana Sahib. But in every case, regard me as at your disposal."[12] But Jinnah replied that "I find that there is no change in your attitude and mentality when you say you would be guided by Maulana Abul Kalam Azad."[13]

Jinnah insisted not only upon full recognition of his League as the "one authoritative" political body in British India representing all Muslims, but he demanded prior acceptance by Gandhi of his equivalent role as spokesman for all Hindus. From Congress's perspective, neither position was tenable—as Jinnah well knew. But what better way of avoiding debate? Reconciliation with Congress was, after all, the last thing he wanted at this juncture. Nothing would do more to undermine his cause of uniting the Muslim community against the clear and present danger of a "Hindu raj." Any form of Congress-League rapprochement in 1938, whether provincial or central, partial or even potential, would have taken the wind out of the full sails of his League's mass recruitment effort and dramatic growth. His entire strategy was, indeed, based on rallying to his ranks every good Muslim who feared for the future of his faith in a land ruled by hostile Hindus. To have agreed to swing his fragile craft round just as it was starting to pick up speed under full wind would have been suicidal to Muslim League prospects. Jinnah might easily have negotiated the concession of a few seats in the Bombay and other provincial cabinets, but he would certainly have lost Pakistan in the process.

Nor should the degenerative affliction of Jinnah's lungs be underestimated in explaining his reluctance to embark on a fresh round of negotiations. He became more testy as the coughing and discomfort increased. He required more privacy, although his tolerance for crowds had never been high, unless he was on stage, orating. "I shall be arriving on the 16th [April] morning with Miss Jinnah by the mail," Jinnah alerted Ispahani in the spring of 1938, adding:

> As to my reception, please see that some proper order is kept and that I get home within a reasonable time, because these long processions, taking hours and hours, have a tremendous strain on one's nerves and physical endurance. Therefore you must try and see that I get home by 12 o'clock and have some rest at any rate in the afternoon. You must have read in the papers how during my tours to Aligarh and Meerut, and other places, I suffered, which was not because there was anything wrong with me but the irregularities and over-strain told upon my health.[14]

Nothing could have been more damaging to his plans for the League than to permit rumors of his fragile health to surface in public. Personal well-being was indispensable to political power. The least suspicion that Jinnah had spots on his lungs that would never disappear would have shattered his charisma. His only hope was to withdraw long enough behind private palatial barricades, to alternate interludes of visibility and frenzied activity with longer periods of convalescence, alone with Fatima as his nursemaid.

To help assure him more privacy, Jinnah remodeled his "palacious residence" on Mount Pleasant Road atop Malabar Hill in Bombay, which was on more than 15,000 square yards of wooded land. This residence was more modern and sumptuous than the smaller bungalow on Little Gibbs Road, where he and Ruttie had lived. He was also in the process of redecorating a sumptuous new mansion he bought at No. 10 Aurangzeb Road in New Delhi's posh diplomatic suburb. That vast establishment, presently serving as the Netherlands Embassy, was furnished by Waring & Gillow in much the same style as his Hampstead home had been. A new car was, moreover, required to go with the New Delhi residence, and Jinnah selected an ivory-colored Packard Eight, with green leather upholstery, a rear curtain, cigar lighter, and custom radio among its many extras. Ever-reliable Ispahani handled all the ordering and paperwork through Khaitan Motor Co. Ltd. in Calcutta, and the total cost of such an elegant imported vehicle then came to only 7,100 rupees. Jinnah at this point was very well off financially. His seven rented flats in Mayfair assured him a handsome monthly income of more than 2,000 rupees. His standard legal fee by then was 1,500 rupees a day, the highest in India; and in addition he earned no less than 40,000 rupees in dividends from stocks alone in 1936,[15] reflecting the value of his ever-growing portfolio of shares in Indian industrial as well as commercial enterprises. Jinnah was one of the elite group of Indian taxpayers whose income required a "super tax" as well as supplementary tax payments, and like many very wealthy people was at times several years late in remitting his taxes.

At this time Jinnah was able to report that Muslim League "parties" were functioning actively within seven of British India's eleven provincial legislatures, "and the membership of those Parties is increasing every day."[16] Jinnah personally organized the League's bloc within the central legislature, and several League candidates had been elected by elections held since the general elections of early 1937. "The Congress is a Hindu body mainly," cried out Jinnah from Calcutta's floodlit amphitheater in mid-April of 1938. "Muslims have made it clear more than once that, besides the question of religion, culture, language and personal laws, there is another question, equally of life and death for them, and that their future destiny and fate are dependent upon their securing definitely their political rights, their due share in the national life, the Government, and the administration of the country. They will fight for it till the last ditch, and all the dreams and notions of Hindu Raj must be abandoned. They will not be submerged or dominated, and they will not surrender so long as there is life in them." Jinnah's strategy was to teach Congress to "respect and fear" the Muslim League, and to teach his own followers to depend primarily on themselves, and to "mobilize" into "one solid people."[17] Muslims, of course, had good reasons to feel aggrieved, and Jinnah and the League decided to collect all complaints against Congress ministries, to publish and publicize them as broadly as possible. The League council appointed a special committee, under Raja Syed Mohamad Mehdi of Pirpur, to seek out such complaints in every Congress-run province, gathering oral as well as written testimony from aggrieved Muslims. Raja Saheb submitted his report to Jinnah a month before the League's annual December session.

Gandhi wrote and wired Jinnah by this time, anxiously seeking to arrange a personal meeting and hoping to have Azad at his side, but Jinnah refused to meet with Azad or any other non-League Muslim. The Mahatma then agreed to come to Jinnah's house in Bombay alone on April 28, after Jinnah refused to break his journey from Calcutta at Wardha. Gandhi reached Jinnah's home before noon. The Mahatma and Quaid-i-Azam remained closeted alone for three and a half hours in late April 1938, during which time Gandhi was too depresed to argue vigorously and merely "jotted down" notes of their talk, which he transmitted to Jawaharlal and Subhas Bose. The sixty-nine-year-old Mahatma emerged from those talks atop Malabar Hill even more depressed, writing to Jawaharlal:

I am carrying on, but it is galling to me to think that I have lost the self-confidence that I possessed only a month ago. . . . I have mentioned this to help you to examine the proposals on their merits. . . . You will not hesitate summarily to reject it if it does not commend itself to you. In this matter you will have to give the lead.[18]

Nehru did, in fact, turn over that task to Congress President Bose, who came to Bombay and met with Jinnah in early May. But those talks resolved nothing, only making the growing distance between Congress and the League more publicly apparent. Jinnah moved forward with his plans for converting the League organizationally into a mirror-image of the Congress. He appointed his own Working Committee "High Command," which met in Bombay on June 4, 1938.[19] It was a strong committee and included Sikander, Fazlul Haq, Khaliquzzaman, and Liaquat Ali. They helped Jinnah magnify the League's status, giving it a "shadow cabinet" like that of Congress or the British Labour party.

Nehru sailed from Bombay just two days before the League's High Command met and reached England before the end of June, where he spent a weekend with Clement Attlee, Stafford Cripps, Aneurin Bevin, Harold Laski, and other members of Labour's shadow cabinet, to discuss "the means by which the next Labour government would transfer power" to India.[20] V. K. Krishna Menon (b. 1896), Nehru's London host, close friend, and publisher, had been one of Laski's disciples at the London School of Economics, and he joined Jawaharlal and his daughter Indira for that fateful weekend at Cripps's country house, Filkins, where so much of India's subsequent political future was charted. With the Spanish Civil War in full blaze and Chamberlain's government so impotent in the face of mounting Nazi atrocities, Labour was confident that its turn at the helm of Westminster could not be delayed much longer. Both at Filkins and in subsequent interviews Nehru was very outspoken in his criticism of Chamberlain's government. "British foreign policy is entirely reactionary and is aiding fascist aggression," he insisted. "As such, it is bringing war nearer, whatever its professions may be. I feel India must reiterate firmly what it has already declared, that it will oppose an imperialist war."[21]

These outspoken attacks against every policy of Chamberlain's government helped make British administrators much more sympathetic and receptive to Jinnah than they had been since the first Round Table conference. Jinnah returned to Simla that August for the Central Assembly's session, and acting viceroy Lord Brabourne, who had been sent to India first as governor of Bombay and then of Bengal, invited Jinnah and soon after Sikander to meet with him. That crucial, secret summit with leaders of Muslim India sealed the fate of the still unimplemented "federation" of autonomous British provinces and princely states that was to have been the keystone of the Government of India Act of 1935. Secretary of State Lord Zetland (1935–40), reported Brabourne's account to him of that important interview on Tuesday evening, August 16, 1938: "Jinnah—ended up with the startling suggestion that 'we should keep the centre as it was now; that we should make friends with the Muslims by *protecting* them in the Congress Provinces and that if we did that, the Muslims would *protect* us at the Centre!"[22] Sir Sikander seconded Jinnah's position, arguing that "we are mad to go ahead with the Federation scheme which is obviously playing straight into the hands of Congress and that the Muslims, given a fair deal by us, would stand by us through thick and thin."[23] That reassurance was crucial to Britain on the eve of its most difficult war, for the British Indian Army still depended heavily on Muslim troops, and the Punjab remained her most fertile source of fresh recruits.

Jinnah helped carry enough votes to allow the government to enact its legisation. More importantly, however, his calm voice in support of martial loyalty on the eve of war may well have tipped the balance toward British survival in India over the next decade; for Subhas Bose soon sided openly with the Axis powers, and with Nehru speaking as he did in London and Gandhi withdrawing his support entirely once the war got underway, there was no Congress leader in Britain's corner. Jinnah inquired rhetorically of his legislative colleagues, "Do you want me to instigate every member of the army from the sepoy upwards to an officer . . . that they should commit acts of insubordination? I am unable to do so. . . . If I instigate the army to-day, it will be only disastrous to me and not to the opponent whom I want to hit."[24] He did not name his opponent. He did not have to. Congress had waited too long to come to terms with him. Jinnah was back in fighting form—in Great Britain's corner—only this time also as *Quaid-i-Azam* of his future Muslim nation.

What made him decide to abandon hope of reconciliation with the Congress? No single incident perhaps, but the cumulative weight of countless petty insults, slights, and disagreements added to the pressures of time and age. Congress insults, stupidity, negligence, venality, genuine and imagined anti-Muslim feeling, fatigue, frustration, fears, doubts, hopes, shattered dreams, passions turned to ashes, pride—all contributed to the change in Jinnah. He would not go softly, or silently, into that dark night. "The struggle that we are carrying on is not merely for loaves and fishes, ministerships and jobs, nor are we opposed to the economic, social and educational uplift of our countrymen as it is falsely alleged," Jinnah told the Sind provincial League in the city of his birth on October 8, 1938.[25] There Jinnah revealed more of his motivation for abandoning hope of Hindu-Muslim unity, at least with the present Congress leadership in power, than he had at any other time during that year of speeches. For what could be more offensive, after all, to a man of his sensibilities and refinements, than to find himself faced with a rabble of ill-clad, untrained "Hindu officials" in province after province—including Bombay and Sind? What better reason for him to return to the side of his British friends and colleagues?

"It is no use relying upon any one else," Jinnah told his Muslim League followers in Karachi, the future capital of Pakistan. "We must stand on our own inherent strength and build up our own power and forge sanctions behind our decisions. . . . If the Musalmans are going to be defeated in *their national goal* and aspirations it will only be by the betrayal of the Musalmans among us as it has happened in the past."[26] This was Jinnah's first public reference to his recently resolved "national goal" for party and people. Nor was it a vagrant, unconsidered remark. He was not quite ready to reveal his long-range strategy, for there was still much organizational work and institution building to be done. But his battle plans were drawn, and surely he protested too much when he added with unconscious irony: "I wish to make it clear that I am not fighting the Hindu community as such nor have I any quarrel with the Hindus generally for I have many personal friends amongst them."[27] Less than six months earlier Iqbal had succumbed to the fatal lung disease that also claimed Jinnah's life a decade later. Sir Sikander alone remained his potential rival to lead the nascent Muslim nation. Jinnah devoted himself unstintingly to the labor of building the League by uniting all Muslims, convinced that he alone could properly guide his "children" out of bondage to Hindudom and the "outcaste" status to which his Brahman rivals traditionally relegated all Muslims.

On the morning of October 9, 1938, Karachi's District Board formally welcomed the Muslim League and its leaders. Sir Sikander hoisted the League's green flag, with its silver crescent moon and star, after which Jinnah was presented with an Urdu address on a silver tray, Karachi's key to its city. "It is a matter of pride for the Town of Karachi that Mr. Jinnah, a person of such great eminence and a well-known statesman, should have been born and bred within her embrace," began that address. He was also called the "great Guide and Commander of the Muslim Community."[28] That afternoon, Jinnah met with Sikander, Fazlul Haq, and Khan Bahadur Allah Bux (Bakhsh), United party premier of Sind, who though a Muslim had earlier refused to join forces with the League. Bux's coalition government relied mostly upon Congress support. Jinnah was determined to add Sind to the League's still paltry provincial list, which consisted as yet only of Bengal and the rather anomalous Punjab, both in fact coalitions. After his arrival in Karachi on October 7, Jinnah had met with no fewer than twenty

Muslim members of the multifactional Assembly, convincing them all to join the League and finally persuading—or so he believed—Allah Bux to join his party as well.

"It was agreed that one solid party of the Muslim members of the Sind Legislative Assembly should be formed as Muslim League Party," Jinnah reported in his irate statement to the Associated Press just a few days later.[29] Allah Bux and all his Muslim ministers promised to resign, Jinnah explained, then a provincial League party election was to have been held to choose the new leader by "unanimous vote," or "in default he should be nominated by Mr. Jinnah and the party would abide by his choice." Early the next morning, however, Jinnah learned that Sind's leader of the Congress party had wired Sardar Vallabhbhai Patel (1875–1950), president of the All-Indian Congress Parliamentary Board, to alert him to the League's intentions, and "When we met at 11 o'clock on the 12th of October 1938 much to the astonishment of every one Khan Bahadur Allah Bux backed out of the agreement." Shocked by such "gross breach of faith in resiling," Jinnah still felt it worth fighting for "unity at any cost" and sent his closest Sind deputy, Haji Sir Abdullah Haroon (1872–1942), to appeal that night to Allah Bux at home but concluded next morning that the latter "was in the hands of the Congress Party." It was a most bitter pill for Jinnah to swallow. He had labored long and hard for an independent province of Sind, since well before the first Round Table conference, being convinced that as a Muslim-majority province it would surely elect a Muslim League government. Now the Sardar, Congress's strong man, the shrewd organizational hand beneath Nehru's idealistic velvet glove, had snatched this plum from Jinnah's lips just as he was about to savor its sweetness.

He would never forget, or forgive, Sardar Patel for having "cheated" him of Sind, "robbing" his home province out from under him at the very meeting of the League. "You had almost achieved a triumph but the dogs of the Congress have snatched from you the cup of victory," wrote Malik Barkat as soon as he heard the bad news. "I have not the least doubt that the Mussalmans of Sindh will teach a lesson this traitor Allah Bakhsh."[30] Bakhsh (Bux) was murdered in May of 1943 and his assassin never caught.

The raja of Pirpur submitted his *Report* in November 1938. It was published in Delhi by Liaquat Ali Khan for the League, a green pamphlet with the Muslim League's flag on its cover. Its "general survey" opening was obviously approved, if not drafted, by Jinnah personally. "The communal problem in India has long defied settlement," it began.

In our humble opinion, however, the problem is a real one and the sooner it is solved the better will it be for the country . . . the com-

munal problem can only be solved when India is free: India can only
be free when the communal problem is solved. Such a circle can lead
us nowhere and will only make the country a prey to any foreign
exploiter.

The communal problem remains unsettled not because of the communalism of the minorities, but because of the communalism of the
majorities.[31]

The report went on to list specific instances of Hindu-Muslim conflict in
most of the Congress-ruled provinces after late 1937. Official Congress policies were blamed for destruction and harm to Muslim property and lives,
though not much detailed evidence could be recorded in that slim pamphlet.

On December 10, 1938, Maulana Mazharuddin Ahmad, editor of the
Muslim Delhi daily *Al-Aman,* proposed in his newspaper that Jinnah be
called Quaid-i-Azam by all Muslims, in recognition of his status as a great
leader. At the annual meeting of the League later that month, Jinnah's new
title would be enthusiastically shouted for the first time by the multitudes
who waited to greet him at Patna's City Railway Station. The seven-mile
journey from the Patna station to the beautiful green silk-decked pandal in
which the League held its three-day session was lined with cheering Muslims, waving flags and shouting "Quaid-i-Azam Zinbabad!" ("Victory to our
Great Leader!"). Syed Abdul Aziz, the popular leader of Bihar's United
party, chaired the reception committee that spared neither money nor time
in organizing that most festive gathering of tens of thousands in the heart
of one of Hindu India's ancient bastions of culture and power, where in the
sixth century B.C. Buddha had taught his noble truths of the all-pervasive
nature of sorrow and universal transience, and several centuries later the
Mauryan Emperor Ashoka ("Sorrowless") echoed the message of pain, advocating love (*ahimsa*) and law (*dharma*) as its best antidotes.

"The Congress has now, you must be aware, killed every hope of Hindu-
Muslim settlement in the right royal fashion of Fascism," said Quaid-i-Azam,
speaking extempore on the night of December 26, 1938, to his enthusiastic
audience.

The Congress High Command makes the preposterous claim that
they are entitled to speak on behalf of the whole of India, that they
alone are capable of delivering the goods. Others are asked to accept
the gift as from a mighty sovereign. The Congress High Command
declares that they will redress the grievances of the Muslims, and
they expect the Muslims to accept the declaration. I want to make it
plain to all concerned that we Muslims want no gifts. The Muslims
want no concessions. We, Muslims of India, have made up our mind

to secure our full rights, but we shall have them as rights. . . . The Congress is nothing but a Hindu body. That is the truth and the Congress leaders know it. The presence of a few Muslims, the few misled and misguided ones, and the few who are there with ulterior motives, does not, cannot, make it a national body. I challenge anybody to deny that the Congress is not mainly a Hindu body. I ask, does the Congress represent the Muslim?

Who is the genius behind it? *Mr.* Gandhi. I have no hesitation in saying that it is *Mr.* Gandhi who is destroying the ideal with which the Congress was started. He is the one man responsible for turning the Congress into an instrument for the revival of Hinduism. His ideal is to revive the Hindu religion and establish Hindu Raj in this Country, and he is utilizing the Congress to further this object. . . . To-day the Hindu mentality, the Hindu outlook, is being carefully nurtured, and Muslims are being forced to accept these new conditions and to submit to the orders of the Congress leaders.[32]

It had been exactly eighteen years since "Mahatma" Gandhi's triumph at Nagpur, and there stood "Quaid-i-Azam" Jinnah on even more sacred Hindu soil, daring not only to call him "Mr." again but openly blaming him for destroying Congress. What sweeter triumph, what more satisfying retribution could he have staged? It was not Congress he addressed, of course, yet his own All-India Muslim League attracted as large, and as loudly cheering, a crowd to Patna as the Mahatma had commanded in Nagpur. This was Jinnah's most vituperative public attack against Gandhi, and as he continued that night he broadened it to include Nehru, Bose, Prasad, and Patel, warning his followers not to believe Congress assurances that it would never accept their federation proposed by the constitution of 1935.

The second day of the Patna session was devoted primarily to discussing Resolution IV, authorizing the Working Committee of the League to resort to "direct action," if and when it decided to do so, to "redress" the grievances and to "protect" the "elementary rights of the Musalmans" of Bihar, the United Provinces, and the Central Provinces, three Hindu-majority provinces from which most "atrocities" against Muslims had been reported. That unanimously carried resolution was what Jinnah called a "revolutionary . . . departure from the past," for until this juncture the League "had been wedded only to the policy of constitutional progress."[33] Though he was authorized to call for direct action, Quaid-i-Azam "pleaded for patience, and asked Muslims to organize the League so that all the 90 million Muslims might come under its banner." Much of the League's third day in Patna was devoted to debating the Palestine resolution. It warned the British government "forthwith . . . [to] stop the influx of Jews into Palestine," declaring "that the problem of Palestine is the problem of Muslims of the whole world; and if the British Government fails to do justice to the Arabs . . . Indian Muslims . . . will be prepared to make any sacrifice . . . to save the Arabs from British exploitation and Jewish usurpation." In discussing this resolution, Abdul Sattar Khairi "said that both the British and the Hindus were Jews to Muslims, that is, their enemies. In India, Mr. Gandhi was the leader of the Hindu Jews."[34] Another League delegate, Abdul Khaliq, insisted that "The real Jews of the West were the British, and those of the East were the Hindus, and both were the sons of Shylock." Jinnah intervened at that point, persuading Khaliq to "withdraw" his "sons of Shylock" remark and insisting that "such statements were not in keeping with the dignity and prestige of the League."[35]

At Patna the Muslim League resolved to create a Muslim women's subcommittee headed by Fatima Jinnah, which would include thirty leading women from every province as well as from Delhi. Several women on that committee, like Begum Shah Nawaz, all their lives had been emancipated from the crippling inhibitions of traditional Islamic purdah and were among the most brilliant, attractive leaders of modern India. A graduate of Queen Mary's College in Lahore and chosen as a delegate to London's three Round Table conferences, Begum Shah Nawaz was the first and only woman to serve on the Muslim League's council from 1931 to 1937, when she drew Jinnah's attention to this serious gap in League membership and appeal. He then nominated a Muslim women's central committee, at the other end of whose spectrum were women like Begum Nawab Siddique Ali Khan of Nagpur who recalled:

> I met the Quaid-i-Azam in 1938 at Patna. . . . I used to wear burqa in those days. At the suggestion of my husband I put off the burqa for the first time in my life before meeting the Quaid-i-Azam. . . . I knew that he was an extremely well-dressed person who was greatly time-conscious. . . . I had an unknown fear of him. When I entered the drawing room, my eyes were fixed on the floor and my feet were trembling. As I looked up, I saw the Quaid-i-Azam standing before me . . . [he] stretched his hand for a hand-shake. I slightly bowed down and shook hands. My husband was very happy to see this, as he knew that I was the daughter of a renowed Qazi and had strong religious convictions; hence he was skeptical if I would shake hands.[36]

Many conversative delegates at Patna protested loudly against the resolution to organize Muslim women, fearing it would put an end to "purdah, which, they said, was sacred to Islam."[37] Jinnah, however, intervened in support of the new subcommittee, diplomatically arguing, strict-constructionist barrister that he was, that "the resolution only stated that women should be given an opportunity to organize themselves under the League in order to support it."

Just as the League was becoming more unified, Congress was confronted with a struggle for power between militant young president, Subhas Chandra Bose, and its conservative old guard led by Gandhi. Bose would, like Jinnah, be hailed as Netaji ("Great Leader") by his growing army of followers, especially young Bengali students who shared none of Gandhi's aversion to violent tactics or martial action. When Gandhi decided it would be best for Congress to replace Bose in 1939 with Maulana Azad, Pattabhi Sitaramayya, or Jawaharlal, Netaji opted to fight for the honor of a second term as president. It was Congress's first internal election battle, and Bose won, mustering 1,580 votes to Sitaramayya's 1,377. He, however, found it impossible to enjoy the power he had won; he received no cooperation from the members of the Working Committee, and his health broke down together with the sudden collapse of support from his party's machine. So Bose resigned and started his own radical Forward Bloc party. Soon after the war began he was imprisoned by the British, escaped to Germany, and thence to Japan, where he led his Indian National Army in martial opposition to the raj. Dr. Rajendra Prasad, Gandhi's loyal Bihar disciple, replaced Bose as Congress president.

The Aga Khan visited Gandhi in January 1939, appealing to him to convince "Congress to settle with Jinnah if it is at all possible."[38] Gandhi was willing to try to reopen negotiations with the League and urged Nehru to seek information from Jinnah about the so-called atrocities in Congress provinces. Jinnah encouraged Fazlul Haq to compile and publish charges of "Muslim Sufferings under Congress Rule," which came to light before the end of 1939 and listed in grim detail more than 100 reports from Bihar, the United Provinces, and the Central Provinces of Muslims who were violently attacked, killed, or looted between July 1937 and August 1939. In all of these cases local officials were charged with aiding Hindus and ignoring the complaints or cries of Muslims under attack. The noted causes of Hindu-Muslim riots were the same as they had always been—conflicts over land, cow slaughter, forms of worship antipathetical to one or the other religion's beliefs—only this time police were controlled by Congress Hindus rather than British Christians. During the Muslim festival of Id on February 1, 1939, for example, in Bihar's Kurwan, Barara, Kaitha, Nayagaon, Hasnauli, Morhaina, and Machhil riots occurred, each of which was supposedly initiated by "an armed Hindu mob" attacking Muslims "assembled for Id prayer in the mosque," where they went to perform that day's ritual cow sacrifice. At some places the Hindu mob allegedly prevented Muslims from carrying out their sacrifice by force, at others they burned or robbed Muslim homes and crops while their owners were at prayer, elsewhere they attacked after the sacrifice ended, reportedly shouting "Gandhi Ki Jai" before killing or injuring the sacrificers. In many villages, Muslim butchers were forced out of business, and "Muslims were coerced into giving up beef-eating." Sometimes raucous marriage parties were the spur, at others it was noisy prayers or the abduction of women. There were reasons enough for conflict in most Indian villages at any time of year. Fazlul Haq's report charged officialdom, however, with consistently taking only one side in such perennial struggles. "A Police Officer took the thumb impression of a Muslim on an 'agreement' waiving the right to perform cow-sacrifice," in Gauspur, for example. "This Muslim and another were subsequently falsely prosecuted."[39]

Some Grievances of the Muslims, 1938–1939, a third report similar to the Pirpur and Fazlul Haq compilations, was published late in 1939 by the Publicity Committee of the Bihar Provincial Muslim League under the chairmanship of Mr. S. M. Shareef of Patna. Confining itself to reports of atrocities against Muslims committed in Bihar, this Shareef report was far more detailed and extensive than both previous ones on which it was based. Some ninety "typical examples of oppression" were detailed in this report, which was studied and recommended to Congress leaders by senior Muslim advocate Khurshad Hasnan of Patna's high court, as affording "opportunity to make enquiries about the correctness or otherwise of the incidents mentioned."[40]

As reports of minority persecution coupled with British official indifference mounted, Jinnah grew more frustrated and angry at his so-called British allies, fearing perhaps that Lord Brabourne's unexpected death of cancer early in 1939 left him without any effective support in New Delhi. Lord Linlithgow, who still had more than a year left to his viceregal term, seemed from Jinnah's perspective partial to Gandhi and was strongly committed to implementing the federation capstone of the Act of 1935 he personally had done so much to formulate. This could be adopted only by a united India, hence Viceroy Linlithgow stressed in every major address his "deep conviction that upon unity depends the position and prestige of India before the nations, and her capacity to take her due place in the world."[41]

Sir Sikander's Unionist party of Punjabi Hindus, Muslims, and Sikhs all pulling together, however, was Linlithgow's provincial model of the federal unity he envisioned at the center, rather than anything Jinnah or his League represented. Given the Punjab's primacy in any British war, moreover, Linlithgow was careful to keep Sir Sikander as happy as possible, courting and flattering him with hospitality whenever he could, and receiving in return repeated assurance that the Punjab would always remain Britain's "sword." More than a hundred million rupees were expended annually by the British raj on martial pay, pensions, and stores in the Punjab alone. Jinnah now felt threatened by Linlithgow as well as by Sikander. Fearing that each might abandon him for perfectly practical political reasons, Jinnah decided with regard to a proposed finance bill in March 1939 to reverse himself once again, if only to remind these two how important his continued support remained to them both.

> Sir, I cannot possibly approve of the Budget as it has been presented to us, because we have no lot or share in it. Now, Sir, the position of the All-India Muslim League Party in this House is a very peculiar one. Fortunately or unfortunately, we hold the balance in the House. If we are supporting the Government, then I think the Finance Member can safely pilot this Bill to his satisfaction and he can carry this Bill without a comma of it being altered. . . . Sir, in the past we have been following the principle that if the Government brought in a measure which was really for the good of the people, then we would support it. . . . But, Sir, I see now that that policy must be altered. . . . Why do you expect us, I ask the Government, to draw the chestnuts out of the fire on your behalf? Why do you expect us to continue to be subservient on the specious pleas which you put forward before us?[42]

It was Jinnah's most forthright explanation of the policy of mutual "support" he and the British central government adopted in 1938. He was, however, open in warning Congress not to misread his message to government, which ended with a curt, "You may go on your own way." "On the other hand, as regards the Congress Party," Jinnah continued, "the Congress Party is not only hostile to the Muslim League but they are inimical. Therefore, I say to them that cooperation between you and us is not possible. . . . But let me tell you—and I tell both of you—that you alone or this organisation alone or both combined will never succeed in destroying our souls. You will never be able to destroy that culture which we have inherited, the Islamic culture, and that spirit will live, is going to live and has lived. You may overpower us; you may oppress us; and you can do your worst. But we have come to the conclusion and we have now made a grim resolve that we shall go down, if we have to go down, fighting."[43]

At this dangerous time Jinnah seems to have sensed his own perilous mortality as well, for on May 30, 1939, he signed his last will and testament, appointing Fatima, Liaquat Ali Khan, and his Bombay solicitor, Mahomed Alli Chaiwalla, joint executors and trustees of his estate. "All shares stocks and securities and current accounts now standing in the name of my sister Fatima Jinnah are her absolute property. I have given them all to her by way of gifts during my life time and I confirm the same, and she can dispose them of [sic] in any manner she pleases as her absolute property."[44] He also left her his houses and their contents, his cars, and a lifetime income of 2,000 rupees a month to be paid from his other properties. To his three other sisters, Rahemat Cassimbhoy Jamal, Mariam Abdinbhoy Peerbhoy, and Shareen Jinnah he left a living of 100 rupees a month, as he did to his brother Ahmed. For his daughter (not named in the will), Jinnah set apart 200,000 rupees to be invested in order to provide her with a living, "which will at 6% bring in income of Rs 1000/—," proving that financially at least he was most unorthodox in never adopting Islam's strict prohibition against charging or accepting any interest. After his daughter's death, the 200,000-rupee corpus was "to be divided equally between her children males or females," though if she had no children that sum would revert to Jinnah's residuary estate to be equally divided among Alighar [sic] University, Peshawar's Islamic College, and the Sindh Madressa of Karachi. Jinnah also left 50,000 rupees to the University of Bombay, and 25,000 each to Bombay's Anjuman-i-Islam School and the Arabic College of Delhi.[45]

On September 3, 1939, Lord Linlithgow broadcast the news of Germany's invasion of Poland. Linlithgow met with Gandhi for almost two hours the following day, after which the viceroy saw Jinnah. Sikander, jealous at not having been invited to the viceregal mansion as well, sent a message asking Linlithgow "that nothing should be done to inflate Jinnah or make him more difficult to deal with. Sikandar [sic] also repeated what he had already said in public, that the Punjab and Bengal were wholly behind the Government in the prosecution of the war whatever Jinnah and his friends might say."[46] Jinnah "regretted" Sikander's attempt to "rush in front of his colleagues in the Muslim League to pledge co-operation" and cautioned Linlithgow that Sir Sikander alone "could not deliver the goods." Jinnah appealed to the viceroy for "something positive" to take back to his party to help him rally Muslim support for the war. Asked if he wanted Congress ministries thrown out, Jinnah replied, "Yes! Turn them out at once. Nothing else will bring them to their senses. . . . They will never stand by you."[47] During this conversation on September 4, 1939, moreover, Jinnah revealed to the viceroy that he now believed the only ultimate political solution for India "lay in partition."

Gandhi initially assured the viceroy of his "full and unconditional" personal support in the war, speaking "with an English heart,"[48] but then explained that he could not commit Congress. Nor would the Mahatma's position be endorsed either by Nehru or the Working Committee. Linlithgow read King George's message to both houses of Delhi's legislature on September 11, 1939, explaining that "the compulsion of the present international

situation" required suspension of all preparations for federation, while retaining that idea "as our objective." India's princes had, in fact, proved
reluctant to commit themselves to federation of any kind, with less than
two-fifths having expressed willingness to participate in the 1935 scheme
that was to have given them one-third of the seats in the Legislature's lower
house and two-fifths of all seats in the upper house. Congress worked hard
at seeking to politicize states, to democratize their representation, which
made Jinnah's League all the more intransigent toward the federation "umbrella" that had begun to sound like just one more "Hindu raj" trap set for
Muslims.

Nehru was in China when the war started. He returned to join the Congress Working Committee, chairing its three-man war committee that included Sardar Patel and Maulana Azad. On September 11, Nehru went to
Wardha to draft the Committee's response to the viceroy's declarations. A
"corrected draft," rewritten next day, was released to the press on September 14 as the Working Committee's Resolution on India and the War.[49]
"Congress has repeatedly declared its entire disapproval of the ideology and
practice of fascism and Nazism and their glorification of war and violence
and the suppression of the human spirit. . . . If the war is to defend the
status quo, imperialist possessions, colonies, vested interests and privileges,
then India can have nothing to do with it."[50] Linlithgow wrote Zetland, reporting on the Congress resolution Jawaharlal had drafted, "It is a tragedy
in many ways that at a time such as this we should have in so important a
position a doctrinaire like Nehru with his amateur knowledge of foreign
politics and of the international stage."[51] They both knew that "the unknown quantity" concerning the war was Gandhi, and on September 26
Linlithgow invited the Mahatma to see him.

"I am off to Simla again," Gandhi wrote Jawaharlal, modestly adding: "I
go only to act as intermediary. You will send me instructions if any. I do
hope you will be ready to answer invitation, if it comes. Love. Bapu."[52]
Aboard his train to Simla on September 25, Gandhi revealed his change of
heart.

My personal reaction towards this war is one of greater horror than
ever before. I was not so disconsolate before as I am today. But the
greater horror would prevent me today from becoming the self-
appointed recruiting sergeant that I had become during the last war.
And yet, strange as it may appear, my sympathies are wholly with
the Allies. . . . But assuming that God has endowed me with full
powers (which He never does), I would at once ask the English to
lay down arms, free all their vassals, take pride in being called "Little
Englanders" and defy all the totalitarians of the world to do their

worst. Englishmen will then die unresistingly and go down to history as heroes of non-violence. I would further invite Indians to co-operate with Englishmen in this godly martyrdom. It would be an in-dissoluble partnership drawn up in letters of the blood of their own bodies, not of their so-called enemies . . . even at the risk of being misunderstood, I must act in obedience to *"the still small voice."*[53]

To Linlithgow, Gandhi explained his decision "to stand aside" from the Working Committee because of his age, noting that had he been "ten or fifteen years younger, 'things might possibly have gone differently.' " The viceroy hoped to convince Gandhi at least to support his idea of a defence liaison committee of leading Congress and League politicians, as well as of princes, to help fashion official policy throughout the war. Indeed, Lin-lithgow invited no fewer than fifty-two leading Indians to Simla at this time, including Jinnah, whom he had hoped would join the meeting with Gandhi. Jinnah, however, dodged the Mahatma, explaining "that he was too busy to come until after 1st October."[54] The viceroy explained to Gandhi that he "could not disregard the legitimate claims of the Muslims and the Princes," though he recognized the "bitterness of communal feeling" and "incompatibility" of the policies of Congress and the League. Gandhi re-plied that Britain should leave Indians to resolve the problem of "achieving unity" themselves. And after three hours of futile discussion, Gandhi "begged" Linlithgow not to consult the Muslim League.

"It is likely that the British Government will try to play off the Congress against the Muslim League and the princes," Nehru wrote his friend Krishna Menon at this time.[55] The day after Gandhi met Linlithgow, Secretary of State Zetland stated in Westminster that "the time has been ill chosen by the leaders of the Congress for a reiteration of their claims." Nehru replied angrily on September 29, and once again his temper proved his own worst enemy, serving Jinnah far better than Congress. He had misread the strength of his Labour party support in London, even as he had long underestimated Jinnah's power. Gandhi's "personal" initial response to Linlithgow, support-ing the war effort with "an English heart" would have proved a far wiser political posture for Congress throughout the war.

On October 5, Jinnah arrived at the viceregal palace, "friendly and co-operative," and "began by thanking Linlithgow for helping to keep the Muslims together and Linlithgow replied that it was in the public interest for the Muslim point of view to be fully and competently expressed."[56] Jinnah pleaded for "more protection" for Muslims, but Linlithgow frankly informed him that after studying the charges of persecution in Congress provinces he "could find no specific instances of oppression." Jinnah argued that "Hindus had a 'subtle intention' to undermine the Muslim position, as for example in the instruction issued in the North-West Frontier Province for compulsory teaching of Hindi." Meanwhile, Labour leader Sir Stafford Cripps was urging Jawaharlal "not to accept anything short of conclusive action and to see to it that the Congress stood firm as a rock," in a letter dated October 11, 1939.[57] That same day Nehru told the All-India Congress Committee, convened at Wardha: "A slave India cannot help Britain. We want to assume control of our government and when we are free we can help the democracies."[58] Gandhi took Jawaharlal's impulsive lead and issued his own statement from Wardha the next day, finding the viceroy's coldly noncommittal declaration of Britain's unchanged "objectives" toward India "profoundly disappointing." "The long statement made by the Viceroy simply shows that the old policy of divide and rule is to continue. So far as I can see the Congress will be no party to it, nor can the India of Congress conception be a partner with Britain in her war with Herr Hitler."[59]

Jinnah said nothing. He waited (one suspects with baited breath) for his rival party's Working Committee to meet, to follow their revolutionary leader helter-skelter into the "wilderness"—out of provincial office. It did meet at Wardha on October 22 and concurred that it could not "possibly give any support to Great Britain, for it would amount to an endorsement of the imperialist policy which the Congress has always sought to end. As a first step in this direction the Committee call upon the Congress Ministries to tender their resignations."[60] Did Nehru and his colleagues believe that by withdrawing their provincial support, Britain's government of India would fall? Or did they hope that in acting so dramatically they might strengthen Labour's leverage in London? Or was this designed as a rallying cry to India's masses to prepare once more for revolutionary struggle?

Jinnah then met with Linlithgow, Gandhi, and Rajendra Prasad in New Delhi on November 1, 1939. They all gathered at his new house at No. 10 Aurangzeb Road, then "drove to Viceroy's House in Jinnah's car."[61] That summit meeting continued, without Nehru, at Jinnah's house after Gandhi and Prasad left the viceroy, but the new round of "communal talks" did not last long—nor did it solve anything—Gandhi concluding, as he had felt before they met, that "*Janab* [Mr.] Jinnah *Saheb* [Sir] looks to the British power to safeguard the Muslim rights. Nothing that the Congress can do or concede will satisfy him."[62]

On November 5, Linlithgow reported the "failure" of the talks as Congress provincial ministries resigned, one after another, obliging British governors to revert to a thoroughly autocratic ordinance raj. "Anonymous placards" passed through the countryside "asking people to cut wires and tear up rails," Gandhi reported to Nehru. "My own opinion is that there is at present no atmosphere for civil disobedience. If people take the law into their own hands I must give up command of civil disobedience movement."[63] To Krishna Menon in London, Jawaharlal wrote the next day: "Our position is one of noncooperation but have not as yet thought of anything more."[64] Then Gandhi appealed to Jinnah through his *Harijan* journal, taking a much more conciliatory tone: "British refusal to make the required declaration of British war aims about India has perhaps come as a blessing in disguise. It removes the Congress out of the way to enable the Muslim League to make its choice, unfettered by the Congress administration in eight Provinces [Assam, Bihar, Bombay, CP, Madras, Orissa, UP and N-W FP], as to whether it will fight for the independence of an undivided India. I hope that the League does not want to vivisect India. . . . Presently the talks between Janab Jinnah Saheb and Pandit Jawaharlal Nehru will be resumed. Let us hope that they will result in producing a basis for a lasting solution of the communal tangle."[65]

But Jinnah had long since decided in favor of a separate and equal nation for Muslim India. Only the precise timing for announcing his intentions remained to be resolved. Great negotiator that he was, he knew how important timing could be for political, as well as legal, advantage. Unlike Jawaharlal he never acted on impulse. If anything, he was more cold-blooded than Linlithgow and Zetland—and more patient. It must have given him great satisfaction after all, to have the viceroy, Gandhi, and Congress president Prasad come to *his* sitting room and drive in *his* Packard Eight to the viceregal palace. Premature slamming of the door to all negotiations would have robbed him of the crowning delight of political gamesmanship. It would have been too easy to come out flatly for Pakistan, moreover, shouting his demand from rooftops, as Rahmat Ali had done in England for the past six years. Indeed, Ali, who first publicized the PAKISTAN demand, was left a lonely man to die in England, with his remains always under foreign soil. Such might easily have been Jinnah's fate as well, but for his unique capacity to make the most of every political option and opportunity. At this time more than ever before, Jinnah's mind focused on Islam and the *Qur'an*. At the end of the Muslim month of fasting, which fell on November 13 in 1939, he was given viceregal permission to broadcast his first Id festival message, addressing himself particularly to "the young . . . for it is they who will henceforth have to bear the burden of our aspirations."[66] Though clearly conscious of how frail his body had become, he was equally determined to keep aloft as he inched forward on the high wire he walked. Jinnah urged his "young friends" to study John Morley's *On Compromise* in this talk, for as he himself had learned from what Morley wrote, "It is worth while to take pains to find out the best way of doing a given task, . . . 'to scorn delights and live laborious days' in order to make as sure as we can of having the best opinion."[67]

Since March of 1939, Jinnah had been chairing a subcommittee of his Working Committee, on which Sir Sikander, Liaquat Ali, and Fazlul Haq sat to consider various schemes for India's political future. Pakistan was one option. Sikander proposed an alternative "Outline of A Scheme of Indian Federation" with seven "zones," the first and last of which were essentially East and West Pakistan. The League had moved closer toward choosing its future course of action by December 1939, but the pressures of war and his own precarious health made Jinnah decide to postpone his party's annual session till the following spring. He did not, however, wish to let the year end without reminding the world of the League's power and without broadcasting its policy. On December 2, 1939, therefore, he issued a dramatic proclamation, announcing his choice of Friday, December 22, as a "Day of Deliverance and thanksgiving as a mark of relief that the Congress regime has at last ceased to function."[68] Jinnah's resolution stated that

> . . . the Congress Ministry has conclusively demonstrated and proved the falsehood of the Congress claim that it represents all interests justly and fairly, by its decidedly anti-Muslim policy.

> . . . the Congress Ministry [sic] both in the discharge of their duties of the administration and in the legislatures have done their best to flout the Muslim opinion, to destroy Muslim culture, and have interfered with their religious and social life, and trampled upon their economic and political rights; that in matters of differences and disputes the Congress . . . invariably have sided with, supported and advanced the cause of the Hindus in total disregard and to the prejudice of the Muslim interests.

> The Congress Governments constantly interfered with the legitimate and routine duties of district officers even in petty matters to the serious detriment of the Musalmans, and thereby created an atmosphere which spread the belief amongst the Hindu public that there was established a Hindu raj, and emboldened the Hindus, mostly Congressmen, to ill-treat Muslims at various places and interfere with their elementary rights of freedom.[69]

Gandhi felt as soon as he read this that any prospect of resolving the Hindu-Muslim problem by further talks was over.[70] Nehru, learning to be less impulsive, wrote Jinnah next day: ". . . what has oppressed me terribly since yesterday is the realisation that our sense of values and objectives in life and politics differs so very greatly. I had hoped, after our conversations, that this was not so great, but now the gulf appears to be wider than ever."[71] Jinnah agreed it was "not possible to carry on talks regarding the Hindu-Muslim settlement . . . till we reach an agreement with regard to the minority problem." High-wire negotiator that he was, however, he never lost his temperate balance and was never to discard the last life line of possible future contact, "I can only say that if you desire to discuss the matter further I am at your disposal."

The Congress press now dubbed Jinnah "Dictator of Malabar Hills."[72] Some of Jinnah's own most trusted lieutenants, including thirty-seven-year-old Ispahani, received a "rude shock" upon reading the resolution.

> I did not expect such a command from you, because you have all along kept politics on a very high and strong pedestal. . . . I, however, felt that some strong reason must have driven you to issue your command for the observance of this day, . . . let me know what prompted you to take the step. . . . The progressive elements in the League who followed you blindly when you actively took up cudgels on behalf of the unfortunate down-trodden Muslims of India, find to their utmost regret and disappointment, that you are gradually drifting more and more into the arms of reactionaries and "jee hoozoors" [yes men]. Those whom we despised, not many years ago, seem to have lined up in the front rank of your supporters and advisers. As a result, the League's policy in general is being based on Sir Sikandar's and Fazlul Huq's dictation. . . . Sir, is it not time that you take stock of the whole situation and put down your foot with firmness?[73]

Sixteen Muslim League members of Bengal's Legislative Assembly, moreover, followed the lead of Abdur Rahman Siddiqi in openly breaking with their quaid over what they considered an irreparable shock to Indian unity.

Jinnah decided to issue a longer statement to the press a few days later, "since the guilty do not admit their guilt and public memory is short."[74] He retraced Muslim grievances against Congress ministries from the start of their tenure, referring to the Pirpur and other League reports. He also reprinted the "direct action" resolution adopted at the Patna League session. As soon as the Congress ministries resigned, Jinnah "immediately decided to appeal for the observance of a day to express our relief and to show its intensity in a matter that would force ears that had hitherto been deaf to listen to us." (What a descriptive way for one whose voice and lungs were fast failing to make himself heard.) He had chosen a Friday so that Muslim shops would, in any event, be closed, and Muslim workers would either stay home or be off to the mosque for communal prayers.

Jinnah won strong support from South India's "Dravidistan" Justice party leader, *Periyar* E. V. Ramaswami Naicker (1880–1974) for his Day of Deliverance. He called upon his party as well as all Dravidians to celebrate December 22 "on a grand scale . . . to rid the country of the menace of the Congress." Similar statements of enthusiastic support were voiced by leaders of the All India Depressed Classes Association and smaller Anglo-Indian groups. It would be impossible to say how many people turned out to celebrate the Day of Deliverance, but many resolutions similar to those originally proposed by Jinnah were adopted. A full-page advertisement of the day ran in the *Times of India,* but Gandhi judged that "it seems to have fallen flat everywhere."[75] At the public meeting in Bombay, Sir Currimbhoy Ebrahim of the Muslim League moved the resolution, and Dr. B. R. Ambedkar, Untouchable leader of the Independent Labour party, seconded it.

Sir Stafford Cripps was in India at this time, having come to test the feasibility of Labour's plan to push Britain's cabinet into proclaiming its immediate willingness to grant dominion status to India and to concede India's right to convene its own constituent assembly "immediately [when] the war is over, or before that time if opportunity occurs."[76] Cripps revealed his scheme to Nehru and Gandhi and soon learned there were other voices in India as well when he met with Liaquat, Sikander, and on December 15 with Jinnah himself. Jinnah insisted that "a Constituent Assembly was not the correct procedure until you had kicked out Great Britain," arguing that "the power factor had to be decided first." Before leaving India, Cripps advised Linlithgow to take a fresh approach to resolving the Hindu-Muslim conflict and urged him to "go in at the right moment, try to get both sides together, and make them write down in so many words precisely what they wanted and in what terms they were prepared to reach an agreement."[77] That was the arbitrator's technique of conflict resolution Cripps would advise Mountbatten to try, effectively, after the war.

Cripps returned home, proposing to Zetland an immediate declaration together with the appointment of national leaders to the viceroy's executive council and the election of a constituent assembly that would take decisions on the principle of a simple majority. This condition was an anathema to Jinnah, who insisted that a two-thirds majority be mandatory for any "communal issue"; Congress though, would not hear of such abandonment of democratic principle. Then Linlithgow toured Bombay in early January and spoke before the Orient Club, announcing that "full Dominion Status . . . of the Statute of Westminster variety" was the goal of His Majesty's Government toward India, and they were prepared immediately to add "a small number" of Indian political leaders to his executive council, to reopen the entire scheme of the Act of 1935 "as soon as practicable."[78] It was the fruit of Cripps's "unofficial" mission and advice, reflecting the growing concern in London over the perils of Indian wartime non-cooperation. Had Linlithgow made such a speech the previous October, Congress might never have withdrawn from provincial administrations and there would have been no Day of Deliverance.

Jinnah seemed increasingly preoccupied from this time till his death with questions of disease and its diagnosis, and thus he was wont to put other ills in terms of "disease." "The constitutional maladies from which India at present suffers may best be described as symptoms of a disease inherent in the body-politic," he wrote for London's *Time and Tide* of January 19, 1940. "Without diagnosing the disease, no understanding of the symptoms is possible and no remedy can suggest itself. Let us, therefore, first diagnose the disease, then consider the symptoms and finally arrive at the remedy."[79] Such was Jinnah's thinking as he braced himself for the final stretch across the high wire, balanced precariously over the abyss of his own mortality. For in March, "As we travelled from Bombay to New Delhi," Fatima recalled, "he had a slight temperature. After dinner, as he lay on his berth, suddenly he gasped with pain and moaned loud enough for me to hear above the noise of the rattling train. I sat up and went to his side. He was in such pain that he could not speak. He pointed with his finger to a spot in the middle of his back, to the right of the spinal cord. His face was contorted with pain, and since we were in a compartmental train I could not rush out for medical aid. I first massaged the spot which he had indicated, but my ministration seemed to do him little good. . . . The train steamed into Delhi station in the early hours of the morning and soon we were at 10 Aurangzeb Road. . . . I phoned his doctor whose diagnosis was that my brother had pleurisy and that he must stay in bed for about a fortnight. As soon as the doctor left, my brother said, 'What bad luck. It is an important session. My participation is essential. And here I am, confined to bed.' Two restless days later he was up and at work."[80] He went to meet Linlithgow on March 13, and "he used the occasion to assure the Viceroy that the Muslims would not retard the war effort if an undertaking was given to them that no political settlement would be reached with the Congress without the previous consent of the Muslims. The Viceroy . . . reacted favourably and said he would communicate his views to London."[81]

Jinnah had little more than a week to recover his strength from the strain of meeting with the viceroy to the start of his journey to Lahore, itself wracked by violent illness on the eve of the League's most momentous meeting. On March 19, 1940, "like a bolt from the blue, Lahore had the impact of a bloody drama in which scores of Khaksars, including their lion-hearted Salar, Agha Zaigham (chest measurement 48″) were mercilessly butchered by the Punjab Police under the command of the Senior Superintendent of Police, Mr. D. Gainsford, who had his nose chopped off in the bargain," Mian Mohammad Shafi, junior reporter at the time, recalled, noting that the ensuing curfew "temporarily converted the gay city of Lahore into a political graveyard."[82] Paramilitary Muslim Khaksars were as hostile toward the Muslim League as they were anti-Hindu and anti-Sikh.

As Khaksar unrest continued to plague Lahore toward the eve of the scheduled meeting, Sir Sikander phoned Jinnah in New Delhi to ask if the session would not best be "postponed to another suitable date?" Quaid-i-Azam's answer was an emphatic no, but he did instruct the premier of the Punjab to "abandon" all "arrangements for taking me out in a procession . . . out of respect to the memory of the Khaksar martyrs."[83] On the morning of March 22, 1940, Jinnah quietly arrived in Lahore by the frontier mail train and motored straight from the railway station to the Mayo Hospital, where he "visited in a general ward each one of the wounded Khaksars," Shafi recalled, insisting that "This had a soothing effect on the lacerated hearts of the people of Lahore." As a whole, however, the Khaksars never were reconciled to Jinnah's leadership and tried more than once in the next few years to assassinate him.

More than 60,000 Muslims gathered inside the gigantic tent erected in Minto (now Allama Iqbal) Park, within view of the lofty marble minarets of the beautiful Badshahi Masjid and Shah Jehan's Great Fort. Lahore, a teeming center of Muslim power in South Asia since the eleventh century, capital of the Punjab, and cultural heartland of Mughal India, was about to give birth to the League's "Pakistan" Resolution. Jinnah wore an achkan and *choridar* pyjamas, traditional Punjabi garb, and entered the packed pandal at 2:25 P.M. on March 22. A regal throne awaited him at center stage. A lower throne to the right was for Fatima clad in a pale, ivory silken sari. They were surrounded by a sturdy cadre of Bombay Muslim League national guards, whose glittering swords remained drawn throughout that Friday session, sharp reminders to all Khaksars inside the pandal to behave themselves in the presence of the Quaid-i-Azam.

Deafening shouts of "Zindabad" welcomed Jinnah as he rose to walk to the microphone. He started speaking in Urdu as the reception committee chairman, the nawab of Mamdot, who introduced him had done, but soon shifted to English, apologizing to the mass audience as he gestured toward the press corps: "The world is watching us, so let me have your permission to have my say in English."[84] At that point there were some murmurs of angry protest, but Jinnah "stood calmly; and while the crowd settled into silence, he lit a cigarette and looked over them with his compelling eye," one witness recalled. "From then, they listened and did not utter a word."[85] "He spoke for nearly two hours," the *Times of India* reported, "his voice now deep and trenchant, now light and ironic. Such was the dominance of his personality that, despite the improbability of more than a fraction of his audience understanding English, he held his hearers and played with palpable effect on their emotions."[86] It was his largest audience, his greatest performance to date. Muslim India's foremost leaders were there, and the overflow crowd filled the park outside, with close to 100,000 Punjabis, Sindhis, Bengalis, Pathans, and Baluchis gathered to hear their Quaid-i-Azam's voice. He must have seemed no less than a Mughal emperor resurrected. Thanks to Associated Press International, Reuters, and UPI, Jinnah's message at Lahore was cabled that evening the world over, and especially perused with tea that same day in London's Atheneum, studied and underlined at Whitehall and Downing Street, discussed in the City, and debated in Westminster.

> The last session of the All-India Muslim League took place at Patna in December 1938. Since then many developments have taken place.

> Now, what is our position with regard to the future Constitution? It is that, as soon as circumstances permit, or immediately after the war at the latest, the whole problem of India's future Constitution must be examined *de novo,* and the Act of 1935 must go once for all. We do not believe in asking the British Government to make declarations. These declarations are really of no use.[87]

Jinnah then reflected on the most recent session of Congress, which had been meeting for the past week in central India's Ramgarh under its newly elected Muslim president, Maulana Azad, and which Gandhi attended. "And this now is what Mr. Gandhi said on the 20th of March, 1940. He says: 'To me, Hindus, Muslims, Parsis, Harijans are all alike. I cannot be frivolous'— but I think he is frivolous—'I cannot be frivolous when I talk of Quaid-i-Azam Jinnah. He is my brother.' " "The only difference is this, that brother Gandhi has three votes and I have only one vote" commented Jinnah acerbically, as he continued, quoting from Gandhi's speech: " 'I would be happy indeed if he could keep me in his pocket.' I do not know really what to say to this latest offer of his," Jinnah remarked smiling wryly. Then speaking to Gandhi, Jinnah added, "Why not come as a Hindu leader proudly representing your people and let me meet you proudly representing the Musalmans? This is all that I have to say so far as the Congress is concerned."[88]

Jinnah felt completely secure, of course, in suggesting this formula for "resolving" their problems, knowing not only that Congress had put its leading Muslim at the pinnacle of the party that year, but also that an *azad* (free) Muslim conference was to be held the next month in Delhi, to which all non-League Muslim parties were invited "to dissociate themselves from Muslim League politics and to assert the general Congress demand," as

Nehru explained it to Krishna Menon, while insisting: "This is not being organized by the Congress as such, though Congress Muslims will take a
leading part."[89] Rather than growing more receptive to admitting "Hindu"
identity, Congress had thus become more determined than ever to prove its
comprehensively national character—and was to remain so—insisting that
religious bias played no role in its deliberations, policies, or programs.

Jinnah and his party were no longer willing to retain mere "minority"
status, and the capital of the Punjab had been chosen purposely as the place
to announce the Muslim League's newborn resolve.

> It has always been taken for granted mistakenly that the Musalmans
> are a minority, and of course we have got used to it for such a long
> time that these settled notions sometimes are very difficult to remove.
> The Musalmans are not a minority. The Musalmans are a nation by
> any definition.

> The problem in India is not of an inter-communal but manifestly of
> an international character, and it must be treated as such. So long as
> this basic and fundamental truth is not realized, any constitution that
> may be built will result in disaster and will prove destructive and
> harmful not only to the Musalmans, but also to the British and
> Hindus. If the British Government are really in earnest and sincere
> to secure the peace and happiness of the people of this Subcontinent,
> the only course open to us all is to allow the major nations separate
> homelands, by dividing India into "autonomous national States."[90]

Jinnah did not use the name Pakistan, nor would it appear in the forthcoming Lahore resolution. He had, nonetheless, obviously given much thought,
not simply to this immediate "solution" for the Hindu-Muslim problem but
also to the long-range international implications of partition. Jinnah no
longer questioned either the wisdom, viability, or aftermath impact of partition but had decided by the spring of 1940 that this was the only long-
term resolution to India's foremost problem.

Jinnah's Lahore address lowered the final curtain on any prospects for
a single united independent India. Those who understood him enough to
know that once his mind was made up he never reverted to any earlier position realized how momentous a pronouncement their Quaid-i-Azam had
just made. The rest of the world would take at least seven years to appreciate that he literally meant every word he had uttered that important afternoon in March. There was no turning back. The ambassador of Hindu-
Muslim unity had totally transformed himself into Pakistan's great leader.
All that remained was for his party first, then his inchoate nation, and then
his British allies to agree to the formula he had resolved upon. As for Gan-

dhi, Nehru, Azad and the rest, they were advocates of a neighbor state and would be dealt with according to classic canons of diplomacy. The crowd went wild with acclamation as he stepped from the microphone and returned to his throne to lead his sister from the pandal. He had crossed the high wire without falling. His hand trembled as he lit a fresh cigarette, but his lungs had held and his voice had remained audible. It had been truly a stellar performance, worthy of the lead role he alone could command in this company.

13

Lahore to Delhi
(1940-42)

The historic Pakistan resolution was hammered into final form at Lahore after Quaid-i-Azam finished speaking. The League's Subjects Committee met to argue over their draft through the early hours of Saturday, March 23, and it was not until late afternoon that unanimity was reached. Sir Sikander found the concept of partition insupportable till the bitter end, for it was at once a repudiation of his Unionist party's basic platform of Hindu-Muslim-Sikh coexistence, and of his potential to win personal leadership over the League. After hearing how enthusiastically Jinnah's speech was received, however, Sikander must have known that his days of aspiring to supreme leadership of the Muslims of India were numbered. Even in the heart of his home province that morning an angry crowd of young Muslim League militants marched round the pandal, while the Subjects Committee met inside, shouting "Sikander Murdabad" ("Death to Sikander"). Hearing that most popular curse connected to his own name in Lahore must have given him pause. When Jinnah appeared, however, the young men changed their cry to "Quaid-i-Azam Zindabad!"[1] Whoever had trained and orchestrated that chorus had done an effective job.

Jinnah presided over the second day's session of the Lahore League. Fazlul Haq, who chaired the Subjects Committee, moved the first resolution, the most famous third paragraph of which stated:

> That it is the considered view of this Session of the All-India Muslim League that no constitutional plan would be workable in this country or acceptable to the Muslims unless it is designed on the following basic principles, viz., that geographically contiguous units are demarcated into regions which should be so constituted, with such territorial readjustments as may be necessary, that the areas in which

the Muslims are numerically in a majority, as in the North-Western and Eastern zones of India, should be grouped to constitute Independent States in which the constituent units shall be autonomous and sovereign.[2]

Pakistan was not explicitly mentioned; nor was it clear from the language of the resolution whether a single Muslim state of both "zones" had been envisioned or two separate "autonomous" independent states, one in the Northwest, the other in the Eastern (Bangladesh) zone. Sher-i-Bengal ("Lion of Bengal") Fazlul Haq at least appears to have had the latter in mind when he drafted the resolution and read it aloud. But Jinnah was the leader; and when asked by reporters if this resolution meant one, or more than one, Muslim nation, his unequivocal answer sealed the fate of Bengal's Muslim majority. India's newspaper headlines next day pronounced the Lahore resolution, a single "Pakistan Resolution," and so it remained.

Sikander held out for some form of federating central government to unite the "sovereign constituent units" and insisted till his death in December 1942 that the Lahore resolution was only a "bargaining point" for the League. For Sikander, indeed it was, but not for Jinnah. Punjab governor, Sir Henry Craik, reported the resolution to Linlithgow as "a very effective riposte to Congress as it torpedoed the Congress claim to speak for India."[3]

A few days later Gandhi was asked: "Do you intend to start general civil disobedience although Quaid-e-Azam Jinnah has declared war against Hindus and has got the Muslim League to pass a resolution favouring vivisection of India into two? If you do, what becomes of your formula that there is no swaraj without communal unity?" To this he replied: "I admit that the step taken by the Muslim League at Lahore creates a baffling situation. But I do not regard it so baffling as to make disobedience an impossibility. . . . The Muslims must have the same right of self-determination that the rest of India has. We are at present a joint family. Any member may claim a division."[4]

Other leaders of Congress reacted more strongly. "I consider it a sign of a diseased mentality that Mr. Jinnah has brought himself to look upon the idea of one India as a misconception and the cause of most of our trouble," argued Chakravarti Rajagopalachari (C.R.) (1879–1972) of Madras, who was to become first Indian governor-general.[5] Nehru wrote of the resolution as "Jinnah's fantastic proposals," reading it as a cat's paw of British imperial duplicity.[6] At Ramgarh, Congress had resolved that "India's constitution must be based on independence, democracy and national unity," repudiating "attempts to divide India or to split up her nationhood."[7]

Liaquat Ali Khan convened the third day's proceedings of the Lahore League shortly before noon, announcing that "the Quaid-i-Azam would arrive a little late." Jinnah, though exhausted, managed to muster strength enough to appear inside the pandal shortly after the meeting commenced. He was in the chair, in fact, when Dr. Mohammad Alam, a recent convert to the League after having left Congress, seconded the resolution moved the day before. The resolution carried by acclamation. Another resolution asserting the League's "grave concern" at British "inordinate delay . . . in coming to a settlement with the Arabs in Palestine," also carried that final day. The session then adjourned and was reconvened by Jinnah at 9:00 P.M., after he had had several hours' rest. He personally moved a resolution on behalf of the Khaksars, urging the Punjab government to remove the "unlawful" ban imposed on that militant Muslim organization, and called for an "impartial committee of inquiry" to investigate the "tragic . . . clash between the Khaksars and the Police" of March 19. Jinnah urged every one to bring "all the evidence" to such an inquiry committee, once it was appointed, adding: "The rest we will see, and God will help us." In winding up the session that night, Jinnah called it a "landmark in the history of India" and concluded that "The more you organize yourself, the more you will be able to get your rights." The session ended just before midnight with shouts of "Quaid-i-Azam Zindabad!" The next day before leaving Lahore, Jinnah told reporters, "I have thoroughly enjoyed my stay in Lahore because of the result; otherwise I was worked to death."[8]

Linlithgow wrote Jinnah in April, reassuring him that "His Majesty's Government are in friendly and sympathetic relations with all Muslim Powers to some of whom indeed they are bound by alliance."[9] Wounded by gunfire in London's Caxton Hall a month before, triggered by young Udam Singh, the Sikh assassin of Sir Michael O'Dwyer, Lord Zetland then opted for early retirement. The War Cabinet's new secretary of state for India was L. S. Amery (1873–1955), Prime Minister Churchill's predecessor as first lord of the admiralty. With Churchill and Amery at the helm in London, Jinnah's stock rose much higher in New Delhi and Simla. *The Hindu's* clever correspondent, B. Shiva Rao, reported from Simla in June on an "outbreak" of "Jinnah complex which seems to obsess the official mind. No step can be taken, however reasonable, lest Mr. Jinnah should be offended."[10]

At this juncture, Sikander tried his best to negotiate a federal scheme settlement with Congress, hoping to short-circuit Jinnah, and working with Linlithgow's tacit support. The viceroy sought a further round of discussions between Gandhi and Jinnah, but Jinnah was not eager to return to futile arguments and waited in any event till he had a chance to meet with his Working Committee and get them to arm him with a tougher set of demands. Gandhi wrote to Linlithgow offering "to go to Germany or anywhere required to plead for peace," since as he noted, "I do not believe

Herr Hitler to be as bad as he is portrayed. He might even have been a friendly power as he may still be."[11] The viceroy did not, however, accept that offer.

Jinnah called his Working Committee to Bombay in mid-June; and after a stormy three-day meeting at which Sikander did his best to wrest leadership of the League for himself, they resolved first of all to endorse the Quaid-i-Azam's position as voiced in late May, reminding the British that "Up to the present moment, we have not created any difficulty nor have we embarrassed the British Government in the prosecution of the war."[12] The League's high command then looked "with alarm at the growing menace of Nazi aggression which has been most ruthlessly depriving one nation after another of its liberty and freedom and regards the unprovoked attack by the Italian Government against the Allies as most unwarranted and immoral at a time when France was engaged in a brave struggle against very heavy odds."[13]

Jinnah visited the viceregal palace at Simla on June 27, 1940, conferring at length with Linlithgow. Afterwards he wrote a memo reaffirming that the Lahore "Pakistan" resolution had become "the universal faith of Muslim India" and that the viceroy had promised him "that no interim or final scheme of new constitution would be adopted by the British Government without the previous approval of Muslim India."[14] They had also agreed that "everything should be done that is possible to intensify war efforts and mobilise all the resources of India for her defence for the purpose of maintaining internal security, peace and tranquility, and to ward off external aggression." Jinnah insisted that "this can only be achieved provided the British Government are ready and willing to associate the Muslim leadership as equal partners in the Government both at the Centre and in all the provinces." Specifically, he recommended that for the duration of the war the Executive Council of the Viceroy be expanded to include at least as many Muslim members as Hindus "if the Congress comes in"; otherwise Muslims, all to be chosen by the League, were to have the majority of additional council membership.

In mid-1940, with Britain braced against German invasion and its populace desperately seeking to survive an endless monsoon of bombs, Jinnah wisely judged that the time was not ripe for a power struggle "show down" with the British. Gandhi at this time published an "open letter" to "every Briton," urging "cessation of hostilities."

> No cause, however just, can warrant the indiscriminate slaughter that is going on minute by minute. . . . I do not want Britain to be defeated, nor do I want her to be victorious in a trial of brute strength. . . . I want you to fight Nazism without arms. . . . I

188 JINNAH OF PAKISTAN

would like you to lay down the arms you have as being useless for saving you or humanity. You will invite Herr Hitler and Signor Mussolini to take what they want of the countries you call your possessions. Let them take possession of your beautiful island, with your many beautiful buildings. You will give all these, but neither your souls, nor your minds. If these gentlemen choose to occupy your homes, you will vacate them. If they do not give you free passage out, you will allow yourself, man, woman and child, to be slaughtered, but you will refuse to owe allegiance to them. . . . I am telling His Excellency the Viceroy that my services are at the disposal of His Majesty's Government, should they consider them of any practical use in advancing the object of my appeal.[15]

The viceroy did not, however, use the Mahatma's "services" in this regard, opting instead to follow Jinnah's advice by expanding his executive council to make it a more effective weapon of war.

Jinnah convened his Working Committee in Bombay early that September. The committee reaffirmed the League's Pakistan demand and noted with satisfaction the viceroy's "clear assurance that no future Constitution, interim or final, will be adopted by the British Government without the Muslim League's approval and consent."[16] It did not, however, accept the viceroy's offer regarding the membership of the Executive Council, resolving later that month to request Linlithgow to "reconsider" his proposal, and authorizing Jinnah to "seek further information and clarification." Sikander tried his best to persuade his committee colleagues to accept the viceroy's August offer, threatening to "withdraw from the League if Jinnah persisted in his obstinacy."[17] Jinnah, however, was never moved by threats from any source, and Sikander did not quit the League. Armed with his Working Committee's support, Jinnah informed the viceroy that a prior condition to the League's willingness to join any expanded executive council or war advisory council was an understanding that "in the event of any other party [Congress] deciding later on to be associated . . . it should be allowed to do so on terms that may be approved of and consented to by the Muslim League." Linlithgow considered Jinnah's escalating demands "obstructive" to the war effort and felt that Jinnah wanted to become "in effect . . . Prime Minister," a goal the viceroy "had no intention whatever" of furthering.

Congress was eager to launch civil disobedience, and the only question Gandhi had to resolve was whether it should be a symbolic individual or mass movement. The individual variety toward which he was predisposed was, of course, easier to control and keep nonviolent. On the eve of his seventy-first birthday, the Mahatma was understandably reluctant to lead another campaign that might provoke major violence. Individual *Satyagraha* was launched in mid-October. Gandhi selected his saintly ashram disciple, Vinoba Bhave, to court arrest first by openly speaking out against the war effort. Vinoba was arrested on October 17 and sentenced to three months in jail. Government ordered all newspapers to stop publishing statements against the war effort. Gandhi "protested" by suspending publication of his *Harijan* journal. The Mahatma next considered the "possibility of a fast, prolonged or unto death" and wrote to warn the viceroy of that possibility, while "waiting on God to find what is to be the case."[18] He also tried to appeal directly to Hitler to stop the war, but the letter he wrote was never permitted to leave India. Nehru argued vigorously against a fast, insisting it was "inopportune" and offering to court jail himself. He was arrested on October 30 and tried for breaking British martial law early in November. Jawaharlal was found guilty as charged and sentenced to four years of rigorous imprisonment, most of it spent in his old cell at Dehra Dun.

Jinnah took pains at this time to remind the British of how loyal Muslims had been and how worthy of partnership. He launched a threefold attack upon "enemies" within the government of India, militant Hindus, and Muslims in Congress. Among the former he included Linlithgow himself, to whose face he was overheard saying, "You have double-crossed me."[19] By then Jinnah considered the viceroy "wooden and ante-diluvian" and had concluded that Linlithgow and his official coterie at Simla merely "want our support on the assurance that we shall be remembered as loyal servants after the war and will even be given a *bakhsheesh!*"[20] Hindu leaders of the Mahasabha wanted to "treat" Muslims, Jinnah argued, "like Jews in Germany." As for Congress Muslims, Jinnah called them mere "show-boys."[21]

Early in February 1941, Shah Nawaz Khan prepared a confidential memorandum for Jinnah on "What is Pakistan," a demographic analysis of each province in the Northwestern and Northeastern Muslim zones of British India, and some strategic advice about "the Indian states." From this date at least, it is clear that Jinnah knew it would be "necessary to readjust" the Punjab's "territorial boundaries"; and Shah Nawaz suggested excluding Ambala Division which was not only mostly Hindu and Sikh in population but also a fiscal "liability and not an asset."[22] In the Northeast, moreover, Jinnah was alerted to the following harsh realities: the Muslim population of Assam was only 31.8 percent of that province's total population, while the Burdwan Division of Bengal was "overwhelmingly Hindu," and the overall Muslim majority of Bengal totalled a scanty 54.8 percent. Shah Nawaz cleverly proposed excluding Burdwan Division from "Pakistan's" Eastern wing but retaining the large and rich region of Assam united to the rest of Bengal, thus raising the Muslim majority in the region as a whole to 57.9 percent. In this confidential memo, Shafi's shrewd son-in-law also recommended a "third federation" of Indian states, since most princes, like Muslims, were "anxious to maintain their integrity and sovereign rights." As for Hyderabad, however, he felt it was large and populous enough to merit "fully independent" status with "direct political relations with the Crown like Nepal." Jinnah was to rely heavily on this memo in the years of strenuous negotiation ahead.

The annual session of the League was scheduled to start on April 12, 1941, in Madras's Peoples Park, where an estimated 100,000 Muslims gathered, filling the pandal to capacity long before their Quaid-i-Azam reached the sweltering scene. "When our train was a few hours from Madras, he got up and suddenly collapsed," Fatima recalled. "I dashed to his side, kneeling on the floor, and asked, 'Jin, what is wrong?'"

> He smiled, a worn out smile, "I suddenly felt very weak, exhausted." He put his hand on my shoulder, slowly lifted himself, and staggered to his berth . . . the train came to a halt . . . and thousands of enthusiastic admirers were on the platform, shouting, "Quaid-e-Azam Zinbabad." I opened the door of our compartment slightly and pleaded, "Don't shout. The Quaid is resting, he has a fever and is fatigued. Please get a doctor."

> Within minutes a doctor arrived, examined him and said, "Sir, you have had a nervous breakdown, nothing serious, but I would advise you not to move about for at least a week. Please stay in bed."

> We were soon in Madras. . . . The Quaid was too weak to address the opening session, but on the following day he insisted that he would deliver his presidential address. I advised him against it, but finding that he was adamant, I begged him to make short speech. "All right, I shall try to be brief," he said. He had no notes . . once he began, he went on speaking for over two hours.[23]

"Ladies and gentlemen, in the first place let me thank you and those who have made enquiries about my indisposition. I have received so many messages and calls that it is not possible for me to reply to them personally. . . . But I hope you will accept my heartfelt thanks. . . ."[24] Behind him on the glittering dais, decked in green silk and flanked by its Muslim League guards, sat the revered leader of South India's anti-Congress non-Brahman Justice party, E. V. Ramaswami Naicker, the *Periyar* ("Great Sage") of the "Dravidistan" movement, and other Tamilnad luminaries, including Jinnah's old friend Sir A. P. Patro. "Since the fall of the Mughal Empire, I think I am right in saying that Muslim India was never so well organized and so alive and so politically conscious as it is to-day." Jinnah kept one hand clutched in the pocket of his loose-hanging white linen jacket as he spoke, bracing himself with the other bony-fingered arm on the speaker's stand, determined not to smoke or to fall. "We have established a flag of our own, a national flag of Muslim India. We have established a remarkable platform which displays and demonstrates a complete unity of the entire solid body of Muslim India." He spoke extempore in a faultless subdued English accent, and his face, though rather skeletal, was brightened by the luminosity of his eyes.

> We have defined in the clearest language our goal about which Muslim India was groping in the dark, and the goal is Pakistan.

> That is our five-year plan of the past. We have succeeded in raising the prestige and reputation of the League not only throughout this country—we have now reached the farthest corners of the world, and we are watched throughout the world. Now what next? . . . No people can ever succeed in anything that they desire unless they work for it and work hard for it. . . . What is required now is that you should think—and I say this particularly to you, Delegates of the All-India Muslim League who have gathered here from all parts of India—we must now think and devise the programme of a five-year plan, and part of the five-year plan should be how quickly and how best the departments of the national life of Muslim India may be built up.[25]

He needed and wanted more brains, more bodies, platoons and brigades of wise, young, and fearless followers to carry on, magnify, actualize his orders. For his own strength, his life's energy was flagging and failing him. He was clearly feeling the strain of speaking in that stuffed, humid, overheated pandal; but instead of quitting, he grit his teeth and forged ahead, drawing energy it seemed from the crowd's attention and palpable devotion. The fever had returned to plague his painfully thin body. Still he would not abandon the podium or turn his back on so huge and receptive an audience.

He meandered over the political history of India since the war had started, returning again and again to his favorite subject,

> . . . what the Congress wants. The Congress has taken up a position about which there is absolutely no doubt. I should like to ask any man with a grain of sense, Do you really think that Gandhi, the supreme leader, commander and general of the Congress, has started this Satyagraha merely for the purpose of getting liberty of speech? Don't you really feel that this is nothing but a weapon of coercion and blackmailing the British, who are in a tight corner, to surrender and concede the Congress demands?[26]

Then Jinnah concluded his Madras address with a

real warning to the British Government, because after all they are in possession of this land and the Government of this Subcontinent. Please stop your policy of appeasement towards those who are bent upon frustrating your war efforts and doing their best to oppose the prosecution of the war and the defence of India at this critical moment. . . . You are not loyal to those who are willing to stand by you and sincerely desire to support you; you desire to placate those who have the greatest nuisance value in the political and economic fields. . . . If the Government want the whole-hearted co-operation of Muslim India, they must place their cards on the table.[27]

"The great enthusiasm of that large gathering had served as a tonic," Fatima remembered, "but only I knew that weakness, exhaustion and fever would follow."[28]

Seeking purer air at higher altitudes for his tubercular lungs, Jinnah went up to the Nandi Hills in Mysore State and Ootacamund to try to recover strength after Madras. What respite he found would only be temporary, for the insidious illness that drained his energy was by now irreversible. Nor could he stop smoking. Jinnah's health remained precarious all that summer, and indeed by July he was still too weak to accept a telephoned invitation from Bombay's governor, Sir Roger Lumley, to come visit him in Poona's Ganeshkhind, the governor's summer house about ninety miles from Bombay, to learn of Linlithgow's plans for constitutional change. Sir Roger wrote "confidentially" to Jinnah on July 20:

He is . . . establishing with the approval of His Majesty's Government, a National Defence Council. This Council will consist of some 30 members, nine of whom will be drawn from Indian States. The Viceroy regards it as essential that the Great Muslim community should be represented on that Council by persons of the highest prominence and capacity. He has accordingly invited the Premier of Assam, Bengal, the Punjab and Sind to serve as members of it. . . . He has considered whether he should invite you to let him have any suggestions as to possible personnel for this Council, but being aware, as he is, of your general attitude, he has concluded that it would be preferable not to embarrass you by inviting you to make suggestions.[29]

Jinnah was not embarrassed; he was infuriated. He read the viceroy's invitations to Sir Sikander, Fazlul Haq, and the League premier of Assam, Sir Muhammad Saadullah, as a direct challenge to his authority and power over each of them as president of the Muslim League. Sikander, in fact, had appealed personally to the viceroy for Punjabi representation on the expanded executive council, and Linlithgow had long found him much easier

Muhammad Ali Jinnah
in his Sindhi costume, 1892

Jinnah, Esquire, Bombay, c. 1900

Jinnah, c. 1910

Ruttie Jinnah around the time of her marriage,
c. 1918

Jinnah and Ruttie's home
atop Malabar Hill in Bombay, c. 1920

Jinnah, c. 1927

Dina with Jinnah's chauffeur and Bentley
in Hampstead, early 1930s

Jinnah and Fatima, Hampstead, c. 1932

Jinnah ("Quaid-i-Azam"), c. 1939

Addressing the Muslim League in Delhi, 1943

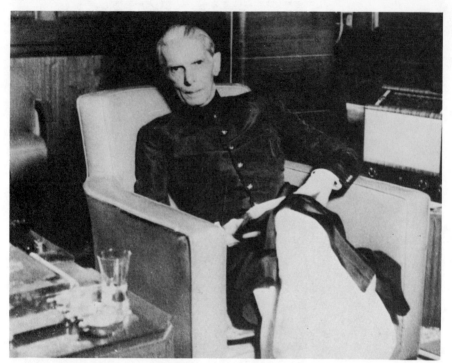

In his New Delhi home, c. 1945

In Simla, c. 1945

Jinnah and Liaquat Ali in Cairo
on the way home from London, 1946

At home in New Delhi, 1945 or '46

Jinnah and Nehru, Simla, 1946

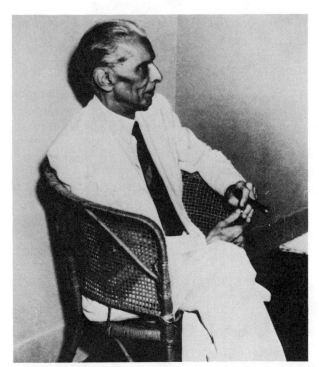

Jinnah, c. 1946

Preparing to address India
on the eve of Pakistan, 1947

Jinnah and his sister in Pakistan's Karachi, 1947

Fatima and others mourning at Jinnah's coffin, 1948

*All photographs courtesy of the Government of Pakistan,
National Archives, Islamabad*

to deal with than Jinnah. That August Jinnah called his Working Committee to Bombay to deal with this challenge from Simla. Sir Sikander, Fazlul Haq, and Saadullah tried in vain to argue that they had joined the viceroy's defence council as provincial premiers, rather than as representatives of Muslim opinion. Jinnah gave them no option but to quit the council or leave the League. Sikander, after a long private talk with Jinnah, agreed to abide by the decision of the committee. Sikander's capitulation was followed immediately by his resignation and that of Sir Saadullah from the viceroy's defence council. Fazlul Haq, however, proved less pliable; and though he promised to resign from the viceroy's council, he was most dilatory about doing it. But he did resign from both the National Defence Council and the Working Committee of the League, "As a mark of protest against the arbitrary use of powers vested in its President," voicing the strongest opposition to Jinnah's leadership and articulating what may in retrospect be viewed as a nascent "Bangladeshi" position against West Pakistani dominance. The Muslim premier of Bengal argued that "recent events have forcibly brought home to me that the principles of democracy and autonomy in the All India Muslim League are being subordinated to the arbitrary wishes of a single individual who seeks to rule as an omnipotent authority even over the destiny of 33 millions of Muslims in the province of Bengal who occupy the key position in Indian Muslim politics."[30]

Begum Shah Nawaz and Sir Sultan Ahmed, unlike Sir Sikander, Fazlul Haq, and Assam's Saadullah, refused to resign from the viceroy's council and were, therefore, expelled from the Muslim League for five years. For the begum it was a particularly bitter pill to swallow, since she had been so close to Jinnah during the Round Table conferences in London. She was later to relent and would return to the League's fold, but only after her half decade of ostracism. "The Government in the teeth of our opposition . . . tried to manoeuvre and wean some of our members by associating them with this scheme," Jinnah remarked during his Id Day message that October.

> Three of them were provincial Premiers of whom two were members of the Working Committee. Well, you know what happened. I am glad, and we have reason to be proud that the British Government have been taught a lesson. Out of evil cometh good! Muslim India from one end to another demonstrated that it was solidly behind the Muslim League. I hope in future our opponents will learn that it is futile to attempt to create disruptions in our ranks. That chapter is now closed.[31]

Jinnah withdrew the League's elected members from the Central Legislature at this time more forcefully to impress upon the viceroy his dissatisfac-

tion with the government's behavior, and he called for a "clear" declaration
of British policy toward all Muslim countries, demanding that Great Britain
affirm its non-intervention policy with regard to universal Muslim "sovereignty and independence." He appointed Ispahani to Fazlul Haq's seat on
the Working Committee.

Japan's startling victories in the wake of Pearl Harbor now raised the
specter of an Axis invasion of India from the East. Since expanding his executive council, Linlithgow had been pressing Churchill's cabinet for permission to release Nehru as well as other key Congress leaders from jail, in
response to demands from his non-official advisers. The viceroy was eager
to show his new members that they could, in fact, "get things done." But
Churchill was reluctant, arguing that "Undoubtedly the release of these
prisoners as an act of clemency will be proclaimed as a victory for Gandhi's
party. Nehru and others will commit fresh offences requiring whole process
of trial and conviction to be gone through again. You will get no thanks
from any quarter."[32] Still, Linlithgow insisted, Amery agreed; most of the
cabinet closed ranks behind them, so that early in December when Churchill convened his War Cabinet to debate the issue he sensed their mood
immediately upon looking "round the room and said somewhat sorrowfully
'I give in,' adding *sotto voce* 'when you lose India don't blame me.' "[33]

Jinnah journeyed to Nagpur on his birthday to address the All-India
Muslim Students Federation on December 26, 1941. "My young friends, to-
day you compare yourselves with what was the position of the Muslims
even three years ago," Jinnah told them.

> Five years ago it was wretched. Ten years ago you were dead. . . .
> The Muslim League has given you a goal which in my judgment is
> going to lead you to the promised land where we shall establish our
> Pakistan. People may say what they like and talk as they like. Of
> course, he who laughs last, laughs best.[34]

Fazlul Haq resigned his League ministry in Calcutta, opting to head a
new coalition of his Proja party members and Hindu Mahasabhites led by
their national vice-president, Dr. Shyama Prasad Mookerjee. He persuaded
the nawab of Dacca to join his new cabinet, which Ispahani called going
"over to the enemy."[35] By that unexpected coup, Haq proved again his political dexterity and durability. "The old fox who is now called the black
sheep of Barisal [Haq's hometown], is playing at one game only and that is
to gain time," bemoaned Ispahani. And Jinnah asked at Nagpur:

> And in Bengal, what is the Congress Party doing? The Congress
> Party has supported this new coalition ministry formed by Mr. Haq,
> and by virtue of it he was able to form a government and continue to

be the Premier. . . . Now I make a Christmas gift of Mr. Haq to Lord Linlithgow! I make another New Year's gift of the Nawab of Dacca to the Governor of Bengal! I am very glad and I am happy that Muslim India is rid of these men who are guilty of the grossest treachery and betrayal of the Muslims.[36]

Both Bengali leaders were expelled from the League, "weeded out" as Jinnah put it.

Linlithgow urged Sir Roger Lumley, the governor of Bombay, to invite Jinnah "to a meal," and he did so in mid-January 1942 when Oxford professor Reginald Coupland arrived on his unofficial tour in search of a "creative" constitutional settlement. "I asked Jinnah to lunch and he came today," Lumley reported, and

> Jinnah was most friendly throughout, and, if there is any effect from this social contact with him, I think it would be favourable. After lunch I had a talk with him, which I had intended would be a short one, so that he could then tackle Coupland: but at the first opening he proceeded to give me an exposition of the Muslim League position which lasted for three quarters of an hour. It was all most friendly, very logical, and well argued from the Muslim League point of view; but there seemed to me to be no indication at all of any change in his position. He appeared quite satisfied with our attitude, although . . . he expressed some fears that the British Press and public opinion would be taken in by Congress and other Hindu propaganda.[37]

Lumley was "considerably impressed" by the logic of Jinnah's arguments, but in the aftermath of their talk saw no prospect for any "solution" to the constitutional "deadlock." "India is hopelessly, and I suspect irremediably split by racial and religious divisions which we cannot bridge, and which become more acute as any real transfer of power by us draws nearer," Linlithgow reported to Amery before the end of January 1942.[38] Attlee was "distinctly disturbed" by Linlithgow's "defeatist" position; he informed Amery, after reading it, that he had lost considerable "confidence in the Viceroy's judgment," suggesting that perhaps "someone" from Home should now be sent to India "charged with a mission to try to bring the political leaders together."[39] Labour's candidate for that job was Sir Stafford Cripps, who just returned from Moscow where he had served as the British ambassador.

Jinnah left Bombay on February 10, taking an all-day and overnight train to Calcutta. A jubilant crowd awaited him at Howrah Station and escorted him in gala procession to Mohammad Ali Park, over which he hoisted the Muslim League flag on February 13, 1942. "Up to the present moment, Muslims were absolutely demoralised," said the Quaid-i-Azam, whose personal preoccupation with death and dying had by now infected most of his political pronouncements, "Our blood had become cold, our flesh was not capable of working and the Muslim nation was, for all practical purposes, dead. To-day we find that our blood circulation is improving. Our flesh is getting stronger and, above all, our mind is getting more clarified."[40] From Calcutta he was driven to Serajganj in East Bengal to preside over the Bengal Provincial Muslim League Conference. "Ladies and gentlemen, the Muslim League has many opponents. We are going through a life and death struggle. . . . We must stand on our own legs and rely on our own strength if we are to achieve anything in this world."[41]

The unexpected fall of Singapore on February 15, 1942, where a British Indian garrison of some 60,000 troops surrendered to Japan with hardly a shot being fired, sent fresh chills of anxiety through New Delhi and Simla as well as through Whitehall. "The really difficult point is how to reconcile our pledge about agreement with the criticism that we are deliberately holding up all progress by giving a blackmailing veto to the minorities," Amery wrote to Linlithgow in late February, briefly setting out what would essentially be Cripps's proposals.

> If there are sufficient Provinces who want to get together and form a Dominion the dissident Provinces should be free to stand out and either come in after a period of option or be set up at the end of it as Dominions of their own. Jinnah could not quarrel with that nor, on the other hand, could Congress feel that it is denied the opportunity of complete independence for that part of India which it controls.[42]

The India Office prepared a "note" for Britain's War Cabinet on the possible impact of constitutional changes in India or her army, which had more than doubled in size since the war's start to over one million. In the prewar Indian army soldiers had expressed anxieties about their own future if the British raj "surrendered" to Congress demands. There was still "a strong feeling that the British officer is the surest guardian of the soldier's interests," Whitehall reported. "It is difficult to say how any concession to Congress would assist the war effort in respect to the Military personnel of the Army. On the other hand it might result in the ruin of the Indian Army as at present constituted."[43] Armed with so formidable a note, Amery advised the prime minister that "Any declaration of Indian policy for the future must make it clear, unequivocally, that we stand by our pledge of 1940, to the Moslems and the Princes, that they are not to be coerced into any system of Indian Government of which they disapprove. This is in any case vital at present, in view of possible effects upon the Moslem element in the Indian Army."[44]

Sir Stafford Cripps was brought into Britain's War Cabinet that February as lord privy seal and made leader of the House of Commons. He was appointed to serve on Deputy Prime Minister Attlee's India committee of the War Cabinet and helped draft what that committee considered an appropriate "declaration" by the month's end, promising "to lay down in precise and clear terms the steps" by which His Majesty's government planned to create a new Indian union, to become a free and equal dominion within the British Commonwealth of Nations. Before agreement could be reached on the proposed declaration, however, Rangoon fell to the Japanese blitz across Southeast Asia. Jinnah wired Churchill to warn against the "plausible subtle and consequently more treacherous" proposals of Sapru and his colleagues, "patrol agents for the Congress. If the British Government is stampeded into the trap laid for them Moslem India would be sacrificed with most disastrous consequences, especially in regard to the war effort,"[45] cautioned the Quaid-i-Azam. On February 22, at a Delhi meeting of the League's Working Committee, Jinnah stated that "direct revolt" would follow any British acceptance of Sapru's proposed unitary constitutional scheme of reforms.

Churchill, therefore, decided that a declaration spelling out the constitutional process for transforming British India into a dominion was too dangerous, opting instead to send Cripps out to India to sound out the "parties" on the spot as to their feelings about a proposal the cabinet approved. "The document on which we have agreed represents our united policy," Churchill informed Linlithgow in early March. "If that is rejected by the Indian parties for whose benefit it has been devised, our sincerity will be proved to the world and we shall stand together and fight on it here, should that ever be necessary."[46]

Prime Minister Churchill rose in the House of Commons at noon on Wednesday, March 11, 1942, to proclaim in his uniquely inspiring baritone that "The crisis in the affairs of India arising out of the advance of Japan has made us wish to rally all the forces of Indian life to shield their land from the menace of the invader."[47] He then announced the decision to send no less distinguished a member of the War Cabinet to India than the lord privy seal, who "carries with him the full confidence of His Majesty's Government and will strive in their name to procure the necessary measure of assent not only from the Hindu majority but also from those great minorities amongst which the Muslims are the most important." Cripps was thus launched on the most frustrating mission of his life.

Cripps flew into Karachi on March 22, was "quaranteened" in isolation overnight, and touched down at New Delhi's airport the following day, "Pakistan Day," the second anniversary of the Lahore resolution that was celebrated in Delhi by a mile-long procession and a mass public meeting addressed by Jinnah. "I can say without fear of contradiction that the Muslim League stands more firmly for the freedom and independence of this country than any other party," the Quaid-i-Azam told a crowd of 50,000 Muslims in Urdu Park. "We are asking for justice and fairplay. We have no designs upon our sister communities. We want to live in this land as a free and independent nation. We are not a minority but a nation."⁴⁸ Referring to Cripps's mission, Jinnah said:

> There is the fear that he is a friend of the Congress. He has enjoyed the hospitality of Pandit Jawaharlal Nehru. . . . That is all true but we should not be afraid on that score. Don't get cold feet. . . . We are prepared to face all consequences if any scheme or solution which is detrimental to the interests of Muslims is forced upon us. We shall not only not accept it but resist it to the utmost of our capacity. If we have to die in the attempt we shall die fighting.⁴⁹

Cripps met with Maulana Azad, then out of jail, on March 25. The Congress president's English, he learned, was not as good as his Persian or Arabic. Azad insisted that to mobilize Indians "effectively" it was "necessary" to give them "control of the defence of their country." Cripps pointed out that strategically India had to be regarded as part of "a much greater theatre of war." Azad reiterated his point, however, and Cripps decided that what Congress really wanted was the "appearance and name of an Indian Defence Minister," not actual control over "the movement of troops or other military arrangements."⁵⁰

Jinnah arrived at the viceroy's palace just as Azad was leaving. Cripps explained that he had not taken the Muslim League or Pakistan "propaganda" very seriously during his last visit two and a half years ago but assured Jinnah that he had "changed" his view because of the "change in the communal feeling in India and the growth of the Pakistan movement." Cripps then handed Jinnah the document he had brought from London, "which I think rather surprised him in the distance it went to meet the Pakistan case. He stated of course that he was not prepared to give any views on it but we had a long discussion as to its effect, especially upon Bengal and the Punjab, and the main thing with which he was concerned was whether they would have the effective right to opt out of the constitution in the event of their so desiring."⁵¹ Jinnah then "promised to lay the matter before his Working Committee in Delhi and to come back and see me immediately afterwards. . . . He was extremely cordial and when we parted expressed the view to me that the one thing that mattered was to be able to mobilise the whole of India behind her own defence and that he was personally most anxious to achieve this."[52] Expert negotiator that he was, Jinnah wisely refrained in his opening meeting with Cripps from any "pernickety criticism."

Cripps's meeting with Gandhi on March 27 did not begin on a happy note. Gandhi considered it "extremely inadvisable" to publish the document and urged Cripps to refrain from doing so, asking what Jinnah thought.

> I told him that he had suggested that, in view of the danger of leakage, it would be wise to publish it before too long; and he interpreted this as being an indication that Jinnah would accept the scheme. . . . I then asked him how, supposing Jinnah were to accept the scheme and Congress were not to, he would himself advise me to proceed. He said that in these circumstances the proper course would be for me to throw the responsibility upon Jinnah and tell him that he must now try to get Congress in either by negotiating direct with them or by meeting them in association with myself. He thought that if it was pointed out to Jinnah what a very great position this would give him in India if he succeeded, that he might take on the job and that he might succeed.[53]

It was one of Gandhi's most brilliant ideas, turning over premier power—and responsibility—to Jinnah, but no British viceroy or cabinet leader had the courage or wisdom to try the idea.

On March 29, Nehru came to breakfast with Cripps, and then both of them went to Birla House to see Gandhi, Azad, and others of the Working Committee of the Congress. Cripps listened and argued for hours. "The general attitude of Nehru, who was tired and not well, was mild and conciliatory and he left me in complete doubt as to whether Congress was more or less decided not to accept it and that it was not worth arguing or pressing for any alteration or whether he was not inclined to press his particular objections in view of the general character of the scheme and its grant of free self-government in India."[54] Less than a week gone by, and Cripps's crisp British confidence was fast dissolving in the miasma of Indian complexity, ambiguity, and transcendental doubt.

Cripps had been counting on his close friendship with Nehru and Krishna Menon as the key to resolving the communal puzzle that had baffled Morley, shattered Montagu, eluded Ramsay MacDonald, flabbergasted Irwin, destroyed Motilal Nehru, and had all but driven Jinnah into permanent exile in Hampstead. He truly believed, or at least desperately hoped he might achieve in a fortnight what the best brains of England and India had failed to accomplish over the past quarter-century of concentrated effort and countless futile hours of intense negotiation. Perhaps it was just that with stakes so high, he could not resist a roll at that fatal game, suspecting as one his confidants put it, that "if he brought this settlement off, Cripps would certainly replace Winston."[55] His fatal flaw was, however, that he believed himself omnipotent. Forgetting what Kipling had written of his well-intentioned forebears, he hoped to "hustle the East."[56]

At this juncture President Franklin D. Roosevelt sent his former assistant secretary of war, Colonel Louis Johnson, out to India as his personal representative, introducing Johnson to Linlithgow as a man of "broad experience with problems relating to military supply," who was selected for "this important mission because of his outstanding ability and high character."[57] Churchill, Amery, and Linlithgow were all anxious about the possible "political" implications of a secret agenda for Colonel Johnson's mission. Linlithgow's representative in Washington wrote that Roosevelt seemed to think that the plan concerning immediate federation did not go far enough and he felt "that complete autonomy, including power to raise armies, should be given to provinces."[58]

As soon as Linlithgow, Amery, and Churchill learned that Johnson and Roosevelt would do nothing to twist their political arms by way of conceding more to a non-cooperating ("shilly-shallying," as Johnson put it) Congress, the Cripps game was over. Only Cripps refused to believe he was finished. He kept meeting with Indian leaders, holding press conferences, sending longer and longer secret telegrams home, and doggedly flogging the horse that had died under him. The once bright and rising star of his political career went into eclipse under India's blinding sun. On April 2, Azad and Nehru handed Cripps the Congress Working Committee's resolution rejecting his offer. Instead of thanking them and flying home, Cripps wired the text of that resolution to Churchill and set up a meeting with Azad, Nehru, and field marshal Sir Archibald Wavell (1883–1950). The tight-lipped commander-in-chief, who replaced Linlithgow as viceroy the following year, was then fighting a losing battle in Malaya and Burma, desperately hoping he could keep the Japanese from smashing through India's Eastern wall of rugged mountainous forests. He had no time, and less talent, for political gamesmanship. With one glass eye, and little to smile about, Wavell's was hardly a personality to appeal to Nehru, Azad, or Cripps. Nor was he ready voluntarily to release any of the military strings he controlled. Still Cripps was determined to try to bring Nehru and Wavell into harness.

Jinnah left Delhi on Thursday, April 2, taking the night train to Allahabad where the annual session of the Muslim League started that Friday. A cheering crowd greeted him with shouts of "Quaid-i-Azam Zindabad!" at

Allahabad's Central Railway Station, then escorted him through more than a hundred green tinsel-decorated arches of triumph that led to the packed pandal in Mahmudabad's garden. Jinnah presented his brief of Cripps's proposals in a clear, succinct manner, saying, now that the scheme was really dead, how "deeply disappointed" all Muslims were to find that the "entity and integrity of the Muslim nation has not been expressly recognized. Any attempt to solve the problem of India by the process of evading the real issues and by over-emphasizing the territorial entity of the provinces, which are mere accidents of British policy, and administrative division is fundamentally wrong. Muslim India will not be satisfied unless the right of national self-determination is unequivocally recognized."[59]

On Easter Sunday of that year, Colonel Johnson met Cripps for the first time at the viceroy's house over lunch and each recognized a potential ally in the other, for both were liberal legal minds who felt as far removed intellectually from the viceroy and his commander-in-chief as they were culturally from Nehru and Azad. Both enjoyed more confidence in high places in London and Washington, moreover, than either did in New Delhi or Simla. And each, in his own way, had fallen under the spell of Nehru's cosmopolitan charm. So in the spirit of Easter Sunday they joined forces, hoping to resurrect the mission that had truly expired on Good Friday. They moved with great energy, resourcefulness, and top secrecy, meeting Nehru, Azad, and other leaders of Congress at all hours of day and night, convincing themselves that there was, indeed, light at the end of India's constitutional tunnel. They came to believe that all Congress really wanted was control over the Ministry of Defence, so they worked out an elaborate, ingenious formula, whereby that ministry could nominally be put under an Indian, while all of its real martial responsibilities would remain under the commander-in-chief, who would instead be called minister of war—and they actually thought that would suffice to solve India's problem. Cripps had even drawn up a list of Indian cabinet ministers for the new "national government" he was going to install, and Congress President Azad was his choice for home minister in charge of police—Azad, whom Jinnah would not speak to and referred to as a "show-boy Muslim." Johnson thought he had convinced Nehru of the wisdom of cooperating, and of the surety that he could "carry" Congress, just as he thought Cripps could "swing" Churchill into line. It was all an illusion, spun out of India's torrid heat.

Many cables were exchanged between London and India in the next few days, including one from Churchill informing Cripps that Johnson was not Roosevelt's representative "in any matter outside the specific mission dealing with Indian munitions and kindred topics on which he was sent."[60] All the cables were unnecessary. Congress turned down the proposal despite its revised form, on April 10, 1942—just as Gandhi had predicted they would the first time he met with Cripps. Explaining his party's rejection of the offer, Congress president Azad wrote Cripps:

> We are yet prepared to assume responsibility provided a truly National Government is formed. . . . But in the present the National Government must be a Cabinet Government with full power, and must not merely be a continuation of the Viceroy's Executive Council. . . . We would point out to you that the suggestions we have put forward are not ours only but may be considered to be the unanimous demand of the Indian people. On these matters there is no difference of opinion among various groups and parties.[61]

"There is no foundation for that assertion," Jinnah told the press as soon as he read Azad's final assertion several days later. "Muslim India has repudiated that claim. We maintain that the Congress does not represent not only the Musalmans of India but even a large body of the Hindus, the Depressed Classes, the non-Brahmins and other minorities." He also repudiated all negotiations that Congress had carried on with Cripps "over the head of all other parties," reiterating what had been his basic position for over two years: "If all parties agree to the Muslim demand for Pakistan or partition and Muslim right of self-determination, details to be settled after the war, then we are prepared to come to any reasonable adjustment with regard to the present."[62]

On April 12, 1942, Cripps wired Churchill, "There is clearly no hope of agreement and I shall start home on Sunday." To Azad he wrote: "You suggest 'a truly National Government' be formed which must be 'Cabinet Government with full power.' Without constitutional changes of a most complicated character and on a very large scale this would not be possible as you realise. . . . The proposals of His Majesty's Government went as far as possible."[63] Roosevelt urged Churchill to "postpone" Cripps's departure, reporting that in the United States "The feeling is almost universally held that the deadlock has been caused by the unwillingness of the British Government to concede to the Indians the right of self-government, notwithstanding the willingness of the Indians to entrust technical, military and naval defense control to the competent British authorities. American public opinion cannot understand why, if the British Government is willing to permit the component parts of India to secede from the British Empire after the war, it is not willing to permit them to enjoy what is tantamount to self-government during the war."[64] Churchill chose to pocket that cable rather than show it to his cabinet or use it to wire Cripps back to New Delhi from Karachi, where he just landed. Churchill had not, after all, become prime minister to preside over the dissolution of His Majesty's Empire.

The Working Committee of the Muslim League issued its resolution on the Cripps offer shortly after Congress resolved upon rejection.

> The Committee, while expressing their gratification that the possibility of Pakistan is recognised by implication by providing for the establishment of two or more independent Unions in India, regret that . . . no alternative proposals are invited. In view of the rigidity of the attitude of His Majesty's Government with regard to the fundamentals not being open to any modification, the Committee have no alternative but to say that the proposals in the present form are unacceptable. . . . The Musalmans cannot be satisfied by such a Declaration on a vital question affecting their future destiny, and demand a clear and precise pronouncement on the subject. Any attempt to solve the future problem of India by the process of evading the real issue is to court disaster.[65]

Once again, Jinnah had raised the minimal terms for negotiating any settlement to the most persistent political problem of recent Indian history. Pakistan was hardly a "pernickety" demand.

14

Dawn in Delhi
(1942-43)

Jinnah's position remained firm throughout the remaining years of World War II. He demanded no less than parity with Congress on any council of government and open recognition of the Muslims' right to Pakistan in any future settlement formula. As Congress became more hostile and non-cooperative, the government of India and His Majesty's government looked more than ever to Muslim soldiers and Muslim League leaders for the support they required to hold India. Jinnah's stock rose to new heights in London as well as in Simla and New Delhi.

Jinnah's political posture was rarely misread at Whitehall. "I don't suppose Jinnah will want to seem less nationalist than Congress and therefore to come in under the existing constitution," Amery wrote Linlithgow, thankful that Cripps was then ancient history and speculating on possible future reforms.

> If he does, I suppose you could give him certain seats, balancing his men with Ambedkar and possibly a new Hindu or two, but still retaining the majority of your existing Executive? Or you may simply decide to drop all idea of bringing in political leaders from either of the two main parties? . . . The Muslim League, I suppose, will still be officially non-co-operative, but probably more co-operative than hitherto in practice in view of the definite concession to the possibility of Pakistan that we have made?[1]

In the wake of Cripps, the governor of the Punjab reported that "the Sikh community were very seriously perturbed by the potentially fissiparous nature of the War Cabinet's proposals." Sikhs were afraid that if the Punjab refused to accede to an all-India confederacy, that wealthy Muslim-majority province once ruled by Sikh Maharajas would be enveloped by "the outer darkness of Pakistan. They regarded themselves as being in danger of everlasting subjection to an unsympathetic and tyrannical Muhammadan Raj."[2] Sikh-Muslim antipathy had roots that went back to seventeenth century mughal imperial rule. "We are doing what we can to deal with the situation," Governor Glancy assured the viceroy. It was a most important warning, passed on to Whitehall by Linlithgow, since martial Sikhs numbered second only to Muslims in the British Indian army.

"Blood and tears are going to be our lot whether we like them or not," Nehru predicted, all too accurately, at a press conference in Allahabad in mid-April after Cripps flew home. "Our blood and tears will flow; maybe the parched soil of India needs them so that the fine flower of freedom may grow again."[3]

Cripps held a press conference in London on April 22 and insisted "The problem now becomes not a political one, but the problem of the defence of India, and in that I have had the assurance from many of the leaders that they are going to co-operate to their utmost."[4] Asked if he had invited Nehru and Jinnah to come to London, he replied negatively, feeling "quite sure" that neither of them would want to leave India in "existing circumstances" even if they were invited.

In Madras, Chakravarti Rajagopalachari (C. R.) now dramatically sought to lead Congress in the direction of co-operation both with the British war effort and the Muslim League. He presided over a meeting of forty-six members of Madras Congress legislators and proposed two resolutions, agreement on which was reached in late April. The first argued that since it was "impossible for the people to think in terms of neutrality or passivity during invasion," it was "absolutely and urgently necessary" for Congress to "remove every obstacle" toward establishing a "National Administration." It therefore urged the All-India Congress Party to "acknowledge" the Muslim League's "claim for separation," thereby removing all doubts and fears in this regard," and to invite the League for "consultation for the purpose of arriving at agreement and securing of national Government to meet present emergency."[5] The second resolution requested permission of the All-India Congress for the Madras Congress to unite with the Muslim League and other provincial parties to restore popular government, as a coalition ministry, to Madras. Both resolutions passed overwhelmingly. It was the first important break in Congress's non-cooperating ranks, a significant victory for Jinnah's policy and the British, and a direct challenge to Gandhi and Nehru.

The All-India Congress met the following week, repudiating C. R. and his Madras resolutions. On April 30, 1942, he resigned from the Working

Committee. Gandhi remained in Wardha, but sent his loving disciple Mira-behn (Madelaine Slade) to Allahabad with a resolution he drafted for presentation to the Congress, stating:

> Whereas the British War Cabinet's proposals sponsored by Sir Stafford Cripps have shown up British imperialism in its nakedness as never before . . . The A.I.C.C. is of opinion that Britain is incapable of defending India. It is natural that whatever she does is for her own defence. There is an eternal conflict between Indian and British interests. . . . The Indian army has been maintained up till now mainly to hold India in subjugation. It has been completely segregated from the general population who can in no sense regard it as their own. . . . Japan's quarrel is not with India. She is warring against the British Empire. India's participation in the war has not been with the consent of the representatives of the Indian people. It was purely a British act. If India were freed her first step would probably be to negotiate with Japan. . . . The A.I.C.C. is, therefore, of opinion that the British should withdraw from India.[6]

Nehru argued that Colonel Johnson and Franklin Roosevelt might help India win freedom if Congress were more supportive of the Allied cause. A compromise resolution was agreed upon by the Working Committee; Gandhi essentially had his way, though the resolution passed on May 1 also professed India's "antipathy to Nazism and Fascism as to imperialism." On June 6, however, Gandhi wrote:

> I see no difference between the Fascist or Nazi powers and the Allies. All are exploiters, all resort to ruthlessness to the extent required to compass their end. America and Britain are very great nations, but their greatness will count as dust before the bar of dumb humanity, whether African or Asiatic. . . . They have no right to talk of human liberty and all else unless they have washed their hands clean of the pollution.[7]

Two American journalists interviewed Gandhi that week in Wardha, and one asked "But what does a free India mean, if, as Mr. Jinnah said, Muslims will not accept Hindu rule?" The Mahatma replied: "I have not asked the British to hand over India to the Congress or to the Hindus. Let them entrust India to God or in modern parlance to anarchy. Then all the parties will fight one another like dogs, or will, when real responsibility faces them, come to a reasonable agreement. I shall expect non-violence to arise out of that chaos."[8] Gandhi was reminded by a reporter for *The Hindu* that until recently he had always said there could be no *Swaraj* without Hindu-Muslim unity, and then he was asked why he had of late insisted there would be "no unity until India has achieved independence?" The seventy-three-year-old Mahatma answered:

> Time is a merciless enemy. I have been asking myself why every whole-hearted attempt made by all including myself to reach unity has failed, and failed so completely that I have entirely fallen from grace and am described by some Muslim papers as the greatest enemy of Islam in India. It is a phenomenon I can only account for by the fact that the third power, even without deliberately wishing it, will not allow real unity to take place. Therefore I have come to the resultant conclusion that the two communities will come together almost immediately after the British power comes to a final end in India.[9]

Jinnah immediately responded to this with, "I am glad that at last Mr. Gandhi has openly declared that unity and Hindu-Muslim settlement can only come after the achievement of India's independence and has thereby thrown off the cloak that he had worn for the last 22 years."[10]

The All-India Congress met again in early August. Gandhi told his followers: "This is a crucial hour. . . . We shall get our freedom by fighting. It cannot fall from the skies. . . . The Britishers will have to give us freedom when we have made sufficient sacrifices and proved our strength. . . . At a time when I am about to launch the biggest fight in my life there can be no hatred for the British in my heart. The thought that because they are in difficulties I should give them a push is totally absent from my mind."[11] Sardar Patel was reported to have said that the British army was ready to abandon India, much the way they had Burma, and that the *Satyagraha* campaign would prove victorious in a week. "If it ends in a week it will be a miracle and if this happens it would mean melting the British heart," Gandhi said, adding:

> Maybe wisdom will dawn on the British and they will understand that it will be wrong for them to put in jail the very people who want to fight for them. Maybe . . . a change may come in Mr. Jinnah's mind after all. He will think that those who are fighting are the sons of the soil and if he sits quiet of what use would Pakistan be for him. . . . God has helped us. . . . When I raised the slogan "Quit India" the people in India who were then feeling despondent felt I had placed before them a new thing. If you want real freedom you will have to come together and such coming together will create true democracy.[12]

The War Cabinet transmitted full authority to Linlithgow to arrest Gandhi and the Congress Working Committee at any time he deemed appropriate. London considered Congress's most recent resolution as "open rebellion" against the government of India. Sikander warned Governor Glancy of his suspicion that Gandhi might try to "make terms with Jinnah by an out-and-out offer of Pakistan and then present a united front to Government."[13] Gandhi did, in fact, write on August 8 that

> Provided the Muslim League co-operated fully with the Congress demand for immediate independence without the slightest reserva- tion . . . the Congress will have no objection to the British Govern- ment transferring all the powers it today exercises to the Muslim League on behalf of the whole of India. . . . And the Congress will not only not obstruct any Government that the Muslim League may form on behalf of the people, but will even join the Government in running the machinery of the free State. This is meant in all serious- ness and sincerity.[14]

Such an offer might have tempted Jinnah if he had believed in or trusted Gandhi, but just a few days earlier, he had told the press: "Mr. Gandhi's conception of 'Independent India' is basically different from ours. . . . Mr. Gandhi by independence means Congress raj. I ask Mr. Gandhi to give up the game of fooling the Musalmans by insinuating that we depend upon the British for the achievement of our goal of Pakistan. . . . Hands off the Muslims."[15] By August 8, all was in readiness within the vast machine of the government of India. The Aga Khan's palace in Poona was chosen as the most secure, comfortable, and convenient "prison" for Gandhi and a select coterie of his family and closest followers, including Sarojini Naidu and Admiral Slade's daughter Mirabehn. The rest of the Congress Working Committee was to be jailed in Ahmednagar Fort.

"Every one of you should, from this moment onwards, consider yourself a free man or woman, and act as if you are free and are no longer under the heel of this imperialism," Gandhi told his Congress colleagues after they passed his "Quit India" resolution on the evening of August 8, 1942. "Here is a *mantra,* a short one, that I give you. You may imprint it on your hearts and let every breath of yours give expression to it. The *mantra* is: 'Do or Die.' We shall either free India or die in the attempt."[16]

Linlithgow waited no longer. Gandhi and the entire Congress Working Committee were arrested next day before dawn. Gandhi's final message to the country was written at 5:00 A.M., shortly before he was taken into cus- tody: "Everyone is free to go the fullest length under ahimsa. Complete deadlock by strikes and other non-violent means. Satyagrahis must go out to die and not to live. They must seek and face death. It is only when individuals go out to die that the nation will survive. *Karenge ya marenge.* ["We will Do or Die."]"[17]

"I deeply regret that the Congress has finally declared war and has launched a most dangerous mass movement in spite of numerous warnings from various individuals, parties and organisations," said Jinnah on August 9, 1942. Unlike Gandhi, he did not expect the war to end swiftly, nor did he think the British would lose. He never believed, moreover, that *Satyagraha* could remain nonviolent. He summoned his Working Committee to Bombay on August 16 to plan the League's strategy. They met in his house for four days and formally resolved to "deplore" the decision of the All-India Congress Committee to launch an "open rebellion" for the purpose of "establishing Congress Hindu domination in India." The result was only "lawlessness and considerable destruction of life and property."[18] The League view the "Quit India" movement as an attempt to "force the Musalmans to submit and surrender to Congress terms and dictation."

The violence started in Bombay a few days after Gandhi's arrest, quickly spreading to the United Provinces, Delhi, and Bihar. The speed and secrecy of the government's predawn sweep initially had a paralyzing impact everywhere. Nor was the press permitted to report any disturbances or strikes. By August 12, however, Linlithgow wrote to Amery, "In Delhi there has been a good deal of trouble. Casualties may be heavy and some damage has been done to property. Here again I attach no importance to it. It is . . . due to millhands on strike, and the Chief Commissioner is quite confident that he can handle the situation."[19]

But by mid-August over thirty people were dead in Bombay, where the police reintroduced whipping as a regular form of punishment. Railway lines all round Patna in Eastern India were torn up, and the British rushed regular army troops to the "affected area," with Linlithgow authorizing "machine-gunning from air of saboteurs."[20] No report of such martial violence unleashed in Bihar was ever permitted to appear in any Indian newspaper. British Indian censors were kept busy keeping secret all movements and operations of the Indian army aimed at "students and riff-raff," as the viceroy called Gandhi's *Satyagrahis*, adding: "I am not disturbed by the situation. Most embarrassing developments are signs of extension of endeavours to interrupt railway, telegraph and telephonic communication. This may develop still further and is of course very difficult to dispose of effectively in a country of the size of India."[21]

A week after Gandhi's arrest, Lord Linlithgow was pleased to note that British action had "tidied up the Bombay position" and was "relieved" that things were relatively "quiet in Delhi, for serious and prolonged rioting in the capital city of a country is not a very good advertisement."[22] Linlithgow's minister of information and broadcasting, Sir C. P. Ramaswami Aiyar, then reported that *"The Muslim League has developed cold feet and desires to negotiate with Gandhi,*" adding: "With my opinion of Jinnah I feel that Government should forestall him. I go further and venture to assert that to speak, as one Governor has spoken, of *crushing* the organisation is to follow the wrong method."[23] Aiyar had earlier appealed to the viceroy to allow him to try to negotiate a settlement with Gandhi. But Linlithgow had refused to permit him to see Gandhi and then tried in vain to convince him to stay in ministerial harness. So Aiyar, formerly Travancore State's prime minister (diwan), returned to his Malabar home, which he hoped would remain under the protection of Britain's paramount power.

"Jinnah has taken advantage of the latest turn in events to raise his terms against us (not that that matters much), and also to raise them against Congress," Linlithgow informed Amery, calling that, "a new and highly ingenious move in Jinnah's game of Poker: for it seemed to me inconceivable that Gandhi could accept the principle of Pakistan by whomsoever it was backed. . . . It remains pretty clear that there is going to be nothing doing with either the Congress or the Muslim League while the war lasts."[24]

Ambassador Lord Halifax (ex-viceroy Lord Irwin) cabled a most secret message from Washington in late August directly to foreign secretary Anthony Eden reliably informing him that the U.S. consul-general (George R. Merrell) in New Delhi had just reported to the State Department that the Muslim League received most of its "financial support" from "the Indian princes, Hindu as well as Mohammedan, the great Mohammedan landlords and the English business community, particularly that of Calcutta." This report went on to explain "that the Indian princes and the British business community support the Moslem League for the same reason that the Government does namely, to prevent the 'representatives of India' from obtaining power . . . to avoid a definite settlement of India's problems and to prolong the present deadlock; and a secondary reason why the Mohammedan landlords are interested in supporting the Moslem League is that they are scared of the Congress Party's belief in the national ownership of all natural resources."[25]

At the end of August, Linlithgow wired Churchill complaining about American "intervention." The viceroy suddenly called the unrest

> by far the most serious rebellion since that of 1857, the gravity and extent of which we have so far concealed from the world for reasons of military security. . . . Mob violence remains rampant over large tracts of the countryside and I am by no means confident that we may not see in September a formidable attempt to renew this widespread sabotage of our war effort. The lives of Europeans in outlying places are today in jeopardy. If we bungle this business we shall damage India irretrievably as a base for future allied operations and

as a thoroughfare for U.S. help to China. . . . These are the circumstances in which I am now threatened by visitations from Wendell Wilkie and Sherwood Eddy. The latter threatens to come to India in the hope of helping by way of mediation. My experience of peripatetic Americans which is now extensive is that their zeal in teaching us our business is in inverse ratio to their understanding of even the most elementary of the problems with which we have to deal.[26]

"Discussing the American invaders in Cabinet this morning much sympathy was expressed for you," Amery assured Linlithgow on September 1, "and a clear conviction that you must obviously refuse flatly to let anyone go and see the prisoners. On the other hand, Eden and others felt that it could only do good your finding time to talk to the better type of American and get our case across. Wilkie is very well disposed and Winston adds especially amenable to the influence of good champagne."[27] Earlier in the same cabinet meeting Churchill had spoken of "the present trouble as completely disposed of and as evidence of the fact, which he has always insisted upon, that Congress really represents hardly anybody except lawyers, moneylenders and the 'Hindu priesthood.' "[28]

By September 5, the Home department of the government of India reported that excluding Bihar, at least 340 Indians had been killed by police fire since August 11 and 630 wounded, adding that the "true total" had to be "considerably higher."[29] Police had sustained twenty-eight deaths. Troops were called out in no less than sixty places, at most of which "they [were] still out." Some fifty-seven battalions worth of regular British army soldiers were used during that most bloody and tragic battle of World War II fought hard against their own people inside India! There was no way of accurately estimating the total number of dead and wounded in Bihar, since British aircraft repeatedly strafed civilians with machine gun fire.

"I always dread a dishonourable settlement between the British Government and the Congress," Jinnah told the international press assembled at his house in New Delhi on September 13. Asked if there was chance of any modification of his party's demand, Jinnah replied: "If you start by asking for sixteen annas [a full rupee's worth!], there is room for bargaining. The Muslim League has never put forward any demand which can by any reasonable man be characterised as unreasonable. The Muslim League stands for independence for the Hindus and for the Mussalmans. Hindu India has got three-fourths of India in its pocket and it is Hindu India which is bargaining to see if it can get the remaining one-fourth for itself and diddle us out of it."[30]

U.S. public pressure, urging Britain to "do something" for India, mounted as the war progressed and American arms, men, and money played an ever greater role in shoring up Allied defenses preparing the launching pads from which to recapture Western Europe and China as well as Southeast Asia. "Harry Hopkins spoke to me last night about this strong pressure now being exerted on the President," Halifax warned Eden, "The Cabinet should realise how strongly public opinion is moving on these lines and I hope it may be possible to say or do something to counteract it. Otherwise I fear American press, which on the whole has stood by us remarkably well in recent Indian crisis, will rapidly and perhaps completely change its attitude much to the detriment of Anglo-American relations."[31]

"What have we to be ashamed of in our Government of India?" Churchill asked Amery at a London garden party that September. "Why should we be apologetic or say that we are prepared to go out at the instance of some jackanapes? . . . For eighty years we have given it peace and internal security and prosperity such as has never been known in the history of that country. . . . We have looked after all classes, and we have protected the interests of all sections, and I am not going to be a party to a policy of scuttle."[32]

Churchill and his cabinet were most concerned about the rapidly mounting sterling balance debt that Britain owed India as a result of wartime production and accelerated export of Indian goods to all fronts. Till this war, India had always been indebted to Britain for rail, telegraph, and other major public works construction schemes that had cost millions in sterling. With half a million Indian troops serving overseas, and Indian industries pouring out every variety of products for the war, the balance was reversed, Great Britain finding itself in sterling bondage to her own colony for an estimated £400 million. Churchill insisted that something must be done quickly to wipe the slate clean, arguing "As Arthur Balfour used to say 'This is a singularly ill-contrived world but not so ill-contrived as that.' "[33] Amery and Linlithgow preferred to "let sleeping dogs lie," knowing what a deafening din of commercial and industrial Indian protest would be raised over any British initiative at this point to change the formula of Indo-British payments now that the balance had tipped in India's favor.

In October of 1942, C. R. unveiled his plan for "resolving" India's deadlock, suggesting "that the Viceroy should act as the Crown would in a crisis in England" and select the "most popular and most responsible" leaders of India to assist him in running what would, in effect, be a "national government."[34] Five "important Congressmen" (including any currently in prison) should first be chosen, and then Jinnah could be invited "to join this Government with as many men of his choice" as he "liked." There might, additionally, be three others to represent the lesser minorities. C. R. believed that neither Congress nor the League could reject his plan without "losing their leadership." Jinnah, however, immediately categorized it with a number of other "kite-flying" schemes and dismissed them all.

Jinnah addressed his party's council in New Delhi on November 9 and warned them of "propaganda to misrepresent the Muslim League . . . as allies of British imperialism in India, obstructing the path of its freedom and independence," which was, he claimed, currently circulating in the United States. "To those who have been correctly following the trend of events in India this allegation about obstructing the path of freedom is not only disgraceful but untruthful," he insisted, adding, "In these days the vicious methods of propaganda are capable of misleading even intelligent people."[35] He knew all the hazards, felt the pressures, and was keenly conscious of the passage of time, adding, "The sands are running out." And two days later, after C. R. and Jinnah had met, Linlithgow, whose twice extended term as viceroy then also had a terminal date of April 1943, wired home to report that Jinnah had conceded nothing, leaving C. R. "rather depressed."

Cripps found himself left with so little influence in Churchill's War Cabinet that he resigned on November 22. He remained till the war's end as minister of aircraft production but would not really return to India's political stage until Attlee came to power. Attlee was Amery's choice to replace Linlithgow; Amery urged Churchill in mid-November to ship his Labour deputy premier to New Delhi, since "He knows the Indian problem and has no sentimental illusions as to any dramatic short cut to its solution."[36] Had Churchill accepted Amery's advice, Attlee's rising domestic star might have followed Cripps's into India's ocean deep, but Churchill obviously mistrusted even the most conservative of Labour leaders too much for any direct imperial responsibility, fearing they were all determined to "scuttle" India. None of his own party colleagues wanted the job. He finally decided to press Linlithgow to stay on half a year longer than his promised April release.

Late in 1942, Linlithgow received what he called a "quite definitely reliable" secret report of a "recent talk with Jinnah," which he passed on to Amery as the "clearest exposition" of Jinnah's views on the "Pakistan issue."[37] Jinnah had insisted he would join an interim government only "on an equal footing" with Hindus, since he viewed that "line" as "the only way in which he could safeguard Pakistan. To accept responsibility in a provisional government on any other terms would be to walk into the trap which Congress and Hindus generally were carefully laying for the unwary or impatient Muslims. It was a deep game; and he, at least, was not prepared to play. The present was a time when Muslims were faced with a 'life and death problem.' He did not say that in an oratorical sense; he meant it lit-

erally. Muslims must either choose to assert themselves and win for themselves a place in the comity of nations or go under and accept a position of
permanent inferiority. It was for them to say what they wanted. If the former,
he was prepared to fight for them till the last; if the latter, he was willing to
'take leave and concern himself with making money at the bar.' "[38]

The U.S. victory at Guadalcanal coming so soon after Rommel's defeat
in North Africa raised Allied spirits the world over, especially in Whitehall
where Amery found "nothing but cheerful faces," predicting that "India
should be entering upon 1943 in much better mood than she began in
1942."[39] But not so in Bengal. Twin specters of Japanese invasion and
famine outdid one another in striking terror among Bengal's population.
"Chittagong is receiving daily attention from enemy airmen," Ispahani reported.

> The food position in the province is growing more and more serious
> each day. In some areas, it is most acute. . . . Tens of thousands
> have died and millions have been rendered homeless and are starv-
> ing. The disaster is really terrible. . . . The Japs have been over-
> loving of late. They have visited us four times. . . . Half of Calcutta
> is on the run.[40]

It was only the start of India's worst famine of the century, a tragedy that
claimed between two and three million Bengali lives during the forthcoming year.

"Government goaded the people to the point of madness," Gandhi
charged, writing from detention to Linlithgow in January 1943. "They
started leonine violence in the shape of the arrests. . . . I must resort to
the law prescribed for satyagrahis, namely, a fast according to capacity. I
must commence after the early morning breakfast of the 9th February . . .
ending on the morning of the 2nd March."[41] Linlithgow wired Amery, soon
after receiving the Mahatma's letter, "I have never wavered that Gandhi,
if he desired to do so, should be allowed on his own responsibility to starve
to death."[42] When Linlithgow informed his council in early February of
Gandhi's intention to fast, he was amazed to find them "unanimously favouring" his release as soon as the fast began. So the government of India
decided to offer to release Gandhi for the duration of his proposed fast,
rather than to risk having him die in detention. Linlithgow wired this decision home. Amery responded how "greatly disturbed" the War Cabinet felt
at the thought of releasing Gandhi "on a mere threat to fast."[43]

An emergency War Cabinet meeting was held on the next Sunday at
which Amery reported:

Winston . . . launched out on the Gandhi subject at once. At first
. . . muttering away his dissatisfaction, but giving me the impression that he was going to agree with a shrug of the shoulder. Presently, however, he warmed up and worked himself into one of his
states of indignation over India. I made efforts to try and bring him
to the point that whatever might or might not be the best method of
handling so peculiar a situation as the Gandhi one, the issue was not
that, but whether you were to override your Council and run the risk
of resignations. That point he simply brushed aside by saying that it
would not matter if they did all resign: we could carry on just as
well without them and this our hour of triumph everywhere in the
world was not the time to crawl before a miserable little old man
who had always been our enemy.[44]

But Gandhi had already been informed of the government of India's offer
to release him and politely refused. "I shall be quite content to take my fast
as a detenu or prisoner," replied the "little old man" on the eve of his
ordeal. "The impending fast has not been conceived to be taken as a free
man."[45] The viceroy heaved a sigh of great relief.

Jinnah felt as adamant about Gandhi's fast as Churchill, telephoning
Ispahani to urge him to keep Bengal's wavering Muslim League members
of the legislature from backing a resolution appealing to the government
for the Mahatma's release. After the first week of Gandhi's fast, Linlithgow
was pleased to report that "Muslims continue to stand apart, and Jinnah's
paper *Dawn* to ridicule and criticise. . . . *Dawn's* leader today is critical
of Gandhi's suggestion in his letter to me of 29th January that he was ready
to see Jinnah form a national government, which is equivalent, it suggests,
to 'a tenancy-at-will as a favour.' "[46]

The League remained aloof from the mounting waves of protest and
unrest throughout India triggered by Gandhi's fast. In New Delhi's legislature, Liaquat Ali Khan reiterated the Muslim League's non-aligned position.
"We have every sympathy for the sentimental concern of our Hindu
friends," said the man who was to be Pakistan's first prime minister. "But
we are unable to join them in this matter."[47] Jinnah was invited by Sapru
to a conference of prominent leaders in New Delhi to discuss the "situation
arising out of Gandhi's fast," but he declined, noting as Linlithgow was delighted to report, that "the situation is really a matter for the Hindu leaders
to consider."[48]

Three British doctors, including the surgeon-general, who observed the
Mahatma, predicted that he would probably not survive another week of
his self-imposed ordeal. Serious signs of organic deterioration were noted,

and with the old man's arteriosclerosis, the doctors expected a heart attack at any moment. Three members of the viceroy's executive council resigned on February 17, 1943, in protest over the viceroy's decision not to release Gandhi "unconditionally, even when danger to his life accrued from the fast."[49] Linlithgow accepted those resignations and found at least three other Indian members of his council "wobbly" but managed to convince them to "stay the course." The viceroy alerted all the governors of the imminent possibility of Gandhi's death, the code word for which was "Rubicon," warning them that "considering Gandhi's position as our prisoner and a declared rebel, there can be no question of half-masting flags or sending official messages of condolence to his widow."[50]

A bulletin signed by six of Gandhi's doctors on February 21 warned that he had "entered a crisis . . . was seized with severe nausea and almost fainted and pulse became nearly imperceptible."[51] Much to every one's amazement, however, the little old man did not die. His stamina surprised the world and delighted his anxious friends, who attributed his survival to divine intervention. Churchill, however, suspected "fraud" and urged Linlithgow to "expose all these Congress Hindu doctors round him" who could so easily "slip glucose or other nourishment into his food."[52] (Churchill himself was just recovering from pneumonia and felt particularly nasty toward Gandhi.) Much as he searched for it, though, Linlithgow could not discover "any firm evidence of fraud" in any of the medical reports issued by Gandhi's physicians, nor in any treatment of that most famous of Indian patients.

Then on the morning of March 3 Gandhi broke his fast. His weight had fallen from 109 to 90 pounds, but the next day Lumley reported from Bombay that "everything is now normal."[53]

Meanwhile Fazlul Haq of Bengal remained Jinnah's worst personnel problem, for as long as he continued presiding over a non-League coalition in that Muslim majority province, he appeared to belie the basic premise of Pakistan. Bengal's foxy premier adroitly survived at the head of a coalition of his own Progressive Muslim League, shifting Mahasabha, Congress, and Forward Bloc members. For sixteen months Haq retained popularity as well as power despite having been ousted from the League. He finally sought reconciliation with Jinnah late in 1942 by going to the Quaid-i-Azam's house in New Delhi in November. But Jinnah's position never altered. He order Fazlul Haq first of all to resign his premiership, then to disband his own Muslim party and pledge allegiance to the Muslim League as prerequisites to readmission to its fold. On February 5, 1943, Haq wrote Jinnah:

I am going to sacrifice all, that I now possess, for the sake of my country and of the solidarity of my community. . . . I have thought carefully over the situation and with a view to facilitate my coming back to the League, I am ready to tender my resignation which will mean the automatic dissolution of the Progressive Coalition Party. May I now get a line from you to tell me that I have understood you alright, and that the ban put on me will be lifted as soon as I tender resignation of my office as Premier? If so, I will take my step I have indicated.[54]

Jinnah reminded Haq that he had heard that promise before, the last November in fact, when Haq had "agreed to carry out these conditions within a fortnight."[55] Ispahani and his friends kept up pressure against Haq's coalition within Calcutta's assembly, which, together with the Japanese pressure mounting from outside shook popular confidence everywhere in Bengal against a government that appeared both incapable of defending its people or feeding them. By mid-March Fazlul Haq phoned Jinnah in Ispahani's presence, trying to clarify his prospects of re-emerging as Bengal's premier if, indeed, he resigned and rejoined the League. After speaking with Haq, Jinnah privately assured Ispahani "that he could not possibly have Mr. Fazlul Haq as leader of the Muslim League in the Legislature."[56]

Fazlul Haq obviously sensed that if he resigned his days of power were over, so he turned elsewhere, desperately working round the clock to shore up support as his forces broke ranks. In the last week of March, however, he survived a no-confidence vote on the "food question" by one vote due to the absence of three Muslim League members. Three days later, Ispahani wired from Calcutta jubilantly to report that "Fazlul Haq has been routed."[57] The League captured six seats contested against Haq's Progressives. Muslims were "crossing the floor" daily to join the once depleted ranks of the Muslim League. "Four Muslims will cross the floor this afternoon," wrote Ispahani. "We are expecting another two to come over by tonight. Inshallah, our wound of having the majority of the Muslim MLAs sitting opposite us, will soon be healed. . . . Fazlul Haq looks a picture of misery."[58] And on March 29, Fazlul Haq's ministry fell; the following month Khwaja Nazimuddin, the leader of Bengal's Muslim League, was invited to form a new government.

That April the League held its annual session in New Delhi. A map of Pakistan adorned the dais, and a banner flew over it reading "Freedom of India lies in Pakistan." Jinnah wore a white sherwani with a gold button engraved with "P" pinned to his starched collar. He was greeted with "tremendous ovation and cheering" as he entered the packed pandal.[59] With his League ministries now running Bengal, the Punjab, Sind, and Assam, Jinnah insisted, "This is only the starting point. . . . In the North-West Frontier Province . . . my information is—and it is based on very reliable sources . . . the Muslim public is entirely with the Muslim League. [That summer a League Ministry under Aurangzeb Khan would come to power in Peshawar.] Don't forget the Minority Provinces. It is they who have spread the light when there was darkness in the majority Provinces. It is they who were the spearheads that the Congress wanted to crush. . . . We have got a great deal to do. . . . Our goal is clear; our demands are clear."[60]

Jinnah then reviewed the history of Hindu-Muslim conflicts from the dawn of the century, after which he indulged in a blistering attack upon Gandhi and his tactics, accusing the Mahatma of wanting to turn the whole of India into his Hindu ashram. He went so far as to suggest a new summit with Gandhi, however, arguing: "Nobody would welcome it more than myself, if Mr. Gandhi is even now really willing to come to a settlement with the Muslim League on the basis of Pakistan. Let me tell you that it will be the greatest day for both Hindus and Musalmans. If he has made up his mind, what is there to prevent Mr. Gandhi from writing direct to me?"[61]

"Jinnah's speeches both in the meetings of the Working Committee and the Subjects Committee (held *in camera*) and in the Open Session have confirmed impressions that of late his mind has been passing through a certain process of change," reported a British spy attending all the League sessions. "He [Jinnah] has become more aggressive, more challenging and more authoritative. The reason appears to be consciousness of power lately acquired and of certain old injuries which can now be avenged therewith."

> He has finally warned the British; he has expressed his profound dissatisfaction with their attitude; he has urged Provincial Leagues now to place themselves on a war footing in preparation for what is to come; he has castigated the Capitalists and pampered the masses (on whose sympathy and goodwill he has to base his future struggle) by his references to "social justice" and "economic reorganisation"; he has tried to impress upon the Provincial Premiers the fact that their own future lies only in following his lead and above all he has, in order to show his *bona fides* to the neutral world, extended an open and almost final invitation to the Congress to approach him for a settlement if it so desires. Inevitably the next stage will be "preparation for the inevitable struggle" and after that the "struggle" itself.[62]

Jinnah's shrewd appreciation of Indian politics and the ever-shifting interaction among its major parties had never been more clearly revealed. His greatly overrated estimate of British postwar power, however, reflected his far less sophisticated appreciation of U.S., Russian, and Chinese potential for more rapid expansion. Anticipating that the war could last "another three years," Jinnah wisely urged his followers to "put our house in order" during that interlude. Ingenious strategist that he was, he concluded with this warning: "The fight being inevitable, we must make our preparations flawless."[63]

Nor was this shrewdest of India's politicians unaware of how carefully his words were recorded, copied, and cabled the world over, to help trouble the sleep of officials in Great Britain's highest echelons of power. Openly, before the mass audience that listened to his presidential address at Delhi, Jinnah said:

If they have got any honest and capable agents they ought to be kept informed in London. I once more draw the attention of the British Government to this fact. It is a very serious situation indeed, and I inform them from this platform that the cup of bitterness, and disappointment—not to use any stronger language—at the shabby treatment meted out to Muslim India is a danger to them. . . . The Muslim League calls upon the British Government to come forward, without any further delay, with an unequivocal declaration guaranteeing to the Musalmans the right of self-determination, and to pledge themselves that they will abide by the verdict of a plebiscite on the lines of the resolution passed at the Muslim League Session in Lahore in 1940.

I say to the Musalmans . . . 100 million Musalmans are with us. When I say 100 million Musalmans, I mean that 99 per cent of them are with us, leaving aside some who are traitors, cranks, supermen or lunatics—an evil from which no society or nation is free. The way in which I see them now is that the phoenix-like rise and regeneration of Muslim India from the very ashes of its ruination . . . is a miracle. The people who had lost everything and who were placed by providence between the two stones of a mill, not only came into their own in a very short time, but became, after the British, socially the most solid, militarily the most virile, and politically the most decisive factor in modern India. Now it is time to take up the constructive programme to build up this nation so that it can march on the path of our goal of Pakistan. . . . The goal is near, stand united, persevere and march forward.[64]

Even before he ended his address, loud and prolonged cheers and cries of "Quaid-i-Azam Zindabad!" "Pakistan Zindabad!" "Muslim League Zindabad!" reverberated from thousands of throats that would carry his message to millions of Muslims beyond range of Jinnah's frail voice. Soon they would all close ranks behind their great leader in the pain-filled march to their Promised Land.

15

Karachi and Bombay Revisited
(1943-44)

Jinnah's challenge to Gandhi in April elicited a letter from the Mahatma, who read the challenge in the *Dawn* early in May. "Dear Qaid-e-Azam, I welcome your suggestion. I suggest our meeting face to face rather than talking through correspondence. . . . But I am in your hands. I hope that this letter will be sent to you and, if you agree to my proposal, that the Government will let you visit me."[1]

Linlithgow's immediate response was to "raise no objection if Jinnah wants to see Gandhi in jail," noting with good reason, "I doubt the Mahatma's move being wholly palatable to Jinnah."[2] Amery was less willing to acquiesce, however, reminding the viceroy that he had refused to permit others, including C. R., to visit Gandhi.

> Although Jinnah is a different case in some respects, refusal has hitherto been based on Gandhi's past behavior and if we once abandon principle that he is kept incommunicado because of his responsibility for rebellion and must remain so until he disassociates himself from that policy, I feel that we may be driven out of our whole position, which is of course Gandhi's object.[3]

Both were loath, moreover, to deliver Gandhi's letter to Jinnah. The matter was to be decided by the cabinet, but Churchill had just sailed off to Washington on the *Queen Mary* with Wavell for an Anglo-U.S. joint chiefs conference code-named "Trident" to coordinate operations against Germany, Italy, and Japan. It was during this trip that Churchill felt he got to know Wavell well enough to believe he was the sort of man to replace Linlithgow.

Precisely how much time the entire British War Cabinet devoted to this

222

single undelivered letter is incalculable, but the secretary of state prepared an elaborate memorandum on the subject which was circulated to the cabinet prior to its first meeting on the question of "Gandhi's request to see Jinnah" on May 18, 1943. A second meeting, also chaired by Attlee in Churchill's absence, was held on the same subject next day. Churchill, of course, remained in telegraphic touch with Amery throughout the whole debate on this vital matter. The secretary of state officially wired a "most immediate" cable to the viceroy after the second meeting, ordering that "Gandhi's letter should not go forward."[4] The ball continued electronically to bounce around the globe over the next week, with Amery even going so far as to wire the man Great Britain considered wise enough to serve as India's viceroy: "It has been suggested to me that possibly situation might be eased if you invited Jinnah to come and see you."[5]

Jinnah during this interval focused his time and energies on the strategy of seeking to make his League more effective and responsive to popular demands and needs in the provinces it ran. "The 'Pakistan' slogan is gaining momentum," reported the Punjab's governor toward the end of May. "There has been a considerable amount of discussion in the Press as to whether Jinnah was justified in suggesting [in Delhi in April] that the Punjab Cabinet is a League Ministry. The Nawab of Mamdot [Punjabi leader of the Muslim League] has sought to improve the occasion by a Press statement that the Sikander-Jinnah Pact has come to an end, the implication being that more active interference by the Muslim League in Punjab politics is to be expected."[6] Sikander's death in December of 1942 had left his Unionist party ministry under the control of a much younger, less experienced Muslim leader, Khizar Hyat Khan Tiwana (1900–75). By early June "Hindu indignation with Jinnah" was reported by Linlithgow as "greater than ever. Jinnah himself is well pleased, so far as one can judge, and there is no question that he has sent his stock up still higher."[7] In his most frank assessment of Jinnah, Linlithgow remarked:

I do not however think he wants a row with Government . . . and his threats do not cause me any sleepless nights! As I have consistently felt and said both to Zetland and to you, Jinnah would be quite as bad a master as Gandhi. But Jinnah is not in as strong a position as Gandhi and Congress, and he is never likely to be, in the near future, since he represents a minority, and a minority that can only effectively hold its own with our assistance. Nor, of course, is his organisation anything like as deeprooted as is that of Congress.[8]

His curse is personal vanity which at his age he is not likely to shake off.[9]

Churchill recommended Field Marshal Wavell to his cabinet in mid-June 1943 as India's next viceroy. General Sir Claude Auchinleck, who had followed Wavell in the Middle East command, was to succeed him as commander-in-chief of India. Labour ministers viewed Wavell as a "safe" or "stopgap" viceroy at a time when India needed creative intelligence, diplomatic skill, and imagination. Churchill's top priority, however, was to hold India militarily at any cost. As Simla's commander-in-chief for the past year and a half, Archie Wavell had proved himself the good soldier, strong and silent.

The one thing King George VI "complained" about to Wavell at a Buckingham Palace lunch was the "length of the Viceroy's telegrams," urging the viceroy-designate to "keep them shorter" than Linlithgow's.[10] Before flying from London to take over in India, Wavell attended several cabinet meetings focused on Indian problems, especially those dealing with England's mounting war debt, which by mid-1943 climbed to over £800 million. Wavell soon recognized, as he noted in his *Diary*, that Churchill "hates India and everything to do with it" and came to appreciate the wisdom of Amery's remark to him that "Winston . . . 'knows as much of the Indian problem as George III did of the American colonies.' "[11] Churchill, of course, instructed Wavell to stay away from political reforms of any sort, warning that "only over his dead body would any approach to Gandhi take place."[12]

Jinnah visited Baluchistan in July and addressed the League's third provincial conference "at the foot of a hill in a tastefully decorated pandal . . . which included all the notables of the city numbered about 25,000."[13] The Quaid-i-Azam "exhorted the Muslims of Baluchistan to shake off their lethargy and march in line with their nation." He urged them to "Give up your mutual jealousies and sectional interests and differences over small things, petty quarrels and tribal notions." The following day he addressed the same conference after it had passed all the resolutions he advocated. Jinnah reiterated his pre-battle plan for Pakistan, seeking first to lay the foundation of reforms and growth, later to press his separatist demands. To the students in his audience he cautioned conservatively, "Do not run after cheap slogans or catchwords. Concentrate your whole attention on education. Get equipped and qualify yourself for action. . . . The better you are equipped the brighter are your chances of success."[14]

Even as Jinnah was speaking on the bleak but well-fed Western border of British India, famine darkened the dismal plains of East Bengal. "We cannot keep Bengal fed (certainly we cannot assume the responsibility of rationing in Calcutta or elsewhere) unless we can get foodgrains into Bengal from outside at once,"[15] Governor John A. Herbert warned the viceroy in July. *"I wonder how far he is right about the Bengal situation,"* Linlithgow noted in that letter's margin. The viceroy remained, however, less preoccupied with the terrible Bengal famine, which had by then claimed over a million lives, than with his own fantasy fears of a fast-unto-death that Gandhi might launch in August.

Jinnah returned to Bombay from his tour of Baluchistan on Friday, July 23. Three days later, on the afternoon of Monday, July 26, a fanatical young Muslim Khaksar from Lahore, Rafiq Sabir Mazangavi, entered the Quaid-i-Azam's Mount Pleasant Road house and appealed to Jinnah's secretary, Mr. M. H. Saiyid, for an interview with the great leader. Just then Jinnah entered his secretary's office and asked who Rafiq was and what he wanted. "I was very busy," Jinnah testified later in Bombay's high court.

> My whole mind was on my correspondence and I was trying to get out of the room. Just as I was about to leave the room, in the twinkling of an eye, the accused sprang on me and gave me a blow with his clenched fist on my left jaw. I naturally reeled back a bit when he pulled out a knife from his waist. . . . It was an open knife. . . . Instinct of self-defence made me put out my hand and catch his wrist, with the result that the momentum of the blow was broken but in spite of this the knife just touched the left side of my jaw. I got a cut near my chin and my coat was cut near the left-shoulder. . . . I also got a wound on my left finger.[16]

Jinnah's watchman helped his secretary disarm the would-be assassin, shortly after which police arrived.

The accused defended himself in court, reporting that he had belonged to the Muslim League in Lahore from 1935–39 but had finally resigned because "the League was not doing anything for the Muslims or for humanity except talking."[17] He insisted that he had gone to appeal to Jinnah for work and help, not to assassinate him, but was found guilty as charged of "attempted murder and hurt" and sentenced to five years in jail. Sub-inspector Abdul Kadir Sheikh, who had been put in charge of the investigation, came to admire Jinnah so much in its aftermath that he opted to join him in Pakistan. The question of conspiracy was closely studied, but no evidence of accomplices was ever clearly established. Though shaken by the violent attack and rather weakened by loss of blood, Jinnah survived the ordeal with no diminution of spirit or stamina. "Don't worry," he wired close friends like Ispahani. "Thank God I am all right."[18] His miraculous escape from serious harm was viewed by many followers as evidence of divine intervention. Muslim India celebrated "A Day of Thanksgiving to God for sparing the most precious life of the Sub-continent."[19] Jinnah publicly appealed to friends and disciples to "remain calm and cool."

Lord Wavell's "secret" assessment of Jinnah in mid-September 1943 was that "It is hardly too much to say that Jinnah is the Muslim League. He is a vain, shallow and ambitious man who would probably think the present time inopportune for any rapprochement with the Hindus."[20] The new viceroy's opinion of Gandhi was not much better. "Gandhi and Jinnah are both dictators. . . . Gandhi because he has built himself up as a saint, and Jinnah because there is nobody in his party who approaches him in ability." Wavell viewed Pakistan as a "serious plan" but noted that "nobody" was "at all definite" about its boundaries. Jinnah held an "inconclusive" series of summit talks with Khizar Tiwana in Simla at this time, which the Punjab's chief minister recounted to his governor as "a series of lectures from Jinnah about the services that he had rendered to mankind."[21]

Ispahani urged Jinnah to come to Calcutta at that time to hold a League council meeting there, feeling Nazimuddin was too weak to counter Hindu Mahasabha attacks against the League ministry, which was, of course, blamed in part for the famine tragedy. "Propaganda and action do not seem to come within the programme of the Ministry," Ispahani moaned. "Our Johnnies have not the guts. . . . It is necessary that . . . you put matters right in Bengal before conditions worsen . . . it is for you, Sir, to please come here . . . and set the house in order."[22] Jinnah dared not risk so arduous and potentially dangerous a trip, however, returning from Simla to Bombay, where he issued a statement on the Bengal famine in late October, insisting that

> the present Ministry working under the present constitution with its limitations cannot be saddled with the responsibility, and further they only came into power after the terrible crisis had overwhelmed Bengal. I am assured that they are doing their very best. But the fact remains that thousands are dying, and I earnestly appeal to His Excellency the Viceroy Lord Wavell to leave no stone unturned and give immediate help and relief to the people of Bengal with all the resources that the Government of India can command. Similarly I appeal to Mr. Churchill. . . . This muddle, whoever is responsible for it, is the greatest blot on the British administration in this country, and it must be wiped off without delay.[23]

Jinnah addressed his Working Committee council in Delhi in mid-November, insisting that "The constitution of the Muslim League is the most democratic that could be framed. There is no Muslim to whom the doors of the Muslim League are not open. If the Musalmans are dissatisfied with the leader, surely the remedy lies in their hand. They can remove him if they so desire by exercising their rights under the constitution of the party, but if they try to settle things by force and violence, nothing but blood-shed would ensue."[24] He was sensitive to the sort of barbed criticism that Khaksars and other Punjabis as well as Bengalis, including chief ministers, often aimed at him. He defended Nazimuddin's ministry in Bengal as a "fire-brigade" called too late to put out the raging famine, yet doing its best to diminish the damage. Three days later he rose to speak on the "food situation" in Delhi's legislative assembly and reprimanded Sir Henry Richardson, the leader of the European party for saying it was "no use" in indulging in "recriminations" against Government for the Bengal disaster.

> Do you call this recrimination when the Government in charge of the country are called upon to explain their conduct, and that we are entitled to examine whether they have discharged their duty and responsibility? Who is the real thief has to be found out. Surely the Government of the country is responsible for the safety of the lives of the people, and that is a fact which nobody can deny. . . . Supposing in England a few hundred people had died or were dying every week of starvation, let alone a few thousands, would Churchill's Government be able to stand . . . for 24 hours? And here we are calmly and coolly told about not indulging in recrimination. . . . It is our misfortune that we are living under a system of Government which is irremovable and irresponsible and, I would add, thoroughly incompetent to handle any big issue.[25]

It was Jinnah's most vitriolic attack against the British government since the post–World War I passage of the Rowlatt acts. Not only were Bengali Muslims dying by the tens and hundreds of thousands, but Muslim League ministries in the Punjab as well as Bengal were being widely blamed for profitting from the famine.

Some 10,000 Muslim delegates gathered in Karachi to attend the thirty-first session of the Muslim League that December. When Jinnah entered the brilliantly lighted tent, he was greeted with thunderous shouts of "Quaid-i-Azam Zindabad" and "Conqueror of Congress Zindabad." He began to speak at 10:50 P.M. on the eve of his sixty-seventh birthday and continued extempore for 100 minutes in English. He was forced to stop "four or five times" by his racking tubercular cough, euphemistically described as "a touch of cold" in the League's official report of that historic address.[26] "Remember the position of Muslim India," Jinnah told his rapt audience. "When a man is sick and almost dying, he has not got the energy either to complain or to ask for anything. . . . That was the condition of Muslim India seven years ago; but to-day, the sick man has recovered from his deathbed. He has acquired consciousness. He is not only convalescent but he is in a position to move about. Now he has got so many suggestions and proposals to make, so many disputes and so many quarrels to settle. It is a good sign, provided it is kept within limits."[27] Jinnah appears at this point to have forgotten he was talking about "Muslim India" as the "sick man" and to have lapsed into a personal reverie: "I get some suggestions which are splendid ones and thoughtful ones and very good, too. I get complaints and petty quarrels, which I do not like. But anyhow it is a healthy sign. In one word, let me put it to you this way. I am thankful to God that Muslim India is awake—I am thankful that Muslim India has regained consciousness. I am thankful that Muslim India is taking interest in things around it, not only in India, but throughout the world."[28]

Jinnah then announced his appointment of a three-man (Liaquat Ali Khan, Khaliquzzaman, and Hussain Imam) parliamentary board as the final arbiter of the League's nationwide candidates for election. He also proposed establishing a new Committee of Action, to be chaired by Nawab Ismail Khan and "convened" by Liaquat Ali, to foster educational, economic, and social planning for Pakistan. This committee was to include the Nawab of Mamdot, G. M. Syed, Haji Sathar Sait, and Qazi M. Isa; and they were all formally appointed by Jinnah on December 27, 1943. After the address ended, Liaquat Ali Khan rose to congratulate Jinnah on his birthday. Quaid-i-Azam and his sister returned to the packed pandal that night for the League's second sitting, "escorted by two bodyguards with drawn swords." Grey uniformed League national guards followed Jinnah everywhere after the attempt on his life and kept close watch over the crowd in attendance. An estimated 2,000 of these League guards, sometimes called Jinnah's "private army" and led by Nawab Siddiq Ali Khan of the Central Provinces, marched round Karachi. Nazimuddin had arrived from Calcutta during the day and joined Khizar and the premiers of Sind, Assam, and the North-West Frontier on stage behind the Quaid-i-Azam, whose glittering silver throne stood apart in front of all other seats on the dais. The frontier premier, Sardar Aurangzeb Khan, prophesied that "The day of reckoning is coming, and when the call from Mr. Jinnah comes to us to get out and fight for Pakistan, we shall not falter."

The strain of his long address in Karachi left Jinnah "prostrate on his bed, gasping for breath. Fortunately," Fatima recalled, "he had the ability to sleep at will. A good night's rest gave him enough energy to cope with the daily crop of letters, requests and important problems for which solutions had to be found. He kept up this tempo . . . in spite of recurring fever which emaciated his body."[29] Jinnah answered most letters requesting his presence in distant corners of the country, like one from Malabar, by explaining "how difficult it is for me to go on touring owing to enormous pressure of work and, therefore, it is not possible for me to make any commitment which I may not be able to fulfill."[30] By minimizing public appearances, while seeing to it that all his statements received maximum press amplification, Jinnah continued to function, presenting a relatively vigorous façade to the world, or else enveloping himself in a cloak of such total isolation that it enhanced his charismatic image by adding auras of mystery and perpetual "pressure of work" to his persona. He had mastered "modern" management techniques of delegating responsibility to trusted lieutenants more brilliantly than any of his Indian contemporaries.

By February 1944 Jinnah was back in Bombay. He urged the Muslim Students' Federation to erect "pillars" of "hard work, industry and perseverance" upon which the "edifice of Pakistan" could be built. He alluded "to suggestions made by some Hindu leaders that he should be made the First Premier of India," calling them mere "camouflage . . . made in order to mislead and confuse the Muslims."[31] Jinnah returned to New Delhi at the end of the month for the opening session of the assembly, where Wavell's maiden speech as viceroy stressed the "geographical unity" of India as central to its postwar constitution. Quaid-i-Azam was outraged by that formulation and viewed it as nothing less than an attempted negation of Cripps's implicit "promise" of Pakistan. He launched a fresh attack in the assembly upon the government's budget to remind Wavell of the League's powers to prevent the government from mustering a Central Legislative Assembly majority. Speaking to the Aligarh Union that month, Jinnah called the viceroy's address "provocative and thoughtless of the Muslim position," adding:

> Lord Wavell like his predecessor has started fishing in the Congress waters. Lord Linlithgow hopelessly failed, but the soldier-Viceroy thinks that he would succeed where his predecessor had failed in landing a big fish or a number of small ones sufficient for his purpose. . . . This has created deep resentment throughout Muslim India.[32]

Wavell sought advice from the governors as how best to proceed, and Sir Henry Twynam of Central Provinces wrote to warn the viceroy against antagonizing Jinnah. "I know that many hard things are said about Jinnah," Twynam noted. "But I often wonder where we should have been had not Jinnah foreseen how fatal it would be to Moslem interests to support Congress."[33] Acting governor Francis Mudie of Bihar reported Khaliquzzaman's opinion that "what Jinnah [was] playing for" was nothing less than "to get Pakistan without giving a *quid pro quo* to the Hindus. . . . Government should make an unequivocal announcement of their unconditional acceptance of Pakistan, Jinnah arguing that a plebiscite would be a waste of time and lead only to riots in the Punjab and Bengal."[34]

Wavell was puzzled by Jinnah and had no appreciation of his complex character or the force of his will or the deep wellsprings of history it drew upon for sustenance. He saw only the surface cosmopolitan appearance; he recalled only Linlithgow's piqued and petty criticism of Jinnah's vanity. "I gather that Jinnah regards me as an enemy of the Muslim League and is determined to be as much of a nuisance as he can," the viceroy confessed to his journal diary in late March. "He does not really represent solid steady Moslem opinion (in fact J. himself is hardly a Muslim) but he can sway opinion, and no one seems to have the character to oppose him."[35] The viceroy was certainly not ready to "concede Pakistan" to such a man,[36] especially while the fighting still raged along India's Eastern front and Bengal remained racked with famine.

One of the things Wavell wanted to do was to talk to Gandhi, but by this time Gandhi's health had seriously deteriorated. After his wife died that February, the Mahatma appeared to have lost any will to survive the last of his long detentions. Every doctor who examined him, British as well as Indian, urged an early release. Wavell recommended unconditional release to Amery in May, warning that "serious difficulties would result if Gandhi died in detention" and agreeing with the medical "opinions" that "Gandhi was unlikely to be an active factor in politics again."[37] This assurance helped win Churchill's approval on May 5, 1944. As soon as Gandhi was transported from the Aga Khan's Poona palace, where he had languished imprisoned to the nearby house of his "old friend" Lady Thackersey, he perked up and received many visitors. The Mahatma's swift recovery reminded Amery of what Lord Byron had written in one of his letters: " 'My mother-in-law has been dangerously ill; she is now dangerously well.' I [Amery] can only hope that that is not going to be true of our old friend Gandhi."[38] Churchill, of course, was outraged at the news of Gandhi's signs of resurrected life and feared his "naked fakir" had outfoxed him.

Within two weeks of his release Gandhi spoke of seeking talks with Jinnah, who had, however, gone to Kashmir to rest and breathe the cool, refreshing air of Srinagar after a frustrating struggle with Khizar in Lahore. Jinnah journeyed to Lahore in late April, hoping to pressure Khizar into abandoning his Unionist label; but with British support the young premier stood firm, refusing to knuckle under to the Quaid-i-Azam. Shaukat Hayat Khan (Sikander's son) was, in fact, the only member of Khizar's provincial cabinet to go along with Jinnah's demand that it proclaim itself a Muslim League, rather than Unionist administration. Khizar then managed to get

Governor Glancy to dismiss Shaukat for some "injustice which had come to light"[39] most conveniently, thus helping strengthen the Unionist Party. The Muslim League's Committee of Action voted to expel Khizar before the end of May. For the remainder of the war, the Punjab could no longer, therefore, be counted among the League's provincial administrative assets. The Jinnah-Sikander pact was finally dead. Glancy and Wavell felt quite "worried about the possible activities of the Muslim League National Guards" in the Punjab, and the viceroy wrote "we shall have to take a very firm line with Jinnah to prevent communal trouble."[40] In June, Khizar warned that Jinnah was "importing into the Punjab a number of Maulvis from the United Provinces to agitate against the Unionist Government on religious lines."[41] Khizar asked the viceroy to keep "these people out, and he would, I think, like to keep Jinnah and other prominent Muslim leaders out of the Punjab too." Wavell liked Khizar very much but recognized he was "not a strong character," and found it "odd that these big Punjab landlords should be so dominated by a down-country lawyer like Jinnah."[42] That ludicrous appraisal of Jinnah glaringly revealed the viceroy's inability to understand his nature or true power.

United Provinces governor Sir Maurice Hallett, who considered Gandhi "cunning as a cartload of monkeys," cautioned Wavell against granting the Mahatma an interview.[43] The viceroy was in no rush to see either Gandhi or Jinnah, suspecting Sir Akbar Hydari, the secretary to his civil supplies department, was correct in his opinion that "no progress was possible till both . . . were underground."[44] But a new round of Gandhi-Jinnah talks was being arranged even as these harsh words were winging toward London on invisible pulses of electric power. C. R. published a political "formula," which he insisted Gandhi was prepared to "accept," if only Jinnah agreed to it. That formula proposed a "plebiscite" for the Muslim-majority "contiguous districts in the north-west and east of India" to "decide the issue of separation from Hindustan. If the majority decide in favour of forming a sovereign State separate from Hindustan, such decision shall be given effect to, without prejudice to the right of districts on the border to choose to join either state."[45] It sounded enough like "Pakistan" to arouse considerable speculation as to the Mahatma's new position.

Jinnah was in no rush to believe C. R.'s assurances of Gandhi's "acceptance," however, and awaited direct word from his old adversary, who finally wrote (the original was in Gujarati) on July 17, 1944:

Brother Jinnah,

There was a day when I could induce you to speak in the mother-tongue. Today I take courage to write to you in the same language.

I had invited you to meet me while I was in jail. I have not written to you since my release. But today my heart says that I should write to you. We will meet whenever you choose. Don't regard me as the enemy of Islam or of the Muslims of this country. I am the friend and servant of not only yourself but of the whole world. Do not disappoint me.[46]

Jinnah replied from Srinagar on the eve of his departure from Kashmir, informing "Mr. Gandhi" that he would be "glad to receive you at my house in Bombay on my return, which will probably be about the middle of August."[47] The War Cabinet was brought into the picture on "Gandhi's recent moves" with a memo circulated by Amery to his busy colleagues. Churchill was beside himself with fury at Gandhi's vigor and the prospect of yet another viceroy "negotiating" with the little old man. Veer Savarkar, leader of the Hindu Mahasabha and the guru to Gandhi's future assassin, was equally upset at the Mahatma's latest move, warning Amery by wire: "Hindu-sabhites can never tolerate breaking up of union of India their fatherland and holyland."[48]

The Muslim League council met in Lahore on July 30, 1944; Jinnah presided and reported on the current state of political developments concerning C. R.'s "formula," and the proposed summit. He was prepared to concede nothing, to accept nothing on faith in his forthcoming meetings with his old adversary. The League's council gave him unanimous support, and Quaid-i-Azam concluded that brief meeting with the promise that "Insha' Allah, Pakistan is coming."

The talks started on September 9; Gandhi and Jinnah posed with broad smiles on the veranda of Jinnah's Malabar Hill house before they went inside for three and a quarter hours of private and secret discussion. Cautious lawyer that he was, Jinnah kept a record of their tête-à-tête. Gandhi reported his version of the first day's talk to C. R., calling the meeting "a test of my patience" and noting, "I am amazed at my own patience. However, it was a friendly talk." He then informed C. R. of Jinnah's "contempt for your Formula and his contempt for you," which Gandhi called "staggering. . . . He says you have accepted his demand and so should I. I said, 'I endorse Rajaji's Formula and you can call it Pakistan if you like.' He talked of the Lahore Resolution. . . ."[49] Gandhi also reported that Jinnah told him that if he conceded Pakistan he stood ready to "go to jail" or even "face bullets. . . . He wants Pakistan now, not after independence. 'We will have independence for Pakistan and Hindustan,' he said. 'We should come to an agreement and then go to the Government and ask them to accept it, force them to accept our solution. . . . The Muslims want Pakistan. The League represents the Muslims and it wants separation.' "[50]

Their second meeting proved no more fruitful than the first, though Gandhi reported to C. R. that Jinnah "drew a very alluring picture of the Government of Pakistan. It would be a perfect democracy."[51] Gandhi then immediately reminded Jinnah of how often he had said "democracy did not suit Indian conditions," but Jinnah insisted "that was with regard to imposed democracy." The press corps waited for Jinnah and Gandhi as they emerged from that morning session, asking "Anything for us?" Gandhi replied: "I have nothing. . . . Yesterday you read something in our faces. . . . I would like you not to read anything in our faces except hope and nothing but hope." Then he turned to ask Jinnah, "Am I right? Have you seen the papers this morning?" Jinnah's response was "Why bother."[52]

Jinnah sensed by this time the futility of the talks. He understood the Mahatma's game too well, writing curtly on September 13:

> Dear Mr. Gandhi, When you arrived here on the morning of September 12 to resume our talks you were good enough to inform me that you had not had time to attend to my letter of September 11. . . . We met again today without having received your reply, and I am still waiting for it. Please, therefore, let me have your reply as soon as possible with regard to the various points mentioned in my letter. . . . Yours sincerely, M. A. Jinnah.[53]

Gandhi answered on September 14. In that letter it was the first time he had written the word Pakistan out of quotation marks, or in any sense other than one of shock or derision, and it may have encouraged Jinnah to think he was making a positive impact on the Mahatma's mind. At any rate, Jinnah wrote a lengthy, rather cordial reply immediately that afternoon.

> Of course, I can quite understand that such a provisional interim government will represent all parties. . . . I can quite understand that when the moment arrives certain things may follow, but before we can deal with this formula in a satisfactory manner I repeat again that, as it is your formula, you should give me a rough idea of the provisional interim government that you contemplate and of your conception.[54]

Gandhi's letter to "Dear Quaid-e-Azam" the following day began by stating: "For the moment I have shunted the Rajaji Formula and with your assistance am applying my mind very seriously to the famous Lahore Resolution of the Muslim League." Then he went on to pick that Lahore resolution apart, arguing "the Resolution itself makes no reference to the two nations theory," which was, in any event "wholly unreal. I find no parallel in history for a body of converts and their descendants claiming to be a nation apart from the parent stock. If India was one nation before the advent of Islam, it must remain one in spite of the change of faith of a very large body of her children."[55] So much then for the Mahatma's readiness to "recognize" Pakistan—it had lasted just one day. Gandhi's true feelings about that "absurd" idea now came pouring forth, and their acidic impact on Jinnah's momentary hope of reaching a settlement may well be imagined.

"It is my duty to explain the Lahore resolution to you today and persuade you to accept it," Jinnah replied two days later. "I have successfully converted non-Muslim Indians in no small number and also a large body of foreigners, and if I can convert you, exercising as you do tremendous influence over Hindu India, it will be no small assistance to me." Jinnah noted, however, that much of Gandhi's letter was "a disquisition" rather than genuine "seeking clarification" and recommended to Gandhi a number of books, including one written by the Untouchable leader Dr. B. R. Ambedkar. "We maintain and hold that Muslims and Hindus are two major nations by any definition or test of a nation," Jinnah said, reiterating the arguments he had made in 1940 in his Lahore presidential address to the League. He then concluded, "By all canons of international law we are a nation. . . . As regards your final paragraph . . . it is quite clear that you represent nobody else but Hindus. . . . I am convinced that the true welfare not only of Muslims but of the rest of India lies in the division of India as proposed in the Lahore resolution. It is for you to consider whether it is not your policy and programme in which you have persisted that has been the principal factor of the 'ruin of the whole of India' and of misery and degradation of the people to which you refer and which I deplore no less than anyone else."[56]

They met again the next day, but the much-touted talks had brought them no closer. Nothing was resolved, and no formula bridged the ever-widening gulf between them. "The more I think about the two-nation theory the more alarming it appears to be," wrote the Mahatma to his "Dear Quaid-e-Azam." Gandhi feared that "Once the principle is admitted there would be no limit to claims for cutting up India into numerous divisions, which would spell India's ruin."[57] Rahmat Ali, who had first publicized Pakistan, was by then advocating no less than ten separate "nations" within the continent of "All-Dinia" as he called India and its oceanic "dependencies." Rahmat Ali's latest pamphlet, "The Millat and Her Ten Nations" was published from his All-*Dinia Milli* ("Religious Nations") Movement headquarters at 16 Montague Road in Cambridge on June 10, 1944, and reissued March 12, 1946.[58] Rahmat Ali's feverish brain conceived of such "nations" as *Siddiqistan, Faruqistan, Haideristan, Muinistan,* and *Maplistan,* which would respectively represent the Muslims of Central India, Bihar and Orissa, Hindustan, Rajistan, and Southern India.

Jinnah had nothing to do with Rahmat Ali or his proliferating plans for "Pakasia," yet many leaders of Congress besides Gandhi feared that mere acceptance of the two-nation theory might give credence to such ten-nation madness. Id fell on September 23 in 1944 and the "summit" was all but over. "In deference to your wishes," Jinnah wrote Gandhi that holiday, "I made every effort all these days, and in the course of our prolonged talks and correspondence, to convert you, but unfortunately it seems I have failed."[59] Gandhi agreed. Still he asked Jinnah to "give me in writing" what precisely "you would want me to put my signature to."

"It is not a case of your being asked to put your signature as representing anybody till you clothe yourself with representative capacity and are vested with authority," Jinnah wrote back the same day. "We stand by, as I have already said, the basis and fundamental principles embodied in the Lahore resolution of March 1940. I appeal to you once more to revise your policy and programme, as the future of this subcontinent and the welfare of the peoples of India demand that you should face realities."[60]

Gandhi answered this with his longest stride toward Jinnah and the League, and it seemed to indicate a change of heart on the Mahatma's part; but next day Jinnah rejected it with almost disdainful hauteur, arguing: "You have already rejected the basis and fundamental principles of the Lahore resolution. . . . You do not accept that the Muslims of India are a nation. . . . You do not accept that the Muslims have an inherent right of self-determination. . . . You do not accept that Pakistan is composed of two zones, north-west and north-east, comprising six provinces. . . . As a result of our correspondence and discussions, I find that the question of the division of India as Pakistan and Hindustan is only on your lips, and it does not come from your heart, and suddenly at the eleventh hour you put forward a new suggestion . . . saying: 'Let it be a partition as between two brothers, if a division there must be.' "[61] This latter point, however, was one that Jinnah himself had recently used in seeking to clarify what he meant by Pakistan. His angry rejection when Gandhi seemed ready to endorse Pakistan appears to indicate that Jinnah really wanted no part in negotiating a formal settlement with the Congress and was caught off guard by Gandhi's swift last moment reversal of position. A Congress-League pact at that point would, after all, have taken the wind out of the League's highly successful organising momentum, which relied for the most part on its passionate popular appeals to Muslim grievances against the Hindu Congress and its raj.

Jinnah did not, however, wish to slam the door absolutely on "unrepresentative" Gandhi's naked toes. He argued, therefore, at the end of his angry letter of September 25: "But now you have . . . made a new proposal of your own on your own basis . . . and it is difficult to deal with it any further, unless it comes from you in your representative capacity. . . . Why not then accept the fundamentals of the Lahore resolution and proceed to settle details?"[62] Gandhi replied by asking Jinnah "to think fifty times before throwing away an offer which has been made entirely in the spirit of service in the cause of communal harmony."[63]

Jinnah responded by rejecting all Gandhi's overtures, including his appeals to address the League council or open session, coldly explaining that "only a member or delegate is entitled to participate in the deliberations of the meeting of the Council or in the open session respectively. Besides, it is a most extraordinary and unprecedented suggestion to make. However, I thank you for your advice. . . . I regret I have failed to convince you and convert you, as I was hopeful of doing so."[64]

"I confess I am unable to understand your persistent refusal to appreciate the fact that the Formula presented to you by me in my letter of the 24th as well as the Formula presented to you by Rajaji give you virtually what is embodied in the Lahore Resolution," Gandhi persisted in his final letter to Jinnah on September 26. "You keep on saying that I should accept certain theses, while I have been contending that the best way for us, who differ in our approach to the problem, is to give body to the demand as it stands in the Resolution and work it out to our mutual satisfaction."[65]

"The Gandhi-Jinnah talks are dragging on and the latest rumour is that they have broken down," Wavell reported to Amery. "Gandhi is going to Wardha for his birthday to receive the fund collected in memory of his wife, and some people think that a statement about his discussion with Jinnah will be issued from Wardha."[66] Jinnah informed the press that day: "I regret to say that I have failed in my task of converting Mr. Gandhi. . . . Nevertheless, we hope that the public will not feel embittered, and we trust that this is not the final end of our effort."[67] Gandhi addressed a larger press corps at Birla House, insisting

> The breakdown is only so-called. It is an adjournment *sine die*. Each of us must now talk to the public and put our viewpoints before them. . . . My experience of the previous three weeks confirms me in the view that the presence of a third power hinders the solution. A mind enslaved cannot act as if it was free. . . . The chief thing is for the Press and the public to avoid partisanship and bitterness.[68]

Asked about his own future plans, Gandhi promised to "act as my inner voice tells me." The next day, Gandhi told the *News Chronicle* in Bombay

that he believed "Mr. Jinnah is sincere, but I think he is suffering from hal-
lucination when he imagines that an unnatural division of India could
bring either happiness or prosperity to the people concerned."[69]

Wavell confessed to his journal, "I must say I expected something better. . . . The two great mountains have met and not even a ridiculous
mouse has emerged. This surely must blast Gandhi's reputation as a leader.
Jinnah had an easy task, he merely had to keep on telling Gandhi he was
talking nonsense, which was true, and he did so rather rudely, without
having to disclose any of the weaknesses of his own position, or define his
Pakistan in any way. I suppose it may increase his prestige with his followers, but it cannot add to his reputation with reasonable men."[70]

16

Simla
(1944-45)

As late as October 1944, Wavell found it "difficult to believe that Jinnah who, whatever his faults, is a highly intelligent man, is sincere about the 'two nations' theory."[1] Pakistan seemed so nebulous, unwieldy, and impractical a proposal that the viceroy had almost as much trouble as did Gandhi in taking Jinnah's advocacy of it seriously. "To take only one example," Wavell noted in his letters to Amery, "the north-eastern Muslim State would amount to very little without Calcutta, but Calcutta is in the main a Hindu city."[2] Jinnah, it seemed, "was arguing for something which he has not worked out." As for Amery, reflecting Churchill's feelings, he feared any "new attempt to wade into the old bog."[3]

Sir Francis Mudie, Home member of the viceroy's executive council, met with Jinnah in New Delhi on November 24, 1944, with the viceroy's "permission," and found him "friendly and talkative. Jinnah said the Muslims would never accept the Cripps procedure for settling the new constitution. . . . He showed no special hostility to a Representative Conference sponsored by Government, and said that he was, as in 1940, prepared to take part in a Coalition Government at the Centre. . . . He did not go into details about the relative strengths of Hindus and Muslims, but made it clear that to him the Mahasabha and the Congress were the same. He was quite prepared to co-operate even if the Congress refused to do so."[4] Wavell rightly suspected that "Jinnah may have got more out of Mudie than he gave away himself."

Jinnah met with Wavell on December 6, and the viceroy found him "quite forthcoming and friendly. . . . He said that India had never been a united nation and never could be. Indian unity was only a British creation, and unity of India under one Native Government would have no historical parallel. It was impossible from a practical point of view, it had been tried for the last 30 years and had completely failed."[5] The viceroy argued "from a practical point of view" that the "unity of India" brought about by British rule ought to be maintained, at least for security and economic purposes.

By mid-December 1944, Bengal's next governor, Richard G. Casey, had talked with enough leaders in Calcutta, to conclude that Pakistan was more a matter of "political wishful thinking" than a potential reality. Casey hoped that "Mr. Jinnah will compromise before Pakistan turns into a tiger that he is riding."[6] He believed it would be easy to "wean" many Bengali Muslims "away from the Pakistan idea," but was sensitive to "the risk of any of us being . . . accused of being partisan," hence wrote Wavell, seeking viceregal approval. "I believe that if the Muslims could be got to realise that the inclusion of Greater Calcutta in 'Pakistan' is a complete impossibility—then the idea of 'Eastern Pakistan' would receive a great blow."[7] Nazimuddin's concept of "Eastern Pakistan" was, in any event, much closer to "the picture of a wholly autonomous sovereign state" such as would, indeed, emerge in Bangladesh after 1971. For Nazimuddin and Suhrawardy, as well as most other Bengali Muslims including Fazlul Haq, the Bengali state of "Eastern Pakistan," as Casey noted, would be one "in which Muslims and Hindus would live in amity and share the responsibility for the business of Government (and all else) in approximate proportion to their numbers."

"Pakistan, or rather the communal suspicion represented by it, is the main obstacle to constructive thinking," Wavell replied.

I do not believe that Pakistan will work. It creates new minority problems quite as bad as those we have now, and the Pakistan State or States would be economically unsound. On the other hand, like all emotional ideas that have not been properly thought out, it thrives on opposition. Some of the abler Muslims may regard it is a bargaining counter, but for the mass of the Muslim League it is a real possibility and has a very strong sentimental appeal. We cannot openly denounce Pakistan until we have something attractive to offer in its place.[8]

Jinnah remained in New Delhi through mid-December, then returned to Bombay, where he celebrated his sixty-eighth birthday without pomp of any sort and left for Karachi immediately afterward. The Muslim chamber of commerce in the city of his birth welcomed him with a banquet on December 27, 1944. There he urged the "Muslim commercial community to be up and doing," reminding them that "the economic position was one of the strongest pillars of a nation. . . . You have got in the Pakistan areas an enormous field and enormous scope if you only look around: if only you will see them properly and seize them."[9] He had gone to Sind to patch up provincial disputes between League premier Sir Ghulam Hussain Hidayatullah and Mr. G. M. Syed, disputes which had almost deposed the League's ministry. It was more a question of a personal power struggle than ideological disputes, but Jinnah's presence was required to settle arguments over ministry appointments and candidates for by-elections. The round of contentious meetings in Sind left him exhausted. Back in Bombay early in January, Quaid-i-Azam issued a statement on Sind, concluding that "it is for the people of Sind now to build up our organisation in harmony, cooperation and unity."[10] Jinnah visited Ahmedabad in mid-January and addressed the Gujarat Muslim Educational Conference that was attended by thousands of young Muslims from all over the Northwest. "I was considered a plague and shunned," he told them. "But I thrust myself and forced my way through and went from place to place uninvited and unwanted. But now the situation was different."[11] As president of the revitalized Muslim League he had "numerous duties to perform and hardly any time to accept invitations. We have reached a stage . . . when we must direct and galvanise our forces for the purpose of some constructive scheme . . . for the educational social and economic uplift of our people." A new school was born that day: Jinnah noted that "Education is a matter of life and death to our nation."

A month's tour, even in India's best weather, left him limp, feverish, and too weak to attend the scheduled League council meeting that was to have been held in New Delhi late in February. He was obliged to cancel all commitments throughout February and March, including a scheduled meeting with Wavell, and retreated behind the walls of his Malabar Hill estate, seeing no one and accepting no calls. The viceroy was told "he has touch of pleurisy and may be laid up for some time."[12] By the end of March he was still dictating short letters such as this:

> I regret to inform you that it is not possible for me to undertake any public engagement for some time as I am ordered strictly to have complete rest. . . . This breakdown was a serious warning to me and my doctor's advice is that in no circumstances am I to depart from what he considers complete rest.[13]

Gandhi also suffered a physical relapse in January 1945, and with both of these aging titans on their backs, the younger leaders of Congress and the League hoped to fashion a new formula of political settlement. Bhulabhai Desai, the adroit Congress leader in the Central Legislative Assembly, and Liaquat Ali Khan supposedly agreed upon that "formula" for an

"*Interim* Government at Centre,"[14] whereby the League and Congress would each choose and control 40 percent of the cabinet, and leave the remaining 20 percent for Sikhs and Untouchables to share, while the viceroy and his commander-in-chief would remain British. Wavell and his secretary, Sir Evan Jenkins, were both assured by Desai that Jinnah and Gandhi "approved" of this formula, but it remains unclear whether or not Liaquat ever actually discussed the matter with Jinnah.

The Desai-Liaquat formula was, however, considered sufficiently important and "ripe" to be argued threadbare by Britain's War Cabinet, which ordered Wavell to refrain from committing himself to any new political "bridge" till its "strength and nature" were most "carefully tested."[15] Wavell was invited home for direct consultations with the cabinet, and Jinnah was reported to have said he "knew nothing of Desai's scheme."[16] Before the end of January, in fact, Jinnah notified the Associated Press that "There is absolutely no foundation for connecting my name with talks which may have taken place between Nawabzada Liaquat Ali Khan and Mr. Bhulabhai Desai."[17] Desai persisted nonetheless in stating privately that "he could guarantee the participation of Jinnah" in his scheme, if the government accepted it, and quoted an old Gujarati proverb "to the effect that Jinnah might grumble about the food, but would eat it."[18]

While Wavell, Amery, and the cabinet fiddled, Bengal and India continued to burn from famine, war, and bureaucratic incompetence that raged unabated across the land. Governor Casey noted most clearly the failure of the British administration in his March 1, 1945, letter to the viceroy, concluding that

> In Bengal at least, after a century and a half of British rule, we can point to no achievement worth the name in any direction. . . . British administration [has been] . . . run on the minimum possible expenditure of public moneys—very low taxation and no expenditure of loan moneys for developmental purposes. The result has been a pinchbeck policy under which the resources and potentialities of Bengal have not been developed . . . a suffocating system of red tape has . . . throttled initiative, and has created in the minds of the services (from whom plans ought to have been forthcoming) a sense of frustration and stultification.[19]

Despite the urgency and wisdom of Casey's criticism, nothing was done about the problems he noted; Wavell never so much as answered his letter. Before the end of March, Nazimuddin's ministry lost a vote of confidence in Calcutta, and Casey took direct control over the province, under Section 93 of the Government of India Act of 1935.

In mid-March the Muslim League's ministry in the North-West Frontier Province under Aurangzeb Khan also lost a vote of confidence, and governor Sir George Cunningham turned to Congress leader, Dr. Khan Sahib, to ask if he wanted to try forming a government with ministers drawn from his own party. A "sealed letter" was reportedly sent by Gandhi from his Wardha ashram to the frontier, apparently instructing Khan Sahib to accept the governor's invitation.[20] For the first time in over five years, after all the Congress ministries had resigned in 1939, the Congress party thus returned to provincial responsibility—in Peshawar. Jinnah was livid, but personal frailty made it impossible for him to journey to the frontier. Several months earlier, he had been requested urgently to come to help heal factional League strife there as he had in Sind. "It is up to you all to realize that you have to put your house in order," Quaid-i-Azam had written League president Taj Ali in December 1944. "The Centre is doing its best to help and guide, but the root is in the Province itself, and it is therefore up to you all to work selflessly for the cause and establish solidarity amongst those who understand . . . and create complete unity and discipline amongst our people."[21] Fine advice, yet hardly enough to avert the daggers that brought the League ministry to its knees along the frontier less than half a year later. "Congress Muslims, under the order from Wardha, have accepted office throwing away all their fundamental principles to the four winds," Jinnah declaimed in his Pakistan Day message to the press that March 23.

> It is not possible to believe that any Musalman, who has got the slightest self-respect and an iota of pride left in him, can tolerate a Ministry in a Muslim majority province, which takes order from and is subject to the control of Mr. Gandhi at Sevagram or the Congress who are deadly opponent [sic] to all Muslim aspirations and their national demand.[22]

Jinnah's same Pakistan Day message contained many images of illness and warnings against conspiratorial "powers," hidden "intrigues," and impending doom—all of which could be overcome only through Muslim unity combined with faith in God.

> I see powers working around us and our enemies are active, but let us go forward undaunted, fearless, without faltering. . . . I have my finger on the pulse of Muslim India, and I feel confident that ten crores of Musalmans will stand as one man at any critical moment, and will not hesitate to make every sacrifice, if we are to be thwarted, ignored or by-passed by those in power. . . . Pakistan is within our grasp. . . . Insha-Allah, we shall win.[23]

Wavell flew out of Delhi on March 20 and arrived in London three days later. Amery had suggested "a small dinner party at 10 Downing Street" to Churchill to "welcome" his viceroy home, but the prime minister coldly replied: "My meeting with him had better be purely official."[24] Addressing the War Cabinet's India committee chaired by Attlee, Wavell requested authority to choose his executive council from among India's political leadership, arguing that "there was a steady political deterioration and a worsening in the administrative and the general position."[25] He reported that Gandhi at seventy-five was "a fairly sick man, who according to some reports could only think consecutively for a few minutes." Wavell judged "Jinnah's control of the Muslim League more uncertain than it had been," reporting on the change of government in the North-West Frontier and the League troubles in Sind, Assam, and the Punjab. He also informed the cabinet that Jinnah "was not very fit, though his brain was as active as ever." And since Jawaharlal was still in jail, he "could not say how Nehru's mind was working, but thought he was still bitter and . . . in the Congress he probably commanded the political Left Wing, but not the industrialists from which Congress drew its financial support."[26]

The war in Europe ended and Churchill's government resigned before the cabinet could reach any conclusion about Wavell and India. "What a crew they are for a perilous voyage!" the tired, frustrated viceroy confessed to his journal.[27] Wavell was, however, granted permission to convene a conference of "Indian leaders" to help him form a new executive council that "would represent the main communities and would include equal proportions of Caste Hindus and Moslems."[28] He returned to New Delhi on June 7, 1945, and informed his current council of the impending changes. Almost all of the Indian members of the council called upon the viceroy to make an immediate declaration of "complete dominion status" for India.

"This is not an attempt to obtain or impose a constitutional settlement," the viceroy announced in his New Delhi broadcast on June 14. "His Majesty's Government had hoped that the leaders of the Indian parties would agree amongst themselves on a settlement of the communal issue, which is the main stumbling-block; but this hope has not been fulfilled."[29] Members of the Congress Working Committee were all released from incarceration. In a press statement on the forthcoming conference, Gandhi called the term "Caste Hindus" offensive, inaccurate, and opposed to the "Modern tendency in Hinduism . . . to abolish all caste distinctions." Jinnah's initial reaction was reflected in *Dawn*'s comment that the "League could not participate in [an] Executive Council in which non-League Moslems were included."[30]

Wavell reserved a suite for Jinnah at Simla's Cecil Hotel, inviting him to the viceregal lodge for a private meeting on the evening of June 24 before the scheduled official opening session of the Simla conference the next morning. Jinnah accepted the invitation but suggested a two-week's postponement of the conference to give him time to consult his Working Committee on the "clarifications" he hoped to receive from the viceroy concerning conference proposals during their private meeting. Wavell refused to be drawn into any such negotiations, insisting that the conference had to start without delay.

"Gandhi and Jinnah are behaving like very temperamental prima donnas," Wavell informed his journal in mid-June, "and the latter is publishing his telegrams in the Press before I even receive them; Gandhi at least had the courtesy to ask whether I agreed to publication."[31] The viceroy was beginning to recognize that his simplistic hopes for a settlement were less realistic than he had assured Britain's cabinet they were. On June 24, Wavell met with Congress president Azad before lunch and with Gandhi after lunch; it was his first conversation with the Mahatma, who was "rather vague and discursive but on the whole gave his blessing to the proposals."[32] As Gandhi left the viceregal lodge, Jinnah arrived to spend an hour and a half alone with the viceroy, who found him "much more direct than Gandhi, but whose manners are far worse."[33]

Lord Wavell officially opened the Simla conference at 11:00 A.M. on June 25, 1945. Twenty-two political leaders of India assembled in the posh ballroom of the viceregal lodge. President Azad spoke for Congress, stressing its "non-communal character." Jinnah spoke next for the League and said "Azad's points were largely irrelevant to the immediate proposals," calling upon the viceroy to address himself exclusively to those. "On the nature of the Congress party I said that there was nothing in the proposals to brand it as a communal organisation," Wavell reported to Amery. "Jinnah interjected here that Congress represented only Hindus, a statement to which Khan Sahib took vehement objection. I remarked that Congress represented its members and both Congress and Jinnah accepted this."[34] Jinnah asked to speak again before that first meeting adjourned, insisting the League would "not agree to any constitution except on the fundamental principle of Pakistan." The League "might well claim," he argued, immediate concession of Pakistan as a prior condition to any cooperation, yet he was willing to participate in this sort of conference thanks to his faith in the "Viceroy's sincerity" and his belief that "the British Government and people really wished to give a fair deal to British India." Wavell felt much relieved and concluded that night that his "Conference has got away to a reasonably good start."

On the morning of June 29 the conference reconvened, and the viceroy asked all party leaders to send him panels of names of candidates for his new council. Azad readily agreed, but Jinnah refused, arguing that he could not submit any list before consulting his Working Committee. And so the conference adjourned until July 14.

Wavell spent an hour and a half arguing with Jinnah on the evening of July 8, "which left us where we began," he reported. "He was obviously in a high state of nervous tension, and said to me more than once; 'I am at the end of my tether'; he also said 'I ask you not to wreck the League.' He is obviously in great difficulties; but they are largely of his own making by his arrogance and intransigence. He fears now to be made the scapegoat for the failure of the Conference; and yet will not give up anything of his claim to represent all Muslims."[35] At the end of their meeting, Jinnah still refused to hand over a list of candidates that Wavell had requested for his council but "left himself a loophole" by requesting a letter from the viceroy spelling out precisely what it was he wanted. That letter came the next day, and Jinnah placed it before his Working Committee on July 9, 1945.

> I fully appreciate your difficulties, but regret that I am unable to give you the guarantee you wish, i.e., that all the Muslim members of the proposed new Council shall necessarily be members of the Muslim League. . . . I have to attempt to form an Executive Council representative, competent, and generally acceptable. . . . It will help me greatly if you will let me have names. . . . I asked for eight, but will certainly accept five if you do not wish to send more.[36]

"The Committee, after giving its very careful consideration to the matter," Jinnah replied the same day, "desires me to state that it regrets very much to note that Your Excellency is not able to give the assurance that all the Muslim members of the proposed Executive Council will be selected from the Muslim League . . . the Committee considers this as one of the fundamental principles, and, in the circumstances, I regret I am not in a position to send the names . . . it is not possible for us to depart from our fundamental principles."[37]

The viceroy remained equally resolved not to "give way on this point" and wired Amery that night to propose his own list of new council members, four of whom were to be Muslim League members (Liaquat Ali, Khaliquazzaman, Nazimuddin, and Eassak Sait) and the fifth, a Muslim landlord from the Punjab, Sir Muhammad Nawaz Khan. The five "Caste Hindus" were to have been Nehru, Patel, Rajendra Prasad, Dr. M. S. Aney, and Sir B. N. Rau. Master Tara Singh was to represent the Sikhs, and Dr. Ambedkar and Muniswami Pillai the Scheduled Castes (Untouchables).

Dr. John Matthai of Madras University (later Nehru's private secretary) was to have been the council's sole Indian Christian, thus bringing the total to sixteen with the viceroy and his commander-in-chief.

The British cabinet, being "rather pernickety,"[38] insisted that Wavell see Jinnah first and tell him the names of the Muslim members he planned to propose, and to "try to persuade Jinnah" to put forward those names as his party's list. Good soldier that he was, Wavell met with Jinnah on July 11, trying again to alter his position. "He refused even to discuss names unless he could be given the absolute right to select all Muslims and some guarantee that any decision which the Muslims opposed in Council could only be passed by a two-thirds majority—in fact a kind of communal veto. I said that these conditions were entirely unacceptable," Wavell recorded, "and the interview ended."[39] The viceroy saw Gandhi an hour later and told him of the conference breakdown. Gandhi took the news "calmly, but said that H. M. G. would have to decide sooner or later to accept the Hindu or the Muslim point of view, since they were irreconcilable."[40]

The utter failure of Wavell's Simla conference served only to underscore the intensity of communal distrust that remained India's key political problem. Many British officials expected that this failure would weaken Jinnah's power over the League, but his presidential position seemed instead to grow stronger as the demand for Pakistan gained credence among Muslims across the land. At the closing session of the conference on July 14, Jinnah stated that "Pakistan and United India were diametrically opposed to each other . . . Musalmans of India were determined to have Pakistan."

"So my efforts to bring better understanding between the parties have failed and have shown how wide is the gulf," noted the weary Wavell. "Whether I have done more good or harm by trying, only time will show."[41] He thought "Jinnah made a tactical blunder in not bringing the matter to an issue," and his final assessment of the Quaid-i-Azam was, "narrow and arrogant . . . actuated mainly by fear and distrust of the Congress . . . constitutionally incapable of friendly cooperation with the other party."[42]

Amery shrewdly reminded Wavell that thanks to Simla, the Congress leaders had, once again, been "brought right up against the fact that it is the Muslim League and not you or I who stand in the way of their aspirations. . . . They must now either acquiesce in Pakistan, or realise that they have somehow or other to win over Muslim support against Jinnah, and that a mere facade of tame Congress Muslims does not help them."[43] The secretary of state suggested holding elections that winter and argued that "It by no means follows that Jinnah will sweep the board in the Muslim Provinces. . . . On the other hand, if he really does, then his claim that the Muslim members should all be members of the League could not so well be resisted." Amery himself had, however, just fought and lost his last election campaign. Britain's postwar Labour landslide brought Attlee and his party to power with a resounding majority of 200 in the House of Commons. When the viceroy learned that his new master in Whitehall was to be Lord Pethick-Lawrence (1871–1961), his initial reaction was to "fear he may have fixed and old-fashioned ideas derived mainly from Congress contacts."[44] That very day in early August of 1945, however, a more awesome explosion at Hiroshima inaugurated an age that was to accelerate the pace of history, bringing World War II to an end within the week and hustling the British raj out of its deep ruts of stately bureaucratic stagnation.

17

Quetta and Peshawar
(1945-46)

The aftermath of the Simla conference debacle was a governors meeting in New Delhi to help Wavell and Whitehall decide their next political move. Winter elections, most agreed, were now required, but the Punjab's Governor Glancy argued vigorously against any elections till an economic planning conference could be called to expose the potential pitfalls of Pakistan. "Unless the Muslim League could be steered away from the crude version of Pakistan," he insisted, "there would be civil war in the Punjab; and immediate Central elections might consolidate the Muslim League position."[1] Glancy feared that Punjab Muslims would vote on what might appear to them simply as a "religious issue," and his concerns reflected Khizar's deepest apprehensions as well. Bengal's governor conceded that none of his leading Muslims "could explain what Pakistan meant. In the last resort they always fell back on Jinnah, e.g., they said that Jinnah was satisfied that Pakistan was economically sound, therefore it must be so."[2] Casey thought time "an important factor," since he doubted that Jinnah had "any real successor" and argued that the "Pakistan idea might go to pieces" without him.

"There are only two major parties in this country," Jinnah insisted, restating Nehru's famous 1937 formula in his first public pronouncement in Bombay following the Simla conference. "Invitations issued to Mr. Gandhi and myself were on the basis that Mr. Gandhi was the recognised leader of one of the parties and myself the leader of the other. The British called them parties, but in fact they are two major nations."[3] No other formula would satisfy him. A quarter of a century after his public humiliation at Nagpur he had risen from the dust of ignominy to stand erect at death's door, proclaiming to the world that *Mr.* Gandhi was no better than Mr. Jinnah, merely his opposite number in a different "major nation." Jin-

nah seemed quite obsessed with Gandhi and his behavior, minutely examining and questioning all facets of his activity.

> When it suits him, he represents nobody, he can talk in individual
> capacity; he is not even a four-anna member of the Congress; he un-
> dertakes fast to decide the political issue; he reduces himself to zero
> and consults his inner voice; yet when it suits him, he is the supreme
> dictator of the Congress! He thinks he represents whole of India. Mr.
> Gandhi is an enigma. . . . How can we come to a settlement with
> him? There was so much venom and bitterness against the Muslims
> and the Muslim League that the Congress were prepared to go to
> any length with two objectives; first, to hammer down, humiliate and
> discourage the Muslim League and every method was adopted to
> bully us, coerce us and to threaten us to surrender; the second was
> to see Muslim League ignored and by-passed and for that purpose,
> they stooped to the lowest point, that they threw up their principles
> to the winds.[4]

Many of the ambivalent fears preoccupying Jinnah's mind then were triggered, as usual, by thoughts of Gandhi—with whom he associated "venom
and bitterness," and what to Jinnah were the two most heinous objectives,
"to hammer down, humiliate, discourage and bully," or to "ignore and by-
pass," him. Whether it was through humiliating action or silent contempt,
nothing could be more shattering to his self-image or more painful to his
sensitivity of heart and mind. He considered it far better to die fighting at
the head of his own smaller party-nation than to live in the shadow of so
insulting an "enigma."

To fill the League's election war chest, Jinnah spoke again in August in
his home city, accusing Congress of trying "by hook or by crook" to lure
Muslims into an "all-India union," and warning that "they look to the British bayonets to perform the task for them and hence they resort to alternating and varying methods, flattering and hurling abuses, cringing and
giving threats to the British Government. . . . But we cannot agree to any
arrangement, which means freedom for Hindus and establishment of 'Hindu
Raj' and slavery for the Muslims."[5] His listeners donated over 300,000 rupees that day, funds which Jinnah called the League's "silver bullets."

"The Labour Party is, of course, both by its convictions and by its public utterances, committed to do its utmost to bring about a settlement of
the India problem," wrote Pethick-Lawrence to Wavell in his first weekly
letter. "I feel sure that my colleagues will welcome your proposal to hold
elections, which I am supporting to them in a paper which should be considered within the next few days."[6] The new secretary of state was "greatly
attracted" to Indian thought and culture; he had visited India with his suf-

fragette wife in 1926–27, served as a member of the Round Table conference in 1931, and was the most empathetic master of the India Office to Indian national aspirations since Montagu or Morley.

Glancy did his best to derail early elections, fearing Pakistan yet finding
that throughout the Muslim districts of the Punjab since the Simla conference Jinnah's "stock has been standing very high. . . . He has been hailed
as the champion of Islam. . . . I must confess that I am gravely perturbed
about the situation, because there is a very serious danger of the elections
being fought, so far as Muslims are concerned, on an entirely false issue. . . . The uninformed Muslim will be told that the question he is
called on to answer at the polls is—Are you a true believer or an infidel and
a traitor? . . . if Pakistan becomes an imminent reality, we shall be heading straight for blood-shed on a wide scale; non-Muslims, especially Sikhs,
are not bluffing, they will not submit peacefully to a Government that is
labelled 'Muhammadan Raj.' "[7] No Englishman so clearly foresaw the
dreadful implications of the partition of the Punjab, yet Glancy's voice
from the hinterland elicited no echo in the rarified corridors of Whitehall.

On August 20, 1945, Wavell was invited home for consultation with the
new cabinet and authorized to announce that elections would be held
throughout British India during the "next cold weather." Before leaving
India, the viceroy sent Pethick-Lawrence his summary analysis of the
Pakistan "problem," first explaining that what Glancy had written about the
Punjab and partition would similarly apply to Bengal, "but the Punjabis are
tougher than the Bengalis, and the Sikhs, who were the rulers in the Punjab
before we annexed it, would fight rather than see their Holy Land pass
under permanent Muslim rule."[8] He then noted the seeming paradox that
support for "the Pakistan idea" was much stronger among Muslims in
Muslim-minority provinces than in the "Pakistan Provinces." Wavell remarked that he had always hoped to be able to "avoid" any full-scale public
inquiry into the feasibility and implications of Pakistan, since he anticipated that Jinnah would "boycott" such a conference or commission and it
might only stir up communal "feeling." He felt, however, that continuing
to ignore the possibility of its birth would not make Pakistan fade away.

Wavell reached London before the end of August and found Pethick-
Lawrence, who "looks old, is pleasant and amiable," waiting to welcome
him home and motor with him to Claridges. They conferred in Whitehall
the next day for an hour and a half. Two days later Wavell met with the
India committee of the cabinet chaired by Attlee. Sir Stafford Cripps, now
president of the Board of Trade, was the committee's most formidable
member. The Viceroy reported that he "thought it most unlikely" that
Jinnah would enter into discussions without a guarantee of acceptance of

Pakistan, at least "in principle." Wavell's own judgment was that "Jinnah spoke for 99 per cent of the Muslim population of India in their apprehension of Hindu domination. . . . The real strength of Mr. Jinnah's position was the widespread and genuine fear among Indian Muslims of Hindu domination and Hindu raj."[9] There had been a "very great hardening" in the positions of the Indian parties since 1942, the viceroy argued, and he saw no readiness on the part of any party in India at present to accept the Cripps offer. As for the Constituent Assembly, Muslims would "boycott it unless the Pakistan issue was conceded." Yet to concede that issue might lead to "a boycott by the Hindus."

Except for Attlee, who had less and less time for India as prime minister, Cripps and Pethick-Lawrence were the only cabinet members to concern themselves deeply with Indian affairs at this time, and Cripps considered his friends Birla and Nehru right in downgrading Jinnah's power or potential. Nor did he take Wavell very seriously. Wavell, on the other hand, fearing from reports of Patel's and Nehru's speeches that Congress was preparing another revolutionary confrontation with the government, inclined more favorably toward Jinnah and the Muslim League, who might prove to be his only allies in the coming struggle for power. So despite Labour's greater sympathy for India and its strongly stated interest in "helping" India resolve its complex political problems, this cabinet, like its predecessor, simply stood behind the Cripps offer of 1942, and ignored the monumental historic changes wrought by three intervening years, self-righteously professing that "If the Indian parties, or any of them, were not prepared to co-operate, the responsibility would be theirs." Wavell and Pethick-Lawrence went back to their drawing boards to seek a better way of informing India that Great Britain's new postwar policy was the same old Cripps position. The viceroy met with Churchill on the eve of the ex-prime minister's departure for Lake Como and was "shocked" to learn that the "only reason" Churchill "had agreed to my political move [the first Simla Conference] was that the India Committee had all told him it was bound to fail!"[10]

Jinnah had taken his pre-election fund-raising tour to Karachi en route to Quetta where the dry cool air was thought to be best for his lungs. His message was simple and the same wherever he spoke—the Muslim League was "the only authoritative and representative" party of Muslims throughout India, and the sole platform of the League was Pakistan. Jinnah began to act like the head of a separate nation, moreover; he wired Attlee at this time to protest any softening of Britain's ban on Jewish refugees being admitted into Palestine, warning the prime minister: "It is my duty to inform you that any surrender to appease Jewry at the sacrifice of Arabs would be deeply resented and vehemently resisted by Muslim world and Muslim India and its consequences will be most disastrous."[11]

With Jinnah obliged to remain in Baluchistan, too weak to travel during the 1945 campaign, Liaquat Ali and other Working Committee members of the Central Parliamentary Board and Committee of Action actually ran the Muslim League from its New Delhi headquarters and ticketed candidates. Much provincial controversy, bickering, and backbiting ensued, especially in Bengal, Sind, and the North-West Frontier. In mid-September, Sir Firoz Khan Noon had resigned his defence seat on the viceroy's executive council to return home to the Punjab to campaign there as a League candidate, but a month later Wavell reported to Pethick-Lawrence that Sir Firoz "has not been universally welcomed, and I doubt if the Party there [in the Punjab] is as united and cordial as it might be. The Muslim League have always suffered from lack of organization as compared with the Congress, and if they waste their time in personal quarrels, they may suffer at the polls."[12]

"Pakistan is the question of life and death for us," Jinnah told a public meeting in Ahmedabad that final week in October, stopping on his way home to Bombay to pick up a check for 200,000 rupees collected from Gujarati Muslims. "I had asked for silver bullets to fight the election campaign, and Ahmedabad had responded next to Bombay which was a richer city. . . . All Muslims believed in one God and were one nation. They wanted Pakistan and would attain it. It was their amulet, their charm which would increase their strength and glory. . . . The moon of Pakistan is shining and we shall reach it,"[13] he assured the cheering crowd.

On November 1, Jinnah predicted a Muslim League "sweep" at the polls, informing a reporter from the Associated Press that he could not agree with critics of his Pakistan plan "who contend it is unworkable. . . . Our next step will be a demand upon Britain for recognition."[14] Congress continued to demand "immediate independence" for India as a whole, under a government selected by the Congress high command. Wavell alerted his officials and prepared to declare "martial law." Politician Pethick-Lawrence, however, read none of Wavell's anxious reports of Congress campaign rhetoric with great alarm, yet cabled the viceroy to ask: "But can Jinnah be induced to accept a modified form of it [Pakistan] which it might be possible to concede?"[15]

Cripps now advised the Cabinet committee to send a parliamentary delegation to India and urge the viceroy to meet with Gandhi, reporting "he understood that Gandhi was ready and willing to influence Indian opinion towards moderation."[16] If, as anticipated after elections, Congress would be "the majority party," it would no longer be possible to treat them irresponsibly, hence Labour's Pethick-Lawrence and Cripps resolved to keep the viceroy in rein on the rugged political road toward India's independent rule, rather than allowing him to bolt off on any smoother martial freeway.

Wavell, however, was losing all patience with India's growing political complexity and penchant for debate. His silences became more ominously eloquent. Boredom and depression settled deep inside the aging marshal's soul, as he had earlier noted in a journal entry of mid-November 1945: "Back this evening from U.P. It was the dullest tour I have done, tiring, depressing and hot." To Whitehall, Wavell wired an "immediate, top secret" reply: "I do not think it advisable that I should invite Gandhi to see me."[17]

Much of Wavell's depression, and that of his commander-in-chief, General Auchinleck, as well as most of the senior British martial and civil officers in India at this time, was immediately associated with the passionate hue and cry raised against British rule that November as soon as the first leaders of Subhas Bose's Indian National Army were brought to trial for treason in New Delhi's Red Fort. Bose had died in a plane crash on Formosa, but three of his leading lieutenants, one Hindu, one Muslim, and one Sikh, all of whom had been serving in the British army in Singapore when it surrendered, emerged now as national heroes. Nehru, Bhulabhai Desai, and Tej Bahadur Sapru volunteered to defend Bose's officers, who were brought home in irons only to be hailed as patriots throughout the land. In Bose's home city, Calcutta, riots of protest raged, leaving over thirty dead, hundreds injured, and countless rupees in property burned and ravaged. Soon after the trial got underway most British officials realized that they had made a terrible mistake in giving the Indian National Army so much publicity and so prominent a platform.

General Sir Claude Auchinleck in a top secret letter to Wavell on November 24, 1945, wrote:

> The evidence reaching us now increasingly goes to show that the general opinion in the Army (as opposed to that of certain units and individuals who have particular reasons for bitterness) is in favour of leniency. If you agree . . . in the case of the present trials, the sentences would be commuted if it was clear from the evidence when the trials are concluded that the accused were carrying out what they believed to be their duty.[18]

To Wavell, more than any message he received from Whitehall, this letter from the "Auck" convinced him that the days of the raj were numbered. The world war may have been won, but India was "lost." Jinnah personally played no part in the great trial of the Indian National Army, though the League associated itself with the defense since, as British Intelligence opined, "the trial of Muslims may make their effect increasingly felt on the Muslim Public and League alike."[19]

For the first time since 1936, Jinnah journeyed to the frontier to campaign for a week. He addressed a Muslim League conference in Peshawar on November 24, 1945: "We have no friends. . . . Neither the British, nor the Hindus are our friends. We are clear in our own minds that we have to fight against both of them. If both (being Banias) are combined against us, we shall not be afraid of them. We shall fight their united might and, Inshaallah, win in the end."[20] When Jinnah asked the crowd if they wanted Pakistan or not, their answer came in deafening shouts of "Allah-o-Akbar" ("God is Great"). To win Pakistan, he assured them, all they had to do was to "vote for the League candidates." Then he became defensive, sarcastic, irate: "They [Hindus] ask: 'What are the sacrifices of Mr. Jinnah and the Muslim League?' It is true that I have not been to jail. Never mind. I am a bad person. But I ask you, 'Who made sacrifices in 1920–21?' Mr. Gandhi ascends the *gaddi* [throne] of leadership on our skulls."[21] This last statement came closest to revealing Jinnah's deepest grievance, reverting to the worst trauma of his political life when he actually appeared to have felt *Mr.* Gandhi step on his "skull" to ascend the throne of Congress national leadership.

In Calcutta, Casey was beside himself with frustration and fear in the face of the pro–Indian National Army riots that left thirty-three dead, hundreds wounded, and all but wrecked the city. Bengal's governor met with Gandhi in Calcutta early in December and reported to Wavell that "His political reasoning lacked realism and balance. However there was no sign of senility."[22] At their second talk, Casey told Gandhi that what was "standing in the way of self-government for India" was not the British but the Muslim League, which was "suffering from Hinduphobia." Casey urged that Congress should make a "public announcement of a substantial list of safeguards" it would be willing to insert in a new constitution for Muslims to "blunt the edge" of League fears and suspicions. Gandhi responded that he had "conceded safeguard after safeguard" to Jinnah, who "constantly raised his price" until he reached what in essence was Pakistan; and Gandhi did not believe "anything less would satisfy him." Gandhi also told Casey that "he believed Jinnah to be a very ambitious man and that he had visions of linking up the Moslems of India with the Moslems in the Middle East and elsewhere and that he did not believe that he could be ridden off his dreams."[23]

The League won all thirty central assembly seats (one of them Jinnah's) that December, a stunning victory that validated Jinnah's prediction and appeared to prove the universal appeal of Pakistan among Muslims of the subcontinent. Congress, though it retained a majority of fifty-five, actually lost four seats. The first round was over. The "day is not far off," Jinnah promised his jubilant followers, "when Pakistan shall be at your feet."[24] He directed more criticism and sarcasm at Nehru, mocking him as "the impetuous Pandit who never unlearns or learns anything and never grows old . . . nothing but Peter Pan."[25]

Pethick-Lawrence wrote to Jinnah and Azad to inform them of the parliamentary delegation's forthcoming visit and asked if they would meet with the British to "discuss matters with them."[26] Jinnah met the ten-member deputation led by Labour's Professor R. Richards in New Delhi on January 10, 1946. Five days earlier Jinnah had talked with Wavell for an hour. But Jinnah's refusal to allow Liaquat to meet with Wavell shows how little he trusted any of his lieutenants to participate in tough negotiations with the government. He alone felt confident in giving nothing away as he wrestled to win Pakistan.

As the provincial election campaigns heated up, reports of Hindu-Muslim riots, and of "poisonous propaganda" especially in the Punjab, increased. Moreover, Pethick-Lawrence had concluded by then that it would be useless to leave another round of political negotiations to the viceroy alone, and nothing less than a cabinet mission to India was required to break the Hindu-Muslim "deadlock." Three ministers with "full authority to decide points at issue" led by the secretary of state would have to fly out shortly before provincial elections were concluded, sometime in March. The cabinet recognized that this mission might, in fact, be its final card in the game of British India spinning so swiftly to its tragic finale. If negotiations broke down, civil disobedience would follow, and things could not long remain nonviolent. The army might even decide not to obey orders. Commutation of Indian National Army trial sentences had accelerated the metamorphosis of "mutineers" into national heroes. The total number of Europeans in all official services was rapidly dwindling, as many more old hands exercised their option of retiring on their pensions back home. Precious little time left.

The cabinet decided in February to send Cripps and first lord of the admiralty, A. V. Alexander to India to be, together with Pethick-Lawrence, their three wise men. Wavell was afraid Cripps would be the "operative element" among those magi and considered Cripps "sold to the Congress point of view" and not quite "straight" in his "methods."[27] A month before the cabinet mission left for India, the parliamentary delegation led by

Richards returned to 10 Downing Street to report what it had found. Most members agreed that some form of Pakistan would have to be conceded— and the sooner the better. Mrs. Muriel Nichol, who admitted that she began her visit to India "impressed by the strong necessity of maintaining the unity of India," found the Punjab "explosive." The Muslim population there was "all worked up in favour of Pakistan," she concluded, and therefore, it "must be conceded." She believed Jinnah would modify his demand, but only if the "principle" were granted "at an early stage."[28] Brigadier Austin Low felt it "would be undersirable that H. M. G. should make a declaration in favour of Pakistan"; he agreed that "it might be necessary" but feared "Pakistan is not a viable proposition." M. P. Reginald Sorensen "regarded Pakistan as wholly irrational—he was not sure that Mr. Jinnah could be regarded as a rational person—but, in his view, necessary." Mr. Arthur Bottomley "did not like Pakistan but thought it would be necessary . . . (a) to avoid widespread bloodshed, (b) to preserve our own trade interests, for whereas the strong tendency in the Congress majority Provinces was to boycott trade with the United Kingdom, the Muslims were eager to do business with us."[29]

Pethick-Lawrence's brilliant private secretary, Francis Turnbull, then prepared a note on the "viability of Pakistan," which helped brief the cabinet mission prior to the start of negotiations. "There is bound to be an economic price to pay for the satisfaction of the Moslem demand for political independence," that weighty document drafted primarily by Mr. Turnbull, warned.

> The division of India will be born in bitter antagonism and it will certainly be rash to assume that this will not be reflected in the efforts necessary to regulate the machinery of communications and of economic intercourse between the Pakistan States and the rest of India. . . . It is hard to resist the conclusion that taking all these considerations into account the splitting up of India will be the reverse of beneficial so far as the livelihood of the people is concerned.[30]

To compound India's problems, drought brought famine to most of the southern provinces of the subcontinent, and grain shortages were starting to spread from Bengal to the frontier. Wavell appealed to Gandhi and Jinnah to nominate deputies to accompany an official food delegation to London and to the United States. Jinnah responded positively. Wavell reported that Gandhi advised him to "send for Azad and talk to him."[31] With food grains rationed to twelve ounces per day, mass protest marches began in many Indian cities starting with Allahabad. Visible "deterioration of health" was widespread. The average Indian's rationed diet provided no more than 1,200 calories, fewer than half the minimal requirement for normal daily activity."[32]

On February 18, 1946, most of the sailors in the Royal Indian Navy in Bombay harbor went on "strike" for higher wages. The next day 3,000 of those "mutineers," as the British considered them, marched around Bombay, stirring tens of thousands of ardent street supporters. The Congress flag flew from both the H.M.I.S. *Talwar* and the H.M.I.S. *Lahore,* as well as from the hats of many jubilant sailors, who called themselves members of the I.N.N. (Indian National Navy), in emulation of Bose's I.N.A. (Indian National Army). On February 22, the mutineers were told that only "unconditional surrender" would be accepted. General Sir R. M. Lockhart, in command of Bombay, had "ample force available," Wavell reported, so that "if ships open fire, they will have to be sunk."[33] Vallabhbhai Patel went out to the ships and persuaded the mutineers to surrender without firing. Sailors in Karachi harbor followed the lead of their Bombay comrades, however, and in the aftermath of both "mutinies" rioting left some 200 civilians dead, as elections continued.

Provincial returns from the Punjab in late February gave the League 75 of 88 Muslim seats, a clear mandate for Pakistan among Muslims of the province, though not enough votes to allow the League to form a ministry, without either Sikh or Congress support. In Sind the League's plight was much the same, with 28 out of 34 seats, while in Assam though even a higher percentage of Muslim League candidates won (31 out of 34), Congress again refused to enter a coalition government with its most hated rival. Jinnah's party soon scored a singular victory in Bengal, however, winning 113 out of 119 Muslim seats. The League lost badly on the frontier, with only 17 out of 38 seats. The overall provincial tally gave the League more than 88 percent of the Muslim vote nonetheless—quite enough to legitimize the Pakistan demand in the eyes of the world.

"The British Government and the British people desire, without reservation, to consummate the promises and pledges that have been made," Pethick-Lawrence stated as he and his Cabinet colleagues touched Indian soil that March 23.[34] Major Woodrow Wyatt returned to India with the Cabinet Mission as Cripps' assistant, and was the first member of the Mission to meet with Jinnah again, visiting him at home in New Delhi on March 27. Major Wyatt had "an old friend . . . who is quite close to Jinnah," the beautiful young "Tazi" (Mumtaz) Shah Nawaz, Sir Muhammad Shafi's granddaughter, who kept him informed of Jinnah's thinking and the internal dynamics of the League, to which she belonged. "The Muslim League seems to be solidly behind Jinnah," Wyatt reported to Cripps on

March 28.[35] Cripps met with Jinnah for an hour on the morning of March 30. "He was calm and reasonable but completely firm on Pakistan."[36] As a result of that conversation, Jinnah agreed to invite Gandhi to meet him. As was so often the case at the start of previous negotiations, Jinnah's opening posture was surprisingly cordial and disarmingly reasonable.

Gandhi appeared before the Mission on April 3, "naked except for a dhoti and looking remarkably healthy."[37] Wavell reported.

> Mr. Gandhi said that he had passed 18 days with Mr. Jinnah. He claimed to be a sincere friend of the Muslims but had never been able to appreciate the Pakistan which Mr. Jinnah says he means. . . . His Pakistan was a sin which he (Mr. Gandhi) would not commit. The substance of Pakistan as he understood it was independence of culture and a legitimate ambition. . . . The two-nation theory is far more dangerous. The Muslim population is a population of converts . . . all descendants of Indian-born people. Jinnah is sincere but his logic is utterly at fault especially as a kind of mania possesses him. He himself was called a maniac and he therefore honoured Jinnah for his mania. . . . He asked Jinnah whether his own son [Harilal Gandhi] who had gone over to the Muslim religion changed his nationality by doing so. . . . Let Mr. Jinnah form the first Government and choose its personnel from elected representatives in the country. The Viceroy would appoint them formally but, in fact, Mr. Jinnah would choose. If he does not do so then the offer to form a Government should be made to Congress. . . . The Interim Government must be absolutely national. Mr. Jinnah could choose who he liked for his Government. They would be subject to the vote of the Assembly from which they were drawn.[38]

Pethick-Lawrence interrupted Gandhi at this point to note that Jinnah's party had not won a majority of the assembly seats, hence he would be asked to preside over a government, most of whose ministers belonged to "parties other than his own." Gandhi said that was "inescapable." The secretary of state pointed out that "Jinnah's government" would, in that case, have to be predominantly Hindu! "Mr. Gandhi said he did not underrate the difficulties of the situation which the Delegation had to face. If he were not an irresponsible optimist he would despair of any solution."

Jinnah arrived for his interview the next morning at ten and spoke to the mission for three hours, "of which at least two were, to my mind," noted Wavell, "entirely wasted."[39] Jinnah began with an historical survey of India, showing how rarely in its long past India had been unified. "A Hindu will wash his hands after shaking hands with a Muslim," he argued, though he personally was probably more scrupulous in that particular habit than any Hindu he knew. It seemed, moreover, that he professed too much when he added: "No Hindu will let Mr. Jinnah have a room in his building. Hindu society and philosophy are the most exclusive in the world. . . . How are you to put 100 millions of Muslims together with 250 millions whose way of life is so different."[40] Cripps then asked whether Jinnah thought the difference between Hindus and Muslims in Bengal was greater than the difference between the Pathans and Muslims of Sind. Jinnah argued that "the fundamentals" were common to all Muslims. He had traveled everywhere, and wherever he met Muslims, they believed "in one God. They believed in equality of men and in human brotherhood. The Hindus believe in none of these principles."

Pethick-Lawrence and Cripps both tackled Jinnah on questions of defense, especially Pakistan's vulnerability from the Northwest, trying their best to get him to admit that some unified joint chiefs structure would be best for all parties concerned; but Jinnah stood his ground on a totally sovereign Pakistan demand, demonstrating the singular tenacity of his advocacy.

Nehru was on tour in Southeast Asia at this time; his visit to Malaya was a great popular success, thanks in no small measure to the warmth of Lord and Lady Mountbatten's welcome there. "In all the public speeches which Nehru made during this visit the central theme was Asiatic unity," a British official reported to the India Office. "He was a little scornful of Jinnah and doubted very much whether he had either the intention or the power to start a revolt in India if he did not secure Pakistan. . . . 'Jinnah' he said, 'rather reminds me of the man who was charged with the murder of his mother and father and begged the clemency of the Court on the ground that he was an orphan.' "[41]

Cripps was then ready with his top secret double-barreled solution for Congress and the League to consider. Proposal A was a three-part "Union of All-India" offer with the Hindu-majority provinces, Muslim-majority provinces, and princely states all under the umbrella of a minimal union government that controlled defence, foreign affairs and communications. Proposal B was that there should be "two Indias formed from the territories of British India, Hindustan and Pakistan, to either of which the Indian States could be invited to federate."[42] The exact limits of Pakistan would be determined from the religious identity of populations in all districts in the Northwest and Northeast regions. Since Pakistan was predicated on the two-nation theory based solely on religion, "It would be wholly inconsistent with this theory if non-Muslim majority areas should be added to Pakistan in order to give a better economic basis nor would it add to its eventual stability if large minorities were to be thus included against their will."[43] There would have to be some form of treaty drawn up between these two "independent sovereign States" to deal with essential economic matters and questions of defense, foreign policy, and communications vital to both nations. Since time was running out, Cripps proposed presenting the details of these two schemes to the leaders of all major parties, insisting that within a few days they notify the mission of their willingness to accept either plan A or plan B. "If neither of the plans meets with general acceptance . . . we must recommend that the one which has the greatest volume of support is immediately acted upon . . . failing that general acceptance we shall use all our influence to put through that scheme which has the greatest measure of support."[44]

Another week of interviews contributed little to what the mission had already learned but helped refine their alternative schemes, which were presented first of all to Jinnah on April 16, 1946. "Before the interview with Jinnah we had 20 minutes Press photography, sitting round a table and very obviously not talking business," Wavell reported. "I dislike this modern craze for publicity."[45] Turnbull, Wavell, and Cripps had each prepared "briefs" on how best to tackle Jinnah, a unique tribute to his powers of debate. Pethick-Lawrence opened the meeting by informing Jinnah that his "full and complete demand for Pakistan" had "little chance of acceptance" and that he could not "reasonably hope to receive both the whole of the territory, much of it inhabited by non-Muslims, which he claimed and the full measure of sovereignty which he said was essential."[46] Hence there was plan A or B, each of which he spelled out. Which did Jinnah prefer?

"Mr. Jinnah asked how Pakistan came in under the proposed all-India Union," the secret record of that interview reported.

> The Secretary of State said that briefly there were two propositions— a small Pakistan with sovereign rights and a Treaty relation, and a larger Pakistan. . . . The latter would come together with Hindustan on terms of equality within an all-India Union. . . . Sir. S. Cripps said that under the second alternative two Federations would be created linked by a Union Centre. . . . The communal balance would be retained at the Centre by some means even if the States came in there. Mr. Jinnah asked how the Union Executive would be formed. Sir S. Cripps said that the Federations would choose the members of the Union Executive. Mr. Jinnah asked how, if there were equal representation, decisions were to be reached. . . . Sir S. Cripps said that . . . responsibility would go back to the two Federations if agreement could not be reached. . . . Mr. Jinnah expressed doubts as to whether this arrangement would work in practice. Matters would have to be decided every day in regard to defence. From what had

been said he had not been able to get anything which would enable him to say that the Union idea was worth considering. . . . Mr. Jinnah said that no amount of equality provided on paper was going to work. . . . Would there, for example, be equality of each community in the Services?

The Secretary of State said that Mr. Jinnah seemed to be turning to the other alternative and asked Mr. Jinnah's views on that. Mr. Jinnah said that once the principle of Pakistan was conceded the question of the territory of Pakistan could be discussed. His claim was for the six Provinces but he was willing to discuss the area. . . . He could not possibly accept that Calcutta should go out merely for the sake of 5 or 6 lakhs of Hindus (largely Depressed Classes who would prefer Pakistan) most of whom were imported labour. . . . The Secretary of State said he wished to emphasise that the Delegation did not consider that either of these two alternatives would be readily acceptable to the Congress. . . . Mr. Jinnah said that he thought with respect that the Congress stood to lose nothing. The unity of India was a myth.[47]

Jinnah's legal adroitness proved more than Pethick-Lawrence, Cripps, or Alexander could outwit, though all three wise British brains tried their best.

Finally "the Secretary of State suggested that Mr. Jinnah should think the matter over further. . . . After the Delegation's return from Kashmir perhaps Mr. Jinnah would let them know his position."[48] Round One was over. Jinnah knocked nobody down but surely won on points before the bell sounded, giving him an interlude of much-needed rest.

18

Simla Revisited
(1946)

Masterful leader that he was, Jinnah marshaled his forces, tightening his grip on the sword arm of his embryonic nation throughout the negotiations with the cabinet mission. All newly elected Muslim League legislators from provincial and central assemblies mustered in Delhi during early April 1946 to take and sign solemn pledges "in the name of Allah, the Beneficent, the Merciful," declaring their conviction that "the safety and security, and the salvation and destiny of the Muslim Nation, inhabiting the Subcontinent of India lies only in the achievement of Pakistan . . . and, believing as I do in the rightness and the justice of my cause, I pledge myself to undergo any danger, trial or sacrifice which may be demanded of me."[1] That pledge was unanimously affirmed by every elected representative of the Muslim League "amidst loud cheers." Armed with those promissory notes on the life of every Muslim League leader in British India, Quaid-i-Azam reminded his followers, "We have made a solemn declaration in this august and historic Convention that while we hope for the best, we are prepared for the worst."[2]

"What next?" asked Bengal's Suhrawardy, moving the pledge resolution that night. "We want to live in peace. We do not intend to start a civil war, but we want a land where we can live in peace. . . . I have long pondered whether the Muslims are prepared to fight. Let me honestly declare that every Muslim of Bengal is ready and prepared to lay down his life"; and turning to Quaid-i-Azam he demanded: "I call upon you to test us."[3] His famine depleted province would soon be saturated with blood. Khaliquzzaman spoke in Urdu, affirming that: "Muslims will now decide their own destiny," and he turned toward his great leader, sitting on the platform in the Anglo-Arabic Hall wearing a cream-colored sherwani, white *shalwar*, and regal fur cap, vowing, "We will lay down our lives for Pakistan."

The Punjab's nawab of Mamdot raised his mighty right arm as he spoke: "We are asked how we will defend Pakistan. I would say that if stalwart soldiers of the Punjab could defend Britain against Nazi aggression, they can also defend their own hearths and homes." From the North-West Frontier rose Pathan leader Khan Abdul Qayyum Khan "amidst thunderous applause" to shout: "Thank God, we have one flag, one leader, one platform and one ideal, Pakistan, to fight for. We are only waiting for the final order to do whatever is considered necessary for the attainment of Pakistan." Young Sardar Shaukat Hayat Khan was there to assure his Quaid-i-Azam: "I speak for the Punjabi soldier, and I say that three-quarter million demobilized soldiers in the Punjab are pledged to achieve Pakistan. . . . You, sir, are holding us back, and we beg of you to give the word of command. Let us prove to the doubting how we can and how we mean to defend our Pakistan." More restrained perhaps because he was older, Sir Firoz Khan Noon said: "Neither the Hindus nor the British know yet how far we are prepared to go in order to achieve Pakistan. We are on the threshold of a great tragedy."[4]

"What are we fighting for? What are we aiming at?" Jinnah asked his band of loyal followers immediately after they pledged him their all, as though suddenly awakening from a dream to find himself at the edge of a dreadful precipice.

> We Muslims have got everything—brains, intelligence, capacity and courage—virtues that nations must possess. But two things are lacking, and I want you to concentrate your attention on these. One thing is that foreign domination from without and Hindu domination here, particularly on our economic life, has caused a certain degeneration of these virtues in us. We have lost the fullness of our noble character. And what is character? The highest sense of honour and the highest sense of integrity, conviction, incorruptibility, readiness at any time to efface oneself for the collective good of the nation. And yet, we have done wonders. In five years our renaissance has been a miracle of achievement. I begin to think it has been a dream. . . .[5]

The mission returned from holiday in Srinagar on April 24 and asked Cripps to meet with Jinnah "informally" that evening to put to him their latest plan. In Kashmir, Nehru and Gandhi had seen—and rejected—a three-tier federation with provinces grouped to embrace the areas of Pakistan demanded by the League, with the rest of British India going to Hindustan and the princely states being permitted to join either. The All-India Union at the top of the federation would have controlled defence, foreign affairs, communications, and minority problems. The federated groups of Hindustan and Pakistan were to have had their own flags and internal security forces, and they would have been governed by central legislatures, each electing equal numbers of representatives to an all-India union. Minority problems and complaints would have been referred to a union court representing the major communities. The Muslim League and Congress would each have appointed drafting committees of their own to draw up group constitutions. Congress leadership argued that such a plan actually created Pakistan before anyone really tested the extent of the desire for such a new state, even among Muslim representatives. The mission then proposed electing a special commission from between 150 to 200 members from all the newly elected representatives of every assembly, and putting Pakistan to a vote in that body. If at least 20 percent of the commission voted for Pakistan, then Muslim representatives of the provincial assemblies of the Punjab, Sind, the North-West Frontier, Bengal, and Assam's Sylhet district could meet separately to vote on whether they wished to opt out of an Indian Union. If at least 75 percent so voted they would remain outside, and if Sind, the Punjab, and the North-West Frontier opted to separate, then Baluchistan would also become part of that Pakistan, as would Bengal and Sylhet. Non-Muslim majority districts within these provinces (as in East Punjab and West Bengal) could vote to remain in the Indian Union, and if 75 percent of their representatives preferred it those border provinces would be so partitioned.

Cripps found Jinnah "in an unreceptive mood."[6] Jinnah did, however, write down the points Cripps proposed and "he said that if Congress would accept these proposals he would put them to his Working Committee." Knowing how cautious and quickly negative Jinnah could be when he disliked a proposal, Wavell believed that Jinnah's mere willingness to present a plan to his followers constituted "provisional, very provisional, acceptance."[7] Cripps was, therefore, authorized to see Nehru "informally" and to "sound him" on the mission's proposition, but Jawaharlal "turned down the new proposal flat." They were back to square one. That evening Cripps returned to Jinnah's house and once again put to him the previous A and B plans. Jinnah definitely rejected the "minimum sovereign Pakistan" embodied in plan B but was "prepared" to put plan A—the three-tiered federal union—before his Working Committee if he could be assured that Congress were "prepared to consider it."[8] Cripps was so heartened by this breakthrough that he took plan A to Azad the next day (though Nehru had just agreed to become his successor as president of Congress the next month), and the Maulana proposed a summit meeting of four Congress and four League leaders to hammer out details of that "solution." Cripps immediately went back to Jinnah with his "good news"; however, Jinnah reminded him that what he had previously expressed was merely his "personal opinion and not necessarily that of the League," though he was willing to put that idea before his Working Committee.[9] The mission and Wavell next drafted a letter to both Jinnah and Azad, proposing a summit meeting—at Simla. New Delhi by then was sweltering, and everyone agreed that chances of reaching closure were bound to be brighter in the cool, rarefied, more rational atmosphere of a Himalayan hill station.

They reconvened at Simla on May 5, Wavell's sixty-third birthday. Jinnah chose Liaquat Ali Khan, Sardar Abdur Rab Nishtar (1899–1958), and Nawab Mohammad Ismail Khan (1886–1958) to join him at the summit. Azad selected Nehru, Patel, and Khan Abdul Ghaffar Khan as Congress's team, thus making it half Muslim and half Hindu. Jinnah refused to shake hands with Azad, but otherwise the meeting got off to what Wavell viewed as a "not too bad" start. The "first point of controversy" arose over union finances; Congress wanted the center to have "powers of direct taxation and to be self-supporting, while Jinnah advocated that it should be given a lump sum and should have to go to the groups if it wanted more."[10] They moved on to controversy over a central legislature; Congress insisted on having one, and Jinnah was negative, "his arguments . . . weaker and more unconvincing," as Wavell noted. Jinnah naturally wanted his legislature at the second-tier "group" level of Pakistan, where Congress was opposed to establishing any form of parliament. The underlying cause of every argument and conflict at Simla remained the basic differences between the League's two-nation and Congress's unitary-government philosophies of political life.

On the morning of May 6, Nehru and Jinnah crossed swords in what was to evolve into the most deadly duel in Indian history.

> Nehru said that . . . The Union of India, even if the list of subjects was short, must be strong and organic. Provinces would not be prevented from co-operating among themselves over such subjects as education and health; but they would not need a Group Executive. He appealed to the League to come into the Constitution-making Body on the assurance that there would be no compulsion. Mr. Jinnah replied that he could not accept that invitation. But if the Congress . . . would accept the Groups, the Muslim League would accept the Union. . . . Nehru pointed out that Mr. Jinnah had accepted no feature of the Union. The Union without a Legislature would be futile and entirely unacceptable.[11]

While Nehru and Jinnah fenced, "Patel's face of cold angry disapproval was a study" worthy of viceregal notice.[12] That afternoon Nehru said that "the question of grouping would arise after the constitution had been formed," insisting that "The first question to decide was the character of the Union. After that Provinces might exercise their autonomy subject to the Union constitution and Provincial representatives might bring up in the All-India Constitution-making Body proposals for grouping."[13]

Cripps drafted a new "points of agreement" document, which he planned to show Gandhi that evening, asking Wavell to tackle Jinnah. The Mahatma was living in Simla's "Chadwick" bungalow with Patel and Ghaffar Khan, but he had not come to any mission meetings. Cripps had hoped to win Gandhi's support, but he struck out. Gandhi argued that "the proposed solution was 'worse than Pakistan,' and he could not recommend it to Congress." He "seemed quite unmoved at the prospect of civil war," Wavell noted, concluding, "I think he [Gandhi] had adopted Patel's thesis that if we are firm the Muslims will not fight."[14] The following evening Wavell met with Jinnah for over an hour. "He was friendly but showed his deep and utter mistrust of Congress and all their works. He is convinced of their intention to split the Muslims and secure Hindu domination. . . . He said finally that we must do what we think just and fair, but not press him too hard."[15] Meanwhile Cripps returned to tackle Gandhi, and this time said the Mahatma gave "full approval" to an outlined proposal of the three-tier system.[16] Wavell, who did "not quite trust Cripps and wholly mistrusted Gandhi," was "not at all persuaded that C. had led G. up to the altar, . . . more likely that G. has led C. down the garden path."[17]

On May 8, 1946, Pethick-Lawrence sent Jinnah and Azad identical copies of nine suggested points of agreement that started with "There shall be an All-India Union Government and Legislature dealing with Foreign Affairs, Defence, Communications, fundamental rights and having the necessary powers to obtain for itself the finances it requires for these subjects," then vested "All the remaining powers in the Provinces," and as point three stated: "Groups of Provinces may be formed and such groups may determine the Provincial subjects which they desire to take in common."[18] Jinnah replied the same day from "Yarrows," the bungalow he occupied in Simla:

> We are of the opinion that the new suggested points for agreement are a fundamental departure from the original formula embodied in your letter of 27th April, which was rejected by the Congress. . . . In these circumstances, we think, no useful purpose will be served to discuss this paper.[19]

Gandhi also rejected the written points of "agreement" for various other reasons, but primarily because 90 million Muslims would enjoy "parity" with over 200 million Hindus, an idea he termed "really worse than Pakistan."[20]

They were back to the drawing board. Cripps went to see Azad; Wavell visited Jinnah. Nehru was with Azad when Cripps saw them, finding them both "reasonable" but "having great difficulty" with "colleagues," presumably meaning Patel. Jinnah assured Wavell that he was "trying to be reasonable" but that he was "already the subject of criticism from his supporters for having yielded" on the "acceptance of a Union of any kind," which he termed "a great concession."[21] Thus he insisted on Pakistan groups meeting to define their own constitution. On the evening of May 9, Nehru proposed that Congress and the League should meet with an "umpire" to settle their points of difference. "Jinnah replied that he would be pleased to meet any *Hindu* representatives of Congress. There was a pregnant silence for a minute or so; and then Nehru suggested that he and Jinnah should meet there and then and see whether they could decide on an umpire."[22] Everyone else left the conference room and strolled round Simla's lawns for forty minutes while Jinnah and Nehru locked horns in single combat. They agreed only to adjourn for two days, however, and resolved to meet again on Saturday, May 11 at 3:00 P.M.

Nehru wrote Jinnah that day on the eve of their meeting to report that he and his colleagues had "given a good deal of thought to the choice of a suitable umpire," deciding that it would "probably be desirable to exclude Englishmen, Hindus, Muslims and Sikhs."[23] The field was thus quite limited, but Congress drew up "a considerable list" that included Americans. Jinnah replied that there were "several points" that remained to be discussed "besides the fixing of any umpire" and informed Nehru that he would be "glad" to meet with him any time after 10:00 A.M. on Saturday. Nehru answered, "I was under the impression that the proposal to have an umpire had been agreed to and our next business was to suggest names."[24] Nonetheless, the two leaders met at Jinnah's residence at 10:30 A.M.

They fought on till after 6:00 P.M., when Pethick-Lawrence asked Jinnah to put his precise conditions in writing for the next round to begin Sunday evening. Jinnah sent a written statement of ten principles to Pethick-Lawrence the next day. There were to be separate constitution-making bodies for the Pakistan and Hindustan groups, and "parity of representation" between the groups in a union executive or legislature that might be established. No "controversial" decision could be taken in the union except by a "three-fourths" majority. Azad also submitted a written proposal of suggested points of agreement on behalf of the Congress. It opened with the formation of a single constituent assembly composed of elective representatives of all provinces and princely states. Pethick-Lawrence asked both parties that evening if they thought, in view of positions they had outlined, that they saw any "chance of reaching agreement?" No one could honestly say yes. The secretary of state, therefore, felt he had no further option but "to close" the conference. The cabinet mission and viceroy planned to return to New Delhi on Tuesday.

That Monday, May 13, Wavell talked with Jinnah, who "looked tired and ill."[25] They talked about the new executive council that the viceroy proposed to appoint. Wavell offered the League parity with Congress, planning to include one Sikh, one Scheduled Caste member, and one "other" minority. He urged Jinnah to accept "so favourable a proportion." Jinnah listened carefully but made "little comment." He said that "whether or not the Muslim League came into the Interim Government would depend on whether our Statement seemed likely to offer a solution of the long-term issue. His fear was that the Congress plan was to get control of the Central Government . . . and concentrate on getting control in the Provinces." Jinnah planned to remain in Simla to "rest and recuperate," Wavell reported, for at least three weeks.

The mission now felt obliged to propose its own settlement, a final move in this stalemated game. It had listened to all the arguments, studied all the documents, and questioned all the witnesses. Judgment could be deferred no longer. The prime minister demanded an account of his mission's progress. The cable between Simla and London was kept hot and humming through many a mid-May night. The Labour government seemed almost ready to break apart, if not topple from power, over the Congress-League struggle.

The cabinet mission broadcast its plan worldwide from New Delhi on Thursday night, May 16, 1946. It was the last hope for a single Indian union to emerge peacefully in the wake of the British raj. The statement reviewed the "fully independent sovereign State of Pakistan" option, rejecting it for various reasons, among which were that it "would not solve the communal minority problem" but only raise more such problems, especially for Sikhs, while irrevocably shattering the military, economic, and administrative unity so arduously developed throughout the last century and more of British rule. The basic form of the constitution recommended was a three-tier scheme with a minimal central Union at the top for only foreign affairs, defence, and communications, and Provinces at the bottom, which "should be free to form Groups with executives and legislatures," with each Group being empowered to "determine the Provincial subjects to be taken in common." Every ten years any Province could by simple majority vote "call for a reconsideration of the terms of the constitution."

Details of the new constitution were to be worked out by an assembly representing "as broad-based and accurate" a cross section of the population of India as possible. An elaborate method of assuring proper representation of all communities was outlined with due consideration given to the representation of states as well as provinces.

"To the leaders and people of India who now have the opportunity of complete independence we would finally say this," the mission's statement concluded.

> We and our Government and countrymen hoped that it would be possible for the Indian people themselves to agree upon the method of framing the new constitution under which they will live. Despite the labours which we have shared with the Indian Parties . . . this has not been possible. We therefore now lay before you proposals which . . . we trust will enable you to attain your independence in the shortest time and with the least danger of internal disturbance and conflict. These proposals may not, of course, completely satisfy all parties, . . . We ask you to consider the alternative to acceptance of these proposals . . . a grave danger of violence, chaos, and even civil war. The result and duration of such a disturbance cannot be foreseen; but it is certain that it would be a terrible disaster for many millions of men, women and children. . . . We appeal to all who have the future good of India at heart to extend their vision beyond their own community or interest to the interests of the whole four hundred millions of the Indian people . . . we look forward with you to your ever increasing prosperity among the great nations of the world, and to a future even more glorious than your past.[26]

"Whatever the wrong done to India by British rule," Gandhi commented next day, "if the statement of the Mission was genuine, as he believed it was, it was in discharge of an obligation they had declared the British owed to India, namely, to get off India's back. It contained the seed to convert this land of sorrow into one without sorrow and suffering."[27] Pethick-Lawrence and Cripps met with Gandhi the following morning for almost three hours and reported to Wavell and Alexander that "At the outset Mr. Gandhi had seemed very content with the Government's Statement, but later he had raised a point over which the Secretary of State felt some difficulty . . . the question whether the procedure laid down for the Constituent Assembly was subject to alteration . . . whether it was open to Congress representatives in the Constituent Assembly at the opening meeting to deal with procedure to raise the question whether the Assembly should in fact divide into the three sections, or whether it should decide the Union's constitution first. . . . Mr. Gandhi indicated that his support for the Statement would hinge on this point."[28] The viceroy "was not very clear" what was "at the back" of Gandhi's mind in raising this question, but argued forcefully, as Jinnah had, that he was "quite convinced" that the primary objective of Congress was "to get power at the centre in the Interim Government" so that it could then "at any time torpedo the Constitution-making Body by raising some crucial communal issue."

Jinnah phoned from Srinagar on May 18 to report that "the reaction of the Muslims against the Statement is very strong,"[29] and requested a month before coming to any "decision" in order to have time to consult his Working Committee. He was obviously fighting for time on two counts: his own fragile health, taxed to its limit by the week's talks; and his concern about extremists in his own party, who were ready to launch jihad without further delay. "If the thing was rushed everything would be spoiled," Jinnah warned Wavell's private secretary in their telephone conversation. Next morning, the mission met with Liaquat Ali Khan and informed him it was "impossible" for them to wait four weeks for Jinnah's response. They "pressed" him to urge Jinnah to return to Delhi "at once" or to "authorize the Nawabzada [Liaquat Ali] to negotiate."[30] Liaquat promised to try but returned that afternoon "after a talk to Jinnah on the telephone, and said that J. was calling the Working Committee . . . for June 3 and 4 and the Council for June 5, and begged not to be hurried as it would take time to persuade his people to accept the proposals."[31] The mission agreed, though "rather reluctantly." Jinnah planned to return to New Delhi on June 2, cutting his much needed vacation in the hills short by a week.

On May 19, the very day Liaquat Ali met with the mission, Gandhi wrote Pethick-Lawrence from "Valmiki Mandir," where he was staying in New Delhi, to ask further clarification on the same sticking point he had raised in earlier conversation with the secretary of state. "Do you regard a recommendation as obligatory on any member of the contemplated Constituent Assembly?" inquired the Mahatma. "I know the legal position," Gandhi added. "My question has reference to the honourableness of opposition to grouping."[32] Wavell read that letter as "the first of the Congress efforts to wreck the Groups of Provinces."[33]

Cripps drafted a reply to Gandhi which explained: "We have stated publicly that we cannot further negotiate these proposals which are—as far as we are concerned—in their final form."[34] On May 20, Gandhi wrote again, this time at greater length.

> I would put on record my conviction that Independence in fact would be a farce, if the British Troops are in India even for peace and order within, or danger from without. . . . If the position about the Troops persists, "Independence next month" is either insincere or a thought-

less cry. Acceptance of "Quit India" by the British is unconditional, whether the Constituent Assembly succeeds or fails. . . . A drastic revision of the attitude is a necessity. . . . As to the Interim Government, the more I think and observe, the more certain is my feeling that a proper National Government responsible in fact, if not in law, to the elected members of the Central Legislative Assembly should precede the summons for the election of members of the Constituent Assembly. . . . Without it, deep and universal corruption cannot end, without it the psychological effect will not be produced. . . . Every day's delay in forming such a government is agony to the famished millions of India.[35]

First Lord Alexander was then convinced that "Gandhi had two objects— to humiliate the British Government and to promote a policy of scuttle, and secondly, to secure power without a constitution coming into being and so to abandon the just claims of the Muslim League."[36]

The mission wired Attlee that the "situation has taken a turn for the worse. . . . Congress propose to make an attack on the grouping proposal and . . . they object to parity in the interim Executive. These two points may be crucial in securing Muslim co-operation. . . . We may therefore be faced before long with threat of direct action by Congress if we do not give way to their demands. We are giving consideration to what our policy should be in that event."[37] While the mission waited for the League to meet, favorable reports of Muslim reactions came in from the Punjab, but communal tensions and fever kept mounting, especially in large cities like Karachi, where "the accidental dropping of an onion from a verandah by a child nearly started a communal fracas," reported the viceroy. "If the Muslim League were to reject the scheme . . . there would undoubtedly be widespread communal riots."[38]

Governor Sir Frederick Burrows of Bengal informed the mission on May 24 that Bengal Hindus and Muslims were both much "relieved" that their province would not have to be partitioned if the plan were accepted. He warned, however, that rejection of the proposals by Jinnah would lead to resignation of the League ministry and serve as a "signal for a Jehad." There had already been "a serious situation in Chittagong started by students protesting against the rejection of Pakistan,"[39] controlled only because of Muslim ministers going personally to that port to exert mollifying influence.

Woodrow Wyatt spoke with Jinnah on Friday, May 24, and was informed by Quaid-i-Azam that "What was required was a surgical operation."[40] Jinnah must have known by then that his lungs were incurable through simple medication. He offered to transmit some advice to the mis-

sion through Major Wyatt "as to how they should proceed," if he thought
the mission "would not breach his confidence." Wyatt reassured him on
the confidentiality point and reported his belief that what Jinnah wanted
to tell the mission was "that the British should remain as the binding forces
in the Indian Centre for some 15 years and deal with defence, and foreign
affairs for Pakistan and Hindustan consulting the Prime Ministers of each
State."[41] This seemed a sensible solution from Jinnah's point of view since
that would have created the least havoc and provided the most security and
stability to all Indians, especially the minorities. He dared not say it in
public, of course, and he did not trust Cripps to keep it from Nehru. Nor
was he certain that Pethick-Lawrence would not tip his hand to Gandhi,
yet with time running out and his energy level as low as it was, Jinnah
obviously felt almost desperate to convey this advice to the mission before
it was too late. He was "very anxious," Wyatt noted, about the strong
"Muslim reaction" against the mission's statement and thus most hesitant
to support it openly.

Wyatt cleverly concluded by "asking" Jinnah, in view of all that he had
said and sensed from his mood and manner, whether the League's Working
Committee might not "possibly pass a resolution on the following lines.

> The British had exceeded their brief in pronouncing on the merits of
> Pakistan. They had no business to turn down what millions of people
> wanted. Their analysis of Pakistan was outrageous. But the Muslims
> had never expected the British to give them Pakistan. They had
> never expected anyone to give them Pakistan. They knew that they
> had to get it by their own strong right arm. The scheme outlined in
> the Cabinet Mission's Statement was impracticable and could not
> work. But nevertheless in order to show that they would give it a
> trial, although they knew that the machinery could not function, they
> would accept the Statement and would not go out of their way to
> sabotage the procedure—*but they would accept the Statement as the
> first step on the road to Pakistan.*

"At this proposition he was delighted and said, 'That's it, you've got it,' and
I am completely convinced that that is what the Muslim League will do,"
Wyatt quite rightly, most presciently, predicted.[42]

"Cripps is still in hospital though better, and Alexander is gone to
Ceylon to inspect the Fleet," Pethick-Lawrence wrote Attlee on May 26.

> What is going to happen I don't know. Gandhi is provokingly enig-
> matic and blows hot and cold. Azad, Nehru and Jinnah I think all
> want a settlement. But already we are up against the second hurdle.
> . . . Azad and Nehru and the Congress generally are willing to waive

any formal or legal change in the interim constitution, but they want
almost absolute power in reality and they want something to be able
to say about it to their people. Jinnah not only does not want the
Viceroy to relinquish his authority but he positively wants him to
retain it. The Viceroy is now I think convinced that he must go to
the limit of what is possible in satisfying the Congress. . . . I have
not . . . abandoned hope that we may surmount this difficulty and
that both Congress and Muslim League may both express a grudging
acquiescence in our plan sufficient to enable us to go ahead with
summoning the Constituent Assembly . . . on or before June 15th.
There are many people who would welcome our positively getting
on with the job.[43]

Not least among them, Pethick-Lawrence himself.

Jinnah returned to New Delhi on June 2, and Wavell met with him the
following morning, finding him "in good heart. He said he could not give
me names for the Interim Government until after he had seen his Council,
but I got the impression that the M. L. would probably come in. . . . He
then went on to complain that the Muslims had not been given parity in
the Union Legislature, and stressed the very great concession he had made
in agreeing to a Union at all. . . . He then asked what we should do if the
M. L. came in and Congress refused. I had anticipated this query and had
consulted S. of S. . . . I told him that the M. L. would certainly not suffer
by its readiness to work the Delegation scheme, and that the intention was
to go ahead . . . with any party who would work for it. He asked for
something more specific before he met his Working Committee at 6 p.m.
and I said I could do nothing more without consulting the Delegation.
He . . . asked me to do so."[44] Wavell got the delegation's "permission to
give Jinnah a verbal assurance" that afternoon.

The League council met on June 5, and a "secret" British Intelligence
report noted that "Mr. Jinnah said that he and other members of the Working Committee were worried as to what would happen if the Muslim
League accepted the proposals and the Congress did not. The Viceroy replied that he would brook no refusal from Congress and that if they decided against acceptance he would hand over the interim government to
the Muslim League and give them all the support they required. This very
point was raised by some members in the Council meeting and Mr. Jinnah
took them into confidence and gave the same reply."[45] Next day, Jinnah
spoke to his League council, informing them "It is now up to you as the
Parliament of the Muslim Nation to take your decision. . . . I repeat . . .
that delay is not good either for the British Government or the Hindus. If
they love freedom, if they love the independence of India, if they want to

be free, then the sooner they realise the better that the quickest way is to agree to Pakistan."[46] Jinnah then discussed both internal and external relations, calling upon the Arabs to "see that not one more Jew landed in Palestine," condemning the "Dutch imperialist hold on Indonesia," and concluding that in India most Hindus had "wind" in their heads. "There is no remedy for a disease of the kind. Where a man is under a delusion, the only place for him is a lunatic asylum. With this delusion, the Hindu is arrogant, tyrannical and oppressive. But I think all this will sober down. If it does not, then we shall have to do something to make it sober down."[47]

Before June 6 ended, the Muslim League council accepted the cabinet mission's plan "by a large majority," Wavell noted. "Now the real battle begins, and the great question is whether the Delegation will stand up to Congress or not. Parity in the Interim Government may be the main issue."[48] Francis Turnbull lunched with Birla on June 6, reporting how "alarmed" he was at Jinnah's demand for Muslim League "parity" in an interim government. Turnbull noted that he thought "Congress had come very near to accepting parity" at Simla last year, but Birla insisted the "situation" had been quite different then, requiring an emergency wartime government, and now with elections having given Congress most of the "general seats" there could be no question of parity for the League.

Jinnah spent an hour with the viceroy on June 7, informing Wavell that he wanted the "Defence Portfolio for himself, and Foreign Affairs and Planning for two of his followers,"[49] in an interim government composed of five Muslim Leaguers, five Congress members, and only two others. It was Jinnah's first positive expression of personal interest in any interim government office and would, unfortunately, be his last. Jinnah asked the viceroy "what would happen to his seat in the Assembly if he became a member of the Interim Government" and "said he hoped there was no objection to his remaining President of the Muslim League if he came into the Interim Government."[50]

Nehru and Azad came to speak to the cabinet mission on June 10, arguing vigorously against parity. Wavell, Alexander and Pethick-Lawrence tried to argue for greater tolerance and more cooperation with the League, but Nehru insisted "it was frankly beyond the power of Congress to agree to parity." Then Gandhi re-entered the scene, letting it be known to Pethick-Lawrence and Cripps through intermediaries that he was willing to see them. Alexander, like Wavell, was "completely mistrustful now of G. and all his ways."[51] Cripps suggested that the viceroy tackle Jinnah and Nehru; Pethick-Lawrence wanted to go off to see Gandhi, but the first sea lord "was dead against it."[52] With his health restored, Cripps came up with the idea of "two vice-presidents" on the interim government cabinet, one from each party—Jinnah and Nehru—rotating office. "It was also possible under this arrangement to have Nehru and Jinnah as Ministers without portfolio. . . . It was agreed that the Viceroy should ask Nehru and Jinnah to come to dinner that evening for a discussion on the position of the Interim Government." Everyone agreed it was essential to get these two leaders to talk before their party positions froze incompatibly.

That night Cripps went personally to "persuade" Jinnah to meet with Nehru and Wavell the following evening. He spent "several hours with Jinnah"[53] alone in his Delhi house, recording an "unsigned" "note" of their "conversation" which has been incorrectly labeled a "Note by Major Wyatt,"[54] but was clearly the record of this most critical Jinnah-Cripps summit conference that failed.

> Mr. Jinnah said that he was not prepared to discuss parity with anyone. He had had great opposition in his own party to accepting the Mission's proposal, he did not think that opposition was fully appreciated, nor what he had gone through. The only way he had been able to persuade the Muslim League Council and Working Committee to accept the Statement was by promising them that he would not join the Interim Government unless the Muslim League had parity with Congress. He was now pledged to that. He could not go back on that. He was not his own master.[55]

A singular confession for Jinnah, yet one he knew would appeal to Cripps. "He was not prepared to meet Nehru or anyone else from Congress to talk about the Interim Government until Congress had accepted the Mission's proposals. Then any such talk would have to be on the basis of parity. The moment that Congress accepted, he would, of course, be willing to meet Nehru and the Viceroy and put before them the names of his nominees with the suggested portfolios."[56] It was one of Jinnah's key techniques for sparing himself and saving energy to carry on important business, by always insisting upon prior acceptance of a principle he deemed vital in any negotiations before taking on the burden of a face to face meeting with the "other side." Especially when he considered the outcome doubtful, or had no faith in his opposite number.

Jinnah next reassured Cripps of how sensible and reasonable he actually was, having just taken so intransigent a stand on this key issue. He expressed "shock" at having "got an impression" (from whom he does not say) that it was being reported that the League's nominees for the interim government would be "any old people from the Muslim League Working Committee." Jinnah insisted "He wanted the best men. This was an important matter. . . . He was not going to put in as his nominees people who were popular or well known in the Muslim League if they could not do the job. He had many able men in the civil service and he would put some of those in even though no one had ever heard of them. The problem was to get the right man for the right job. He was quite prepared to talk over the portfolios with Nehru and make adjustments with him so that they could get a workable team which was what was needed."[57] Could anything be more reasonable? Now that barrister Jinnah re-established his image of sensible moderation in management matters, he could return to his parity demand, but this time he put the onus of having *abandoned* "parity" on Congress.

"He seemed slightly interested in an idea that had been put to him of an inner cabinet of six with parity for Congress and the Muslim League. (Something based on these lines may be the way out.)"[58] The parenthetic was Cripps's note to himself and his Mission colleagues, for he was always coming up with such brilliant solutions to what everyone else found "insoluble" problems. Cripps concluded this important "note" with an indication of how much he personally had been swayed and moved by Jinnah's unique advocacy, and how open his own mind remained to every shred of information: "I have now heard . . . from different sources (apart from Mr. Jinnah), that Jinnah *did* promise the Muslim League Council and Working Committee that he would not go into an Interim Government without parity. I believe that he really did have to deal with a great deal of resentment in his party."[59] That closing comment sounds positively sympathetic to Jinnah's position and the pressures under which he was fighting. He had weaned Cripps a long way from Nehru's side without really budging one inch from the position to which he clung so tenaciously.

Just when Jinnah scored in this tête-à-tête with the mission's most brilliant, pro-Congress member, Nehru, Patel, and Gandhi were leaving negative personal impressions on the cabinet mission as well as the viceroy, who viewed them alternately as petulant or pettifogging hagglers. Nehru brought a list of fifteen names for the interim council, but only four were from the League; five were Congress Hindus, one non-Congress Hindu, one Congress Scheduled Caste, and one Congress woman. Wavell rightly informed Nehru that "this list would be quite unacceptable to Mr. Jinnah." Next morning Jinnah arrived and gave the viceroy "some names for the Government if the League came in." Nehru returned that afternoon and "seemed depressed, worked himself up to one outburst about Jinnah's refusal to meet Azad and described Jinnah as a wrecker."[60] Later that evening Patel returned and "talked volubly without listening to any argument and sung a continuous hymn of hate against Jinnah and the League. He said . . . that no Government formed by the Viceroy would be acceptable." That day, Gandhi wrote to Wavell, urging him to "Dare to do the right" in choosing between Congress's list of nominees and the League's. "You must make your choice of one horse or the other," the Mahatma advised the field marshal. "So far as I can see you will never succeed in riding two at the same time. Choose the names submitted either by Congress or the League. For God's sake do not make an incompatible mixture and in trying to do so produce a fearful explosion. Anyway fix your time-limit and tell us all to leave when that limit is over. I hope I have made my meaning clear."[61] Wavell, however, was thoroughly disenchanted with Gandhi, whom he judged to be "an exceedingly shrewd, obstinate, domineering, double-tongued, single-minded politician; and there is little true saintliness in him."[62]

In London, the British cabinet considered the "military implications" of a proposed breakdown in Indian negotiations. It rejected a proposal, should Congress refuse to cooperate with the mission's plan, to grant independence ("scuttle") to Central and Southern India and fall back to the North-West and North-East, seeking to hold "Pakistan." The prime minister authorized working out plans for the "evacuation" of Europeans but stressed the importance of "safeguarding against leakage" the fact that any such plans were underway. The cabinet resolved "in principle" that "no further women and children should be embarked for India."

The British cabinet considered the foreign policy implications of "any action by His Majesty's Government which appears to suggest that we are abandoning our position in India" and was warned by Foreign Minister Ernest Bevin that

> As regards American public opinion, such sympathy as we might hope to get—and it would not be much—from liberal internationalist circles for a policy of abandonment would be infinitely outweighed to our disadvantage by the confirmation that far wider circles would see in such a policy of their assumption that we no longer had the means or resolution to face our responsibilities. . . . To sum up . . . any appearance of abandonment of our position in India without a solution would weaken our world position.[63]

In New Delhi, Britain's cabinet mission continued laboring to put a new interim government in place before India's summer heat melted the hearts and minds of those three exhausted wise men. On June 16, Wavell noted "the Delegation's final (?) attempt to induce the children to play together is launched. . . . All this huckstering and bargaining by Congress has shown their complete inability to take a broad or statesmanlike view. Jinnah has shown up well in comparison."[64] Azad kept sending him long, detailed, demanding letters. Gandhi kept meeting with Pethick-Lawrence, Nehru with Cripps, Wavell with Jinnah. They were arguing over one or two names on an interim cabinet that never met—designed to keep a land of 400 million from drowning in an ocean of blood and poverty. Was it that all of them understood how hopeless a task they would face once they agreed to take "power?" Wavell was bored sick of them all by now, including Jinnah, with whom he reported a "not very pleasant" interview on June 18, commenting "The more I see of these Indian politicians, the more I despair of India. . . . He said that the Working Committee were meeting tonight . . . but indicated that he thought we were being very weak with Congress and giving way to them on every point, and that he himself was being 'ground down' beyond endurance. . . . Jinnah gave me the impression of being rather depressed and tired, and of feeling that he had been rather let down."[65]

Cripps was prepared to ask Jinnah "for a list of names" for an entire interim government if Congress opted to reject the mission's plan. Wavell, however, "would be very chary of giving Jinnah responsibility for forming the whole Government. He would prefer to ask Jinnah to come in on the basis that he would get the same share as now proposed. The responsibility for this Interim Government would be the Viceroy's and Jinnah would not be Prime Minister," argued the offended viceroy, who thus proved his ability to "play" the game as well as any of the other "children."[66] Cripps responded that "it seemed to him reasonable that Jinnah should have the opportunity of expressing his views as to . . . the composition of the Government. If Jinnah declined to serve on reasonable terms, his view was that we should then ask Congress to form a Government. The Viceroy said he could not agree. He would rather have a Government of officials." The first lord of admiralty agreed with Wavell. Pethick-Lawrence "sympathised somewhat with Sir S. Cripps" but did not want to ride roughshod over the viceroy, and he decided if it came to choosing Jinnah he would have to consult Attlee and his colleagues back home.

The mission met with Nehru, Azad, Patel, and Rajendra Prasad on Sunday, June 23. Pethick-Lawrence explained that he and his colleagues "quite appreciated the importance which Congress attached to the recognition of their national character, but they did hope that in this particular instance Congress would see their way not to make a demand for the inclusion of a Muslim among the Congress representatives in the Interim Government, though without in any way creating a precedent or approving a principle."[67] Nehru protested that "the Delegation appeared to start with the presumption that progress could only be made with the co-operation of the Muslim League. The Congress disagreed." Cripps tried to argue that Con-

gress Muslims being included in provincial governments, sufficed to dem-
onstrate the "national character of Congress," but Nehru would not budge,
nor would Patel or Azad. Pethick-Lawrence quite cogently remarked that

> The greatest obstacle to India going forward towards independence
> was the inability to get started. . . . Suppose that the Congress rep-
> resentatives persuaded the Delegation to agree to the inclusion of a
> Congress Muslim. If that occurred he did not believe that Mr. Jin-
> nah would accept it, and there would be no Coalition Government.
> He believed it was really in the best interests of Congress and of In-
> dia to act courageously and to begin by accepting the conditions
> under which a coalition would be possible. A solution of the com-
> munal problem in India had to be found, and for the parties to work
> together on practical problems provided the best hope.[68]

The wisdom of Pethick-Lawrence's final plea made no positive impact however. Nehru replied that the leaders of Congress had been seeking a solution of the communal problem "for thirty years" but had always been
"undermined" by the League's refusal to recognize any "Muslims who supported the national ideal, and the Congress could not desert those Muslims
who had done so." Patel added that to capitulate on this point "would force
all the Muslims out of the Congress." But on June 25, 1946, the Congress
Working Committee finally resolved to "accept" the mission's plan of the
last month, while expressing grave reservations about "The limitation of the
Central authority, as contained in the proposals, as well as the system of
grouping of Provinces."[69]

"We are now precluded from trying to form an Interim Government
with the participation of the Muslim League, but without that of the Congress," Wavell noted in his "top secret" memo to the mission after receiving
the Congress response, "and Congress will claim that in any fresh attempt
all the original bases and the assurances given to Mr. Jinnah have disappeared. We have in fact been outmanoeuvred by the Congress and this
ability of Congress to twist words and phrases and to take advantage of
any slip in wording is what Mr. Jinnah has all along feared, and has been
the reason for his difficult attitude. The success of the Congress, which he
will feel has been mainly due to their continuous contacts with the Mission . . . will increase his distrust, both of the Congress and the Mission,
and of the Viceroy. . . . Tempers are frayed; the Muslim League feel that
they have been betrayed; and the Congress feel that they have gained an
advantage of which they will not be slow to make capital."[70] Wavell would
soon be left to form a caretaker government of officials, an alternative far

more congenial to his nature and experience than trying to preside over a coalition cabinet would have been.

That evening the Mission and Wavell met with Jinnah to show him the Congress resolution. That final meeting lasted almost three hours, till after 8:00 P.M. Wavell informed Jinnah that he would appoint a "caretaker government" for a "short interval" and they could "go ahead with the Constituent Assembly and constitution-making" during that interlude since the cabinet mission was returning to England. Jinnah was thoroughly shocked by what he heard, asking "Did he understand that the Delegation did not now wish to form an Interim Government? He had understood that if one party rejected the offer of June 16th we should go ahead with the other. . . . The Muslim League had accepted. . . . Mr. Jinnah said he disliked the suggestion for a postponement of the question of the Interim Government. He thought it was bad for the prestige of the Delegation and also for his own prestige. It would destroy both."[71] How ego shattering that moment of "truth" must have been for him, how frustrating after all these years, all these decades. Once more to be told "Not yet! Still not quite ready for you, Sir. Next month, perhaps, or next year." Would he live another year? It was "a deplorable" interview, Wavell reported, noting that "by the time we got down to real business . . . J. was in a thoroughly evil mood; accused us of bad faith and of giving way to Congress, and considered that he should be given the opportunity of entering the Government."[72]

Next day, Alexander went round to see Jinnah to tell him how "anxious" he was not to "part" with bad feelings between them. But Jinnah's feeling of friendship, empathy, and trust for the British and all they had always stood for since his first trip to London, would never quite be put back together again—after that fatal fall.

19

Bombay to London
(1946)

"If there is not sufficient power, create that power," Jinnah charged his League council in Bombay in late July. "All efforts of the Muslim League at fairplay, justice, even supplication and prayers have had no response of any kind from the Congress. The Cabinet Mission have played into the hands of the Congress. It has played a game of its own."[1] In 1920 he had lost faith in Congress. Then, more than a quarter-century later, he abandoned hope and trust in the British, whose postwar problems and pressures obliged them to "play" into Congress's hand.

"Throughout these negotiations the Cabinet Mission and the Viceroy were under terror and threats of the Congress," Jinnah told his 450 followers, who were packed into a sweltering hall crowded with members of the press, both foreign and domestic, as well as delegates from every province.

> The Cabinet Delegation and the Viceroy . . . have gone back on their plighted word and abandoned what was announced as their final proposals. . . . Congress really never accepted the long-term plan. Its conditional acceptance was communicated to the Cabinet Mission by the Congress President on June 25. . . . The Cabinet Mission like a drowning man ready to catch hold of a straw treated this conditional acceptance . . . as genuine. . . . Pandit Jawaharlal Nehru as the elected President . . . at a Press conference in Bombay on July 10, made the policy and attitude of the Congress towards the long-term proposal clear . . . that the Congress was committed to nothing. . . . What is the use of imagining things and dreaming.[2]

Jinnah convened his council to re-examine "the whole position" in the light of broken British "pledges" and of Congress's defiance of the League

and rejection of the mission's plan. "I can tell you this without fear of contradiction that of the three parties, throughout the negotiation the Muslim
League behaved as an honourable organization," Jinnah assured his backers. "We worked with clean hands. The Muslim League is the only party
that has emerged from these negotiations with honour and clean hands."[3]
Clean hands had always been a prime virtue to him, and they seemed then
to symbolize a political surgeon's final preparation before entering the op-
erating room where the hopelessly sick patient lay waiting to be cut. Nothing short of radical surgery would suffice, when even the "great" British
mission "went back on its words . . . cowed down and paralysed" before
a Congress which had neither "decency" nor "any sense of honour and
courage."

"All these facts prove clearly beyond a shadow of doubt," Quaid-i-Azam
continued, "that the only solution of India's problem is Pakistan. So long
as the Congress and Mr. Gandhi maintain that they represent the whole
of India . . . so long as they deny true facts and the absolute truth that
the Muslim League is the only authoritative organization of the Muslims,
and so long as they continue in this vicious circle, there can and will be no
compromise or freedom. . . . Mr. Gandhi now speaks as a universal adviser. He says that the Congress . . . is the trustee for the people of India. . . . We have enough experience of one trustee that has been here for
150 years. We do not want the Congress to become our trustee. We have
now grown up. The only trustee of the Muslims is the Muslim nation."[4]

Jinnah now accused Cripps of trying to "wriggle out" of simple defini-
tions in his Commons talk about the mission, resorting "to jugglery of words
and misleading the house," and adding in what for Jinnah was perhaps the
deepest cut of all, "I am sorry to say that Sir Stafford Cripps debased his
legal talents." To Pethick-Lawrence, who had informed London's House of
Lords "that he [Jinnah] could not have a monopoly of Muslim Nomination," Jinnah shouted, "I am not a trader. I am not asking for concessions
for oil, nor am I higgling and haggling like a *banya*." His fierce rejection
of the business of his fathers and their commercial community underscores
how betrayed he felt in the aftermath of the negotiations that ended the
mission. To orthodox fellow Muslims, for whom commerce, trade, and interest were almost as execrable as pork and wine, he had proudly professed
himself as antipathetic to "higgling *banyas*" as the strictest Sunni mullah.
The bridge of faith in the British common law that had hitherto linked him
to Cripps, Pethick-Lawrence, Ramsay MacDonald, Morley, and Gladstone
was shattered, swept away by torrents of self-interest that gushed from
Simla's Himalayan heights, dissolving like his trust in all of them in a flood
of frustrated despair.

Next day the Muslim League council met to consider over a dozen resolutions that had been tabled by members, trying to decide "what steps" the League should take in view "of the Cabinet Mission having gone back on their word," as Jinnah told them. Liaquat Ali read each of the resolutions aloud, and then general discussion began, lasting two whole days. "The best for us is frankly to admit that we made a mistake in accepting a Union of some sort proposed in the Scheme and go back to our Pakistan ideal," urged Sir Firoz Khan Noon. "The path of wisdom lies in the total rejection of the constitutional proposals . . . let there be one guiding beacon before us—a fully sovereign, separate State of Pakistan."[5] Maulana Hasrat Mohani rose to shout amidst wild cheering, "If the Quaid-i-Azam will only give his word, the Muslims of India will rise in revolt at a moment's notice." Other maulanas, khans, and mullahs reiterated those chants, and Raja Ghazanfar Ali promised that "If Mr. Jinnah gave the call, Muslims from all walks of life would come forward to carry on the struggle for the attainment of Pakistan."

On July 29, 1946, Jinnah and his Working Committee presented two resolutions hammered out after hearing the council's opinions. The first withdrew League acceptance of the cabinet mission's May proposals; the second charted the League's course of future direct action.

> Whereas Muslim India has exhausted, without success, all efforts to find a peaceful solution of the Indian problem by compromise and constitutional means; and whereas the Congress is bent upon setting up Caste-Hindu Raj in India with the connivance of the British; and whereas recent events have shown that power politics and not justice and fair play are the deciding factors in Indian affairs; and whereas it has become abundantly clear that the Muslims of India would not rest contented with anything less than the immediate establishment of an Independent and fully sovereign State of Pakistan . . . the time has come for the Muslim nation to resort to Direct Action to achieve Pakistan to assert their just rights, to vindicate their honour and to get rid of the present British slavery and the contemplated future Caste-Hindu domination.[6]

After both resolutions were enthusiastically adopted, Jinnah concluded: "We have taken a most historic decision. Never before in the whole life-history of the Muslim League did we do anything except by constitutional methods and constitutional talks. We are to-day forced into this position by a move in which both the Congress and Britain have participated. We have been attacked on two fronts. . . . To-day we have said good-bye to constitutions and constitutional methods. Throughout the painful negotiations, the two parties with whom we bargained held a pistol at us; one with power and machine-guns behind it, and the other with non-co-operation and the threat to launch mass civil disobedience. This situation must be met. We also have a pistol."[7]

Pethick-Lawrence urged Wavell to meet Jinnah as soon as possible and to "press him even now" to permit members of the Muslim League to join an interim coalition government with Congress. Wavell underestimated Jinnah's anger and the imminence of violent League action. He wired home on August 1 that there was "no indication of any immediate attempt at a mass movement" and asked Pethick-Lawrence to inform the cabinet that "it would not be advisable to send for Jinnah immediately. . . . If I send for Jinnah at once it will be regarded as a panicky reaction to a threat and will put up Jinnah's stock. . . . I should propose to leave Jinnah alone."[8] So the game continued, move by Machiavellian move.

After the League council had met, a correspondent for the *Daily Telegraph* interviewed Jinnah to ask what he meant by "direct action," and Jinnah at first replied that "there would be a mass illegal movement"; but when the correspondent showed him the text of his article before cabling it home, Jinnah changed "illegal" to "unconstitutional."[9] Jinnah's secretary reported that the Working Committee set the date for a "univeral Muslim hartal" for Friday, August 16, 1946. The viceroy's deputy private secretary felt a strike had "possibilities of working up mass hysteria," yet Wavell remained unperturbed, mistakenly believing that "J. has no real idea what to do."[10]

On August 6, 1946, with Pethick-Lawrence's approval, Wavell wrote Nehru, as president of the Congress, inviting him "to submit to me proposals for the formation of an Interim Government. . . . It will be for you to consider whether you should first discuss them with Mr. Jinnah. . . . I am sure you agree with me that a Coalition government can best direct effectively the destinies of India at this critical time. Time is short."[11] Nehru replied from Gandhi's ashram at Wardha on August 10, accepting the "responsibility" offered. On August 13, Nehru wrote Jinnah from Wardha to "seek your cooperation in the formation of a coalition provisional Government."[12] Jinnah's response was acute surprise.

> I know nothing as to what has transpired between the Viceroy and you, nor have I any idea what agreement has been arrived at between you two. . . . If this means the Viceroy has commissioned you to form an Executive Council . . . and has already agreed to accept and act upon your advice . . . it is not possible for me to accept such a position. . . . However, if you care to meet me, on behalf of Congress, to settle the Hindu-Muslim question and resolve the serious deadlock, I shall be glad to see you today at 6 p.m.[13]

That was August 15, 1946, precisely one year before the birth of India and Pakistan. Nehru responded the same afternoon from Bombay, "I am prepared to come to your place at 6 p.m."

After their meeting, Nehru reported to Wavell that he had "offered Jinnah assurances" that no "major communal issue" would be acted upon in the constituent assembly except by a majority of both parties, that any disputed points would be referred to the federal court for decision, and that "while Congress did not like the idea of grouping and preferred autonomous provinces under the Centre they would not oppose grouping by provinces if the provinces wished it."[14] Nehru offered Jinnah five Muslim League seats on a cabinet of fourteen but "did not see" how the League could possibly object to a nationalist Muslim being included among the Congress party quota—which would also be five. Jinnah not only objected but thereupon refused to participate in the interim government, and his "only proposal," as Nehru reported it, was to defer "all action . . . for six months." Jawaharlal refused to wait any longer, however, leaving Jinnah's Malabar Hill estate as the sun went down on the eve of India's bloodiest year of civil war.

"There was a curious stillness in the air" over Calcutta, Major L. A. Livermore reported from his perch atop Fort William that hot, sticky, monsoon morning of Friday, August 16, 1946, as dawn broke over Kipling's City of Dreadful Night. Muslim workers from the Howrah jute mills had begun pouring into the city, headed toward Ochterlony's "needle" Monument for the mammoth meeting to "celebrate" Direct Action Day. Chief minister Suhrawardy and other leaders of Bengal's Muslim League were scheduled to address that meeting. Reports that "Hindus had erected barricades at the Tala and Belgachia bridges to prevent Muslims from entering the city" reached British headquarters at the fortress by 7:30 A.M., but the brigadier in command of Calcutta, J. P. C. Mackinlay, had "ordered" all of his troops to be "confined to barracks" that day. India's largest, most crowded, most communally volatile city was left virtually naked. Suhrawardy had given the government servants an extraordinary three-day weekend off.

"Communal trouble started as early as 7 a.m. in Maniktolla area in north-east Calcutta and has continued and spread throughout the day," Governor Burrows wired Wavell that night.

> Situation up to 6 p.m. is that there have been numerous and widespread communal clashes . . . accompanied by some looting of shops, arson. Weapons employed appear to have been chiefly brick bats but in a number of cases shot guns have been used by members of both communities and some cases of stabbing have been reported.

. . . A marked feeling of panic, especially among Hindu traders in north Calcutta, has been feature of situation since early in the day and has given rise to many wild reports far exceeding actualities. . . . Disturbances so far have been markedly communal and not, repeat not, in any way anti-British.[15]

Lieutenant-general Sir Francis Tuker, in charge of India's eastern command, received intelligence reports that Suhrawardy told "an immense Muslim crowd" gathered round Ochterlony's Monument that afternoon that

the Cabinet Mission was a bluff, and that he would see how the British could make Mr. Nehru rule Bengal. Direct Action Day would prove to be the first step towards the Muslim struggle for emancipation. He advised them to return home early and said . . . that he had made all arrangements with the police and military not to interfere with them. Our intelligence patrols noticed that the crowd included a large number of Muslim *goondas* [hoodlums], and that . . . their ranks . . . swelled as soon as the meeting ended. They made for the shopping centres of the town where they at once set to work to loot and burn Hindu shops and houses. . . . At 4.15 p.m. Fortress H.Q. sent out the codeword "Red" to indicate that there were incidents all over Calcutta.[16]

Curfew was proclaimed in the "riot-affected districts" at 6:00 P.M.; but by 8:00 P.M., when the area commander called in the 7th Worcesters and the Green Howards from their barracks in the north, they found College Street Market "ablaze" and the "few unburnt houses and shops completely sacked," in Amherst Street the litter of mass looting, in Upper Circular Road the rubble left by "fire-bugs," on Harrison Road, the cries of wounded and terrorized residents, and many bodies of "newly dead." "Calcutta was the battlefield"; Major Livermore recalled, "the battle was mob rule versus civilisation and decency; the casualties of that stricken field were for the most part the poor, the low-caste illiterates and those too weak to defend their property from the looter, the vulture of the mob."[17]

"February's killings had shocked us all but this was different:" General Tuker noted, "it was unbridled savagery with homicidal maniacs let loose to kill and kill and to maim and burn. The underworld of Calcutta was taking charge of the city. . . . The police were not controlling it. Daylight showed not a sign of bus or taxi: rickshaws were battered and burnt: there were no means for clerks to get to their work . . . all the more idle men loafing about the town . . . rioters carrying loaded sticks and sharpened iron bars . . . it was obvious that their mood was thoroughly dangerous . . . a man . . . beaten to death less than a hundred yards [from] . . .

police . . . slow to get out of their vehicles and before they had come into action three people were beaten down and lay dead on the road."[18]

On Monday, August 19, one of Major Livermore's platoons removed 150 dead bodies from a single street crossing.

> The stench in this area had become appalling and one citizen was so grateful for the removal of at least part of the cause that he pressed two bottles of champagne on the platoon responsible. . . . At about 9 p.m. that night we received orders that the main streets at least must be clear of bodies by the time the curfew lifted at 4 a.m. next morning. Stench masks and gas capes would be sent to aid us in lifting the decomposing corpses; the location of Muslim burial grounds and Hindu burning ghats would reach us as soon as possible. . . . "How the hell do I tell a Muslim from a Hindu when they've all been dead three days?" . . . It took two more days and nights to finish my own area—a total of five hundred and seven corpses in the one Company sector, most of which came from a locality less than four hundred yards square. . . . Already there was a threat of a cholera epidemic.[19]

By the night of August 19, rotting corpses posed so serious a threat to Calcutta that Bengal's government offered to pay troops "five rupees for each body collected." One of those who pitched in was Major Dobney of the Calcutta Fortress Staff.

> Except for the occasional band of British troops the city was literally a City of the Dead. . . . All the streets were well lit, showing the rotting piles of humanity and rubbish. Handcarts were piled high with bodies and had been left abandoned at the curb-side. . . . Once it was known that the mad Englishmen were collecting the dead, more bodies appeared from the labyrinth of houses and hovels. . . . All night the horrible task went on.[20]

No one knows exactly how many people were slaughtered during the Great Calcutta Killing, but General Tuker estimated the toll ran "into thousands." Unofficial sources claimed that as many as 16,000 Bengalis were murdered between August 16–20, 1946, and many times that number fled over the bridge across the Hughli, which for days remained "a one-way current of men, women, children, and domestic animals headed toward the Howrah railroad station," Margaret Bourke-White reported. Finding the trains could not carry them all, the people settled down to wait on the concrete floor, dividing themselves automatically into Hindu and Muslim camps."[21] It was only the beginning of partition.

On August 21, Wavell informed Pethick-Lawrence that "the present estimate" of casualties was 3,000 dead and 17,000 injured. Congress was "convinced that all the trouble was deliberately engineered by the Muslim League Ministry" but the viceroy had as yet seen no "satisfactory evidence to that effect." The latest estimate of casualties was that "appreciably more Muslims than Hindus were killed."[22]

Jinnah was asked about the Great Calcutta Killing by a foreign news agency later in August and replied:

> If Congress regimes are going to suppress and persecute the Musalmans, it will be very difficult to control disturbances. . . . In my opinion, there is no alternative except the outright establishment of Pakistan. . . . We guarantee to look after non-Muslim and Hindu caste-minorities in Pakistan, which will be about 25 millions, and protect and safeguard their interests in every way. . . . That is the quickest way to India's real freedom and to the welfare and happiness of all the peoples inhabiting this sub-continent.[23]

On August 24, Wavell announced that Nehru and thirteen colleagues of his choice would form a new interim government starting early in September. "The recent terrible occurrences in Calcutta have been a sobering reminder that a much greater measure of toleration is essential if India is to survive the transition to freedom," stated the viceroy.[24] A week later, Sir Shafaat Ahmed Khan, one of three non-League Muslims named to Nehru's cabinet was stabbed seven times by two young Muslim League fanatics in Simla.

Two days after Wavell's broadcast, Jinnah announced that the viceroy "has struck a severe blow to the Muslim League and Muslim India, but I am sure that the Muslims of India will bear this with fortitude and courage and learn lessons from our failure to secure our just and honourable position in the interim Government. . . . I still maintain that the step he has taken is most unwise and unstatesmanlike and is fraught with dangerous and serious consequences and he has only added insult to injury by nominating three Muslims who, he knows, do not command either the respect or confidence of Muslim India."[25]

Wavell now appealed to Nehru and Gandhi to accept a new formula on "grouping," threatening not to convene the constituent assembly until they did so. "Several times last evening," Gandhi wrote the viceroy on August 28,

> you repeated that you were a "plain man and a soldier" and that you did not know the law. We are all plain men. . . . It is our purpose, I take it, to devise methods to prevent a repetition of the recent terrible happenings in Calcutta. The question before us is how best to do it. Your language last evening was minatory. As representative of

the King you cannot afford to be a military man only, nor to ignore
the law. . . . Nor can the Congress be expected to bend itself and
adopt what it considers a wrong course because of the brutal exhibition recently witnessed in Bengal. . . . I say this neither as a Hindu
nor as a Muslim. I write only as an Indian. . . . You will please convey the whole of this letter to the British Cabinet.[26]

"The strong reaction by Gandhi to my suggestion that Congress should
make their assurance about the Grouping categorical shows how well justified Jinnah was to doubt their previous assurances on the subject," Wavell
wrote Pethick-Lawrence as his cover letter enclosing Gandhi's missive, adding, "It is to my mind convincing evidence that Congress always meant to
use their position in the Interim Government to break up the Muslim
League and in the Constituent Assembly to destroy the Grouping scheme
which was the one effective safeguard for the Muslims."[27] The secretary of
state and the prime minister disagreed. "We fully appreciate gravity of the
danger of serious and widespread communal trouble," Pethick-Lawrence
wired in response. "At the same time we must ask you not to take any
steps which are likely to result in a breach with the Congress."[28] Wavell
was now tempted to resign and deeply regretted having abandoned Jinnah
in June, sensing that to work in harness with Nehru would prove more
galling and less congenial.

"As long as Jinnah feels he can get his veto through the Viceroy, he will
not drop his intransigence," G. D. Birla wrote Cripps the next day. "There
were signs of a feeling among the followers of the League that Jinnah was
leading them to the wilderness," Birla noted.[29] And in his Id message from
Bombay on August 29, Jinnah appealed to his followers to "rally round the
Muslim League . . . let us stand as one united nation under our flag and
on one platform and be determined and prepared to face the worst as a
completely united and great people with our motto: unity, faith and discipline. God is with us and we are bound to succeed."[30]

A few days later on September 1, the eve of Congress taking over the
interim government, communal rioting rocked Bombay as Muslim houses
all along Sandhurst Road flew black flags of mourning. Curfew was imposed, troops were called out, but in that one orgiastic night of violence 35
people were killed and 175 injured. Sporadic rioting in Bombay would
continue for over a week, and by September 10 more than 200 Hindus and
Muslims were dead as a result of communal violence. There was violence
in Karachi as well, but League premier Shaikh Ghulam Hussain broadcast
an "appeal for calm and tolerance" which helped subdue Muslim passions
in that city. "The horrors of Calcutta have begotten an attitude of sullen
resentment on the one side and imbecile panic on the other," Sind's British

chief secretary reported, noting that both communities were busy surreptitiously arming themselves.[31]

The "door to Purna Swaraj has at last been opened," Mahatma Gandhi told his prayer meeting at Birla House in New Delhi, on September 2, 1946, as their "uncrowned king, Jawaharlal," and his colleagues took oaths of office in that flower-decked capital. Nehru was now virtually the prime minister of India, and he placed Patel in charge of home affairs (police) and Baldev Singh in charge of defence (or war). "A new Government came into being in this ancient land," Nehru broadcast from New Delhi a few days later, "the Interim or Provisional Government we called it. . . . India, this old and dear land of ours, is finding herself again through travail and suffering. She is youthful again with the bright eyes of adventure, and with faith in herself and her mission.[32]

On September 8, Wavell "very urgently" transmitted his "breakdown plan" for India to Pethick-Lawrence, estimating that "we could not govern the whole of India for more than a year and a half."[33] The viceroy's plan of withdrawal depended, as he put it, "on absolute firmness by H.M.G.," and Wavell requested permission to announce his plan publicly before January 1. He wanted all Indians to know that the British were ready to pull back their troops from south to north, disembarking from the subcontinent through Karachi and Calcutta, with select elite officials flying out of New Delhi. Approximately 100,000 European civilians and another 100,000 British troops would have to be evacuated from India.

Wavell dined with Jinnah's old friend, Sarojini Naidu, on September 10, "and we had a long talk on politics and of the necessity of getting Jinnah and the M.L. in and the difficulties of Jinnah's character. Mrs. N. spoke of Jinnah rather as of Lucifer, a fallen angel, one who had once promised to be a great leader of Indian freedom, but who had cast himself out of the Congress heaven."[34]

The *Daily Mail*, whose correspondent in Bombay interviewed Jinnah, reported his remarking:

> The wound is too deep and the negotiations have led to too much bitterness and rancour for us to prolong the present arguments. The slate must be wiped clean and we must begin from the beginning again. I shall never plead my case, but were the British Government to invite me to London to start a new series of conferences on an equal footing with other negotiators I should accept. . . . If the British insist on doing nothing more than support the present interim Government with their bayonets all I can say is the Moslems can endure it. If they want to arrest me now I am ready to go to prison immediately.[35]

With riots in Bombay, Calcutta smouldering, and Nehru running the show in New Delhi, the prospect of a visit to London must have looked quite appealing to Jinnah through sultry monsoon haze atop Malabar Hill. Or if not London, why not prison? Rather one extreme of glory or the other than the limbo of obscure uncertainty, cut off from power, from the glitter of the viceroy's magic circle, where he had once held center stage, and from the achievement of Pakistan, which hardly anyone mentioned nowadays except with a shudder or shrug.

The viceroy met alone with Jinnah on September 16 for seventy-five minutes, and earlier that same day with Nehru and Patel, both of whom disliked his overtures to Jinnah. Congress leadership by now mistrusted Wavell and advised Pethick-Lawrence, Cripps, and Attlee to remove him from power, considering the viceroy too supportive of Muslim League demands and dangerously limited in background and training to the resolution of military, rather than political problems. The cabinet in the aftermath of its mission's bitter failure, however, was hardly ready to take any radical leap inside India's political jungle. At Nehru's insistence, Wavell agreed "provisionally" to convene the constituent assembly on December 9, by which time the viceroy hoped a settlement with the League would be reached.

The mission ministers met with Attlee at 10 Downing Street on September 23 to consider the viceroy's breakdown plan. The prime minister expressed "strong objections" to Wavell's proposals, which he considered alarmist. Cripps agreed, saying that "the moment our withdrawal was announced everyone in India would start scrambling for position. . . . Civil war would come upon us at once."[36] He favored convening the constituent assembly at once, with or without the Muslim League. Pethick-Lawrence felt that "the Viceroy's proposal would make an administrative breakdown a certainty." Attlee could not understand why Wavell wanted to abandon Madras and Bombay, "two of the best places from which to withdraw Europeans," leaving the British troops to hold "the most difficult part of India" where "an attempt to set up Pakistan . . . would cause civil war."

Wavell spent almost two hours with Jinnah on September 25, reporting him "very quiet and reasonable" and "anxious for a settlement if it can be done without loss of prestige."[37] Jinnah hoped Congress would refrain as a "gesture of good-will" from appointing any Muslim, and he was interested in rotating the vice-president's position in the cabinet with Nehru. The next afternoon, Nehru and Gandhi came in tandem, each talking for an hour with the viceroy and convincing him "they do *not* want Jinnah and the League in, and Gandhi at the end exposed Congress policy of domination more nakedly than ever before. The more I see of that old man," Wavell admitted, "the more I regard him as an unscrupulous old hypocrite."[38]

By October 1, Wavell was convinced that "it is no use trying to squeeze the Congress any further on the nationalist Muslim issue." The viceroy then decided his "best tactics" would be to "induce Jinnah simply to give me five names for the Muslim seats."[39] It was in the "obvious interest of the Muslim League" to come into the government as soon as possible, Wavell now believed.

So Wavell met Jinnah next day and spelled out his strategy for bringing the League into the interim government. "Mr. Jinnah said nothing at all on the nationalist Muslim issue and did not attempt to argue it"; the viceroy noted, "but he said that if he was to have any chance of success with his Working Committee he must have some success to show them on the other points he had raised." Wavell explained "that the only function of the Vice-President was to preside at Cabinet meetings in my absence, and that I could arrange for the leader of the Muslim Party to be appointed as Vice-Chairman of the C.C.C., which was really a more influential position."[40] He understood well how important matters of prestige were to Jinnah's mind and clearly revealed here the unpublicized powers retained by himself as governor-general. By the end of their meeting he "got the impression" that Jinnah was "anxious" to "come in." Jinnah, moreover, by then must have been at least equally impressed at how much the viceroy wanted "him" as the League's comforting countervailing influence to Nehru, Patel, and the others inside the viceregal council chambers of Delhi and Simla.

Whether it was Wavell's ardor in wooing him or Jinnah's current frustrations at having missed the maiden voyage of the interim government that imbued Nehru with so much seeming power and pomp, those October negotiations in New Delhi swiftly accomplished what had eluded the labors of the cabinet mission for three months earlier in the year. Perhaps it was the tragic, sobering reality of the Great Calcutta Killing and the bloody Bombay riots, or his council's impatience, or his own deteriorating health that made Jinnah far more flexible in reaching a settlement that was to bring the League into an interim coalition government with Congress in a record-breaking mere two weeks of negotiation. Nor did Nehru and Congress court him or pander to his ego. Such negative signals from old adversaries may have served only to convince Jinnah that it was, indeed, high time for him to scuttle excess baggage and climb aboard while there was still a rope to catch and a ship's master, to welcome him so warmly.

The nawab of Bhopal, Jinnah's old friend and chancellor of the Chamber of Princes since 1944, then entered the act (or "shoved in a rather intrusive oar," as Wavell put it[41]), inviting Jinnah and Nehru to meet in his palace to discuss their residual differences. "I have consulted some of my colleagues about the matters discussed by us yesterday," Nehru wrote Jinnah on October 6.

> We all agreed that nothing could be happier and better for the country than that these two organisations [Congress and the League] should meet again as before, as friends having no mental reservations and bent on resolving all their differences by mutual consultation, and never desiring or allowing the intervention of the British Government through the Viceroy or some other. . . . We would therefore welcome the decision of the League to join the interim Government for it to work as a united team on behalf of India as a whole.[42]

Nehru then noted a number of problems and concerns he had with various "points put forward" by Jinnah in their conversation. Jinnah responded next day: "I appreciate and reciprocate your sentiments. . . . With regard to the second paragraph," he countered the points noted in Nehru's letter, concluding "I am anxious that we should come to . . . settlement without undue delay."[43] Nehru's response to Jinnah's letter was less cordial; and Wavell reported on October 9, "There has evidently been some hitch."

Two days later, the viceroy wired a "secret" report he had just received from Bhopal as to what went wrong. Jinnah and Gandhi apparently "accepted a formula which spoke of the Muslim League as representing 'the overwhelming majority of Muslims.' Then at the instance of the Patel group he (Gandhi) added a rider to the effect that the two parties would agree to work as a team and would never invoke or permit the intervention of the Governor General. Inevitably the rider was unacceptable to Jinnah. . . ."[44] Wavell had earlier been at pains to assure Nehru that he was not calling in Jinnah to push him and the League into a coalition cabinet in order to create a "King's party" inside the new government, but now he admitted fearing that "Gandhi and the Congress" were seeking "to secure Muslim League compliance in an arrangement to eliminate the Governor-General's influence in the Cabinet and reduce him to a figure-head."[45]

The viceroy had what he called "a crucial interview with Jinnah" the next afternoon, when he learned that the League was ready to join the interim government but that Jinnah was going to pitch "a surprise fast ball" at Congress by proposing a member of the Scheduled (Untouchable) Caste as one of his five "Muslim" names for the cabinet. "I said that it would look rather like 'tit for tat,'" Wavell noted, "a counter to the Congress nomination of a nationalist Muslim, and would therefore be rather an embarrassment to me. . . . I gathered that the man they had in mind to nominate was . . . at present a Minister in Bengal."[46] J. N. Mandal was then minister of law in Bengal, an advocate whose greatest attraction to the League appears to have been that he was born "untouchable." Jinnah personally decided to remain outside, leaving Liaquat to head his party's team, with I. I. Chundrigar of Bombay, Abdur Rab Nishtar from the frontier, and Ghazanfar Ali Khan of the Punjab to complete the League's interim government slate. Nehru dropped two of his Muslims, Shafaat Khan and Syed Zaheer, and Subhas Bose's brother, Sarat Bose, from his cabinet, thus making room for Jinnah's choices. The new coalition was officially announced on October 15. But as communal rioting spread from Bengal to the North-West Frontier, the Congress-League coalition was off to a most precarious start. A major stumbling block was that the League insisted on preempting at least one of the three most powerful cabinet positions—foreign affairs, home, or defence—held by Nehru, Patel, and Baldev Singh, respectively. Congress was unwilling to relinquish any of those jobs. Nehru was also upset about reports of a speech Liaquat made in Karachi on October 20, when he reportedly said the League had decided to enter the government because "Congress in its heart was adverse to the League's entry" and that, as before, Muslims must continue to prepare to "fight" for "the winning of their goal—Pakistan."[47] Nehru demanded retraction of both statements and wanted clarification of the League's long-range intentions as well as "a definite assurance by them that there will be cooperation and team work."[48] Wavell feared that Congress resolved to "do all they can to prevent the League coming in."[49] Nehru had earlier indicated that Congress was ready to turn over finance, then headed by South Indian Christian Dr. John Matthai, to the League. A harried Wavell insisted, whatever the outcome, that "I must . . . come home at once for consultation."

On the evening of October 24, Nehru confirmed that Congress had decided to resign if Patel's Home ministry portfolio went to the League. The viceroy called in Jinnah at 7:30 P.M. to ask if he would accept finance.

> J. was not in a very accommodating mood, . . . but he agreed . . .
> with the usual proviso that it was subject to the decision of his Working Committee. I then sent for Nehru at 9.30 p.m. and told him that the League would accept Finance, and asked him to let me know what alternative portfolio he proposed for Matthai. Nehru, who looked very tired and worn, accepted this quietly, and said he would let me know after consulting his colleagues. . . . Neither party has the least trust in the other. . . . It is all very wearing; and for almost the first time in my life I am really beginning to feel the strain badly—not sleeping properly and letting these wretched people worry me.[50]

The new members of the government were sworn in October 26, but there would be no harmony or true spirit of unity in that short-lived central government. Jinnah permitted himself to be persuaded by Wavell to join up, only as a tactical strategem, to buy time for the League to marshal all its forces, gathering strength in this brief period of seeming cooperation with Congress for the final phase, the last charge up the perilous hill of partition to Pakistan. There was no reconciliation, no solution to the problems of fundamental mistrust, suspicion, fear, and hatred. Too much blood had been let, too many knives buried in too many backs, too many unborn babies had been butchered in their mother's wombs, too many women raped, too many men robbed; people were fired to irrational hatred by the sick reflections of their communal neighbors in the house or village next door.

India's newly elected legislative assembly met on October 29, with Nehru and Liaquat Ali Khan seated side by side on the government's front bench, neither smiling or saying a word to each other all day. They sat the way most Hindu and Muslim Indians lived, in sullen, silent, angry proximity, resenting, fearing, and distrusting one another. Next morning Nehru took to his bed, exhausted more by depression than overwork though his daily schedule had been grueling. Jinnah spent over an hour with Wavell on October 30, and the viceroy found him "at his most Jinnah-ish . . . completely unsatisfactory."[51] "I told Mr. Jinnah that I hoped he would call his Council at once to accept the Statement of May 16," Wavell reported, since that cabinet mission statement "was a condition of the League's acceptance of office at the Centre" and had been rejected the previous month by the League's council in Bombay.

Wavell flew in to Calcutta on October 31. Sarat Bose was threatening to call a new strike. Governor Burrows warned the viceroy that he could not "carry Bengal" for more than one more year. Nehru and Patel, and Liaquat and Nishtar flew to Calcutta early in November to see for themselves how India's premier metropolis was faring. Burrows briefed them on arrival, pointing out that the army had been directing traffic in the streets in Calcutta for approximately ten weeks, while trade was "stagnating" and workers as well as businessmen were "very injuriously affected." Bengal, with 33 million Muslims and 25 million Hindus, desperately needed an "all-party government" to help bring "tranquillity" to the province, yet no coalition was even being discussed. Nehru and Liaquat could hardly accomplish for Bengal, however, what they found impossible to do among themselves in New Delhi.

Governor Sir Hugh Dow of Bihar reported his "appreciation" of the communal riots in his province on November 9, by which time nine battalions of troops had been ordered into the rural regions most seriously affected. "Roving Hindu mobs have sought to exterminate the Moslem population wherever they could find them," wrote the governor. "Almost all casualties have been Moslems and it is estimated that of these 75% have been women and children."[52]

Dawn headlined a mid-November interview given by Jinnah to the foreign press on its front page, "ABSOLUTE PAKISTAN THE ONLY SOLUTION," reporting:

> Muslim League President Qaed-e-Azam Mohammed Ali Jinnah declared . . . that in his view "the only solution" to India's present communal situation "is Pakistan and Hindustan," . . . anything else would be artificial and unnatural. . . . Of the Interim Government, Mr. Jinnah said . . . the Muslim League Ministers were there "as sentinels" who would watch Muslim interests in the day to day administration. . . . Asked if he favoured abandoning the Interim Government, Mr. Jinnah replied: "I have said this: It was forced upon us. The present arrangement I don't approve of."[53]

Congress insisted, and Pethick-Lawrence agreed, that the constituent assembly must be called on December 9, as planned. Official invitations were issued, and soon after, on November 21, *Dawn* led off with "The Viceroy seems to think that the play of *Hamlet* can be staged with only half a Hamlet: he has summoned the Constituent Assembly to meet, . . . although the Muslim League's decision not to participate in it still stands. There are reasons to believe that he has been jockeyed into this decision by Congress pressure. . . . For some days past all 'guns' have been trained on him. . . . Whatever his gallantry on the battlefields might have been, he seems to have put that virtue in cold storage along with his Field-Marshal's uniform."[54]

Wavell met with all four Muslim League members of the cabinet that afternoon, and "Liaquat put to me quite bluntly the question whether I and His Majesty's Government intended to keep order in India and protect minorities while we remained here or not. He said that the responsibility was still ours, but that we were not carrying it out. . . . I felt bound in honesty to tell them that our ability to carry out our responsibility had very greatly weakened. Since the British Government had announced its intention of handing over power in India shortly, we could not expect the same degree of co-operation and support from the officials and police that we formerly enjoyed. The recent troubles had shown that the police in many parts of India were affected with communalism and were no longer to be relied on for firm action against their own community."[55]

Jinnah announced to the press on November 22 that "No representative of the Muslim League will participate in the Constituent Assembly." Wavell sent for Liaquat next day and "argued" with him for over an hour, trying to persuade his finance member to get his party to attend the assembly. "I completely failed to convince him," Wavell wired Pethick-Lawrence, "as I had previously failed . . . with Jinnah."[56] It was finally clear to Lord Wavell that his last great push, getting the League into government, was only a Pyrrhic victory. Nothing had changed.

The secretary of state invited Wavell to return home at once with two representatives of the Congress and two from the League to discuss the entire situation and seek a new settlement formula. The viceroy suggested adding a Sikh, proposing Baldev Singh, his defence member. Nehru consulted colleagues on the Working Committee and on behalf of Congress turned down the invitation. Baldev also declined a day later. Jinnah, however, was pleased to accept and agreed to fly to London with Liaquat and the viceroy. Attlee then wired a personal appeal to Nehru, pleading with him to reconsider, "to help in this way to make rapid and smooth progress towards the goal of Indian Freedom."[57] Congress met again for a full day's discussion, and Nehru and Baldev Singh decided to go to London after all. On the eve of their departure, Jinnah changed his mind after learning that Nehru and Baldev were coming. "What an impossible set of people they are!" Wavell noted. "I sent Ian Scott off to see Liaquat; and by midnight he returned to say that we had got this far, that Liaquat had agreed to come with us to Karachi tomorrow to see Jinnah and try to persuade him to come."[58] The next day when they flew from Delhi, Liaquat was "dressed for Europe." Jinnah received a midnight cable from Attlee, personally pressing him to come, and though "rather late," he finally climbed aboard the viceroy's plane in Karachi. The crowd that had come to see him off at the airport shouted "Pakistan Zindabad."

20

London—Final Farewell
(1946)

London in December was cold, wet, and bleak. How redolent it must have been of his first arrival there fifty-four years ago. So much had changed, yet so many feelings were the same. Jinnah still felt lost and alone, cut off from all those who once loved him, forced out to fight treacherous battles with hated strangers all of whom wanted to cheat him of the starring role. How different his life would have been had he remained with the company of Shakespearean thespians with whom he had performed years ago. The company he traveled with in 1946 was a far less congenial troupe. And how bitter the final act had become. He wore his black Jinnah cap, but the rest of his emaciated body was clothed in a double-breasted British wool suit and a heavy gray coat.

Wavell had prepared a "top secret" note for discussion with the cabinet, handing it to Attlee, Pethick-Lawrence, and Alexander at the start of their first meeting on December 3.

> Present situation is that Congress feel that H.M.G. dare not break with them unless they do something quite outrageous. Their aim is power and to get rid of British influence as soon as possible, after which they think they can deal with both Muslims and Princes; the former by bribery, blackmail, propaganda, and if necessary force; the latter by stirring up their people against them, as well.[1]

Woodrow Wyatt had arranged a luncheon for Jinnah that day with a number of other M.P.s; he reported that Jinnah was "still harping" on the mission's betrayal.

> [He] feels very bitterly that he should have been allowed to form a Government when Congress turned down the short-term plan. He

vehemently sticks to the view that Congress have *never* accepted the long-term plan, never meant to accept it and never will accept it. . . . He says repeatedly that all they are after is to seize power . . . he will do all he can to prevent that. He now refers to the Cabinet Mission plan as a fraud and a humbug. . . . He has now returned to the proposition that only the creation of Pakistan can deal with the situation. Any lingering thoughts that he had at Simla of a central government with three subjects appear to have gone for ever. . . . "You don't realise," he said, "how far the situation has gone in India since you were there." His theme song on this issue is what he calls the deliberate butchery of Muslims by Hindus in Bihar. When asked for a constructive proposition, he said that the only thing that could be done immediately was to restore law and order. . . . They must all co-operate, particularly the British, in restoring law and order. . . . Then, for Pakistan. . . . I do not ever remember seeing him before in a worse mood. . . . His last words to me as he got into his car were: "There is no time any more for argument."

The *only* hope now, I am sure, is to frighten him badly and to say that if he won't accept the Constituent Assembly, then his people must leave the government, and he will get no support from the British.[2]

Pethick-Lawrence tackled Jinnah and Liaquat after lunch and reported much the same about Jinnah's attitude.

The cabinet mission trio met with Wavell and Attlee at 10 Downing Street the next morning. Cripps "said that he felt that the position had now come to the stage where the course of events would depend on the action taken by the British Government. It looked as if it had got beyond the British Government. It looked as if it had got beyond the possibilities of compromise. If Jinnah was in the frame of mind indicated there would be no chance of an adjustment or of Jinnah accepting one. . . . Jinnah was playing for full Pakistan which he expected to get as the outcome of a breakdown. . . . He [Cripps] thought the vital thing now was for H.M.G. to make a declaration of what they were going to do. He thought that the Opposition would agree that our position in India was now becoming untenable."[3]

Alexander was not sure of this latter point, remarking that at a dinner for Jinnah and Liaquat, "Mr. Eden had expressed the view . . . that possibly we ought to say that we had gone too fast and that, while we adhered to our pledges, it was necessary to give a breathing space for law and order to be restored and for constitution-making to proceed in a calm atmosphere. Otherwise we should be unable to fulfil our obligations to minorities." This Conservative party line was, of course, the same argument Jinnah had used with Pethick-Lawrence. Alexander suggested "that this general line might be taken by the Opposition and might command some support in the country. Moreover, the case might be made that we were allowing India to fall into chaos and that this would be a danger to world peace."[4]

Attlee left the cabinet meeting to see Jinnah and Liaquat, immediately after which he reported to his colleagues that "the burden of Mr. Jinnah's discourse had been that it was a mistake to have tried to introduce self-government into India. . . . Mr. Jinnah seemed convinced that the Congress did not mean business in regard to the Constituent Assembly; his own aim was simply that of Pakistan, within the British Commonwealth. He held out no prospect of coming to an arrangement with the Congress."[5]

While the prime minister met with the Muslim League leaders at 10 Downing Street, the mission and the viceroy went across Whitehall to reconvene inside the secretary of state's old office for a meeting with Nehru. Pethick-Lawrence opened that meeting by saying how "anxious" they all were to "help to enable India to achieve independence smoothly."[6] The secretary of state confessed that the cabinet mission's three-tier "solution" seemed to be "losing its hold on the thought of both parties." He added, dropping something of a bombshell to Nehru, that "The question now was whether that broad general basis was any longer sufficiently accepted to make it worth while to proceed upon it. Pandit Nehru said that he thought that that was the basis on which everything was proceeding. Naturally there was tension. . . ."

Here Wavell jumped in to say "that a total of several thousand killed indicated something more than tension." But Nehru argued that the reason for so many deaths was that "steps had been taken which encouraged violence. He had thought that the essence of the Cabinet Mission's proposals was that they were to be put through. Was it now suggested that the essence was that if one party objected the proposals did not go forward?" Pethick-Lawrence tried to explain "that it was not H.M.G.'s policy that one party should have a veto on progress, but clearly if one major party declined to participate, that raised a very difficult situation." Nehru had been caught off guard, never expecting this intimation that his British hosts, his good British friends, his Labour comrades, might suddenly turn their backs on him, simply cutting their losses.

Cripps then asked what Nehru thought were the "fundamental reasons" the League would not come into the constituent assembly. Nehru insisted that the League had "never been prepared to co-operate," being totally negative about everything, wanting only "a veto." The Congress wanted "co-operation" because everyone knew that nothing could be done "socially or politically" if co-operation among Hindus or Muslims was lacking. Nehru argued, however, that the Muslim League was "not interested" in either social or political "advance." Cripps next asked whether Nehru thought that if the Muslims could "be assured that a three-tier system would eventuate" out of a constituent assembly, that might induce them to come in? Nehru said he thought the Muslims would come in anyhow "sooner or later," provided that they felt the assembly was going to be convened. But even if the Muslim League came in, Nehru predicted, it would not be to work harmoniously with Congress, but merely as "a step in a conflict," the way it had done in the interim government.

The longer Jawaharlal talked, the clearer it became to all of them that Nehru and Congress would not be able to work harmoniously with Jinnah and the League—not in the same cabinet and probably not in the same country. Still they tried, for another hour to convince Nehru that it might just possibly be better to reassure the League of a free hand in its sections to form the groups that would have satisfied it—three months ago—than to embark upon trying to draft a constitution without one-quarter of its population represented. But Nehru "could not see why the Muslim League should not come in and put any questions of interpretation to the Federal Court. The only other test was the test of battle."[7]

That same afternoon, Pethick-Lawrence, Cripps, and Alexander met with Jinnah and Liaquat. Cripps asked Jinnah if he would join the constituent assembly if the federal court handed down an interpretation "favourable to the Muslim League" about "procedure in the Sections?" Jinnah replied that his League "could not be a party" to any such judicial appeal, concluding that it "would be unwise to plunge India into constitution-making in the present atmosphere."[8] Cripps and Alexander argued that the British would stand firm behind their mission plan. But they did not set Jinnah's mind at ease or budge him from his intransigent position.

At this time Cripps favored a public declaration that the British would leave India in a year or, at the most, eighteen months, insisting it would be necessary to hand things over to any government set up by the constituent assembly. Pethick-Lawrence believed that Nehru was anxious to reach a settlement "fair to the Muslims" but suspected many "more communal elements" within Congress would not let him do so. Wavell agreed, insisting there was "no chance at all" of Congress showing "generosity" toward Muslims. They discussed the possibility and wisdom of referring the "Indian problem" to the United Nations, with Attlee suggesting that it might be brought up as a matter "endangering world peace." Wavell reminded them that "Jinnah had always emphasised that Pakistan would remain

within the Commonwealth and presumably hoped to get British assistance
to deal with the Frontier problem."

Friday, December 6, 1946, was the last day of London's India conference, since Nehru had insisted on returning to New Delhi for the opening
session of the constituent assembly on December 9. Jinnah and Liaquat,
however, were in no rush to get home and opted to remain in London a
few more weeks. The Cabinet met by themselves and approved a statement, which began: "The conversations held by His Majesty's Government
with Pandit Nehru, Mr. Jinnah, Mr. Liaquat Ali Khan and Sardar Baldev
Singh came to an end this evening . . ." concluding that "Should a Constitution come to be framed by a Constituent Assembly in which a large section of the Indian population had not been represented, His Majesty's Government could not of course contemplate—as the Congress have stated they
would not contemplate—forcing such a Constitution upon any unwilling
parts of the country."[9] That evening, Prime Minister Attlee informed his
Indian guests:

> The British Government had done their part. They had secured ac-
> ceptance in this country for a line of policy urged for many years by
> leading Indians. They were entitled now to ask for Indian coopera-
> tion. In the present series of meetings they had been unable to get
> acceptance by either side of the view held by the other. They pro-
> posed therefore to issue tonight a Statement.[10]

Nehru flew home the next morning. Kanji Dwarkadas, who had just
arrived in London from New York after six months in the United States
studying "labor problems," called on Jinnah at Claridge's.

> I found him sick and depressed. . . . I told him that I was away
> from India for about seven months and I was, therefore, not able to
> understand what was happening to the country. "Country, what
> country?" Jinnah asked. "There is no country. There are only Hindus
> and Mussalmans." I found that Jinnah wanted no settlement except
> on basis of Pakistan. He wanted to keep the fight on because he was
> badly handled and treated and abused by the Congress leaders. . . .
> I put it to Jinnah that the Muslim League and the Congress could
> carry on their quarrels outside the Government . . . but was it not
> essential that they should work together inside the Government and
> do as much as they possibly could for the country? Jinnah replied:
> "What do you mean? How can it be possible? Do you mean to say
> that you and I can kiss each other in this room and go out of the
> room and stab each other?" . . . I felt that if the Congress leaders
> had not broken away from him in personal relationship, he would
> not have been so embittered. His self-esteem, his pride and his feel-

ing of being personally hurt had embittered him and he had created ghosts of suspicion and distrust all round him. At the same time he had kept his shrewdness and he knew the art of not speaking too much as also of upsetting his opponents. He had found in the impetuous and conceited Nehru, an easy victim.[11]

Pethick-Lawrence's parliamentary undersecretary, Arthur Henderson, who met with Kanji that December, also remarked about Jinnah being "a sick man," which must have been common knowledge by then in the higher echelons of the British raj as well as among the leadership of both Congress and the League. "Henderson . . . told me that he had sat next to Jinnah at the King's Lunch and was surprised to see that Jinnah did not touch the food at all," noted Kanji. "He conceded that Jinnah was a sick man and promptly added: 'Don't think that your troubles would be over if Jinnah disappeared. Liaquat and Suhrawardy are worse. . . .' I agreed. But neither Liaquat nor Suhrawardy would be able to keep the Muslim League together . . . as Jinnah had been able to do."[12]

That ninth December day the constituent assembly met for the first time in New Delhi "with dignity and decorum," acting viceroy Sir John Colville reported to Wavell, who also had lingered in London. Dr. Satchidananda Sinha was the convening president till the assembly elected Dr. Rajendra Prasad, who was to be the Indian republic's first president, to chair its deliberations. The Hindu press generally hailed this "historic occasion" as the culmination of "that popular awakening to a sense of national solidarity and high destiny which began nearly a century ago."[13] The Muslim League boycott, however, proved totally effective, with 79 of the seats in that assembly hall remaining empty, while almost 300 congressmen and women took their places as representatives of their inchoate nation.

Begum Shah Nawaz and Ispahani had gone to New York to present the League's case to as many delegates of the UN as they could meet, returning through London to spend mid-December with Jinnah and Liaquat. Shafi's shrewd Punjabi daughter recalled how

Ispahani was talking about the Punjabi Muslims, the so-called sword-arm, who had done nothing to achieve Pakistan. I listened quietly for two or three days and then I could not stand it any more. I said that it was not the rank and file, but the leaders, who were responsible for it. The Quaid asked at once, "What do you mean by leaders? Today, every Muslim Leaguer is a leader." I said if that is so, then Punjab will not lag behind other provinces. . . .

While in London, Dr. Buchman, founder of the Moral Re-Armament Movement, invited the Quaid-i-Azam and Nawabzada Liaquat Ali Khan to see their play and have supper with him, and wanted me to persuade the Quaid to accept the invitation. [Ispahani] and I had seen the play in New York and liked it immensely. Mr. Jinnah agreed, and after the play when we went to Dr. Buchman's house, I said that I had asked the Quaid to attend the supper because I wanted Londoners to know him. On that one of the guests said, "London knows Mr. Jinnah." How that perked him up! Mr. Jinnah was the life of the party, talked of his grand-children and gave us a number of anecdotes.[14]

Jinnah was there with Liaquat Ali, Ispahani, and the begum on December 11, when the prime minister informed the Commons that "the conversations with Indian leaders which took place during last week have unfortunately ended without agreement. . . . I am sure I am speaking for all parties in this House in making appeal to all communities in India to co-operate in framing a Constitution."[15] Winston Churchill rose, however, to note that "His Majesty's Opposition have shown over all these long months great forbearance and restraint in not raising a Debate upon India, but I must give the Leader of the House notice that we feel a Debate must now take place. Matters are assuming so grave an aspect that it is necessary that the nation at large shall have its attention concentrated upon them."

The India Debate ran for the next two days. Cripps kicked off at 3:52 P.M., moving "That this House . . . expressed its hope that a settlement of the present difficulties between Indian Parties will be forthcoming."[16] At 4:39 P.M. Churchill rose to respond:

> I warned the House as long ago as 1931 . . . that if we were to wash our hands of all responsibility, ferocious civil war would speedily break out between the Muslims and Hindus. But this, like other warnings, fell upon deaf and unregarding ears.

> Indeed, it is certain that more people have lost their lives or have been wounded in India by violence since the interim Government under Mr. Nehru was installed in office four months ago by the Viceroy, than in the previous 90 years. This is only a foretaste of what may come. It may be only the first few heavy drops before the thunderstorm breaks upon us. These frightful slaughters over wide regions and in obscure uncounted villages have, in the main, fallen upon Muslim minorities.

> I must record my own belief . . . that any attempt to establish the reign of a Hindu numerical majority in India will never be achieved

without a civil war, proceeding, not perhaps at first on the fronts of armies or organised forces, but in thousands of separate and isolated places. This war will, before it is decided, lead through unaccountable agonies to an awful abridgement of the Indian population. . . . The Muslims, numbering 90 million, . . . comprise the majority of the fighting elements in India . . . the word "minority" has no relevance or sense when applied to masses of human beings numbered in many scores of millions. . . .[17]

These remarks of Churchill made Jinnah take even a tougher line than he had with Attlee and Cripps as well as with Woodrow Wyatt. This final London visit helped reassure him of the strength of Conservative party support he still enjoyed, and it confirmed his resolve to let Nehru and Congress race round the constituent assembly track alone, stirring animosity among British officialdom as well as among the Muslims who watched from smouldering sidelines. For that same December 13, 1946, Nehru rose in New Delhi to move that: "This Constituent Assembly declares its firm and solemn resolve to proclaim India as an Independent Sovereign Republic. . . . Wherein all power and authority . . . are derived from the people."[18]

On the evening of December 18, Prime Minister Attlee called Lord Louis Mountbatten to 10 Downing Street and invited him to succeed Wavell. Attlee and his colleagues were "most unfavourably impressed" with India's political "trends," and they feared that "If we were not very careful, we might well find ourselves handing India over not simply to civil war, but to political movements of a definitely totalitarian character. Urgent action was needed to break the deadlock, and the principal members of the Cabinet had reached the conclusion that a new personal approach was perhaps the only hope."[19] Everyone agreed that "Dickie" Mountbatten alone possessed the requisite charisma. Mountbatten's "fatal charm" was by now known the world over; his liberal ideas made him generally acceptable to Labour and his royal blood more than acceptable to Conservatives. As Empress Victoria's great grandson, Mountbatten was viewed as the perfect last viceroy for India. His ambition and desire, however, was to return to active duty with the navy, and his appointment as rear-admiral-in-command of the First Cruiser Squadron was to have started in April. Mountbatten knew enough about India, moreover, to appreciate how impossible his new assignment was, so he "put up a stiff fight against the Prime Minister's pressure and blandishments, stressing his extreme tiredness, and the folly of wearing him out too young," his trusted press secretary and Boswell, Campbell-Johnson recalled. It bought him some time, but it did not alter Attlee's decision.

Jinnah and Liaquat flew into Cairo for a few days of Pan-Islamic meetings en route to India. "It is only when Pakistan is established that Indian and Egyptian Muslims will be really free," the Quaid-i-Azam insisted to Egypt's prime minister Nokrashy Pasha on December 17. "Otherwise there will be the menace of a Hindu Imperialist Raj spreading its tentacles right across the Middle East."[20] Jinnah was a guest of the Arab League in Cairo and told a press conference on December 20: "If India will be ruled by Hindu imperialistic power, it will be as great a menace for the future if not greater, as the British imperialistic power has been . . . the whole of the Middle East will fall from the frying pan into the fire."[21] Asked about his talks with Egyptian and Palestinian Arab leaders, Jinnah explained:

> I told them of the danger that a Hindu empire would represent for the Middle-East and assured them that Pakistan would tender co-operation to all nations struggling for freedom without consideration of race or colour. . . . If a Hindu empire is achieved, it will mean the end of Islam in India, and even in other Muslim countries. There is no doubt that spiritual and religious ties bind us inexorably with Egypt. If we were drowned all will be drowned.[22]

On December 22, 1946, Jinnah was back on Karachi's soil. He had come full circle in the seven decades of his life, home again from London to the city of his birth, which was soon to emerge as the capital of his nation and then to remain his final resting place. Fatima was waiting to take him home, to nurse and care for him properly, as she alone could do. But some of the longest and toughest negotiations still lurked up the steep road ahead. His heaviest battle had yet to be won.

21

New Delhi
(1947)

As the new year dawned practically every one seemed to know it was time for dramatic change in Great Britain's relationship with India; but *what* was to be done? And how? Jinnah had returned home a sick man, too exhausted to say anything, lacking energy even to meet with his Working Committee before January 29. "I hope that Jinnah does not interpret our Statement of December 6th to mean that if he only sits back and does nothing he will get his Pakistan," Pethick-Lawrence wrote Wavell on January 2, probably suspecting that his letter would be called to Jinnah's attention. "It may also be interpreted to mean a Provincial autonomy which would be far less to his liking. I agree with you that Pakistan is a quite unworkable proposition."[1]

Again on January 1, Attlee appealed to Mountbatten to take up the viceroy's burden, and Mountbatten replied two days later:

I have thought over very earnestly all that you said. . . . It makes all the difference to me to know that you propose . . . terminating the British "Raj" on a definite and specified date; or earlier . . . if the Indian Parties can agree. . . . I could not have gone out there with confidence, if it had been possible to construe my arrival as a perpetuation, at this moment, of the viceregal system. . . . I deeply appreciate your offer to give me every assistance in forming my new staff. I told Sir Stafford . . . how honoured and touched I was that he should have offered to come to India with me, but I made it clear to him that I felt the presence of a man of his prestige and experience could not fail to reduce me to a mere figure head in the eyes of the people he would be negotiating with. . . . I feel it is essential that I should be allowed to fly home as often as I feel it really necessary to do so. . . . Although it would be our intention to observe the Protocol necessary to uphold the position of Viceroy and Vicereine, my wife and I would wish to visit Indian Leaders, and representative British and Indian people, in their own homes and unaccompanied by staff; and to make ourselves easier of access than the existing protocol appears to have made possible.[2]

Lady Edwina Mountbatten's charm was at least as potent as her husband's, and Nehru's romantic fascination for her was to play a role in the frantic last minute negotiations that often kept at least one of the Mountbattens in touch with Jawaharlal "unaccompanied by staff."

The British director of central intelligence, Sir Norman P. A. Smith, informed Wavell that from the "British angle,"

the game so far has been well played . . . both Congress and the League have been brought into the Central Government. . . . The Indian problem has been thereby thrust into its appropriate plane of communalism . . . an opportunity for orderly evacuation now presents itself. . . . The fullest advantage should be taken of our present breathing space. . . . Secretary of State's control over civil officers should be abrogated at the earliest possible moment. This is only fair to the officers and has the political advantage that a decisive gesture of this kind will help to keep the problem on its correct communal plane. . . . Grave communal disorder must not disturb us into action which would reintroduce anti-British agitation. . . . The former is a natural, if ghastly, process tending in its own way to the solution of the Indian problem.[3]

Such neo-Malthusian cynicism was rarely put into written form by any twentieth-century British officials.

A few days before the League's Working Committee was scheduled to meet in Karachi, Khizar ordered his Punjab police to crack down on the active League national guards in his province. The Muslim guards were viewed as a "party army on lines familiar in Germany and Italy before the war" and compared to "Mosley's Black Shirts" in England by Governor Jenkins, in explaining the official ban to Pethick-Lawrence.[4] More than a thousand steel helmets were found in national guard headquarters at Lahore, and the general commanders of the guard were all arrested. The League responded with "direct action" protests in the streets, demanding an end to Khizar's coalition government and thus finally bringing the Punjab's Muslim "swordarm" into violent operation, as Begum Shah Nawaz promised Jinnah in Claridge's. The next day Khizar withdrew his ban, fearing he could not hope to restore provincial peace otherwise. Too late. League leaders now angrily demanded Khizar's immediate resignation; mass meetings were attended by huge crowds in Lahore and other Punjab cities. Shaukat Hayat proclaimed that the Muslim League was ready to "put out 15 million Muslims to break [the] law," if Khizar's ministry refused to resign.[5] At midnight, Khizar struck again, arresting all the most powerful provincial League leaders, including the nawab of Mamdot, Firoz Khan Noon, and Mian Mumtaz Daultana. Riots erupted in every district of the Punjab. On January 31, the League's Working Committee resolved against calling the council to reconsider its rejection of the mission's plan, thus removing any residual possibility of the League opting to enter the constituent assembly.

Nehru saw Wavell the next day and vowed that the constituent assembly would carry on, saying he would have to consult his colleagues as to their next move, though Wavell rightly anticipated that "Congress can now hardly fail to demand the dismissal or resignation of the League Members of the Cabinet."[6] Before that request of February 6 came, however, Attlee wrote Wavell to ask him to resign, notifying him that his successor had been chosen. The British cabinet recognized that the "danger of civil war in India could not be ruled out" and feared that perhaps "it was Mr. Jinnah's intention to bring it about . . . there was no telling what the consequences of their [Muslim League] actions in the Punjab might be. It seemed that they were developing the technique of civil disobedience. . . . In the long run the extent to which the League would be able to cause serious trouble would depend on whether their activities caused the Indian Army to disintegrate."[7] In New Delhi, astute observers like V. P. Menon now considered India's partition "inevitable."[8]

On February 20, 1947, Prime Minister Attlee informed his peers in the Commons that:

> His Majesty's Government desire to hand over their responsibility to authorities established by a constitution approved by all parties in India . . . but unfortunately there is at present no clear prospect that such a constitution . . . will emerge. . . . His Majesty's Government wish to make it clear that it is their definite intention to take the necessary steps to effect the transference of power into responsible Indian hands by a date not later than June 1948. . . . It is therefore essential that all parties should sink their differences in order that they may be ready to shoulder the great responsibilities which will come upon them next year."[9]

Congress and the League both welcomed the new statement. "The British Government have at last seen the light and taken a historic decision which will finally end the Indo-British conflict in a manner worthy of civilized nations," wrote the *Hindustan Times* next day. "The Muslim League and Mr. Jinnah are now face to face with reality. No Indian wishes to deny the Muslim community its rightful place in India; it is not possible to do so now that the third party is quitting. There is no alternative to a mutual settlement."[10] But *Dawn* did not agree, arguing in its lead article the same day: "Mr. Attlee and his colleagues appear to have realised at last what the Muslim League has repeatedly asserted that the hope of framing an agreed constitution for a united India was an idle dream. All attempts made to that end have failed because they were based on an unreal approach."[11]

Wavell met with Nehru and Liaquat on February 21. "Nehru was obviously impressed by the Statement and conscious of the responsibility thrown on the Congress," reported the viceroy. "He spoke of the possible partition of the Punjab and Bengal, if agreement was not reached."[12] Liaquat was not prepared to react for the League, and Wavell suggested it might be best for him to invite Jinnah "to come to Delhi." A week later, Liaquat informed Wavell that "Jinnah was a sick man [had gone to Bombay] and would not be in Delhi before the middle of the month [March]."[13]

During the last week in February, the Punjab erupted with intensified violence in half a dozen major cities, including Lahore and Amritsar, with mobs of young League followers "invading courts and private houses and endeavouring to hoist Muslim League flag in place of Union Jack."[14] Several deaths, of police as well as civilians, and hundreds of injuries shook Khizar's resolve and made him decide to "settle" with the League by releasing all prisoners, removing the month-long ban on public meetings, and hoping to organize an all-party coalition government, which Governor Jenkins viewed as "most improbable." The League had also begun direct action in the North-West Frontier province; "unruly mobs" surrounded and broke most of the windows of the Congress premier, Dr. Khan Sahib's house in Peshawar, while police stood by and "refused to obey orders to open fire."[15]

Khizar resigned on March 2, after consulting with Zafrullah Khan and other friends he trusted in Lahore. He concluded to Governor Jenkins

> that the Muslim League must be brought up against reality without delay. . . . They [League leaders] had no idea of the strength of Hindu and Sikh feeling against them and so long as he and his Muslim Unionist colleagues acted as a buffer, they would not change their fantastic and arrogant ideas. . . . The outlook for Mamdot [Punjabi League leader] was very bleak, and . . . if he failed to secure adequate support from the Hindus or Sikhs or both, it would be my duty to go into Section 93 [Governor's Raj].[16]

This marked the end of Punjabi unity; the political demise of the "Land of Five Rivers." Sikh leader Swaran Singh told the governor that his party had "no intention" of joining a coalition government with the League since they had no intention of allowing themselves to be "treated as serfs under Muslim masters, and felt that they were strong enough to defend themselves."[17] Anti-League meetings spread the following week; and Congress and the Akali Sikhs announced plans for mass rallies for March 11 and proclaimed "anti-Pakistan Day," to be held throughout the Punjab. Violence spread and more deaths were reported daily.

The India debate was launched in the Commons on March 5 by Cripps, who defended the government's policy and noted how "unfortunate" it was that

> just at the moment when the Muslim League was about to reconsider the situation with a view, possibly, to coming into the Constituent Assembly at Karachi, events in the Punjab boiled up. . . . We can only hope that tolerance and good sense will bring about some settlement. . . . This is just another one of those factors which make it so difficult to predict the course of events . . . in India today.[18]

Winston Churchill rose the next day to speak the opposition's mind. He affirmed his continued adherence to the 1942 Cripps offer and accused the present government of having departed in several basic respects from the 1942 formula. He launched a bitter attack on the "Government of Mr. Nehru," which he called "a complete disaster," insisting that "It was a cardinal mistake to entrust the government of India to the caste Hindu." Turning to "the new Viceroy," Churchill argued:

> India is to be subjected not merely to partition, but to fragmentation, and to haphazard fragmentation. A time limit is imposed—a kind of guillotine—which will certainly prevent the full, fair and reasonable discussion of the great complicated issues that are involved. These 14 months will not be used for the melting of hearts and the union of Muslim and Hindu all over India. They will be used in preparation for civil war; and they will be marked continually by disorders and disturbances such as are now going on in the great city of Lahore.[19]

Attlee, in a tepid attempt at rebuttal, admitted that "There is gross inequality of wealth in India, but unfortunately, that social and economic system was continued during all the time of our rule. We did not go in for the revolutionary business of turning out the landlords who do nothing whatever. We did something to repress the moneylenders, but not much.

We accepted that social and economic system. Why are we told now, at the very end of our rule, that we must clear up all these things before we go, otherwise we shall betray our trust? If that trust is there, it ought to have been fulfilled long ago."[20] The House of Commons divided late that night in March strictly along party lines, with a majority of 337 Labourites closing ranks behind their prime minister and 185 Conservatives walking the other way with Churchill. Mountbatten with his brilliant staff of experts were soon to be launched on the fastest mission of major political surgery ever performed by one nation on the pregnant body politic of another.

Communal rioting in Multan left twenty dead and many more injured, as Jenkins took direct control of his Punjab province under Section 93 of the fast-fading Act of 1935. The nawab of Mamdot worked frantically to put a Muslim League ministry together but could win the support only of several Scheduled Caste and Indian Christian members of his assembly as well as three non-League Muslims, to add to his block of eighty party stalwarts. This left the solid Hindu-Sikh opposition almost equally balanced against him. Meanwhile, in New Delhi's interim cabinet, finance member Liaquat Ali accepted official "advice" and presented a tax-heavy budget designed to squeeze Indian industrial and commercial capitalists heavily enough to meet skyrocketing deficits caused by abandoning the salt tax and by paying retiring service pensions in unprecedented numbers. Wavell noted to Pethick-Lawrence, "The Budget is a clever one, in that it drives a wedge between Congress and their rich merchant supporters, like Birla."[21]

"Amritsar was my main anxiety yesterday," Jenkins wrote Wavell on March 7. "By the evening the city was completely out of control. . . . The death-roll does not seem to be very high, but the figures we have are only for the corpses which have passed through the hospital mortuary. Most of the population seem to have produced arms . . . many buildings are burning. Masses of people . . . running away from the city added to the confusion and . . . looting . . . Police reinforcements were despatched by midnight and two British Battalions. . . . Bad rioting is reported from Rawalpindi with 25 dead and perhaps 100 injured. Rioting has continued in Sialkot and Jullundur. These affairs always go through three stages— frenzy, funk and recrimination. . . ."[22] The frenzy was to continue all year.

The Congress Working Committee met in emergency session on March 8 and resolved that

The transfer of power, in order to be smooth, should be preceded by the recognition in practice of the Interim Government as a Dominion Government with effective control over the services and administration. . . . The Central Government must necessarily function as a

Cabinet with full authority and responsibility. Any other arrangement is incompatible with good government and is peculiarly dangerous.

In this hour when final decisions have to be taken . . . the Working
Committee earnestly call upon all parties and groups . . . to discard
violent and coercive methods, and co-operate peacefully. . . . The
end of an era is at hand and a new age will soon begin. Let this
dawn of the new age be ushered in bravely, leaving hates and dis-
cords in the dead past.[23]

When forwarding these Congress resolutions to the viceroy the next day,
Nehru explained "our intention" to urge the Muslim League to join Congress in the assembly and to work together amicably toward reaching a
final settlement. He added with an almost audible sigh of resignation:

If unfortunately this is not possible, we . . . have also suggested the
division of the Punjab into two parts. This principle would, of course,
apply to Bengal also . . . not pleasant for us to contemplate, but
such a course is preferable to an attempt by either party to impose
its will upon the other. Recent events in the Punjab have demonstrated . . . that it is not possible to coerce the non-Muslim minority
in the Province, just as it is not possible or desirable to coerce the
others. . . . In the event of the Muslim League not accepting the
Cabinet Delegation's scheme and not coming into the Constituent
Assembly, the division of Bengal and Punjab becomes inevitable.[24]

Congress was now ready to concede Pakistan, including only Muslim-
majority districts, but Pakistan nonetheless! It was early March of 1947.
Jinnah had won. "We have got to stand on our own legs," Quaid-i-Azam
told Muslim journalists in Bombay on March 12, insisting that "our ideology, our goal, our basic and fundamental principles . . . are not only
different from the Hindu organisations but are in conflict. . . . There is no
common ground for co-operation. . . . There was a time when the idea of
Pakistan was laughed at, but let me tell you this there is no other solution
which will do credit and bring honour to our people. . . . *Insha Allah*
("God Willing"), we shall have Pakistan."[25]

Communal "tension," Jenkins reported was "acute in almost all districts"
of the Punjab, with the major cities, Lahore, Amritsar, Multan and Rawalpindi, key "danger points." But the "trouble" was spreading to villages,
fanning out across the once prosperous countryside like cancerous cells of
fanatical hatred cut loose and growing at so alarming a rate there seemed
to be no control possible, no inhibiting force available to stop them.

In Amritsar, Master Tara Singh was reported to have told his Sikh fol-

lowers that the "Civil War" had "already begun."[26] Sikh defence member
Baldev Singh wrote Wavell, "I make no secret of my conviction that Muslim League's onslaught on the Coalition Ministry had been engineered in
the way it was because the League had despaired of being able to defeat it
by constitutional methods."[27] There were as yet no firm casualty figures for
the Punjab, but Jenkins estimated that about 1,000 persons had been killed
in the last month of rioting and many multiples of that figure wounded.
The rains would be late that year, but the Punjab's fields were to be
flooded with blood.

Mountbatten met almost daily with the cabinet in London, seeking answers to thorny problems from those who had grown old failing to solve
them. His youth was his armor; his innocence of Indian politics garbed him
in hope. He thought, as he informed the cabinet in early March "that the
Indian leaders themselves would sooner or later realise that the retention
of the Indian Army under central control was vital both to the external
security of India and to the maintenance of internal law and order."[28] He
planned to "warn the Interim Government that he would not allow them
to use British bayonets to keep law and order, but only to protect British
lives." That evening they met at 10 Downing Street. The viceroy-designate
needed flying orders, and there were still many "amendments" to be considered.

Nehru's old friend, roving ambassador V. K. Krishna Menon, also met
with Mountbatten that March 13, briefing him on the current situation in
India and Congress's suggested solutions. On the question of Muslim
League demands, Krishna Menon proposed two "Pakistans," one in the
Northwest, partitioning the Punjab as well as Sind, the other in the Northeast,

> to include the districts of Eastern Bengal which are predominantly
> Moslem, and certain areas of Assam, thus partitioning Bengal. . . .
> I believe that partition is the price that will have to be paid for any
> stability in Bengal . . . any solution which hands over Calcutta to
> Pakistan will be unstable and impractical. . . . On the other hand,
> the League has to be given a port on the East, and the solution is
> that as part of the compromise settlement India should build a large-
> sized city and port in Chittagong, that is, provide the money for it
> however many millions it may cost.[29]

Calcutta financial interests thus were prepared to pay for retention of their
capital, and this formula was ultimately accepted by all parties.

Tens of thousands of refugees began pouring into Rawalpindi from
ravaged villages in the countryside. "Attacks on non-Muslims have been

organized with extreme savagery," Jenkins wired on March 17. "Deputy Commissioner Rawalpindi believes that in his district alone there may be 5,000 casualties."[30] As information flowed in from outlying regions of the Punjab a pattern of "organisation and conspiracy" seemed to emerge, wrote the governor, "in parts of Rawalpindi outbreaks . . . have occurred almost simultaneously . . . carefully planned and carried out. All Muslims in the affected districts seem to be involved in or sympathetic to the movement. The Commander 7th Division told me when I saw him yesterday that attacks on non-Muslims had been led in some cases by retired Army officers— some of them pensioners. . . . The Muslim section of the local notables, to whom I spoke . . . were extremely sulky . . . non-Muslims are vehemently bitter against the civil services and particularly against the Police."[31] The League's "Swordam" was being wielded now with a vengeance.

On March 18, Mountbatten received his predeparture orders from the prime minister:

> My colleagues of the Cabinet Mission and I have discussed with you the general lines of your approach to the problems which will confront you in India. It will, I think be useful to you to have on record the salient points. . . . It is the definite objective of His Majesty's Government to obtain a unitary Government for British India and the Indian States, if possible within the British Commonwealth, through the medium of a Constituent Assembly . . . and you should do the utmost in your power to persuade all Parties to work together to this end. . . . If by October 1 you consider that there is no prospect of reaching a settlement on the basis of a unitary government . . . you should report to His Majesty's Government on the steps which you consider should be taken for the handing over of power on the due date. . . . You will do your best to persuade the rulers of any Indian States in which political progress has been slow to progress rapidly.
>
> It is essential that there should be the fullest co-operation with the Indian leaders in all steps that are taken as to the withdrawal of British power so that the process may go forward as smoothly as possible.[32]

On March 22, 1947, Mountbatten reached New Delhi, where he met with Wavell.

> There was some discussion of the failure of the Indian politicians to appreciate how little time there was to arrange the transfer of power before June, 1948, and the question was raised whether the partition of Punjab and Bengal could take place inside the Cabinet Mission's plan. LORD MOUNTBATTEN . . . said he thought there must be

some strong authority to which to hand over in India, and that any solution must be based on the Indian Army.[33]

Wavell quit New Delhi early the next morning but remained viceroy till he flew out of Karachi the following day. "I went round to Mountbatten's suite and had a discussion with the Viceroy designate, clad in his underpants and vest," press attaché Alan Campbell-Johnson recalled. "He showed me this morning's masterpiece on the front page of *Dawn*. It is a photograph of Ronnie Brockman [of Mountbatten's staff] and Elizabeth Ward, Lady Mountbatten's private secretary, in which they are, of course, described as 'Lord and Lady Louis arriving.'"[34]

The nineteenth and last of the British viceroys was sworn in by Lord Chief Justice Sir Patrick Spens on the morning of March 24, 1947, with a streamlined version of pomp and panoply for New Delhi's royal ceremony-loving audience. Mountbatten delighted his audience by speaking "in an easy and pleasant manner" for several minutes after his investiture,[35] nodding to Nehru and the Congress ministers seated to his right, and to Liaquat and his League cabinet colleagues on the other side. That afternoon he got to work, meeting first with Nehru and then with Liaquat. He had already written personally to Gandhi and Jinnah asking each of them to come to New Delhi at their earliest convenience to meet with him. Jinnah was still recuperating in Bombay.

Nehru had spent some time with the Mountbattens in Malaya during the war and admired Dickie's natural elegance, unpretentious manner, aristocratic urbanity, and conviviality. They had "hit it off" beautifully. Mountbatten used Nehru as his primary Indian sounding board for vital information, asking, for example, "his own estimate" of Jinnah.

Nehru said the essential thing to realise about Jinnah is that he is a man to whom success has come very late in life—at over sixty. Before that he had not been a major figure in Indian politics . . . was a successful lawyer, but not an especially good one. . . . The secret of his success—and it had been tremendous, if only for its emotional intensity—was in his capacity to take up a permanently negative attitude. . . . He knew that Pakistan could never stand up to constructive criticism, and he had ensured that it should never be subjected to it.[36]

This negative analysis of his leading rival reveals Nehru's intense hatred of Jinnah more than it helps illuminate the true source of Jinnah's powers. Mountbatten's own rather negative assessment of Jinnah was, in some measure, probably influenced by Nehru's singular aversion to the Quaid-i-Azam and all he represented.

The new viceroy next met with Liaquat Ali Khan, whose attempt to solve India's economic problem had met with such strong Congress opposition that he had finally agreed to cut his proposed excess profits tax from 25 to 16 percent. But Mountbatten did not find Liaquat as intellectually stimulating or personally appealing as Nehru, and no bond of real intimacy ever developed between them.

Mountbatten spent over ten hours talking in private with Gandhi at five separate meetings from March 31 through April 4, during which the Mahatma proposed that

> Mr. Jinnah . . . be given the option of forming a Cabinet. . . . If Mr. Jinnah accepted this offer, the Congress would guarantee to cooperate freely and sincerely, so long as all the measures that Mr. Jinnah's Cabinet bring forward are in the interests of the Indian people as a whole . . . sole referee of what is or is not in the interests of India as a whole will be Lord Mountbatten. . . . Mr. Jinnah must stipulate, on behalf of the League . . . that, so far as he or they are concerned, they will do their utmost to preserve peace throughout India. . . . There shall be no National Guards or any other form of private army. . . . Within the framework hereof Mr. Jinnah will be perfectly free to present for acceptance a scheme of Pakistan, even before the transfer of power, provided, however, that he is successful in his appeal to reason and not to the force of arms which he abjures for all time for this purpose. Thus, there will be no compulsion in this matter over a Province or part thereof. . . . If Mr. Jinnah rejects this offer, the same offer to be made mutatis mutandis to Congress.[37]

When Gandhi initially proposed this ingenious formula, Mountbatten admitted it "staggered me. I asked 'What would Mr. Jinnah say to such a proposal?' The reply was 'If you tell him I am the author he will reply "Wily Gandhi." ' I [Mountbatten] then remarked 'And I presume Mr. Jinnah will be right?' To which he replied with great fervour 'No, I am entirely sincere in my suggestion.' "[38] Gandhi's offer would never be conveyed to Jinnah. Mountbatten opted first to discuss the matter with Nehru, whose reaction was totally negative. Nehru was shocked to learn that his Mahatma was quite ready to replace him as premier with the Quaid-i-Azam. After telling Mountbatten how "unrealistic" Gandhi's "solution" was, Jawaharlal said "he was anxious for Mr. Gandhi to stay a few days longer in Delhi, as he had been away for four months and was rapidly getting out of touch with events at the Centre."[39] Nehru and Patel hoped quickly to bring the unpredictable old man back into "touch" with their conclusions on how best to handle Jinnah and the Muslim League. Perhaps even if Jinnah were offered the entire central government on a platter with the whole cabinet under his personal control, he might have dismissed it with a negative wave of his long-fingered hand. Yet it was an exquisite temptation to place before him. It was a brilliant solution to India's oldest, toughest, greatest political problem. The Mahatma alone was capable of such absolute abnegation, such instant reversal of political position. Gandhi understood Jinnah well enough, moreover, to know just how potent an appeal to his ego that sort of singularly generous offer would have been. It might just have worked; surely this was a King Solomon solution. But Nehru had tasted the cup of power too long to offer its nectar to any one else—last of all to that "mediocre lawyer," the "reactionary-Muslim Baron of Malabar Hill" as so many good Congress leaders thought of Jinnah. Nehru notified Mountbatten that the scheme was "quite impracticable . . . even less realistic now than a year ago" when Gandhi had suggested the same idea to the cabinet mission.

Mountbatten met Jinnah for the first time on April 5, finding him "most frigid, haughty and disdainful."[40] The only light moment came before discussion started, when the cameramen photographed Jinnah with Lord and Lady Mountbatten in the garden, and Mountbatten recalled, "He had obviously prepared his quip for the press, expecting Edwina to pose *between* us, you see, but when we insisted on having him stand in the middle, his mind wasn't quite fast enough to shift gears, so he said what he'd rehearsed, 'A rose between two thorns!' "[41] Was Jinnah's mind perhaps working a bit faster than Mountbatten suspected? The Mountbattens invited Jinnah and Fatima to dinner the next evening and the Jinnahs obviously enjoyed it, staying till well after midnight, by which time "the ice was really broken."

> Mr. Jinnah claimed that there was only one solution—a "surgical operation" on India, otherwise India would perish altogether. I replied by reiterating that I had not yet made up my mind, and pointed out that an "anaesthetic" must precede any "surgical operation." He gave me an account (which worries me a great deal) about his previous negotiations with Mr. Gandhi. . . . He emphasized, and tried to prove from this account, that on the Muslim side there was only one man to deal with, namely himself. . . . But the same was not true of the representatives of Congress—there was no one man to deal with on their side. Mr. Gandhi had openly confessed that he represented nobody . . . had enormous authority with no responsibility. Nehru and Patel represented different points of view within Con-

gress—neither could give a categorical answer on behalf of the party as a whole. . . . He also spoke of the emotionalism of the Congress leaders. . . . He accused Congress leaders of constantly shifting their front. . . . They would stoop to anything. . . . At the end of our interview, after he had told me a succession of long stories about how appallingly the Muslims had been treated, I informed him that what fascinated me was the way that all the Indian leaders spoke with such conviction.[42]

The conviviality of that intimate dinner party, which obviously loosened Jinnah's tongue and "worried" Mountbatten "*a great deal,*" seems to have so diminished his confidence in Jinnah that he decided irrevocably against transmitting Gandhi's offer, thus shattering the last hope of preserving Indian unity. Jinnah's own negative assessment of Gandhi's powers to "deliver" Congress contributed, no doubt, to that most tragic decision, yet fundamentally it was based on Mountbatten's personal judgment of Jinnah's state of mind and body, both of which he considered dangerously and undependably "infirm" after that first marathon meeting. It was not simply that he did not "like" Jinnah as much as he liked Nehru. It went deeper. He really did not *trust* Jinnah's judgment and appears to have found those "long stories" symptomatic of senility.

They met again on April 7, with Lord Ismay joining the discussion that afternoon. Mountbatten "tried by every means" to get Jinnah to say he "would accept the Cabinet Mission plan and enter the Constituent Assembly."[43] Jinnah remained adamant, however.

Next evening they met for two more hours, and Mountbatten explained his resolve to recommend to the British government how best to transfer Britain's power after hearing the views of all major parties. Unlike the cabinet mission, he did not wait for the parties to reach "agreement" since the terminal date had been set.

> I then asked him what, if he were in my place, his solution would be; and he repeated once more the demand for Pakistan. . . . I invited Mr. Jinnah to put forward his arguments for partition. He recited the classic ones. I then pointed out that his remarks applied also to the partition of the Punjab and Bengal, and that by sheer logic if I accepted his arguments in the case of India as a whole, I had also to apply them in the case of these two Provinces . . . he expressed himself most upset at my trying to give him a "moth eaten" Pakistan. He said that this demand for partitioning the Punjab and Bengal was a bluff on the part of Congress to try and frighten him off Pakistan. He was not to be frightened off so easily; and he would be sorry if I were taken in by the Congress bluff.[44]

On April 9, Mountbatten and Jinnah talked again for over an hour. Jinnah insisted that the "Begin all and end all" of Pakistan was to have its own army.

> I told him that I regarded it as a very great tragedy that he should be trying to force me to give up the idea of a united India. I painted a picture of the greatness that India could achieve. . . . I finally said that I found that the present Interim Coalition Government was every day working better and in a more co-operative spirit; and that it was a day-dream of mine to be able to put the Central Government under the Prime Ministership of Mr. Jinnah himself. . . . Some 35 minutes later, Mr. Jinnah, who had not referred previously to my personal remark about him, suddenly made a reference out of the blue to the fact that I had wanted him to be the Prime Minister. There is no doubt that it had greatly tickled his vanity, and that he had kept turning over the proposition in his mind.

> Mr. Gandhi's famous scheme may yet go through on the pure vanity of Mr. Jinnah! Nevertheless he gives me the impression of a man who has not thought out one single piece of the mechanics of his own great scheme, and he will have the shock of his life when he really has to come down to earth and try and make his vague idealistic proposals work on a concrete basis.[45]

And after three more hours alone with Jinnah on April 10, Mountbatten reported to his staff that he considered "Mr. Jinnah was a psychopathic case."[46] The viceroy had

> brought all possible arguments to bear on Mr. Jinnah but it seemed that appeals to his reason did not prevail. . . . Mr. Jinnah had not been able in his presence to adduce one single feasible argument in favour of Pakistan. In fact he had offered no counter arguments. He gave the impression that he was not listening. He was impossible to argue with. . . . He was, whatever was said, intent on his Pakistan— which could surely only result in doing the Muslims irreparable damage . . . until he had met Mr. Jinnah he [Mountbatten] had not thought it possible that a man with such a complete lack of sense of responsibility could hold the power which he did.[47]

Ismay expressed his own belief that "the dominating feature in Mr. Jinnah's mental structure was his loathing and contempt of the Hindus. He apparently thought that all Hindus were sub-human creatures with whom it was impossible for the Muslims to live."[48]

All the while communal rioting had continued to rack the Punjab. By mid-April, official estimates of some 3,500 dead in little more than a month of mayhem counted approximately six Hindus and Sikhs for every Muslim murdered. "One of my troubles has been the extreme complacency of the League leaders in the Punjab who say in effect that 'boys will be boys,'" reported Jenkins, who estimated by then that "Every British official in the I.C.S. and I.P. in the Punjab, including myself, would be very glad to leave it tomorrow . . . we feel now that we are dealing with people who are out to destroy themselves."[49] The North-West Frontier was also ablaze with at least half of Dera Ismail Khan razed by "flames" that blood-drenched spring. Bombay was placed under dusk-to-dawn curfew, as was Benares. Calcutta, too, simmered in the heat of communal violence, which daily, grew more intense, fired by rumors of imminent partition.

Chief Minister Suhrawardy hoped to save Bengal the agony of a second partition in less than half a century by proposing a coalition government to his Congress and Forward Bloc opponents, advocating independent national status for united Bengal. With Bengal enjoying the virtual world monopoly of jute and having Calcutta's highly developed international port, Suhrawardy sought British as well as American capital to develop his "nation's" economic potential. "We Bengalis have a common mother tongue and common economic interests," Suhrawardy argued. "Bengal has very little affinity with the Punjab. Bengal will be an independent state and decide by herself later whether she would link up with Pakistan."[50] Jinnah would have welcomed the emergence of an independent, united Bengal with open arms; but Nehru and Patel considered it an anathema to Congress and Indian interests and feared that a unified "Bangladesh," led by a Muslim premier, would form closer alliances to Pakistan than India.

Mountbatten found Liaquat Ali Khan much easier to deal with than Jinnah in that he was more like Nehru in his urbanity and relative reasonableness. He met with Liaquat for two hours on the evening of April 10, taking him into confidence, as to

> how my mind was beginning to work towards a solution. . . . I started off with Pakistan and complete partition of the Punjab and Bengal and Assam. I told him that I had no doubt that the Indian leaders and their peoples were in such an hysterical condition that they would all gladly agree to my arranging their suicide in this way. He nodded his head, and said "I am afraid everybody will agree to such a plan; we are all in such a state." I told him that the worst service I could do to India, if I were her enemy or completely indifferent to her fate, would be to take advantage of this extraordinary mental condition to force the completest partition possible upon them, before going off in June 1948 and leaving the whole country in the most hopeless chaos.[51]

That talk with Liaquat sealed India's tragic fate. Mountbatten was completely sincere in what he said after Liaquat mournfully admitted that even Jinnah would accept the triple-partition plan, for Mountbatten was wise enough to anticipate the horrors of slashing a subcontinent so tortured by religious pluralism into competing national fragments. He understood, indeed too well, the pitfalls and dangers of dividing the army, of withdrawing the foreign troops and impartial leaders, and of leaving the unlettered, prejudiced, fearful, superstitious masses to battle it out, to fall onto one another venting their fears and spleen on neighboring village and urban ward. He sensed, in fact, that *"the worst service* I could do to India, *if I were her enemy or completely indifferent to her fate,"* was precisely what he *would* do—just a few months after voicing those dread words. He did not want to do this. Quite the contrary, of course! He had gone out to save India, to heal its wounds, to offer peace not the sword of partition. He and Lady Mountbatten loved India and the Indians. They were ready to risk their lives—and did so, in fact, daily in the service of these impassioned, mercurial, mostly impoverished people. But there was *no other solution.*

Gandhi's "mad plan," the only exception, would have meant turning the very land and all the people Mountbatten loved most in it, including Nehru, over to Jinnah, whom he considered "psychopathic." Partition alone remained the viable option, but Pakistan demanded, by the sheer logic of its premise, partition of the Punjab and Bengal as well. The best "servant" Britain ever sent out to India would soon thus find himself *obliged* to perform "the worst service I could do to India." And that night after Liaquat left him, Mountbatten sought some consolation in hope, writing, "I have an impression that Mr. Liaquat Ali Khan intends to help me find a more reasonable solution than this mad Pakistan."[52]

A British journalist who saw Jinnah at this time reported to the viceroy's private secretary his "most disturbed state of mind," which made George Abell advise Mountbatten, "It was possible that Mr. Jinnah was ill but more probable that he was bewildered by the impact of events."[53] Deputy private secretary Ian Scott also got "the impression that Mr. Jinnah was indeed becoming seriously troubled by the prospect opening out before him. He felt that this process should be allowed to take its course; there would be a psychological moment at which to take advantage of it." All wishful thinking. None of those "clever" strategies worked.

Krishna Menon continued to keep in touch with Mountbatten, who found he had "very shrewd views" on world politics, warning Mountbatten against America's "object in India . . . to capture all the markets, to step in and take the place of the British, and finally . . . to get bases in India for ultimate use against Russia."[54] Mountbatten was at least equally "shrewd" in return, however, cautioning Nehru's closest adviser on foreign affairs that unless India remained in the British Commonwealth, Pakistan, which was most anxious to do so, might soon build up its "armed forces immensely superior to those of Hindustan . . . and I presumed that places like Karachi would become big naval and air bases within the British Commonwealth." Krishna Menon "absolutely shuddered" at that prospect and promised to do all he could to help convince Nehru and Patel to request dominion status for India—as in fact they soon did, despite "firm" previous Congress commitments that India would become a completely "independent sovereign State."

Viscountess Edwina Mountbatten tried to befriend Fatima, inviting her to tea and seeking to "steer the conversation" on such occasions away from politics, but Fatima always returned to her favorite subject "and made violent attacks on Congress and the Hindu community as a whole," Lady Mountbatten reported. "She seemed almost fanatical . . . made frequent references to the fact that 'the Muslims would fight for separation and their rights if these were not agreed to.' . . . Like Mr. Jinnah, she has, of course, a persecution mania, and is obviously convinced that the Hindu intends to subjugate and dominate the Muslim completely."[55] Lady Mountbatten tried to get Fatima to explain to her how Pakistan "would really work," but "Miss Jinnah refused to give any definite answer, saying all the time that the problems involved would be quite easy once Muslim demands had been agreed to."

By the end of April, the Muslim League had a clear majority in the Punjab, and the nawab of Mamdot demanded that Governor Jenkins call upon him to form a ministry instead of continuing autocratically to rule under Section 93 of the 1935 act. Jinnah finally went to Mountbatten to reiterate that demand, but the viceroy, like his governor, refused to install one-party rule in the Punjab, fearing it would incite "civil war" as threatened by the Sikhs. During this same interview, the viceroy informed Jinnah of Suhrawardy's recently expressed hope that "he might be able to keep a united Bengal on condition that it joined neither Pakistan nor Hindustan. I asked Mr. Jinnah straight out what his views were about Bengal united at the price of its remaining out of Pakistan."

> He said, without any hesitation; "I should be delighted. What is the use of Bengal without Calcutta; they had much better remain united and independent; I am sure that they would be on friendly terms with us."
>
> I then mentioned that Mr. Suhrawardy had said that if Bengal remained united and independent, they would wish to remain within the Commonwealth. Mr. Jinnah replied "Of course, just as I indi-

cated to you that Pakistan would wish to remain within the Commonwealth." I corrected him and said, "No, you told me that if the Pakistan Government was formed, its first act might well be to ask to be admitted to membership of the British Commonwealth." He corrected me, and said I completely misunderstood the position; it was not a question of asking to be admitted, it was a question of not being kicked out. He said that Mr. Churchill had told him. "You have only to stand firm and demand your rights not to be expelled from the British Commonwealth, and you are bound to be accepted. The country would never stand for the expulsion of loyal members of the Empire."[56]

Whatever Mountbatten and his staff thought of Jinnah's mental state, he clearly retained the unique sharpness of his legal faculties and proved perfectly correct in his brilliant legal opinion of the much confused and belabored issue of commonwealth membership.

"Mr. Jinnah told me that he had asked Sir Stafford Cripps what form legislation on the transfer of power was likely to take"; Mountbatten continued to report on that late April meeting, "could he count on the fact that it would be in the form that India or parts of India would be granted the same privilege as other members of the British Commonwealth; i.e., the right to secede if they so wished, failing which they would automatically still be in the Empire. Sir Stafford Cripps replied that he was not in a position to answer that question at that time. Mr. Jinnah said 'Thus like a true lawyer he evaded the question; but it is quite clear to me that you cannot kick us out; there is no precedent for forcing parts of the Empire to leave against their will.' "[57] Jinnah could hardly have paid Cripps a higher compliment, of course, than to call him "a true lawyer."

Jinnah explained that his reasons for insisting that Pakistan must remain within the British Commonwealth were not merely legalistic, however, arguing that "the leaders of Congress are so dishonest, so crooked, and so obsessed with the idea of smashing the Muslim League, that there are no lengths to which they will not go to do so; and the only way of giving Pakistan a chance is to make it an independent nation of the British Commonwealth, with its own army, and the right to argue cases at any Central Council on this basis." That was to be his trump card in defence of his newborn nation, no matter how "moth-eaten" a state it might be.

Jinnah's hopes for Bengal remaining united were shared by Liaquat, who informed Sir Eric Mieville "that he was in no way worried about Bengal as he was convinced in his own mind that the province would never divide. He thought it would remain a separate state, joining neither Hindustan nor Pakistan."[58] Liaquat also "hinted" to Mieville that "there was a chance that 'Sikhistan' might join up with Pakistan, and that the Muslim League would offer them very generous terms."[59] Jinnah had several secret meetings with Sikh leaders, including the maharaja of Patiala and Baldev Singh, and tried to induce them to join Pakistan. Nehru and Patel were in position to offer more, however, keeping Baldev and his troops, as well as Master Tara Singh, loyal to India; and Baldev was to retain control over India's ministry of defence in Nehru's cabinet. Jinnah thus tried his utmost and actually believed till the bitter end that he might be able to avert the bloody disaster of subdividing both Bengal and the Punjab while extricating Pakistan's Northwestern provinces from the Indian union, thus leaving a unified Eastern Bangladesh on its own.

"The more I look at the problem in India the more I realise that all this partition business is sheer madness and is going to reduce the economic efficiency of the whole country immeasurably," Mountbatten wrote home on May 1. "No-one would ever induce me to agree to it were it not for this fantastic communal madness that has seized everybody and leaves no other course open . . . one small horrifying example: my wife had Miss Jinnah to tea again. . . . She told Miss Jinnah that she had spent that morning at the Lady Irwin College, and was so delighted to find how happily that institution was working and on what excellent terms the Hindu and Muslim girls were. . . . To this Miss Jinnah replied: 'Don't be misled by the apparent contentment of the Muslim girls there; we haven't been able to start our propaganda in that college yet.' . . . The Hindus are nearly as bad. . . . The most we can do . . . is to put responsibility for any of these mad decisions fairly and squarely on the Indian shoulders in the eyes of the world, for one day they will bitterly regret the decision they are about to make."[60]

The Mountbattens flew up to Simla for a week's holiday, taking Nehru and his daughter, Indira, as house guests. "Having made real friends with Nehru during his stay here," Mountbatten wired his chief of staff, Lord Ismay, "I asked him whether he would look at the London draft [of the plan for voting on partition], as an act of friendship and on the understanding that he would not utilise his prior knowledge or mention to his colleagues that he had seen it. He readily gave this undertaking and took the draft to bed."[61] Next morning Nehru wrote Mountbatten that the plan he had previewed "frightened me . . . much that we had done so far was undermined and the Cabinet Mission's scheme and subsequent developments were set aside, and an entirely new picture presented—a picture of fragmentation and conflict and disorder, and . . . of a worsening of relations between India and Britain. . . . If my reactions were so powerful, you can well imagine what my colleagues and others will think and feel

. . . it will be a disaster."[62] Mountbatten reported Nehru's "bombshell" to Ismay, suggesting that in view of this reaction some "redrafting of the plan" would be required. At this point, Attlee asked Mountbatten to fly home unless he preferred having Cripps, Alexander, or the new secretary of state, Lord Listowel, fly out to New Delhi to consult with him on the spot. Mountbatten chose to go to London.

Before flying from New Delhi in mid-May, Mountbatten showed his revised proposed plan to Liaquat. "I then asked him whether the Muslim League was going to accept partition of the Punjab and Bengal, to which he replied: 'We shall never agree to it, but you may make us bow to the inevitable.' I told him it was essential that, if it did become inevitable, all parties should give their public agreement to avoid bloodshed, and that I proposed to raise this with Mr. Jinnah."[63]

Jinnah's reaction to the Mountbatten plan was even more negative than Nehru's. "The Muslim League cannot agree to the partition of Bengal and the Punjab," Jinnah wrote. "It cannot be justified historically, economically, geographically, politically or morally. These provinces have built up their respective lives for nearly a century . . . and the only ground which is put forward for the partition is that the areas where the Hindus and Sikhs are in a majority should be separated from the rest of the provinces . . . the results will be disastrous for the life of these two provinces and all the communities concerned . . . if you take this decision—which in my opinion will be a fateful one—Calcutta should not be torn away from the Eastern Bengal . . . if worst comes to worst, Calcutta should be made a free port."[64]

At 10 Downing Street, on the evening of May 19, 1947, Mountbatten informed Prime Minister Attlee and his Cabinet colleagues that "It had become clear that the Muslim League would resort to arms if Pakistan in some form were not conceded."[65] Jinnah was interviewed by Reuters the next day and demanded an 800-mile long "corridor" to link West and East Pakistan, promising a "really beneficial" relationship between Pakistan and Britain, and offering "Hindustan" a "friendly and reciprocal" alliance.[66] Congress reactions to the "corridor" demand proved so strongly negative that it never became a serious issue, receiving even less attention than the idea that Calcutta should emerge as a free port. Then Jinnah wired the cabinet demanding that before Bengal and the Punjab were partitioned, a referendum should be held in each province to determine the will of its people in this vital regard. Mountbatten, however, spoke against that proposal, insisting it "would merely result in delay."[67] The cabinet "agreed," and the imperial steamroller moved ahead in high gear.

Krishna Menon flew to London to inform Mountbatten on May 21 that

Nehru and Patel were "ready to accept" dominion status if it were offered to India in 1947. "As I am anxious that there should be no misunderstanding, I am writing to you even though I have seen you this morning!" Nehru's confidant wrote Mountbatten from India House that same day. "If Mr. Jinnah wants a total separation, and that straight away, and if we agree to it for the sake of peace and dismember our country, we want to be rid of him, so far as the affairs of what is left to us of our country are concerned. I feel sure you will appreciate this, and also that it is not a matter of detail, but is fundamental."[68] Congress had begun to fear that in another six months they would lose the Eastern Punjab and Sikh support, as well as Calcutta and Western Bengal, possibly more of the princely states also, especially Hyderabad and Bhopal, for the longer Jinnah argued the stronger and greater his demands became. Nehru was sick and tired of arguing, ready, as he put it "privately," to concede Pakistan on the theory that by "cutting off the head we will get rid of the headache."[69]

Attlee's final hurdle remained Churchill and the Conservative opposition in Parliament, who could easily have held up the Independence of India Bill in a prolonged and acrimonious Commons debate that would have made transfer of power in 1947 impossible. Mountbatten went round to visit "Mr. Churchill in bed" and soothed the ex-prime ministers' anxieties and fears with his "fatal" charm. He understood the forensic powers of this cigar-smoking old man who looked so deceptively frail in his sick bed. "I then asked him if he would advise me how I should proceed if Jinnah was intransigent," Mountbatten reported. "He thought about this for a long time and finally said: 'To begin with you must threaten. Take away all British officers. Give them military units without British officers. Make it clear to them how impossible it would be to run Pakistan without British help.'" Mountbatten "agreed to try and follow some such policy," but more important he actually managed to get Churchill to give him a "personal message" for Jinnah, stating "This is a matter of life and death for Pakistan, if you do not accept this offer with both hands."[70] Churchill's words carried more weight with Jinnah than those of any other living person, as Mountbatten well knew. The final obstacle was now removed from the path to partition. With Churchill on board, it was "full ahead" for the Mountbatten plan, which was to bring two "moth-eaten," wretched, impoverished, embattled, bitter new dominions into the British Commonwealth.

On Monday morning, June 2, 1947, India's leaders drove into the North Court of the viceroy's house in New Delhi: Liaquat and Nishtar accompanying Jinnah; Patel and J. B. Kripalani (Congress president for the year), and Baldev Singh, with Nehru. That meeting, at which those leaders were briefed on the plan brought back from London, lasted only two hours.

"The atmosphere was tense," reported Mountbatten, "and I got the feeling that the less the leaders talked the less the chance of friction and perhaps the ultimate breakdown of the meeting. . . . I reported on the most helpful attitude of His Majesty's Government and the Opposition. . . . I asked the leaders to let me have their replies before midnight. . . . Jinnah said he would come in person at 11 p.m. after they had seen their Working Committee. I kept back Jinnah after the meeting . . . to impress on him that there could not be any question of a 'No' from the League."[71] That must have been when Mountbatten delivered Churchill's message. The viceroy, by now thoroughly disenchanted with Gandhi (possibly thanks to an undelivered "message" from Churchill), wrote "He may be a saint but he seems also to be a disciple of Trotsky." The Mahatma arrived at Mountbatten's study door half an hour after the others had gone off to read their copies of the plan. It was Gandhi's day of silence, so he wrote his comments on bits of paper. Jinnah had also done some doodling that morning, leaving a scrap behind that seemed to show rockets, tennis rackets, and balloons going up and had "Governor General" written in quotes across the center page—the Quaid-i-Azam apparently enjoying the sight of his future title.[72]

> At 11 o'clock that night Jinnah came round. He spent half an hour conveying the protest of his Working Committee against the partition of the Provinces. . . . I then asked him straight out whether his Working Committee were going to accept the plan. He replied that they were "hopeful." I then asked him whether he intended to accept it himself, to which he replied that he would support me personally and undertook to use his very best endeavours to get the All-India Muslim League Council to accept. . . . He had called an urgent meeting next Monday. . . . I finally asked him whether he felt I would be justified in advising the Prime Minister to go ahead and make the announcement, to which he replied very firmly "Yes."[73]

Mountbatten met to confer with his staff the next morning and reported his futile efforts to get Jinnah to accept the plan in writing, but "no amount of pressure" would make him agree prior to his council's meeting.

> Mountbatten then reminded Jinnah that the Congress Party were terribly suspicious of this particular tactic, which he always used, whereby he waited until the Congress Party had made a firm decision about some plan, and then left himself the right to make whatever decision suited the Moslem League. . . . Nothing Mountbatten could say would move him. . . . "If that is your attitude, then the leaders of the Congress Party and Sikhs will refuse final acceptance at the meeting in the morning; chaos will follow, and you will lose your Pakistan, probably for good." "What must be, must be," was his

only reaction, as he shrugged his shoulders. . . . "Mr. Jinnah! I do not intend to let you wreck all the work that has gone into this settlement. Since you will not accept for the Moslem League, I will speak for them myself. . . . I have only one condition, and that is that when I say at the meeting in the morning, 'Mr. Jinnah has given me assurances which I have accepted and which satisfy me,' you will in no circumstances contradict that, and that when I look towards you, you will nod. . . ." Jinnah's reply to the proposition itself was to nod.[74]

The formal announcement was made on the night of June 3. Bhopal, Patiala, and the prime ministers of a dozen major princely states joined the viceroy in his oval office to get their copies of the plan before it was broadcast to the world. At 7:00 P.M. All-India Radio carried the public announcement made first by the viceroy then followed by separate speeches from Nehru, Jinnah, and Baldev Singh. The viceroy announced,

> On February 20th, 1947, His Majesty's Government announced their intention of transferring power . . . by June 1948 . . . [we had] hoped that it would be possible for the major parties to co-operate. . . . This hope has not been fulfilled . . . the procedure outlined below embodies the best practical method of ascertaining the wishes of the people . . . to determine the authority or authorities to whom power should be transferred.[75]

Then followed a provincial and district breakdown of "Pakistan" with specifications as to how legislative assembly referenda would be held to decide by "a simple majority" for or against "partition," provincial as well as national. To "avoid delay," different provinces or parts of provinces would "proceed independently," and the existing constituent assembly as well as the new constituent assembly (if formed) should "proceed to frame Constitutions." These bodies would be "free to frame their own rules." His Majesty's Government were now willing to "anticipate" the June of 1948 deadline and envisioned setting up an independent Indian government "or governments" by an even earlier date. Accordingly, His Majesty's Government proposed introducing legislation "during the current session for the transfer of power this year on a Dominion Status basis to one or two successor authorities according to the decisions taken as a result of this announcement," Mountbatten concluded.[76]

"I am glad that I am afforded an opportunity to speak to you directly through this radio from New Delhi," Jinnah remarked that evening after Mountbatten and Nehru had finished their speeches. "It is the first time I believe that a non-official has been afforded an opportunity to address people through the medium of this powerful instrument on political matters. It augurs well, and I hope that in the future I shall have greater facilities to enable me to voice my views and opinions which will reach you directly, life-warm, rather than in the cold print of the newspapers."[77] How pleased he must have been, how proud to be seated there addressing millions of listeners—a veritable viceroy at long last.

Jinnah's speech had a mollifying impact, and as one "expert" in League "dialectic" wishfully put it, "This . . . means peace."[78] Mountbatten's press secretary was, however, more cautiously wise in assessment, noting, "Nehru's last words had been 'Jai Hind,' Jinnah closed with 'Pakistan Zindabad' . . . said in such a clipped voice that some startled listeners thought at first that . . . [he] pronounced 'Pakistan's in the bag!' "

On the morning of June 5, Mountbatten met with the political leaders again round the oval table in his office to discuss the administrative consequences of partition, using an official brief as their point of departure. "Jinnah was at pains to explain that both States would be independent and equal in every way. Nehru pointed out that the whole basis of approach must be different; India was continuing in every way the same, but the fact that dissident Provinces were to be allowed to secede must not interrupt the work of the Government of India or its foreign policy. Feeling was very tense."[79]

The last meeting of the All-India Muslim League was held in New Delhi's magnificent Imperial Hotel on June 9–10, 1947. Some 425 Muslim delegates gathered in that ornate grand ballroom overlooking the lush grounds with their picket of royal palms distancing the hotel from the spacious King's Way outside. The hotel was one of those sumptuous islands of peace and quiet that long helped British residents in Delhi to survive with minimal pain. At first it seemed that the League council might also enjoy the tranquillity of this civilized retreat during its historic deliberations on the Mountbatten plan of partition that hot June day. But not for long. Militant Muslim opposition from every province, orthodox mullahs and mighty landed barons with the most to lose from the Punjab's partition, as well as mercantile magnates who hated the thought of giving Calcutta to their Hindu rivals, cried out angrily inside the ballroom against the plan, calling it "betrayal," and a "tragedy for Pakistan." Khaksars rushed in through the once-tranquil garden, entering the hotel lounge "brandishing *belchas,* or sharpened spades . . . shouting 'Get Jinnah!' . . . half-way up the staircase leading to the ballroom where Jinnah and the Council were . . . in session before . . . League National Guards could grapple with them and turn them back. It took police with tear-gas to bring the disturbance to an end."[80] Some fifty Khaksar would-be assassins were arrested, and hotel guests in the lounge "ran helter-skelter," while those in the "din-ing-hall sat down for their dinner with tearful eyes as the tear-gas spread in the hall. Mr. Jinnah, however, continued the proceedings of the meeting untrammelled by the disturbances on the ground floor. A few demonstra-tors, who found their way into the meeting-hall were soon ejected. On the top floor of the Hotel, Muslim League National Guards and Khaksar dem-onstrators clashed . . . broke furniture and smashed glass panes . . . a few persons sustained injuries,"[81] morning news reported.

Inside the grand ballroom, Jinnah was hailed as *"Shahenshah-e-Pakistan"* (literally, "Emperor of Pakistan") in the Persian style of Iran's monarch, but he was quick to disclaim that title, urging his supporters not to repeat it and insisting, "I am a soldier of Pakistan, not its Emperor." Though the council met "in camera," Vallabhbhai Patel sent a "transcript of shorthand notes on the proceedings, presumably taken by a Congress spy!" to Mount-batten soon after the meeting ended.[82] The League's council gave "full au-thority to President Quaid-i-Azam M. A. Jinnah, to accept the fundamental principles of the Plan as a *compromise,* and to leave it to him, with full authority, to work out all the details of the Plan in an equitable and just manner. . . ." [Italics added][83]

That League resolution "caused a howl of indignation" from the Con-gress press and "violent letters of protest from Nehru and Patel," who wrote Mountbatten to express "fears that they would not be able to manage the All India Congress Committee in view of the failure of the League to make a definite announcement that they accepted the plan as a *settlement.*" [Italics added][84] Muslim zealots were, however, even more outraged at how far from the original Pakistan demand Jinnah had gone toward accept-ing the plan, and Rahmat Ali's Pakistan National Movement in Cambridge now denounced it as "The Greatest Betrayal" to the "whole Millat (Muslim Community)," writing:

It has now been completely betrayed, bartered, and dismembered by Mr. Jinnah, whose act of accepting the British Plan shatters the foundations of all its nations and countries and sabotages the future of all its 100 million members living in the Continent of Dinia . . . unless nullified, it will forever cripple the life of the Pak Nation, blight the existence of the Millat in Dinia, and compromise the free-dom of the Fraternity throughout the world. . . . We will carry on the fight to the end. . . . We will never quit or capitulate. . . . It shall never be said of us that, when the time came to choose be-tween the greatest battle for the Millat and the greatest betrayal . . . we too followed the quislings and chose betrayal. . . . *Long Live The Millat!*[85]

The first meeting of the interim government's cabinet following the announced plan almost led to a fight between Nehru and Liaquat over Jawaharlal's appointment of his sister, Madame Pandit, to be an ambassador; at which point Mountbatten shouted, "Gentlemen, what hopes have we of getting a peaceable partition if the first discussion leads to such a disgraceful scene as this?"[86] The answer, of course, was *"None!"*

22

Karachí-"Pakistan Zindabad" (1947)

On June 20, 1947, members of the Bengal legislative assembly voted for partition of their province by a large majority. Three days later the Punjabi assembly members opted for a similar Caesarian solution to the communal problem that had burned much of Lahore and Amritsar to the ground. Sind's legislature also voted, 33 to 20, to join Pakistan. "Thus we can now look upon the creation of Pakistan on the 15th August as legally decided upon," Mountbatten reported on June 27.[1]

Jinnah was invited into the viceroy's office that day to sit with Nehru and Patel, as well as Liaquat and Baldev, on a new "partition council," which addressed itself to the creation of boundary commissions. Four high court judges, two chosen by Congress and two by the League were to sit on each commission for partitioning the Punjab and Bengal. Jinnah suggested Britain's distinguished barrister, Sir Cyril Radcliffe, to chair those boundary commissions. Radcliffe, who had never even visited India and expressed no known opinions on its problems was unanimously accepted and would soon decide the destiny of millions of Hindus, Sikhs, and Muslims by the power of his repeatedly required casting vote. Nehru subsequently expressed grave misgivings about Radcliffe because of his close Conservative associations, and he urged that the federal court serve instead as final arbitrator, but Jinnah was adamantly opposed. Radcliffe reached New Delhi on July 8, giving him precisely five weeks to draw new national boundaries across whose lines, bitterly disputed by both countries, approximately 10 million refugees would run terrified in opposite directions.

Separate committees went to work to partition the army and other elements of the vast administrative machine that had kept British India running for some ninety years. Mountbatten hoped and indeed expected to be asked to stay on as joint governor-general over both new dominions, at once symbolizing their friendly and continued cooperation while expediting the process of the final division of assets in an equitable manner. Jinnah would hear nothing of that, however, insisting he must become governor-general of Pakistan himself. Jinnah suspected both Mountbattens of open favoritism to Congress, knowing how intimate they were with Nehru, and feared that Pakistan might be compromised or possibly suffer as a stepchild under Mountbatten. Jinnah was also acutely conscious of the tuberculosis consuming his lungs and knew little time remained to his life. He was eager to enjoy at least a taste of power, to which he had given so much of his energy. As prime minister, however, he would have been saddled with daily political as well as administrative responsibilities and preferred to leave those to a younger man. Being governor-general would raise him eye-to-eye with Mountbatten, Attlee, Smuts, and all the other heads of dominions of the Commonwealth the world over. It was clearly the only rank worthy of a Quaid-i-Azam. And it seemed a fitting first and only position for him to hold in the nation he had sired.

"It will be remembered that I reported to the Cabinet Committee that Nehru had put in writing a request to me to remain on as the Governor General of India," Mountbatten wrote on July 4. "Before I went to London Jinnah said that although he thought two Governor Generals would be better than one, he asked me specifically to stay on as a Super Governor General over the other two."[2] Mountbatten could not get cabinet approval for that proposal, however; nevertheless he and his staff continued to press Jinnah for "an answer" to the joint governor-general idea they were all so anxious to initiate.

India, like Pakistan, depended initially on British officers to head all three military services, while Field Marshal Auchinleck actually continued in overall command of both dominion armies for almost half a year following August 15. Nehru, like Jinnah, depended on several British governors, inviting Sir John Colville of Bombay and Sir Archibald Nye of Madras to serve independent India in their same official capacities. Nothing Mountbatten could say made Jinnah budge from his resolve to take direct control of Pakistan. After much soul-searching, considerable misgivings, and further consultation with London, the Mountbattens decided, nonetheless, to remain in New Delhi for almost another year, as originally planned.

"In moving the Third Reading of this Bill," Cripps informed the Commons on July 15, when he opened the final debate of the Indian Independence Bill, "I am introducing what will be the last Debate in this House on

Indian affairs. . . . This Bill will launch . . . a new and, let us hope, a happier era."³ Attlee concluded the debate that passed this historic measure, thus setting up two "Independent Dominions" of India and Pakistan on August 15, 1947. On Friday, July 18, King George VI added his talismanic seal of assent to the new act.

Jinnah held a press conference in mid-July and "assured" minorities in his inchoate dominion that they would have "protection with regard to their religion, faith, life, property and culture. They would, in all respect, be citizens of Pakistan without any discrimination. . . . The same principle . . . would apply to the minorities in India as well. . . . Mr. Jinnah sincerely hoped that the relations between Pakistan and India would be friendly and cordial.⁴

"I resigned myself fatalistically to the coming disaster," Penderel Moon wrote that July. "It was easy to predict disaster but what was the exact form that it would take? . . . The Senior Superintendent of Police, Delhi . . . asked for his opinion as to what would happen . . . replied crudely but tersely: 'Once a line of division is drawn in the Punjab all Sikhs to the west of it and all Muslims to the east of it will have their———chopped off.' "⁵ Until August 14 thousands of Sikhs and Hindus continued to believe that Lahore would fall to India, so instead of moving their valuables from that capital of the Punjab, they left most of what they owned behind when the boundary line was finally made public, racing east in panic and seeking only to save their lives. Mountbatten flew to Lahore on Sunday, July 20, and met with the Punjab partition committee, suggesting that the new government of east Punjab's "unessential personnel" all be moved out to Simla by August 10, but Radcliffe's final award would remain top secret till the eve of partition and independence.

In New Delhi the interim coalition government virtually ceased to function. Nehru and Liaquat were barely speaking to one another. Separate provisional administrations for India and Pakistan functioned virtually independently during those last frantic weeks when the assets of a subcontinent were divided in the most hasty, haphazard fashion—much the way a hostile divorcing couple might of an evening sort out their possessions. Governor general-designate Jinnah was busy selling his houses, with the mansion in New Delhi bringing a handsome profit from a Marwari merchant, and the estate atop Malabar Hill in Bombay going to a Western European consulate. Fatima supervised the packing, for all had to be ready August 7, when the Jinnahs flew off to Karachi to prepare their new mansion for the following week of historic ceremony. Meanwhile, Mountbatten also preoccupied himself with matters of vital interest to an admiral of the fleet.

I got both Jinnah and Nehru to agree that the Navies would fly the white ensign at the ensign staff and the Dominion Flag at the jack-staff, and that the Governors General would fly the regular Dominion Governor General's Flag, with the King's crest and the name of the Dominion. When I showed Jinnah the design of his new flag he announced that he had changed his mind and he intended to design his own flag with his own monogram on it, and he regretted that he could not allow his ships to fly the white ensign. He was only saved from being struck by the arrival of the other members of the Partition Council at this moment. However, I sent Ismay round to beat him up as soon as possible, and Jinnah claimed that I must have misunderstood him as of course he was keen that the Pakistan Navy should fly the white ensign, and talked glibly about the "brotherhood of the seas."[6]

The Mountbattens invited Jinnah and Fatima to dine with them on Friday, July 25, and as Campbell-Johnson recalled, "It was quite a small and informal affair, comprising only House guests and some of Mountbatten's staff. Jinnah completely monopolised the conversation by cracking a series of very lengthy and generally unfunny jokes. When Mountbatten tried to even out the conversation by talking to the guests next to him and leaving Jinnah to tell one of his stories to Lady Mountbatten, Jinnah broke off and interrupted across the table with, 'I think Mountbatten would like to hear this one.' It is customary for the Viceroy, representing the King, to precede his guests to and from the dining-room, but immediately this dinner was over the Jinnahs got up at the same time as Their Excellencies and walked out with them."[7] Jinnah, of course, considered himself no less than Lord Mountbatten at this point, the governor-general of his own dominion—the first person of Asian birth ever to achieve so exalted a rank of Commonwealth power.

The rulers of the princely states all knew that by August 15 they had to accede to one or the other dominion, since British paramountcy and its protective umbrella would disappear from their lands on that day; yet many a maharaja, nawab, and nizam found it almost impossible to decide which way to jump. Bhopal, in Central India, chafed at the bit of integration into a dominion toward which its nawab felt the strongest personal antipathy. Kashmir and Hyderabad were to prove the most difficult problems. The Hindu maharaja of Kashmir, Hari Singh, refused to join either dominion, fearing he would be dethroned by Jinnah for religious reasons, yet "hating Nehru with a bitter hatred" because of his socialist proclivities and democratic demands. The nizam of Hyderabad preferred to join Pakistan, if he was not allowed to remain independent, but surrounded as he was by Indian territory and with 85 percent of his state's population Hindu, he was forced the following September by "Operation Polo" to integrate his domain within the Indian union.

Mahatma Gandhi trekked off to Noakhali in Bengal to seek to calm communal passions there on the eve of partition, and much to Mountbatten's delight

> Gandhi has announced his decision to spend the rest of his life in Pakistan looking after the minorities. This will infuriate Jinnah, but will be a great relief to Congress for, as I have said before, his influence is largely negative or even destructive and directed against the only man who has his feet firmly on the ground, Vallabhbhai Patel.[8]

Jinnah picked Lieutenant-General Sir Frank W. Messervy, the commander of the northern army of British India, to serve as Pakistan's first commander-in-chief, and Messervy submitted a "most disturbing" report to Mountbatten, warning that the North-West Frontier defence forces would fall from sixty-seven battalions to forty-five, a number of which would only be at "half strength," immediately after August 15, 1947. To "mitigate the immediate danger," Messervy suggested re-enlisting "up to 10,000 demobilised Punjabi Mussalman and Pathan infantrymen," while warning Afghanistan against seeking any border changes.[9]

Jinnah and his sister flew out of New Delhi in the viceroy's Dakota on the morning of August 7. Thousands of admirers were waiting at the airport in Karachi, and cheers of "Pakistan Zindabad" reverberated across the sands of Sind and echoed over the Arabian Sea. Refugees kept pouring into Karachi along every road as the provincial port grew overnight into a national capital with its population doubling within a matter of months. Throngs of cheering onlookers lined most of the road from the airport to government house, formerly the residence of the governor of Sind and now about to become Jinnah's last bungalow. Walking up the steps of that white Victorian mansion, Jinnah turned to naval Lieutenant S. M. Ahsan, transferred from Mountbatten's staff to the Quaid-i-Azam's, confessing: "Do you know, I never expected to see Pakistan in my lifetime. We have to be very grateful to God for what we have achieved."

Two days later, Sind's governor-elect, Sir Ghulam Hidayatullah, Jinnah's old Bombay companion, gave a posh party in honor of his great leader at the elegant Karachi Club, where Jinnah said: "Yes, I am Karachi-born, and it was on the sands of Karachi that I played marbles in my boyhood. I was schooled at Karachi. . . . Let us trust each other . . . let us judge by results, not by theories. With the help of every section—I see that every class is represented in this huge gathering—let us work in double shift, if necessary, to make the Sovereign State of Pakistan really happy, really united and really powerful."[10]

Pakistan's constituent assembly met in Karachi for the first time on August 11 and unanimously elected Jinnah to preside over its meetings, amid thunderous applause, as its first business. Jinnah took the chair, thanking the assembled delegates for

> the greatest honour that is possible for this Sovereign Assembly to confer—by electing me as your first President. . . . I sincerely hope that . . . we shall make this Constituent Assembly an example to the world. The Constituent Assembly has got two main functions to perform. The first is the very onerous and responsible task of framing our future Constitution of Pakistan and the second of functioning as a full and complete Sovereign body as the Federal Legislature of Pakistan. We have to do the best we can. . . .[11]

Then he seemed suddenly to awaken from a dream, looking around at the packed and steaming hall filled with eager, perspiring faces all turned to him for inspiration, orders, instruction on every minute question of how to build a new state. "You know really that not only we ourselves are wondering but, I think, the whole world is wondering at this unprecedented cyclonic revolution which has brought about the plan of creating and establishing two independent Sovereign Dominions in this sub-continent. As it is, it has been unprecedented; there is no parallel in the history of the world. This mighty sub-continent with all kinds of inhabitants has been brought under a plan which is titanic, unknown, unparalleled. . . ." He could not quite believe it yet. He had won. The highest court had returned another verdict in his favor—*Pakistan* was to be born in just a few days. But *what* exactly was it? And *how* was it going to work? There had never been time to consider details, after all, never strength enough, nor help. Not even time to write out a single speech in advance.

> Dealing with our first function in this Assembly, I cannot make any well-considered pronouncement at this moment, but I shall say a few things as they occur to me. The first and the foremost thing that I would like to emphasise is this—remember that you are now a Sovereign Legislative body and you have got all the powers. It therefore, places on you the gravest responsibility as to how you should take your decisions. The first observation that I would like to make is this. . . . You will no doubt agree with me that the first duty of a Government is to maintain law and order, so that the life property and religious beliefs of its subjects are fully protected by the State.
>
> The second thing that occurs to me is this: One of the biggest

curses from which India is suffering . . . is bribery and corruption. That really is a poison. We must put that down with an iron hand and I hope that you will take adequate measures as soon as it is possible. . . . Black-marketing is another curse. . . . I know that black-marketeers are frequently caught and punished. Judicial sentences are passed or sometimes fines only are imposed. Now you have to tackle this monster which today is a colossal crime against society, in our distressed conditions, when we constantly face shortage of food. . . . A citizen who does black-marketing commits, I think, a greater crime than the biggest and most grievous of crimes. These black-marketeers are really knowing, intelligent, and ordinarily responsible people. . . . I think they ought to be very severely punished, because they undermine the entire system of control . . . and cause wholesale starvation and want and even death.

The next thing that strikes me is this: Here again it is a legacy which has been passed on to us . . . the evil of nepotism and jobbery. This evil must be crushed relentlessly. I want to make it quite clear that I shall never tolerate any kind of jobbery, nepotism or any influence directly or indirectly brought to bear upon me. . . . I know there are people who do not quite agree with the division of India and the partition of the Punjab and Bengal. Much has been said against it, but now that it has been accepted, it is the duty of everyone of us to loyally abide by it and honourably act according to the agreement, which is now final and binding on all. But you must remember, as I have said, that this mighty revolution that has taken place is unprecedented.

But the question is, whether it was possible or practicable to act otherwise than what has been done. . . . A division had to take place. On both sides, in Hindustan and Pakistan, there are sections of people who may not agree with it, who may not like it, but in my judgement there was no other solution and I am sure future history will record its verdict in favour of it. And what is more it will be proved by actual experience as we go on that that was the only solution. . . . Any idea of a United India could never have worked and in my judgement it would have led us to terrific disaster. May be that view is correct; may be it is not; that remains to be seen.[12]

He seemed unable to move his mind from that awesome question. For the first time he openly challenged his own judgment, wondering aloud if it might *not* have been correct, sensing perhaps that the worst part of the dream—the true tragic nightmare of partition was about to begin, the hurricane waiting behind this "cyclonic revolution." "All the same," he continued in this uncharacteristic troubled monologue of reflection before the perplexed mullahs, pirs, nawabs, rajas, shahs, and khans trying to fathom as well as follow his every word, "in this division it was impossible to avoid the question of minorities being in one Dominion or the other."

Now that was unavoidable. There is no other solution. Now what shall we do? Now, if we want to make this great State of Pakistan happy and prosperous we should wholly and solely concentrate on the well-being of the people, and especially of the masses and the poor. If you will work in co-operation, forgetting the past, burying the hatchet you are bound to succeed. If you change your past and work together in a spirit that everyone of you, no matter to what community he belongs, no matter what relations he had with you in the past, no matter what is his colour, caste or creed, is first, second and last a citizen of this State with equal rights, privileges and obligations, there will be no end to the progress you will make.

I cannot emphasise it too much. We should begin to work in that spirit and in course of time all these angularities of the majority and minority communities, the Hindu community and the Muslim community—because even as regards Muslims you have Pathans, Punjabis, Shias, Sunnis and so on and among the Hindus you have Brahmins, Vashnavas, Khatris, also Bengalees, Madrasis, and so on—will vanish. Indeed if you ask me this has been the biggest hindrance in the way of India to attain the freedom and independence and but for this we would have been free peoples long long ago.[13]

What a remarkable reversal it was, as though he had been transformed overnight once again into the old "Ambassador of Hindu-Muslim Unity" that Sarojini Naidu loved. His mind was racing too swiftly for logical coherence, almost freely associating as he rambled extemporaneously. Was it, in fact, over now? Or was it all just about to begin?

You are free; you are free to go to your temples, you are free to go to your mosques or to any other place of worship in this State of Pakistan. . . . You may belong to any religion or caste or creed— that has nothing to do with the business of the State. . . . We are starting in the days when there is no discrimination, no distinction between one community and another, no discrimination between one caste or creed and another. We are starting with this fundamental principle that we are all citizens and equal citizens of one State. The people of England in course of time had to face the realities of the situation and had to discharge the responsibilities and burdens placed upon them by the government. . . . Today, you might say with justice that Roman Catholics and Protestants do not exist; what exists now is that every man is a citizen, an equal citizen of Great Britain . . . all members of the Nation.[14]

What was he talking about? Had he simply forgotten where he was? Had the cyclone of events so disoriented him that he was aruging the opposition's brief? Was he pleading for a united India—on the eve of Pakistan—before those hundreds of thousands of terrified innocents were slaughtered, fleeing their homes, their fields, their ancestral villages and running to an eternity of oblivion or a refugee camp in a strange land? "Now," the governor-general-designate continued, "I think we should keep in front of us as our ideal and you will find that in course of time Hindus would cease to be Hindus and Muslims would cease to be Muslims, not in the religious sense, because that is the personal faith of each individual, but in the political sense as citizens of the State. . . . I shall always be guided by the principles of justice and fairplay without any, as is put in the political language, prejudice or ill-will, in other words, partiality or favouritism. My guiding principle will be justice and complete impartiality, and I am sure that with your support and co-operation, I can look forward to Pakistan becoming one of the greatest Nations of the world."[15]

Yet even as he concluded on so optimistic a note, rumor had reached Liaquat Ali as well as Jinnah that the strategic Muslim-majority Gurdaspur district of the Punjab, affording the only all-weather road access to Kashmir, was going to be awarded to East Punjab by Radcliffe. Liaquat warned Ismay that such a "political" decision would be viewed by Muslims as "so grave a breach of faith as to imperil future friendly relations between Pakistan and the British."[16] Mountbatten insisted, however, that he had "resolutely" kept himself "out of the whole business" of the boundary commission and had not so much as seen the final maps, which were only brought to his office by Radcliffe after he and his wife had flown from Delhi to Karachi on August 13 to help celebrate the formal transfer of power there by conveying His Majesty's as well as his own official greetings to the new Dominion.

Jinnah and Fatima awaited the Mountbattens not at Karachi airport but inside the entrance hall of government house, "which had been decked up to look just like a Hollywood film-set, and all four were subjected to takings and re-takings under the dazzling light and sizzling heat of the arc-lamps."[17] Jinnah remained strangely "aloof" at the banquet which he hosted for the Mountbattens there that night. Liaquat and the other League leaders who had listened to his disjointed ramblings before the constituent assembly then insisted that he read from a prepared text, since the entire diplomatic corps as well as world press would be represented in the banquet hall. He rose to adjust his monocle to his eye, unfolding the text, reading softly, slowly, "Your Excellency, Your Highness, and Ladies and Gentlemen, I have great pleasure in proposing a toast to His Majesty the King."[18] The words had been fashioned for him by the best of his bright young clerks. Nothing of this toast was Jinnah's—only the frail voice that read it aloud in such perfect upper-class English accent. "Here I would like to say, Your Excellency Lord Mountbatten, how much we appreciate your having carried out whole-heartedly the policy and the principle that was laid down by the plan of 3rd June. . . . Pakistan and Hindustan will always remember you. . . ." Perhaps he did inject the word "Hindustan," insisting upon using it, as so many of his followers would do, feeling it a more appropriate appellation for Pakistan's neighbor than "India," which was, after all, just an English corruption of the name of Pakistan's major river artery, the Indus.

Mountbatten sat at dinner between Miss Jinnah and Begum Liaquat Ali Khan and reported, "They both pulled my leg about the midnight ceremonies in Delhi saying that it was astounding that a responsible Government could be guided by astrologers. . . . I refrained from retorting that the whole Karachi programme had had to be changed because Jinnah had forgotten that it was Ramazan and had had to change the lunch party he had himself suggested to a dinner party."[19]

Next morning the Jinnahs drove from the government house to the legislative assembly hall along a carefully guarded route, lined with soldiers as well as police alerted to watch for possible assassins, since reports of a Sikh plan to assassinate Jinnah on the day Pakistan was born had reached Mountbatten and Jinnah several days earlier. But only shouts of "Pakistan Zindabad" and "Quaid-i-Azam Zindabad" were hurled at his carriage. The Mountbattens followed in a separate carriage, and inside the crowded semicircular chamber of Pakistan's parliament, which had been Sind's legislative assembly, Lord Mountbatten graciously felicitated Jinnah and read the message from his cousin, King George, welcoming Pakistan into the Commonwealth. Jinnah replied, reading again from the carefully hammered out words of a text prepared by his staff.

> Your Excellency, I thank His Majesty on behalf of the Pakistan Constituent Assembly and myself. I once more thank you and Lady Mountbatten for your kindness and good wishes. Yes, we are parting as friends . . . and I assure you that we shall not be wanting in friendly spirit with our neighbours and with all nations of the world.[20]

"Lady Mountbatten pressed Miss Jinnah's hand affectionately as Jinnah sat down after giving his address," a witness reported. "If Jinnah's personality is cold and remote, it also has a magnetic quality—the sense of leadership is almost overpowering. . . . Here indeed is Pakistan's King Emperor, Archbishop of Canterbury, Speaker and Prime Minister concentrated into one formidable Quaid-e-Azam."[21]

Mountbatten was still worried about a possible assassination attempt and feared that if it was going to be tried against Jinnah, then was the time when he, as governor-general, should be driven back to the government house in an open carriage. "It occurred to me that the best way for me to protect him would be to insist on our riding in the same carriage, you see," Mountbatten recalled, smiling. "I knew that no one in that crowd would want to risk shooting *me!* And luckily it worked beautifully, but such was Jinnah's vanity, you know, that no sooner did we get inside the gates of Government House than he tapped my knee and said, 'Thank God *I* was able to bring you back alive!' "[22]

The Mountbattens flew to New Delhi that afternoon for another round of gala independence celebrations at India's constituent assembly and Red Fort, where the tricolor of India's dominion was raised at midnight. "Long years ago we made a tryst with destiny," Nehru informed his nation, "and now the time comes when we shall redeem our pledge. . . . At the stroke of the midnight hour, when the world sleeps, India will wake to life and freedom. A moment comes, which comes but rarely in history, when we step out from the old to the new, when an age ends, and when the soul of a nation, long suppressed, finds utterance."[23]

The next morning Radcliffe's "awards" were revealed, and all celebration ended; then the slaughter began. In and around Amritsar bands of armed Sikhs killed every Muslim they could find, while in and around Lahore, Muslim gangs—many of them "police"—sharpened their knives and emptied their guns at Hindus and Sikhs. Entire trainloads of refugees were gutted and turned into rolling coffins, funeral pyres on wheels, food for bloated vultures who darkened the skies over the Punjab and were sated with more flesh and blood in those final weeks of August than their ancestors had enjoyed in a century.

In Bengal, Gandhi fasted on Independence Day, knowing how many were condemned to premature death by that double-dominion birthday. In Calcutta all businesses closed in terror for two days, August 15–16; the latter deemed so "inauspicious" by Hindu astrologers that no religious Brahman dared to leave the safety of his home. The Mahasabha raised black flags in opposition to partition, the vivisection of Mother India, *Akhand Hindustan.* Calcutta Muslims fled, shrank, and hid in panic, "crowding together for sanctuary in certain predominantly Muslim areas of the city," General Tuker reported, "deserted, leaderless, depressed and on the defensive." Sanity was restored to that premier city of eastern India only after Gandhi undertook a fast-unto-death to help stop the killing of innocents.

The austere Muslim month of Ramazan ended on August 18, and Jinnah broadcast an Id day message to his nation, announcing that

> This day of rejoicing throughout the Muslim world so aptly comes immediately in the wake of our national State being established, and therefore, it is a matter of special significance and happiness to us all. . . . I fervently pray that God Almighty make us all worthy of our past and hoary history and give us strength to make Pakistan truly a great nation amongst all the nations of the world. No doubt we have achieved Pakistan but that is only yet the beginning of an end. Great responsibilities have come to us, and equally great should be our determination and endeavour to discharge them.[24]

But the strength had gone out of him. He could carry on only after longer and longer interludes of rest in his lonely west wing of the government house, where only Fatima, the secretaries, and servants were permitted.

Fatima saw it most clearly. She alone was close enough to see that

> even in his hour of triumph the Quaid-e-Azam was gravely ill. . . . I watched with sorrow and pain. He had little or no appetite and had even lost his ability to will himself to sleep. All this coincided with reports from both sides of the border of harrowing tales of massacre, rape, arson and looting. He began his day discussing these mass killings with me at breakfast and his handkerchief furtively often went to his moist eyes. . . .
>
> The Constitution had to be framed, and he applied his mind to this as often as he could. . . . He worked in a frenzy to consolidate Pakistan. And, of course, he totally neglected his health, and his coughing and slight temperature were beginning to worry me more and more. At my insistence, he agreed to be examined by Colonel Rahman, his personal physician, who diagnosed a slight attack of malaria. The Quaid, who had an aversion to medicine, said . . . "I don't have malaria. I am just run down." Asked to rest, he replied flatly, "I have too much to do."[25]

He did not, in fact, have malaria. He had consumption, soon to be compounded by cancer of the lungs.

In Karachi his working day usually started at 8:30 A.M. when he seated himself behind the large table on which his papers were stacked, with his "tin of Craven 'A' cigarettes" always at his finger tips and his box of "high quality Cuban cigars, the aroma of which also pervaded the room," Jinnah's aide-de-camp, Brigadier Husain recalled.

Jinnah's frugality had been, of course, well known, but since the birth of Pakistan he had better reason perhaps than ever to guard each rupee, for he found, as he told Begum Shah Nawaz, "only twenty crores [200 million] rupees in the treasury and nearly rupees forty crores of bills lying on the table."[26] Nor was India willing to part with substantial funds vouchsafed to Pakistan by the formula agreed upon for sharing all pre-partition assets of the British raj. Patel and Baldev were specially loathe to "arm" Pakistan with the wherewithal to fight India—whether in the Punjab, Sind, Kashmir, or Bengal.

Jinnah knew how precarious Pakistan's position, like his own health was, and issued a statement to the press on August 24, 1947, urging calm in the face of the "grave unrest" created by the daily news of the "outrages" perpetrated against Muslims in India's East Punjab. He assured his people that Pakistan was doing all in its power to "give succour and relief to the victims" and to help evacuate Muslims from terrorized districts and States.

In the last week of August, the Mayor of Karachi and his councillors presented an "address of welcome" on vellum encased in silver to their Quaid-i-Azam, who responded in the old Municipal Corporation Building near his birthplace. Jinnah said how proud he was that people in Karachi "have kept their heads cool and lived amicably" amidst so much "disturbance" in other parts of the subcontinent. Bureaucrats, refugees, workers, merchants and their businesses and capital flowed into Karachi from every direction, by sea and air as well as along dusty roads. Property values soared, goods and services were in such demand that prices skyrocketed. For Jinnah's hometown, the boom was of magnificent proportions, and even as the Punjab withered and writhed in post-partition torment and pain, Sind began to blossom with Karachi itself in the vanguard of growth and development. Pakistan's entire navy, consisting initially of a single frigate and a few minesweepers and smaller craft, was based at Karachi, for Chittagong was still a village lit by kerosene lanterns, a "port" with dock space only for two ships at a time, at the landing of the British Club in East Bengal, the one building as yet capable of generating its own electricity.

Even as remoteness from the Punjab border offered Karachi breathing space in which to prosper, proximity left Lahore a shambles, the target of endless streams of destitute refugees, much as Amritsar and Delhi then became. The sick and dying brought every need, demand, and physical blight with their battered bodies to a city whose housing shortage had been tripled by arson and whose water supply was infested with the worst diseases of dead and disintegrating corpses thrown into its arteries. Its spacious mosques and once beautiful Mughal gardens were turned into crowded camps for Muslim refugees fleeing Sikh persecution. Much to "everyone's surprise"[27] Jinnah attended a Joint Indo-Pak Defence Council meeting chaired in Lahore by Mountbatten at the end of August. His doctor's orders and fever notwithstanding, the Quaid-i-Azam flew into the Punjabi capital to see for himself how much dreadful damage had been done since his last visit. Governor Sir Francis Mudie, formerly the governor of Sind, had been appointed by Jinnah to replace Sir Evan Jenkins on the eve of independence. Jinnah liked Mudie and lived with him in Lahore.

Jinnah insisted on dismantling the Punjab Boundary Force that Mountbatten had created a month earlier, which had proved virtually useless in the face of the tragic events that ensued. He preferred to have the Muslim troops of that 50,000-man unit back inside Pakistan's borders, should they be required elsewhere in the near future. Kashmir still hoped to remain independent, its vacillating maharaja playing a waiting game that was to prove tragically expensive to his 3 million voiceless subjects, 75 percent of whom were Muslim. Hyderabad had also refused to join India, and Congress "intelligence" reported early in September that the nizam's government was trying to purchase "armaments in Czechoslovakia and in general to build up its separate sovereignty."[28] Whether or not that information was accurate, Jinnah hoped to bring the nizam into close alliance with, if not actually under the sovereignty of, Pakistan.

Hyderabad financier and later prime minister, Mir Laik Ali, Jinnah's most intimate disciple in the nizam's inner circle, recalled:

> On more than one occasion we discussed the Pakistan Plan . . . and what would happen to the rest of the Muslims and the Muslim States, particularly the State of Hyderabad. One evening, early in September [1947], I received a long-distance call from Karachi . . . the Governor-General. . . . He . . . told me that the first delegation of Pakistan to the United Nations would be leaving shortly for Lake Success and he had included me. . . . I mildly protested that I . . . was too involved in my affairs and suggested that it would be more appropriate if some one from Pakistan takes my place. . . . I met Mr. Jinnah in Karachi, he at the very start elaborated that Pakistan . . . was in urgent need of finances. . . . He was aware of my personal contacts with the financial circles . . . in the USA and some parts of Europe. . . . He said Pakistan would accept any reasonable terms and offer "quid pro quo" short of affecting its hard earned sovereignty . . . when I returned towards the end of October, I . . . managed to journey to Lahore, and saw him ailing in bed. The doctors had forbidden visitors but I was allowed to meet him for no more than half an hour. I briefly reported the situation to Mr. Jinnah. . . . Pakistan was faced with another serious situation . . . India had withheld the agreed share of . . . Reserve Bank's

cash balances amounting to some Rs. 55 crore. There was hardly any money to meet the day-to-day expenses and the position was really critical. India . . . believed that this very first blow would finish Pakistan. Could Hyderabad state or the Nizam advance adequate loan to Pakistan to tide over the crisis?

. . . Never in my life had I seen Mr. Jinnah emotional except on that day. He asked me if I had seen the . . . refugees as I drove from the airport. . . . I had of course. Tears rolled down his cheeks several times as he spoke of the mass human misery. . . . Soon after that the Nizam sanctioned a loan of Rs. 20 crore to Pakistan. Mr. Jinnah lost no time in publicly announcing that Pakistan had received a loan of that sum from Hyderabad and . . . had no further financial problems . . . the leaders of India were just wild and furious over it.[29]

Jinnah had also sent Ispahani to the United States as Pakistan's ambassador and deputy leader of the UN delegation, which future foreign minister Sir Mohammed Zafrullah Khan led. Ispahani purchased a building in Washington for $150,000 to serve as Pakistan's "Chancery" and wrote Jinnah from New York in mid-September to report having

met the top executives of General Motors Company who have taken prompt note of your requirement of a Cadillac super-limousine. . . . General Motors has assured me that arrangements would be made for the delivery of the car at Karachi as soon as possible, and will override all other prior bookings. . . . In regard to the special aeroplane, my friends and I have contacted some leading manufacturers. . . . I hope you are keeping good health.[30]

The super-limousine cost $6,000 and was "cavern green." A converted B-23 Beechcraft was to cost more than the embassy building, so Jinnah decided on a Vickers Armstrong instead, the price of which was "not unreasonable."[31]

Jinnah ordered Liaquat to move his cabinet secretariat to Lahore in September and joined him there the following month, as relations with India deteriorated to the point of virtual "war."[32] Armed "convoys" of Muslim refugees leaving India could pass through hostile Sikh territory only with special instructions from Nehru and official Indian "escorts." Ismay flew to Karachi in mid-September to meet with Jinnah for no less than eleven hours during his two-day visit, reporting himself to have been "the first guest at Government House since the 15th August," winning over Jinnah enough to be called "a good fellow" by the Quaid-i-Azam to his face.[33] But the more disturbing part of Ismay's report to his chief was that "Jinnah was full of wrath against Congress, saying that he could never understand these men's hatreds and was now beginning to feel that there was no alternative but to fight it out."

The Muslim nawab of Junagadh, a small princely state on the coast of Kathiawar, acceded to Pakistan that September, though his domain was surrounded by India and the vast majority of his state's population was Hindu. The apolitical nawab's shrewd diwan was Sindi landowner Sir Shah Nawaz Bhutto (the enterprising father of Pakistan's late prime minister, Zulfi Bhutto), who drafted the documents of accession and personally delivered them to Jinnah. Nehru and Patel were outraged when they learned of Junagadh's "treachery" and delayed martial invasion only till November, driving Muslim courtiers like the Bhuttos to sail from Veraval port to Karachi, with their treasure and talents placed at Pakistan's service.

Before the end of September, Jinnah appealed directly to his Commonwealth colleagues for help in Pakistan's tragic disputes with its closest neighbor. The flood of refugees continued to deluge the Punjab, and each new arrival brought blood-curdling tales of tragedy that fired the hatred of Muslims throughout the Northwest, leading many to cry out for revenge against the "infidels," igniting passions with pain, stimulating pressures for retaliation, and drowning caution in an ocean of bitter fury. Sir Archibald Carter, permanent undersecretary of the Commonwealth Relations Office, visited Karachi at this time, and London became more conscious of the urgency of Pakistan's plight and the potential imminence of Indo-Pak war. Liaquat flew to Delhi and remained for several nights as Mountbatten's guest in the government house, portentously warning Ismay before he flew back to Lahore, "Let India go ahead and commit an act of war, and see what happens."[34] Ismay understood Liaquat's thinly-veiled threat as apparently aimed at Kashmir. Mountbatten's chief-of-staff returned to London in early October, putting up overnight again with Jinnah in Karachi, on October 2, Gandhi's seventy-eighth birthday.

The procrastinating maharaja of Kashmir, Sir Hari Singh, signed a "standstill agreement" with Pakistan that permitted petrol supplies and other vital needs of that northernmost state of South Asia to continue flowing over the Pakistan roads that served as its major highways to the world. Hari Singh knew that time was running out. Muslim peasants in Kashmir's southern province of Poonch were the first to revolt. That September and early October, neighboring Pakistani Muslims crossed the Poonch border to help their co-religionists fight against the maharaja's forces sent to put down the revolt. By mid-October Pakistan stopped all shipments of vital

348

JINNAH OF PAKISTAN

supplies to Kashmir. New Delhi then "decided to step into the breach and try to send such things as salt, kerosene and sugar" to "blockaded" Srinagar.[35]

On October 23, British trucks and jeeps of the Pakistan army loaded with some 5,000 armed Pathan Afridi, Waziri, and Mahsud tribesmen of the North-West Frontier crossed the Kashmir border and headed east along the Muzaffarabad-Baramula road that led to Srinagar itself. That "invasion" of Kashmir from Pakistan would long be called by Pakistan a purely "volunteer" action undertaken "spontaneously" by irate "tribals" rushing to the aid of oppressed Muslim brothers. But the trucks, petrol, and drivers were hardly standard tribal equipment, and British officers as well as Pakistani officials all along the northern Pakistan route they traversed knew and supported, even if they did not actually organize or instigate, that violent October operation by which Pakistan seems to have hoped to trigger the integration of Kashmir into the nation, whose acrostic name gave its "K" central prominence. Reports of the raiders burning and seizing Muzaffarabad reached New Delhi unofficially on the night of October 24, and the next morning, Pakistan army headquarters officially informed New Delhi's sister-dominion command that "tribal volunteers" had "entered" Kashmir, "Their advance guard . . . only 35 to 40 miles from Srinagar."[36] Mountbatten summoned an emergency meeting of the Indian Defence Committee that Saturday morning, and they agreed to assemble all the arms and aircraft they could find for possible immediate despatch to Srinagar. V. P. Menon was sent flying over Himalayan heights to see if he could convince Hari Singh to sign an accession agreement at this point. Menon returned early Sunday morning, October 26, to report to Mountbatten, Nehru, and Patel that the maharaja "had gone to pieces completely" and could "come to no decision." His state's prime minister, M. C. Mahajan (later chief justice of India), however, proved "receptive" to Menon's mission and returned with him to New Delhi, where he met with Nehru and Patel.

"I requested immediate military aid on any terms," Mahajan recalled, urging Nehru to "Give us the military force we need. Take the accession and give whatever power you desire to the popular party. The army must fly to save Srinagar this evening or else I will go to Lahore and negotiate terms with Mr. Jinnah."[37] Mahajan reported that Nehru "became upset" and "angry" at the mention of Jinnah's name and ordered him "away," but Patel detained him, whispering "Of course, Mahajan, you are not going to Pakistan." Then Sheikh Abdullah, who appears to have been "listening" from an adjoining bedroom in Nehru's Delhi house, sent in a "message" to second Mahajan's advice, which instantly changed Nehru's "attitude."

The next morning the defence council met and decided to airlift the First Sikh Battalion from New Delhi to Srinagar. "In the early hours of the morning of the 27th," Mahajan wrote, "I could hear the noise of the planes flying over Sardar Baldev Singh's house [where Mahajan spent the night] and carrying the military personnel to Srinagar. At about 9 a.m. I got a message from . . . Srinagar that troops had landed there and had gone into action. On receipt of this message, I flew to Jammu with Mr. V. P. Menon. . . . Mr. Menon and myself met His Highness [Hari Singh had driven down from Srinagar the previous night to his Winter capital] at the palace. . . . After some discussion, formal documents were signed which Mr. Menon took back to New Delhi. . . . I stayed at Jammu. This was a narrow shave."

Mahajan's autobiographical account of this most important sequence of events is at critical variance with previous reports published by V. P. Menon and others close to Nehru and Patel and associated with the Government of India at the time. Menon insists that Kashmir's "instrument of accession" was signed and delivered to New Delhi *before* any Indian troops were flown into action in Srinagar;[38] Mahajan reports the reverse. The actual sequence is of more than academic interest, since India's claim to Kashmir was, in legal terms, based on having secured a legitimate instrument of accession prior to airlifting any troops into the Vale. Mountbatten, of course, understood that "the risk of Pakistan also sending troops would be considerable." and if that occurred then two Commonwealth armies, each trained and led by British commanding officers, would have had for the first time in history to face one another on the field of battle. It would have been so ignominious, so utterly intolerable a conclusion to his "last Chukka in India,"[39] that Mountbatten had to move heaven and earth to avoid so tragic a denouement. He had, in fact, assembled over a hundred transport planes, civil as well as military, at Delhi's airport with less than a day's notice, and packed India's best Sikh regiment inside those planes, fueled up and kept ready to take off before dawn on October 27. All that he lacked was the signed accession, which would, he rightly reported to his royal cousin, "fully regularise the position, and reduce the risk of an armed clash with Pakistan forces to the minimum. I shall relate a little further on how lucky it was that this accession was accepted."[40] The crisis situation Mountbatten faced during that last terrible week in October obviously did not permit the luxury of holding a plebiscite or referendum. The tribals were burning, looting, raping, shooting, and within a day's march of Srinagar—where hundreds of thousands of people were virtually unprotected or, as Mountbatten quite accurately put it, "time did not, of course, permit the will of the people being ascertained first," prior to lifting those guardian troops over the Himalayan wall that separated Delhi from Srinagar. By the same token, then, should time permit the indecision of an autocratic maharaja who had "gone to pieces," fled Srinagar, and abandoned his own subjects to a fate worse than death, to stand in the way of their salvation?

"Even after this decision had been reached Lord Mountbatten and the three British Chiefs of Staff of the Indian Army, Navy and Air Force pointed out the risks involved in the operation," V. P. Menon reported. "But Nehru asserted that the only alternative to sending troops would be to allow a massacre in Srinagar, which would be followed by a major communal holocaust in India. Moreover, the British residents in Srinagar would certainly be murdered by the raiders, since neither the Pakistan Commander-in-Chief nor the Supreme Commander was in a position to safeguard their lives."[41] What else could Lord Mountbatten possibly have done in the face of such dire warnings, threats, and advice? To hesitate for even an hour might have proved fatal to so precarious an operation.

On October 27, as soon as Governor-General Jinnah learned of India's airlift to Srinagar, he ordered his "acting" British commander-in-chief (General Messervy was on leave), General Sir Douglas Gracey, to "move two brigades of the Pak army into Kashmir . . . one from Rawalpindi and another from Sialkot. The Sialkot army was to march to Jammu, take the city and make the Maharaja a prisoner. The Rawalpindi column was to advance to Srinagar and capture the city."[42] Such strategic action could have secured Kashmir for Pakistan while saving Srinagar from "tribal anarchy." General Gracey refused, however, to accept those orders from his governor-general, informing Jinnah that "he was not prepared to issue instructions which would inevitably lead to armed conflict between the two Dominions and the withdrawal of British Officers, without the approval of the Supreme Commander" [Field Marshal Auchinleck].[43]

Having just flown in from Karachi, Jinnah was in Lahore at this time and stayed with Mudie, who was "most aggressive and abusive" to Gracey over the phone, wanting to know "Why the hell Gracey was not carrying out Mr. Jinnah's orders. What had it got to do with the Supreme Commander? What did it matter if the British Officers were withdrawn? Could he not send the troops on without British Officers? Mr. Jinnah insisted on the orders being issued at once." Gracey informed Auchinleck the next day that he thought "Mudie had been drinking," and Mountbatten added in his report of this unpleasant incident to the King, that Sir Francis had apparently "lived up to his reputation." General Gracey informed Field Marshal Auchinleck from Rawalpindi by phone at 1:00 A.M. on October 27–28 that he had "received orders from Jinnah which if obeyed would entail issue 'Stand Down' order,"[44] Auchinleck wired his chiefs of staff in

London on October 28. A "stand down" order meant the automatic withdrawal of all British officers from a dominion army.

The "Auk" flew into Lahore from Delhi that fateful morning of October 28 and was met at the airport by Gracey, who stated that the orders Gracey had *not* obeyed were nonetheless issued to Pakistani troops "to seize Baramula and Srinagar also Banihal Pass and to send troops into Mirpur district of Jammu."[45] The supreme commander and General Gracey went to confront Jinnah immediately to explain the "situation *vis-à-vis* British officers very clearly," Auchinleck reported to London. "Gracey also emphasized military weakness of Pakistan while I pointed out incalculable consequences of military violation of what now is territory of Indian Union in consequence of Kashmir's sudden accession." "His approach to Jinnah," Mountbatten reported of Auchinleck's crucial confrontation in Lahore, "was based on the fact that India's acceptance of the accession of Kashmir was just as legally proper and correct as Pakistan's acceptance of Junagadh's accession; that India had a perfect right to send troops to the State in response to the Maharajah's request; and on the extreme weakness of the Pakistan Army, and its virtual uselessness without British Officers."[46] Jinnah "withdrew orders," Auchinleck was able to report at the end of his longest day in India's service.

Mountbatten and Ismay flew to Lahore without Nehru on November 1, 1947, and met with Liaquat, who was quite sick with an ulcer that morning in his bedroom.

He was sitting up with a rug round his knees, looking very ill. . . . I began by giving Liaquat a copy of a statement which had been signed by the three India Commanders-in-Chief . . . intended to dispel the impression, in the minds of the Pakistan Government, that India had planned the sending of military assistance to Kashmir before the tribal invasion began. . . . I then went on to explain . . . the whole position of Junagadh . . . and of Kashmir, as I saw it. I used the same arguments as I later expanded to Jinnah whom I saw in the afternoon. The burden of Liaquat's reply was that the Maharajah had . . . brought about a serious situation by allowing his Hindus, and in particular his State forces, to massacre Muslims particularly in, and across the border of, Jammu. . . . Liaquat appeared to be very depressed and almost disinclined to make any further effort to avoid war. Ismay and I did our best to cheer him up . . . he . . . bade us a very friendly au revoir.[47]

Mountbatten and Ismay went off directly to lunch with Jinnah, and after finishing their food, accompanied the Quaid-i-Azam to his room and had 3½ hours of the most arduous and concentrated conversation, of which Kashmir formed the main theme. . . . I handed to Jinnah a further copy of the Chiefs of Staff statement of events . . . he expressed surprise at the remarkable speed at which we had been able to organize sending troops into the Srinagar plain. . . . Jinnah's principal complaint was that the Government of India had failed to give timely information to the Government of Pakistan about the action they proposed to take in Kashmir. I pointed out, in reply, that Nehru had telegraphed to Liaquat Ali Khan on the 26th, immediately the decision to send in troops had been taken. . . . Ismay agreed that the Government of Pakistan should have had the earliest possible notification. . . . To the best of his recollection, Nehru had told him on the 28th that he had kept Liaquat Ali Khan in touch with what was happening. . . . If this had not been done, the oversight must have been due to the pressure of events, and not because the Government of India had anything to hide.

Jinnah looked up his files and said that the telegram had arrived after the troops had landed, and that it did not contain any form of an appeal for co-operation between the two Dominions in this matter; it merely informed him of the accession and the landing of troops. Continuing, he said that the accession was not a bona fide one since it rested on "fraud and violence" and would never be accepted by Pakistan. I asked him to explain why he used the term "fraud," since the Maharajah was fully entitled in accordance with Pakistan's own official statement about Junagadh . . . to make such accession. It was therefore perfectly legal and valid. Jinnah said that this accession was the end of a long intrigue and that it had been brought about by violence. I countered this by saying that I entirely agreed that the accession had been brought about by violence; I knew the Maharajah was most anxious to remain independent, and nothing but the terror of violence could have made him accede to either Dominion; . . . the violence had come from tribes for whom Pakistan was responsible. . . . Jinnah repeatedly made it clear that in his opinion it was India who had committed this violence by sending her troops into Srinagar; I countered as often with the above argument, thereby greatly enraging Jinnah at my apparent denseness.[48]

Jinnah told Mountbatten and Ismay that he had "lost interest in what the world thought of him since the British Commonwealth had let him down when he asked them to come to the rescue of Pakistan." "At the end Jinnah became extremely pessimistic and said it was quite clear that the Dominion of India was out to throttle and choke the Dominion of Pakistan at birth, and that if they continued with their oppression there would be nothing for it but to face the consequences . . . he was not afraid; for the situation was already so bad that there was little that could happen to make it worse. . . . Ismay tried to cheer him up out of his depression but I fear was not very successful. . . . We parted on good terms."[49]

A mood of lonely resignation and fatalism shrouded Jinnah throughout the rest of that last bitter year of his life. His hopes of breathing the cool, healthful air of Srinagar faded with each passing day of prolonged fighting as more and stronger Indian forces kept flying in to push back the tribals and regular Pak "volunteers" who managed, without British support, to hold a line east of Muzaffarabad but would never reach the coveted Vale. Dark "forces," both inside and out of Pakistan, were "after" him, seeking to snuff out his own feeble life and to choke his political offspring. Only a week earlier, on the eve of his leaving Karachi, "an apparent attempt on Jinnah's life" had been made by "Two men with the lower parts of their faces masked and wearing moon and crescent hats," who rushed the guard at the government house, whipped out "revolvers," and wounded one police officer before they could be frightened off by his "whistle."[50] Were they Khaksars? Or were they a different, still more fanatical, sect of ortho-dox Muslims who considered him the "enemy?" While Liaquat nursed his bleeding ulcer, and Mudie drowned both his sorrows and the Punjab's with whiskey and water, Jinnah, longer and longer through every night, racked his body with coughing and dislodged more blood from his scarred and tired lungs.

"That freedom can never be attained by a nation without suffering and sacrifice, has been amply borne out by the recent tragic happenings in this sub-continent," Jinnah told a mass rally of his compatriots from the plat-form of Lahore's University stadium on October 30.

We are in the midst of unparalleled difficulties and untold suffer-ings; we have been through dark days of apprehension and an-guish. . . . The systematic massacre of defenceless and innocent people puts to shame even the most heinous atrocities committed by the worst tyrants known to history. We have been the victims of a deeply-laid and well-planned conspiracy executed with utter disre-gard of the elementary principles of honesty, chivalry and honour. We thank Providence for giving us courage and faith to fight these forces of evil. . . . Do not be afraid of death. Our religion teaches us to be always prepared for death. We should face it bravely to save the honour of Pakistan and Islam. There is no better salvation for a Muslim than the death of a martyr for a righteous cause.[51]

"It was in this speech that I first heard him speak of death," Fatima recalled. "The sufferings of the refugees affected him deeply and he went to bed again, exhausted and feverish. But files kept pouring in, ministers and secretaries came to seek his instructions, so peace and rest were impossible."[52]

23

Ziarat
(1948)

The "all India" Muslim League council met for the last time in Karachi on December 14–15, 1947. Some 300 members, 160 from India, assembled in the capital of Pakistan and voted to do to the Muslim League what that party had been so instrumental in accomplishing throughout British India— splitting it into "independent and separate" Pakistan and India parties. Jinnah left his sick bed to preside over this final session of his party's council; he addressed them in English, and his speech was later translated into Urdu—Pakistan's national language—by Sardar Abdur Rab Nishtar, the minister of communications. "As you know, the Muslim League has achieved and established Pakistan," Quaid-i-Azam told them. "The Muslims were a crowd, they were demoralized, and they had to suffer economically. We have achieved Pakistan, not for the League, not for any of our colleagues, but for the masses."[1]

Not everyone was satisfied, however. Maulana Jamal Mian angrily rose to protest that "Pakistan could hardly take pride in calling itself a 'Muslim State.' He found many un-Islamic things in the State from top to bottom. . . . The behaviour of the Minister is not like that of Muslims. The poor cannot enter the houses of the Ministers; the needy and the lowly cannot see them. Only the courtiers can enter, those who possess large bungalows can enter. The name of Islam has been disgraced enough." "We are only a four-month-old child," Jinnah responded, feeling not much stronger himself. "You know somebody would like to overthrow us. I know you would say we have not done such and such a thing, but we are only four months old."

In addition to resolving to divide itself and electing Liaquat Ali Khan "convenor" of the Pakistan Muslim League, the Council placed on record its deep sense of sorrow and its feelings of horror at the widespread acts of organized violence and barbarity which have taken place, resulting in the loss of hundreds of thousands of innocent lives, colossal destruction of property, wanton outrages against women, and mass migration of populations, whereby millions of human beings have been uprooted from their hearths and homes and reduced to utter destitution.

The Council also views with grave concern the rising tide of communal antagonism against the Muslim minority in the Indian Union where, in spite of the repeated declarations by the Congress that minorities will be dealt with justly and fairly . . . Muslim life and property continue to be insecure.[2]

Liaquat flew to Delhi for a meeting of the Joint Defence Council on December 22, at which time Nehru handed him a letter charging that the tribal "raiders" of Kashmir "have free transit through Pakistan. . . . Food and other supplies are also secured from Pakistan; indeed, we have reliable reports that the raiders get their rations from military messes in Pakistan."[3] The government of India demanded an end to all such aid, access, supplies, and training. Liaquat promised to reply; and on December 31, when Nehru had as yet received no official response from Pakistan, India submitted its formal complaint to the UN Security Council, an action urged by Mountbatten but one which Nehru and his cabinet would long regret having initiated. India's complaint requested the security council to "call upon Pakistan to put an end immediately" to all "assistance" it was providing frontier tribal invaders of Kashmir, "a State which has acceded to the Dominion of India and is part of India," or "the Government of India may be compelled in self-defence, to enter Pakistan territory, in order to take military action against the invaders."[4]

Pakistan replied to India's complaint on January 15, 1948, and in a sound legal fashion, Prime Minister Liaquat Ali Khan cross-complained. Liaquat's first brief argued: "the Pakistan Government emphatically deny that they are giving aid and assistance to the so-called invaders or have committed any act of aggression against India."[5] And "Pakistan's Complaint Against India," filed the same day in the security council, and an even longer document called "Particulars of Pakistan's Case" served to place a number of broader issues and problems still festering between the newborn neighbors on the Council's agenda.

. . . an extensive campaign of "genocide" directed against the Muslim population of East Punjab, Delhi, Ajmer . . . (etc) was undertaken by the non-Muslim Rulers, people, officials, police and armed

forces of the States concerned and the Union of India . . . still in
progress . . . large numbers of Muslims—running into hundreds of
thousands—have been ruthlessly massacred, vastly larger numbers
maimed, wounded and injured and over five million . . . driven
from their homes. . . . Brutal and unmentionable crimes have been
committed against women and children. Property worth thousands
of millions of rupees has been destroyed.[6]

Concluding its cross-complaint, Pakistan asked the security council to call
upon India to "desist from acts of aggression against Pakistan" and to appoint a commission or commissions of the UN to investigate all of its
"charges" and to arrange for "cessation of fighting in the State of Jammu
and Kashmir" and elsewhere in the subcontinent. A bill of "particulars"
added documentation to support these various charges.

Jinnah had no strength to fly to New York for the UN debate on India
and Pakistan, but foreign minister Sir Mohammed Zafrullah Khan performed brilliantly as Pakistan's advocate before the security council; he
was judicious, articulate, and often eloquent in presenting his case while
refuting India's charges. The security council appointed its commission,
initially of three and later five members, who managed to effect a cease-
fire by year's end; but it never won agreement to withdrawal of all the
martial forces that kept pouring into that war-torn State, and it could
never inaugurate a State-wide plebiscite.

"The first World War of 1914–18 was fought to end war," Jinnah recalled on January 23, 1948, launching the H.M.P.S. *Dilawar* ("Sword"),
Pakistan's first modern destroyer.

This led to the birth of the League of Nations and the idea of col-
lective security, but the League of Nations proved only a pious
hope. . . . The destruction caused by the first world war pales into
insignificance as compared to the devastation and havoc resulting
from the last world war and now with the discovery of the Atom
Bomb, one shudders to think of the pattern of future wars. . . .
Pakistan must be prepared for all eventualities and dangers. The
weak and the defenceless, in this imperfect world, invite aggression
from others. . . . Pakistan is still in its infancy and so is its Navy.
. . . But this infant means to grow up and God willing will grow up
much sooner than many people think. . . . You will have to make
up for the smallness of your size by your courage and selfless devotion to duty for it is not life that matters but the courage fortitude
and determination you bring to it.[7]

A few days earlier, Mahatma Gandhi won the last of his fasts-unto-
death, persuading India's cabinet to pay its debt of 55 crores of rupees to

Pakistan, helping to put an end to the slaughter and looting of Muslims in and around Delhi, which had become so tragic a scandal. Angry Sikhs and militant Hindus marched round Birla House with black flags, shouting "Let Gandhi die!," calling him "Mohammad Gandhi," since he so often advocated Pakistan's cause at prayer meetings and read from the *Qur'an*. And on January 20, a bomb exploded in Birla House compound, but Gandhi had already finished his prayer meeting.

Ten days later, his assassin did not miss. At his last prayer meeting on January 29, Gandhi said:

> If a man was in distress, the key to his happiness lay in labour. God did not create man to eat, drink and make merry. . . . Millionaires who ate without work were parasites. Even they should eat by the sweat of their brow or should go without food. The only permissible exception was the disabled. . . . Gandhiji then spoke about peasants. If he had his say, our Governor-General and our Premier would be drawn from the *kisans* [*peasants*]. . . . As real producers of wealth, they were verily the masters while we have enslaved them. . . . It was true, we were all labourers. In honest labour lay our salvation and the satisfaction of all vital needs.[8]

The next evening, before he could reach his prayer platform, Mahatma Gandhi was shot to death by a hate-crazed Hindu Brahman named Nathuram Godse.

"He was one of the greatest men produced by the Hindu community," wrote Jinnah, in his brief message of condolence. How ironic it must have seemed to him that an orthodox Hindu should have killed his most intransigent opponent, believing the Mahatma an "Agent of Pakistan" and a "Muslim-lover." Norbert Bogdan, a vice-president of Schroeders' Banking Group in New York, met with Jinnah in Karachi just a few days after Gandhi's assassination and reported that "Jinnah" . . . spoke of Gandhi in much more generous terms than he saw fit to use in his message, acknowledging . . . how great was the loss for the Moslems. Jinnah added that . . . the real trouble was with the extremist groups, and he had been favourably impressed by the Indian Government's firm handling of these following on Gandhi's assassination."[9] New Delhi outlawed the *Rashtriya Svayam Seva Sangh* and Hindu Mahasabha, putting many of their leaders under immediate "preventive detention" arrest.

Mir Laik Ali now became premier of Hyderabad, and India's government was most unsettled by news of the nizam's 20-crore loan to Pakistan. Because of that loan, of course, Pakistan remained solvent, and its first annual budget was presented to Karachi's assembly by finance minister

Ghulam Mohammed on February 28. Defence expenditure was projected to be no less than £27.8 million out of the total estimated expenditure of only £39.4 million. Revenues were so meager moreover, that a deficit of £25.1 million was expected.[10] Similarly, the government of India allocated over 50 percent of its total budget to arms and projected a deficit of some £20 million. Pakistan did its best to encourage imports from the sterling bloc and the United States, but because of its minimal industrial development, the continuing influx of refugees, and poor agricultural output in 1948, revenues fell below anticipated totals with its deficits soaring higher. Ispahani appealed urgently for U.S. support, private as well as public. General Motors "are interested in installing plants in Pakistan," Ambassador Ispahani reported to his great leader that March, but "threatening war clouds" over Kashmir kept "holding them back."[11] The World Bank and Export Bank were less worried about international instability but required proper surveys and reports by "first-class concerns" of carefully worked out "schemes regularly broken down to the minutest items of expenditure and income" before doling out any loans. Pakistan was as yet unprepared to present such detailed proposals.

Jinnah himself had no energy left to work on such matters. He could not even answer Ispahani's letters anymore. An old Parsi friend from Bombay visited him in Karachi at this time and found him "dozing" in his garden at the government house. When Jinnah finally woke up, he whispered, "I am so tired, Jamshed, so tired."[12] At seventy-two he had not only won his greatest suit but had outlived his foremost rival. It was high time for him to rest, was it not?

Nonetheless, his government insisted that he fly to Dacca that March to address the majority of Pakistan's population from their own "group" soil. He had not even gone to the East, or set foot in Dacca, the second "capital" of his nation. Great leader that he was, Jinnah answered the call of his cabinet and addressed a crowd estimated to be over 300,000 in Dacca's maidan on March 21, 1948. That was his last major public address; ironically, he delivered it in English, though he spoke to a Bengali-language audience and informed them "in the clearest language" that "the State Language of Pakistan is going to be URDU and no other language."[13] This was, of course, the most volatile, divisive issue in Pakistani politics.

> Any one who tries to mislead you is really the enemy of Pakistan. Without one State Language, no Nation can remain tied up solidly together and function. Look at the history of other countries. Therefore, so far as the State Language is concerned, Pakistan's language shall be URDU. . . . I tell you once again, do not fall into the trap of those who are the enemies of Pakistan. Unfortunately you have

fifth-columnists and I am sorry to say they are Muslims—who are financed by outsiders . . . you must have patience. With your help and with your support we will make Pakistan a mighty State. . . . No amount of trouble, no amount of hard work or sacrifice is too much or to be shirked. . . . I wish you God speed.[14]

He did not live to return, however, or to see East Pakistan metamorphosed through fire into the separate nation of Bangladesh, where Bengali would become and remain the sole official language.

The Frontier grew more restive as well. Pathans continued talking about a state of their own, "Pashtunistan," and even the Baluchis kept murmuring about a "Greater Baluchistan." So in April Jinnah was flown to Peshawar where he had to speak at Islamia College, and to air force cadets at Risalpur, and to the civil officers at the government house, and then at an open-air meeting in Peshawar, where "He was drenched to the bone," Fatima recalled. "That night it was obvious that he had caught a chill, but he refused to send for a doctor. 'It's nothing,' he said to me, 'just a cold.' This cold was the beginning of the end. In Karachi, his cough continued, and only when I forced a doctor on him did we learn that he had bronchitis. . . ."[15] Jinnah knew it was much worse than either a cold or bronchitis but did not wish to alarm Fatima more than was absolutely necessary. He understood too well by then that there was no cure for his sickness, no simple patent medicine to take his pain away or make the coughing stop.

Jinnah's relations with his closest colleagues deteriorated rapidly in the final months of his life. As he grew weaker and daily more conscious of the imminence of death, he was less patient with inefficiency and ineptitude, more easily angered by the usual excuses for not getting anything done. Before dying, he naturally wanted to see significant progress in his struggling infant land. In mid-April at a "private and exclusive lunch" at the nawab of Bahawalpur's House, Jinnah called Liaquat "mediocre"[16] in luncheon conversation with M. A. Khuhro, the then chief minister of Sind. Relations between the governor-general and his prime minister could hardly have been less than strained perhaps in that era of unrelieved national calamity and stress, financial stringency, and virtual war. Liaquat reportedly wrote Jinnah in January and offered to "resign" as prime minister after learning from his begum of Jinnah's angrily and openly expressed dissatisfaction with his work. Jinnah expressed equal frustration and disgust at the way the nawab of Mamdot, then chief minister of the Punjab, "was uninterested in the fate of the refugees." He called Mamdot and Governor Mudie to Karachi in May and told Mamdot, who had been his right arm in winning the Punjab for the League, that "he was useless as a Prime Minister, which," Mudie reported, "was only too true. He [Jinnah], therefore, nominated Mian Mumtaz Daultana" to take control of the Punjab ministry,[17] but Daultana "refused, protesting that he had complete confidence in Mamdot. . . . I [Mudie] knew and he [Daultana] knew that if he did become Prime Minister Mamdot would just about cut his throat. Jinnah was very angry and the meeting was adjourned. . . . Jinnah . . . rounded on me. . . . 'Your policy is weak. You've lost your nerve.' I asked what his orders for me were. He said 'None.' I then asked what his advice to me would be as a friend. He replied 'Wash your hands of them, as I am going to do.' . . . It was clear . . . that Jinnah was far from well. Indeed he had to lie down immediately after our meeting."[18]

In June, Jinnah and Fatima flew to Quetta, where he could breathe the cool bracing air of Baluchistan mountain country. "Within a few days of our arrival . . . he was able to sleep and eat well; the coughing subsided and his temperature came down to normal," Fatima recalled. "For the first time in many years he seemed relaxed."[19] On June 14, Jinnah addressed the officers of Quetta's Staff College, reflecting perhaps his own deepest anxieties about the growing strain in his relations with the cabinet and other official colleagues.

> You, along with other Forces of Pakistan, are the custodians of the life, property and honour of the people of Pakistan. The Defence Forces are the most vital of all Pakistan Services and correspondingly a very heavy responsibility and burden lies on your shoulders. . . . I want you to remember and if you have time enough you should study the Government of India Act, as adapted for use in Pakistan, which is our present Constitution, that the executive authority flows from the Head of the Government of Pakistan, who is the Governor-General, and, therefore, any command or orders that may come to you cannot come without the sanction of the Executive Head.[20]

The next day he told the Quetta municipality, which presented him with a handsome Relief Fund purse, that "luckily Baluchistan was spared the tragedy which the Punjab went through on the establishment of Pakistan. . . . Quetta may be as great a civil station as a cantonment. . . . For a large part of Western Pakistan it will be the natural summer resort. . . . It naturally pains me to find the curse of provincialism holding sway over any section of Pakistanis. Pakistan must be rid of this evil. It is a relic of the old administration . . . British control. . . . We are now all Pakistanis—not Baluchis, Pathans, Sindhis, Bengalis, Punjabis and so on . . . and we should be proud to be known as Pakistanis and nothing else."[21]

Fatima tried to "talk him out of" agreeing to fly back to Karachi to speak at the opening ceremony of the State Bank of Pakistan on July 1, 1948, but Jinnah insisted on going. The flight so "exhausted him" that "he could hardly get out of bed" to deliver the speech that was written for him. As Fatima noted: "Those who saw and heard him must have realised that he was not in good health; his voice was scarcely audible and he paused and coughed his way through his speech. When we returned home he collapsed into bed with his shoes on."[22] He had earlier accepted an invitation from the Canadian commissioner of trade to attend a reception that evening to celebrate the eighty-first anniversary of the dominion; that was to be the last social function Jinnah would ever attend.

On July 6, Jinnah and his sister flew back to Quetta, but he continued to run "a slight fever," so the doctors advised moving him to even more rarefied an atmosphere. Ziarat, a lonely Baluchi hill station forty miles and several thousand feet above Quetta, boasted a residency bungalow built by the British. That hill station was perched like an eagle at the top of the timber line. It was Jinnah's last retreat in the search of air pure enough to save his dying lungs. "A cluster of fruit trees and beds of flowers add to the beauty of the place," Fatima recalled, noting how her brother, whose "condition was deteriorating," liked "its quiet charm."

Lieutenant Colonel Ilahi Bakhsh of the Indian Medical Service was "sitting out on [his] lawn" in Lahore after dinner on July 21, when Muhammad Ali, the secretary general to the government of Pakistan, phoned from Karachi ordering him to fly "immediately" to Quetta. Dr. Bakhsh was met at the airport there on Friday afternoon by Major General M. A. Khan and Colonel K. Jilani, who drove with him in the governor-general's car to Ziarat. "Nobody knew what he was suffering from," recalled Bakhsh. "All I could gather was that he abhorred injections and patent medicines and preferred to be addressed as 'Sir' and not as 'Your Excellency.' "[23]

Fatima brought him to his great leader's bedroom the next morning.

I found the Quaid-i-Azam lying in bed facing the door. He looked shockingly thin and weak and had an ashen grey complexion . . . his appearance that morning frightened me. He must have guessed what was in my mind, for he diverted my attention by motioning me to a chair and enquiring if I had a pleasant journey. I sat down and asked for a detailed account of his present and previous illnesses. . . . "There is nothing much wrong with me," he told me, "except that I have got stomach trouble and exhaustion due to overwork and worry. For forty years I have worked for 14 hours a day, never knowing what disease was. However, for the last few years I have been having annual attacks of fever and cough. My doctors in Bombay regarded these as attacks of bronchitis, and with the usual treatment and rest in bed, I generally recovered within a week or so. For the last year or two, however, they have increased both in frequency and severity and are much more exhausting." While I was listening to him I found him losing breath after every sentence and sometimes pausing in the middle. His mouth was dry and he moistened his lips many times while talking. The voice lacked tone and was . . . almost inaudible. He had a couple of fits of coughing . . . which left him exhausted. . . . After a short pause during which he closed his eyes and looked more dead than alive, he continued, "About three weeks ago I caught a chill and developed fever and a cough for which the Civil Surgeon of Quetta prescribed penicillin lozenges. I have been taking these since; my cold is better, the fever is less, but I feel very weak. I don't think there is anything organically wrong with me . . . if my stomach can be put right I will recover soon. Many years ago I had a rather bad stomach trouble for which I consulted two or three London specialists, but they failed to diagnose my illness, and one of them even advised operation. . . . I didn't submit to the operations and on the advice of another London doctor went to Germany and consulted a famous doctor. He told me that I had no organic trouble and only needed rest and a regulation of diet. I stayed in his clinic for a few weeks and recovered completely. In 1934 I was diagnosed by the Bombay doctors to be suffering from heart disease, but a heart specialist in Germany assured me that my heart was perfectly normal."

The doctor asked the governor-general to remove his silk pyjama top so that he could listen to his heart; "I observed with distress that he was much thinner than he appeared with clothes on and could not make out how he had managed to survive and work in such an advanced stage of emaciation. . . . I had seen equally severe cases among the prisoners of war at Singapore. . . . The physical examination . . . dimmed my hopes, although I did not reveal my fears to the patient. . . . I expressed a desire to have him investigated further before I could give my final diagnosis, but hinted that the root cause of the trouble appeared to me to be lung disease and not his stomach. The Quaid-i-Azam still believed, however, that his primary trouble was the stomach, and urged me to pay more attention to it. . . ."[24] Bakhsh did not ignore his patient's concern and prescribed a "high caloric . . . low residue diet." Fatima "appeared to doubt" the "advantage" of inflicting such a diet on her brother but said nothing, and for a day or two Jinnah seemed to eat better, for the wise doctor also prescribed "a digestive mixture."

Bakhsh did the best, in fact, that any medical practitioner could have done. He "rang up" the civil surgeon from Quetta, who drove up to Ziarat

next morning with his clinical pathologist and brought along his micro-
scope and reagents to test Jinnah's blood sputum and do the usual labora-
tory work. Their lab "findings" confirmed the colonel's "suspicions." With
so important a patient, however, further corroboration was considered essential before surrendering hope to the fatal disease that was consuming
his lungs. So Bakhsh wired his own hospital in Lahore and ordered three
of its best specialists to fly to Ziarat, telling one of them to bring his por-
table x ray along. Then he wired Karachi for special medicines. Within the
week most of Pakistan's advanced medical people were flown or driven
8,500 feet above sea level to Ziarat; they concentrated on the dying old
man who coughed without respite in that remote spot, whose strange name
means "burial tomb," like the ancient ziggurat mound of Mesopotamia
erected at the dawn of civilization to house the remains of a god-king.
Bakhsh recalled.

> While I was telling him the grave news I watched him intently.
> He . . . remained quite calm and all he said after I had finished
> was, "Have you told Miss Jinnah?" I replied, "Yes, Sir . . . I had to
> take her into confidence." The Quaid-i-Azam interrupted me and
> said, "No, you shouldn't have done it. After all she is a woman." I
> expressed regret for the pain caused to his sister. . . . The Quaid-i-
> Azam listened patiently and in the end said, "It doesn't matter, what
> is done is done. Now tell me all about it. How long have I had this
> disease? What are the chances of my overcoming it? How long will
> the treatment last? I should like to know everything and you must
> not hesitate to tell me the whole truth." . . . I replied that I . . .
> felt confident that with the aid of the latest drugs there should be a
> fair chance of a considerable improvement.[25]

Ispahani flew in from New York that week and offered to arrange for
any "medical aid from America" that might be needed, which he was
ready to bring in a "special plane" if Dr. Bakhsh thought it advisable. "He
enquired about the nature of the illness—which, of course, I could not
reveal," Bakhsh noted, allowing Jinnah's friend to see him alone. However, "After his interview he came downstairs visibly moved. I hoped he
had not betrayed his anxiety before the patient. In his evident concern he
repeated his offer of medical help from America. . . ." But there was nothing any American doctor could have done that Bakhsh was not trying to
do. No cure had been discovered for the tuberculosis-turned-to-lung-can-
cer that had by then almost totally consumed both of his lungs.
    Liaquat arrived shortly after Ispahani left and spent about half an
hour alone with Jinnah. He must have seen what anyone allowed close
enough to look could have seen—the governor-general was dying. The

Quaid-i-Azam would soon to be no more, and the burden of leading Pakistan would fall upon his shoulders, his ulcer, his life. Fatima, who had never really liked either Liaquat or his begum—(perhaps she blamed them both for helping lure Jinnah back to India from his Hampstead retreat, where she and her beloved brother might have lived their lives out in peace and quiet contentment), subsequently reported that after Liaquat left, Jinnah told her with trembling voice, "Do you know why he has come? He wants to know how serious my illness is, how long I will last."[26] It was doubtless true, yet hardly as opprobrious as Fatima considered it, under the circumstances. There was, after all, still a nation to be run—millions of displaced persons to be fed and cared for, an undeclared war in Kashmir to be fought, a constitution to be drafted, dissident Bengalis, Pathans, Baluchis, Punjabis, and Sindis somehow to be satisfied. To Liaquat, a displaced Nawabzada from the United Provinces and Oxford, it must have seemed odd to be there in Ziarat, still a mere "courtier" to that imperious regal couple, though he was almost fifty-three. The prime minister would have little more than three years after Jinnah died before a hired assassin's bullet claimed his life in mid-October 1951, in Rawalpindi. Dr. Bakhsh remarked of Liaquat:

> Downstairs in the drawing room I met the Prime Minister. He anxiously enquired about the Quaid-i-Azam, complimented me on having won the first round by securing the patient's confidence, and expressed the hope that it would contribute to his recovery. He also urged me to probe into the root cause of the persistent disease. I assured him that despite the Quaid-i-Azam's serious condition there was reason to hope that if he responded to the latest medicines which had been sent for from Karachi he might yet overcome the trouble, and that the most hopeful feature was the patient's strong power of resistance. I was moved by the Prime Minister's deep concern for the health of his Chief and old comrade.[27]

Streptomycine arrived and was administered, but "miracle" drug that it was, it could not achieve the impossible. Nor did the Id prayers of Jinnah's nation, voiced from every mosque in Pakistan and elsewhere throughout the Muslim world on August 7, suffice to turn the inexorable tide of the insidious disease that silently consumed his lungs. By August 9 edema of the feet set in, and the medical staff surrounding the Quaid decided it would be best to remove him to a lower altitude. Ziarat's rarefied atmosphere appeared to be imposing too great a strain on his failing heart and kidneys. Injections of coramine and ultraviolet therapy proved useless. Jinnah, however, was reluctant to move anywhere, especially on the eve of Independence Day, which was precisely when Bakhsh advised driving

him down to Quetta. "This is impossible," the governor-general replied.
"The earliest would be the 15th." They feared that date might be too late,
enlisting Fatima's support in pressing him till at last he agreed.

Jinnah's final journey home began on August 13 at 3:30 P.M. He insisted on wearing "a brand new suit with a tie to match, and a handker-
chief in his vanity pocket," Fatima recalled. "I helped him put on his
polished pump shoes. He was brought down on a stretcher and was placed
in a semi-reclining position in the back of the big Humber car, in which
we travelled to Quetta."[28] Though many "precautions" had been taken to
keep the move "top secret," cheering crowds lined the road along their
winding descent. The Humber had escort cars and a jeep front and rear,
so it was quite a convoy with the governor-general's handsome blue flags
flying as they bumped over the rocky ill-surfaced road that had never
borne so important or imposing an entourage before. They stopped for tea
about a mile past the Rest House, since Jinnah had noticed "about a dozen
men" standing around there and wanted no intrusive eyes seeing how
weak he was. Dr. Bakhsh remembered:

> We reached Quetta just before sunset after about four hours' driv-
> ing. The Residency had been cleared of all visitors, and we shifted
> him on stretcher to his bed-room on the first floor. . . . I examined
> his pulse and found that every tenth or fifteenth beat was missing. . . .
> I ascribed the abnormality in the pulse to the exhaustion of the jour-
> ney and hoped it would disappear with rest. . . . Next morning,
> August the 14th, was the Anniversary of the establishment of Paki-
> stan. We visited the Quaid-i-Azam at about 8.30. . . . I said: "Sir,
> we are very fortunate in having brought you down to Quetta with-
> out any mishap. It was risky to shift you from Ziarat in such a weak
> state. . . ." The Quaid-i-Azam smiled, saying, "Yes, I am glad you
> have brought me here. I was caught in a trap at Ziarat."[29]

A statement published that morning in Pakistan's daily newspapers was
entitled the Quaid-i-Azam's "Message" to the "Citizens of Pakistan" but
was obviously composed in Karachi not Ziarat:

> Today we are celebrating the first anniversary of our freedom. We
> have faced the year with courage, determination and imagination,
> and the record of our achievements has been a wonderful one in
> warding off the blows of the enemy. . . . I congratulate you all—my
> Ministers under the leadership of the Prime Minister.[30]

Jinnah had written none of it, of course. He wrote nothing any longer and
barely glanced at the morning newspapers. How remote that glorious carriage ride with Mountbatten must have seemed to him on this first anni-

versary—the air ringing with shouts of "Pakistan Zindabad" and his most pressing fear of death then from an unknown assassin's bullet. The countless "traps" set for him, some baited so handsomely—provincial governor, prime minister, knighthood—he had eluded them all. Daggers, guns, bombs, all of them had missed the Grey Wolf. He had proved himself too fast, too elusive, too strong for them.

The third week in August, Jinnah's appetite improved slightly. He asked for halva and purées, two delicacies his doctor initially had feared might be too "heavy" for him to digest, but Fatima wisely fed her brother his favorites, and they seemed to cheer him up. The doctors tried to get him to move as much as possible by sitting him up in bed for his meals, then standing him on his feet, walking him a bit, trying to keep his muscles from atrophying, and trying to help his digestive system to function. He became more irritable; he yelled at everyone for not being more "punctual," and Fatima explained that "her brother attached a great deal of importance to punctuality, and had all his life been most punctual himself."[31]

Jinnah's doctor was "shocked" to find that his patient weighed only eighty pounds. It was clear to all those at the Quaid-i-Azam's bedside that if he was ever to return alive to his capital he would have to be flown back there very soon. Jinnah asked for permission to resume smoking. (He had smoked an average of fifty or more Craven A cigarettes a day over the last thirty years.) The doctor permitted him to have one cigarette a day, ordering him not to inhale. Soon, however Bakhsh agreed to double his "ration."

It did us good to see him enjoying it, . . . since in a habitual smoker the first sign of recovery was commonly a craving for and pleasure in smoking. . . . Next morning I noticed four cigarette stumps in the ashtray on the table by his bedside . . . the patient had exceeded his allowance. . . . Looking at the ashtray, I remarked that he appeared to have enjoyed his cigarettes. The Quaid-i-Azam took the hint, and ingeniously replied: "Yes, but didn't you tell me there was no harm in smoking if I didn't inhale?" . . . his mind was regaining its old legal quality, and we welcomed this additional sign of recovery.[32]

Cigarette smoke did not help heal his lungs, however, so the doctors continued advising him to moderate his smoking and return to Karachi. But Jinnah did not want to go "home" to the governor-general's mansion as an "invalid." He suggested a few quieter places on the plains, Sibi and Malir, but both of those were hot, dusty, and remote.

He said to Bakhsh: "Don't take me to Karachi on crutches. I want to go there when I can walk from the car to my room. You know, from the porch you have to pass the A.D.C.'s room and then the Military Secretary's before you reach mine. I dislike being carried on a stretcher from the car to my room." He wanted none of his Karachi staff to see him this way, too weak to stand up. Jinnah practically stopped eating after August 28, and whenever Bakhsh urged him to take some food, he was told, "Doctor, you are overfeeding me. I have never taken so much food before, even when I was quite well. . . . Some years ago we had a European diplomat to dinner in Bombay. He did not take the soup when it was served. I noticed this but thought perhaps he was not fond of soup. When the fish was brought he refused that also. I was surprised but kept quiet. But when the joint was served and he didn't touch it, I couldn't refrain from asking him the reason of this abstinence. Our guest replied that he had been living on lettuce for six months. We were all the more surprised because he appeared to be in very good health. Now do you think a man can live for such a long time on lettuce and maintain good health?"[33]

Jinnah lived on a few cups of tea and coffee, and some plain water to swallow his pills. He "lay in bed quietly all day," listless, apathetic, depressed. "Fati, I am no longer interested in living. The sooner I go the better," he confessed before the month ended. "It does not matter whether I live or die," he told Bakhsh on August 29. Bakhsh "noticed tears in his eyes, and was startled by this manifestation of feeling in one generally looked upon as unemotional and unbending. . . . I had always felt that he had been kept going, despite his low vitality, by an indomitable will. . . . I knew from experience that when a patient gave up the fight no treatment, however perfect, could achieve much, and was, therefore, greatly distressed to find that the man of iron will had given up the fight.[34]

By September, Jinnah had pneumonia as well as tuberculosis and cancer of the lungs. His temperature rose to about 100° with his pulse disproportionately higher and his heartbeat was irregular, occasionally missing. Oxygen was required to help him breathe. Ispahani was cabled to call Dr. Hinshaw of the Mayo Clinic in Minnesota to fly immediately to Quetta for consultation.[35] Bakhsh also sent for Dr. M. A. Mistry from Karachi. Mistry arrived the next morning, September 9. Mistry and Bakhsh had been classmates at Guy's Hospital in London, where both had received their M.D.s in 1931. After examining the patient, Mistry confirmed his friend's diagnosis, treatment, and advice, judging that there was really nothing more any American doctor could do. Jinnah was heard muttering aloud as he tossed about uncomfortably in bed . . . "The Kashmir Commission have an appointment with me today, why haven't they turned up? Where are they?"[36]

The governor-general's Viking and two Dakota airplanes to carry his staff and luggage arrived at Quetta airport and were ready to take off by 2:00 P.M. on September 11, 1948. "As his stretcher was taken into the Viking's cabin," Fatima recalled, "the pilot and crew lined up and saluted him. He in turn lifted his hand feebly. . . . A bed had been improvised in the front cabin and I sat with him, along with Dr. Mistry. . . . Oxygen cylinders and a gas mask were ready. . . . After about two hours flying, we landed at the Air Force base at Mauripur at 4:15 pm. Here he had landed just over a year ago, full of hope and confidence that he would help build Pakistan into a great nation. Then thousands had thronged to welcome him. But today, as instructed . . . there was no one at the airport. Colonel Knowles . . . greeted us as we came out of the plane."[37] Knowles was Jinnah's military secretary and had brought the army ambulance into which the governor-general was carried on his stretcher. Fatima and a Quetta nurse, Sister Dunham, sat inside the rear of the ambulance with Jinnah, while the doctors followed in the governor-general's new Cadillac limousine.

"After we had covered about four or five miles, the ambulance coughed and came to a sudden stop. Five minutes later," Fatima reported, "I got out only to be told that it had run out of petrol, but the driver was also fidgeting with the engine . . . there was no breeze, and the humid heat was oppressive. To add to his discomfort, scores of flies buzzed around his face, and he did not have the strength to brush them away. . . . Sister Dunham and I fanned him in turns, waiting for another ambulance to arrive. . . . Every minute was an eternity of agony. He could not be shifted to the Cadillac as it was not big enough for the stretcher."[38]

"Wondering what had happened," wrote Bakhsh, "I got out and found that there had been a breakdown due to engine trouble. The driver assured us that he would soon put it right, but he fiddled with the engine for about twenty minutes, and the ambulance would not start. Miss Jinnah sent the Military Secretary to fetch another ambulance. Dr. Mistry went with him. . . . I examined him [Jinnah] and was horrified to find his pulse becoming weaker and irregular. I ran . . . and brought back a thermos flask containing hot tea. Miss Jinnah quickly gave him a cup. . . . What a catastrophe if, having survived the air journey, he were to die by the road-side."[39]

It was a lonely stretch of highway leading south toward Karachi. "Nearby stood hundreds of huts belonging to the refugees," noted Fatima, "who went about their business, not knowing that their Quaid, who had given them a homeland, was in their midst, lying helpless. Cars honked their way past, buses and trucks rumbled by, and we stood there immobilized in an ambulance that refused to move an inch. . . . We waited for over one hour, and no hour, in my life has been so long and full of anguish."[40]

The trip from the airport to the government house took half as long as the entire flight from Quetta. They reached the governor-general's mansion at 6:10 P.M. "He slept for about two hours," Fatima noted, "then he opened his eyes and . . . whispered, 'Fati. . . .' His head dropped slightly to the right, his eyes closed. I ran out of the room crying, 'Doctor, doctor. Come quickly. My brother is dying. Where are the doctors?' In a few moments they were there, examining him and giving him injections. I stood there, motionless, speechless. Then I saw them cover his body, head to foot, with the sheet . . . and fainted on the floor."

Quaid-i-Azam Jinnah died at 10:20 P.M. on September 11, 1948. All that remained of him weighed only seventy pounds. Wrapped in a simple shroud, he was buried the next day in Karachi, where a handsome domed monument of pink marble now stands, housing the remains of one of history's most remarkable, tenacious, enigmatic figures.

Fatima Jinnah, who inherited most of her brother's estate, remained in Pakistan till her death on July 9, 1967. In 1964–65, the *Madar-i-Millat* ("Mother of the Nation"), tried to follow in her brother's political footsteps by running for president of Pakistan against Field Marshal Ayub Khan. She ran a vigorous campaign as the candidate for Ayub's united opposition and won great support in the east; but she was defeated because of Ayub's "basic democracy" technique of undemocratic elections. After that she resumed her former life of luxurious isolation, spending her final years in virtual solitude and reflecting on the remarkable man to whom she had devoted herself.

Jinnah's daughter Dina never joined her father in Pakistan while he lived; she came to Karachi only for his funeral. When Dina married Neville Wadia, a Parsi-born Christian, Jinnah tried his best to dissuade her, going almost as far as Sir Dinshaw Petit had with his daughter. As Justice Chagla recalled: "Jinnah, in his usual imperious manner, told her that there were millions of Muslim boys in India, and she could have anyone she chose. Then the young lady, who was more than a match for her father, replied: 'Father, there were millions of Muslim girls in India. Why did you not marry one of them?' "[41] Jinnah never spoke to his daughter after she married. And though they did correspond, he always addressed her formally as "Mrs. Wadia" and never talked of her to his friends, insisting, indeed, that he had "no daughter."[42]

Dina and Neville Wadia kept house in Bombay and had two children, soon after which they separated. Neville, who presided over the Wadia commercial and textile empire there, passed control of his business on to his son Nusli, who chairs the board of Wadia Industries, Ltd. and has two sons, Jinnah's only great grandchildren, who live in Bombay as citizens of India. Dina and Neville had a daughter as well, who apparently lives in Manhattan as something of a "recluse" but was "too young to remember [Jinnah] and saw little of him," according to her father. Neville Wadia left India after divorcing Dina, choosing to reside in Switzerland. Dina moved to New York City and lived alone in a splendid apartment on Madison Avenue until at least 1982. Thus, none of Jinnah's direct descendants ever opted for Pakistan.

Notes

CHAPTER 1: KARACHI

1. Fazlur Rahman, *Islam* (Garden City: Doubleday, 1966), pp. 213–19; S. A. A. Rizvi, "Islam in Medieval India," in *A Cultural History of India*, ed. A. L. Basham (Oxford: Clarendon Press, 1975), chap. 19.

2. G. Allana, *Quaid-i-Azam Jinnah: The Story of A Nation* (Lahore: Ferozsons Ltd., 1967), p. 3.

3. Jinnah's sisters, Rahmat, Maryam, Fatima, and Shireen, followed in that order, while the youngest of his siblings were his two brothers, Ahmed Ali and Bundeh Ali.

4. M. A. Harris, "Quaid-i-Azam, What is his date of birth?," in M. A. Harris, *Quaid-i-Azam* (1950; reprint, Karachi: Times Press, 1976), pp. 35–53, is the best primary source evidence concerning the puzzling question of Jinnah's actual birth date.

5. Fatima Jinnah, "My Brother," an unpublished personal memoir preserved in the National Archives of Pakistan, Islamabad, F/143.

6. Alexander F. Baillie, *Kurrachee: Past, Present and Future* (Karachi: Oxford University Press, 1975), p. 4.

7. M. H. Saiyid, *Mohammad Ali Jinnah* (Lahore: S. M. Ashraf, 1945), p. 2.

8. Jinnah, "My Brother."

9. Hector Bolitho, *Jinnah, Creator of Pakistan* (London: John Murray, 1954), p. 7.

10. Jinnah, "My Brother."

11. Ibid.

12. Ibid.

13. Sir John Evelyn Wrench, *The Immortal Years, 1937–1944* (London: Hutchinson, 1945), p. 132.

14. Ibid.

15. Jinnah, "My Brother."

16. Ibid.

17. India Office Library and Records, London. *IOR: Photo Eur* 127.

18. Bolitho, *Jinnah*, p. 7.

19. President Dadabhai Naoroji's address to the Calcutta Congress, December 1886, in *The Indian National Congress*, 2d ed. (Madras: G. A. Natesan & Co., 1917), p. 19. Hereafter cited as *INC*.

20. Jinnah, "My Brother."

21. Ibid.

22. Stanley Wolpert, *Morley and India, 1906–1910* (Berkeley and Los Angeles: University of California Press, 1967), p. 19.

23. President Alfred Webb's address to the Madras Congress, 1894, *INC* [19], p. 187.

24. Bolitho, *Jinnah*, p. 13.

25. Jinnah, "My Brother."

26. Syed Sharifuddin Pirzada, *Some Aspects of Quaid-i-Azam's Life* (Islamabad: National Commission on Historical and Cultural Research, 1978), p. 11.

27. *IOR: Photo Eur 127.*

CHAPTER 2: BOMBAY (1896–1910)

1. Jinnah, "My Brother."

2. Sarojini Naidu, "Mohammad Ali Jinnah-Ambassador of Hindu-Muslim Unity," in *Quaid-i-Azam as Seen by His Contemporaries*, comp. Jamil-ud-din Ahmad (Lahore: Publishers United Ltd., 1966), p. 159.

3. There were several influential and wealthy Peerbhoy families settled in Bombay, most famous of which was Sir Adamji Peerbhoy's (1863–1913) Borah Muslim family. Jinnah's aunt was not related to Sir Adamji, but her three sons, Akbar, Ayaz, and Yusuf, attained prominence in their own right; Akbar was a barrister. I am indebted to my good friend and colleague, Professor D. R. Sar Desai of Bombay and Los Angeles, for the above information.

4. Saiyid, *Jinnah*, p. 8.

5. Allana, *Quaid-i-Azam*, p. 27.

6. Jinnah, "My Brother."

7. President Badruddin Tyabji's address to the Madras Congress, 1887, *INC* [I, 19], p. 25.

8. G. Allana, ed., *Pakistan Movement: Historic Documents* (Karachi: Department of International Relations, University of Karachi, 1967), p. 1.

9. Ibid., p. 3.

10. A contemporary Bombay "advocate" of Jinnah's quoted in Bolitho, *Jinnah*, p. 18.

11. Joachim Alva, *Leaders of India* (Bombay: Thacker & Co. Ltd., 1943), pp. 63*ff*.

12. M. C. Chagla, *Roses in December, An Autobiography* (Bombay: Bharatiya Vidya Bhavan, 1974), p. 53.

13. President Pherozeshah Mehta's address to the Calcutta Congress, 1890, *INC* [I, 19], p. 68.

14. Ibid., p. 72.

15. C. Y. Chintamani, ed., *Speeches and Writings of the Honourable Sir Pherozeshah M. Mehta, K.C.I.E.* (Allahabad: The Indian Press, 1905), pp. 818–19.

16. Ibid., p. 823.

17. B. R. Nanda, *Gokhale: The Indian Moderates and the British Raj* (Princeton: Princeton University Press, 1977), pp. 187–89.

18. Sarojini Naidu's words, quoted in Sharif Al Mujahid, *Quaid-i-Azam Jinnah; Studies in Interpretation*, 2d rev. ed. (Karachi: Quaid-i-Azam Academy, 1981), p. 8.

19. President Gopal K. Gokhale's address to the Benares Congress, 1905, *INC* [I, 19], p. 796.

20. Allana, *Pakistan Movement*, pp. 7–10.

21. Mary, Countess of Minto, *India, Minto and Morley, 1905–10* (London: Macmillan, 1934), pp. 47–48.

22. *Amrita Bazar Patrika*, October 4, 1906, quoted in M. N. Das, *India under Morley and Minto* (London: George Allen & Unwin, 1964), p. 173.

23. Aga Khan to Dunlop Smith, October 29, 1906, S. S. Pirzada, ed., *Foundations of Pakistan: All-India Muslim League Documents*, vol. I (1906–24) (Karachi: National Publishing House Ltd., 1969), p. 4. The next quote is from ibid., p. xliv.

24. Ibid., p. 5.

25. Ibid., p. 6.

26. H. H. The Aga Khan, *The Memoirs of Aga Khan* (New York: Simon & Schuster, 1954), pp. 122–23.

27. President Dadabhai Naoroji's address to the Calcutta Congress, 1906, *INC* [I, 19], pp. 837–38.

28. Ibid., p. 853–54.

29. Sarojini Naidu's title for him in Naidu, "Ambassador."

30. Ibid., pp. 158–59.

31. Minto to Morley, November 11, 1909, in Wolpert, *Morley*, p. 198.

32. Morley to Minto, December 6, 1909, ibid., p. 199. The following quote is from ibid.

33. Saiyid, *Jinnah*, p. 64.

34. Resolution XVI, Allahabad Congress, 1910, *INC* [I, 19], pt. II, p. 142.

CHAPTER 3: CALCUTTA (1910–1915)

1. Mary Minto, *India*, pp. 371–72.

2. Resolution IX, Lahore Congress, 1909, *INC* [I, 19], pt. II, p. 135.

3. February 25, 1910, Calcutta, in Fazal Haque Qureshi, ed., *Every Day with the Quaid-i-Azam* (Karachi: Sultan Ashraf Qureshi, 1976), p. 66. The following quote in the same paragraph is also from this source.

4. Mohammad Yusuf Khan, *The Glory of Quaid-i-Azam* (Lahore: Caravan Book Centre, 1976), pp. 23–24.

5. Pirzada, *Foundations*, vol. I, p. 258.

6. Ibid., p. 272.

7. Sarojini Naidu, ed., *Mohammad Ali Jinnah: His Speeches and Writings, 1912–1917* (Madras: Ganesh, 1918), p. 11.

8. Ibid.; Naidu, "Ambassador."

9. Bolitho, *Jinnah*, p. 58.

10. Resolution V, Karachi Congress, 1913, *INC* [I, 19], pt. II, pp. 159–60.

11. Resolution IV, ibid., p. 159.

12. Pirzada, *Foundations*, vol. I, 316.

13. Lord Crewe to Lord Hardinge, 14 May 1916, in *Viceroy Lord Hardinge Papers*, Reel 11, 37. Cambridge University Library, Cambridge, Hereafter cited as *HP*.

14. At a reception for him in the Cecil Hotel, London, August 14, 1914, *India* (London: British Committee Weekly of Indian National Congress), p. 71.

15. Bombay, January 14, 1915, *The Collected Works of Mahatma Gandhi*, vol. XIII (Ahmedabad: Navajivan Trust, 1964), p. 9. Hereafter cited as *CWMG*.

16. Pirzada, *Foundations*, vol. I, pp. 330–1.

17. Ibid., p. 350.

18. Ibid., p. 353.
19. Ibid., p. 352.
20. Chagla, *Roses in December*, p. 25.
21. Pirzada, *Foundations*, vol. I, pp. 353–54.
22. Ibid., p. 361.

CHAPTER 4: LUCKNOW TO BOMBAY (1916–1918)

1. L. F. Rushbrook-Williams, "The Evolution of the Quaid-i-Azam As Observed," in *Papers Presented at the International Congress on Quaid-i-Azam*, 19–25 December 1976, 5 vols. (Islamabad: Quaid-i-Azam University, 1976), vol. I, p. 115. Hereafter cited *Papers*.

2. S. M. Edwardes, *Memoir of Sir Dinshaw Manockjee Petit* (Oxford: Oxford University Press, 1923), p. 3.

3. Kanji Dwarkadas, *Ruttie Jinnah* (Bombay: Kanji Dwarkadas, 1963), p. 9.

4. Saiyid, *Jinnah*, append. II, p. 842.

5. Ibid., p. 846.

6. Ibid., p. 851.

7. Ibid., pp. 854–55.

8. Allana, *Pakistan Movement*. All quotations in the following paragraph are from Saiyid, *Jinnah*, pp. 33–39.

9. Saiyid, *Jinnah*, pp. 41–42.

10. Pirzada, *Foundations*, vol. I, pp. 371–73.

11. This portion of Jinnah's address does not appear in ibid., which used the Muslim League's "Official Pamphlet" report of Jinnah's presidential address as its primary source. The quoted passage was deleted from that pamphlet but has been preserved in Saiyid, *Jinnah*, append. III, pp. 872–89, esp. 873.

12. Saiyid, *Jinnah*, pp. 878–79.

13. Ibid., pp. 879–80.

14. President A. C. Mazumdar's address to the Lucknow Congress, 1916, *INC* [I, 19], p. 1274.

15. Quoted in Stanley A. Wolpert, *Tilak and Gokhale* (Berkeley and Los Angeles: University of California Press, 1962), p. 275.

16. Chagla, *Roses in December*, p. 119.

17. Edwin S. Montagu, *An Indian Diary*, ed. Venetia Montagu (London: William Heinemann, 1930), November 26, 1917, pp. 8–10.

18. Ibid., November 10, 1917, pp. 8–10.

19. Ibid., November 29, 1917, p. 58.

20. Qureshi, *Every Day*, p. 394.

21. Saiyid, *Jinnah*, p. 159.

22. Pirzada, *Foundations*, vol. I, p. 427.

23. Budget Debate, 1917–18, Proceedings of the Indian Legislative Council, Government of India, p. 388.

24. Raja of Mahmudabad, "Some Memories," in *The Partition of India*, ed. C. H. Philips and M. D. Wainwright (London: George Allen & Unwin Ltd., 1970), p. 385.

25. M. K. Gandhi, *The Story of My Experiments With Truth* (*Gandhi's Autobiography*), trans. Mahadev Desai (Washington: Public Affairs Press, 1948), p. 539.

26. Ibid., pp. 541–42.

27. Ibid., p. 543.

28. April 24, 1918, Saiyid, *Jinnah*, p. 181.

29. Willingdon to Montagu, April 30, 1918, *Montagu Papers*, 1917–18, p. 50.

30. Chelmsford to Montagu, September 17, 1918, *Chelmsford Papers,* v. 4, Reel 2. 379.
31. Saiyid, *Jinnah,* p. 184.
32. Ibid., p. 188.
33. Bolitho, *Jinnah,* p. 75.
34. Saiyid, *Jinnah,* pp. 199–200.
35. Gandhi to Jinnah, July 4, 1918, in Syed Sharifuddin Pirzada, ed., *Quaid-e-Azam Jinnah's Correspondence,* 3d. rev. ed. (Karachi: East and West Publishing Company, 1977), p. 82.
36. Gandhi, *My Experiments,* p. 545.
37. Gandhi to Maffey, August 9, 1918, *Chelmsford Papers,* 20, 46.
38. Gandhi, *My Experiments,* pp. 551–54.
39. C. H. Philips, ed., *The Evolution of India and Pakistan, 1858 to 1947. Selected Documents* (London: George Allen & Unwin Ltd., 1962), pp. 267–68.
40. Saiyid, *Jinnah,* pp. 223–25.
41. Ibid., p. 211.
42. Ibid., p. 213.
43. The marble plaque inscription on the wall, Syed Hashim Raza, "The Charisma of Quaid-i-Azam," in *Papers* [IV, 1], vol. V, p. 207.

CHAPTER 5: AMRITSAR TO NAGPUR (1919–1921)

1. Mohammad Yusuf Khan, *The Glory of Quaid-i-Azam* (Lahore: Caravan Book Centre, 1976), pp. 30–31.
2. Saiyid, *Jinnah,* pp. 238–39.
3. Pirzada, *Foundations,* vol. I, p. 475.
4. Chaman Lal, "The Quaid-i-Azam As I Knew Him," in Ahmad, *Quaid-i-Azam,* p. 167.
5. Lloyd to Montagu, June 12, 1919, *Montagu Papers,* Reel 5, MSS EUR D 523/24.
6. This and the following quotes from the same interview were reported in the *Bombay Chronicle,* November 17, 1919, in the *Chelmsford Papers,* Reel 2.
7. Gandhi to Jinnah, June 28, 1919, *CWMG,* [III, 15] vol. XV, pp. 398–99.
8. Lady Dhanavati Rama Rao's personal recollection of Ruttie related to the author in Los Angeles, March 14, 1979. Another old friend of Ruttie, Mrs. P. Jayakar, reported much the same characteristics as dominant in an interview in Los Angeles on May 15, 1981.
9. Pirzada, *Foundations,* vol. I, pp. 517–27.
10. Ibid., p. 543–44.
11. Ibid., p. 544.
12. Judith Brown, *Gandhi's Rise To Power: Indian Politics, 1915–1922* (Cambridge: Cambridge University Press, 1972), p. 273.
13. Jinnah's letter dated 27–10–20 is reproduced in M. R. Jayakar, *The Story of My Life* (Bombay: Asia Publishing House, 1958), vol. I, p. 405.
14. Gandhi to Jinnah, October 25, 1920, *CWMG* [III, 15], vol. XVIII, p. 372.
15. Saiyid, *Jinnah,* pp. 264–65.
16. *CWMG* [III, 15], vol. XIX, pp. 159–62.
17. *Times of India,* January 13, 1921, in Harris, *Quaid-i-Azam,* p. 128.
18. Dr. Naeem Quershi, *Papers,* [IV, 1] vol. V, p. 229.
19. Jamil-ud-Din Ahmad, *Glimpses of Quaid-i-Azam* (Karachi: Education Press, 1960), p. 2.
20. Sly to Viceroy Chelmsford, Nagpur, January 1, 1921, *Chelmsford Papers,* XXVI, 2–4.

CHAPTER 6: RETREAT TO BOMBAY (1921–1924)

1. Chagla, *Roses in December,* p. 120.
2. Ibid.
3. Saiyid, *Jinnah,* pp. 269–72. The quotes that follow are from Chagla, *Roses in December,* pp. 276–79.
4. *Young India,* 18–8–21, in *CWMG* [III, 15], vol. XX, p. 527.
5. Jayakar, *Story,* vol. I, p. 504.
6. "Notes," December 20, 1921, *CWMG* [III, 15], vol. XXII, pp. 66–67.
7. Pirzada, *Foundations,* vol. I, p. 557.
8. *Bombay Chronicle,* January 14, 1922, *CWMG* [III, 15], vol. XXII, p. 178.
9. *Young India,* 19–1–21, ibid., p. 218.
10. *Young India,* 16–2–22, ibid., pp. 415–16.
11. Jayakar, *Story,* vol. I, p. 555.
12. Ibid.
13. Ibid., p. 567.
14. Dwarkadas, *Ruttie,* pp. 24–25.
15. Ibid., p. 26.
16. Chagla, *Roses in December,* pp. 118–19.
17. Raja of Mahmudabad, "Some Memories," p. 385.

CHAPTER 7: NEW DELHI (1924–1928)

1. K. M. Panikkar and A. Pershad, eds., *The Voice of Freedom: Selected Speeches of Pandit Motilal Nehru* (London: Asia Publishing House, 1961), p. 101.
2. M. Rafique Afzal, *Quaid-i-Azam Mohammad Ali Jinnah: Speeches in the Legislative Assembly of India, 1924–30* (Lahore: Research Society of Pakistan, 1976), p. xxi.
3. February 14, 1924, ibid., p. 8.
4. February 11, 1924, ibid., p. 5.
5. February 14, 1924, ibid., p. 9.
6. Ibid., pp. 21–22.
7. Ibid., p. 56.
8. Ibid., p. 57.
9. Pirzada, *Foundations,* vol. I, pp. 576–77.
10. Ibid., p. 577.
11. Ibid., p. 581.
12. Gandhi to Motilal Nehru, August 9, 1924 *CWMG* [III, 15], vol. XXIV, p. 536.
13. Pattabhi Sitaramayya, *The History of the Indian National Congress (1885–1935)* (Bombay: Padma Publications Ltd., 1935), vol. I, p. 269.
14. Jawaharlal Nehru, *Toward Freedom* (New York: The John Day Company, 1941), pp. 108, 25.
15. Sitaramayya, *Indian National Congress,* vol. I, pp. 272–73.
16. August 31, 1924, *CWMG* [III, 15], vol. XXV, p. 6.
17. Dwarkadas, *Ruttie,* p. 27.
18. Ibid., pp. 27–28.
19. Ibid., pp. 29–30. The next quote is on p. 30.
20. April 7, 1925, ibid., pp. 31–32.
21. April 12, 1925, ibid., pp. 33–35.
22. June 5, 1925, ibid., p. 38.

23. Ibid., p. 41.

24. December 19, 1925, Qureshi, *Every Day*, p. 394. ". . . Plain Mr. Jinnah" is the title of vol. I of selections from *Shamsul Hasan Collection* by Syed Shamsul Hasan, secretary to the Muslim League (Karachi: Royal Book Company, 1976).

25. Dwarkadas, *Ruttie*, p. 43.

26. Ibid., pp. 45–46.

27. Hasan, *Collection*, p. 83.

28. Only Clement Attlee, one of the two Labour members on the commission, attained great distinction.

29. Second Earl of Birkenhead, *F. E. The Life of F. E. Smith, First Earl of Birkenhead* (London: Eyre & Spottiswoode, 1960), p. 514.

30. July 4, 1927, National Archives of Pakistan, F/15, 20.

31. Pirzada, *Foundations*, vol. II, p. 114.

32. Ibid., p. 127.

CHAPTER 8: CALCUTTA (1928)

1. Chagla, *Roses in December*, p. 94.

2. *Young India*, February 2, 1918, *CWMG* [III, 15], vol. XXXVI, p. 15.

3. Birkenhead to Irwin, January 19, 1928, Second Earl of Birkenhead, *F. E. Smith*, p. 515.

4. Ibid., p. 516.

5. Report of the Committee, *All Parties Conference, 1928* (Allahabad: All-India Congress Committee, 1928), p. 21.

6. Nehru to Gandhi, February 23, 1928, *CWMG* [III, 15], vol. XXXVI, p. 58.

7. The proposals are in Jinnah's pamphlet, "History of the Origin of 'Fourteen Points,'" in Ahmad Saeed, *Writings of the Quaid-E-Azam* (Lahore: Progressive Books, n.d.), pp. 48–49.

8. Ibid., p. 54.

9. Irwin to Birkenhead, March 15, 1928, IOL, MSS EUR C 152/29, in Waheed Ahmad, *Jinnah-Irwin Correspondence (1927–1930)* (Lahore: Research Society of Pakistan: 1969), p. 9.

10. Second Earl of Birkenhead, *F. E. Smith*, p. 519.

11. Ruttie's letter was written on Taj stationery, 30–3–28, National Archives of Pakistan, 29.

12. Saiyid, *Jinnah*, pp. 400–2.

13. Lal, "Quaid-i-Azam," p. 172.

14. Ibid.

15. Ibid.

16. Chagla, *Roses in December*, p. 95.

17. Ibid., p. 96.

18. *All Parties Conference*, p. 42.

19. Press conference, October 26, 1918, in Qureshi, *Every Day*, p. 337.

20. Saiyid, *Jinnah*, p. 413.

21. Motilal Nehru to Jinnah, October 28, 1928, National Archives of Pakistan F/15.

22. Jinnah to Motilal Nehru, November 2, 1928, Pirzada, *Quaid-e-Azam*, p. 289.

23. Mohammed Ayoob Khuhro, "My Personal Contacts and Impression About Quaid-i-Azam Mr. M. A. Jinnah," *Papers* [IV, 1], vol. V, p. 36.

24. Motilal Nehru's "Confidential Note" in M. R. Jayakar Papers, File No. 442, *All Parties Conference, 1928*, pp. 238–39.

25. Calcutta, December 26–30, 1928, Pirzada, *Foundations*, vol. II, p. 139.

26. Chagla, *Roses in December,* p. 96.
27. Saiyid, *Jinnah,* p. 419.
28. Ibid., pp. 426–27.
29. Saiyid, *Jinnah,* pp. 428–29.
30. Ibid., pp. 432–35.

CHAPTER 9: SIMLA (1929–1930)

1. Aga Kahn, *Memoirs* [II, 26], p. 221.
2. Ibid., p. 222.
3. Dwarkadas, *Ruttie,* p. 56.
4. Lal, "Quaid-i-Azam," pp. 172–73.
5. Dwarkadas, *Ruttie,* p. 57.
6. Ibid., p. 58.
7. Chagla, *Roses in December,* p. 121.
8. March 12, 1929, Qureshi, *Every Day,* pp. 85–86.
9. Hasan, *Collection,* p. 48.
10. Though originally fifteen in number, the last two points were merged in order to limit the number to that which echoed President Wilson's famous "Fourteen Points."
11. Hasan, *Collection,* p. 48.
12. Saiyid, *Jinnah,* pp. 437–38.
13. Hasan, *Collection,* pp. 48–49.
14. Irwin to Dawson, May 20, 1929, Ahmad, *Correspondence,* p. 13.
15. Panikkar and Pershad, *Voice of Freedom,* p. 62n18.
16. Ibid., p. 54n11.
17. Saiyid, *Jinnah,* pp. 450–51.
18. Ibid., p. 453. The following quotes are from ibid., pp. 456–59.
19. Irwin's report quoted in Second Earl of Birkenhead, *F. E. Smith,* p. 522.
20. Ibid., p. 523.
21. MacDonald to Jinnah, August 14, 1929, National Archives of Pakistan, F 15/5.
22. Jinnah to MacDonald, September 7, 1929, National Archives of Pakistan, F 15/7.
23. Irwin to Jinnah, October 1929, National Archives of Pakistan, 15/15-17. The following quote is ibid., p. 18.
24. Saiyid, *Jinnah,* p. 465.
25. Gandhi to Nehru, November 8, 1929, *CWMG* [III, 15], vol. XLII, p. 116.
26. Minutes of that meeting taken by Sir George Cunningham, Irwin's private secretary, were mailed to Jinnah on December 27, 1929 (National Archives of Pakistan, F/15, 53–9, from which all quotes of the meeting are taken). The bomb that rocked the viceroy's train was planted and ignited by the revolutionary Yashpal (1903–76), a leader of the Hindustan Socialist Republican Army, whose autobiography, edited and translated by Corinne Friend, was recently published as *Yashpal Looks Back* (Delhi: Vikas Publishing House, 1981).
27. National Archives of Pakistan, F/15, 54.
28. Ibid., F/15, 55–56.
29. Ibid., p. 57.
30. Ibid., F/15, 58–59.
31. Sitaramayya, *Indian National Congress,* vol. I, p. 363.
32. Saiyid, *Jinnah,* p. 469.
33. Sapru to Jinnah, January 5, 1930, National Archives of Pakistan, F/15, 47.
34. May 20, 1930, Ahmad, *Correspondence,* pp. 38–39.

35. Gandhi to Irwin, May 18, 1930, *CWMG* [III, 15], vol. XLIII, pp. 411–16.

36. Ibid., p. 416.

37. Jinnah to Irwin, June 24, 1930, Ahmad, *Correspondence*, p. 41–42.

38. July 23, 1930, *CWMG* [III, 15], vol. XLIV, pp. 42–43.

39. Ibid., p. 44.

40. Jinnah to Irwin, August 6, 1930, Ahmad, *Correspondence*, pp. 43–44.

41. *CWMG* [III, 15], vol. XLIV, p. 81.

42. Jinnah to Irwin, August 19, 1930, Ahmad, *Correspondence*, pp. 46–47.

43. Appen, III, *CWMG* [III, 15], vol. XLIV, pp. 470–71.

44. Jinnah to Irwin, September 9, 1930, Ahmad, *Correspondence*, p. 51.

CHAPTER 10: LONDON (1930–1933)

1. The *Times* (London), Thursday, November 13, 1930, p. 14.

2. Hailey to Irwin, November 14, 1930, Indian Office Library, London, MSS EUR E. 220–34.

3. R. J. Moore, *The Crisis of Indian Unity, 1917–1940* (Delhi: Oxford University Press, 1974), p. 126.

4. Aga Khan, *Memoirs* [II, 26], p. 228.

5. *Indian Round Table Conference, 12 November 1930–19 January 1931: Proceedings* (Cmd. 3778) (London: His Majesty's Stationery Office, 1931), p. 32.

6. Wrench, *Immortal Years*, p. 133.

7. *Round Table* [X, 5], p. 146.

8. Ibid., p. 147.

9. Ibid., p. 149.

10. *Round Table* [5] November 21, 1930, p. 182.

11. Hailey to Irwin, December 13, 1930, India Office Library, London, MSS EUR E. 220–34.

12. Hailey to Irwin, December 15, 1930, ibid.

13. MacDonald to Bennett, December 23, 1930, "India Round Table Conference, 1930," *MacDonald Papers*, Public Record Office, Kew, 30/69/1/578 II.

14. Pirzada, *Foundations*, vol. II, p. 159.

15. *MacDonald Papers*, Public Record Office [X, 13].

16. Kanji Dwarkadas, *India's Fight for Freedom, 1913–1937* (Bombay: Popular Prakashan: 1966), p. 385.

17. Ziauddin Ahmad, ed., *Mohammad Ali Jinnah: Founder of Pakistan* (Karachi: Ministry of Information & Broadcasting, Government of Pakistan, 1976), p. 89.

18. *Round Table* [5], January 19, 1931, p. 512.

19. Simon to Dube, National Archives of Pakistan, February 26, 1931, F/15, 92.

20. Bolitho, *Jinnah*, p. 101.

21. E. C. Mieville, Willingdon's private secretary, to Jinnah, March 17, 1931, National Archives of Pakistan, F/15, 109.

22. Sir A. P. Patro to Jinnah, March 19, 1931, ibid., p. 110.

23. MacDonald to Jinnah, June 18, 1931, ibid., p. 141.

24. Henderson to Jinnah, May 5, 1931, ibid., p. 135.

25. Raza, "The Charisma of Quaid-i-Azam" in *Papers* [IV, 1], vol. V, p. 209.

26. Haroon to Jinnah, March 24, 1931, National Archives of Pakistan. F/15, 115–16.

27. Patro to Jinnah, March 19, 1931, ibid., p. 112.

28. Gandhi to Willingdon, August 27, 1931, *CWMG* [III, 15], vol. XLVII, p. 365.

29. Ibid., p. 366n1.

30. Willingdon to "My dear Prime Minister," May 29, 1931, *MacDonald Papers,* Public Record Office, Kew 30/69/1/578 II.

31. Rushbrook-Williams, "Evolution," vol. I, p. 121.

32. "Statement of Mr. M. A. Jinnah on the Prime Minister's Declaration," National Archives of Pakistan, F/15, 163.

33. *Round Table* [5], p. 359.

34. Ibid., p. 361.

35. Ibid., p. 368.

36. Ibid., p. 390–98.

37. Aga Khan to Jinnah, March 29, 1931, National Archives of Pakistan, F/15, 117.

38. Durga Das, *India, From Curzon to Nehru and After* (London: Collins, 1969), p. 155.

39. *Round Table* [5], p. 416.

40. National Archives of Pakistan, F/15, 163–64.

41. Chagla, *Roses in December,* p. 103.

42. Das, *India,* p. 154.

43. Begum Liaquat Ali Khan in an interview in Karachi, February 1980, at her home.

44. Bolitho, *Jinnah,* p. 102.

45. K. K. Aziz, ed., *Complete Works of Rahmat Ali* (Islamabad: National Comission on Historical and Cultural Research, 1978), vol. I, p. 4.

46. Ibid., p. 10.

47. Sir Michael O'Dwyer, June 15, 1933, to the Joint Committee on Indian Constitutional Reforms (sess. 1932–33), *Minutes of Evidence* (London: His Majesty's Stationery Office, 1934), vol. IIA, pp. 74–75.

48. Ibid., vol. IIC, p. 1496, q. 9598. Following quotes are from ibid., q. 9599–600.

49. National Archives of Pakistan, F/17.

50. Jinnah to Choudhury, March 30, 1933, Allana, *Pakistan Movement,* pp. 91–92.

CHAPTER 11: LONDON-LUCKNOW (1934–1937)

1. Hasan, *Collection,* p. 55.

2. Pirzada, *Foundations,* vol. II, p. 226.

3. Ibid., p. 233.

4. Joint Committee on Indian Constitutional Reforms (sess. 1933–34), *Report* (Cmd. 4268), vol. I, pt. 1 (London: His Majesty's Stationery Office, 1934), p. 320.

5. Muslims were promised one-third of the Central Legislative Assembly seats and the following provincial legislative allocations: *Assam,* 34 out of a total of 108 seats; *Bengal,* 119 out of 250; *Bihar,* 42 out of 175; *Bombay,* 30 out of 175; *CP,* 14 out of 112; *Madras,* 29 out of 210; *NWFP,* 38 out of 50; *Punjab,* 86 out of 175; *Sind,* 34 out of 60; and *UP,* 66 out of 228.

6. Pirzada, *Foundations,* vol. II, p. 233.

7. Hasan, *Collection,* p. 60.

8. Speech of February 7, 1935, in Jamil-ud-din Ahmad, ed., *Some Recent Speeches and Writings of Mr. Jinnah* (Lahore: Ashraf, 1952), vol. I, p. 9.

9. Ibid., pp. 4–6.

10. Chagla, *Roses in December,* p. 103.

11. Winston Churchill, February 11, 1935, in the House of Commons, Philips, *Evolution*, p. 316.

12. Saiyid, *Jinnah*, p. 529.

13. Ahmad, *Recent Speeches*, vol. I, pp. 12–15.

14. Ibid., p. 19.

15. Waheed Ahmad, ed., *Diary and Notes of Mian Fazl-I-Husain* (Lahore: Research Society of Pakistan, 1977), p. 201.

16. Pirzada, *Foundations*, vol. II, p. 258.

17. Ibid., p. 262.

18. Nehru to Subhas C. Bose, March 26, 1936, S. Gopal, ed., *Selected Works of Jawaharlal Nehru* (New Delhi: Orient Longmans, Ltd., 1973), vol. VII, p. 407.

19. John Glendevon, *The Viceroy at Bay: Lord Linlithgow in India, 1936–1943* (London: Collins, 1971), p. 23. The following quote is in ibid., p. 25.

20. "All India Muslim League, Central Board, Policy and Programme," in Ahmad Saeed, *Writings of the Quaid-e-Azam* (Lahore: Progressive Books, n.d.), p. 66.

21. Hasan, *Collection*, p. 65.

22. M. A. H. Ispahani, *Quaid-e-Azam Jinnah As I Know Him*, 2d. ed. (Karachi: Forward Publications Trust, 1966), p. 1.

23. Ispahani to Jinnah, August 9, 1936, Z. H. Zaidi, ed., *M. A. Jinnah–Ispahani Correspondence, 1936–1948* (Karachi: Forward Publishing Trust, 1976), p. 76.

24. Saeed, *Quaid-e-Azam*, pp. 80–81.

25. Aziz, *Rahmat Ali*, pp. 23–25.

26. Nehru at Ambala, January 1937, Gopal, *Nehru*, vol. VIII, pp. 7–8.

27. Jinnah in Calcutta, January 1937, quoted by S. R. Mehrotra, "The Congress and the Partition of India," in *Partition*, ed. Philips and Wainwright, p. 194.

28. Gopal, *Nehru*, vol. VIII, p. 119.

29. Ibid., p. 121.

30. Ibid., p. 8.

31. Das, *India*, pp. 181–82.

32. Nehru, March 22, 1937, quoted by Z. H. Zaidi, "Aspects of the Development of Muslim League Policy, 1937–47," in *Partition*, ed. Philips and Wainwright, p. 256.

33. Dwarkadas, *India's Fight*, p. 467.

34. Das, *India*, p. 182.

35. Choudry Khaliquzzaman, *Pathway to Pakistan* (Lahore: Pakistan Longmans, 1961), p. 161.

36. Dwarkadas, *India's Fight*, pp. 466–67. The following quote is ibid.

37. Gandhi to Jinnah, May 22, 1937, *CWMG* [III, 15], vol. LXV, p. 231.

38. Interview with Mr. Ispahani in his London home, summer of 1978.

39. Muhammad Yusuf Saraf, "Quaid-i-Azam in Kashmir," *Papers* [IV, 1], vol. I, p. 84.

40. Ahmad, *Glimpses*, p. 11.

41. Khaliquzzaman, *Pathway*, p. 170.

42. Pirzada, *Foundations*, vol. II, pp. 265–73.

CHAPTER 12: TOWARD LAHORE (1938–1940)

1. Resolution II, adopted October 17, 1937 at Lucknow, Pirzada, *Foundations*, vol. II, p. 274.

2. Resolution VI, ibid., p. 278. On November 1, 1937, Congress's Working Committee explained its position on *Bande Mataram,* stating:
This song appears in Bankim Chandra Chatterji's novel "Anandamatha", but it . . . was written independently of, and long before the novel, and was subsequently . . . set to music by Rabindranath Tagore in 1896. The song and the words "Bande Mataram" were considered seditious by the British Government. . . . At a famous session of the Bengal Provincial Conference held in Barisal in April 1906 . . . a brutal lathi charge was made by the police on the delegates and volunteers and the "Bande Mataram" badges worn by them were violently torn off. . . . The words "Bande Mataram" became a slogan of power which inspired our people, and a greeting which ever remind us of our struggle for national freedom.
Reprinted in *Muslims Under Congress Rule, 1937–1939: A Documentary Record,* ed. K. K. Aziz (Islamabad: National Commission on Historical and Cultural Research, 1978), vol. I, p. 120.

3. Resolution XIV, Lucknow League, Pirzada, *Foundations,* vol. II, p. 280.

4. Mukhtar Zaman, *Students' Role in the Pakistan Movement* (Karachi: Quaid-i-Azam Academy, 1978), p. 25.

5. Ibid., p. 29.

6. February 5, 1938, Ahmad, *Recent Speeches,* vol. I, p. 42.

7. Ibid., pp. 43–45.

8. Nehru to Jinnah, January 18, 1939, quoted in Kailash Chandra, *Tragedy of Jinnah* (Lahore: Varma Publishing Company, 1943), p. 140.

9. Jinnah to Nehru, January 25, 1938, ibid., p. 141.

10. Nehru to Jinnah, February 4, 1938, ibid., pp. 146–47.

11. Jinnah to Nehru, February 17, 1938, ibid., p. 149.

12. Gandhi to Jinnah, February 24, 1939, Saiyid, *Jinnah,* p. 586.

13. Jinnah to Gandhi, March 3, 1938, ibid., pp. 586–87.

14. Jinnah to Ispahani, April 12, 1938, Zaidi, *Correspondence,* p. 106.

15. National Archives of Pakistan, F/77, quoted by Z. H. Zaidi, "M. A. Jinnah—The Man," *Papers* [IV, 1], vol. III, p. 45.

16. Pirzada, *Foundations,* vol. II, p. 292.

17. Ibid., pp. 293–95.

18. Gandhi to Nehru, April 30, 1938, ibid., p. 56.

19. Jinnah presided over the Working Committee, whose first twenty-two members were his personal choices in mid-1938: Liaquat Ali Khan, who served as secretary; Haji Abdullah Haroon of Sind; Maulana Shaukat Ali of UP; Abdul Majid Sindhi of Sind; Malik Barkat Ali of Punjab; Sir Currimbhai Ibrahim of Bombay; Choudhry Khaliquzzaman of UP; Abdul Matin Choudhari of Assam; Sayed Abdul Rauf Shah of CP; Sardar Aurangeb Khan of NWFP; Sir Sikander Hyat Khan of Punjab; Nawab Mohammad Ismail Khan of UP; Haji Abdul Sattar Seth of Madras; Sir A. M. K. Dehlavi of Bombay; Fazlul Haq of Bengal; Sir Nazimuddin of Bengal; Sayed Abdul Aziz of Bihar; K. B. Sadullah of NWFP; Raja Amir Ahmad Khan of UP; Abdul Rahman Siddique of Bengal; and Mohammad Ashiq Warsi of Bihar.

20. R. J. Moore, *Churchill, Cripps, and India, 1939–1945* (Oxford: Clarendon Press, 1979), p. 4.

21. June 29, 1938, ibid., p. 29.

22. Second Marquess of Zetland, *"Essayez," The Memoirs of Lawrence, Second Marquess of Zetland* (London: John Murray, 1956), p. 247. National Archives of Pakistan, F/1095 confirms the appointment with Mr. Jinnah at the vice-regal lodge in Simla on Tuesday, August 16, 1938, at 6:30 P.M.

23. Zetland, *"Essayez."*

24. Legislative Assembly, August 23, 1938, Ahmad, *Recent Speeches*, vol. I, pp. 56–57.
25. Karachi, October 8, 1938, Aziz, *Muslims*, pp. 161–62 (italics added).
26. Saiyid, *Jinnah*, pp. 623–24 (italics added).
27. Ibid., p. 624.
28. "English Translation of Original Address of Welcome," October 9, 1938, from the Urdu, National Archives of Pakistan, F/160, 339–40.
29. Karachi, October 13, 1938, ibid., pp. 238–40.
30. Ali to Jinnah, October 14, 1938, ibid., p. 216.
31. Mehdi, *Report*, pp. 1–2.
32. Pirzada, *Foundations*, vol. II, pp. 304–6.
33. Ibid., p. 324.
34. Ibid., p. 317.
35. Ibid.
36. Khurshid Ara Begum Nawab Siddiq Ali Khan, "Women and Independence," in *Quaid-i-Azam and Muslim Women* (Karachi: National Book Foundation, 1976), p. 55.
37. Pirzada, *Foundations*, vol. II, p. 319.
38. Gandhi to Mirabehn, January 16, 1939, *CWMG* [III, 15], vol. LXVIII, p. 303.
39. Aziz, *Muslims*, p. 403.
40. Ibid., append., p. 565.
41. Associated Chambers of Commerce of India, annual meeting in Calcutta, December 19, 1938, Marquess of Linlithgow, *Speeches and Statements* (New Delhi: Bureau of Public Information, 1945), p. 152.
42. Ahmad, *Recent Speeches*, vol. I, pp. 90–93.
43. Ibid., p. 94.
44. May 30, 1939, Little Gibbs Road, Bombay, National Archives of Pakistan, F/76, 2.
45. Ibid., p. 3.
46. Glendevon, *Linlithgow*, pp. 136–37.
47. Ibid., p. 138.
48. Ibid., p. 136.
49. All three drafts are in Gopal, *Nehru*, vol. X, pp. 122–38.
50. Ibid., pp. 124–29.
51. Linlithgow to Zetland, September 18, 1939, Moore, *Churchill*, pp. 18–19.
52. September 24, 1939, *CWMG* [III, 15], vol. LXX, p. 197.
53. September 25, 1939, ibid., pp. 205–6.
54. Glendevon, *Linlithgow*, p. 142.
55. Nehru to V. K. Krishna Menon, September 26, 1939, Gopal, *Nehru*, vol. X, pp. 163–64.
56. Glendevon, *Linlithgow*, p. 150.
57. Sarvepalli Gopal, *Jawaharlal Nehru*, vol. I (Cambridge, Mass: Harvard University Press, 1976), p. 253.
58. Gopal, *Nehru*, vol. X, p. 185.
59. October 18, 1939, *CWMG* [III, 15], vol. LXX, pp. 267–68.
60. Append. III, ibid., pp. 419–20.
61. Rangaswami Parthasarathy, *A Hundred Years of The Hindu* (Madras: Kasturi & Sons, Ltd., n.d.), p. 512.
62. October 30, 1939, *CWMG* [III, 15], vol. LXX, pp. 318–19.
63. November 4, 1939, ibid., p. 328.
64. Gopal, *Nehru*, vol. X, p. 226.
65. November 7, 1939, *CWMG* [III, 15], vol. LXX, p. 335.

66. Ahmad, *Recent Speeches*, vol. I, p. 105.

67. John Morley, *On Compromise* (London: Macmillan & Co., 1921), p. 56.

68. Ahmad, *Recent Speeches*, vol. I, p. 110.

69. Ibid., pp. 110–11.

70. December 8, 1939, *CWMG* [III, 15], vol. LXXI, p. 16.

71. Nehru to Jinnah, December 9, 1939, Pirzada, *Quaid-e-Azam*, p. 271.

72. *Bombay Sentinel*, December 9, 1939, quoted by M. A. H. Ispahani, "Non-Muslim Reaction" in *Reminiscences of The Day of Deliverance* (Islmabad: National Committee for Birth Centenary Celebrations of Quaid-i-Azam Mohammad Ali Jinnah, 1976), p. 13.

73. Ispahani to Jinnah, December 12, 1939, Zaidi, *Correspondence*, pp. 132–33.

74. Ahmad, *Recent Speeches*, vol. I, p. 112. The next six quotes are all from ibid., pp. 113–17.

75. Gandhi to Nehru, December 28, 1939, *CWMG* [III, 15], vol. LXXI, p. 65.

76. Moore, *Churchill*, p. 9. The following quote is from ibid., p. 13.

77. Glendevon, *Linlithgow*, p. 160.

78. January 10, 1940, append. II, *CWMG* [III, 15], vol. LXXI, pp. 433–35.

79. "Constitutional Maladies of India," in Gopal, *Nehru*, vol. I, pp. 128*ff*.

80. Jinnah, "My Brother."

81. Glendevon, *Linlithgow*, p. 194.

82. M. M. Shafi, "The Historic League Session," in Ahmad. *Quaid-i-Azam*, pp. 124–25.

83. Ibid., p. 125.

84. Ibid., p. 126.

85. Bolitho, *Jinnah*, p. 128.

86. Pirzada, *Foundations*, vol. II, p. 327.

87. Ibid., pp. 327–30.

88. Ibid., pp. 332–33.

89. February 27, 1940, Gopal, *Nehru*, vol. X, pp. 337–38.

90. Pirzada, *Foundations*, vol. II, pp. 335–37. All of the following quotes, till the end of this chapter are from ibid., pp. 337–39.

CHAPTER 13: LAHORE TO DELHI (1940–1942)

1. Pirzada, *Foundations*, vol. II, p. 340.

2. Ibid., p. 341.

3. Glendevon, *Linlithgow*, p. 167.

4. April 1, 1940, *CWMG* [III, 15], vol. LXXI, pp. 387–88.

5. Parthasarathy, *The Hindu*, p. 533.

6. Nehru to Krishna Menon, April 12, 1940, Gopal, *Nehru*, vol. XI, p. 16.

7. Maulana Abul Kalam Azad, *India Wins Freedom* (New York: Longmans, Green & Co., 1960), p. 38.

8. Ahmad, *Recent Speeches*, vol. I, p. 182.

9. Linlithgow to Jinnah, April 19, 1940, Pirzada, *Quaid-e-Azam*, p. 201.

10. Parthasarathy, *The Hindu*, p. 534.

11. May 26, 1940, *CWMG* [III, 15], vol. LXXII, pp. 100–101.

12. Pirzada, *Quaid-e-Azam*, p. 202.

13. Ibid., p. 203.

14. Jinnah to Laithwaite, Simla, July 1, 1940, ibid., p. 204. The following quote is from ibid., pp. 205–6.

15. July 2, 1940, *CWMG* [III, 15], vol. LXXII, pp. 229–31.

16. Tej Bahadur Sapru et al., *Constitutional Proposals of the Sapru Committee* (Bombay: Padmar Publications, 1945), September 2, 1940, p. 47.

17. Glendevon, *Linlithgow,* p. 184. The following quotes are from ibid.

18. October 24, 1940, Gopal, *Nehru,* vol. XI, p. 193n3.

19. Kanji Dwarkadas, *Ten Years To Freedom* (Bombay: Popular Prakashan, 1968), p. 55.

20. Ahmad, *Recent Speeches,* vol. I, p. 204.

21. Ibid., p. 205.

22. Shah Nawaz Khan, "What is Pakistan?," National Archives of Pakistan, F/1099, pp. 18*ff.*

23. Jinnah, "My Brother."

24. Pirzada, *Foundations,* vol. II., p. 359.

25. Ibid., pp. 360–61.

26. Ibid., pp. 368–70.

27. Ibid., p. 371.

28. Jinnah, "My Brother."

29. Lumley to Jinnah, July 20, 1941, Pirzada, *Quaid-e-Azam,* pp. 215–16.

30. September 8, 1941, Zaidi, *Correspondence,* append. III, pp. 650–51.

31. Ahmad, *Recent Speeches,* vol. I, p. 341.

32. November 13, 1941, Glendevon, *Linlithgow,* p. 210.

33. December 2, 1941, ibid., p. 212.

34. December 26, 1941, Ahmad, *Recent Speeches,* vol. I, p. 348.

35. Ispahani to Jinnah, December 8, 1941, Zaidi, *Correspondence,* p. 222.

36. December 26, 1941, Ahmad, *Recent Speeches,* vol. I, p. 364.

37. Lumley to Linlithgow, January 15, 1942, Nicholas Mansergh, ed., *The Transfer of Power, 1942–7* (London: Her Majesty's Stationery Office, 1970), vol. I, pp. 25–26.

38. January 21, 1942, ibid., p. 48.

39. January 24, 1942, ibid., p. 75.

40. Ahmad, *Recent Speeches,* vol. I, p. 368.

41. February 15, 1942, ibid., pp. 370–71.

42. February 21, 1942, Mansergh, *Transfer of Power,* vol. I, p. 218.

43. Note by Major General Lockhart, India Office, February 25, 1942, ibid., pp. 238–39.

44. Ibid., p. 240.

45. Quoted by "Former Naval Person" (Churchill) to Roosevelt, March 4, 1942, ibid., p. 310.

46. March 10, 1942, ibid., p. 395.

47. Ibid., pp. 406–7.

48. March 23, 1942, Ahmad, *Recent Speeches,* vol. I, p. 400. The following quote is ibid., pp. 401–2.

49. Ibid., pp. 401–2.

50. March 25, 1942, Mansergh, *Transfer of Power,* vol. I, p. 479.

51. Ibid., pp. 480–81.

52. Ibid., p. 484.

53. March 27, 1942, ibid., p. 500.

54. Ibid., p. 530.

55. A. D. K. Owen's statement, quoted in Moore, *Churchill,* p. 82.

56. "And the end of the fight is a tombstone white,
          with the name of the late deceased,
    And the epitaph drear: 'A fool lies here
          who tried to hustle the East."
                                    Rudyard Kipling

57. March 19, 1942, Mansergh, *Transfer of Power*, vol. I, p. 445.
58. Bajpai to Linlithgow, April 2, 1942, ibid., p. 619.
59. April 3–6, 1942, Pirzada, *Foundations*, vol. II, pp. 383–84.
60. April 9, 1942, Mansergh, *Transfer of Power*, vol. I, p. 704.
61. April 10, 1942, ibid., pp. 729–30.
62. April 13, 1942, Ahmad, *Recent Speeches*, vol. I, pp. 415–19.
63. April 10, 1942, Mansergh, *Transfer of Power*, vol. I, p. 733.
64. Roosevelt to Hopkins, for Churchill, April 11, 1942, Moore, *Churchill,*
p. 130.
65. April 11, 1942, Mansergh, *Transfer of Power*, vol. I, pp. 748–50.

CHAPTER 14: DAWN IN DELHI (1942–1943)

1. April 11, 1942, Mansergh, *Transfer of Power*, vol. I, pp. 757–58.
2. Glancy to Linlithgow, April 14, 1942, ibid., pp. 772–73.
3. April 16, 1942, ibid., pp. 789–90.
4. Ibid., p. 815.
5. Ibid., p. 842.
6. April 24, 1942, *CWMG* [III, 15], vol. LXXVI, pp. 63–65.
7. June 6, 1942, ibid., p. 187.
8. Ibid., p. 197.
9. June 11, 1942, ibid., p. 213.
10. Ahmad, *Recent Speeches*, vol. I, pp. 422–24.
11. All-India Congress Committee, August 7, 1942, *CWMG* [III, 15], vol.
LXXVI, pp. 377–81.
12. Ibid.
13. Glancy to Linlithgow, July 17, 1942, Mansergh, *Transfer of Power*, vol.
II, p. 404.
14. August 8, 1942, *CWMG* [III, 15], vol. LXXVI, p. 382.
15. July 1942, Ahmad, *Recent Speeches*, vol. I, pp. 432–33.
16. August 8, 1942, *CWMG* [III, 15], vol. LXXVI, pp. 391–92.
17. Ibid., p. 403.
18. Pirzada, *Foundations*, vol. II, pp. 395–96.
19. Linlithgow to Amery, August 12, 1942, Mansergh, *Transfer of Power*,
vol. II, p. 669.
20. Ibid., p. 708.
21. Linlithgow to Amery, August 15, 1942, ibid., pp. 708–9.
22. August 17, 1942, ibid., pp. 740–41.
23. Aiyar to Linlithgow, August 19, 1942, ibid., p. 749.
24. August 24, 1942, ibid., pp. 810–11.
25. Halifax to Eden, August 28, 1942, ibid., p. 839.
26. Linlithgow to Churchill, August 31, 1942, ibid., pp. 853–54.
27. September 1, 1942, ibid., p. 877.
28. Ibid., pp. 874–75.
29. September 5, 1942, ibid., p. 908.
30. September 13, 1942, Ahmad, *Recent Speeches*, vol. I, pp. 449*ff*.
31. Halifax to Eden, September 16, 1942, Mansergh, *Transfer of Power*, vol.
II, p. 970.
32. Churchill to Amery, in Enclosure No. 2 from Sir A. R. Mudaliar to Sir
G. Laithwaite, September 21, 1942, ibid., vol. III, p. 3.
33. Churchill to Linlithgow, September 24, 1942, ibid., p. 37.
34. Append. A to No. 153, October 21, 1942, ibid., pp. 213–15.
35. November 9, 1942, Ahmad, *Recent Speeches*, vol. I, p. 464.

36. November 13, 1942, Mansergh, *Transfer of Power,* vol. III, p. 243.
37. Linlithgow to Amery, November 16, 1942, ibid., p. 266.
38. Annex to No. 187, "Report by a Reliable Informant," ibid., pp. 268–70.
39. Amery to Linlithgow, November 17, 1942, ibid., pp. 278–79.
40. Ispahani to Jinnah, December 17 and 26, 1942, Zaidi, *Correspondence,* pp. 313–14.
41. Gandhi to Linlithgow, January 29, 1943, *CWMG* [III, 15], vol. LXXVII, pp. 55–56.
42. Linlithgow to Amery, February 2, 1943, Mansergh, *Transfer of Power,* vol. III, p. 570.
43. Amery to Linlithgow, February 8, 1943, ibid., p. 617.
44. Ibid., pp. 631–32.
45. Gandhi to Sir Richard Tottenham, February 8, 1943, *CWMG* [III, 15], vol. LXXVII, p. 61.
46. Linlithgow to Amery, February 15, 1943, Mansergh, *Transfer of Power,* vol. III, pp. 667–68.
47. February 16, 1943, ibid., p. 670.
48. *Times of India,* February 16, 1943, ibid.
49. Linlithgow to Amery, February 17, 1943, ibid., p. 683.
50. February 18, 1943, ibid., pp. 684–85.
51. *CWMG* [III, 15], vol. LXXVII, p. 69n1.
52. Churchill to Linlithgow, February 25, 1943, Mansergh, *Transfer of Power,* vol. III, p. 730.
53. Lumley to Linlithgow, March 4, 1943, ibid., p. 760.
54. Haq to Jinnah, February 5, 1943, Pirzada, *Quaid-e-Azam,* pp. 79–80.
55. Jinnah to Haq, February 10, 1943, ibid., p. 81.
56. Ispahani's note of their telephone conversation, March 17, 1943, Zaidi, *Correspondence,* p. 328.
57. Ispahani to Jinnah, March 26, 1943, ibid., p. 334.
58. Ibid.
59. Pirzada, *Foundations,* vol. II, p. 399.
60. Ibid., p. 407.
61. Ibid., p. 420.
62. "Strictly Secret Note" on the proceedings at Delhi, April 24–6, 1943, Mansergh, *Transfer of Power,* vol. III, pp. 918–20.
63. Ibid., p. 922.
64. Pirzada, *Foundations,* vol. II, p. 422.

CHAPTER 15: KARACHI AND BOMBAY REVISITED (1943–1944)

1. Gandhi to Jinnah, May 4, 1943, *CWMG* [III, 15], vol. LXXVII, p. 75.
2. Linlithgow to Amery, May 8, 1943, Mansergh, *Transfer of Power,* vol. III, p. 953.
3. Amery to Linlithgow, May 9, 1943, ibid., p. 955.
4. Amery to Linlithgow, May 19, 1943, ibid., p. 996.
5. Amery to Linlithgow, May 24, 1943, ibid., p. 1004.
6. Glancy to Linlithgow, May 29, 1943, ibid., pp. 1025–26.
7. Linlithgow to Amery, June 6, 1943, ibid., p. 1045.
8. June 10, 1943, ibid., p. 1053.
9. Lord Linlithgow's marginal note in ibid., vol. IV, p. 36.
10. Penderel Moon, ed., *Wavell: Tthe Viceroy's Journal* (Karachi: Oxford University Press, 1974), p. 11.
11. Ibid., p. 12.

12. Ibid., p. 23.

13. July 3, 1943, Ahmad, *Recent Speeches,* vol. I, p. 567. The following quote is from ibid., p. 568.

14. Ibid., pp. 570–71.

15. Herbert to Linlithgow, July 5, 1943, Mansergh, *Transfer of Power,* vol. IV, pp. 44–45.

16. A. A. Peerbhoy, *Jinnah Faces An Assassin* (Bombay: Thacker & Co., 1943), trial transcript, pp. 60–61.

17. Ibid., p. 77.

18. Jinnah to Ispahani, August 3, 1943, Zaidi, *Correspondence,* p. 365.

19. July 26, 1943, Qureshi, *Every Day,* p. 223.

20. September 15, 1943, Mansergh, *Transfer of Power,* vol. IV, p. 260. The following quote is from ibid., p. 261.

21. Glancy to Linlithgow, September 16, 1943, ibid., p. 269.

22. Ispahani to Jinnah, September 8, 1943, Zaidi, *Correspondence,* pp. 372–73.

23. October 31, 1943, Ahmad, *Recent Speeches,* vol. II, p. 3.

24. November 15, 1943, ibid., p. 4.

25. November 8, 1943, ibid., pp. 6–10.

26. Pirzada, *Foundations,* vol. II, p. 461.

27. Ibid., pp. 450–51.

28. Ibid., p. 466.

29. Jinnah, "My Brother."

30. Jinnah to Abdul Aziz, January 2, 1944, *Syed Shamsul Hasan Collection,* Karachi, Madras, vol. I. Hereafter cited as *Hasan Collection.*

31. February 2, 1944, Ahmad, *Recent Speeches,* vol. II, pp. 52–53.

32. March 4, 1944, ibid., pp. 71–72.

33. Twynam to Wavell, April 9, 1944, Mansergh, *Transfer of Power,* vol. IV, p. 873.

34. Mudie to Jenkins, April 14, 1944, ibid., p. 879.

35. Moon, *Wavell,* p. 63.

36. Wavell to Amery, April 16, 1944, Mansergh, *Transfer of Power,* vol. IV, p. 883.

37. May 5, 1944, ibid., p. 952.

38. Amery to Wavell, May 11, 1944, ibid., p. 965.

39. Wavell to Amery, May 1, 1944, ibid., p. 941.

40. June 12, 1944, ibid., pp. 1022–23.

41. June 20, 1944, ibid., p. 1035. The following quote is from ibid.

42. Moon, *Wavell,* p. 81.

43. Hallett to Wavell, June 29, 1944, Mansergh, *Transfer of Power,* vol. IV, p. 1058.

44. Moon, *Wavell,* p. 73.

45. April 8, 1944, Ahmad, *Recent Speeches,* vol. II, p. 128.

46. Gandhi to Jinnah, ibid., p. 148.

47. Jinnah to Gandhi, July 24, 1944, ibid.

48. July 26, 1944, Mansergh, *Transfer of Power,* vol. IV, p. 1123.

49. September 9, 1944, *CWMG* [III, 15], vol. LXXVIII, pp. 87–88.

50. Ibid., pp. 88–89.

51. September 12, 1944, ibid., p. 96. The following quotes are from ibid.

52. *CWMG* [III, 15], vol. LXXVIII, p. 98.

53. Ahmad, *Recent Speeches,* vol. II, p. 167.

54. Jinnah to Gandhi, September 14, 1944, ibid., pp. 171–72.

55. Gandhi to Jinnah, September 15, 1944, *CWMG* [III, 15], vol. LXXVIII, p. 101.

56. Ibid., pp. 101–3.
57. September 22, 1944, *CWMG* [III, 15], vol. LXXVIII, p. 122.
58. "The Millat and Her Ten Nations," Aziz, *Rahmat Ali,* vol. I, pp. 149–60.
59. Jinnah to Gandhi, September 23, 1944, Ahmad, *Recent Speeches,* vol. II, p. 194.
60. Ibid., p. 196.
61. Jinnah to Gandhi, September 25, 1944, ibid., pp. 198–201.
62. Ibid., pp. 204–5.
63. September 25, 1944, *CWMG* [III, 15], vol. LXXVIII, pp. 130–31.
64. Jinnah to Gandhi, September 26, 1944, Ahmad, *Recent Speeches,* vol. II, pp. 207–8.
65. September 26, 1944, *CWMG* [III, 15], vol. LXXVIII, pp. 131–32.
66. Wavell to Amery, September 27, 1944, Mansergh, *Transfer of Power,* vol. V, p. 47.
67. September 27, 1944, *CWMG* [III, 15], vol. LXVIII, append. XII, p. 418.
68. September 28, 1944, ibid., pp. 136–37.
69. Ibid., p. 142.
70. September 29, 1944, Mansergh, *Transfer of Power,* vol. V, pp. 56–57.

CHAPTER 16: SIMLA (1944–1945)

1. Wavell to Amery, October 3, 1944, Mansergh, *Transfer of Power,* vol. V, p. 75.
2. Ibid.
3. Amery to Wavell, October 10, 1944, ibid., p. 96.
4. Wavell to Amery, November 29, 1944, ibid., p. 252.
5. December 6, 1944, ibid., pp. 279–80.
6. Casey to Wavell, December 17, 1944, ibid., p. 308.
7. Ibid., p. 309. The following quote is from ibid.
8. Wavell to Casey, January 1, 1945, ibid., p. 345.
9. December 27, 1944, Ahmad, *Recent Speeches,* vol. II, p. 345.
10. January 7, 1945, ibid., p. 347.
11. January 14, 1945, ibid., p. 350.
12. Moon, *Wavell,* p. 115.
13. Jinnah to I. A. K. Qaisar, March 25, 1945, *Hasan Collection,* vol. III, U. P.
14. Wavell to Amery, January 14, 1945, Mansergh, *Transfer of Power,* vol. V, p. 400.
15. Enclosure no. 202, January 17, 1945, ibid., p. 408, and pp. 411–12.
16. January 19, 1945, ibid., p. 423.
17. Ibid., p. 473.
18. V. P. Menon's report of dinner with Desai and Jenkins, January 27, 1945, ibid., p. 476.
19. Casey to Wavell, March 1, 1945, ibid., pp. 637–42.
20. Wavell to Amery, March 20, 1945, ibid., p. 712.
21. Jinnah to Taj Ali, December 18, 1944, *Hasan Collection,* vol. I, NWFP.
22. March 23, 1945, Ahmad, *Recent Speeches,* vol. II, p. 361.
23. Ibid., pp. 360–62.
24. March 25, 1945, Mansergh, *Transfer of Power,* vol. V, p. 733.
25. March 26, 1945, ibid., p. 735.
26. Ibid., pp. 738–40.
27. May 11, 1945, Moon, *Wavell,* p. 129.
28. Mansergh, *Transfer of Power,* vol. V, p. 1078.
29. June 14, 1945, ibid., p. 1122.

30. Wavell to Amery, June 15, 1945, ibid., pp. 1126–27.

31. June 16, 1945, Moon, Wavell, p. 142.

32. June 24, 1945, ibid., pp. 144–45.

33. Ibid., p. 146. The following quote is from ibid., pp. 146–47.

34. Wavell to Amery, June 25, 1945, Mansergh, *Transfer of Power*, vol. V, pp. 1155–56. The following quotes are from ibid., pp. 1156–57.

35. July 9, 1945, Moon, *Wavell*, pp. 152–53.

36. Wavell to Jinnah, July 9, 1945, Pirzada, *Foundations*, vol. II, pp. 502–3. The following quote is from ibid., p. 503.

37. Ibid., p. 503.

38. Amery to Wavell, July 10, 1945, Mansergh, *Transfer of Power*, vol. V, p. 1224.

39. July 11, 1945, Moon, *Wavell*, p. 154.

40. Ibid.

41. July 14, 1945, ibid., p. 155.

42. Wavell to Amery, July 15, 1945, Mansergh, *Transfer of Power*, vol. V, p. 1262.

43. July 12, 1945, ibid., p. 1237. The following quote is from ibid.

44. August 6, 1945, Moon, *Wavell*, p. 161.

CHAPTER 17: QUETTA AND PESHAWAR (1945–1946)

1. August 1, 1945, Mansergh, *Transfer of Power*, vol. VI, p. 6.

2. August 2, 1945, ibid., pp. 22–23. The following quote is from ibid.

3. August 6, 1945, Ahmad, *Recent Speeches*, vol. II, p. 387. The following quote is from ibid.

4. Ibid., pp. 390–91.

5. Pethick-Lawrence to Wavell, August 11, 1945, Mansergh, *Transfer of Power*, vol. VI, p. 57. The following quote is from ibid., p. 58.

6. Wavell to Pethick-Lawrence, August 12, 1945, ibid., p. 59.

7. Glancy to Wavell, August 16, 1945, ibid., pp. 71–72.

8. Wavell to Pethick-Lawrence, August 21, 1945, ibid., p. 113. The following quote is from ibid.

9. Cabinet minutes, August 29, 1945, ibid., pp. 174–75.

10. August 31, 1945, Moon, *Wavell*, p. 168.

11. Ahmad, *Recent Speeches*, vol. II, p. 411.

12. Wavell to Pethick-Lawrence, October 16, 1945, Mansergh, *Transfer of Power*, vol. VI, p. 348.

13. October 27, 1945, Ahmad. *Recent Speeches*, vol. II, pp. 423–24.

14. November 1, 1945, ibid., pp. 426–28.

15. Pethick-Lawrence to Wavell, November 8, 1945, Mansergh, *Transfer of Power*, vol. VI, p. 463.

16. Cabinet minutes, November 19, 1945, ibid., p. 501.

17. Wavell to Pethick-Lawrence, November 23, 1945, ibid., p. 524.

18. November 24, 1945, ibid., pp. 531–34.

19. "Secret" Intelligence Bureau enclosure, November 20, 1945, ibid., p. 513.

20. November 24, 1945, Ahmad, *Recent Speeches*, vol. II, pp. 438–39.

21. Ibid., pp. 440–43.

22. Casey to Wavell, December 2, 1945, Mansergh, *Transfer of Power*, vol. VI, p. 589.

23. December 3, 1945, ibid., pp. 590–91.

24. December speech to Punjab Muslim Students, Ahmad, *Recent Speeches*, vol. II, p. 363.

25. December 21, 1945, ibid., p. 364.

26. Pethick-Lawrence to Jinnah, December 21, 1945, Mansergh, *Transfer of Power,* vol. VI, pp. 672–73.

27. February 12, 1946, Moon, *Wavell,* p. 211.

28. February 13, 1946, Mansergh, *Transfer of Power,* vol. VI, p. 948.

29. Ibid., pp. 949–50.

30. "Viability of Pakistan," February 13, 1946, ibid., pp. 951–55.

31. Wavell to Pethick-Lawrence, February 13, 1946, ibid., pp. 967–68.

32. February 18, 1946, ibid., p. 1006.

33. February 22, 1946, ibid., p. 1048.

34. March 23, 1946, ibid., vol. VII, p. 1.

35. Note by Wyatt, March 28, 1946, ibid., pp. 22–24.

36. Note by Cripps, March 30, 1946, ibid., pp. 59–60.

37. April 3, 1946, Moon, *Wavell,* p. 236.

38. Secretary's report of Gandhi interview, April 3, 1946, Mansergh, *Transfer of Power,* vol. VI, pp. 117–18.

39. April 4, 1946, Moon, *Wavell,* p. 237.

40. April 4, 1946, Mansergh, *Transfer of Power,* vol. VII, pp. 119–21. Following quotes are from ibid.

41. "Secret" note by Duckworth, April 4, 1946, ibid., p. 136.

42. "Top Secret" note by Cripps, ibid., p. 176.

43. Ibid., p. 179.

44. Ibid., p. 180.

45. April 16, 1946, Moon, *Wavell,* p. 246.

46. April 16, 1946, 11 A.M., Mansergh, *Transfer of Power,* vol. VII, pp. 281–82.

47. Ibid., pp. 283–84. Following quotes are from ibid.

CHAPTER 18: SIMLA REVISITED (1946)

1. April 7–9, 1946, Pirzada, *Foundations,* vol. II, pp. 522–23.

2. Ibid., p. 523.

3. Ibid., pp. 514–15.

4. Ibid., pp. 516–20.

5. Ibid., pp. 523–24.

6. Record of meeting, April 25, 1946, Mansergh, *Transfer of Power,* vol. VII, p. 330.

7. April 25, 1946, Moon, *Wavell,* p. 252.

8. April 26, 1946, Mansergh, *Transfer of Power,* vol. VII, p. 342.

9. April 27, 1946, Moon, *Wavell,* p. 253.

10. May 5, 1946, ibid., p. 257. Following quote is from ibid., p. 258.

11. May 6, 1946, Mansergh, *Transfer of Power,* vol. VII, p. 437.

12. Moon, *Wavell,* p. 258.

13. Mansergh, *Transfer of Power,* vol. VII, p. 440.

14. May 6, 1946, Moon, *Wavell,* p. 260.

15. Ibid.

16. May 7, 1945, Mansergh, *Transfer of Power,* vol. VII, p. 452.

17. May 7, 1945, Moon, *Wavell,* p. 261.

18. May 8, 1946, Mansergh, *Transfer of Power,* vol. VII, pp. 462–63.

19. Ibid., pp. 464–65.

20. Ibid., p. 466.

21. Record of meeting, ibid., p. 480.

22. Moon, *Wavell,* p. 263.

23. Nehru to Jinnah, May 10, 1946, Mansergh, *Transfer of Power,* vol. VII, p. 502.

24. May 11, 1946, ibid., p. 507.

25. May 13, 1946, Moon, *Wavell,* p. 267. Following quote is from ibid., p. 268.

26. Mansergh, *Transfer of Power,* vol. VII, p. 591.

27. *Harijan,* May 17, 1946, quoted in ibid., p. 615.

28. Record of meeting, May 18, 1946, ibid., p. 616.

29. Note by George Abell, May 18, 1946, ibid., p. 619.

30. Record of meeting, May 19, 1946, 11:00 A.M., ibid., p. 623.

31. May 19, 1946, Moon, *Wavell,* p. 273.

32. May 19, 1946, Mansergh, *Transfer of Power,* vol. VII, p. 622.

33. Moon, *Wavell,* p. 273.

34. Mansergh, *Transfer of Power,* vol. VII, p. 634.

35. Gandhi to Pethick-Lawrence, May 20, 1946, ibid., pp. 636–37.

36. Ibid., p. 638.

37. May 20, 1946, ibid., p. 644.

38. Ibid., p. 655.

39. Record of meeting, May 24, 1946, ibid., pp. 675–78.

40. Note by Wyatt, May 25, 1946, ibid., p. 684.

41. Ibid., pp. 685–86.

42. Ibid., pp. 686–87 (Italics in original).

43. May 26, 1946, ibid., pp. 705–6.

44. June 3, 1946, Moon, *Wavell,* pp. 285–86.

45. Note by Intelligence Bureau, June 5, 1946, Mansergh, *Transfer of Power,* vol. VII, pp. 819–20.

46. June 6, 1946, Ahmad, *Recent Speeches,* vol. II, pp. 402–4.

47. Ibid., p. 406.

48. June 6, 1946, Moon, *Wavell,* p. 288.

49. June 7, 1946, ibid.

50. Wavell's Note of interview with Jinnah, Mansergh, *Transfer of Power,* vol. VII, p. 839.

51. June 11, 1946, Moon, *Wavell,* p. 290.

52. Record of meeting, June 11, 1946, Mansergh, *Transfer of Power,* vol. VII, p. 863n2.

53. June 12, 1946, Moon, *Wavell,* p. 290.

54. Mansergh, *Transfer of Power,* vol. VII, pp. 866–67; see heading and footnote, p. 867.

55. Ibid., p. 867.

56. Ibid., p. 866. This was clearly Jinnah's position from the start, and Wavell's account of it is jumbled and inaccurate, where he first notes (June 12, 1946, Moon, *Wavell,* p. 290) that "Cripps has spent several hours with Jinnah last night and said that he had agreed to this." (By "this" was meant a meeting with Nehru.) The viceroy later wrote in his journal (Moon, *Wavell,* p. 292): "At 3:40 P.M., when I was due to see Nehru and Jinnah at 4 P.M., Cripps came in and told me that Jinnah would not come; he had written a letter earlier to say that he did not feel he could meet Nehru, unless the parity basis was conceded." With so much changing every hour those days, Wavell obviously found it impossible to keep clear in his mind the exact sequence of events, even with daily diary notes.

57. Mansergh, *Transfer of Power,* vol. VII, p. 866.

58. Ibid., p. 867.

59. Ibid.

60. June 13, 1946, Moon, *Wavell*, p. 292.
61. Mansergh, *Transfer of Power*, vol. VII, p. 910.
62. Moon, *Wavell*, p. 314.
63. June 14, 1946, Mansergh, *Transfer of Power*, vol. VII, pp. 931–33.
64. Moon, *Wavell*, p. 294.
65. Ibid., p. 296.
66. Record of meeting, June 21, 1946, Mansergh, *Transfer of Power*, vol. VII, p. 995. Following quotes are from ibid., pp. 996–97.
67. June 23, 1946, ibid., pp. 1012–13. Following quote is ibid., p. 1014.
68. Ibid., p. 1017. Following quotes are ibid., pp. 1017–18.
69. Ibid., p. 1037.
70. Note by viceroy, June 25, 1946, ibid., p. 1039.
71. Ibid., pp. 1044–47.
72. June 25, 1946, Moon, *Wavell*, p. 306.

CHAPTER 19: BOMBAY TO LONDON (1946)

1. July 28, 1946, Ahmad, *Recent Speeches*, vol. II, p. 407.
2. Ibid., pp. 408–11.
3. Pirzada, *Foundations*, vol. II, pp. 546–48.
4. Ibid., pp. 548–49. Following quotes are from ibid.
5. Ibid., p. 551. Following quotes are ibid., pp. 551–52.
6. Ibid., pp. 557–58.
7. Ibid., p. 560.
8. Pethick-Lawrence to Wavell, Mansergh, *Transfer of Power*, vol. VIII, p. 162.
9. Minute by Scott, August 1, 1946, ibid., p. 174.
10. Wavell's minute, ibid., p. 175.
11. Ibid., p. 188.
12. Nehru to Jinnah, August 13, 1946, ibid., p. 238.
13. Jinnah to Nehru, ibid.
14. August 18, 1946, ibid., p. 248.
15. Burrows to Wavell, August 16, 1946, ibid., p. 239.
16. Francis Tuker, *While Memory Serves* (London: Cassell, 1950), p. 158.
17. Ibid., append. V, pp. 597–98.
18. Ibid., pp. 160–61.
19. Ibid., append. V, pp. 599–600.
20. Ibid., pp. 601–3.
21. Margaret Bourke-White, *Halfway To Freedom* (New York: Simon & Schuster, 1949), p. 20.
22. Wavell to Pethick-Lawrence, August 21, 1946, Mansergh, *Transfer of Power*, vol. VIII, p. 274.
23. Ahmad, *Recent Speeches*, vol. II, p. 433.
24. August 24, 1946, Mansergh, *Transfer of Power*, vol. VIII, p. 307.
25. Ahmad, *Recent Speeches*, vol. II, p. 444.
26. August 28, 1946, Mansergh, *Transfer of Power*, vol. VIII, p. 322.
27. Ibid., p. 323.
28. Ibid., p. 332. The following quote is ibid., p. 334.
29. August 29, 1946, ibid., p. 344.
30. Ahmad, *Recent Speeches*, vol. II, pp. 423–25.
31. A. P. Le Mesurier's report, September 2, 1946, Mansergh, *Transfer of Power*, vol. VIII, p. 385.

32. Nehru's broadcast, September 7, 1946, in Dorothy Norman, ed., *Nehru: The First Sixty Years* (London: The Bodley Head, 1965), vol. II, pp. 248–51.

33. September 8, 1946, Mansergh, *Transfer of Power,* vol. VIII, pp. 455–59.

34. September 10, 1946, Moon, *Wavell,* pp. 348–49.

35. Mansergh, *Transfer of Power,* vol. VIII, p. 478.

36. Record of meeting at 10 Downing Street, September 23, 1946, 10:30 A.M., ibid., pp. 570–72. Following quotes are from ibid.

37. Wavell to Pethick-Lawrence, September 26, 1946, ibid., p. 588.

38. September 26, 1946, Moon, *Wavell,* pp. 352–53.

39. Wavell's note, October 1, 1946, Mansergh, *Transfer of Power,* vol. VIII, pp. 631–32.

40. "Top Secret Note" of interview with Jinnah, October 2, 1946, ibid., pp. 643–44.

41. Ibid., p. 683.

42. Nehru to Jinnah, October 6, 1946, ibid., p. 671.

43. Jinnah to Nehru, October 7, 1946, ibid., p. 673.

44. October 11, 1946, ibid., p. 694.

45. October 11, 1946, Moon, *Wavell,* p. 356.

46. Wavell's note, October 12, 1946, Mansergh, *Transfer of Power,* vol. VIII, p. 704.

47. *Hindustan Times,* October 21, 1946, ibid., p. 779n4.

48. Nehru to Wavell, October 23, 1946, ibid., p. 785.

49. Wavell to Pethick-Lawrence, October 23, 1946, ibid., p. 785.

50. October 24, 1946, Moon, *Wavell,* p. 363.

51. October 30, 1946, ibid., p. 367.

52. Dow to Wavell, November 9, 1946, Mansergh, *Transfer of Power,* vol. IX, p. 39.

53. *Dawn,* November 15, 1946, ibid., pp. 73–75.

54. Ibid., p. 125.

55. November 21, 1946, ibid., p. 128.

56. Wavell to Pethick-Lawrence, November 23, 1946, ibid., p. 153.

57. Pethick-Lawrence to Wavell, November 27, 1946, ibid., p. 187.

58. November 29, 1946, Moon, *Wavell,* p. 385. The final quote is from ibid., December 1, 1946.

CHAPTER 20: LONDON—FINAL FAREWELL (1946)

1. Wavell's note, December 2, 1946, Mansergh, *Transfer of Power,* vol. IX, pp. 240–42.

2. Note of conversation with Jinnah by Wyatt, December 3, 1946, ibid., pp. 246–47.

3. Cabinet meeting, December 4, 1946, ibid., pp. 252–53.

4. Ibid., pp. 253–55.

5. Cabinet minutes, December 4, 1946, 12:15 P.M., ibid., pp. 260–61.

6. Meeting, December 4, 1946, 10:30 A.M., ibid., pp. 255–56. Following quotes are from ibid.

7. Ibid., p. 259.

8. Meeting with Jinnah and Liaquat Ali, ibid., pp. 262–64.

9. Cabinet meeting, 10 Downing Street, December 6, 4:00 P.M., ibid., p. 295.

10. Cabinet meeting, 6:00 P.M., p. 297. Following quotes are from ibid., pp. 298–300.

11. Dwarkadas, *Ten Years To Freedom,* pp. 190–91.

12. Ibid., p. 192.

13. Parthasarathy, *The Hindu,* p. 629.
14. Begum Shah Nawaz, "Reminiscences," in Ahmad, *Quaid-i-Azam,* p. 99.
15. *Parliamentary Debates,* House of Commons, Fifth Series, vol. 431, pp. 1175–76. Following quote is from ibid., p. 1178.
16. Ibid., p. 1346.
17. Ibid., pp. 1360–67.
18. Norman, *Nehru,* vol. II, pp. 278–86.
19. Alan Campbell-Johnson, *Mission With Mountbatten* (New York: Dutton & Co., 1953), December 19, 1946, pp. 17–18.
20. Reuter's "Report of Jinnah's Meeting in Cairo," in Atique Z. Sheikh and M. R. Malik, eds., *Quaid-e-Azam and the Muslim World: Selected Documents* (Karachi: Royal Book Co., 1978), p. 166.
21. Cairo, December 20, 1946, ibid., p. 168.
22. Ibid., p. 169.

CHAPTER 21: NEW DELHI (1947)

1. January 2, 1947, Mansergh, *Transfer of Power,* vol. IX, pp. 444–45.
2. Mountbatten to Attlee, January 3, 1947, ibid., pp. 451–52.
3. Enclosure to No. 304, January 24, 1947, ibid., pp. 542–43.
4. Jenkins to Pethick-Lawrence, January 26, 1947, ibid., p. 557.
5. January 29, 1947, ibid., p. 572.
6. Wavell to Pethick-Lawrence, February 1, 1947, ibid., p. 593.
7. Cabinet minutes, February 5, 1947, ibid., p. 618.
8. February 6, 1947, Moon, *Wavell,* p. 418.
9. "Indian Policy" (Cmd. 7047), February 20, 1947, Mansergh, *Transfer of Power,* vol. IX, p. 774.
10. *Hindustan Times,* February 21, 1947, ibid., pp. 775–76.
11. *Dawn,* February 21, 1947, ibid., pp. 777–78.
12. Wavell to Pethick-Lawrence, February 22, 1947, ibid., pp. 785–86.
13. February 28, 1947, Moon, *Wavell,* p. 424. For inset, see Mansergh, *Transfer of Power,* vol. IX, p. 824n3.
14. Jenkins to Pethick-Lawrence, February 25, 1947, ibid., p. 815.
15. Wavell to Pethick-Lawrence, February 26, 1947, ibid., p. 819, recounting what had been reported in Caroe to Wavell, February 22, 1947, ibid., p. 788.
16. Jenkins to Wavell, March 3, 1947, ibid., p. 830.
17. Ibid., p. 832.
18. *Parliamentary Debates,* House of Commons, Fifth Series, March 5, 1947, vol. 434, pp. 502–5.
19. Ibid., pp. 669–73.
20. Ibid., pp. 673–74.
21. February 28, 1947, Moon, *Wavell,* p. 424.
22. Jenkins to Wavell, March 7, 1947, Mansergh, *Transfer of Power,* vol. IX, p. 879.
23. Enclosure of Resolutions Passed, March 8, 1947, ibid., pp. 899–900.
24. Nehru to Wavell, March 9, 1947, ibid., p. 898.
25. M. H. Shahid, ed., *Quaid-i-Azam Muhammad Ali Jinnah (Speeches, Statements, Writings, Letters)* (Lahore: Sang-e-Meel Publications, 1976), pp. 50–51. The final segment of this quote is from Mansergh, *Transfer of Power,* vol. IX, p. 927n3.
26. Jenkins to Wavell, March 10, 1947, ibid., p. 912.
27. Baldev Singh to Wavell, March 11, 1947, ibid., pp. 914–16.
28. Cabinet meeting, March 13, 1947, 5:15 P.M., ibid., p. 940.

29. Krishna Menon to Mountbatten, March 13, 1947, ibid., pp. 948–49.
30. Jenkins to Abell, March 17, 1947, ibid., p. 962.
31. Ibid., pp. 967–68.
32. Attlee to Mountbatten, March 18, 1947, ibid., pp. 972–74.
33. Minutes of meeting, March 22, 1947, 10:30 P.M., ibid., pp. 1011–12.
34. Campbell-Johnson, *Mountbatten,* March 23, 1947, p. 41.
35. Parthasarathy, *The Hindu,* p. 646.
36. Campbell-Johnson, *Mountbatten,* March 25, 1947, p. 44.
37. Annex I to Mountbatten's "Personal Report," no. 2, April 9, 1947, India Office Library, London, L/P.O./433/31. Hereafter cited *Mountbatten's Personal Report.*
38. Record of Mountbatten-Gandhi interview, April 1, 1947, Mansergh, *Transfer of Power,* vol. X, p. 69.
39. Record of Mountbatten-Nehru interview, April 1, 1947, ibid., p. 70.
40. "Top Secret" interview, Mountbatten-Jinnah, April 5–6, 1947, ibid., p. 137.
41. Mountbatten's personal recollection in an interview at his home, summer of 1978.
42. Record of interviews, April 5 and 6, 1947, Mansergh, *Transfer of Power,* vol. X, pp. 138–39.
43. April 7, 1947, ibid., p. 149.
44. April 8, 1947, ibid., pp. 159–60.
45. Ibid., p. 164.
46. "Top Secret," April 11, 1947, ibid., p. 190.
47. Ibid.
48. Ibid.
49. Note by Jenkins, April 16, 1947, ibid., pp. 282–83.
50. Parthasarathy, *The Hindu,* p. 649.
51. Record of Mountbatten-Liaquat Ali interview, April 10, 1947, Mansergh, *Transfer of Power,* vol. X, pp. 331–32.
52. Ibid., p. 333.
53. "Top Secret" record of discussion, ibid., p. 349.
54. Record of interview with Krishna Menon, April 22, 1947, ibid., p. 372. The following quote is from ibid.
55. April 24, 1947, ibid., p. 388. The following quote is from ibid., p. 389.
56. Record of interview with Jinnah, April 26, 1947, ibid., pp. 452–53.
57. Ibid., p. 453. The following quote is from ibid., p. 454.
58. Mieville to Mountbatten, April 29, 1947, ibid., p. 479.
59. Mountbatten's Personal Report, No. 5, May 1, 1947, ibid., pp. 537–38.
60. Ibid., p. 540.
61. Mountbatten to Ismay, May 10, 1947, ibid., p. 776.
62. Nehru to Mountbatten, May 11, 1947, ibid., p. 756.
63. Record of interview with Liaquat Ali, May 15, 1947, ibid., p. 825.
64. Jinnah's note, May 17, 1947, ibid., pp. 852–53.
65. Cabinet minutes, May 19, 1947, ibid., p. 896.
66. Reuter's report, May 21, 1947, p. 929.
67. Cabinet minutes, May 20, 1947, ibid., p. 922.
68. Krishna Menon to Mountbatten, May 21, 1947, ibid., p. 940.
69. Campbell-Johnson, *Mountbatten,* June 1, 1947, p. 98.
70. Record of Churchill-Mountbatten interview, May 22, 1947, Mansergh, *Transfer of Power,* vol. X, pp. 945–46.
71. June 5, 1947, *Mountbatten's Personal Report,* no. 8, p. 115. Following quote is from ibid.

72. That doodle is reproduced in a photograph in Campbell-Johnson, *Mount-batten*, facing p. 97.

73. June 5, 1947, *Mountbatten's Personal Report*, no. 8, p. 117.

74. Campbell-Johnson, *Mountbatten*, June 3, 1947, pp. 102–3.

75. June 3, 1947 Plan, append., ibid., pp. 364–68.

76. Ibid., p. 367.

77. Jinnah's broadcast of June 3, 1947, Shahid, *Quaid-i-Azam Speeches*, pp. 77–79.

78. June 3, 1947, Campbell-Johnson, *Mountbatten*, p. 107. Following quote is from ibid.

79. June 5, 1947, *Mountbatten's Personal Report*, no. 8, pp. 122*ff*.

80. Campbell-Johnson, *Mountbatten*, June 9, 1947, pp. 115–16.

81. *Morning Herald*, June 10, 1947, and *Morning News*, June 11, reported in Pirzada, *Foundations*, vol. II, pp. 566–67. Following quote is from ibid., p. 567.

82. June 12, 1947, *Mountbatten's Personal Report*, no. 9, p. 125.

83. Pirzada, *Foundations*, vol. II, p. 568.

84. June 12, 1947, *Mountbatten's Personal Report*, no. 9, p. 125.

85. "The Greatest Betrayal," Aziz, *Rahmat Ali*, vol. I, pp. 291–301.

86. June 12, 1947, *Mountbatten's Personal Report*, no. 9, p. 127.

CHAPTER 22: KARACHI—"PAKISTAN ZINDABAD" (1947)

1. June 27, 1947, *Mountbatten's Personal Report*, no. 10, p. 139.

2. July 4, 1947, ibid., no. 11, p. 160.

3. *Parliamentary Debates*, House of Commons, Fifth Series, vol. 440, pp. 227–29. The Attlee quote is from ibid., pp. 283–84.

4. July 13, 1947, Shahid, *Quaid-i-Azam Speeches*, p. 82.

5. Penderel Moon, *Divide and Quit* (Berkeley and Los Angeles: University of California Press, 1962), p. 88 (Deletion in original).

6. July 25, 1947, *Mountbatten's Personal Report*, no. 14, pp. 202–3.

7. Campbell-Johnson, *Mountbatten*, July 26, 1947, p. 143.

8. August 8, 1947, *Mountbatten's Personal Report*, no. 16, p. 228.

9. Ibid., pp. 233–34.

10. Karachi Club, August 9, 1947, *Speeches of Quaid-i-Azam Mohammad Ali Jinnah as Governor General of Pakistan* (Karachi: Sind Observer Press, 1948), pp. 4–5.

11. August 11, 1947, ibid., p. 6.

12. Ibid., pp. 7–9.

13. Ibid., pp. 9–10.

14. Ibid., p. 10.

15. Ibid.

16. August 16, 1947, *Mountbatten's Personal Report*, no. 17, p. 247.

17. Campbell-Johnson, *Mountbatten*, August 13, 1947, p. 154. Following quote is from ibid., p. 155.

18. August 13, 1947, *Speeches of Quaid-i-Azam*, p. 11. Following quote is from ibid.

19. August 16, 1947, *Mountbatten's Personal Report*, no. 17, p. 249.

20. August 14, 1947, *Speeches of Quaid-i-Azam*, pp. 14–15.

21. Campbell-Johnson, *Mountbatten*, August 14, 1947, p. 156.

22. Mountbatten's recollection to the author in the Summer of 1978.

23. Norman, *Nehru*, vol. II, p. 336.

24. *Speeches of Quaid-i-Azam*, p. 16.

25. Jinnah, "My Brother."

26. Begum Shah Nawaz, "The Quaid As I Knew Him," in *Quaid-i-Azam and Muslim Women,* p. 18.

27. Campbell-Johnson, *Mountbatten,* August 30, 1947, p. 176.

28. Ibid., September 8, 1947, p. 183.

29. Mir Laik Ali, "Reminiscences of the Quaid," in Ahmad, *Jinnah,* pp. 61–70.

30. Ispahani to Jinnah, September 19, 1947, Zaidi, *Correspondence,* pp. 525–26.

31. Jinnah to Ispahani, October 1, 1947, ibid., p. 569.

32. Master Tara Singh reportedly said, "This is War," by September 12, 1947, Campbell-Johnson, *Mountbatten,* p. 188.

33. Ibid., September 14, 1947, p. 190. Following quotes are from ibid., pp. 190–94.

34. Ibid., September 29, 1947, p. 210.

35. November 7, 1947, *Mountbatten's Personal Report,* p. 339.

36. Ibid., p. 340. The following quote is from ibid., p. 341.

37. Mehr Chand Mahajan, *Looking Back* (London: Asia Publishing House, 1963), pp. 151–52. Following quotes are from ibid., pp. 152–54.

38. V. P. Menon, *The Story of the Integration of the Indian States* (London: Longman, Green & Co., 1956), pp. 399–400.

39. Mountbatten's polo term for his Viceroyalty, mentioned in his letter to King George VI on the eve of his acceptance, January 4, 1947, Mansergh, *Transfer of Power,* vol. IX, pp. 5452–54.

40. November 7, 1947, *Mountbatten's Personal Report,* p. 342. The following quotes are from ibid.

41. Menon, *Integration of States,* p. 400.

42. Mahajan, *Looking Back,* p. 154.

43. November 7, 1947, *Mountbatten's Personal Reports,* p. 343.

44. John Connell, *Auchinleck* (London: Cassell, 1959), p. 931.

45. Ibid. The following quote is from ibid.

46. November 7, 1947, *Mountbatten's Personal Report,* p. 343.

47. Ibid., p. 347. Following quotes are from ibid.

48. Ibid., pp. 347–52.

49. Ibid.

50. Campbell-Johnson, *Mountbatten,* October 27, 1947, pp. 221–22.

51. "The Tasks Ahead," October 30, 1947, *Speeches of Quaid-i-Azam,* pp. 29–30.

52. Jinnah, "My Brother."

CHAPTER 23: ZIARAT (1948)

1. Pirzada, *Foundations,* vol. II, p. 569. Following quotes are from ibid., p. 571.

2. Ibid., pp. 573–74.

3. Menon, *Integration of States,* p. 410.

4. S. L. Poplai, ed., *India, 1947–50* (London: Oxford University Press, 1959), vol. II, p. 345.

5. January 15, 1948, ibid., pp. 351–52. Following quotes are from ibid., pp. 352–53.

6. Ibid., pp. 353–58.

7. January 23, 1948, *Speeches of Quaid-i-Azam,* pp. 58–60.

8. M. K. Gandhi, *Delhi Diary* (Ahmedabad: Navajivan Publishing House, 1948), pp. 390–92.

9. Campbell-Johnson, *Mountbatten,* February 5, 1948, p. 283.

10. *Indian Affairs* (London, March 4, 1948), vol. VII, no. 5, p. 1.
11. Ispahani to Jinnah, March 31, 1948, Zaidi, *Correspondence,* p. 582.
12. Bolitho, *Jinnah,* p. 210.
13. March 21, 1948, *Quaid-e-Azam Speaks: Speeches of Quaid-e-Azam Mohammad Ali Jinnah* (Karachi: Ministry of Information & Broadcasting, 1950), p. 133.
14. Ibid., pp. 133–36.
15. Jinnah, "My Brother."
16. S. S. Pirzada, "The Last Days of Quaid-i-Azam," *The Pakistan Times,* October 17, 1979. A typescript of this memoir written by Pakistan's Minister of Justice was given to the author in Islamabad in 1980.
17. Sir Francis ("Frank") Mudie's "Report" was dictated shortly before his death and is preserved at the India Office Library in London, MSS EUR, 33.
18. Ibid.
19. Jinnah, "My Brother."
20. June 14, 1948, *Quaid-e-Azam Speaks,* pp. 154–55.
21. "Provincialism, A Curse," June 15, 1948, ibid., pp. 156–58.
22. Jinnah, "My Brother." The following quotes are from ibid.
23. Ilahi Bakhsh, *With the Quaid-i-Azam During His Last Days* (Karachi: Quaid-i-Azam Academy, 1978), p. 2. The following quotes are from ibid., pp. 3–5.
24. Ibid., p. 5.
25. Ibid., p. 8. The following quotes are from ibid., pp. 9–10.
26. Pirzada, "Last Days of the Quaid," p. 6.
27. Bakhsh, *Last Days,* p. 11. The following quote is from ibid., p. 15.
28. Jinnah, "My Brother."
29. Bakhsh, *Last Days,* pp. 18–19.
30. August 14, 1948, *Quaid-e-Azam Speaks,* pp. 247–49.
31. Bakhsh, *Last Days,* p. 24. The following quote is from ibid., p. 25.
32. Ibid., p. 26.
33. Ibid., pp. 28–31.
34. Ibid., pp. 32–33.
35. Wire no. 405, September 1948, Zaidi, *Correspondence,* p. 617.
36. Bakhsh, *Last Days,* p. 40.
37. Jinnah, "My Brother."
38. Ibid.
39. Bakhsh, *Last Days,* pp. 47–48.
40. Jinnah, "My Brother."
41. Chagla, *Roses in December,* p. 120.
42. Lady Rama Rao's recollection in an interview with the author in Los Angeles, 1979.

Bibliography

PRIMARY SOURCES

Letters and Documents: Public and Private

PAKISTAN

Islamabad The National Archives of Pakistan (*NAP*)
Some 80,000 pages of "Quaid-i-Azam Papers," the primary archive for Jinnah's entire life, are preserved by the Education Division of Pakistan's Ministry of Education and Scientific Research. *Accession Lists* and *Descriptive Catalogues* of most of these papers have been published under the direction of Dr. Atique Zafar Sheikh, director of Archives, who has also edited a *Descriptive List* of the Ahmed Hamid Lakha Collection, twenty-three volumes of newspaper and periodical clippings about Quaid-i-Azam Jinnah, also deposited in *NAP*.

Karachi
Archives of the Freedom Movement, preserved at the University of Karachi, contain more than 35,000 documents relating to the All-India Muslim League and Pakistan Muslim League, and sixteen other private collections of political significance, dealing with the "Muslim Freedom Movement." Dr. M. H. Siddiqi, director of these important archives, has compiled a *Hand-List of Classified Volumes,* noting the more than 320 bound volumes to date (1976), as well as a *Progress Report* on the state of the "Archives of the Freedom Movement" as of 1978.
Syed Shamsul Hasan Collection, a private collection of some thirty bound volumes of Jinnah letters and papers compiled by Muslim League Secretary Shamsul Hasan, long a close friend of Jinnah and now deceased, is preserved at the National Bank of Pakistan by Vice-President Khalid Shamsul Hasan, present owner of this fine collection.
A complete set of microfilm of The Quaid-i-Azam Papers at *NAP* is preserved in the Quaid-i-Azam Academy under the direction of Prof. Sharif al Mujahid, whose excellent library also contains the best general collection of newspaper articles, pamphlets, pictures, and published works on Quaid-i-Azam Jinnah's life

and times, outside of *NAP*. Five volumes of important *Papers Presented at the International Congress on Quaid-i-Azam,* held at Quaid-i-Azam University, Islamabad, from 19–25 December 1976, have been compiled for private circulation by the organizing committee of the Congress, and are also preserved at this academy.

ENGLAND

London

India Office Library (IOL):

Brabourne Collection. MSS Eur. F. 97.
Chelmsford Papers. MSS Eur. E. 264.
Christie Collection. MSS Eur. D. 718.
Cunningham Collection. MSS Eur. D. 670.
Curzon Papers. MSS Eur. F. 111 & 112.
Fleetwood Wilson Papers. MSS Eur. E. 224.
Hailey Collection. MSS Eur. E. 220.
Halifax Collection (Irwin Papers). MSS Eur. C. 152.
Hallett Collection. MSS Eur. E. 251.
Hamilton Papers. MSS Eur. D. 510.
Linlithgow Collection. MSS Eur. F. 125.
Montagu Papers. MSS Eur. D. 523.
Mudie Diary. MSS Eur. 28–34.
Reading (Lady) Collection. MSS Eur. E. 316.
Templewood (Hoare Papers) Collection. MSS Eur. E. 240.
Zetland (Lawrence Papers) Collection. MSS Eur. D. 609.

India Office *Records:*

India. The War Series. L/P & J/8/524.
Mountbatten "Top Secret" Personal Reports as Viceroy. L/P.O./433.
Private Secretary to the Viceroy on the Transfer of Power. R/3/1.
Rahmat Ali Pamphlets. L/P & J/8/689.

*Public Record Office—*Kew *(PRO):*

Cripps Collection. CAB 127/57–154.
Ramsay MacDonald Papers. PRO 30/69.

Cambridge

Alexander Papers.
Baldwin Papers.
Hardinge Papers.

Bibliographies

Anwar, Muhammad, *Quaid-i-Azam Jinnah:* A Selected Bibliography (Karachi: National Publishing House, 1969)
Khurshid, Anis, *Quaid-i-Azam Mohammad Ali Jinnah: An Annotated Bibliography,* Vol. 1 (Karachi: Quaid-i-Azam Academy, 1978)

Books and Articles

Afzal, M. Rafique, ed. *Quaid-i-Azam Mohammad Ali Jinnah: Speeches in the Legislative Assembly of India, 1924–30.* Lahore: Research Society of Pakistan, 1976.

Aga Khan, H. H. *The Memoirs of Aga Khan*. New York: Simon & Schuster, 1954.
Ahmad, Jamil-ud-din, ed. *Some Recent Speeches and Writings of Mr. Jinnah*. 2 Vols. Lahore: Ashraf, 1952.
————. *Glimpses of Quaid-i-Azam*. Karachi: Education Press, 1960.
————. *Quaid-i-Azam as Seen by His Contemporaries*. Lahore: Publishers United Ltd., 1966.
Ahmad, Riaz, ed: *Iqbal's Letters to Quaid-i-Azam*. Lahore: Friends Educational Service, 1976.
Ahmad, Rizwan, ed. *The Quaid-E-Azam Papers, 1940*. Karachi: East and West Publishing Co., 1976.
Ahmad, Waheed, ed. *Jinnah-Irwin Correspondence, 1927–1930*. Lahore: Research Society of Pakistan, 1969.
————. *Diary and Notes of Mian Fazl-I-Husain*. Lahore: Research Society of Pakistan, 1977.
Ali, Mir Laik. "Reminiscences of the Quaid." In *Mohammad Ali Jinnah*, edited by Ziauddin Ahmad. Karachi: Ministry of Information & Broadcasting, 1976.
Allana, G., ed. *Pakistan Movement: Historic Documents*. Vol. I. Karachi: Department of International Relations, University of Karachi, 1967.
All Parties Conference, 1928. Allahabad: All-India Congress Committee, 1928.
Alva, Joachim. *Leaders of India*. Bombay: Thacker & Co., Ltd., 1943.
Ambedkar, B. R. *What Congress and Gandhi Have Done to the Untouchables*. Bombay: Thacker & Co., 1945.
Azad, Maulana Abul Kalam. *India Wins Freedom*. New York: Longmans, Green & Co., 1960.
Aziz, K. K., ed. *Complete Works of Rahmat Ali*. Islamabad: National Commission on Historical and Cultural Research, 1978.
————. *Muslims Under Congress Rule, 1937–1939: A Documentary Record*. Islamabad: National Commission on Historical and Cultural Research, 1978.
Bakhsh, Ilahi. *With the Quaid-i-Azam During His Last Days*. Karachi: Quaid-i-Azam Academy, 1978.
Campbell-Johnson, Alan. "Reflections on the Transfer of Power." Address delivered to East India Association meeting jointly with the Overseas League at Over-Seas House, March 27, 1952, with the Right Hon. Earl Listowel in the chair.
————. *Mission With Mountbatten*. New York: Dutton & Co., 1953.
Chagla, M. C. *Roses in December: An Autobiography*. Bombay: Bharatiya Vidya Bhaven, 1974.
Chintamani, C. Y., ed. *Speeches and Writing of the Honourable Sir Pherozeshah M. Mehta, K.C.I.E.* Allahabad: The Indian Press, 1905.
Collected Works of Mahatma Gandhi. Vols. XIII–LXXXIV. Ahmedabad: Navajivan Trust, 1964–82.
Dar, B. A., ed. *Letters of Iqbal*. Lahore: Iqbal Academy Pakistan, 1978.
Desai, M. H., ed. *Day to Day with Gandhi*. Vol. II. Varanasi: Sarva Seva Sangh Prakashan, 1968.
Dwarkadas, Kanji. *Ruttie Jinnah*. Bombay: Kanji Dwarkadas, 1963.
Full & Authentic Report of the Tilak Trial, 1908. Poona: N. C. Kelkar, Sept. 1908.
Gandhi, M. K. *The Story of My Experiments With Truth*. Translated by Mahadev Desai. Washington: Public Affairs Press, 1948.
Gopal, S., ed. *Selected Works of Jawaharlal Nehru*. 14 Vols. New Delhi: Orient Longman Ltd., 1972–81.
Harris, M. A. *Quaid-i-Azam*. Karachi: Times Press, 1976.
Hasan, Syed Shamsul. ". . . *Plain Mr. Jinnah*." Vol. I of *Selections from Shamsul Hasan Collection*. Karachi: Royal Book Company, 1976.

Indian National Congress, 2d ed. Madras: G. A. Natesan & Co., 1917.
Ispahani, M. A. H. *Quaid-e-Azam Jinnah As I Knew Him*. 2d ed. Karachi: Forward Publications Trust, 1966; 2d Rev. Ed., 1967.
Jafar, Malik Muhammad et al. *Jinnah as a Parliamentarian*. Lahore: Afzar Publications, 1977.
Jafri, S. Q. Hussain, ed. *Congress Leaders Correspondence with Quaid-i-Azam*. Lahore: Aziz Publishers, n.d.
Jayakar, M. R. *The Story of My Life*. Vol. I. Bombay: Asia Publishing House, 1958.
Joint Committee on Indian Constitutional Reforms, *Report* (Cmd. 4268). Vol. I., pt. 1. London: His Majesty's Stationery Office, 1934.
Khaliquzzaman, Choudhry. *Pathway to Pakistan*. Lahore: Pakistan Longman, 1961.
Linlithgow, Marquess of. *Speeches and Statements*. New Delhi: Bureau of Public Information, 1945.
Mahajan, Mehr Chand. *Looking Back*. London: Asia Publishing House, 1963.
Mahmudabad, Raja of. "Some Memories." In *The Partition of India*. Edited by C. H. Philips and Mary D. Wainwright. London: George Allen and Unwin Ltd., 1970.
Mansergh, N. and Lumby, E. W. R., eds. *Constitutional Relations Between Britain and India: The Transfer of Power*. 11 Vols. London: Her Majesty's Stationery Office, 1970–82.
    Vol. I: *Cripps Mission, January–April 1942* (1970).
    Vol. II: *"Quit India," 30 April–21 September 1942* (1971).
    Vol. III: *Reassertion of Authority, Gandhi's Fast and the Succession to the Viceroyalty, 21 September 1942–12 June 1943* (1971).
    Vol. IV: *The Bengal Famine and the New Viceroyalty, 15 June–31 August 1944* (1973).
    Vol. V: *The Simla Conference, Background and Proceedings, 1 September 1944–28 July 1945* (1974).
    Vol. VI: *The Post-War Phase: New Moves by the Labour Government, 1 August 1945–22 March 1946* (1976).
    Vol. VII: *The Cabinet Mission, 23 March–29 June 1946* (1977).
    Vol. VIII: *The Interim Government, 3 July–1 November 1946* (1979).
    Vol. IX: *The Fixing of a Time Limit, 4 November–22 March 1947* (1980).
    Vol. X: *The Mountbatten Viceroyalty, Formulation of a Plan, 22 March–30 May 1947* (1981).
    Vol. XI: *The Mountbatten Viceroyalty Announcement and Reception of the 3 June Plan, 31 May–7 July 1947* (1982).
Mary, Countess of Minto. *India, Minto and Morley, 1905–10*. London: Macmillan, 1934.
Montagu, Edwin S. *An Indian Diary*. Edited by Venetia Montagu. London: William Heinemann, 1930.
Naidu, Sarojini. *Mohammad Ali Jinnah, an Ambassador of Unity: His Speeches and Writings, 1912–1917*. With a biographical appreciation by the author. Madras: Ganesh, 1918.
Nehru, Jawaharlal. *Toward Freedom*. New York: The John Day Company, 1941.
————. *A Bunch of Old Letters*. New York: Asia Publishing House, 1960.
Nehru-Jinnah Correspondence: includes Gandhi-Jinnah Correspondence. Allahabad: A-I Central Committee of Congress, 1938.
Noon, Firoz Khan. *From Memory*. Lahore: Feroz Sons, 1966.
Norman, Dorothy, ed. *Nehru: The First Sixty Years*. Vol. I (through 1939), and Vol. II (1940–50). London: The Bodley Head, 1965.

Panikkar, K. M. and Pershad, A., eds. *The Voice of Freedom: Selected Speeches of Pandit Motilal Nehru*. London: Asia Publishing House, 1961.

Peerbhoy, A. A. *Jinnah Faces An Assassin*. Bombay: Thacker & Co., 1943.

Philips, C. H., ed. *The Evolution of India and Pakistan, 1858 to 1947. Select Documents*. London: George Allen and Unwin Ltd., 1962.

Pirpure, Raja Syed Mohamed Medhi. *Report of the Inquiry Committee appointed by the Council of the All-India Muslim League to inquire into Muslim Grievances in Congress Provinces*. Delhi: Liaquat Ali Khan, 1938.

Pirzada, Syed Sharifuddin, ed. *Foundations of Pakistan: All-India Muslim League Documents*. Vol. I (1906–24) and Vol. II (1924–27). Karachi: National Publishing House Ltd., 1969.

———. *Quaid-e-Azam Jinnah's Correspondence*. 3d Rev. Ed. Karachi: East and West Publishing Company, 1977.

Poplai, S. L., ed. *India, 1947–50*. Vol. II. *External Affairs*. London: Oxford University Press 1959.

Prasad, Rajendra. *Autobiography*. Bombay: Asia Publishing House, 1957.

Proceedings of the Indian Round Table Conference (Cmd. 3778). 12 November 1930–19 January 1931. London: His Majesty's Stationery Office, 1931.

Quaid-e-Azam Speaks: Speeches by Quaid-e-Azam Mohd. Ali Jinnah, Founder of Pakistan from June 1947 to August 1948. Karachi: Pakistan Publicity, n.d.

Quaid-e-Azam Speaks: Speeches of Quaid-e-Azam Mohammad Ali Jinnah. Karachi: Ministry of Information and Broadcasting, 1950.

Quaid-i-Azam and Muslim Women. Islamabad: National Committee for Birth Centenary Celebrations of Quaid-i-Azam Mohammad Ali Jinnah, 1976.

Qureshi, Fazal Haque, ed. *Every Day with the Quaid-i-Azam*. Karachi: Sultan Ashraf Qureshi, 1976.

Reminiscences of the Day of Deliverance. Islamabad: National Committee for Birth Centenary Celebrations of Quaid-i-Azam Mohammad Ali Jinnah, 1976.

Report of the Indian Statutory Commission (Cmd. 3569) Vol. II. May 1930. London: His Majesty's Stationery Office 1930.

Saeed, Ahmad, ed. *Writings of the Quaid-E-Azam*. Lahore: Progressive Books, n.d.

Saiyid, M. H., *Mohammad Ali Jinnah*. Lahore: S. M. Ashraf, 1945.

Sapru, Tej Bahadur et al. *Constitutional Proposals of the Sapru Committee*. Bombay: Padmar Publications, 1945.

Shahid, M. H., ed. *Quaid-i-Azam Muhammad Ali Jinnah*. Lahore: Sang-e-Meel Publications, 1976.

Speeches of Gopal Krishna Gokhale. 3d Ed. Madras: Natesan & Co., 1920.

Speeches of Quaid-i-Azam Mohammad Ali Jinnah as Governor General of Pakistan. Karachi: Sind Observer Press, 1948.

Templewood Viscount (Sir Samuel Hoare). *Nine Troubled Years*. London: Collins, 1954.

Wavell, Archibald. *Wavell: the Viceroy's Journal*. Edited by Penderel Moon. Karachi: Oxford University Press, 1974.

Zaidi, A. Moin, ed. *Evolution of Muslim Political Thought in India*. 6 Vols. New Delhi: S. Chand, 1975–79.

Zaidi, Z. H., ed. *M. A. Jinnah–Ispahani Correspondence, 1936–1948*. Karachi: Foward Publishing Trust, 1976.

Zetland, Marquess of. *"Essayez"—The Memoirs of Lawrence, Second Marquess of Zetland*. London: John Murray, 1956.

SECONDARY SOURCES

Ahmad, Ziauddin. *Liaquat Ali Khan, Leader and Statesman.* Karachi: Ministry of Information & Broadcasting, 1970.

————, ed. *Mohammad Ali Jinnah: Founder of Pakistan.* Karachi: Ministry of Information & Broadcasting, 1970.

Akhtar, Jamnadas. *Political Conspiracies in Pakistan.* Delhi: Punjab Pustak Bhandar, 1969.

Ali, Chaudhri Muhammad. *The Emergence of Pakistan.* New York: Columbia University Press, 1967.

Ali, Mahmud. *Quaid-e-Azam and Muslim Economic Resurgence.* Lahore: Amir Publications, 1977.

Allana, G. *Quaid-E-Azam Jinnah: The Story of a Nation.* Lahore: Ferozsons, Ltd., 1967.

Ambedkar, B. R. *Ranade, Gandhi and Jinnah.* Bombay: Thacker, 1943.

Amery, L. S. *India and Freedom.* London: Oxford University Press, 1942.

Aziz, K. K. *The Making of Pakistan.* London: Chatto & Windus, 1967.

Baillie, Alexander F. *Kurrachee: Past, Present and Future.* Karachi: Oxford University Press, 1975.

Baldwin, A. W. *My Father: The True Story.* London: George Allen & Unwin, 1956.

Beg, Aziz, ed. *Quaid-i-Azam Centenary Bouquet.* Islamabad: Babur and Amer Publications, 1977.

Bhargava, G. S. *Pakistan in Crisis.* 2d Ed. London: Vikas Publications, 1969.

Birkenhead, the Second Earl of. *F. E., The Life of F. E. Smith, First Earl of Birkenhead.* London: Eyre & Spottiswoode, 1960.

Bolitho, Hector. *Jinnah: Creator of Pakistan.* London: John Murray, 1954.

Bose, Subhash Chandra. *The Indian Pilgrim and Letters, 1897–1942.* New Delhi: Manobar, 1980.

Brown, Judith. *Gandhi's Rise to Power: Indian Politics, 1915–1922.* Cambridge: Cambridge University Press, 1972.

————. *Gandhi and Civil Disobedience: The Mahatma in Indian Politics, 1928–34.* Cambridge: Cambridge University Press, 1977.

Bourke-White, Margaret. *Halfway To Freedom.* New York: Simon & Schuster, 1949.

Chandra, Kailash. *Tragedy of Jinnah.* 2d Ed. Lahore: Varma Publishing Co., 1941.

Chopra, P. N. *Role of Indian Muslims in the Struggle for Freedom.* New Delhi: Manohar, 1979.

Coatman, John. *India: The Road to Self-Government.* London: George Allen & Unwin, 1941.

Collins, Larry and La Pierre, Dominique. *Freedom At Midnight.* New York: Simon & Schuster, 1975.

————. *Mountbatten and the Partition of India.* New Delhi: Vikas, 1982.

Cooke, Colin. *The Life of Richard Stafford Cripps.* London: Hodder & Stoughton, 1957.

Dalton, Dennis. *Indian Idea of Freedom.* New Delhi: Manohar, 1982.

Das, Durga, *India, From Curzon to Nehru and After.* London: Collins, 1969.

Das, M. N. *India Under Morley and Minto.* London: George Allen & Unwin, 1964.

————. *Partition and Independence of India: Inside Story of Mountbatten Days.* New Delhi: Manohar, 1982.

Dwarkadas, Kanji. *India's Fight for Freedom, 1913–1937.* Bombay: Popular Prakashan, 1966.

————. *Ten Years To Freedom.* Bombay: Popular Prakashan, 1968.

Edwardes, S. M. *Memoir of Sir Dinshaw Manockjee Petit.* Oxford: Oxford University Press, 1923.

Ellinwood, DeWitt C. and Pradhan, S. D., eds. *India and World War I.* New Delhi: Manohar, 1978.

Feldman, H. *Karachi Through a Hundred Years.* Karachi: Oxford University Press, 1970.

Friend, Corinne, ed. *Yashpal Looks Back.* New Delhi: Vikas, 1981.

Glendevon, John. *The Viceroy at Bay: Lord Linlithgow in India, 1936–1943.* London: Collins, 1971.

Gopal, Sarvepalli. *Jawaharlal Nehru.* Vol. I (1889–1947). Cambridge, Mass.: Harvard University Press, 1976.

————. *Jawaharlal Nehru.* Vol. II (1947–56). New Delhi: Manohar, 1979.

Gordon, Leonard A. *Bengal: The Nationalist Movement, 1876–1940.* New Delhi: Manohar, 1979.

Hardy, Peter. *The Muslims of British India.* Karachi: Pakistan Publishing House, 1973.

Hasan, Khalid, ed. *Quaid-i-Azam Mohamed Ali Jinnah: A Centenary Tribute.* London: Information Division, Embassy of Pakistan, 1976.

Hasan, Mushirul. *Nationalism and Communal Politics in India, 1916–1928.* New Delhi: Manohar, 1979.

————, ed. *Communal and Pan-Islamic Trends in Colonial India.* New Delhi: Manohar, 1981.

————. *Mohamed Ali: Ideology and Politics.* New Delhi: Manohar, 1981.

Hodson, H. V. *The Great Divide.* Karachi: Oxford University Press, 1969.

Husain, Azim. *Fazil-i-Husain: A Political Biography.* Bombay: Longmans, Green & Co., 1946.

Hyde, H. Montgomery. *Lord Reading: The Life of Rufus Isaacs, First Marquess of Reading.* London: Heinemann, 1967.

Iqbal, Afzal. *The Life and Times of Mohamed Ali.* Lahore: Institute of Islamic Culture, 1974.

Jafri, S. Q. H., ed. *Articles on Quaid-e-Azam.* Lahore: Aziz Publishers, 1977.

Kabir, Humayun. *Muslim Politics, 1906–47.* New Delhi: Manohar, 1969.

Kaura, Uma. *Muslims and Indian Nationalism: The Emergence of the Demand for India's Partition, 1928–40.* New Delhi: Manohar, 1977.

Khan, Khurshid Ara Begum Nawab Siddiq Ali. "Women and Independence." In *Quaid-i-Azam and Muslim Women,* Edited by Khurshid Khan. Karachi: National Book Foundation, 1976.

Khan, Mohammad Yusuf. *The Glory of Quaid-i-Azam.* Lahore: Caravan Book Centre, 1976.

Khan, Shaukat Hayat, "The Commander I Served Under." In *Quaid-i-Azam as Seen by His Contemporaries,* Edited by Jamil-ud-din Ahmad. Lahore: Publishers United Ltd., 1966.

Kulkarni, V. B. *M. R. Jayakar.* New Delhi: Publications Division, Government of India, 1976.

Kumar, H. L. *The Apostle of Unity: A Biographical Study of Maulana Abul Kalam Azad.* Lahore: Hero Publications, 1942.

Lateef, S. Abdul. *The Great Leader.* Lahore: Lion, 1947.

Liaquat Ali Khan (retrospective volume, n.d.)

Lelyveld, David. *Aligarh's First Generation.* Princeton: Princeton University Press, 1977.

Low, D. A., ed. *Soundings in Modern South Asian History.* Berkeley and Los Angeles: University of California Press, 1968.

————, ed. *Congress and the Raj: Facets of the Indian Struggle, 1917–47.* London: Heinemann, 1977.

Lumby, E. W. R. *The Transfer of Power in India, 1945–47.* London: Allen & Unwin, 1954.

MacDonald, J. Ramsay. *The Awakening of India.* London: Hodder & Stoughton, 1910.

McDonough, Sheila, ed. *Mohammed Ali Jinnah: Maker of Modern Pakistan.* Lexington, Ky.: D. C. Heath and Company, 1970.

McPherson, K. *Jinnah. In the Leaders of Asia Series.* University of Queensland Press, 1980.

Majumdar, S. K. *Jinnah and Gandhi.* Calcutta: Firma K. L. Mukhopadhyaya, 1966.

Malik, Hafeez, ed. *Iqbal: Poet-Philosopher of Pakistan.* Washington, D.C.: Public Affairs Press, 1963.

————. *Muslim Nationalism in India and Pakistan.* Washington, D.C.: Public Affairs Press, 1963.

————. *Sir Sayyid Ahmad Khan and Muslim Modernization in India and Pakistan.* New York: Columbia University Press, 1980.

May, Lini S. *Iqbal: His Life and Times.* Lahore: Sh. Muhammad Ashraf, 1974.

Mehrotra, S. R. *India and the Commonwealth, 1885–1929.* New York: Praeger, 1965.

————. "The Congress and the Partition of India." In *The Partition of India.* Edited by Philips and Wainwright.

————. *Towards India's Freedom and Partition.* New Delhi: Vikas, 1979.

Menon, K. P. S. "A College Friend's Tribute." In *Liaquat Ali Khan* (retrospective volume).

Menon, V. P. *The Story of the Integration of the Indian States.* London: Longman, Green & Co., 1956.

————. *The Transfer of Power in India.* Bombay: Orient Longman, 1957.

Merriam, Allen Hayes. *Gandhi vs. Jinnah: The Debate over the Partition of India.* Calcutta: Minerva, 1980.

Minault, Gail. *The Khilafat Movement: Religious Symbolism and Political Mobilization in India.* New York: Columbia University Press, 1982.

Mody, Homi. *Sir Pherozeshah Mehta.* New York: Asia Publishing House. 1st Ed., 1921; rpt., 1963.

Moore, R. J. *The Crisis of Indian Unity, 1917–1940* New Delhi: Oxford University Press, 1974.

————. *Churchill, Cripps and India, 1939–45.* Oxford: Clarendon Press, 1979.

————. *Escape From Empire: The Attlee Government and the Indian Problem.* Oxford: Clarendon Press, 1979.

Morley, John. *On Compromise.* London: Macmillan, 1921.

Mujahid, Sharif al. *Founder of Pakistan, Quaid-i-Azam Mohammad Ali Jinnah 1876–1948).* Islamabad: National Committee for Birth Centenary Celebrations of Quaid-i-Azam Ali Jinnah, 1976.

————. *Ideological Orientation of Pakistan.* Islamabad: NCBCC, 1976.

————. *Quaid-i-Azam Jinnah: Studies in Interpretation.* Karachi: Quaid-i-Azam Academy, 1978.

Mukhtar, Zaman. *Students' Role in the Pakistan Movement.* Karachi: Quaid-i-Azam Academy, 1978.

Naim, C. M., ed. *Iqbal, Jinnah, and Pakistan: The Vision and the Reality.* Syracuse: Maxwell School of Citizenship & Public Affairs, 1979.

Nanda, B. R. *Gokhale: The Indian Moderates and the British Raj.* Princeton: Princeton University Press, 1977.

Nawaz, Begum Shah. "The Quaid As I Knew Him." In *Quaid-I-Azam and Muslim Women*, edited by Kurshid Khan. Karachi: National Book Foundation, 1976.

Nichols, Beverley. *Verdict on India*. New York: Harcourt, Brace & Co., 1944.

Noman, Muhammad. *Muslim India: Rise and Growth of the All-India Muslim League*. Allahabad: Kitabistan, 1942.

Page, David. *Pakistan: Past and Present*. London: Stacey International, 1977.

———. *Prelude to Partition: The Indian Muslims and the Imperial System of Control, 1920–1930*. New Delhi: Manohar, 1982.

Pandey, B. N. *Nehru*. London: Macmillan, 1976.

———, ed. *Leadership in South Asia*. New Delhi: Vikas, 1977.

Panikkar, K. M. (Kerala Putra). *The Working of Dyarchy in India, 1919–1928*. Bombay: D. B. Taraporevala, 1928.

Pannoun, N. A. *Jinnah the Lawyer*. Lahore: Mansoor Book House, n.d.

Parthasarathy, Rangaswami. *A Hundred Years of The Hindu*. Madras: Kasturi & Sons, Ltd., n.d.

Philips, C. H. and Wainwright, Mary D., eds. *The Partition of India: Policies and Perspectives, 1935–1947*. London: George Allen & Unwin Ltd., 1970.

Prakasa, Sri. *Pakistan: Birth and Early Days*. Meerut: Meenakshi Prakashan, 1965.

Prasad, Beni. *The Hindu-Muslim Question*. London: George Allen & Unwin, 1946.

Qureshi, I. H. *The Pakistani Way of Life*. London: Heinemann, 1957.

———. *The Struggle for Pakistan*. Karachi: University of Karachi, 1965.

Qureshi, Saleem. "Mohammad Ali Jinnah: Concept of Self-Determination." *Secrutiny* 5, nos. 4–5 (1979): 1–13.

Rahman, Fazlur. *Islam*. Garden City, N.Y.: Doubleday, 1966.

———. "Quaid-i-Azam as I Saw Him." In *Q-i-A as Seen By His Contemporaries*. Edited by Jamil-ud-din Ahmad. Lahore: Publishers United Ltd., 1966.

Rajagopalachari, C. *The Way Out*. London: Oxford University Press, 1944.

Rajput, A. B. *Muslim League, Yesterday and Today*. Lahore: Sh. Muhammad Ashraf, 1948.

Rao, P. Kodanda. *The Right Honourable V. S. Srinivasa Sastri: A Political Biography*. London: Asia Publishing House, 1963.

Ravoof, A. A. *Meet Mr. Jinnah*. Madras: Deccan Times Press, 1944.

Ray, P. C. *Life and Times of C. R. Das*. London: Oxford University Press, 1927.

Reading, the Second Marquess of. *Rufus Isaacs: First Marquess of Reading (1914–35)*. London: Hutchinson, 1945.

Rizvi, S. A. A. "Islam in Medieval India." In *A Cultural History of India*. Edited by A. L. Basham. Oxford: Clarendon Press, 1975.

Robertson, John Henry. *Auchinleck*. London: Cassell, 1959.

Robinson, Francis. *Separatism Among Indian Muslims: The Politics of the United Provinces' Muslims, 1860–1923*. Cambridge: Cambridge University Press, 1974.

Saeed, Ahmad. *The Green Titan: A Study of Quaid-i-Azam Mohammad Ali Jinnah*. Lahore: Sang-e-Meel, 1976.

Sayeed, Khalid Bin. *Pakistan: The Formative Phase*. Karachi: Pakistan Publishing House, 1960.

———. *The Political System of Pakistan*. Karachi: Oxford University Press, 1967.

———. "Political Leadership and Institution Building Under Jinnah, Ayub and Bhutto." In *Pakistan: The Long View*. Edited by Lawrence Ziring et al. Durham: Duke University Press, 1977.

Shafi, Mian Ahmad. *Haji Sir Abdoola Haroon: A Biography*. Karachi: Begum Daulat Anwar Hidayatullah, n.d.

————. "The Historic League Session." In *Quaid-i-Azam as Seen by His Contemporaries*, edited by Jamil-ud-din Ahmad. Lahore: Publishers United Ltd., 1966.

Shiekh, Atique Z. and Malik, M. R., eds. *Quaid-e-Azam and the Muslim World*. Karachi: Royal Book Co., 1978.

Siddiqui, Misbah-ul-Haque and Gilani, T. K., eds. *Essays on Quaid-e-Azam*. Lahore: Shahzad, 1976.

Sitaramayya, Pattabhi. *The History of the Indian National Congress*. Vol. I (1885–1935). Bombay: Padma, 1935; rpt., 1944.

Smith, Ray T. *The 'Liberals' in the Indian Nationalist Movement, 1918–1947: Their Role as Intermediaries*. Ann Arbor, Mich.: University Microfilms, 1964.

Smith, W. C. *Pakistan as an Islamic State*. Lahore: Sh. Muhammad Ashraf, 1951.

Stephens, Ian. *Horned Moon*. London: Chatto & Windus, 1954.

————. *Pakistan*. London: Ernest Benn, 1967.

Suleri, Ziauddin A. *My Leader*. Lahore: Lion, 1946.

Syed, Anwar H. *Issues of Bureaucratic Ethic*. Lahore: Progressive Publishers, 1974.

Symonds, Richard. *The Making of Pakistan*. London: Faber & Faber, 1950; reissued in National Book Foundation edition at Islamabad: National Committee for Birth Centenary Celebrations of Quaid-i-Azam Mohammad Ali Jinnah, 1976.

Tendulkar, D. G. *Mahatma*. 8 vols. Bombay: The Publication Division, 1953–54.

Toosy, M. S. *My Reminiscences of Quaid-i-Azam*. Islamabad: National Committee for Birth Centenary Celebrations of Quaid-i-Azam Ali Jinnah, 1976.

Tuker, F. I. S. *While Memory Serves*. London: Cassell, 1950.

Von Vorys, Karl. *Political Development in Pakistan*. Princeton: Princeton University Press, 1965.

Waheed-uz-Zaman. *Towards Pakistan*. Lahore: Publishers United, 1954.

————. *Quaid-i-Azam Mohammad Ali Jinnah, Myth and Reality*. Islamabad: National Committee for Birth Centenary, 1976.

————. *Quaid-i-Azam Mohammad Ali Jinnah, Myth and Reality*. Islamabad: National Committee for Birth Centenary Celebrations of Quaid-i-Azam Ali Jinnah, 1976.

Wasti, Syed Razi. *Lord Minto and the Indian Nationalist Movement, 1905–1910*. London: Oxford University Press, 1965.

Weekes, Richard V. *Pakistan, Birth and Growth of a Muslim Nation*. Princeton: D. Van Nostrand Co., 1964.

Wheeler, Richard S. *The Politics of Pakistan: A Constitutional Quest*. Ithaca, N.Y.: Cornell University Press, 1970.

Wilber, Donald N. *Pakistan, Yesterday and Today*. New York: Holt, Rinehart, 1964.

Wilcox, Wayne A. *Pakistan, Consolidation of a Nation*. New York: Columbia University Press, 1963.

Wolpert, S. A. *Tilak and Gokhale*. Berkeley and Los Angeles: University of California Press, 1962.

————. *Morley and India, 1906–1910*. Los Angeles: University of California Press, 1967.

————. *A New History of India*. 2d Ed. New York: Oxford University Press, 1982.

————. *Roots of Confrontation in South Asia*. New York: Oxford University Press, 1982.

Wrench, John Evelyn. *The Immortal Years*. London: Hutchinson, 1954.

Wriggins, Howard, ed. *Pakistan in Transition*. Islamabad: University of Islamabad Press, 1975.

Young, Kenneth. *Stanley Baldwin*. London: Weidenfeld and Nicolson, 1976.

Zaidi, Z. H. "Aspects of the Development of Muslim League Policy, 1937–47." In *The Partition of India*. Edited by Philips and Wainwright.

Ziring, Lawrence, Braibanti, Ralph, and Wriggins, W. Howard, eds. *Pakistan: the Long View*. Durham: Centre for Commonwealth & Comparative Studies, 1977.

Index